Editor	Nils Anderson
Developmental Editor	Gay L. Pauley
Production Manager	A. Colette Kelly
Sales & Marketing	Don DeLong
Cover Design	Cynthia Maliwauki

Gorsuch Scarisbrick, Publishers
8233 Via Paseo del Norte, F400
Scottsdale, Arizona 85258

Printed in the United States of America.

10 9 8 7 6 5 4 3 2 1

Goodwin, John R., 1929-
Hotel and hospitality law: principles and cases. — 4th ed./
John R. Goodwin, Jolie R. Gaston.
p. cm.
Rev. ed. of: Hotel law. c1987.
Includes bibliographical references and index.
ISBN 0-942280-60-1
1. Hotels, taverns, etc.—Law and legislation—United States.
2. Hospitality industry—Law and legislation—United States.
I. Gaston, Jolie R. II. Goodwin, John R., 1929- Hotel law.
III. Title.
KF951.G65 1992 91-47616
CIP

This one, once again, is for
Elizabeth Ann Paugh, with love
JRG

Many thanks to JRG
from JRG

11

12

13

14

15

16

Preface

Hotel and Hospitality Law: Principles and Cases, Fourth Edition, is designed to meet the legal needs of students in such courses as hotel law, travel law, travel agent law, and the laws of innkeepers and hotel managers. This new edition of the textbook has been revised according to suggestions offered by individuals who have used the book during its life of more than thirty class semesters.

The objectives of this new edition are, first, to examine the laws that regulate the travel and lodging industry and, second, to set forth management principles that must be developed and followed in that industry. In serving this dual purpose, the book emphasizes the direct relationship between the science of business management and the laws governing the hospitality industry. A few words about how this approach evolved will assist in a better understanding of its form.

In the late 1970s, a colleague and I were asked to create a new-style law book for hospitality students in courses such as those mentioned above. A literature search revealed that the majority of books used in these courses were essentially compilations of court cases with little or no relevant explanation provided for the student. Upon further research, we determined that a more appropriate approach would set forth traditional business-law topics as they related to the travel and lodging industry *in an applied manner.*

As readers have confirmed, the text is not a "mini" business-law book but an effective application of relevant business law to a particular industry. The text presents legal concepts and management ideas seldom introduced in traditional business-law courses and presents them in a readable, understandable style. Students who study from the book use this legal material to assist them in virtually all of their hospitality courses—in other words, they *learn how to apply it.*

We believe that this book will contribute to the professional success of those who use it. In this manner it should contribute

FOREIGN AND LEGAL WORDS AND PHRASES FOUND IN THE CASE DECISIONS

Ad hoc: For this special purpose.

Appellant: The one taking an appeal in court.

Appellee: The one against whom an appeal is taken.

Arguendo: In the course of the argument.

Bifurcated: The splitting of a trial into separate issues.

Bill of lading: A transportation document that lists goods received for shipment.

Bona fide: In good faith.

Causa mortis: In contemplation of approaching death.

Caveat emptor: Let the buyer beware.

Circa: About, around, with relation to.

Common law: That body of law that has grown from the rulings of courts over the centuries.

Cum testamento annexo: With the will annexed.

De bene esse: Conditionally, provisionally.

Dehors: Out of, without, beyond.

Denovo: Anew, fresh, a second time.

Ejusdem generis: Of the same kind, class, or nature.

En masse: In a mass or lump.

Estoppel: Stopping or closing one's mouth; a technique that can be used by the courts to correct an inconsistent position that one may attempt to use against another.

Et al.: Abbreviation for *et alia;* "and others."

Ex contractu: From the contract.

Fiat: A sanction or decree; an order "let it be done."

Habeas corpus: "You have the body."

In camera: In chambers, in private.

Infra hospitium ("hospis-e-em"): Within the inn.

In limine: In the very beginning. On or at the threshold.

Innamium: In old English, a pledge.

In personam: Against the person.

In rem: Against the thing (property).

Inter alia enactatum fuit: "Among other things, it was enacted." This is an ancient phrase found in the old pleadings (court papers) to refer to statutes.

Inter vivos: Between the living.

Judex: A private person appointed by the praetor, with the consent of the parties, to try a case brought before that person in ancient Rome.

Judex ad quem: A judge to whom an appeal was taken in ancient Rome.

Jurisprudence: A word of the legal profession that describes the legal system and its supporting laws.

Jus: Right, justice, law.

Laus deo: "Praise be to God." A phrase used as a heading on old bills of exchange.

Liability: Responsibility under law.

Malfeasance: Evil doing. The commission of some act that is unlawful. Ill conduct.

Misfeasance: The improper performance of an act that a person has the legal power to do.

Mote: A meeting or assembly.

Moteer: A service or payment at the court of the lord, from which some were exempt by charter or privilege.

Nexus: Bound persons. Obligation or bond.

Nonfeasance: Nonperformance of an act that should be performed.

Non obstante verdicto: Not withstanding the verdict. In spite of the verdict.

Per curium: By the court.

Per se: By himself or herself.

Praetor: A municipal officer of the ancient city of Rome.

Prima facie: Such as will prevail until contradicted. On the face of it.

Prohibition: Inhibition, intradiction.

Pro se: For himself (or herself) in his or her own behalf.

Quasi-contract: Not a true contract but close to it.

Quid pro quo: What for what, something for something. Used in law for giving one valuable thing for another.

Qui facit per alium facit per se: "He who acts through another, acts himself." (The basis for the law of agency.)

Quo warranto: An ancient writ used to force one to show by what authority he or she holds a public office.

Remittitur: A subtraction from a jury verdict.

Res ipsa loquitur: The thing speaks for itself.

Respondent: The party who must reply or answer an appeal in court.

Scienter: Knowingly.

Sequester: To separate or isolate.

Stare decisis: To abide by or adhere to decisions. Let the decision stand.

Statute: An act of a legislative body.

Statutory law: That body of law that comes from acts of legislative bodies.

Subjudice: Under judicial consideration.

Summary judgment: Judgment given to one party where the other fails to reply to the complaint filed in court.

Supercedas: A writ commanding a stay of proceedings at law.

Suzerainty (French): A nation that exercises potential control over nations in relation to which it is sovereign.

Venditor: Seller.

Venire facias de novo: A fresh or new trial where some error has occurred that prevents a judgment being entered.

1

Travel and Lodging Law: An Overview

There was also a pragmatic reason for the addresses in London and Zurich. Weinberg had learned from other con men that the Hotel Zurich and the Hilton Hotel in London shared a unique custom. Neither hotel would tell a caller that the person he was calling was not registered at the hotel. Both hotels would simply accept messages for an unregistered guest on the assumption that the guest would arrive later. The caller was left with the impression that his party was registered at the hotel, a valuable aid to confidence men who thrive on the impression that they are flitting through Europe from one big business deal to another.

The Sting Man, Robert W. Greene[1]

OVERVIEW

In this chapter we identify some of the features of this specialized body of law, become acquainted with its basic terminology, and place it in its historical perspective.

The principles of travel and lodging law have been recognized for centuries as a unique, specialized body of jurisprudence, designed to control a specific industry. Yet the subject has only recently—as legal history goes—made its formal appearance in the colleges of hotel administration. The prototypes of this subject were found in the "Business Law" and other similar courses in colleges of business administration. These courses have been recognized for years as being of key importance to students in business schools because they provide a necessary understanding of the nature of law and the part that it plays in the regulation of business.

THIS BUILDING outside of Las Cruces, New Mexico, at Mesilla, once housed the Capitol of Arizona and New Mexico and was the courthouse in which Billy the Kid was sentenced to be hanged.

This general treatment of law in the business schools was in turn called upon by the colleges of hotel administration to meet *their* legal needs. Many of these colleges used traditional business-law textbooks in their hotel-law courses. While "hotel-law" textbooks have been available for many years, they are almost always a treatment of the laws of innkeepers and thus quite narrow in scope.

Litigation over the past decade has made it increasingly clear that those who are preparing for a career in the hospitality field must study law as it is applied to the various segments of this field. This particular industry has special requirements that have been forced upon it by court decisions.

It is the purpose of this book to provide the means by which this study can be undertaken in a meaningful, understandable manner. That it is necessary to study the legal requirements of all segments of this industry is illustrated by a full-page ad that appeared in a national law journal published for the legal fraternity.[2] First comes the following heading set in type almost one inch high:

> FOR YEARS LAWYERS HAVE THOUGHT OF TRAVEL LITIGATION AS UNREWARDING. IT'S JUST NOT TRUE.
>
> [These paragraphs follow:]
>
> For years lawyers have operated under the illusion that they should avoid travel litigation as not worth the time and trouble. Nothing could be further from the truth! Increasingly, attorneys

> and the courts are discovering that spoiled travel plans involve more than superficial injuries. Awareness of consumer rights has resulted in sizeable recoveries against those responsible for destroying the travel plans of vacationers and businessmen.
>
> Consider: A vacation is ruined because an individual was "bumped" from his airline flight, his baggage was lost, his hotel was overbooked, and the hotel he was forced to stay in was unfinished and miles from the area he wanted to visit. Do you take the case?

The legal upshot is clear: The travel and lodging business has become a "legal-target industry." This has happened in the past against other industries, including automobile-injury cases aimed at the insurance industry; the products-liability cases against manufacturers of defective products, and malpractice cases against medical doctors. It is now the turn of the hospitality industry and it is necessary for future hospitality managers to prepare themselves to minimize or avoid this assault by the legal profession.

THE HRI INDUSTRY AS A "LEGAL TARGET"

Since the HRI industry has become a "legal target," it follows that those in this industry must begin to get its terms in mind as well as the titles of those who make the industry thrive.

A Matter of Titles

In this look at the laws that regulate the HRI industry, we will be examining a variety of "traveler-oriented" businesses. Included will be hotels, motels, inns, bed-and-breakfast inns, boardinghouses, lodginghouses, condominiums, and even trailer and RV (recreational vehicle) parks.

Thus, to facilitate our discussion the decision was made to sweep all of the above under the broad heading of "innkeeping" and to call those who manage such endeavors "innkeepers" or "hotel managers."

To avoid excessive wordage, we will also use an abbreviation throughout the text. In some of the leading nonlegal textbooks in use in the hotel schools,[3] the hospitality industry is referred to as the "HRI industry." We will use the notation "HRI" but, when it is used, we will understand that it includes not only hotels, restaurants, and "institutions," but also bars, travel agencies, carriers, casinos, and other businesses that make up the hospitality industry.

today come from "court-made" law and not from acts of legislative bodies. The relatively late establishment of the English Parliament can also be cited as a reason for this. Examine Figure 1.1.

The courts began the creation of a body of unique law that is still being developed in the modern courts and legislatures. The creation of these laws placed upon those in the "travel chain" increasing legal responsibilities for the safety of travelers, for their comfort, and for protection of their goods and valuables. In this manner the law began to forge inn and tavern practices.

Many of these practices have come down to us today in the form of custom. To illustrate, when a modern innkeeper greets a guest, the innkeeper is acting out an age-old policy that was forced upon inns by early court decisions. These decisions made the innkeeper an "insurer" of the property of the guest and so the guests were greeted for security purposes and escorted personally to their rooms for the night.

In this legal process, another feature of HRI law had its birth. Since the inn and the tavern were so important to the needs of the traveling public, the courts came to treat them as public houses. Since the inn was now a public house—even though privately owned—it was required to receive all who presented themselves there; to safeguard not only the traveler but the traveler's horse and other property; to provide "refreshment" or "entertainment"; and many other duties and policies that we will encounter.

The author of a hotel-law text said it this way: "The supply of food and shelter to a traveler was a matter of public concern, and

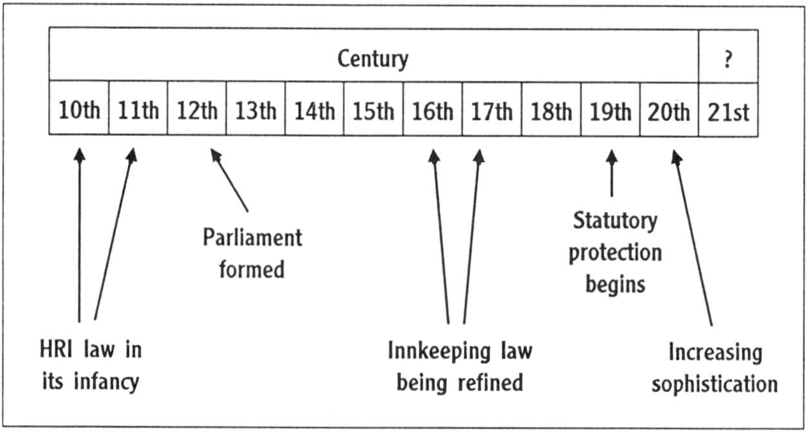

FIGURE 1.1 Development of HRI laws.

the house which offered such food and shelter was [recognized to be] engaged in a public service. The law must make injustice to the individual traveler impossible: the caprice of the host could not be permitted to leave a subject of the king hungry and shelterless. In a matter of such importance the public had an interest, and must see that, so far as was consistent with justice to the innkeeper, his [her] inn was carried on for the benefit of the whole public, and so it became in an exact sense a public house."[6]

Shaped by the courts, nurtured by the public need, the law of innkeeping developed into a finely honed body of law that forms the basis of our study. As an example of the fine balance of HRI law, one can look at what the courts had to say about those who lacked the capacity to contract, such as infants. Were they too extended the protection of the law?

Infants and Innkeeping

In establishing the legal duty of those in the HRI industry to receive travelers, the early courts were never concerned with whether the traveler had the legal capacity to form a binding contract. If that had been the test, infants and others under common-law disabilities would have been denied HRI services. Thus the duty to receive was extended to infants and others regardless of their legal capacity.

Today it is useful to keep the historical perspective in mind while thinking of the "chain of travel." This chain is made up of those who carry the traveler from one point to another, those who provide the "home-away-from-home" for the night, and those who feed that person and provide other entertainment while he or she is on the journey. So long as the chain is maintained in a safe, certain, reasonable manner, with reasonable fees being charged, and so long as the sojourner can travel with a minimum of inconvenience or loss, the ancient desire to promote travel is fulfilled.

Looking back, we can conclude that the early courts met the challenge that was placed upon them to meet the needs of the traveling public. The result of this legal process is that body of HRI common law that forms the greatest part of our study. Outside of this body of law, the HRI industry is relatively uncontrolled today. There is an almost total absence of legislation directed toward this industry.

One definition states: "A hotel is a building held out to the public as a place where all transient persons who come will be received and entertained as guests for compensation and it opens its facilities to the public as a whole rather than limited accessibility to well-defined private groups."[8]

The definition of a hotel under New Jersey law is important to those who want to enter the casino business at Atlantic City. Such persons must, as a condition precedent to the issuance of a gaming license, construct a hotel that meets the specifications of New Jersey law. A portion of the New Jersey casino-control law follows:

> A hotel is:
>
> A single building under one ownership, located within the limits of the city of Atlantic City as said limits were defined as of November 2, 1976, and containing not fewer than 500 sleeping units, each of at least 325 square feet measured to the center of perimeter walls, including bathroom and closet space and excluding hallways, balconies and lounges; each containing private bathroom facilities; and each held available and used regularly for the lodging of tourists and convention guests and conforming in all respects to the facilities requirements contained in this act. For the purpose of exceeding the maximum casino size specified in section 83 of this act, an approved hotel may, by means of physical connection, annex additional buildings or facilities. "Physical connection" for the purposes herein means an enclosed permanent pedestrian passageway. In no event shall the main entrance or only access to an approved hotel be through a casino.

Under Virginia law, a hotel is an inn or public lodging house that can accommodate five or more transient guests. A "transient guest" is one who puts up for less than one week.[9]

The courts by legal interpretation have even expanded the word "hotel" to include private schools. In *Blair Academy et al. v. Patricia Q. Sheehan*,[10] the Superior Court of New Jersey had this to say:

> The hearing examiner who conducted the Department hearing on the requests for an administrative determination made findings and conclusions and recommended to the Commissioner that the three appellant schools "be ordered to permit the Department to inspect their dormitories as 'multiple dwellings,'" and that they "be ordered to register their buildings with the Department and pay the required fee." The Commissioner modified the first part of "the recommended decision and order of [the] hearing examiner," by providing that the schools "be ordered to permit the Department to inspect their dormitories as 'hotels' rather than 'multiple dwellings,'" and adopted the recommended decision and order as thus modified.

> From our review of the record submitted on this appeal we are entirely satisfied that the Commission's determination is "supported by substantial credible evidence on the whole record, allowing for agency expertise and evaluation of the credibility of witnesses." *Parkview Village Ass'n. v. Collingswood,* 62 N.J. 21, 34, 297 A.2d 842, 848 (1972). We discern no reason or justification for disturbing it. *State v. Johnson,* 42 N.J. 146, 162, 199 A.2d 809 (1964). The Commissioner's announced conclusion is sound. It is obviously designed to effectuate the essential purpose and intent of the Hotel and Multiple Dwelling Law. See N.J.S.A. 55:13A-2; *Rumson Country Club v. Community Affairs Comm'r,* 134 N.J. Super 54, 338 A.2d 219 (App. Div.), certi. den. 68 N.J. 482, 348 A.2d 523 (1975). Appellants' dormitories come within the definition of the term "hotel" as defined by N.J.S.A. 55:13A-3(j).

In Nevada, the statutory definition enlarges the word *hotel* to include roominghouses and lodginghouses that solicit transient trade:

> Every building or structure kept as, used as, maintained as, or held out to the public to be, a place where sleeping or rooming accommodations are furnished to the transient public, whether with or without meals, shall, for the purpose of this chapter, be deemed to be a hotel; and whenever the word "hotel" shall occur in this chapter it shall be deemed to include a lodginghouse or roominghouse where transient trade is solicited.[11]

A word closely associated with "hotel" is that of "motel."

Motel

This word is a product of the last forty years and is a contraction of "motorist" and "hotel." As the motel industry began to develop, notably in the 1950s, the word identified a small hotel-type structure with rooms for hire by the day, with a minimum amount of service provided by management.

Today, the word "motel" is associated with some of the most luxurious travel accommodations on the face of the earth. It has been noted recently that some of the larger motel chains are advertising their units as "hotels."

The forerunner of the hotel and the motel was, of course, the inn.

Inn

"An inn is a house where all who conduct themselves properly, and who are able and ready to pay for their entertainment, are received, if there is accommodation for them, and who, without any stipulated engagement as to the duration of the stay or as to the rate of compensation, are, while there, supplied at a reasonable charge for their meals, their lodging, and such services and attention as are necessarily incident to the use of the house as a temporary home."[12]

Another word of the industry that needs definition is that of "traveler."

Traveler

A person crossing the country or going to another nation is certainly a "traveler" in the ordinary sense. So is a local who stays a night at a local hotel in order to catch a plane the following morning. The definition is important in HRI law because it is for the benefit of this person that this body of law was designed. The courts approach situations in which the definition becomes important on a case-by-case basis. The word has further legal significance in that it is "travelers" who become "guests" at the inns.

Guest

One who is a "guest" at a lodging facility is given greater rights by law than one who is not a guest. To determine if one is a "guest" in the innkeeping sense, the courts will look *to the intention of the parties.* An innkeeper and a "guest" may form a "boardinghouse" or "landlord and tenant" relationship. If this happens, the "guest" is not a "guest" in the innkeeping sense. A townsperson who stops at the cigar stand in the lobby to buy a newspaper would not be a guest. This intention of the traveler to become a guest is treated at law as being an "offer." If this offer is accepted by the innkeeper, the innkeeper-guest relationship has arisen. The offer of the traveler is most often accepted by front-desk personnel as agents of the innkeeper.

Yet the status of "guest" at an inn can never be established unilaterally by the traveler. Thus, if a traveler, intending to pay later, takes a room key from an unattended front desk and gains admittance to a room, he or she would not be a guest at that inn. For the inn-guest relationship to arise there must be an opportunity for the innkeeper to receive or reject that person. If received, the innkeeper-guest relationship comes into being. The law of innkeeping will then control the relationship until the guest status ends.

Guest status may end in a variety of ways: A guest may check out and end it, or an innkeeper may eject a guest for immoral conduct. A problem in determining the beginning rather than the ending of the relationship arises in those instances where travelers use the services of an inn for food and drink but not for lodging. The courts may say that if such use is in furtherance of the travel and if the innkeeper knowingly serves the traveler, the inn-guest relationship *is* in being until the traveler moves on.

If a family (husband, wife, and children) checks into an inn, each member of the family gains guest status even though only one member of the family checks in and pays.

As mentioned, locals generally cannot gain guest status since they are not "travelers." Yet if a local is received by the innkeeper with the intention of having that person as a guest, the status has arisen.[13]

Does the inn-guest relationship apply to an *employee* who, as part of his or her employment contract, occupies a room at the inn? Or how about an employee who stays overnight at an inn because of a severe snowstorm? In both instances the courts have held that there is no inn-guest relationship. The reason is, of course, the employee does not meet the "traveler" test.[14]

A "guest" must be distinguished from a "tenant."

Tenant

A tenant, under landlord and tenant law, gains a right of exclusive possession of the leased premises. This right is an enforceable property interest and it takes legal process to terminate the status. A guest at an inn, on the other hand, gains a mere license or right to *use* the inn room. This is a temporary right and ends as the guest resumes his or her travels. Of course, a guest who remains at an inn on an extended basis could become a tenant and would then have a property interest in the room. The counterpart of the tenant is the landlord.

Landlord

Landlords, as distinguished from innkeepers, serve those who intend to remain in a certain locale on an extended basis. Such persons have not traditionally needed the same legal protection that was needed by travelers. For this reason the law allows a landlord to bargain, select, and use his/her own judgment in deciding who will or will not be acceptable as a tenant.

In addition, the rates charged by landlords are a matter of contract between the parties. There is no rule, in the absence of rent controls, that says the rates charged by a landlord must be reasonable.

Tavern

At common law, a "taverner" was a person who sold wines to the public. From that word came the word "tavern." While inns and taverns share common points, legally they are not the same. An inn is an establishment designed to provide rest, shelter, and entertainment for the traveler. A tavern, on the other hand, primarily serves those who live in the immediate area and thus have access to their own homes at night.

An important definition is found in the legal meaning of the word "innkeeper."

Innkeeper

An innkeeper is one who assumes the responsibilities of operating an inn, as that word developed at common law. In practice, there have been cases in which the keeper of rooms has denied that he or she was in fact an innkeeper. This could happen where there was an attempt to escape innkeeping liability to a guest or roomer. The defense often seen in such cases is that only shelter was furnished, not food and drink; at common law, to be an innkeeper within the legal meaning of that word, both shelter and food and drink had to be furnished.[15]

In *Doe v. Bridgton*,[16] the judge provided a summary of what an innkeeper is:

> He (the innkeeper) was bound by the common law to receive and lodge all comers in the absence of a reasonable ground of refusal. 21 *Halsbury's Laws of England* 445–446, 3d ed. (1957). A valid refusal had to be related to the inn's operations as an inn. *Whites's Case*, 2 Dyer 158, 73 Eng. Reports 343 (K.B. 1558). Full occupancy or the traveler's condition, such as drunkenness, which might offend other guests, constituted good cause for exclusion. On the other hand, arrival at a late hour or on a Sunday was held to be insufficient to deny lodging. *Rex v. Ivens*. There had to be a rational relationship, a causal nexus, between the reason for the refusal and the function of the inn.

This definition of an innkeeper raises a related question: Who is *not* an innkeeper?

Who Is Not an Innkeeper?

One who only occasionally receives travelers and provides food and shelter for them is not an innkeeper. In addition, one who receives and provides for those who are not travelers or transients is not an innkeeper and cannot be held to innkeeper liability.

To render one responsible as an innkeeper, ". . . a person must make [innkeeping] to some extent a regular business, a means of livelihood. He should hold himself out to the world as an *innkeeper*. It is not necessary that he should have a sign, or a license (although he will usually have both), provided that he has in any other manner authorized the general understanding that his was a public house, where strangers had the right to require accommodation."[17]

An innkeeper must be distinguished from those who manage common carriers, such as ship lines or Amtrak.

Common Carriers

A common carrier which furnishes rooms and food and drink as part of the act of carriage is not an innkeeper. The function of the carrier is to provide *transportation*–the shelter and food and drink are ancillary to that purpose.

The standard of care that the law imposes on a common carrier is that of the highest degree of care and diligence for the safe arrival of the passengers. The innkeeper, on the other hand, is held to the standard of ordinary, reasonable care. This distinction arises because of inherent dangers in the operation of airlines, passenger trains, and cruise ships. Common carriers share one thing in common with innkeepers, however: They are both engaged in serving the public. The carrier is in a position of public employment and is regulated by public administrative bodies. The inn is a public house, but is *not* regulated by administrative agencies.

The carrier is an insurer of the safety of the passengers and their goods, while an innkeeper no longer is. Examine Figure 1.2.

While carriers are administratively controlled, they enjoy the protection of some statutes as well as treaties. For example, The Warsaw Convention limits the liability of international air carriers for both death of passengers and the loss of their goods. The Warsaw Convention will be examined in Chapter 24. Another lim-

law and give a client an opinion of what it means; a legislature may enact laws of all types; the people in turn are affected by these laws—yet it is only in a court that law can be enforced.

The ALI definition falls short of what the law is in fact because law never exists in a vacuum. It must in some manner involve the will of the people, and in addition, other forces must come to bear upon it. Justice Oliver Wendell Holmes alluded to this when he defined law as ". . . a statement of the circumstances in which the public force will be brought to bear through the courts."[2]

Other definitions encountered in the law books tell us that law can be "predictions of what a court will do"; that it is "commands from the state"; that, while it can be demands, it can at the same time be "prohibitions from the state."

CHARACTERISTICS OF LAW

Law is a liberal art and, as stated by Harry T. Allan, ". . . is the most important liberal art if liberally taught—in any free society that truly practices what it preaches. It is of importance to both future managers and future poets."[3]

The law is pervasive for it permits, forbids, regulates, and moderates. It is not an exact science nor is it necessary that it should be. The law is more concerned with "what will work" than what something *should* be. It does not address high idealism for the simple reason that that would not work as a norm in law. It is the guarantor of many rights enjoyed by citizens in free nations. Without law, there could be no promises of liberty, property rights, free speech, and other rights that have come down to us from medieval England.

While the law is not an exact science, it draws upon techniques of science. Examples can be found in the use of the deductive method of reasoning by the judges as they seek resolutions of disputes by the use of reason and logic. At times, the courts use the inductive method of reasoning as the judge builds on experience in arriving at decisions. At other times a judge may look to the intuitive method and proceed upon the basis of ethics, morals, or social welfare. In addition, all of these scientific methods may be blended in the court process.

Law represents a struggle of human beings to have a viable (workable) set of rules by which society can be regulated. Constant changes, modifications, or repeal of laws become necessary, for the law must flow with the changing needs of society. This often results in the law lagging behind these needs and then being outdated when it does catch up. This is true because law is not self-creating or self-adjusting but requires "justiciable controversies" in courts before such adjustments can be made there. This is a slow process and, if this fact is not understood, one expects too much from the law and becomes impatient with it.

Natural-law precepts provide us with a reliable guide for much of our modern law since it is established that each of us is entitled to basic rights, many of which were set forth for the first time in the Magna Carta in 1215 and in its later reissues.

As to how law grew, we believe that it all began at a primitive or tribal stage, although few records exist upon which to base this premise. We do know that next came the beginning of the common law that is now so much a part of our legal system. This was followed by a natural law or "equitable" step in its development. This stage is seen historically as a period of refinement and increasing sophistication and, during this time, "equity"—the brother of law—was born.

The law (and equity) is not static nor will it ever be so as long as free societies remain on earth. Therefore, it is incorrect to assume that law is in full bloom or final form for it is not and cannot be. While it can be argued that we are in a stage of maturity of law, this presumes too much. The law is simply in a continuing stage of development, just as it has been for centuries.

"Law is not a game of chance where the spoils go to the alert and crafty. It is rather a system devised by civilized society to settle peaceably and equitably disputes between human beings." A district court judge said that perhaps fifty years ago. And Felix Frankfurter ten years later said, "Law isn't something that exists as a closed system within itself, but draws its juices from life. A system—but not a closed system. A living, evolving system that grows as the world grows. The law is life, organizing the new and integrating it as well as possible with the old." Another source spoke of law this way: "The law deals mainly with how we relate to other people, to our parents, our children, the people we buy from, the people we sell to, our guests, our hosts, and whole nations of other people. The law grows to encompass new relationships and to affirm the old. As it guides us, may it secure in all of us generosity of spirit and a joy in the possibilities of the future" (*Everyday Law,* December, 1988, The Association of Trial Lawyers of America, 1050 31st St. N.W., Washington, D.C. 20007-4499, front page).

To acquire a better feel for the subject, it is helpful to become acquainted with the primary sources of law.

Rejecting Stare Decisis

If a common-law principle becomes "too old" or if it no longer serves a rational purpose, a court can reject it. However, in the area of "public law" the doctrine is frequently ignored. This often happens in cases involving prior interpretations of a constitution, as the following illustrates:

> A judge looking at a constitutional decision may have compulsions to revere past history and accept what was once written. But he remembers above all else that it is the Constitution which he swore to support and defend, not the gloss which his predecessors may have put on it. So he comes to formulate his own views, rejecting some earlier ones as false and embracing others. He cannot do otherwise unless he lets men long dead and unaware of the problems of the age in which he lives do his thinking for him.
>
> This reexamination of precedent in constitutional law is a personal matter for each judge who comes along. When only one new judge is appointed during a short period, the unsettling effect in constitutional law may not be great. But when a majority of a Court is suddenly reconstituted, there is likely to be substantial unsettlement. There will be unsettlement until the new judges have taken their positions on constitutional doctrine. During that time—which may extend a decade or more—constitutional law will be in flux. That is the necessary consequence of our system and to my mind a healthy one. The alternative is to let the Constitution freeze in the pattern which one generation gave it. But the Constitution was designed for the vicissitudes of time. It must never become a code which carries the overtones of one period that may be hostile to another.
>
> So far as constitutional law is concerned *stare decisis* must give way before the dynamic component of history. Once it does, the cycle starts again. Today's new and startling decision quickly becomes a coveted anchorage for new vested interests. The former proponents of change acquire an acute conservatism in their new *status quo.* It will then take an oncoming group from a new generation to catch the broader vision which may require an undoing of the work of our present and their past. . . .[7]

A fifth source of law is found in the rulings of administrative agencies on cases that come before them.

Administrative Agencies and Their "Law"

One hundred-twenty-five years ago, the population of the United States was a fraction of what it is today. Business was agriculture-oriented and, for the most part, localized. Our nation was only partially settled and life still had a rural, local, personal atmosphere to it. All of this changed with the coming of the first war "to end all wars."

An industrial expansion started that has not ceased in growth. Life changed to one of increasing complexities, and perhaps something was lost in the process. The courts and law were caught up in the change. While the courts had been adequate to regulate society in that other age of 125 years ago, it became increasingly evident that they could no longer fill this role in such changing times.

When this came to pass, large gaps existed in the regulations needed to make certain that an orderly process of business—life itself—would be available to our society today and tomorrow. A hundred years ago, one could challenge a business practice or seek protection by bringing a law suit and then patiently waiting for the legal process to run its course. But today it would be impossible for our courts to regulate the growing airline, travel, radio, television, computer, video, and other industries that have had their inceptions in recent times. Something else was needed to provide such regulation.

Solution

The device selected had its beginning when legislative bodies began to enact laws that were designed to create "administrative agencies." These laws would grant certain powers to a "commission," the membership of which would then be filled by the executive officer such as the governor of a state.

Today

At the federal level, we find the Federal Trade Commission (FTC), Interstate Commerce Commission (ICC), and numerous other "alphabet agencies." At the state level we find public service commissions, departments of public safety, banking commissions, alcohol control commissions, insurance commissions, and others. At the municipal level we find water and sanitation commissions, parking authorities, and police forces.

As a practical matter, the day-to-day impact of such agencies and commissions is much greater than that of the courts, and they play a direct and important part in the regulation of business. Administrative agencies and their rulings have been challenged as an unconstitutional intrusion upon the three-part separation of powers. But the courts uphold them as *an extension of the legislative power* since it is there that they are created in the first instance.

There are other sources of law such as executive orders at the state and federal levels, and rulings of attorney generals. They will not be discussed but we will look at a final source that involves the wishes of the people.

Public Policy

Public policy can find expression through political actions. To illustrate, the voters of a state reject a candidate for governor who campaigns on the grounds of legalization of gambling. The rejection expresses the wishes of the voters; thus, this becomes part of the "public policy" of that state. The courts will give effect to this policy when matters involving gambling come before them.

Other matters of public policy involve things that are against the interests of the public. Some examples include contracts that restrain trade, agreements that affect the administration of justice, contracts never to compete in a certain business, and similar areas.

To conclude, we will examine an administrative-law case that was appealed to a state supreme court. It contains matters of importance and gives us a chance to see how administrative actions create "law" in the broad sense.

CASE INTRODUCTION

Two brothers in Portland applied to the Oregon Liquor Control Commission for a license to sell alcoholic beverages at their restaurant. To qualify for the license, the brothers had to produce sufficient evidence to convince the commission that the granting of a liquor license would be "a judicious use" of the limited licenses that the commission could issue. The evidence they produced did not convince the hearings officer, however. They then went before the commission, where the findings of the hearings officer were confirmed. The brothers then appealed to the courts in an attempt to overturn the ruling of the commission. They failed here, too, thus probably ending their restaurant venture.

As the case is read, pay close attention to the conclusions of the administrative agency because these rulings create law. Also ask this question: What additional evidence might the brothers have brought before the commission to have increased their chances of getting the license?

MARKANTONATOS V. OREGON LIQUOR CONTROL COMMISSION
Or. App. 562 P. 2d 570 (1977)

THORNTON, Judge.

Petitioners seek judicial review of the Oregon Liquor Control Commission's (OLCC) refusal to grant them a Dispenser Class "A" (DA) license for their restaurant, Zorba the Greek. Petitioners assert that the OLCC's findings of fact and ultimate findings of fact are not supported by substantial evidence and that therefore the conclusions of law, on which the license refusal ultimately depends, are unsupported.

Petitioners at the hearing before the hearings officer introduced, in support of their application for a DA license, a petition signed by about 650 supporters, various documents indicating that petitioners' credit is sound, photographs of the decor of the restaurant, an Economic Analysis of the Portland Downtown Guidelines Plan conducted by a Portland consulting firm, a letter from the mayor of Portland indicating a need for more downtown liquor licenses and testimony by eight favorable witnesses. OLCC presented evidence in opposition in the form of testimony by three witnesses and the results of an informal survey.

After a hearing, the hearings officer recommended denial of a DA license. At the hearing before OLCC, the denial was affirmed based on the following ultimate findings of fact, which are generalized restatements of findings of fact, and conclusions of law:

"ULTIMATE FINDINGS OF FACT

"1. There is some opposition in the community to the issuance of the license, and there is likewise some support.

"2. The area in which applicants' outlet is located is heavily saturated with DA outlets, with seven in a radius of 1½ blocks. These outlets offer reasonably adequate service to the public. Applicants' witnesses referred in significant numbers to the shortcomings of only three of the outlets, and a generalized statement to the effect that 'all the outlets' in the area have similar problems does not adequately demonstrate that the witness was in fact aware of the existence of each of the seven outlets' names. The fact that three outlets in the area have replaced seven previously licensed is as indicative of lack of demand leading to the closure of the other outlets, as it is an opportunity for additional licenses in the area. Issuance of licenses to Rian's and L'Omelette was made on the basis of saturation at that time, together with all other factors present, and these outlets are more centrally located.

"3. A gross volume of food sales averaging approximately $60 a day is indicative of the lack of demand at the location, and the adequacy of present outlets to meet the public demand. A change of menu may possibly increase food sales, but the fact and extent of this change cannot be determined on the present record.

"4. Demand for Dispenser outlets in the downtown Portland core area in general may well continue to be present, and increase in the future, but there is no basis in the record that this demand requires an additional DA outlet at this time, or if so, such demand exists at applicants' specific location. The testimony of a small number of witnesses is not persuasive on the issue of demand by the entire public, especially when the sales of the establishment indicate that large numbers of persons choose not to patronize the outlet.

"5. The fact that the number of DA licenses in downtown Portland exceed its ratable allocation indicates that the citizens of the state would be better served by issuance of the license to establishments better able to serve a greater number of the citizens of the community and state.

"From the foregoing Findings of Fact, the following Conclusions of Law are entered:

"CONCLUSIONS OF LAW

"1. Seven premises licensed to serve liquor by the drink are available within a radius of 1½ blocks from applicants' premises, [10–715(1)].

"2. Applicants' low gross food sales indicate a lack of demand at that location, and the adequacy of the seven outlets mentioned previously to provide service to the public, [10–720(5)].

"3. The granting of a Dispenser license to applicants' outlet would not be a judicious use of the limited number of such licenses available statewide, [10–715(10)].

"* * * ."

Since the actual grounds for denial of the license in this case are the conclusions of law, findings of fact not relevant to those conclusions are superfluous and we need not consider them on appeal.

Petitioners maintain that the findings of saturation in the area and that other outlets adequately serve the public are not based on substantive evidence. The evidence is uncontroverted that there are seven DA licensed outlets within one and one-half blocks of applicants' premises. Applicants and six of their supporting witnesses testified that other establishments in the area generally provided bad service, were overcrowded and charged high prices. The OLCC found that the applicants had failed to establish that the other outlets were inadequate and gleaned the opposite conclusion from the testimony, i.e., the fact that the witnesses patronized the other establishments was evidence that the prices were not too high and the service was adequate. The applicants in this case did not introduce specific evidence tending to establish the inadequacy of other outlets in the area. The OLCC's conclusions that there is a heavy saturation in the area and that these outlets offer reasonably adequate service to the public, are rationally supported by the evidence.

Petitioners challenge the OLCC's findings on food sales but do not contend that they are not based on the evidence. They maintain that the average per day food sales figure is misleading because petitioners are only open six days a week and not seven days a week. The commission's arithmetical method may have been questionable, but that does not affect the operative fact that the applicants' food sales are low and that fact led the OLCC to conclude that there is a lack of demand for a DA license at the subject location. The finding that applicants' food sales are low is supported by the evidence.

Petitioners also object to the commission's rejection of their argument that present food sales are not pertinent since petitioners intend to change their menu to offer specialty Greek cuisine which would, according to their testimony, increase food sales by 100 percent to 400 percent. The OLCC need not accept petitioners' speculative predictions.

Contrary to petitioners' argument, the OLCC's third conclusion of law referred to above was not a holding that the 1:2000 ratio (ORS 472.110(4)) precludes issuance of the license, but that issuance of the license to these applicants would not be judicious given low food sales and a saturation in the immediate area.

Prior to the hearing, petitioners were told by the referee that he had access to the entire file of the OLCC, including material relevant to a refusal of a prior application by petitioners for a DA license. Petitioners assign as error the consideration of this material in violation of ORS 183-450(2). As petitioners were fully apprised that the referee had access to the prior material and that material did not form the basis for the commission's decision in this case, the error of the OLCC was not prejudicial. [Annotation.]

In their third assignment of error, petitioners maintain that the decision of the OLCC must be reversed because the members of the commission did not personally hear the case or consider the record, contrary to the provisions of former ORS 183.460. That portion of former ORS 183.460 on which petitioners rely was deleted from the statute by Oregon Laws 1975, ch. 759, §13, p. 2092, effective October 8, 1975. The final order in this proceeding was issued November 18, 1975. The requirement that the OLCC members personally consider the record before issuing a final order does not, therefore, apply in this case.

Affirmed.

QUESTIONS

1. How would *you* define law after having read this chapter? Write it out.

2. Explain how some modern rules of law could be over 1,000 years old.
3. Explain how something can be unconstitutional.
4. Explain how something could be unlawful but not unconstitutional.
5. Why must a judge wait for a justiciable controversy before a matter can be declared unconstitutional or unlawful?
6. Give an example of lawmaking in each of the three branches of government.
7. Give an example of how interpretation by a court may change a statute. (Make up a fictitious statute. "It shall be unlawful to. . . .")
8. Why do we have so few uniform laws when compared with all of the laws that we do have?
9. Make up a fictitious court ruling to show how common law is created.
10. True or false. In the area of public law, the doctrine of *stare decisis* is seldom ignored.

ENDNOTES

1. J. Bryan III and Charles J. V. Murphy, *The Windsor Story.* Dell Publishing Company, New York, p. 43.
2. *American Banana Co. v. United Fruit Co.,* 213 U.S. 347 (1909).
3. "Law as a Liberal Art Versus Law as a Professional Discipline: A False Dichotomy," *American Business Law Journal,* Spring 1977, Vol. 15/1, p. 68.
4. U.S. Constitution, Article IV.
5. *McCullough v. Maryland,* 4 Wheat 316, 407, 4 L. Ed. 579 (1819).
6. *Myers v. United States,* 272 U.S. 52.
7. Justice William O. Douglas, Eighth Annual Benjamin Cardozo Lectures.

3

Classifications of HRI Law

The eighteenth century was famous for taverns and its coffee houses. London inns at which the coaches and post-chaises were wont to call were also places where traders and their customers met to transact business. It was at this time that the furnishings of public-house rooms graduated from the rough and ready benches and high-backed settles to the more elaborate joinery furniture which became a feature of both the town and country inn. The leading stylists in the creation of the new furniture were Sheraton, Chippendale and Hepplewhite, but the coming of the Industrial Revolution produced a lower grade of craftsman who relied on mechanized production to produce vast quantities of indifferent furniture for the blossoming public houses and clubs of the time.

Tavern Treasures, Charles Tresise

OVERVIEW

We want to learn the classifications of law, see what they mean to the HRI industry, and examine the role that understanding them can play in the operation of the modern inn.

The laws that regulate the HRI industry, as well as general business, come from the common law, acts of the legislatures of our states, and from other sources, as we have seen. Many of these laws form the general laws of business, while some take on a distinct substance of their own as they are applied by the courts. HRI laws fall in the latter category. As we proceed, we will have ample opportunity to see how HRI laws are distinguished from the general laws of business, for they are not the same. There are common areas, of course, but there are also vast differences. Once law is created–from whatever source–it will be of a certain type or will fit into a category that allows us to classify it. These classifications

Summertime Scene at Vail, Colorado.

are important for one must see where one law stands in relation to another. If we do not have this awareness, the law can be difficult to comprehend. To assist in gaining this understanding, we will examine several classifications in this chapter.

The chapter has been divided into the following classifications:

1. Judicial and administrative law.
2. Common and statutory law.
3. Common and civil law.
4. Public and private law.
5. Substantive and procedural law.
6. Contract and property law.
7. Tort and criminal law.
8. Law and equity.

Judicial and Administrative Law

Many things become the subject matter of court action, and they involve matters that are "legal" or judicial in nature. They involve law that is created in our constitutions, in the statutes, by common-law rulings, or by interpretations by judges. On the other hand, "administrative law" has as its source an agency that exists outside of the legal system.

This means that we have "judicial law" and we have "administrative law." These classifications can better be understood if we reflect on our discussion of administrative law in Chapter 2 and the Markantonatos case.

Common and Statutory Law

Again, these classifications were previously identified and discussed at length. The former is created by court rulings, the latter by acts of lawmaking bodies. A classification of the common law that varies from this, however, is found in the next category.

Common and Civil Law

While the former exists because of court decisions, the latter exists because of legislative acts. Where we find a civil-law system, ancient Roman law has had an influence on that system. The law of Europe and South America is civil—a statutory or "codified" system as contrasted with one that uses precedent from case decisions to create new law. Thus a civil-law system operates primarily on statutes—a common-law system operates on case precedent.

Louisiana, Texas, California, and a few other states follow a civil-law system. If a common-law state would reduce its law to a "code" (codification), it would be a civil-law state.

Public and Private Law

Public law affects us collectively as a "people." This heading can be subdivided into constitutional law, administrative law, and criminal law. Private law, on the other hand, is law that relates directly to legal relationships between one individual and another. Examples include contract, tort, and property.

A ruling of a Public Service Commission is a public-law ruling. An interpretation of a constitutional principle—even if it concerns only one person, is also public. This is true since that interpretation will affect society *en masse* just as the constitution itself does. If A kills B, that act is public in nature even though it is a highly personal matter to B. If C enters into a contract with D, or if E injures F in a car accident, those acts are private between C and D, and E and F.

Substantive and Procedural Law

"Substantive" law is the substance of the law itself. It may be a statutory or civil-law rule of law. It may be a common-law precedent. It is the law itself. Statutes that set forth health regulations for lodging facilities are substantive. (See Chapter 5 for an example.) So are case decisions that establish liability standards for innkeepers. Likewise, rulings of an administrative agency are substantive since they are part of the matrix or substance of the law.

Procedural law, on the other hand, concerns matters *other* than substantive law. Here we encounter the methods by which lawsuits are started, the way that wages are attached, and countless other matters of procedure including actions of administrative agencies.

Thus, one must look to substantive law to determine if a "cause of action" exists–the right to use a court in an attempt to obtain relief. If a cause of action does *not* exist, or if in the opinion of a lawyer it does not exist, then in most instances the matter ends there. If a cause of action does exist, or if in the opinion of a lawyer there is at least a fair chance of success, then one can begin to use procedural law in a court.

Procedural law includes filing suits, serving papers, calling jurors, serving subpoenas on witnesses, taking testimony in court, enforcing judgments, and all of the other functions carried out by courts and administrative bodies. Procedural law may be thought of as the "machinery" of the legal system. The appeal in the Markantonatos case in Chapter 2 was based on procedural points.

The next classifications of contract and tort, and tort and crime, involve substantive law since these are part of the principles of law itself.

Contract and Property Law

Contract law is that body of law that regulates the creation of private agreements between individuals and firms. These agreements almost always arise from promises. These promises may be to build a motel, to remodel a restaurant, or to serve as a manager in a travel agency. The promises may be to supply materials, to construct specially designed equipment, or to pave a parking lot.

The principal feature of a contract is that two persons, firms, or any combination of persons and firms have brought into play an obligation on the part of each that had no existence before the contract was made. Thus a contract is a voluntary relationship since one can never force a contract upon another—or if it is in fact forced, a court will not enforce it.

By the use of the contract, we can buy hotels, construct restaurants, hire employees, buy and sell stock, have a bank account, buy and sell inventory, and do the endless matters that become involved in travel and lodging functions. The contract will be examined in detail in Chapters 6 and 7.

"Property," in the simplest sense, is the earth and everything permanently affixed to it, and all other items that are loose upon the earth or which are recognized as being property at law. A motel is affixed to the earth "permanently" (although it may be removed at some future time) and is "real property." An automobile is loose upon the earth and is "personal property." Property can be invisible, such as a debt obligation that one owes another. A debt is a "property right" of the one to whom it is owed.

Property is perpetually the subject matter of contract for it is by the contract that property is acquired. It is by the contract that property is sold and transferred. It is by the contract that property is constructed in the first place. Therefore, contract and property are inseparable in the private and business community. Contract law sets forth the rules for owning, transferring, improving, and doing countless other things with property. Property law, on the other hand, provides the rules of ownership, title, rights, and duties of possession of property. The principles of property law will be examined in detail in Chapters 7 and 8.

Tort and Criminal Law

A tort is a negligent, careless, or deliberate act of one person that results in injury to another person, his or her reputation, the other person's property, or all three.

The word evolved from the French word "torquere" which means "twisted" or wrong. A tort can be distinguished from a contract because it will seldom involve a voluntary act by *both* parties. In addition, the parties often do not intend for a tort to come into being. Therefore one is involuntary, the other voluntary. An exception exists when one *intends* to harm another. In a deliberate assault by C on D, it can be assumed that C intended to injure D or the assault would not have occurred. But, regardless of the intention, the assault or attack is a tort. In addition, since the act was deliberate, it would also be a "crime."

A crime then is some conduct that is recognized as being undesirable to society collectively. Therefore, the law of crime—criminal law—involves duties that are owed to the state. It is for this reason that the state prosecutes those who commit crimes.

In the absence of intention to commit harm, torts are treated as violations of duties owed to the injured party. Thus they are private between those parties. A owes a duty to the *state* not to rob B with a gun. C owes a duty to D not to operate his (C's) car in such a careless manner as to injure D. Thus tort and crime can be distinguished by the duties owed. Tort liability can arise in a variety of ways.

Negligence is the most common basis upon which tort actions are based. Negligence or "neglect" is the failure to use due care in doing an act, such as driving a car. Or it can be the failure to do something that a reasonable person *should* have done under the same circumstances. An example would be the failure to replace burned-out lights in a motel parking lot. See the Rappaport case in Chapter 1.

There are other grounds for tort actions; they will be discussed at appropriate places in later chapters.

Law and Equity

Law, as we have looked at it up to this point, is concerned with legal matters—matters of litigation in the law courts. While equity is administered in the courts by judges, it is not "law" in the broad sense. A historical illustration will help put this into perspective.

A thousand years ago, the English courts used a writ system. This was a procedural arrangement whereby the litigants had to fashion their pending cases to match the available writs. There were writs in contract, tort, conversion, debt, covenant, and other areas that are still a part of our modern court systems. Today they are called "common-law forms of action." In those early centuries it often happened that a potential litigant could not fit his or her case into one of the established writs. When this happened, there could be no court relief in that case. This was the old doctrine of "no writ, no remedy." In short, the law was deficient in certain areas.

At some point in history, such matters began to come to the attention of the King or Queen who in turn would refer them to the spiritual advisor, the "chancellor." When the King or Queen began issuing orders based upon the chancellor's advice, "equity" was born. This then became that side of our courts that deals in what is just or right: in short, what is "equitable."

From the birth of equity until today, equitable actions were handled by the issuance of orders from an appropriate person. Today the same is true and all equitable matters are heard and decided by a judge sitting without a jury. Some examples of modern equity matters include specific performance (ordering one to do an act promised), rescission (canceling a contract), injunctions (an order to someone to stop doing something), and divorces (reversing the marriage contract).

If one refuses to obey an equitable order, that person can be held in "contempt of court" and may be jailed until the order is obeyed. Many courts today list their equity cases on the "chancery" docket, a modern remembrance of the ancient chancellor who had a hand in the development of equity.

Today, most courts call both legal and equitable cases "civil actions," yet all modern courts handle equitable matters without a jury. Figure 3.1 presents a summary of the relationship of law, equity, and rulings of administrative agencies.

Final mention is made here of a category that was not mentioned at the beginning of this chapter: that of "constitutional and statutory" law. The subject of constitutional law was covered adequately in the last chapter and statutory law was classified above. Thus the subject is eliminated here. A quote in reference to the nature of constitutional law seems appropriate, however, since constitutional rights do arise in HRI operations from time to time.

		Purpose	Who hears?	Enforcing rulings
Civil actions	Law	Recover damages (dollars)	Jury and (or) judge	Levy of execution
	Equity	To force action or inaction	Judge (no jury)	Contempt of court
	Administrative agencies	Regulation of business	Hearing examiner	Denial of or loss of license
				Cease and desist orders and corrective orders

FIGURE 3.1

> Constitutional questions are rarely topics of burning interest to the general public. The rather mundane principles that comprise the practical structure of American government are overshadowed in the popular mind by the more striking issues arising from the Bill of Rights, such as racial discrimination, free speech, and the death penalty. It is only in the unique cases, like tests of strength between branches of government or breakdown of governmental functions (such as Watergate), that the fundamental building blocks and organizational patterns of government are examined.[1]

Examine Figure 3.2 for a summary of HRI legal areas that are of concern to the HRI manager. Leaving our general discussion of classifications of law, it is helpful to examine two HRI cases so as to see these classifications in use.

INTRODUCTION TO CASE NUMBER ONE

In the first case, we see several of the classifications of law in use. First, there is the contract by which the old hotel structure was to be demolished. This is followed by the tort that damaged the res-

- I. Contract Law
  - A. Conventional contracts
    - 1. Front of the house contracts
      - a. Room reservations
      - b. Check-in
    - 2. Realty contracts
    - 3. Employment contracts
  - B. Sales contracts, Article 2, UCC
    - 1. Back of the house contracts
      - a. Ordering supplies
      - b. Buying food and drink
    - 2. Selling food and drink
- II. Tort Law
  - A. Law of Negligence
    - 1. Contributory negligence
    - 2. Comparative negligence
  - B. Breach of common-law duty to receive
  - C. Injury to person, property, or reputation
- III. Property Law
  - A. Real estate law
  - B. Personal property law
- IV. Law of Business Organizations
  - A. Corporation law
  - B. Partnership law
- V. Bailment Law
  - A. Gratuitous bailments
  - B. Bailments for hire
  - C. Professional and nonprofessional bailments
- VI. Treaties
  - A. Warsaw Convention
  - B. Travel compacts
  - C. "Unidroit"
- VII. Criminal Law
  - A. Felonies
  - B. Misdemeanors
  - C. Petty offenses
    - 1. Assault
    - 2. Assault and battery
    - 3. Invasion of privacy
    - 4. False imprisonment
    - 5. Robbery
- VIII. Labor Law

FIGURE 3.2 HRI law in a nutshell.

taurant. The whole project was being carried out under a federal statute. Then came the administrative action of the appraisers in setting values on the land and building. The matter went first to a trial court in New Mexico. The case ends up in a higher court where the error of the two lower courts is corrected. This is done by "directing a verdict" to the lower judge. This means that the lower court must do what the higher court has told it to do.

The case illustrates how something that started out as a routine business matter developed into a legal tangle. A good question to ask is, "How could the litigation have been avoided in the beginning?"

OWEN V. BURN CONST. CO.[2]

EASLEY, Justice.

Plaintiffs A. A. Owen and his wife, Rubye, (Owen), owners of a restaurant building in Las Cruces, sued Burn Construction Company, Inc. (Burn) in damages for the negligent destruction of the building. The jury returned a verdict of $3,500 in favor of Owen. Both parties filed motions for judgment notwithstanding the verdict and both motions were denied by the trial court. [This means that in spite of the verdict, neither party is satisfied with the verdict and wants it set aside, or adjusted to favor one or the other of the parties. In the usual case, only one party to a case makes this motion for the winning party is usually satisfied. This motion is seen in other cases under the abbreviation "N.O.V."–*non obstante verdicto.*]

Both parties appealed to the Court of Appeals and that court reversed the trial court, directing that judgment be entered in favor of defendant notwithstanding the verdict. Owen petitioned for *certiorari.* We reverse the Court of Appeals and the trial court.

Burn held a contract with Las Cruces Urban Renewal Agency (Agency) to demolish a two-story hotel building immediately adjacent to Owen's restaurant building. While the work was in progress part of the second story of the hotel toppled onto Owen's structure completely destroying its usefulness. The Agency agreed to complete the demolition of the Owen building and to remove the debris. Part of the agreement was that the action of the Agency in clearing Owen's lot would not prejudice Owen's right to seek damages against Burn for the destruction of the building.

Two months after the hotel collapsed on the Owen structure and after the debris had been removed, the Agency filed suit to condemn the vacant lot. The Agency and Owen stipulated to the entry of judgment whereby Owen would receive $59,072.00 for the vacant lot. The judgment signed by the court specifically set forth that the settlement was based on the value of the lot at the time the condemnation action was filed, i.e., without the building, and that the settlement would in no way affect any claim which Owen might have against Burn for the prior damage to the building.

Owen later filed this case against Burn to recover $26,000.00 in damages for the total destruction of the building. It was undisputed that the damage to the building was the fault of Burn. The evidence was also uncontested that the value of Owen's building at the time the damage occurred was $26,000.00.

On the theory that Owen had already been fully compensated by the Agency for both the lot and the building, Burn induced the trial court to take judicial notice of the entire file in the prior condemnation action. Over Owen's objections and in derogation of the express terms of the judgment entered pursuant to the stipulation of the parties, testimony and written opinions of the court-appointed appraisers were admitted into evidence to attempt to prove that the $59,072.00 appraised value included both the building and the land.

The jury returned a verdict for Owen in the inexplicable amount of $3,500.00. Both parties moved for judgment which motions were denied; judgment was entered; both parties appealed.

The Court of Appeals held that the trial court should have entered judgment n. o. v. in favor of Burn, and remanded with instructions to set aside the $3,500.00 judgment for Owen and to enter judgment for Burn. This court granted Owen's petition for writ of *certiorari*.

Owen makes three contentions: (1) the judgment in the condemnation matter was clear and unambiguous; therefore, it was error for the trial court to permit evidence which varied and contradicted the judgment and it was error for the court to refuse an instruction that the building had not been paid for in the condemnation case; (2) the admission of written appraisals made by persons who were not called as witnesses and were not subject to cross-examination was violative of N.M.R. Evid. 802 [§20-4-802, N.M.S.A. 1953 (Supp. 1975)]; and (3) the Court of Appeals' direction of a verdict for Burn was improper because the record shows that Owen was entitled to that relief.

Owen first contends that the two lower courts were in error in deciding that evidence of the condemnation suit and the appraisals made in conjunction therewith were admissible in this cause for the purpose of proving that Owen had already been paid for his building.

The consent judgment entered by stipulation of the Agency and Owen was in no way ambiguous. It provided:

> The compensation is based upon the value of the premises . . . on the date of the commencement of this action, and such award is not intended to affect any claim which the defendants, Owen may have against any person, firm or corporation who may have damaged said premises prior to the commencement of this proceeding, and the stipulation on

> file herein and this judgment shall not constitute a settlement or release of any claim which the defendants may have by reason of damage that may have occurred to the condemned premises prior to the commencement of this action; . . .

The written stipulation that was filed was even more explicit as to the parties' intent that the $59,072.00 be considered payment for the vacant lot.

However, the trial court permitted testimony and written opinions from the appraisers that their evaluations in the condemnation suit included both the land and the building. The Court of Appeals held that the consent judgment was binding on the Agency and Owen but was not binding on Burn, that since the appraisers considered the value of the land and the building in arriving at their evaluations that Owen had already been justly compensated, that assessment of damages is the exclusive function of the jury and that "duplication of damages is not proper." We disagree that these principles of law are dispositive of the case.

It is true, as pointed out by the Court of Appeals, that a stipulated judgment is not considered to be a judicial determination; "rather it is a contract between the parties," *State v. Clark*, 79 N.M. 29, 439 P.2d 547 (1968); but this legal principle is not controlling and does not diminish the legitimacy of the claim or preclude the relief prayed for by Owen.

The rules to be followed in arriving at the meaning of judgments and decrees are not dissimilar to those relating to other written documents. Where the decree is clear and unambiguous, neither pleadings, findings nor matters *dehors* the record may be used to change or even to construe its meaning. *Chavez v. Chavez* 82 N.M. 624, 485 P.2d 735 (1971).

Considering this consent judgment as a mere contract between Owen and the Agency affords no comfort to Burn. "It is well settled in New Mexico that where the language of a contract is clear and unambiguous, the intent of the parties must be ascertained from the language and terms of the agreement." *Hondo Oil & Gas Co. v. Pan American Petroleum Corp.*, 73 N.M. 241, 245, 387 P.2d 342, 345 (1963). It is not the province of the court to amend or alter the contract by construction and the court must interpret and enforce the contract which the parties made for themselves.

[Citations omitted.]

In this case the words cannot be misconstrued; they spell out clearly that the parties intended that Owen should have the right to preserve this action against Burn for damages. There can be no legitimate claim of ambiguity; therefore, there was no need for the court to resort to evidence extrinsic to the agreement.

We are confronted with the specious reasoning of Burn, which corporation was not a party to the suit, that we should go behind the judgment and the specific stipulation signed by the parties and adopt unsworn testimony to emasculate these solemn documents. Who would know what was bought and sold and at what price better than the buyer and seller; and how much better can the bargain be sealed than by a lucid stipulation and judgment?

We hold that it was error to admit the evidence *dehors* the record to vary the terms of the judgment in condemnation; and, as a necessary corollary, we hold that it was error for the court to refuse Owen's instruction that he had not received compensation for his building in the first suit.

Owen claims that the trial court was in error in admitting into evidence written appraisals of the property in question without the appraisers being present for cross-examination. The trial court held that the evidence was admissible under N.M.R. Evid. 803(6), [§20–4–803(6), N.M.S.A. 1953 (Supp. 1975) as an exception to the hearsay rule because it was a record of a regularly conducted activity. The rule provides that a report setting forth an opinion in the course of a regularly conducted activity, "as shown by the testimony of the custodian or other qualified witness," is admissible even though the declarant is not available.

The evidence shows that the written appraisals were prepared for use in the condemnation proceedings, i.e., for purposes of litigation. The Agency did not prepare them but engaged outside parties, whom they did not supervise, to make the appraisals. The Agency would not vouch for the accuracy of the reports and did not know what factors were considered by the appraisers. The evaluation of one of the appraisers was based on the erroneous assumption that the building was forty years old rather than ten years old. There was no opportunity for Owen to cross-examine, the appraisers not being present at the trial.

Owen claims that the circumstances under which the appraisals were prepared and presented provide none of the circumstantial guarantees of trustworthiness which are normally required to justify an exception to the hearsay rule. We agree.

[Citations omitted.]

The prejudice inherent in the admission of such hearsay evidence is readily apparent. It is even questionable, although we need not decide, that the evidence qualifies as a "record of a regularly conducted activity."

Therefore, even if Burn had the legal right to challenge the efficacy of the judgment in question, the entire evidentiary basis of his challenge was inadmissible hearsay. The trial court and the Court of Appeals were in error in holding otherwise.

(3) Owen's third issue on appeal is that the two lower courts were in error in failing to hold that Owen's motion for judgment n.o.v. should have been granted, and was in error in giving the same relief to Burn. We agree. The issues as to Burn are heretofore set forth. There is no rational basis to support the $3,500.00 verdict awarded by the jury. Furthermore, as to Burn's liability and the amount of $26,000.00 as the damages suffered by Owen there are no issues of material fact disclosed by the record.

In a case such as this where the evidence on an issue of fact is undisputed, and the inferences to be drawn therefrom are plain and not open to doubt by reasonable men, the issue is no longer one of fact to be submitted to the jury, but becomes a question of law. If reasonable minds cannot differ, then a directed verdict is not only proper but the court has a duty to direct a verdict.

We have no hesitancy in holding that reasonable minds could not differ as to the liability of Burn or as to the amount of damages, since there literally is no evidence disputing either of these factual issues. The same holding pertains to the wholly unsubstantiated award of damages in the verdict of the jury.

It necessarily follows that we dismiss the cross-appeal of Burn, reverse the Court of Appeals and the trial court on issues above indicated, affirm the Court of Appeals' decision ordering that the award to Owen of $3,500.00 be set aside, and direct that judgment be entered, notwithstanding the verdict, awarding Owen $26,000.00 in damages plus his costs.

IT IS SO ORDERED.

McMANUS, C.J., and SOSA and PAYNE, J.J., concur.

INTRODUCTION TO CASE NUMBER TWO

In the next case, we have the opportunity to see how criminal law can become blended with innkeeping law. Note what the court had to say about the accused being a transient guest and the importance of that decision to this man's freedom. This also points out the importance of statutory terminology to the outcome of a case. The case raises warnings. After this decision, the accused has a good cause of action against the inn for injury to his name. The defendant is anonymous in the case style and probably was a person under the age of majority.

STATE OF CONNECTICUT V. ANONYMOUS[3]

DAVID M. SHEA, Judge.

The defendant was found guilty by the court of larceny in the third degree by theft of services in violation of General Statutes §53a-124.[4] Although the defendant filed twelve assignments of error, he has abandoned all except that relating to the failure of the court to warn him adequately about the hazards in his decision to act as his own attorney at the trial and that relating to the conclusion of guilt reached by the trial court upon the evidence. Since our resolution of the latter is dispositive of the appeal, we need not consider the former issue.

General Statutes §53a-119(7) provides, in pertinent part: "A person is guilty of theft of services when: (1) With intent to avoid payment . . . for services rendered to him as a transient guest at a hotel, motel, inn, tourist cabin, rooming house or comparable establishment, he avoids such payment by unjustifiable failure or refusal to pay, by stealth, or by any misrepresentation of fact which he knows to be false. . . ." The question which is decisive of this appeal is whether there was sufficient evidence that the defendant was a "transient guest" within the meaning of this statute.

There was testimony that the defendant rented an efficiency apartment at a motel on a weekly basis for four weeks. The efficiency apartments of the motel were not rented on a daily basis, as were the regular motel rooms. They were provided with cooking facilities and did not receive maid service, unlike the other units. There was no provision for renting the efficiency apartments for a period of less than one week. The rent of $58.35 per week was payable in advance on the first day of each weekly period. The defendant paid the rent as it fell due each week. On the day when the next weekly payment was due and was not made, the room of the defendant was checked and some of his belongings were still in the room. Two days later a woman came to the motel, removed the remaining property of the defendant and left the key at the motel office. The next day the complainant telephoned the defendant at an address which was obtained from his room registration card and informed him that he owed the rent for one week. The defendant claimed that he had vacated his motel room and was not responsible for rent for an additional week.

Who Is a "Guest" at Law?

It is fundamental that the state had the burden of proving every element of the offense charged beyond a reasonable doubt. *State v. Brown*, 163 Conn. 52, 64, 301 A.2d 547. Proof that the defendant was a "transient guest" at the motel was essential for a conviction under the statute. The word "transient" means "[a] person passing through a place or staying there only temporarily." *Ballentine's Law Dictionary*, p. 1293 (3d Ed.). "To be a guest of an inn or hotel it is essential, at least at common law, that the person should be a transient, that is, that he should come to the inn for a more or less temporary stay, for if he comes on a permanent basis he will be deemed a boarder or lodger rather than a guest." 43 C.J.S. Innkeepers §3, p. 1140. Although it has been said that a guest must be a traveler, that is meant in a broad sense to include anyone away from home who enjoys the same accommodations which are offered to travelers. *Walling v. Potter*, 35 Conn. 183, 185. The length of stay, the existence of a special contract for the room, the fact that a person has another abode and the extent to which he has made the room his home for the time being are material circumstances in determining whether the relationship is that of a guest or a lodger. 43 *C.J.S., supra*, p. 1138.

The defendant, who acted as his own counsel,[5] never raised any claim that he was not a "transient guest." It was essential, nevertheless, that the evidence establish beyond a reasonable doubt that he had that status. That standard has not been met in this case. The testimony bearing upon this issue indicates that the defendant may have been a roomer rather than a "transient guest." Apparently he was not a traveler in the literal sense. The rental arrangement and the nature of the accommodations differed from those pertaining to the regular motel rooms. The duration of the occupancy was not so brief as to justify a conclusion that it was merely temporary in character. Whether the defendant intended the room to be a more or less permanent residence or whether he had a home elsewhere are questions unanswered by the testimony. In sum, there is insufficient evidence to support a conclusion that the defendant was a "transient guest."

There is error, the judgment is set aside, and the case is remanded with directions to render a judgment of not guilty.

In the opinion PARKSKEY and SPONZO, J.J., concurred.

QUESTIONS

1. Give examples of "substantive" law and "procedural" law.
2. What docs a "cause of action" mean?
3. Explain why a contract has to be voluntary.
4. Give five examples of personal property and five of real property.
5. Historically, tort grew out of crime. Explain why.
6. Give an example of negligence not mentioned in this chapter.
7. What did "no writ, no remedy" mean 900 years ago?
8. In the Owen case, in this chapter, why did the court set aside the verdict of $3,500?
9. What does *dehors* mean?
10. Give another example of how "public policy" could have an effect on a court action.

ENDNOTES

1. James R. Silyenat, reviewing *The Tides of Power,* Bob Eckhart and Charles Black, Yale Press, 225 pages.

2. 563 P. 2d 919 (1977).
3. 34 Conn. Sup. 603, 379 A. 2d 1 (1977).
4. Section 53a-124 provides, in pertinent part, that: "(a) A person is guilty of larceny in the third degree when: (1) The value of the property or service exceeds fifty dollars. . . ."
5. Although we do not reach the issue of waiver of counsel, we note that the defendant has raised a serious question of whether his waiver was knowledgeable under the constitutional standards established in *Von Moltke v. Gillies*, 332 U.S. 708, 68 S.Ct. 316, 92 L.Ed. 309.

4

Lawyers, Judges, and Juries: Their Role in HRI Law

I went into the bathroom and splashed some water on my face. I didn't care much for what I saw in the mirror, the haunted-looking countenance of a Holocaust survivor, but I attributed it in part to the neon lighting, which in Vegas hotels tends to age you a month a day. Or perhaps it was just the air of the place. I remember Dawn once telling me that living in Las Vegas was equivalent to being mummified. "After you're here for a while," she said, "if you try to leave, you just crumble into dust. We're like those people in that old movie about Shangri-La, frozen in time." She was right; it's what I call the place's unreality factor.

When the Fat Man Sings, William Murry

OVERVIEW

Our purpose here is to learn enough about the legal role of lawyers, judges, and juries to give us a better understanding of the cases that we will be working with as we go along.

About the only time the typical citizen goes near a courthouse is as a party or witness to litigation, or when called for jury duty. In these instances, which are infrequent, one finds himself or herself in a foreign world of armed guards, court reporters, upset jurors, and in an arena where the watchwords are "tort," *habeas corpus*, "depositions," "cross examination," and countless other unusual words. There is nothing comparable to it in our society and

COUNTY COURTHOUSE, Brookfield, Missouri.

thus no way to prepare oneself for it. It has just not been part of our lives nor have we been taught very much about it.

This is all unfortunate, of course, because what happens in our courts plays a material part in the regulation of our businesses and society itself. The courts shape the form of our lives and this is especially true in all businesses, including the HRI industry.

As lawyers, judges, and juries go about their legal business, the law takes on a viable substance that is of concern to the HRI industry. The industry has become a target of the legal profession, as we have stated before, and mismanagement that leads to loss or injury to guests, patrons, and third parties can trigger the legal process against them.

The cases are brought under the American "adversary process," which means that for every lawyer who would seek money damages from an HRI component, there is another who would just as forcibly deny that recovery. That brings the judges and juries into the picture as these disputes go to court for resolution. This means that there are different points of view in the legal process. The plaintiff's (the party bringing the suit) lawyer sees things one way, the defense lawyer another. Quite frequently the judge disagrees with both, and what juries do in court is almost always unpredictable.

The interplay of the three–judge, jury, and lawyers–is a meshing of interests, and the results are often unsatisfactory. Such results are more often than not a detriment to the HRI facility involved. Let's first learn something about lawyers.

LAWYERS

> Money is a subject Solomon tries to avoid. He's made it, sure. He and his wife Lilli Ann live on the edge of Beverly Hills. They're comfortable.
>
> "If I wanted to make millions," Max says, "I would have gone into civil law. If I were rich, I'd refuse to die."
>
> Not that Max worked for nothing. When he asked for a trial continuance by saying "My material witness, Mr. Green, did not show up," the judges understood and granted the delay. It meant that Max hadn't been paid.
>
> —From "It Takes Style, Flare to Defend the Folks on Life's Shady Side," *Las Vegas Review Journal*, November 15, 1981, 15D.

A lawyer is a person who is learned in the law: ". . . who for fee or reward, prosecutes or defends causes in courts of records or other judicial tribunals of the United States, or of any of the states, or whose business it is to give legal advice in relation to any cause or matter whatever."[1] Thus we see at the outset that lawyers function both in and out of court. In England, lawyers are divided into solicitors and barristers. The former confine their legal activities to their offices and are rarely seen in court. The latter specialize in trial work.

While there is no such formal distinction in the United States, as a practical matter we have "office lawyers" and we have "trial lawyers." Many of our 600,000 plus lawyers engage in both activities—others specialize in office consultation and some in trial work. A few have gained national reputations for criminal defense work. Some are recognized for their abilities in airline tort work.

About one-half of the American lawyers belong to the American Bar Association (ABA), and all practicing lawyers are members of their state-bar associations. In addition, all states have local bar associations. Through these organizations, standards of conduct are established and rules of court procedure are developed. Thus, practicing lawyers tend to be a close-knit group and are quite liberal in their beliefs and attitudes. In addition, they tend to be a highly intelligent group collectively, although they have not been spared criticism in the past or at the present time.

Legal Profession Under Fire

In recent years, the profession has been subjected to closer scrutiny than ever before by the public as well as by the courts. For example, the U.S. Supreme Court in *Goldfarb v. Virginia State Bar*, ruled that fee schedules used by local bar associations are a form of price fixing and are thus illegal.[2] In addition, many of the practices of the profession have been successfully challenged, and this can be expected to continue in the future. Although there has been considerable publicity directed toward lawyers who have plundered estates, or who have been held to be incompetent in the courts, the vast majority of American lawyers are intelligent, honest, hard-working men and women, who give value for the fees that they are paid.

Rules of Professional Conduct

While there have been other codes of conduct for lawyers, the primary one is the Rules of Professional Conduct. Set forth in the RPC are detailed guidelines establishing standards of conduct for lawyers. While the RPC is a product of the ABA, which represents only about 50 percent of American lawyers, it is understood that all lawyers must comply with its standards. The supreme courts of most of our states have approved the RPC, in effect making it state law. Some states have adopted the Code of Professional Responsibility which is based on the Canons of Ethics. Failure to so comply with the rules can result in disciplinary action, such as a reprimand, or, in severe cases, disbarment of the offending lawyer.

It is next important to become acquainted with the services that the legal profession provides. Lawyers provide services in their offices, in the courts, and before administrative agencies.

SERVICES OF LAWYERS

The greatest part of a practicing attorney's time is spent in the office. Consulting touches all phases of business activities and is perhaps the most important service that the legal profession can provide. Proper legal advice, timely sought and wisely given, can avoid the necessity of going to court.

Lawyers who consult with business persons will admit that the necessity of using the courts often means that something went wrong along the line. Of course, if one's business is sued, it is necessary to use lawyers for defensive purposes. As part of the court function, lawyers will prepare the papers needed to start and defend lawsuits; research and prepare trial briefs; develop evidence to be produced at trial; present and defend cases before judges and juries; and file appeals if they are warranted.

Related to court work is the handling of matters before administrative agencies. Perhaps an inn has been cited for a violation of the Occupational Safety and Health Act (OSHA), or for a violation of the Equal Employment Opportunity Act (EEOA) that the client intends to contest, or wishes to be granted a liquor-dispenser permit.

The lawyer will prepare the forms and see that they are filed within the required time. At appropriate times, testimony may be required before the agency. These proceedings are similar to court proceedings. Records are made, transcripts are prepared, and appeals are taken as required. As a general rule, administrative procedures are more informal than court proceedings. The rules of evidence do not apply and paper work is carried out by the exchange of notices and letters. It is the practice of administrative agencies to issue their rulings in opinion form, in which the findings of fact and the conclusions of law are set forth. A good example of this is seen in the Markantonatos case in Chapter 2.

PARALEGAL MOVEMENT

There has been a growing tendency in recent years to delegate "lawyer-like" duties to legal assistants. These persons are *not secretaries* but rather persons who have been trained to handle legal matters. They are frequently business-trained persons who have no formal legal training. Instead, they have degrees from paralegal schools or they are provided special training by the law firms. They are being used to make investigations, to prepare corporate minutes and resolutions, to handle filing work in the courts, and to do legal matters that have become a drain on the lawyers' time. They do not try cases, except in limited situations. In California, for example, paralegals are permitted to make limited court appearances.

Some of the paralegal programs being offered at the universities require a candidate to have completed an undergraduate degree in some other program.

Leaving paralegals, we want to learn something about legal fees, because one who contemplates the use of legal services will naturally be interested in what those services are going to cost.

FEES

Before the Goldfarb case, it was a practice for local bar associations to publish and circulate "minimum bar fee schedules." The fees set forth were the *least* that could be charged for the services listed. For example, a name change might be listed at $200, a will at $100, and a deed at $100. Now, because of the Goldfarb decision, lawyers charge what they feel clients will bear, which is often *higher*

A FORMER HOTEL at Green River, Colorado, now a travel center.

than the minimum fees. However, a vestige of the minimum fees remain in "flat fees."

Flat Fees

In all bar associations, certain legal services become so standardized that lawyers tend to charge a flat fee for them. This is true in adoption, divorce, and title-search fees. These fees often remain uniform in spite of abolition of the fee schedules.

As another way of charging fees, many lawyers work on an hourly basis.

Hourly Fees

Many lawyers and legal firms provide legal services on a straight hourly rate basis. At appropriate times, the hours are billed at a rate that may begin at $50 per hour or may exceed $250 per hour. Surprisingly enough, this is often the cheapest way that legal services can be provided. The client can obtain a constant stream of lawyer contact, split into a series of relatively short time periods, that may add up to only an hour or two. Administrative matters, such as OSHA or EEOC complaints, or worker's compensation matters, are usually best handled on an hourly basis.

Some business persons, however, prefer to place lawyers on "retainers."

Retainers

A "retainer" is the "act of a client in employing his attorney or counsel, and also denotes the fee which the client pays when he retains the lawyer to work for him, and thereby prevents him from acting for his adversary."[3] Retainers can be general or special.

General Retainers

A "general retainer" gives one the right to expect legal services when requested. It binds the one retained not to take a fee from another that would be contrary to that retainer.[4]

Special Retainers

A "special retainer" is an engagement for a designated purpose, such as to defend one on a criminal charge.[5]

Annual general retainers may run into the hundreds of thousands of dollars, or be as low as $100 in small-business situations. Their value is in gaining the assurance that the services of a particular lawyer or firm will be available if needed. If services are provided, the client will pay for services beyond the amount of the retainer. In criminal defense work, it is the practice for a retainer to be paid at the outset.

Many legal fees are based upon the "contingency of recovery."

Contingent Fees

One of the more spectacular arrangements between attorneys and their clients for the payment of legal fees is found in the agreement to pay fees out of future recoveries. Such arrangements pose a serious legal threat to the HRI industry, since they enable the poorest member of the traveling public to acquire the services of the best in plaintiff's counsel.

These arrangements are encountered most frequently in tort (negligence) cases but are seen from time to time in contract actions. They are *not* used in criminal cases since this would violate public policy. For example, a court will not allow a lawyer to recover a percentage of the wealth of a client whom that lawyer successfully defends in a murder trial. Contingent fees are otherwise permitted by the Rules of Professional Conduct.

Without contingent fees, lawyers would require retainers which many litigants could not afford to advance. Contingent fees have led to some spectacular results. In the MGM fire case, recoveries reached $138 million. This means that the lawyers took at least $41 million of that to their banks.

One final way in which legal fees can be charged and paid is by the use of "prepaid legal service plans." Such plans are relatively new and provide a means by which a wage earner can obtain legal services much like wealthier persons who have the means to retain counsel of their choice.

Prepaid Plans

These plans are a product of the 1970s. When they are in operation, covered employees contribute so much per hour, week, or month toward a prepaid legal service plan. This is matched by employer contributions. The plan is administered by a board of trustees usually made up of company employees elected for that purpose.

To implement these plans, prearrangements are made with lawyers in "closed plans" or the general bar in "open plans." The scope of the services available per year are spelled out, such as six hours of office consultation, one will, one contested court action. As an employee draws upon his or her plan, the fees are paid out of the fund. Some plans have deductibles. These plans have found wide acceptance and can now be bargained for collectively just as other fringe benefits.

Leaving the lawyers (or attorneys), we come to the person who, while often a lawyer, is given by law a position of power and consequent respect that rivals the governors of our states and even the president of our nation: the judge.

JUDGES

> There once was a judge who preferred to use a silver dollar instead of a gavel. When a lawyer asked him why, the judge explained that it was simple.
>
> "Note that clear, metallic ring," the judge said, rapping the dollar on the bench. "Restores order every time. And it's the first dol-

lar I ever earned. Besides," the judge continued, flipping the coin in the air, "sometimes I have to make a decision."

—Harry Rodenberry, quoted by Judy Wells Martin in Jacksonville *Florida Times: Union*

Function of Judges

The primary function of judges is to decide questions of law. An example would be determining what statutes apply to the inn case at hand. Judges might be thought of as "secondary innkeepers" in that their decisions provide guidelines that must be followed at the inns in the future.

Orders and Judgments

While judges can never bring matters before themselves by unilateral action, once a controversy is there, they can hold hearings, issue orders, and render judgments.

When a court enters an "order" directing that something be done, that order must be obeyed. Failure to obey court orders permits judges to issue contempt citations in both legal and equitable matters. This can lead to a fine or imprisonment, or both. This power gives our courts "teeth" or power over the matters that come before them.

Other orders issued by the courts are routine, such as those that overrule motions, those that permit papers and motions to be filed in the case, and many others. The nature of the judgment must be understood.

A "judgment" has been defined as "the official and authentic decisions of a court of justice upon the respective rights and claims of the parties to an action or suit therein litigated and submitted to its determination."[6] "The conclusion (of the judge) is a syllogism having for its major and minor premises issues raised by the pleadings and the proofs thereon."[7]

Forms of Judgments

Various forms of judgments are found in our courts, and a few will be mentioned. A "confession of judgment" means that one admits the truth of the charges against her or him. A "consent judgment" is one for which the parties have agreed upon terms. A "default judgment" is one that is entered by the court when one of the parties fails to defend. A "final judgment" puts an end to a lawsuit; an "interlocutory judgment" is of a preliminary nature with something yet to be done in the court.

Following are some terms that relate to judgments in court.

Judgment Terms

A "judgment book" is where judgments are recorded and indexed. A "judgment debtor" is one who has had judgment entered against him or her. A "judgment creditor" is the one to whom the judgment debt is owed. Judgments can be *in personam*—against the person, or *in rem*—against a particular thing or subject matter. The latter would take the form of a "judgment lien" against the property once the judgment is placed on record.

Turning from forms and terms of judgments, it is important to look at qualifications of judges and the legal reasoning applied by them in the courts.

Qualifications of Judges

The qualifications of judges will vary from state to state, but most state constitutions set minimum age and residency requirements. In most states it is *not* a requirement that judges be lawyers. At the federal level, since judges must be nominated by the President and confirmed by the U.S. Senate, it is mandatory that they be lawyers.

Schools of Thought

Some judges are influenced by historical thought and give weight to the evolutionary process of ideas and prior case decisions. They tend to be influenced by custom and prior usages, and frequently do *not* exercise independent judgment.

Other judges are "natural-law" thinkers. Such a judge views humanity as a grouping of persons who seek ideal rights and justice and are concerned about "good" and "evil." Law rests on reason and is something more than what humans made as law. The latter may be held by such a thinker to be unfair, unjust, or unreasonable. One who thinks this way may find ways to circumvent laws when rendering decisions.

An "analytical thinker" views law as something that is made up of those rules and principles that the *state* feels is mandatory for its citizens—even if those rules may seem unjust or unreasonable to the judge. For one influenced by this type of thinking, there is a need for certainty, and law is considered to be a series of commands or orders from the state. Under such thinking, the less control by law, the wider latitude those in business have in which to conduct their affairs. If the state does not consider certain acts to be unjust, the judge will not interfere with those acts. Such judges often say, "If that should be the law, then it is for the legislature to say so, not me."

Other judges are "sociological thinkers." Law to them is a means to an end–it is a matter of striking a balance between conflicting interests. Law thus becomes a generalization and is based on experience.

Many judges are, of course, affected by different combinations of the above "schools of legal thought" as different facts are confronted by them in different cases. This tells us that the "law" can be what a judge says it should be. In practice, some judges become identified with certain forms of thinking, and are sought by some litigants for that reason. Other litigants avoid certain judges for the same reason.

Leaving judges, a few words are in order about the companion of the judges in our courts: the jury.

JURIES

The word *jurata* in old English law referred to those persons chosen by their peers to hear and decide questions of fact in court. After being sworn to "truly try the facts," they would hear evidence from all parties involved and then "declare the truth" of the matter before them. The term "jury" today includes grand juries, trial or petit juries, coroner's juries, and others.

A jury is selected by the parties to the suit and, at common law, was made up of twelve persons. Today the six-person jury is used in Florida and in the federal courts in civil cases.

Trial by Jury

This phrase means a trial by the designated number of " . . . competent men and women, disinterested and impartial, not of kin, nor personal dependents of either of the parties, having their homes within the jurisdictional limits of the court, drawn and selected by officers free from all bias in favor of or against either party, duly empaneled and sworn to render a true verdict according to the law and the evidence."[8] These are the trial juries as contrasted to the grand juries, and their function is to decide "questions of fact"—not law. The latter is reserved for the judges.

Grand Juries

A grand jury is one that hears preliminary evidence in a pending criminal case and must decide if "probable cause" has been produced before it that the person or business entity has committed a crime. If the grand jury so believes, it can return a "true bill," commonly known as an "indictment." These juries do not decide questions of fact for that is the function of the trial jury.

Trial Juries in Court

Once trial juries are selected, empaneled, and sworn, they will hear the evidence as it is given to them by the testimony of witnesses. They will examine photos and other documents that the judge allows to "come into evidence."

Fact Finders

The role of our trial or petit juries as "finders of fact" presents an interesting situation. If A claims that facts UV&W control the oral contract that he has entered into with B, but if B claims that facts XY&Z control, then a finding must be made of the "true facts." This is done by the presentation of evidence to the jury under the judge's guidelines. Once the evidence is in (meaning that it has been heard by the jury), the judge will issue his or her "instructions" or "charge" to the jury.

Following are two instructions given in a restaurant and motel case, along with their citations.

HRI Court Instructions

> "The duty of the owner or operator of a business that is open to the public is to exercise reasonable care in keeping that part of the sidewalk in proper condition for the passage of customers rightfully using it."
>
> The appeals court approved the trial judges instruction, concluding: "The duty of reasonable care owed by an inviter to an invitee should in no way be diminished by the presence of natural

accumulations of ice and snow . . . " *Poe v. Tate*, 315 N.E. 2d 392 (Indiana, 1974).

"It was the duty of the (inn) not only to exercise reasonable care to keep this walkway free from stones that might cause one using it to fall, but it was also their duty to provide sufficient light to enable guests to use the walkway in safety. (The motel's) failure to sufficiently illuminate the walkway was not excused by the fact that the summer season at Myrtle Beach had not commenced nor by the fact that the Bowlings were the only guests at that time. . . . It is true that there is no evidence that (the motel) knew of the presence of the stone on which Bowling twisted his ankle on the walkway. . . . However, (the motel's) negligence was predicated, not solely on the presence of the stone on the walkway, but also on the breach of their duty to provide sufficient illumination to enable a guest to use the walkway in safety. . . ." *Bowling v. Lewis*, 261 F. 2d 311 (South Carolina, 1958).

On appeal by the losing party, if the upper court (appellate court) believes from the record brought before it that the case was presented fairly and impartially to the jury, the upper court will seldom set aside that verdict or amend it.

Thus the higher court gives recognition to the work done by the trial jury. On the other hand, if the trial jury is misled or makes errors of its own, the upper courts have a duty to make necessary adjustments leading to justice in the matter at hand.

QUESTIONS

1. Do American lawyers have anything in their legal system that compares to England's barristers and solicitors?
2. Why is the document, Rules of Professional Conduct, a new document rather than a revised one?
3. True or False. Paralegals are trained to make legal decisions on their own.
4. Give an example of a special retainer; a general retainer.
5. Give one reason why a plaintiff might complain about a contingent-fee arrangement.
6. Give an example of how one could become a "judgment debtor."
7. Distinguish a grand from a petit jury.
8. True or False. Trial juries are triers of the law, not the facts.

9. Why do appellate courts tend to refuse to meddle with jury verdicts in the absence of error?

ENDNOTES

1. Act of July 13, 1866, sec. 9, 14 St. at Large 121.
2. *Goldfarb v. Virginia State Bar,* 421 U.S. 773 (1975).
3. *Bright v. Turner,* 205 Ky. 188, 265 S.W. 627, 628.
4. *Rhode Island Exch. Bank v. Hawkins,* 6 R.I. 206.
5. *Agnew v. Wolden,* 84 Ala. 502, 4 So. 672.
6. *Bullock v. Bullock,* 52 N.J. Eq. 561, 30 A. 676, 27 L.R.A. 216.
7. *Barlow v. Scott,* Mo. Sup., 85 S.W. 2d 504, 517.
8. *Shafer Motor Freight Service,* 4 N.Y.S. 2d 526, 167 Misc. 681.

5

HRI Cases and Statutes: How They Are Applied in Court

Pub signs have a very long pedigree, going back to the days of Pompeii, when pictorial signs were first used, one of the earliest being that of the chequer board, as I have mentioned previously. Furthermore, inn signs were a necessary form of identification in an age when most people were illiterate. Excavations at Pompeii have brought to light signs appropriate to various trades: a goat was the sign for a dairy, a mule the sign for a mill or baker, and two men carrying a large amphora of wine was the sign for the vintner.

The first inn sign noted in England was the ale stake–a long pole protruding from the front of the house. Later, the simple stake was improved to include a bush and, still later, a sign. Early signs were simply painted on a board and suspended from the front of the house. Later they were hung from a sign post set up in the street.[1]

OVERVIEW

We want to learn more about legal liability and what it can mean when it arises. In this chapter we will examine a state statute and see what happened when that law became involved in two federal court actions. We will then look at a guest-death case brought against an inn under common-law principles.

As each cause of action goes into our judicial system, it becomes known as a "case" or lawsuit. A court has said that " . . . the word 'case' or 'cause' means a judicial proceeding for the determination of a controversy between parties wherein rights are enforced or

POSTVILLE COURTHOUSE, Lincoln, Illinois. Abe Lincoln practiced law near here.

protected, or wrongs are prevented or redressed."[2] The amount in controversy is not always a determinative factor and this should be understood. Our American courts will give the same attention to the small cases as they will to the large.

The phrase "cases and controversies" is found in the U. S. Constitution. It means ". . . controversy of a justiciable nature, excluding advisory decrees on hypothetical facts."[3] A "case sufficient to go to a jury" is one that ". . . has proceeded upon sufficient proof to that stage where it must be submitted to jury and not decided against the state (or other) as a matter of law."[4]

At some trial-court levels, and at the appellate level of most state and all federal courts, case decisions are reduced to typed form. Afterward, these decisions are placed into printed volumes, as will be explained in a moment. Once in printed form, they are available to the public and wide use is made of them by law schools, hotel schools, lawyers, agencies, judges, and others. Thus the "case study" of law is one that makes use of the decisions found in printed volumes: a "reporter system."

REPORTER SYSTEM

West Publishing Company has divided the United States into "reporter regions." This company accumulates the decisions from all appeals courts in these regions and places them in bound volumes. The reporter areas are as follows:

ATLANTIC (A.)

Connecticut, Delaware, District of Columbia, Maine, Maryland, New Hampshire, New Jersey, Pennsylvania, Rhode Island, and Vermont.

NORTHEASTERN (N.E.)

Illinois, Indiana, Massachusetts, New York, and Ohio.

NORTHWESTERN (N.W.)

Iowa, Michigan, Minnesota, Nebraska, North Dakota, South Dakota, and Wisconsin.

PACIFIC (P.)

Alaska, Arizona, California, Colorado, Hawaii, Idaho, Kansas, Montana, Nevada, New Mexico, Oklahoma, Oregon, Utah, Washington, and Wyoming.

SOUTHEASTERN (S.E.)

Georgia, North Carolina, South Carolina, Virginia, and West Virginia.

SOUTHWESTERN (S.W.)

Arkansas, Kentucky, Missouri, Tennessee, and Texas.

SOUTHERN (SO.)

Alabama, Florida, Louisiana, and Mississippi.

In addition, New York has the *New York Supplement* (NYS) and California the *California Reporter* (Cal. Rep.) These extra reporters were created because of the large volume of litigation carried out in those states.

Federal Reporters

At the federal level are found the *Federal Supplement* (F. Supp) that reports some, but not all, of the decisions of the federal district courts; the *Federal Reporter* which reports cases in the U.S. Courts of Appeal, and the *Supreme Court Reporter*, whose name tells us what cases it contains.

To make use of this immense body of cases, which grows larger each day, one must understand something about legal research.

LEGAL RESEARCH

As one begins to search for relevant cases, it is necessary to identify areas in which the search should be conducted. This is done by the use of the "TAP" rule: "things," "acts," and "places." To illustrate, A is injured by a dog kept in an adjoining room of an inn. A seeks legal advice and the lawyer wants to know if the innkeeper is liable. "Things" include "pets," "animals," "injury to inn guests," and others. "Acts" include "animals in inn rooms," "travel," "boarding of animals," "innkeepers liability," and others. "Places" include "motels," "hotels," "inns," and "lodging facilities." Armed with these terms, the lawyer can use the indexes to cases, reporters, and other legal treatises to find cases and thus establish the extent of legal liability–if any, as developed by prior case law. Also, appropriate statutory law will be researched. The latter is found in the state codes and "annotations" that accompany each statute. The latter are citations to cases that have been decided under court decisions. Through this process, items may be found that lead to different sources. Legal research is one of the arts of the legal profession. We need to understand how to read case citations.

A Case Citation Example

Examine the following case citation: *Gray v. Zurick Hotel Co.*, 65 Cal. 2d 263, 419 P. 2d 168, 54 Cal. Rep. 104 (1966).

The title tells us the names of the parties to the lawsuit. It does *not* tell us who was the plaintiff or defendant since the names may be reversed, depending upon who takes the appeal. The case can be found in the *California Reports,* Second Series, volume 65, beginning on page 263. It can also be found in the *Pacific Reporter,* Second Series, volume 419 beginning on page 168, as well as in the *California Reporter,* volume 54 beginning on page 104. The case was decided in 1966.

Our Use of Cases

In the following and previous chapters, "cases" have been inserted to illustrate points and should be read carefully. To assist in understanding them, it is good policy to create a "case brief" for each. An example follows.

Case Briefs

As each case is encountered, "brief" it, answering the following questions:

1. What was the citation of the case?
2. What state or federal court was it decided in?
3. Briefly state the facts of the case—how or why did it get into court?
4. What was the decision of the court?
5. How could this decision be summarized so it could be stated as a point of law in one short sentence?

In addition to cases, we will work with statutes in the coming chapters.

STATUTES

To illustrate what a statute looks like, and to see how some of them are used in the lodging industry, examine Figure 5.1.

Next, let's find out something about the place where cases originate—the courts.

COURTS

A "court" has been defined as " . . . a tribunal officially assembled under authority of law at the appropriate time and place for the administration of justice"[5]; " . . . an agency of the sovereign created by it directly or indirectly under its authority, consisting of one or more officers, established and maintained for the purpose of hearing and determining issues of law and fact regarding legal rights and the alleged violations thereof, and of applying the sanctions of law, authorized to exercise its powers in due course of law at times and places previously determined by lawful authority."[6] A characteristic of courts that must be understood is that "it is a passive forum for adjusting disputes and has no power to investigate facts or to initiate proceedings."[7] It must wait until "justiciable controversies" are brought before it by lawyers and their clients.

Classifications

Courts can be "courts of record" or "not of record." In the former, court reporters record testimony and proceedings and later transcribe this testimony into "transcripts" for use in the appeal process where appeals are taken. Courts "not of record" do not record proceedings.

Courts can be "superior" or "inferior," pointing out that some have powers over those below them. Courts can be "civil," and

THE RATE PER DAY OF THIS ROOM

Room No. ______

For 1 Person	__________	For 3 Persons	__________
For 2 Persons	__________	For 4 Persons	__________

NOTICE

Check-Out Time Is 12 Noon
Kindly Notify The Office If Your Departure Will Be Delayed.

CODE OF VIRGINIA

Sec. 35-10—Duties of Inn-Keepers; Limitation of Liability

It shall be the duty of keepers of hotels. inns, and ordinaries to exercise due care and diligence in providing honest servants and employees, and to take every reasonable precaution to protect the person and property of their guests and boarders. No such keeper of hotel, inn or ordinary shall be held liable in a greater sum than three hundred dollars, for the loss of any wearing apparel, baggage or other property not hereinafter mentioned, belonging either to a guest or boarder, when such loss takes place from the room or rooms occupied by said guest or boarder, and no keeper of a hotel, inn or ordinary shall be held liable for any loss by any guest or boarder of jewelry, money or other valuables of like nature belonging to any guest or boarder if such keeper shall have posted in the room or rooms occupied by guests or boarders in a conspicuous place, and in the office of such hotel, inn or ordinary a notice stating that jewelry, money and other valuables of like nature must be deposited in the office of such hotel, inn or ordinary unless such loss shall take place from such office after such deposit is made. The keeper of any such hotel, inn or ordinary shall not be obliged to receive from any one guest for deposit, in such office, any property hereinbefore described, exceeding a total value of five hundred dollars.

Sec. 35-11—Liability Where Guest Failed to Lock or Bolt Doors

If the keeper of such hotel, inn or ordinary shall provide suitable locks or bolts on the doors of the sleeping rooms used by his guests, and suitable fastening on the transoms and windows of said rooms, and shall keep a copy of this and the preceding section conspicuously posted in each of said rooms, together with a notice requiring said guests or boarders to keep said doors locked or bolted, and transoms fastened, and if said guests or boarders fail to lock or bolt said door or doors, or to fasten said windows and transoms, then the said keeper of such hotel, inn or ordinary, shall not be liable for any property taken from such room or rooms in consequence of such failure on the part of such guest or boarder; but the burden of proof shall be upon such keeper to show that he has complied with the provisions of this section, and that such guest or guests have failed to comply with these requirements. Nothing in this section shall be construed to in any wise exempt the keeper, or keepers, of hotels, inns and ordinaries from being liable for the value of any property of guests taken or stolen from any room therein by any employee or agent of said keeper or keepers.

FIGURE 5.1

thus handle civil matters, and others, "criminal." Some are "equity" courts and others "law" courts. In smaller, rural jurisdictions, one court may have many of these classifications. There are many specialized courts such as courts of admiralty, bankruptcy, claims, and others.

As to the names by which our top state courts are known, there are similarities yet differences. Maine calls its top state court the "Supreme Judicial Court"; Massachusetts, the "Full Court of the Supreme Judicial Court"; Maryland, the "Court of Appeals"; New York, the "Court of Appeals"; and West Virginia the "Supreme Court of Appeals." All other states call their top court the "Supreme Court." Texas and Oklahoma also have a Court of Criminal Appeals at the top of their system.

The Delaware Supreme Court has three members, as does the Oklahoma Court of Criminal Appeals. The Connecticut Supreme Court has six members. Seven state supreme courts have nine members; eighteen have five members and twenty-two have seven members.

Turning from our examination of lawyers, judges, and the courts, let's take a look at two case situations. The first involves a statute in Nevada that limits innkeepers' liability for the loss of property and money and valuables at inns in that state.

The second case involves the death of a guest at an inn in North Carolina.

NEVADA STATUTE

The statute, involved in the first situation, reads as follows:

> 651.010 Civil liability of innkeepers limited.
>
> 1. No owner or keeper of any hotel, inn, motel, motor court, boardinghouse or lodginghouse in this state is civilly liable for the theft, loss, damage or destruction of any property left in the room of any guest of such an establishment because of theft, burglary, fire or otherwise, in the absence of gross neglect by the owner or keeper.
>
> 2. If an owner or keeper of any hotel, inn, motel, motor court, boardinghouse or lodginghouse in this state provides a fireproof safe or vault in which guests may deposit property for safekeeping, and notice of this service is personally given to a guest or posted in the office and the guest's room, the owner or keeper is not liable for the theft, loss, damage or destruction of any property which is not offered for deposit in the safe or vault by a guest unless the owner or keeper is grossly negligent. An owner or keeper is not obligated to receive property to deposit for safekeeping which exceeds $750 in value or is of a size which cannot easily fit within the safe or vault.

3. The liability of the owner or keeper under this section does not exceed the sum of $750 for any property of an individual guest, unless the owner or keeper receives the property for deposit for safekeeping and consents to assume a liability greater than $750 for its theft, loss, damage, or destruction in a written agreement in which the guest specifies the value of the property. [1:256:1953]–(NRS A 1979, 1114)

The following from Volume 2-2 of the *Hotel and Casino Law Letter,* published at the College of Hotel Administration, University of Nevada, Las Vegas, is a summary of two federal cases in which this statute became involved. As it turned out, both courts held that the liability of the hotels in question was limited.

> The "money and valuables" statutes found in all fifty states represent the granting of a legislative grace to innkeepers and replace the harsh common-law rule of strict liability. The state of Nevada has such a law and features of it have been the subject of litigation in the federal courts in Louisiana and New York. The cases involved the Sands Hotel and Desert Palace, Inc. (Caesar's Palace), located near each other on the Strip in Las Vegas.[8]

Would this statute be enforced and deny recovery for loss of money and valuables stolen from Las Vegas hotel rooms? How were appellate courts in two separate parts of the United States going to interpret a law created in Carson City, Nevada?

The Nevada Law

Nevada Revised Statutes, 651.010, as just quoted (enacted originally in 1953), provides, in part, as follows:

> No owner or keeper of any hotel, inn, motel, motor court, or boarding house or lodging house in this state shall be civilly liable after July 1, 1953, for the loss of any property left in the room of any guest of any such establishment by reason of theft, burglary, fire or otherwise, in the absence of gross neglect upon the part of such keeper or owner.

In 1979, this statute was amended and the following paragraph was added:

> If an owner . . . of any hotel . . . provides a fireproof safe or vault in which guests may deposit property for safekeeping, and notice of this service is personally given to a guest or posted in the office and the guest's room, the owner . . . is not liable for the theft . . . of any property which is not offered for deposit in the safe or vault by a guest unless the owner or keeper is grossly negligent.

Two Legal Questions

First, what is the meaning of "left in the room"? Does it mean left in the room while the guests are away from the room, or does it mean valuables left in the room while the guests are, in fact, in the room? In the following two cases, the guests were asleep in their rooms when the valuables were stolen. If the statute does not apply, the common-law rule of strict liability will be in effect, and the innkeepers will be responsible for the value of the stolen valuables.

The second question involves the meaning of "in the absence of gross neglect upon the part of such keeper or owner." Was there negligence on the part of the innkeepers in each case? Was there an absence of gross neglect, or was there gross neglect?

The Cases

In both cases, the guests checked into their hotels with a considerable amount of jewelry. Both hotels maintain safes for the storage of valuables and so informed the guests. Both hotels had notices of the availability of the safes posted at the front office and in the rooms.

On the night of both thefts, jewelry was taken to the rooms. Dead bolts were fastened and the couples retired in the presence of their jewelry. In both cases, however, the dead bolts did not function. The Caesar's Palace maintenance staff was in the process of replacing malfunctioning bolts, but the particular door in question had not yet been repaired. No repair or replacement of bolts had been planned at the Sands Hotel.

The rooms were entered in the early hours of the morning by use of a passkey, and jewelry was stolen while the couples were asleep. One couple, William J. and Simone Levitt, sued in the federal courts in New York, and the other couple, Chris and Sol Owens, sued in the U.S. District Court for the Eastern District of Louisiana.

"Left in the Room" or Not?

In answering this question, the court ruled against the plaintiffs, stating, "We believe that the statute's reference to 'property left in the room of any guest' distinguishes between property left in the room and property given to the hotel for safekeeping, rather than between property left in the room while the guests are out and property that they keep with them while they sleep."

Absence of "Gross Negligence"?

The Nevada courts had construed the phrase "gross negligence" in a previous case. Since federal courts must apply state law in this instance, they adopted the rule of this case which held, "Gross negligence is substantially and appreciably higher in magnitude and more culpable than ordinary negligence. . . ." It is " . . . manifestly a smaller amount of watchfulness and circumspection than the circumstances requires of a prudent man."

The court said, "The issue before us is simply whether the hotel exercised even slight care to insure the safety of its guests' property." Both courts held there was more than ample care in both instances.

Summary

The value of the cases is to be found in guidelines that can be summarized as follows:

1. Comply strictly with the money and valuables and property statutes.
2. Include notification of the availability of safes on the registration forms and on notices in the front office, the guest rooms and in the elevators. Also, tell all guests that the service is available.
3. If guests possess valuables, offer to escort them to and from their rooms when using the front-desk safe.
4. Employ guards in hotel hallways and tell them to report suspicious persons.
5. Take full advantage of the protection offered by the statutes. If the statutes are not strictly followed, a court may hold the common-law rule of strict liability has been revived.

CASE INTRODUCTION

To assist in understanding the case of *Page v. Sloan* that follows, it is helpful to understand what is meant by a "pretrial conference," "stipulations," and "depositions." A *pretrial conference* is a meeting held prior to trial at which the judge and lawyers for both sides will:

1. Attempt to settle the case.
2. Make "stipulations" in order to shorten trial.
3. Take care of other routine matters in order to expedite trial.

Stipulations are agreements by both sides on facts or documents to be used in the trial. For example, if a deed is to be used and both sides stipulate the deed, it can be used in trial without the necessity of calling authenticating witnesses from the county clerk's office.

Depositions are oral statements of witnesses taken under oath. It works this way: The attorney wanting to take the deposition of a witness will serve notice upon opposing counsel. This notice will set the time and place for the deposition. At that time, the deponent (witness) is sworn and the questioning begins. Objections can be made, thus reserving them for later ruling in trial. Cross examination follows direct examination. After the session is completed, the testimony is transcribed (typed) and the original filed in the case file.

If this witness is not able to be at the trial, the deposition can be read to the jury. This is subject, however, to objections raised previously. If a deponent should change his or her testimony later at trial, the deposition can be used to impeach that testimony.

In the following case, the person bringing the suit is the widow of a guest killed at a motel. She brought the suit as the Administratrix CTA—"cum testamento annexo"—"with the will attached." This tells us that her deceased husband had not executed a formal will but had left some document that evidenced his wishes in the event of his death.

The suit was brought in tort to recover for the loss to the estate of the services and earnings of the deceased.

The issue in the case is this: "Were there questions of fact that should have been decided by a jury in the lower court?"

PAGE V. SLOAN[9]

In this case, the plaintiff was the administratrix CTA *(cum testamento annexo)* of the estate of Channing Nelson Page, who was killed on August 29, 1964. The death resulted by the explosion of an 82-gallon electric hot water heater located in a utility room of the Ocean Isle Motel in Brunswick County, North Carolina. She alleged that Mr. Page was a paying guest in said motel which was owned and operated by the defendants as co-partners and that Mr. Page was assigned a corner room adjoining the utility room which contained the motel's hot water heater. This electric hot water heater was installed, used, and operated by defendants for the purpose of furnishing hot water to the various guest rooms of the Ocean Isle Motel. She alleged that the explosion of the electric hot water heater was the direct and proximate cause of the death of Page and that at all times the said water heater was in the exclusive possession and control of the defendants. She further alleged that the explosion of said electric hot water heater was caused by, or due to, the actionable negligence of the defendants.

Defendants answered admitting allegations of residence, the death of Channing Nelson Page, their ownership and operation of Ocean Isle Motel, their acceptance of Page as a paying guest and assigning him a corner room adjoining the utility room containing the electric hot water heater, the water heater serving the function of furnishing hot water to various guest rooms in the said motel, and said electric hot water heater exploding at the alleged time and place. However, the defendants specifically denied negligence on their part.

Pursuant to the provisions of Rule 16 of the Rules of Civil Procedure and Rule 7, General Rules of Practice in the Superior and District Courts, a final pretrial conference was held in this action on the 7th day of January, 1971. It was stipulated that all the parties were properly before the court, and that the court had jurisdiction over the parties and the subject matter. The parties stipulated and agreed with respect to the following salient facts:

* * * * * * * * * * * * *

"(i) This hot water heater unit installed by Shallotte Hardware Company at Ocean Isle Motel remained in operation and use in the new units at that place from approximately April, 1962, until the explosion in August, 1964.

* * * * * * * * * * * * *

"(k) In June or July, 1964, George Sloan and Rea Sloan had Olaf Thorsen check the hot water unit here in question due to a complaint of no hot water or insufficient hot water by motel guests. Olaf Thorsen removed the lower heating element of the water heater and obtained a replacement from Shallotte Hardware Company. The original heating element was of the size of 2500 watts. After the explosion it was determined that the lower heating element in the heater at the time of the explosion was an element of 4500 watt size.

"(l) The water heater in question was rated by an inscription on a plate attached thereto at 3000 watts for the upper element, at 2500 watts for the lower element, and at 3000 watts maximum.

* * * * * * * * * * * * *

"(p) Olaf Thorsen was a licensed plumber in Brunswick County, North Carolina.

* * * * * * * * * * * * *

"(r) The 82 gallon electric hot water heater was manufactured by State Stove and Manufacturing Company and installed in the Ocean Isle Motel by Shallotte Hardware Company and worked on by Olaf Thorsen and was the hot water heater which exploded in the utility room adjacent to the motel room occupied by Channing Nelson Page.

* * * * * * * * * * * * *

"(s) There was no inspection of the installation of the hot water heater at the time of its installation in 1962 by the N. C. Department of Labor Boiler Inspection Division as required by North Carolina General Statutes.

The installation was inspected by the Brunswick County inspector who was not with the Department of Labor."

* * * * * * * * * * * *

In addition to the foregoing stipulations, several depositions were considered by the trial judge at the hearing on motion for summary judgment. These depositions, which were considered by consent, included depositions of each of the defendants, the deposition of Olaf Thorsen (the plumber-repairman), and the depositions of each of the three partners in Shallotte Hardware (the original installer of defendants' electric hot water heater).

The deposition of Olaf Thorsen tends to show that he is a licensed plumber, and that he has no license or experience as an electrician. It tends to show that defendants called him to adjust or repair the electric hot water heater because there was no hot water. It tends to show that he removed a 2500 watt heating element and replaced it with a 4500 watt element, and reset the thermostat to a higher temperature reading. The stipulations show that the water heater was rated for a 2500 watt heating element, and a maximum of 3000 watts. The deposition of Alton Milliken, a licensed electrician, tends to show that the introduction of a 4500 watt heating element would heat the water faster and would draw a larger current through the thermostat which would tend to cause its points to melt and thereby freeze the thermostat so that it would no longer control the temperature. The deposition of Glenn Williamson tends to show that the tank of defendants' electric hot water heater was blown some two hundred to three hundred feet by the explosion.

Defendants' motion for summary judgment was heard during the 18 January 1971 Session of Superior Court held in Moore County. It was stipulated that Judge Long might enter judgment out of the District and after expiration of the Session. After consideration of the pleadings, depositions, and stipulations, Judge Long by judgment filed 31 March 1971 found that there was no genuine issue of any material fact as to liability and that defendants' motion for summary judgment should be granted. Plaintiff appeals.

BROCK, Judge.

Plaintiff-appellant insists that the doctrine of *res ipsa loquitur* is applicable in this case and, being entitled under that doctrine to have the case submitted to the jury, that summary judgment for defendant was error. We agree.

Summary judgment is proper only where movant shows that there is no genuine issue as to any material fact and that he is entitled to judgment as a matter of law. Application of the doctrine of *res ipsa loquitur* recognizes that common experience sometimes permits a reasonable inference of negligence from the occurrence itself. In other words, the application of the doctrine of *res ipsa loquitur* recognizes a genuine issue as to the material fact of defendants' actionable negligence and precludes summary judgment for defendants.

The rules governing the application of the doctrine of *res ipsa loquitur* in North Carolina have been stated as follows: "When a thing which causes injury is shown to be under the exclusive management of the defendant and the accident is one which in the ordinary course of events does not happen if those in control of it use proper care, the accident itself is sufficient to carry the case to the jury on the issue of defendant's negligence."

In this case, the evidence before the trial judge clearly shows that the electric hot water heater was under the exclusive management and control of defendants, and that they had undertaken the maintenance of it. It is a matter of common knowledge that electric water heaters are widely used to fill the hot water requirements of residential, commercial, and industrial users. When in a safe condition and properly managed, electric hot water heaters do not usually explode; therefore, in the absence of explanation, the explosion of an electric hot water heater reasonably warrants an inference of negligence.

[Innkeepers' Modern Law Standard]

A hotel or motel keeper, from the nature of his occupation, extends an invitation to the general public to use his facilities. When a paying guest goes to a hotel or motel the very thing he bargains for is the use of safe and secure premises for his sojourn. Although the hotel or motel keeper is not an insurer of the guest's personal safety [in modern times], he has the duty to exercise reasonable care to maintain the premises in a reasonably safe condition; and if his negligence in this respect is the proximate cause of injury to a guest, he is liable for damages.

[Defendant's Argument]

Defendants argue that *res ipsa loquitur* does not apply because the evidence leaves the cause of the explosion a matter of conjecture. The depositions of the two defendants which were before the trial judge indicated that a thunderstorm was in the area during the night preceding the explosion of the electric hot water heater. This testimony may constitute evidence for consideration by the jury as a possible explanation of the cause of the explosion, but its probative value is for jury determination and it does not remove the more reasonable inference that the cause of the explosion was negligence of defendants in the management and control of the electric hot water heater.

Defendants further argue that they lack the knowledge and skill to inspect and regulate the heater, that they reasonably relied upon an independent contractor for proper installation, and that they reasonably relied upon an independent contractor for repairs. The evidence before the trial judge discloses that defendants hired one Olaf Thorsen to adjust and repair the electric hot water heater. The evidence before the trial judge discloses that Olaf Thorsen is not a licensed electrician and is not experienced as an electrician, but is licensed and experienced only as a plumber. The evidence before the trial judge further discloses that the repair and maintenance on the electric hot water heater required working with, installing, and adjusting electrical wiring, electrical heating elements, and a thermostat to control the flow of electrical current. At the time of the accident in question, G.S. §87-43 provided in part as follows: "No person, firm or corporation shall engage in the business of installing, maintaining, altering or repairing within the State of North Carolina any electric wiring, devices, appliances or equipment unless such person, firm or corporation shall have received from the Board of Examiners of Electrical Contractors an electrical contractor's license. . . ."

[The Independent Contractor Rule]

Plumbers who are answerable only for the result of their work are generally regarded as independent contractors. The general rule is that an employer or contractee is not liable for the torts of an independent contractor committed in the performance of the contracted work. However, a condition prescribed to relieve an employer from liability for the negligent acts of an independent contractor employed by him is that he shall have exercised due care to secure a competent contractor for the work. Therefore, if it appears that the employer either knew, or by the exercise of reasonable care might have ascertained that the contractor was not properly qualified, then the employer may be held liable for the negligent acts of the contractor. "An employer is subject to liability for physical harm to third persons caused by his failure to exercise reasonable care to employ a competent and careful contractor (a) to do work which will involve a risk of physical harm unless it is skillfully and carefully done, or (b) to perform any duty which the employer owes to third persons." Restatement, Second, Torts, §411. The evidence of the repairs and maintenance performed on the electrical system of defendants' electric hot water heater by Olaf Thorsen tends to affirm the incompetence of defendants' independent contractor as an electrician.

This evidence before the trial judge tends to show a specific act of negligence on the part of defendants in failing to secure the services of a competent independent contractor and tends to strengthen the inference that the cause of the accident was defendants' negligence. The application of the doctrine of *res ipsa loquitur* to this case should not be denied because the evidence tends to show a specific act of negligence on the part of defendants.

The entry of summary judgment was error.

Reversed.

VAUGHN and GRAHAM, J.J., concur.

The decision of the North Carolina Court of Appeals was upheld (affirmed) by the Supreme Court of North Carolina in 1972.[10] This cleared the way for the case to be returned to the trial court for a jury trial on the points raised in the case itself.

QUESTIONS

1. Why do New York and California have extra reporter volumes?
2. Explain what a case citation tells us.
3. How can an innkeeper in Nevada lose the protection of the statutes that limit liability for the money and valuables of guests as well as a guest's property?
4. In the Levitt case (Caesar's Palace money and valuables case) the court found an absence of gross negligence on the hotel. What was the significance of this finding?
5. How do we know that Mr. Page, in *Page v. Sloan*, died without a will?
6. Where in your inn would you have notices of the statutory limitations on liability posted? Could any harm come from *extra posting* in places not specified in the statutes?
7. How do "statutes" differ from "cases"?
8. What do the words "left in the room" mean under the Nevada property statutes?
9. True or False. At one time, the innkeeper was an insurer of the goods and valuables of guests but this is no longer true.
10. What was the principal defense set up by the inn in *Page v. Sloan*?

ENDNOTES

1. Charles Tresise, *Tavern Treasures,* p. 121.
2. *Ex Parte Chesser,* 93 Fla. 590, 112 So. 90 (1920).
3. *John P. Agnew Co. Inc. v. Hooge,* 69 App. D.C. 116, 99 F. 2d 349, 351.
4. *State v. McDonough,* 129 Conn. 483, 29 A. 2d 582, 584.
5. *In re Carter's Estate,* 254 Pa. 518, 99 A. 58.
6. *Isbill v. Stoval,* Tex. Civ. App., 92 S.W. 2d 1067, 1070.
7. *Sale v. Railroad Commission,* 15 Cal. 2d 612, 140 P. 2d 38, 41.
8. *Levitt v. Desert Palace, Inc.,* 601 Fed. Rpt. 2d 684 (1979), and *Owens v. Summa Corporation and XYZ Insurance Co.,* 625 Fed. Rpt. 2d 600 (1980).
9. 12 N.C. App. 433, 183 S.E. 2d 813 (1971).
10. 281 N.C. 697, 190 S.E. 2d 189 (1972).

6

Conventional Contracts and the HRI Industry

It was easy to find Jensen's motel; Foxx Jensen's Chinook Inn was the largest and newest in Iiwaco and had a fine view of the fishing harbor. The windows of the Inn's restaurant were steamed from the warmth inside; it looked charming, welcoming, a cozy refuge from the cold mist. I shook the rain off my Irish walking hat and opened the door to the smell of frying Walla Walla sweets and the muted clunk clunk of dishes in the kitchen. The tables and chairs were made of varnished knotty pine; there were elks' antlers on the walls, stuffed pheasants, stuffed mallards and chukkers, mounted chinooks and silvers. Some of the fried onions were crammed inside cheeseburgers on the tray of a waitress on her way to a table of fishermen.[1]

OVERVIEW

First we want to learn the requirements of the formation of conventional contracts at HRI operations. Then we will find out what happens when contract promises are not kept.

In this chapter we will examine the basic principles that are found in one of the most extensive and well-developed bodies of our substantive law—the law of contract. At the outset, however, we must recognize that what is discussed in this chapter must be supplemented by what we will learn in the next chapter about "sales contracts." Here we will be concerned with all contracts *other* than those that apply to the *sale of goods between merchants,* the subject matter of the next chapter. Examine Figure 6.1.

CONTRACTS IN THE COURTS

When deciding legal controversies, the courts are always watchful to see if a contract was involved in the dispute. If so, the terms of that agreement come to the front and the court will use those terms in deciding the matter. By making a contract, the parties set their own standards. The courts will not change those standards in the absence of fraud or other criminal activity that may have given rise to the contract. The courts do not write contracts–they only use them to resolve disputes. A good way to begin is by an examination of the definition of contract.

DEFINITION

A leading authority on the subject tells us that "a contract is a promise, or set of promises, for the breach of which the law gives a remedy, or the performance of which the law in some way recognizes as a duty."[2] This definition points out that a promise or promises are needed and that the "law" is involved. A contract creates legal obligations when it comes into being; it usually concerns property or something of value, and it creates rights that can be addressed to a court for enforcement. If the contract requires

Innkeepers and Contract Law	
Conventional Contracts (This Chapter)	Sales Contracts (Chapter 7)
• Avoiding breach. • Acceptance required. • Inn reservations. • Hiring inn employees. • "Consideration" needed. (Reasons to enforce the promises.) • Mutual promises are required. • The front desk is involved. • All reservations at inns fall under this topic. • Custom and usage will be looked to by judges in some disputes.	• Good faith is required. • Acting "seasonably" is a legal requirement. (A matter for the court to decide). • Paying an invoice is an acceptance. • Acting inconsistently is an acceptance. • Failing to inspect and reject seasonably is an acceptance. • A "sale" triggers the warranties of Article 2, UCC.

FIGURE 6.1

skill, exercise of special knowledge, or judgment, it is a "personal service contract." If it concerns property, it is a "property contract."

Contract Definition and Reservations

Travel Group X makes prepaid reservations at Zero Inn for 50 rooms, two weeks in advance. When attempting to check in, the group is told that no rooms are available. The translation of the above contract definition follows: "A contract is the promise of Zero Inn to have 50 rooms available for Travel Group X on the agreed day. The promise was not kept, thus giving the travel group the right to seek damages (dollars) in court, or a remedy in equity. If the promise had been kept, the law would recognize that as having been a duty."

Next, it is useful to examine the basic contract classifications.

CLASSIFICATIONS

Contracts can be joint or several; bilateral or unilateral; executory or executed; express or implied; and void, voidable, and unenforceable.

Joint or Several

A joint contract is one in which A and B bind themselves to C so that both are responsible for the obligations assumed. Both must be sued by C if they fail to meet their obligations. A "several contract" is one in which either A or B may be sued for breach, at the election of C.

Bilateral or Unilateral

If A and B enter into a contract and each makes binding promises to the other, the contract is "bilateral"–or two-party. If an "offeror"–the one who makes an offer–does not want a promise in return, the situation is "unilateral." For example, A says "cut down that tree at the inn and carry away all debris and I will pay you $200." This is a *promise for an act* and does not create a binding obligation on either–at least not at that point. If B cuts down the tree and removes the debris, the act requested is completed and A must pay the sum promised. The same situation often arises in the making of room reservations.

A Unilateral Reservation Contract

For example, it is late afternoon and the inn is nearing capacity. Ninety percent of the guests have checked in, and an additional 8 percent of the available rooms are out on guaranteed reservations. Assuming the inn has 300 rooms, six rooms remain available.

If a walk-in requests a room, the common-law duty to receive requires acceptance assuming that person is in acceptable condition and able to pay. Five vacancies now exist.

A phone caller then requests a "room for tonight, down and out, arrival at 5:30 P.M." The caller is an American Express card holder who offers to guarantee payment by use of the card number.

Two options now are available. One can accept the reservation unconditionally, reducing the available rooms to four, or accept the reservation with the condition that the traveler arrive by a specified time. The latter is an option since the common-law duty to receive does *not* extend to phone reservations.

One could reply, "We will hold the room for you if you arrive no later than 6 P.M. If you don't, we will sell the room if someone wants it."

A unilateral offer has been created. We have promised to have the room available if that person performs the act of arriving by the stated time. If he or she arrives on time, the sale is made–if not, the room is available for a potential guest, and bookings can reach 100 percent.

Unilateral Contracts: Another Example at the Inn

An employee handbook created by an inn sets forth duties, rights, responsibilities, penalties, and the like. This is an example in which there is only one set of promises and they have been made by the inn. As the employees go about their duties, those acts constitute an acceptance and the terms of the handbook become contractual.

Closely related to the making of reservations in unilateral form is the using of *conditions* when taking reservations.

Conditions on Inn Reservations

When making a reservation contract, it is permissible for the innkeeper to place conditions on that contract. Some examples would be a "cash deposit received in advance," a "minimum stay of three days," and "subject to cancellation if the guest does not arrive by 6:00 P.M." If such conditions are not met, the reservation contract does not come into being. As a judge once said, "Conditions are the arch enemy of the promise," for the more conditions one makes, the less the promise is worth. Thus, their use in HRI operations makes good business sense. Conditions can be "precedent" (meaning something must first happen), "concurrent" (meaning some event must occur at the same time as another event), or "subsequent" (meaning that some event must follow an event).

Another classification is that of executory and executed contracts.

Executory and Executed

An executory contract is one in which one or both parties must yet perform. An executed contract is one that has been performed with nothing left for either to do. A promise to sell land is an executory contract. After the deed is transferred and the price paid, the contract is executed.

Express or Implied

An express contract is one in which the promises and terms are stated by the parties. Implied contracts arise "from mutual agreement and intent to promise but where the agreement and promise have not been expressed in words. Such contracts are true contracts and have sometimes been called contracts implied in fact."[3]

Void, Voidable, and Unenforceable

A void contract is technically no contract at all. It may be a contract that the parties felt was valid but that has been held by a court to be invalid. "Void contract" is thus a redundancy. A "voidable" contract is one that is valid but has built within it the right of one or both of the parties to avoid all obligations under the contract. A, a minor, buys an item from B, an adult. A can void the contract because of A's age and B can do nothing about it. However, until A voids, B is bound to perform with A.

An unenforceable contract is one that, for some reason, cannot be enforced by one against another. A contract may be unenforceable in part and enforceable in the balance. For example, A contracts with B and the contract contains six provisions. Two of these provisions are illegal but the other four are not. The contract is unenforceable as to the two provisions and valid as to the balance. This brings into play the "blue pencil doctrine." If such a contract gets before a court, the judge can "blue pencil" the illegal provisions and enforce the others.

Turning from classifications, it becomes necessary to examine the legal requirements for the creation of a binding conventional contract sometimes called "common-law contracts."

THE STATUTES OF FRAUDS

The first factor to consider in contract making is the "statutes of frauds," which require certain contracts to be in written form and "signed by the party(ies) to be charged."

Historically such laws were called "Statutes of Frauds," because they were designed to prevent fraud in the use of contracts and they are called this now. Examples of contracts that must be in writing and signed include:

1. Contracts involving the sale of real estate or any interest in real estate.
2. Contracts that cannot be performed in one year.
3. Promises of one person to pay the debt of another.
4. Leases for more than one year.
5. Contracts in which one person promises another money or property if that person will enter into marriage with the other.
6. Promises of those who handle deceased persons' estates to pay the debts of creditors out of their own pockets if there is not enough in the estate for that purpose.

A helpful way to gain an understanding of the statutes of frauds is to ask oneself, "What *isn't* covered?" If a pending contract does not fall into one of the six areas, then the contract *does not have to be in writing to be binding.* A sampling of noncovered areas follows:

1. Personal-service contracts, even though they are to last for more than one year.
2. Providing a service as contrasted to a sale.
3. Leases of real estate for less than one year.
4. The sale of items of real estate which are to be removed from the real estate by the seller.
5. Inn reservations on a short-term basis.

This brings us to the *form* of contracts.

Form of the Contract

No particular words are necessary to show contractual promises or the intention of the parties as they relate to those promises. With the exception of those contracts that must be in writing under the statute of frauds, oral contracts are as binding as written contracts. For example, a hotel manager can hire an assistant manager orally and the terms agreed upon are binding. Employment contracts are an exception to the statute of fraud's one year provision. Even if the employment may last for years, it *could* have ended in the first year by the death of the employee. Therefore, it is *not* a contract that *cannot be performed* in one year–a technical point.

Related to form are time periods in which contracts can be enforced in court.

Statute of Limitations

In each state, a statute of limitations controls the time within which one may sue for breach of contract. The period of five to ten years is typical and starts when the breach occurs, not from the date of the contract.

Turning from the statutes of frauds and the form of contracts, we next examine the legal requirements of a contract that can be enforced in court.

JEFFERSON COUNTY COURTHOUSE, Mt. Vernon, Illinois.

REQUIREMENTS OF A BINDING CONTRACT

The conventional contract has six requirements that must come into being before it becomes legally enforceable. These requirements are offer, acceptance, mutuality (or meeting of the minds, sometimes called "manifestation of mutual assent"), consideration, competent parties, and legal purpose. We will examine each in turn.

Offer

An offer is made by the "offeror" ("promisor") and is most often a statement of what that person is willing to do if the other is willing to do what is requested. While an offer is a promise, it is conditional. The promise may lapse if not accepted within a reasonable time, or it may be revoked by the one who made it, provided the revocation comes before an acceptance. It must come to the mind of the offeree–the one to whom it is directed. An offer may be rejected by the offeree, or the offeree may make a "counteroffer" which is treated as a rejection of the offer. Mere silence on the part of the offeree is nothing at law and thus the offer will lapse after the passage of a reasonable time.

An offer must be definite in its terms. If there is an offer and an acceptance, but the terms are so indefinite that they cannot be determined, the court will hold that there is no contract.

To assist in understanding the process under discussion, the main steps have been placed into a drawing. Examine Figure 6.2, Step 1.

The offer will not last indefinitely and, if made face to face, ends when the parties part. It can lapse after the passage of time; it can be revoked by the one who makes it so long as this happens

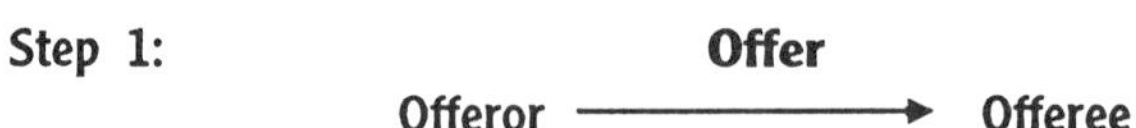

The offeror (or promisor) has made an offer, the form of which is a question: "Here is my offer (or promise). Do you want the benefits of it?"

At this point, the offer is a mere inquiry. In the absence of a standing relationship between the parties, there is no obligation on the part of the offeree to reply. He or she may stand silent and the silence will not constitute an acceptance.

FIGURE 6.2

before it is accepted; it can be rejected by the one to whom it is made, thus bringing it to an end; it can end by the making of a counteroffer; it can end by destruction of the subject matter of the offer, by illegal interventions, and by acceptance. An offer also ends upon the death or insanity of the offeror if either event occurs before acceptance. An offer cannot be assigned unless it takes the form of a written option. The brother of the offer is the "acceptance."

Acceptance

Acceptance occurs when there is some assent that the offeree wants to be bound in a contract with the offeror. If the offer specifies a time by which acceptance must be made, an acceptance after that time is ineffective. If no time limit is specified, an offer must be accepted within a reasonable time. Acceptance comes too late if an offer lapses, is revoked, or is rejected. If a dispute arises as to whether or not an offer was accepted, it becomes a question of fact for a jury to determine.

Just as with the offer, an acceptance must be communicated. If the offer is revoked before an acceptance is received, the acceptance fails.

An acceptance can be made in the form in which the offer is made. That is, if an oral offer is made, the acceptance can be oral. If the offer is in writing, the acceptance should be in writing. If an offer is made by mail and acceptance is also made by mail, the acceptance is effective when mailed. The offeror chose the mail, so when the acceptance was mailed it was in the hands of the offeror's agent and thus effective at that time. The rule that acceptance made by mail is good when mailed was laid down in the case of *Adams v. Lindsell.*[4] Thus the rule is part of the common law.

Acceptance can come about by signing a document, by acts where the offer is in unilateral form, by conduct, by trade usage, and even by custom. If the offeror specifies that the acceptance will not be effective until received, then that provision controls. In a face-to-face situation a nod of the head may be a good acceptance.

An acceptance must conform to the offer, and if it varies the terms of the offer, it will fail. The offer must also be accepted in its totality or not at all. An attempt to accept part would vary the terms of the offer and is not permitted. If parties exchange letters and the terms in those letters are not on "all fours," there is no contract. The letters are merely proposals of each to contract with the other. The court will treat them as "negotiations." If the terms in the letters agree, a contract will result. Examine Step 2, Figure 6.3.

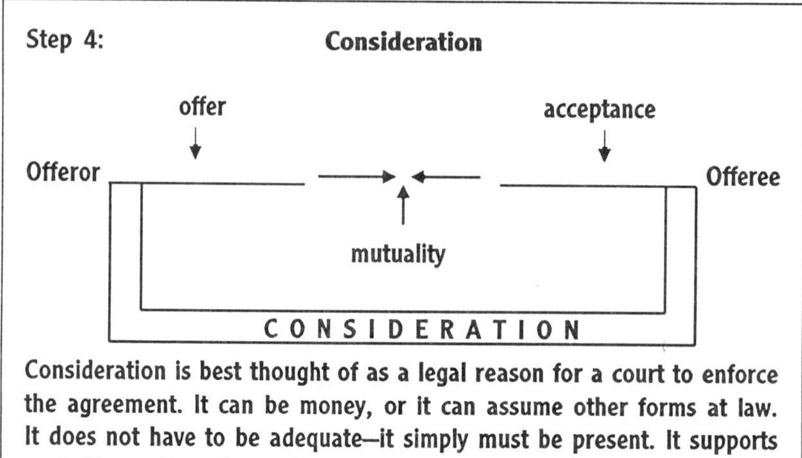

Consideration is best thought of as a legal reason for a court to enforce the agreement. It can be money, or it can assume other forms at law. It does not have to be adequate—it simply must be present. It supports or holds up the offer and acceptance.

FIGURE 6.5

Competent Parties

Both parties to a contract must be of the age of majority; functioning free from duress, fraud, or mistake; and have no mental disabilities that would render them incapable of knowing the nature and consequences of their acts. An incompetent party can cause a contract to be void or voidable, depending upon the circumstances. The following are considered to be incompetent to contract: infants; those who are adjudicated insane; intoxicated persons; those under the influence of narcotics; and those who, because of the nature of the surrounding circumstances, are not capable of exercising normal, rational judgment.

Legal Purpose

A contract must be for a legal purpose. Courts will not force parties to do illegal acts even if they contract to do them. Thus if a so-called contract is for an illegal purpose, it cannot and will not be enforced in court. Illegal bargains, which often involve violations of statutes, include contracts of bribery, extortion, gambling, usury, and contracts to violate licensing laws.

Following is a list of inn situations that involve conventional contracts.

Conventional-Contract Inn Examples

1. A requests a room at the inn and the inn accepts.
2. A reserves a room at the inn but it is conditioned upon arrival before 6:00 P.M. A arrives at 5:45 P.M.
3. C agrees in writing to sell her inn to D for $10,000,000.
4. Guest X at Zero Hotel gives his suit to a bellboy for cleaning and pressing and return the next day.
5. Travel Agent Z books T on a trip around the world.
6. Guest H deposits valuables at the front desk of the inn.
7. Traveler Jim leaves his auto with the inn valet.
8. At a restaurant, patron U checks her valuable fur at the check room and pays a $1.00 fee.

It is next necessary to learn something about contract "performance" and "breach."

PERFORMANCE AND BREACH

In the countless contracts entered into yearly, most are performed without problems arising. It is to those contracts about which disputes arise that we will briefly turn.

ABRAHAM LINCOLN'S LAW OFFICES, Springfield, Illinois.

Breach

A breach of contract has been defined as anything so material and important as in truth and fairness will defeat the essential purposes of the parties to a contract.[7]

Where a breach occurs, damages to compensate the other party for loss are generally available. However, the other party may not be able to prove loss and thus recover nothing. It should also be understood that a breach of contract is not a criminal act. It is simply a violation of the civil duty to honor one's promises. The Thirteenth Amendment prohibits "involuntary servitude" and this keeps civil debts from being criminal in nature.

Anticipatory Breach

If one party to a contract has made it clear that he or she will not perform when the time arises, the other party can "anticipate" the breach and sue at once.[8]

Refusal to Perform

If, when time of performance arrives, one party refuses to perform, that party is guilty of the first breach and can be held responsible for loss caused by the refusal. But if one refuses to perform a minor part of a contract, this may not excuse the other party from performing.

If a breach occurs because of fraud on the part of one party, the injured party may sue in tort or contract. If one proceeds in a contract action for the loss suffered, a later tort action will be barred since an "election" has been made. One cannot sue twice on one civil cause of action.

Damages Recoverable

What can be recovered because of a breach of contract are damages that fairly, reasonably, and naturally arise in the course of such breach.[9] One will not be allowed to escape liability where the loss will be substantial but not capable of precise determination. The court will allow a "reasonable standards" measurement to be used with the matter being a question of fact for a jury to determine. If proof of damages must be based on pure speculation, however, the proof will fail. The courts will not permit guessing in the proof of contract damages.

What About Damages to Punish?

Punitive (exemplary—to make an example of) damages are not allowed in breach of contract cases. Yet if the breach is accompanied by a willful or malicious tort, this may create an independent claim for punitive damages that may be allowed by a court.

If a breach of a reservation contract is caused by no-shows, the inn has the right to seek damages. For a case in which a hotel recovered for the cost of 120 rooms not occupied, see *Hotel Del Coronado v. Qwip Systems.*[10]

As a general rule, damages in a court action cannot exceed the assets of the defendants, whether a hotel corporation, chief executive officers at an inn, directors of inn personnel, or others.

What About Custom and Usage?

Can custom and usage be used to defeat a contract action for breach of a reservation contract? A federal judge in Pennsylvania had this to say: "The plain terms of the contract prevail over trade usage or custom. . . . Custom and usage evidence cannot create an ambiguity where none exists."[11]

Nominal Damages

Another type of damages are known as "nominal damages." When such damages are awarded, it means that the winning party has proved liability but has failed in his or her proof of loss. The typical nominal-damages verdict is $1.00. Such an award has the practical effect of placing the costs of the litigation on the losing party. The *USFL v. NFL* litigation ended with such an award.

Liquidated Damages

The parties to a contract may agree in advance as to what the damages will be in the event of a later breach. Such provisions are enforceable provided that they bear a reasonable relationship to actual loss and are not in the form of a penalty. The term "liquidated" tells us that the damages are "set" and thus not a subject of speculation.

To illustrate, Motel Zero contracts with Ace Construction to remodel the pool. The price agreed upon is $200,000, which includes all costs and labor. The work is to be completed no later than May 31, the customary pool opening date in Eastern states.

The parties agree that, if the work is not completed by that date, the construction firm will forfeit $500 for each day the firm is late. Since the motel sells pool memberships at $100 per family, the agreed-upon damages would be reasonable and would be enforced by the court. If the pool is 30 days late in the completion, the motel can deduct $15,000 from the final payment.

If a liquidated-damage clause is not included in a contract, and even if a completion date is spelled out, the passage of that time without completion of the contract will generally *not* be held to be a breach. The exception to this would be if the contract makes "time of the essence," and contains those words or words to the same effect.

"Time Is of the Essence"

If these or similar words are included in a contract, the courts will treat the date specified as the time by which performance must be completed. Otherwise, the completion date will be treated as an approximate date.

In some contract situations, the legal remedy of damages (dollars) may not be sufficient. A second remedy is provided by "equity."

SPECIFIC PERFORMANCE

If the subject matter of a contract is unique, upon breach by one party the other party may ask a judge to specifically require the breaching party to perform. This remedy is available in real estate contracts where one refuses to perform as promised. Since each parcel of real estate is unique, the remedy of specific performance can be used.

Specific performance cannot be used in personal-service contracts or in any situation in which supervision of the court would be needed to carry out the contract. A court will not place itself in the position of an overseer. The only remedy would be an action for damages in such cases.

To conclude our discussion of conventional contracts, we will examine implied contracts, illegal contracts, and contracts that violate public policy.

IMPLIED CONTRACTS

An express contract must be distinguished from a contract implied in fact and one implied in law. The principle involved in implied contracts is an equitable one that holds that one should not unjustly enrich oneself at the expense of another.

A contract implied in fact is a true contract, the terms of which will be inferred from the circumstances. When one confers benefits upon another, which the other knows of and should pay for, the law implies an agreement that such payment will be made. An express contract is thus distinguishable from one implied in fact. In the former, the terms are agreed upon. In the latter, the terms are implied from the conduct of the parties.

Contracts *implied in law* are not true contracts and are resorted to by the courts for purposes of remedy only. Such situations are often referred to as "quasi-contracts." The widest application would be in situations where, if they were not used, an injustice would occur.

As a general rule, where there is an express contract, an implied contract in fact or in law will never arise. The express contract controls.

ILLEGAL CONTRACTS

An illegal contract is one that has as its object an illegal purpose. As a general rule, an illegal contract is void–not voidable–and cannot be the subject of a court action for breach of that contract. There can be no enforcement of an illegal contract in law or equity whether the illegality existed at the outset or "intervened" later. For example, a subsequent statute may make the terms of a prior contract unlawful. In addition, "when an illegal modification of a lawful contract is attempted, the modification is a nullity and the contract is unscathed."[12]

An illegal contract should be distinguished, however, from one that is against "public policy."

CONTRACTS AGAINST PUBLIC POLICY

"Public policy" relates to the requirements of the public welfare. "Whatever tends to injustice or oppression, restraint of liberty, commerce, and natural or legal rights; whatever tends to obstruction of justice, or to the violation of a statute; and whatever is against good morals, when made the object of a contract, is against public policy and therefore void and not susceptible of enforcement."[13] Thus, while a contract against public policy may be illegal, it is not so limited because, otherwise, legal contracts may violate public policy.

Whenever a court must look at such a matter, the court will not look for a precise definition of "public policy" and will not hesitate in its practical application to the law of contracts.[14] An example of a contract against public policy would be one in which "a party stipulates for his exemption from liability for the consequences of his own negligence."[15] Such a contract is not permitted at law. Other examples include contracts to influence legislation, the joining of companies to circumvent the effect of restrictive statutes, and a contract by a servant promising to release the master *before* injury occurs to others.

To conclude the chapter, we will examine an old HRI case that still carries an important message.

Ms. Aaron entered into a contractual relationship with a bathhouse at Coney Island, paying 25 cents as the consideration for that contract. The contract was then breached by those in charge of the bathhouse and Ms. Aaron sought damages. The ALI definition of contract told us that, for a breach of contract, the law gives a remedy. That "remedy" is the subject matter of the case.

AARON V. WARD[16]

APPEAL, by permission, from a judgment of the Appellate Division of the Supreme Court in the second judicial department, entered March 21, 1910, affirming a judgment of the Municipal Court of the city of New York in favor of plaintiff.

The nature of the action and the facts, so far as material, are stated in the opinion.

In all cases of breach of contract (breach of promise of marriage excepted) the plaintiffs loss is measured by the benefit to him of having the contract performed, and this is, therefore, the true measure of damages. The cases where actions *ex contractu* have been brought against carriers and transportation companies wherein damages have been allowed for humiliation, indignities and mental suffering or anguish are highly exceptional in their character, and arise altogether out of the peculiar nature and character of the particular contract under consideration.

The business conducted by the defendant was purely private in its nature, and the ticket of admission by the plaintiff was entirely revocable at the pleasure of the defendant, and the latter could, if necessary, expel the plaintiff from the premises with all reasonable force.

The trial court having found for the plaintiff it had a right to award the plaintiff compensatory damages and was not limited to the actual loss of money sustained which in this case was twenty-five cents, the price of the ticket. The case at bar is analogous to that of a passenger for wrongful treatment by a common carrier and to that of a guest for injuries to feelings by an innkeeper. The claim that the business of keeping bathing houses for hire is not of the same public nature as that of a common carrier or an innkeeper and may be said to be a private enterprise may be sound without, however, affecting the rule as to the measure of damages.

[The Opinion of the Court Now Follows:]

CULLEN, Ch. J. The defendant was the proprietor of a bathing establishment on the beach at Coney Island. The plaintiff, intending to take a bath in the surf, purchased a ticket from the defendant's employees for the sum of twenty-five cents, and took her position in a line of the defendant's patrons leading to a window at which the ticket entitled her to receive, upon its surrender, a key admitting her to a bathhouse. When she approached the window a dispute arose between her and the defendant's employees as to the right of another person not in the line to have a key given to him in advance of the plaintiff. As a result of this dispute plaintiff was ejected from the defendant's premises, the agents of the latter refusing to furnish her with the accommodations for which she had contracted. It is not necessary to discuss the merits of the dispute or narrate its details as the questions of fact involved in that matter have been decided in plaintiff's favor by the Municipal Court, in which she subsequently brought suit, and that judgment has been unanimously affirmed by the Appellate Division. The plaintiff was awarded $250 damages against the defendant's contention that she was not entitled to any recovery in excess of the sum paid for the ticket, and the correctness of the defendant's contention is the only question presented on this appeal.

The action is for a breach of the defendant's contract and not for a tortious expulsion. It is so denominated in the complaint and was necessarily so brought as the Municipal Court has no jurisdiction over an action for tort. It is contended for the defendant that as the action was on contract, the plaintiff was not entitled to any damages for the indignity of her expulsion from the defendant's establishment. It may be admitted that, as a general rule, mental suffering resulting from a breach of contract is not a subject of compensation, but the rule is not universal. It is the settled law of this state that a passenger may recover damages for insulting and slanderous words uttered by the conductor of a railway car as a breach of the company's contract of carriage. (*Gillespie v. Brooklyn Heights R. R. Co.*, 178 N.Y. 347.) The same rule obtains where the servant of an innkeeper offers insult to the guest. (*de Wolfe v. Ford,* 193 N.Y. 397.) *And it must be borne in mind that a recovery for indignity and wounded feelings is compensatory and does not constitute exemplary damages.* (*Hamilton v. Third Ave. R. R. Co.,* 53 N.Y. 25.)

It is insisted, however, that there is a distinction between common carriers and innkeepers, who are obliged to serve all persons who seek accommodation from them, and the keepers of public places of amusement or resort, such as the bathhouse of the defendant, theaters and the like. That the distinction exists is undeniable, and in the absence of legislation the keeper of such an establishment may discriminate and serve whom he pleases. [It must be kept in mind that there is no longer an "absence of legislation" because of the *Civil Rights Act* of 1964/72]. Therefore, in such a case a refusal would give no cause of action. So, also, it is the general rule of law that a ticket for admission to a place of public amusement is but a license and revocable. But granting both propositions, that the defendant might have refused the plaintiff a bath ticket and access to his premises, and that even after selling her a ticket he might have revoked the license to use the premises for the purpose of bathing, which the ticket imported, neither proposition necessarily determines that the plaintiff was not entitled to recover damages for the indignity inflicted upon her by the revocation. We have seen that in the case of a common carrier or innkeeper, a person aggrieved may recover such damages as for a breach of contract, while on the other hand, on the breach of ordinary contracts, a party would not be so entitled, and the question is, to which class of cases the case before us most closely approximates. In several of the reported cases the keeping of a theater is spoken of as a strictly private undertaking, and it is said that the owner of a theater is under no obligation to give entertainment at all. The latter proposition is true, but the business of maintaining a theater cannot be said to be "strictly" private. In *People v. King* (110 N.Y. 418) the question was as to the constitutionality of the Civil Rights Act of this state which made it a misdemeanor to deny equal enjoyment of any accommodation, facilities and privileges of inns, common carriers, theaters or other places of public resort or amusement regardless of race, creed or color, and gave the party aggrieved the right to recover a penalty of from fifty to five hundred dollars for the offense. The statute was upheld on the ground that under the doctrine of *Munn v. Illinois* (94 U.S. 113) theaters and places of public amusement (the case before the court was that of a skating rink) were affected with a public interest which justified legislative regulation and interference. In *Greenberg v. Western Turf Assn.* (140 Cal. 357) a statute making it unlawful to refuse to any person admission to a place of public amusement and giving the person aggrieved the right to recover his damages and a hundred dollar penalty in addition thereto, was upheld on the authority of the cases we have cited—a decision plainly correct, because if the legislature can forbid discrimination by the owners of such resorts on the ground of race, creed or color, it may equally forbid discrimination on any other ground. Our statute has since been amended so as to expressly include keepers of bathhouses. On the other hand, no one will contend that the legislature could forbid discrimination in the private business affairs of life–prevent an employer from refusing to employ colored servants, or a servant from refusing to work for a white or for a colored master. So, it has been held that a bootblack may refuse to black a colored man's shoes without being liable to the penalty prescribed by our statute. (*Burks v. Bosso,* 180 N.Y. 341.) Such conduct may be the result of prejudice entirely, but a man's prejudices may be part of his most cherished possessions, which cannot be invaded except when displayed in the conduct of public affairs or quasi public enterprises. That public amusements and resorts are subject to the exercise of this legislative control shows that they are not entirely private. Therefore, though under the present law the plaintiff might have been denied admission altogether to the defendant's bathhouse, provided she were not excluded on account of race, creed or color (*Grannan v. Westchester Racing Assn.,* 153, N.Y. 449), the defendant having voluntarily entered into a contract with her admitting her to the premises and agreeing to afford facilities for bathing, her status became similar to that of a passenger of a common carrier or a guest of an innkeeper, and in case of her improper expulsion she should be entitled to the same measure of damages as obtains in actions against carriers or innkeepers when brought for breach of their contracts. The reason why such damages are recoverable in the cases mentioned is not merely because the defendants are bound to give the plaintiffs accommodation, but also because of the indignity suffered by a public expulsion. In a theater or other place of public amusement or resort the indignity and humiliation caused by an expulsion in the presence of a large number of people is as great, if not greater, than in the case of an expulsion by a carrier or innkeeper, as it is the publicity of the thing that causes the humiliation.

The judgment of the Appellate Division should be affirmed, with costs.

GRAY, WERNER, WILLARD BARTLETT, HISCOCK, CHASE and COLLIN, JJ., concur.

Judgment affirmed.

QUESTIONS

1. True or False. A "several" contract is one that can be held to be binding on A and B or A or B.
2. Explain the danger inherent in a unilateral contract situation.

3. Under what legal theory may a court imply a contract at law?
4. What evil was the statute of frauds designed to avoid?
5. True or False. "Consideration" must always have a dollar and cent value.
6. Why do mutual promises standing alone provide consideration?
7. Why must one be careful when contemplating or anticipating a breach of contract?
8. Explain what "liquidated damages" are.
9. What legal impact do the words "time is of the essence" have on a contract?
10. Under what circumstances might a jury award nominal damages in an inn case?

ENDNOTES

1. Richard Hoyt, *Fish Story*. Viking Press, New York.
2. 1. *Williston on Contracts,* sec. 1, p. 1.
3. 1. *Williston on Contracts,* sec. 3. p. 6.
4. 1. *Barn and Alp.* 681, 106 *Eng. Reg.* 250 (K.B. 1818).
5. *Bott v. Wheller,* 183 Va. 643, 33 S.E. 2d 184.
6. *Roller v. McGraw,* 63 W. Va. 462, 60 S.E. 410.
7. *F. A. D'Andrea, Inc. v. Dodge,* 15 F. 2d 1003.
8. *Burke v. Shaver,* 92 Va. 345, 23 S.E. 749.
9. *Krikorian v. Dailey,* 171 Va. 16, 197 S.E. 442.
10. *Hotel Del Coronado v. Qwip Systems,* N.Y.L.J., July 16, 1981, page 13, col. 4 (N.Y. Sup.).
11. *King of Prussia v. Greyhound Lines, Inc.,* 457 F. Supp. 56 (E.D. Pa.)
12. *Tearney v. Marmison,* 103 W. Va. 394, 137 S.E. 543.
13. *Williams v. Board of Education,* 45 W. Va. 199, 31 S.E. 985.
14. *O'Dell v. Appalachian Hotel Corp.,* 153 Va. 283, 149 S.E. 487, 68 A.L.R. 629.
15. *Johnson v. Richmond & D.R. Co.,* 86 Va. 975, 11 S.E. 829.
16. 203 N.Y. 351 (1911).

7

Sales Contracts in the HRI Industry

The boy behind the registration desk of the Doyle Hotel was about ten years old and looked Indian. The smell of cigarettes was heavy in the air. He was reading a math book, and he ignored me the first two times I addressed him. On the third try he looked up. "What did you say?" he snapped.

"I said, 'Excuse me, I need some help.'"

He shrugged and went back to the book. The hotel lobby was no better or worse than any other in the neighborhood: cracked vinyl couch repaired with duct tape, broken TV set in one corner, broken cigarette machine in another, and registration counter shoved under the stairs with a wall of empty pigeonholes behind it. On the wall hung a calendar from a Mexican restaurant, with a busty woman in a torn skirt waving the Mexican flag.

The House of Blue Lights, Robert J. Bowman

OVERVIEW

Here we encounter the contract law designed to cover the purchase and sale of goods between merchants. Since *all* purchases of food, drink, and supplies at all American hotels, motels, bars, and other HRI components are controlled by this law, it is imperative to gain a working understanding of it.

The subject matter of this chapter is Article 2 of the Uniform Commercial Code, Sales. This law is a product of the National Commission on Uniform State Laws. The UCC is the most significant law created by the NCUSL and has been adopted in full or amended form by forty-nine states, and in part (including Article

2) by Louisiana. Article 2 is a rewrite of the Uniform Sales Act, which was created in 1908, so the subject matter is not completely new. Yet, in relation to conventional contract rules that go back for centuries, it is quite new.

Three techniques have been used in the preparation of this chapter. First, a nonlegal narrative is presented in which the features of Article 2 are set forth in nonlegal terms. This is followed by a law school-type presentation of the law. Finally, examples are offered with accompanying drawings, questions, and answers to demonstrate what this law means in practice.

The following was taken from the *Hotel and Casino Law Letter,* Volume 2-3, April 1983.

THE PURCHASE OF GOODS

Let's walk toward the "back of our house" with the idea of taking a legal look at what goes on in our purchasing department. You say that the purchasing department isn't in the "back of the house"? Little worry because we want to look at it wherever it is. But while there, we might as well also take a look at our receiving department.

There are a lot of goods coming into the inn each day and these items are worth a bundle. Thus we need to pay the same attention to them as we would if it was cash that we were receiving and not goods.

So we have taken a look at the physical receipt of our goods and what have we seen? A rather nondescript location with some peeling paint and hand-cart gouges in the plaster, but other than that we are in good shape. Well we certainly hope so, but that is our reason for a look at our receiving and purchasing departments in the first place. There could be legal problems in both and these problems could be serious indeed.

What Law Governs?

The law that governs the buying and selling of goods between merchants in all fifty states, including Louisiana, is Article 2 of the Uniform Commercial Code, known in legal circles as "Sales." Since innkeepers, restaurateurs, bar operators, and others in the hospitality industry are merchants as that word is defined in Article 2, and since they most assuredly purchase goods from other merchants, this particular law applies to them. But are HRI managers really "merchants" as that word is used at law?

UCC 2-104 defines a "merchant" as ". . . a person who deals in goods of the kind or otherwise by his occupation holds himself out as having knowledge or skill peculiar to the practices or goods involved in the transaction or to whom such knowledge or skill may be attributed by his employment of an agent who . . . holds himself out as having such knowledge or skill." So there it is: if the HRI manager in fact does not have the knowledge or skill of a merchant, he or she must hire a purchasing agent who does.

What this means is that Article 2, UCC, *does* apply and that the HRI manager will be expected to measure up to the standard of a "reasonable merchant."

What Kind of Law Is Article 2 of the UCC?

First, it is a complicated body of contract law. Second, it is new as legal matters go, being a product of the past four decades. Finally, it must be distinguished from that age-old body of contract law that we can trace back to the ancient Egyptians. If we are buying land or an inn, or hiring employees, the law of the ancients is there to guide us. If we are buying linens, foodstuffs, lamps, chairs, and other supplies, we must look to Article 2, Sales, for guidance.

Thus we see that our sales contracts involve the back of our house since that is where we receive and store our goods, and that is why we decided to take a look there in the beginning.

To facilitate our discussion of our buying and receiving department, let's assume that we need to purchase 10,000 sheets for immediate and future use in our inn.

Easy Enough

First, should we look for catalogs of suppliers of sheets? Not necessarily so. It is better to look to state statutes to see if our legislature has directed its attention to such matters. As it turns out, the legislatures have done just that in many states. To illustrate, Nevada Revised Statutes, 447.090, subsection 3 provides: "Sheets shall be at least 98 inches long and of sufficient width to cover the mattress and spring completely." Other states, such as Virginia, specify the size and also the substance from which they must be made.

So, being an "HRI legal manager," and wanting to comply with laws that are binding upon us, we first go to the statutes. *Now* we turn to the catalogs and find a source for what we need.

Our Purchase Order

We are in a hurry as usual so let's get on the phone and place the order direct. That way, we will get our linens shipped faster. This is alright, but there is a legal problem to consider since Article 2 does have a Statute of Frauds. Such statutes have not only been around since 1677 in conventional contract law, they also have a way of causing legal problems when least expected.

Statute of Frauds

Article 2-201, UCC, states: "A contract for the sale [purchase] of goods for the price of $500 or more is not enforceable by way of action or defense unless there is some writing sufficient to indicate that a contract for the sale has been made between the parties and signed by the party against whom such enforcement is sought or by his authorized . . . agent." Does the law really say that? It certainly does. While there are three exceptions to it, the basic rule remains. So back to that oral order. Since our 10,000 sheets will cost more than $500, must we use a writing? We had better do so because the seller is going to insist that we do—and, in the end, we will want to do so too. There are two ways we can do it.

First Choice

We can place our order by use of a written purchase order, signed by our authorized agent. That will solve the problem. We will have our purchase order forms prepared by counsel and will use multiple copies for receiving, accounting, and one for the boss. Or we may use computer forms. But it would still be nice if we could use the phone in order to speed things up and there is a way we can do this so long as we do it right.

Second Choice

So we place the order by phone: "Please ship us 10,000 sheets, size 100" x 96", catalog item XYZ, at a per-unit price of $16.00 each, FOB our inn, delivery needed by June 1." So this speeds it up—but what about UCC 2-201? It is still there and we do need to comply with it.

Written Confirmation

There is a way we can comply with the statute of frauds and it is simplicity itself: We *confirm* the oral order, in writing, and *our agent signs it.* Now under UCC 2-201 (2), if we send the confirmation within a reasonable time, it satisfies the Statute of Frauds, unless the seller gives ". . . written notice of objection to its contents" within 10 days after it is received.

Our Policy in Purchasing Goods

First, we are going to place our orders of goods of $500 or more in writing.

Second, if we do place orders by phone, we are going to confirm them in writing, over our agent's signature, and we are going to do this in due course.

So now that our order has been placed, where are we? Well, we might receive a written acknowledgment of our order, and if our seller is being careful we can be certain that we will receive one. Does it matter if we do? It certainly does, because the acknowledgment may change our order and if this occurs, the UCC places responsibilities upon the buyer.

What Must the Buyer Do?

Once we receive notice of a nonconforming shipment, we have two choices: (1) object and tell why we cannot use the substituted goods or (2) pay the price.

Are we saying that we may be held responsible for goods *that we did not order*? That is exactly what we are saying and the law that creates this particular situation will be explored in a moment. So suffice it to say that we must take a look at our acknowledgments as we receive them, and check them against our purchase orders. To do otherwise is to court legal problems. For example, what if the price is *higher* on the acknowledgment than it is on the purchase order?

We must remember that the acknowledgment is a written confirmation of *our* order. Thus we have to object to it within 10 days. If our objection arrives before the goods are shipped, then no harm has been done if what we object to is corrected. But change the facts and assume that we do not receive an acknowledgment. We must now await the arrival of the goods.

The Shipment Arrives

Assume that the delivery is different from what we ordered and is thus "nonconforming." Now what? Several things can happen. First, if we were to become angry about the misdelivery, we might instruct our sales personnel to set the goods aside and not let the seller have them back. That would teach them a lesson, wouldn't it? Not at all, because "acting inconsistently" with someone else's merchandise *constitutes an acceptance*. Thus we now must pay for something that we did not order! So we would be the ones who learned a lesson. Thus we cannot act inconsistently with goods that belong to someone else.

A second choice is to place the goods in stock and use them. We might well decide to do that if the goods are an acceptable alternate to what was ordered. But hold on a minute. The goods we received are *cheaper* than what we ordered. What now? No problem because, by accepting the goods, we have bought them at the lower price so that is what we must pay. But if the nonconforming goods had been at a *higher price* and we accept them, we do so at the higher price. Since this is something that we usually do not want to do, what now?

How to Handle Nonconforming Goods?

The answer to this question is important and it brings into play one of the more interesting parts of Article 2 of the Uniform Commercial Code. The Code makes it clear that, if nonconforming goods are received, we must do three things. First, we must inspect the goods, second, we must reject the goods if we do not want them, and, third, we must state why we cannot use the goods.

The reason for this provision will be explored in a moment but back to our inspection and rejection. If we fail to meet this three-part test, *then we have accepted the goods!* It is another way that an acceptance can come about in a sales-of-goods situation. But why such a rule?

The reasoning behind the rule is this: Since Article 2 applies to merchants, such persons should have knowledge of what types of goods can be substituted for others that have been ordered. If such a substitution is made and the other merchant does not object, then why shouldn't there be an acceptance? If the seller is incorrect about the substitution, then that person has a right to be told why the substitution is not acceptable. That is the reason for the requirements of rejection accompanied with an explanation. Once the seller is told why the nonconforming goods are unacceptable, the seller has the right to "cure"—that is, send conforming goods.

In legal circles, this process is known as the "perfect tender-cure" rule. The buyer is entitled to a "perfect tender": exactly what was ordered. But if this is not received, the seller has the right to "cure." The only way a seller can cure is to be told why the goods are not acceptable.

Does this mean that if we receive nonconforming goods and fail to inspect, reject, and state why, we have accepted those goods and must pay for them? The answer is "yes" as the U.S. Army found out with a large amount of hams (*Max Bauer Meat Packer, Inc. v. United States*, 458 Fed. 2d 88, 10 UCC Rep. 1056 (U.S. Court of Claims, 1972)), and Eastern Airlines with nonconforming 727 jet aircraft (*Eastern Airlines, Inc. v. McDonnell Douglas Corp.*, 532 F.2d 957, 19 UCC Rep. 353 (5th Cir. 1976)). So the law applies to big orders of goods as well as small and it applies to our inn as well.

So if all of this is the law, how quickly must we inspect, reject, and state why? In the ham case, the army rejected the hams in less than five hours. The court held that *that was too long* and thus the army had to pay for hams it did not order, did not want, and could not use. In the airline case, Eastern waited a few weeks before it discovered that its new fleet of jet aircraft was not what was wanted. The court held that a few weeks was too long and Eastern wound up with jet aircraft that did not meet its specifications.

The Code says that the rejection must be "seasonable" and that seems to mean "in due course." With food that is going to be placed into preparation, such as the U.S. Army hams at Thanksgiving time, it would mean a short time indeed.

Thus it is clear that our policy on all incoming goods must be to inspect in due course. If any items are nonconforming, we must reject and state why as part of the same time frame. Having done that, we have not accepted the goods and have no contract obligation to pay for them.

But What About the Goods?

True, we still have the goods in our possession, but we now hold them under the law of bailment and not the law of Sales. As a bailee, we must use ordinary, reasonable care to protect and safeguard them for disposition by the owner, namely the seller. If we use ordinary care and the goods are stolen or destroyed by fire, the loss falls on the seller and not us. This makes the rejection rules even more important to us, as can be seen.

If the rejected goods are perishable and we cannot safeguard them, then we should tell the seller at once. The seller may instruct us to sell them at a loss or to ship them elsewhere. We are expected to follow such orders, but *at the expense of the seller*. So all is well and good, but does this law mean we are going to have to spend every minute of every hour looking at each item we receive to make sure each is conforming? For example, there is our stack of new sheets packed three to a box. Do we have to open each box and inspect each linen for size and quality?

Scope of Inspection

All we have to do is to inspect *by sample*. A box or two from different parts of the shipment will meet the legal requirement of inspection.

But what if our shipment is in sealed containers that we cannot open until we are ready to use them, such as canned food stuffs? If we open them later and find that the contents are nonconforming, are we stuck with them? Not at all, because the Code covers this situation too.

Revoking an Acceptance

If defects are hidden or sealed and are not likely to be discovered until use, which may not come until later, then we can revoke our acceptance. By revoking our acceptance, and doing so seasonably, the seller then has the right to cure. If the seller cannot cure, the goods belong to the seller and we hold them as a bailee.

In Sum

Thus we have had a look at the laws that control our buying at the back of the house. And when one considers that merchants are involved, the rules are not unreasonable at all. These rules represent a special contract law that has been designed to cover the sale of goods between merchants. If we conduct ourselves in our buying as a reasonable merchant would be expected to do, then in most instances we would be complying with the rules.

Good faith and honesty are of course involved because merchants should so conduct themselves. Failure to so act can trigger many surprising rules of Article 2 as we have tried to illustrate.

In our discussion we have left many topics unmentioned such as late delivery, insolvency of a buyer, recapture of goods, and others. Suffice it to say that Article 2 covers all of these and more, and if they become involved in our buying and receiving, legal advice must be sought.

Otherwise, if we act in good faith and honesty and watch what we are doing in our buying and receiving department, and provide instruction in the form of house policies, we can get along nicely in the company of a contract law called "Sales."

With the above in mind as an introduction, let's turn to the more technical aspects of the law.

All orders for supplies and shipment of goods of all types, both to and from a place of business, will be covered or affected by this article. Article 2 covers "transactions in goods" and is not limited to "sales," nor is it intended to be.[1] It *does not* apply to sales that are intended to be "secured transactions." In that event, Article 9 controls.

A helpful way to continue is by an examination of key terms encountered in Article 2.

KEY TERMS

A *buyer* is any person who buys or *contracts to buy* goods. (This distinction is important.) A *seller* is one who sells or contracts to sell goods. A *merchant* is one who deals in goods and has knowledge or skills of those goods and practices of the transaction. A merchant can also be one who has this skill and knowledge attributed to him or her because of the use of agents. In short, a merchant is one who knows, or should know, more about the goods than an ordinary, untrained person. An innkeeper ordering food supplies for the restaurant would be a merchant. So would the supplier of those goods. This would be a transaction "between merchants." This brings us to the definition of "goods," and related terms.

What Are "Goods" and Terms Related to Them?

Goods means all items *that are movable* at the time they become the subject of a sales contract. The definition includes the unborn young of animals, growing crops, and, in some cases, items attached to real estate that are to be severed from the realty.[2] Goods must be *existing* and *identified* before a property interest in them can pass. Goods which are not existing and identified are *future goods* and can be the subject only of a contract to sell—not a present sale. The following are quoted from Article 2.

Lot means a parcel or a single article which is the subject matter of a separate sale or delivery, whether or not it is sufficient to perform the contract.[3]

Commercial unit means such a unit of goods as by commercial usage is a single whole for purposes of sale and division of which materially impairs its character or value on the market or in use.

A commercial unit may be a single article (as a machine) or a set of articles (as a suite of furniture or an assortment of sizes) or a quantity (as a bale, gross, or carload) or any other unit treated in use or in the relevant market as a single whole.[4]

Contract and *agreement* are limited to those relating to the present or future sale of goods. *Contract for sale* includes both a present sale of goods and a contract to sell goods at a future time. A *sale* consists in the passing of title from the seller to the buyer for a price. A *present sale* means a sale which is accomplished by the making of the contract.[5]

Goods or conduct including any part of a performance are "conforming" or conform to the contract when they are in accordance with the obligations under the contract.[6]

Termination occurs when either party pursuant to a power created by agreement or law puts an end to the contract otherwise than for its breach. On "termination," all obligations which are still executory on both sides are discharged but any right based on prior breach or performance survives.[7]

Cancellation occurs when either party puts an end to the contract for breach by the other and its effect is the same as that of "termination" except that the canceling party also retains any remedy for breach of the whole contract or any unperformed balance.[8]

A contract for the sale of timber, minerals, or the like or a structure or its materials to be removed from realty is a contract for the sale of goods if they are to be severed by the seller, but until severance, a purported present sale thereof which is not effective as a transfer of an interest in land is effective only as a contract to sell.

A contract for the sale apart from the land of growing crops or other things attached to realty and capable of severance without material harm thereto is a contract for the sale of goods whether the subject matter is to be severed by the buyer or by the seller even though it forms part of the realty at the time of contracting, and the parties can by identification effect a present sale before severance.

These provisions are subject to any third party rights provided by the law relating to realty records, and the contract for sale may be executed and recorded as a document transferring an interest in land and shall then constitute notice to third parties of the buyer's rights under the contract for sale.[9]

Turning from terms, it is important to find out how a sales contract is created.

FORMATION OF A SALES CONTRACT

Just as with conventional contracts, sales contracts have a statute of frauds and thus certain sales contracts, just as some conventional contracts, must be in writing and signed.

Statute of Frauds

A contract for the sale of goods for $500 or more requires that there be some writing sufficient to indicate the contract, and it must be signed by the one against whom enforcement is sought. It can be signed by an agent. Such writing is not insufficient if it omits a term agreed upon. If it incorrectly states a quantity of goods, the writing is not effective beyond that quantity.[10] This statute of frauds is quite flexible. The statute does not apply at all if specially manufactured goods are involved, or if one admits in court that a contract had been made, or if one receives the goods and pays for them. These acts standing alone would be sufficient to prove the contract. If a sales contract is in written form and is then modified, the modification should also be in writing and signed. Article 2 makes it clear that an oral modification *does not* satisfy the statute of frauds, although it may constitute a waiver.[11] But it is not a good idea to rely upon the waiver.[12]

Examples

Certain Alabama farmers contracted to sell their crop of cotton one year for prices in the 3 cents to 35 cents per pound range. At the time the crop was in, the price was 80 cents on the market and the farmers refused to honor the contract to sell. Since the original contract had been oral, the court ruled that the statute of frauds governed and the farmers were free to sell as they pleased.[13]

In a case that arose in Minnesota, a supplier on the witness stand stated in part ". . . I was interested in buying up to fifty million gallons a year (of heating oil). I said we were interested in selling the product and we agreed to sell it–or to put it in the singular, I agreed to sell it, subject to credit clearance and other clearances back at the home office." The court held that this admission was sufficient to hold the supplier to the oral sales contract.[14]

Avoiding Statute of Frauds

If one is in a situation in which the other party refuses to place anything in writing, can something be done to avoid the statute of frauds problem? Under UCC Article 2-201(2), if one party sends the other a letter of confirmation of the oral deal, and if the other party does not object within ten days, then that letter meets the requirements of the statute. Thus the sales statute of frauds can be met by the party who wants to play safe by getting the agreement in writing—even if the other party does not.

As a matter of good business practice, all contracts for the sale of goods of $500 or more should be reduced to writing at the outset or confirmed by a letter that sets forth the terms of the contract. If the one who receives the letter does not want to be bound, that person must say so, in writing, and must do so promptly.

Related to the statute of frauds is the "parol-evidence rule."

Parol-Evidence Rule

This rule is based upon the common-law principle that, when two persons reduce their agreement to writing, neither can vary or alter that agreement later by oral testimony. This rule has been carried into sales contracts in a modified form. What is reduced to writing cannot be altered by oral testimony—but it can be explained by course of dealing, usage of trade, and prior performance between the parties. The rule does not prohibit oral testimony as to terms not included in the written contract.

A contract for the sale of goods may be made in any manner sufficient to show agreement, including conduct that recognizes the existence of the contract.[15] But one must not forget the effect of the statute of frauds or the parol-evidence rule.

The precise time of the making of the contract is not essential[16] and the fact that one or more terms are left open does not cause it to fail for indefiniteness.[17] These rules are contrary to conventional-contract principles.

OFFER AND ACCEPTANCE

A sales offer invites acceptance in any reasonable manner. If one offers to buy goods that must be shipped, a prompt shipment or promise to ship will be an acceptance. If the offer indicates that the offer is to be accepted by beginning to perform, and the other person does not begin the performance, the offeror may treat the offer as having lapsed before acceptance.[18]

An offer can become "firm"—that is, cannot be revoked—if a merchant promises another in writing to hold the offer open for a period not to exceed three months. Such an offer takes the form of an "option," and no consideration is required.[19]

If Acceptance Changes Offer

If one accepts an offer but changes the terms, *it may still be a good acceptance.* The additional terms are treated as a proposal to make additions to the contract and become part of the contract unless:

a. The offer limited the terms of the acceptance.
b. The changes *materially* alter the offer.
c. The other party gives prompt notification of objections to the changes. Silence would allow the contract to come into being as altered.[20]

If the writings of the parties do not establish a contract, yet the parties recognize the existence of one, then the contract will be treated as one that contains the terms upon which there is agreement. The UCC will then provide the lacking terms. Course of performance controls, supplemented by course of dealing and usage of trade.

Article 2 contains provisions for modification, rescission, and waiver of a sales contract, and all of these should be reduced to writing.[21]

Battle of the Forms

Quite often the inn buyer uses a written purchase order when ordering goods, and the seller in turn uses a written acknowledgment. This is good business-legal practice on both sides for it removes the statute of frauds from any future legal disputes. The use of such documents, which should be initialed or signed by the parties or their agents, satisfies the sales statute of frauds. But what happens if the forms do not agree as to terms?

For example, the buyer on his or her form says "you (the seller) pay the freight." On the seller's acknowledgment is found the phrase "FOB our warehouse." This means the buyer must pay the freight from the seller's warehouse to the destination. Thus the

To: Zero Corporation

Ship: 10,000 units ABC,
Model S, 1½" x 8"
at $9.00 per unit

Terms: 1. A
2. B
3. C
4. D
5. E

Hotel,

s/s Ace/, Inc.

FIGURE 7.1 An HRI purchase order.

forms do not agree. This is not unusual in sales contract situations and has become known as the "battle of the conflicting forms." Does such a state of facts destroy the sales contract? It certainly would destroy a pending conventional contract.

As it turns out, Article 2 covers this situation, and here is how it works. First, examine Figures 7.1 and 7.2. Notice that the number of units has been reduced on the acknowledgment; the size and price are different; and while terms 1 and 2 are the same on both forms, terms 3, 4, and 5 are not.

Hotel

To: ACE/, Inc.

Thanks

Will ship 9,000 units
ABC, Model S, 1¼"
x 8" at $9.50 per unit.

Terms: 1. A
2. B
3. F
4. G
5. H

s/s Zero Corporation

FIGURE 7.2 An acknowledgment of the HRI purchase order.

The UCC says that there *is* a contract as to the terms upon which the parties agree. As to the terms upon which they disagree, then "course of performance controls," supplemented by "course of dealing" and "usage of trade." Thus there is not only a contract between the parties, but its terms are there even if those terms have to be determined by a court.

Such situations often arise in HRI operations. Carpeting at an inn may stretch, causing a dispute over quality. Glass in windows may stain and have to be replaced. Air conditioners may fail when placed into use. What did the contracts have to say about such contingencies? Probably nothing at all, yet the law provides the terms to cover these situations.

When merchants come to understand the nature of Article 2, they tend to adjust their differences by subsequent agreements, for they know that if they do not the courts will do it for them. This feature of Article 2 tends to make it self-regulating in practice and this too gives legal effect to its purposes.

Revocation of Sales Offer

One who makes a sales contract offer can revoke it before acceptance. The exceptions would be when it was a "firm offer" or when the other party had timely started performance. The UCC does not change prior contract law in this area. Unless displaced by the particular provisions of Article 2, the principles of law and equity, including the law merchant and the law relative to capacity to contract, principal and agent, estoppel, fraud, misrepresentation, duress, coercion, mistake, bankruptcy, or other validating or invalidating cause shall supplement its (Article 2) provisions.[22]

OBLIGATIONS OF THE PARTIES

Tender of Delivery

The seller has a duty to make a proper tender of delivery under the terms of the contract. This is done by placing conforming goods at the disposal of the buyer and by notifying him or her so the buyer can take delivery. It is important that tender be at a reasonable hour and under reasonable circumstances. The goods must be held by the seller or seller's agent for a reasonable time to give the buyer the opportunity to take possession.

Stopping Goods in Transit

Under certain conditions, a seller can stop goods that are in transit to the buyer. If it is learned that the buyer is insolvent or has missed a payment due the seller, shipment can be stopped. If the goods are in the hands of a common carrier, shipment cannot be stopped unless it is a truckload, carload, or planeload. A seller cannot stop a UPS truck and demand that the driver shift through a thousand packages to find one. The order to stop shipment must be made timely. If it is made after the goods are delivered, it comes too late.

When a proper stop shipment order has been made, the one who has the goods (bailee or shipper) must hold the goods and deliver them according to the instructions of the seller.

The right to stop shipment applies only between seller and buyer. If the buyer has resold the goods to others, those goods cannot be stopped in transit.

In a Missouri case, A sold goods to B, who assigned the shipment to C on a nonnegotiable bill of lading. (A "bill of lading" is a list of goods received for shipment. A nonnegotiable bill is one that cannot be transferred to others cutting off the original shipper. A negotiable bill can do just that.) The check from B to A bounced and A stopped shipment to C. The court held that since C was not a bona fide purchaser for value, A could stop the shipment.[23] But if C had been a bona fide purchaser for value, A could not have stopped the shipment. If a stop shipment is unlawful in any respect, the seller must bear the responsibility for any loss to the buyer caused by the improper stop order.[24]

Buyer's Right of Inspection

Once the goods are tendered, the buyer has the right (and duty) to inspect them before accepting them.[25] This must be done at a reasonable time and place and in a reasonable manner. If a buyer waives the right to inspect, that in itself is an acceptance *even if the goods are nonconforming.*

If the parties agree that payment is to be made before inspection, then the buyer must pay before inspection even if the goods are nonconforming. This occurs in COD[26] payments against documents of title and CIF[27] contracts. The burden is now shifted to the buyer, who must pay the price and then sue for any loss. Buyers should resist efforts to make them pay before inspection for this reason, and this should be a policy at the inn.

Improper Delivery

If an improper delivery is made, such as a shipment of nonconforming goods, the buyer must do one of three things:

1. Reject all of the goods.
2. Accept all of the goods.
3. Accept any commercial unit or units and reject the rest.[28]

If the buyer decides to do 2, above, prompt notice should be given to the seller that the buyer demands an allowance for the failure to conform.[29]

If the buyer decides to reject the goods, two extremely important principles must be followed:

1. After prompt inspection, the buyer must notify the seller in a reasonable time that the goods are being rejected.[30] A wait of as long as an hour may be too long in some deliveries. Failure to so notify is treated as an acceptance.[31]

2. If the defects are such that they can be "cured" (corrected), the buyer must also tell the seller what these defects are.[32]

After rejection and notification, the buyer must act reasonably with the goods and follow reasonable instructions from the seller as to their disposal. Such instructions might be to reship to the seller or a third party, or even to sell the goods as salvage. If the goods are perishable, the buyer has a duty to sell them promptly to protect the seller. The buyer is entitled to compensation for services performed with rejected goods.[33] If the seller fails to provide instructions in a reasonable time, the buyer can store, ship, or sell the goods for the account of the seller.[34] These are the options of the merchant-buyer. A nonmerchant-buyer has only the duty to hold the goods for the seller.

In any rejection, the buyer should never do anything that could be construed as the buyer treating the goods as being his or her own property. A court might treat such acts as an acceptance. For example, if an inn rejects an air conditioner, then refuses to allow the seller to pick it up, that would be an acceptance and render the inn liable for the price.[35]

Revoking an Acceptance

In instances where defects cannot be discovered by an immediate inspection, and where such defects are uncovered later, sometimes years later, is the buyer stuck because of the prior acceptance? No, since the buyer can, in some cases, revoke an acceptance.[36] In an Arkansas case, a court held that a defective air conditioner could be rejected three years after purchase, since it had not worked properly all along and efforts had been made to repair it, which had not been successful. Thus the right existed to revoke the acceptance.[37]

SELLER'S RIGHT TO CURE

If a seller makes an improper delivery, the seller has the right to be told why the delivery is improper. For example, a delivery of 1000 cruise ship excursion tickets arrives and it is discovered by the buyer that the name of the ship is wrong. The buyer must reject and tell why. The seller now has the right to "cure" or remedy the defect by delivering new tickets.[38] If the cured goods arrive by the deadline for their use, the contract is complete and the price must be paid. If goods cannot be cured timely, then the defective delivery and the rejection keeps a binding contract from coming into being.

If the goods arrive late in the beginning, must the buyer still reject timely and tell the seller why? A Florida case involving jet airliners answered this question "yes."[39] So the two steps of rejection should be made for *any* improper delivery that the buyer does not want to accept—even a delivery that comes too late for use.

PASSING OF TITLE

"Passing of title" (ownership) was an abstract legal concept that caused many problems prior to the UCC. Now, Article 2 does not refer to the passing of title but leaves the various sections of the Code to be used to determine the rights and obligations of the parties. However, the Code does contain specific provisions that regulate "passing of title."

Title cannot pass on goods that are not in existence and identified to the contract.[40] Title cannot pass until goods are made, if they are to be manufactured. And even after they are completed, title does not pass until the seller indicates that these goods are intended for the buyer.[41] Subject to such rules as these, the parties are free to agree at which point title is to pass.[42]

RISK OF LOSS

The parties are free to make any agreement between them as to risk of loss.[43] However, the agreement cannot be unconscionable. The risk can be divided if they choose.[44] If a shipment contract is involved, the risk of loss normally passes to the buyer when the goods are delivered to the carrier.[45] Examples of shipment contracts include FOB,[46] point of shipment, FOB vessel or car, FAS,[47] CIF,[48] or C and F[49] (see the endnotes for definitions).

If the contract is a "destination agreement," then risk of loss shifts to the buyer when a proper tender is made at that point.[50] "FOB destination" is a destination agreement. Common sense tells us that both buyers and sellers must be conscious of risk of loss, because it means just that. If the goods are lost, stolen, damaged by fire, or other cause, someone must bear the loss. As a policy matter it is sound business practice to agree on the risk and then buy appropriate insurance to cover that risk.

RECAPTURE RIGHTS

If goods are sold on credit, tender is made, and acceptance follows but the buyer refuses to pay for the goods, can the seller "recapture" the goods? If goods are delivered to a buyer who is found to be insolvent, recapture is limited to the following 10 days unless there is proof of misrepresentation of insolvency; then it is extended to three months.[51] What happens after these time periods is that the Code shifts the "goods" to a "debt," leaving the seller the right to take legal action on the debt—not the happiest thing for the seller. With the recapture rights lost, the seller may have to wait a year or two to recover in court for the loss.

MISCELLANEOUS SALES-CONTRACT CASES

Because of the importance of the law of sales, an examination of a variety of situations in which merchants have found themselves in court because of such contracts is in order.

Statute of Frauds

As we have seen, contracts for the sale of goods of $500 or more must be in writing. If not, and if one of the exceptions does not arise, the contract cannot be enforced. One court has gone beyond the exceptions and has ruled that where one party has so changed his position in reliance on the oral contract that an unconscionable loss would result to the other, that person should be "estopped" to deny the contract,[52] thus enforcing the oral agreement.

Can a down payment satisfy the statute of frauds if made by check? Article 2 provides that it can only do so with respect to goods for which payment has been made and accepted.[53] It is best not to rely on such payments but rather to use the written contract.

In a Maryland case,[54] a party to an oral contract wound up on the witness stand and then admitted the contract. That satisfied the statute.

Turning from the statute of frauds, does the UCC have a "statute of limitations"?

Statute of Limitations

A glass wall had been installed in 1966. In 1972, a boy fell through the glass and was killed. The court held that the breach of warranty occurred at the time of installation, if it occurred at all, and since more than four years had passed, the manufacturer of the glass had no liability. This left the responsibility squarely on the buyer of the glass.

The UCC normally allows a four-year period in which to bring a suit for breach of sales contract.[55] This does not always mean what it says. Martin Becker bought a car in 1969 and sued for breach of warranty within four years. The California court held that, in that state, action for injuries caused by a wrongful act or neglect must be brought in one year.[56] It should be pointed out, however, that there is a split of the courts in such instances. In other words, do other state statutes of limitations supersede those in the UCC? The question has not been settled.

Trade usage can severely shorten the statute of limitations. Thus, since a sales contract not only means what it says, but is supplemented by trade custom and practices, the result can be surprising. A buyer purchased certain glass and insisted on a 100% guarantee against "staining." After resale to others, the glass stained and the buyer refunded the price to *his* buyers. He then turned to the seller for recovery on the guarantee. The court held that it was too late because, in the trade of glass selling, it was customary for such complaints to be made between seven and thirty days. The contract was silent on the period of limitations, so trade practice controlled.[57]

Turning from periods of limitations, how definite must a sales contract be?

Definiteness

In a Georgia case, the buyer agreed to buy over $58,000 worth of goods and made a down payment of over $4,000. It was in writing and all seemed in order. However, there was no payment schedule, no time for performance, and other terms were lacking. Did it fail for "indefiniteness" when the buyer wanted out? The court said no, pointing out that since the parties had intended to make a contract, that Article 2 will supply the price,[58] decide when payment is due,[59] and provide for the method and place of delivery.[60] Thus the contract did not fail for indefiniteness although these terms were missing.[61]

Next, is there a material difference between a "sales" and a "service" contract?

Sales Versus Service

Warranty liability arises only if a "sale of goods" is involved. This requires a merchant to stand behind the goods sold. If a mere "service" is involved, the warranties do not apply—at least so it has been in prior years.

A Michigan electric company installed electrical wiring in a building, which subsequently suffered an electrical fire. The installer claimed that this was an installation (service); thus warranties did not apply. The court held that since the installer supplied the goods, which carried the warranties, the court would imply a warranty of fitness as to the manner in which the goods were installed. The old distinction between sales and service is no longer as clear as it was in the past.[62]

After a sales contract comes into being, can it be modified, or changed in some material provision?

Article 2 permits modification of a sales contract, so long as the parties both agree.[63] The only requirement is that each act in good faith with the other.

Leaving the technical discussion of Article 2, some examples provide a way to place the material of this chapter into perspective. In the drawings, the following symbols are used:

MB—Merchant-buyer. (This would be the innkeeper.)
MS—Merchant-seller.

C–Consumer
IRS–The obligation to "inspect, reject, and state why."

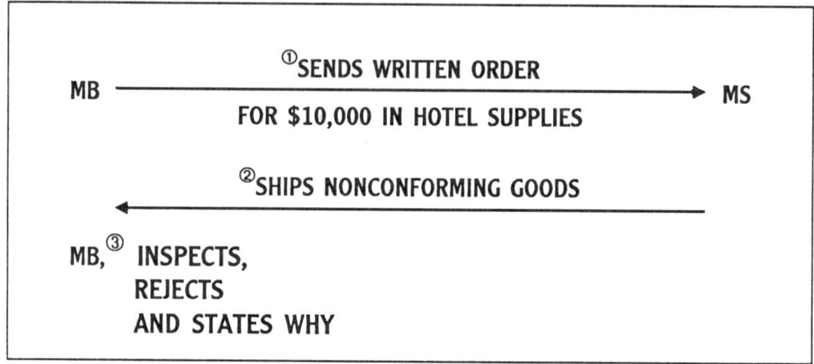

FIGURE 7.3

Looking at Figure 7.3 the goods are now on the loading platform of MB, where they had been inspected and found to be nonconforming.

1. As a matter of law, what is the legal relationship of MB and MS as of this point in time?
2. Is there a contract as to the goods?
3. The goods are now stolen and there is no fault on the MB. Who must bear the loss?

(Answers: (1) MB is a bailee and must exercise ordinary care for the safety of the goods; (2) there is no contract at this point, but the MS now has the right to cure by shipping conforming goods; (3) MS must bear the loss since MB was not at fault.)

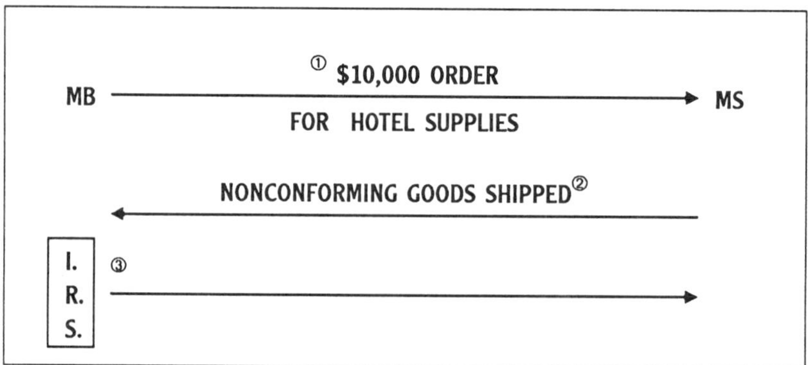

FIGURE 7.4

Examine Figure 7.4.

1. Is there a contract?
2. What are the rights of MS?
3. What if MS cannot cure for the reason that conforming goods are not available?

(Answers: (1) There is no contract at this point; (2) MS now has the right to cure; (3) if MS cannot cure, the matter is at an end and MB is free to go on the market and deal with another MS.)

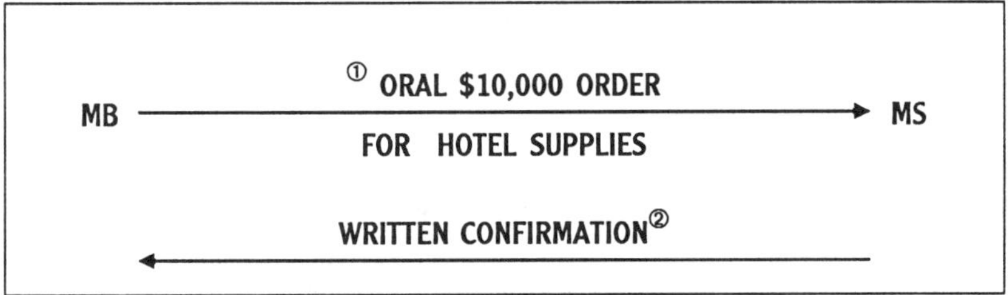

FIGURE 7.5

Examine Figure 7.5. Assume that the confirmation lists nonconforming goods that MB does not want. What is the danger to MB if he or she remains silent?

(Answer: If MB does not object to the confirmation and ten days pass, the confirmation not only satisfies the statute of frauds but may be held by a court to be an acceptance of the nonconforming goods for failure to object to them.)

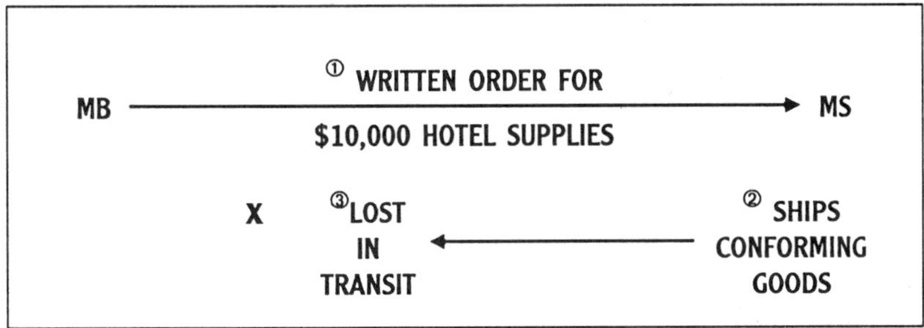

FIGURE 7.6

Examine Figure 7.6. Who bears the loss? The answer will depend upon varying factors. If the goods had become identified

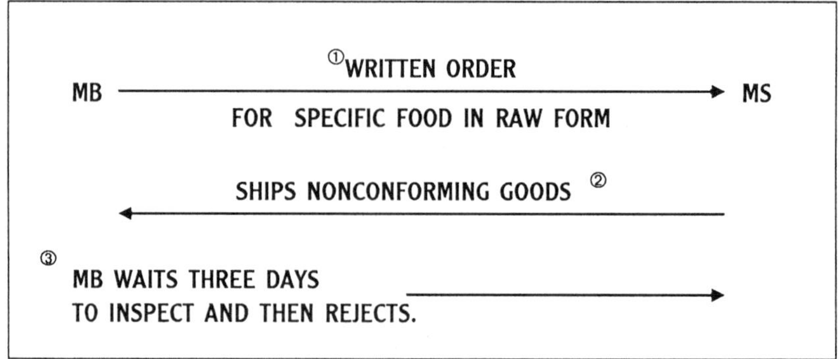

FIGURE 7.7

with the contract, the loss will probably fall upon MB. If FOB terms are involved, such terms could affect the answer. The thing to learn here is to always provide for risk of loss and cover it accordingly, one way or the other.

Since food in raw form was involved, a court might hold, as in the Max Bauer case, that the rejection was not seasonable. Thus the delay in inspection could well be an acceptance of the goods (Figure 7.7).

SOME REFLECTIONS ON ARTICLE 2

The practical legal effect of Article 2 is that it treats the merchant buyer and the merchant seller as equals. It gives no edge or preference to either. That assumes, of course, that both are equally knowledgeable about the law and that may not always be true. This fact makes it important for the HRI manager to have a working knowledge of Article 2.

An understanding of this law by the HRI manager will have another effect in practice: It will allow "educated guesses" to be made. It is a matter of asking one's self, "What would merchants be expected to do in the situation at hand?" Hotel students who have been exposed to this law will have a greater chance of avoiding losses in the future because of this concept of "educated guessing."

Perhaps the Sales law of Article 2 could have been written in some other form. But the fact that it was not means that the HRI manager is going to have to live with it for the balance of her or his career in both the United States and Canada, where it has also been adopted. The lawyer for the inn is not going to be running the purchasing department.

As a parting shot, let's ask a question: Since inns receive large amounts of frozen goods and frozen meats and vegetables, why should care be taken to see that these items do not begin to thaw before the inspection of them is completed? (This is an example of an "educated guess.")

QUESTIONS

1. Why must goods be existing and identified before a present legal interest in them can pass to another?
2. Name the three exceptions to the sales statute of frauds.
3. Compare the sales statute of frauds with the conventional contracts statute of frauds in Chapter 6. How do they differ?
4. What must a buyer do who receives nonconforming goods?
5. Under what conditions may a seller stop goods that are in transit?
6. Under what conditions may one revoke an acceptance?
7. Write out the meanings of FOB, FAS, CIF, and C and F. What is the importance of knowing which of these controls a sales contract?
8. Why does the law require that a written confirmation be objected to quickly?
9. List three ways in which a sales contract can be accepted.
10. Name one way that custom may become involved in a sales case.

ENDNOTES

1. UCC 2-102.
2. UCC 2-107.
3. UCC 2-104 (5).
4. UCC 2-104 (6).
5. UCC 2-106 (1).
6. UCC 2-106 (2).
7. UCC 2-106 (3).
8. UCC 2-106 (4).
9. UCC 2-107.
10. UCC 2-201.
11. UCC 2-209 (4).

12. *Double E. Sportswear Corp. v. Girard Trust Bank,* 488 F. 2d 292 (3d. Cir. 1973).
13. *Cox v. Cox,* 289 So. 2d 609, 14 UCC Rep. 330 (1974).
14. *Oskay Gasoline & Oil Co. v. Continental Oil Co.,* 19 UCC Rep. 61 (1976).
15. UCC 2-204.
16. UCC 2-204 (2).
17. UCC 2-204 (3).
18. UCC 2-206.
19. UCC 2-205.
20. UCC 2-207.
21. UCC 2-209.
22. UCC 1-103.
23. UCC 2-703 (b).
24. *Clock v. Missouri–Kansas–Texas Railroad Co. v. Crawford,* 407 F. Supp. 448 (E.D. Mo. 1976).
25. UCC 2-513.
26. "Cash on delivery"
27. "Cost of goods, insurance and freight."
28. UCC 2-601.
29. UCC 714 (2).
30. UCC 2-602 (1).
31. UCC 2-606.
32. UCC 2-605 (1) (a).
33. UCC 2-603 (2).
34. UCC 2-604.
35. UCC 2-709 (1) (a).
36. UCC 2-608.
37. *Dapierlla v. Arkansas Louisiana Gas Co.,* 225 Ark. 150, 12 UCC Rep. 468 (1973).
38. UCC 2-508.
39. *Eastern Airlines, Inc., v. McDonnell Douglas Corp.,* 532 F2. 957, 19 UCC Rep. 353 (5th Cir. 1976).
40. UCC 2-401 (1).
41. UCC 2-501.
42. UCC 2-401 (1).
43. UCC 2-509 (4).
44. UCC 2-303.

45. UCC 2-509 (1).
46. FOB, "Free on board." (This can be at shipping point or at destination).
47. FAS. "Free alongside," referring to shipping vessel or other means of transportation.
48. CIF. This means that the quoted price includes the cost of goods, insurance to the designated destination, and freight charges to that destination.
49. C&F. This means the quoted price includes costs of goods and freight to destination, but not insurance.
50. UCC 2-509 (1) (b).
51. UCC 2-702 (2).
52. *Dangerfield v. Marhel,* 222 N.W. 2d 373, 15 UCC Rep. 915 (N.D. 1974).
53. UCC 2-201 (3) (c).
54. *Lewis v. Hughes,* 346 A 2d 231, 18 UCC Rep. 52 (MD. App. 1975).
55. UCC 2-725 (1).
56. *Becker v. Volkswagen of Am., Inc.,* 18 UCC Rep. 135 (Cal. App. 1975).
57. *Jazel Corp. v. Sentinel Enterprises, Inc.,* 20 UCC Rep. 837 (N.Y. Sup. Ct. 1976).
58. UCC 2-305 (1).
59. UCC 2-310.
60. UCC 2-309.
61. *Deck House, Inc. v. Scarborough, Sheffield & Gastin, Inc.,* 228 S.E. 2d 142, 20 UCC Rep. 278 (Ga. App. 1976).
62. *Insurance Co. of North America v. Radiant Elec. Co.,* 222 N.W. 2d 323, 15 UCC Rep. 261 (Mich. App. 1974).
63. UCC 2-209.

8

HRI Agents and Independent Contractors

The motel looked like it had been built during the postwar automobile boom, forty years earlier, when U.S. Route 1 funneled vacationers from Boston and Hartford and even New York City to resorts in Hampton and Ogunquit and Kennebunkport, and truckers steamed up and down the coast, and businesses boomed everywhere. Then along came Interstate 95, all eight lanes of it, and Route 1 was left to the locals and the occasional aimless tourist. The motels and gas stations and ice cream stands that had sprouted along the roadside like goldenrod in the forties and fifties were mostly boarded up or torn down or converted into shops selling automobile parts and carpet remnants.

Dead Winter, William G. Tapply

OVERVIEW

The law of agency plays a major role in the operation of all business, especially those that are "people-oriented" such as in the HRI industry. This is true because of the day-to-day need to deal with third parties by the use of agents. It is a law that forces many management principles upon the HRI industry because it is here that the use of agents, both "in-house" and "professional," comes to the front.

Some basic points of agency law are set forth and should be of assistance in understanding the discussion that follows.

PRELIMINARY POINTS

1. Agents normally do not assume personal liability for contracts entered into on behalf of their principals (employers).

2. Both principals and agents may become jointly liable for torts committed by an agent when carrying out the authority granted by the principal.

3. Principals are seldom liable for criminal acts committed by an agent.

4. One business may have more than one principal and the number of agents may be in the hundreds or even thousands, depending upon the size of the business.

5. The authority granted to an agent is not permanent in that it will end at some point as the agent completes that day's work.

6. Employees are not necessarily agents although they may become so if they have contact with and deal with third parties.

7. The usual agents found in business are often also employees of that business. These agents must be distinguished from professional agents such as lawyers, accountants, insurance men and women, and others who serve the same business.

8. Innkeeping is "people-intensive" and at the same time, it is "agent-intensive."

9. Liability in contract, vicarious liabilities under agency law in tort, and liability under public policy are all different and can reach different results.

10. Agency law will cause liability to attach to an innkeeper even though the innkeeper in fact did not know of the acts that were being done by the agent. That is why the liability is "vicarious" or indirect.

11. Innkeeper P hires Agent A to accomplish duties at the inn that we will label "AB&C." To accomplish these duties, Agent A must also do "DE&F." Thus A has express authority to do "AB&C" and implied authority to do "DE&F." Both sets of authority are "real authority," since one is required to achieve the other.

12. Those who carry out room-service duties at the inn are agents and have direct contact with third parties. Any acts committed by them, such as theft or tort, can well bind the innkeeper.

Leaving these preliminary points, it is next useful to look at some basic legal points about the law of agency.

PRELIMINARY OBSERVATIONS

If an agent plans and carries out a robbery, the principal has no responsibility for the crime.[1] However, if in the scope of the agent's employment, the agent robs or commits fraud upon an innocent third party, such as a guest at a motel, the principal is liable for the damage done—but not for the crime itself[2] (The principal pays for the loss, the agent goes to jail.)

Generally, once an agent leaves work, the responsibility of the principal ends. Examine Figure 8.1. In a car-bailment case, the employee left work at the parking lot, returned, stole a parked car, and wrecked it. The court held that the principal was not liable even though the agent had a criminal record and was on probation at the time.[3]

In a hotel case, a guest turned over his car to a bellhop who parked it in a hotel parking lot. The bellhop went off duty, returned, took the car, and wrecked it. The facts are almost identical to the above situation, yet here the court held that "misdelivery to the bellhop imposed absolute liability on the hotel for damages, regardless of whether the misdelivery was in good faith, through negligence, or otherwise." The court further said this was a bailment for hire and the bailee hotel promised to redeliver the car in good shape and failed to do so.

These preliminary situations are offered to allow one to see at the outset that the law of agency has fine distinctions within it.

A good place to begin is by an examination of the traditional reach and scope of the law of agency.

AGENCY

Agency has been defined as the relationship which results from the manifestation of consent by one person to another that the other shall act on his or her behalf and subject to his or her control and the agreement by the other so to act. The definition leads itself to an outline:

1. P consents that A shall act for P.
2. A agrees to act for P.
3. A agrees that P shall control A while A is so acting.

In practice, P is called the "principal," A the "agent." These letters will be used in the chapter. It follows that the acts of the agent will in some manner involve "third parties," which we will call T.

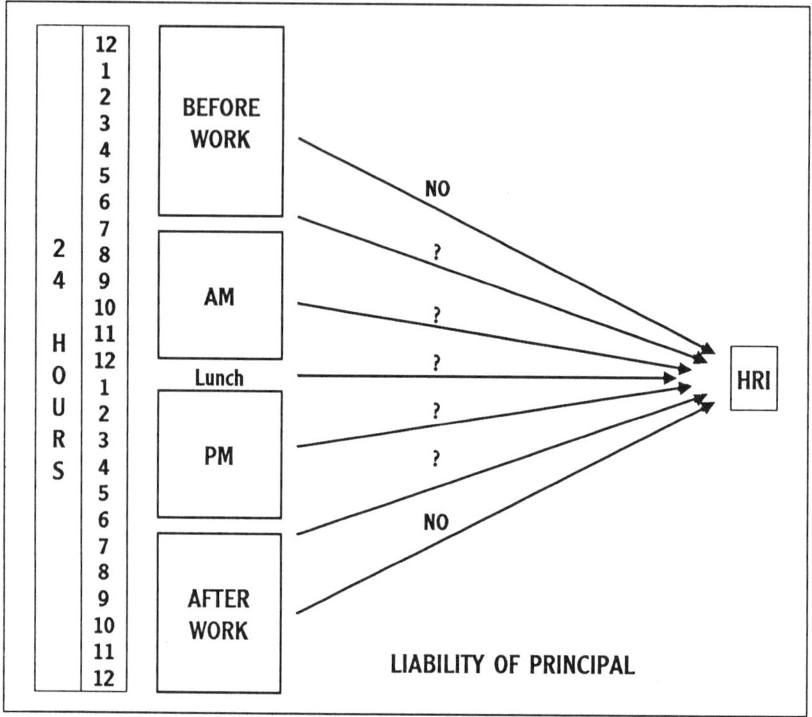

FIGURE 8.1 Timing in agency law.

The relationship brings into being four legal consequences:

1. A "contract of agency" is created between P and A.
2. When A acts with T, a contract may come into being between P and T—even though P did not deal with T personally.
3. When A acts for P, and while so doing causes injury to a third party, P may be held responsible for that injury.
4. When A contracts with T for the benefit of P, A incurs no personal responsibility on the contract.

Therefore an agent is one who acts for another, who must account to the other, who binds the other in contract and tort, and who usually does not benefit personally from the specific act performed. Rather, the agent is compensated by the principal for the act, or a continuous series of acts, as is so often the case. Examples of agents include lawyers, bank cashiers, brokers, insurance agents, front-desk clerks, waiters, auctioneers, agents of corporations, and employees who deal with third parties.

Examine Figure 8.2, the "circle view of agency law."

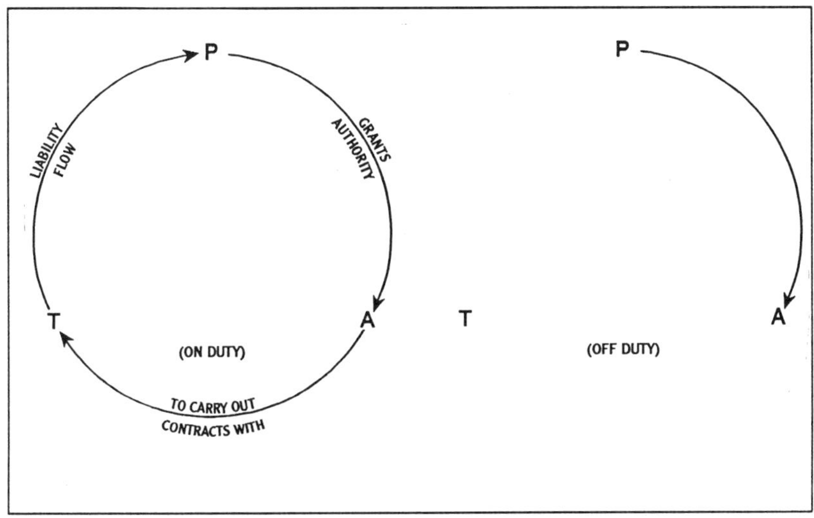

Figure 8.2 The "circle view of agency law."

Agents and "Servants" Are Different

An agent, by the nature of the law of agency, acts with third parties, while a servant performs mechanical or manual acts under the direct control of the principal-master. Servants can create liability upon the master, just as the agent can upon the principal. Many employees seem to have the characteristics of servants–while others could well act with third parties and thus be agents.

Types of Agents

Agents are classed as "special" or "general" agents. The former performs a single act or tries to accomplish a single objective. The latter handles continuing, general affairs of the principal. One authorized to purchase all goods needed to keep an inn in operation would be a general agent. One who is authorized to sign one deed for a principal is a special agent.

Another Classification

A "private" agent may bind the principal even when the agent acts beyond the scope of the authority given to A. A "public" agent, such as the governor of a state, binds the principal (state) only if the acts are within the authority granted. Examples of public agents include governors, police officers, deputy sheriffs, sheriffs, and fire marshals. Thus one who is injured by a tort or breach of contract committed by a public officer may find the scope of recovery sharply reduced because of the limit of liability upon the state. On the other hand, one injured by a private agent can almost always look directly to P.

Agents Distinguished from Trustees

In most instances a trustee has no principal. Such a person handles estates or "powers" and is in a fiduciary (high position of trust) capacity. The agent does have a principal, as we have seen.

FORMATION OF THE RELATIONSHIP

An agency relationship is most often formed by a contract between P and A. Such relationships are said to be "express agencies" since they arise from the terms expressed orally or placed in writing by the parties. In addition, agencies can be "implied" and, in rare cases, may arise by estoppel. We will begin by looking at the express agency–the most common type found in HRI businesses.

Express Agency

The agency contract may be oral or written. There is no specific legal form required other than that there be a clear statement of the authority granted by P and an assent on the part of A to act as an agent. If, however, the authority granted will require a formal legal act by A, such as the execution of a deed for P, then the authority granted must have the same "dignity" as the act to be performed. That is, the grant of authority must also be written and signed by P.[4]

In earlier times, such as the last century, a formal grant of authority to an agent had to be sealed–that is, the word "seal" or "L.S.," had to appear following the signature of P. This requirement has been abolished in most states and under the Uniform Commercial Code as well, when the "sale of goods" is involved.[5] Today, when agency agreements are placed in writing, they are seldom sealed.

If a court is called upon to construe (decide what the parties intended) a written agency contract, the subject matter of the contract, the acts of the parties, and the surrounding circumstances will be examined in determining the intent of the principal and agent.

An agency can be implied by the business acts of the parties.

Implied Agency

An agency may be implied from the conduct of P and A, and from the nature and circumstances surrounding that conduct. This means that an agency may exist even though neither party expressly stated that one was in existence. What the parties call themselves is immaterial. The courts will look to the actual relationship between them[6] and, if that relationship is in fact an agency, the courts will apply agency law to it.

Agency by Estoppel

An estoppel can be used by a court in those instances where one has misled another in an "agency-type" situation to a degree that harm will result if the misled party is not provided some legal protection. This protection comes in the form of a court stopping (estopping) the one who misled the other, from denying that the two of them were in fact bound in an agency relationship. In short, a court can "close a person's mouth" in certain situations.

To illustrate, assume that P, in some manner, leads T to believe that A is P's agent. In fact, there is no express or implied relationship between P and A. If T is misled, and consequently assumes a position of liability, then P will be "estopped" to deny the agency. The effect of this is that T can look to P just as though an agency had in fact existed between P and A. However, if A leads T to believe an agency exists between P and A and P in fact knows nothing about it, the estoppel principle would have no application. This is true because an agency cannot be proven by statements of the alleged agent standing alone.

A hybrid type of agency is found in those that are created by statutes.

Statutory Agencies

A good example of agencies created by statute is found in the "long-arm statutes." These permit nonresident HRI businesses to be sued in a state where they have transacted substantial business but who are headquartered in another state. In such cases, these "foreign" corporations can be sued in a local court and served process through the secretary of state of that state. The nonresident corporations, by doing business in the state, have by statute appointed the secretary of state their agent for this purpose.

Another statutory example is found in laws that require a newly forming corporation to name in the corporate application an agent for service of legal process.

Leaving the types of agencies, let's examine the scope of an agent's authority and see what the law has to say about that authority.

SCOPE OF AGENT'S AUTHORITY

An agent's authority to act for a principal may be express, implied, or "apparent"–sometimes called "ostensible." Express authority presents no problems. It simply involves the doing of those things that P expressly gave A the authority to do. But the law does not stop there. With any grant of express authority, there must also go authority that can be "implied" from the express grant itself. To illustrate, if P grants A the authority to lease apartment units in Zero Condominium, then A would have the implied power to advertise the rentals, enter into lease agreements, and collect rent for the benefit of P. Conversely, A would *not* have the implied power to sell the building. A coal mine superintendent would have the implied power to hire employees; an accountant would have the implied power to charge P for the books necessary to carry out the bookkeeping. On the other hand, a hotel manager would have no authority to enter into a contract to sell a hotel van in the absence of an express grant of such authority from the hotel owner.

The duties to be carried out and the nature of the acts and the surrounding circumstances become relevant in determining whether or not implied authority exists on behalf of an agent, and the courts will take such factors into consideration.

Apparent Authority

An implied grant of authority falls within the real scope of the authority granted. Apparent, or ostensible, authority, however, falls outside the express and real scope of the authority granted. Examine Figure 8.3. The test of apparent authority is whether a third party, knowing the usages of business, is justified in supposing that A is authorized to perform the act because of the nature of the known duties.[7] Such a rule is necessary in the laws of agency to cover those fringe matters that may arise as agents carry out their duties.

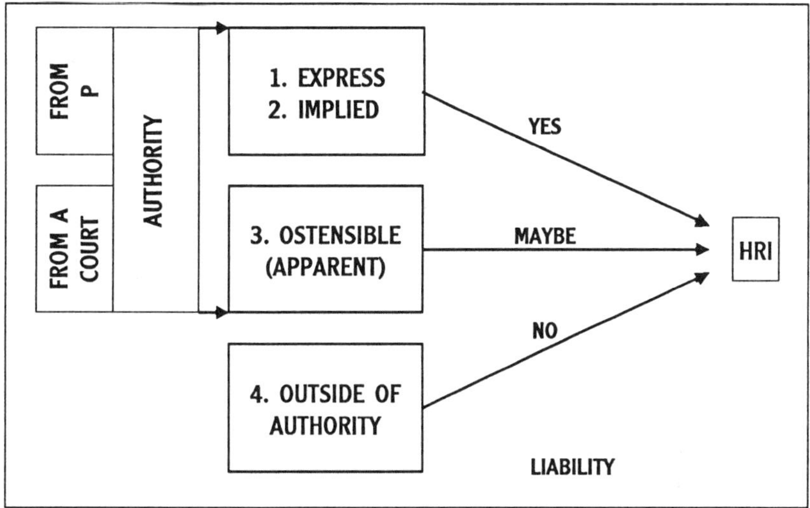

FIGURE 8.3 Agent's authority.

Third-Party Peril

When one deals with an agent, it is that person's duty to determine the nature and extent of the authority of the agent. The law presumes that the third party knows the scope of the authority granted to A. If the third party is wrong in its estimation of the authority of A, then that party must bear the risk of loss. To translate this principle into commonsense terms, anyone who deals with any agent and who is in doubt of the authority of that agent should immediately make inquiry to the principal. If T is confronted by A, who is asking that the debt owing to P be paid in cash–not check–T obviously has a duty to make inquiry.

In many instances, an agent will act outside the range of actual, implied, or apparent authority. In such instances, upon learning of this, P should repudiate such acts of A. In so doing, P will not be bound by those acts. In other instances, however, P may want to adopt such acts of A. Now P must take a different action at law, called "ratification."

Ratification

If P learns that A has done acts with T that are totally outside of all authority granted to A, and if P wants to gain the benefits of such acts, those acts must be "ratified." To accomplish this, the

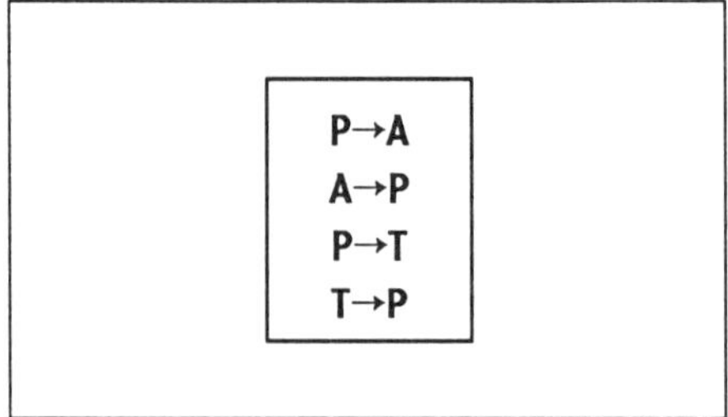

Figure 8.4 Flow of duties.

principal must expressly or impliedly adopt these acts. This can be done by express statements, by payments, by retention of goods involved–and often by mere silence, depending upon the circumstances. It follows that P cannot ratify acts of A that P in fact knows nothing about. The effect of ratification is that P is now bound to T on the unauthorized acts of A, and conversely T is bound to P. One cannot ratify and thus adopt only beneficial parts of an unauthorized act but rather must adopt all of it or none.

In the agency relationship, a multitude of rights, duties, and liabilities arise between the parties involved. Examine Figure 8.4.

RIGHTS, DUTIES, AND LIABILITIES

Duties of A to P

The agent must follow reasonable instructions of P. In the event of emergencies, agents are permitted–and expected–to deviate from instructions. For example, P may expressly tell A "under no circumstances are you to borrow money in my name." If P should be absent on vacation, and floodwaters have damaged the carpets in P's motel, A could borrow money in the name of P and do other reasonable acts necessary to correct the problem. In fact, A would, as a matter of law, often be expected to do such acts.

An agent must exercise a reasonable amount of care, caution, and discretion. The "reasonable person" test is applied. If an agent acts as he or she would have if the subject had been his or her property, that person will generally not be held personally responsible for subsequent loss if such should occur.

An agent must act in good faith with the principal and be loyal to P. An agent must not profit personally from the acts done for P. If this were done, such profits would be held by A, in trust, for

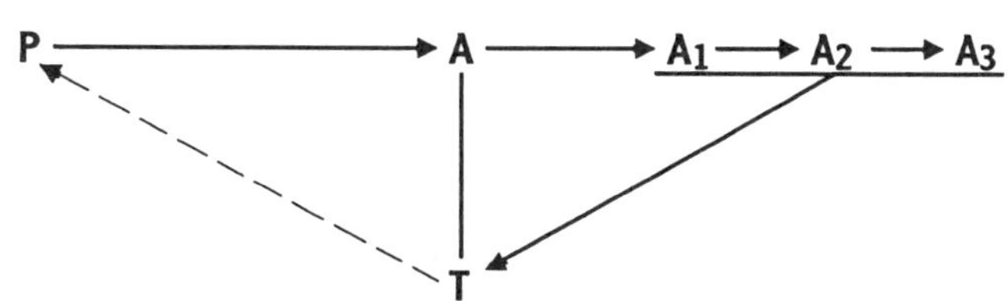

The formula of subagents: P to A to A1, to A2 to A3 to T to P. Agency law always places someone in the middle.

FIGURE 8.5

the benefit of P. An agent must at all times make full disclosures to P and not withhold information of value to P. This disclosure is best carried out by periodic written reports to P, which, by the way, is a good management practice. Examine Figure 8.5 for an "agency formula."

An agent should never sell the goods of P to himself or herself except upon express authority of P. A position of delicacy arises in such cases and the agent must be careful. There is nothing wrong, however, with one agent buying P's goods from another agent of the same principal. Most principals insist that this pattern be followed.

It follows that an agent should never represent a second principal so as to be in conflict with the interests of the first principal. Nor should an agent commingle P's funds with A's. Separate accounts must always be maintained. Collections made by A on behalf of P and deposited into A's account could conceivably lead to a charge of embezzlement. Care is in order. In instances where A collects and maintains accounts for P, A must be ready at all times to give a full accounting to P. If A acts for P but does not disclose P, then the agent is personally liable on any contract entered into.

In retrospect, these duties of A to P are reasonable, designed to strip A of temptations to take advantage, and represent rules that a reasonable person would conclude should be the duties of A to P.

Duties of P to A

The principal has a duty to compensate A for services rendered. The rate is usually set at the time of creation of the relationship. Further, P has a duty to *reimburse* A for expenses and advances made by A while carrying out the scope of authority granted. If P fails to compensate or reimburse, A would have a lien (claim) against goods or property of P that are in the hands of A. In such circumstances, legal advice should be sought by A before enforcing the lien against such goods.

Duties of A to T

Generally an agent is *not* liable to T on any contract entered into on behalf of P. An agent *may* be bound if the agent intended to be bound, but the presumption is otherwise. If a principal remains hidden, or unknown to T (referred to as an undisclosed principal), the agent would be bound on any contract made with T. This is true even though it had been made for the benefit of P, and it is true for the reason that A is the contracting party in such instances. Once P is disclosed, T can also look to P for performance of the contract.

If an agent acts within the limits of the authority granted and is not aware that an apparent wrong or tort is being caused to others, the principal will be responsible for the tort. If P commands A to commit a tort, such as a trespass, both P and A will share the liability. If A commits a tort knowingly, and without any participation by P, A can be looked to for any loss suffered by T. If the intentional tort occurs within the scope of the authority granted by P to A, then P may also be held accountable for the tort.

Duties of P to T

As long as an agent acts within the scope of the authority, as discussed previously, the principal has a duty to T to fulfill any and all obligations created by A with T.

In an undisclosed agency, when T enters into a contract with A, not knowing of the existence of P, both A and P have a duty to T on the contract—but only after P is disclosed. T can then look to either for performance—but not both. If T sues P on such a contract, P has a duty not to establish any greater claim against T than A could have. For example, T may have a set-off claim against A. Thus P would be subject to this set-off, and have a duty to extend to T the benefits of this set-off.

To illustrate a set-off, assume that T buys, for $10,000, an item that A is selling as an agent for an undisclosed P. At the time of the sale, A owed T $5,000 for some outside transaction. P now comes forward and seeks payment of $10,000 from T. T has the legal right to off-set the $5,000 owed by A and is thus responsible to P for only $5,000.

P has a duty to compensate third parties who are injured by tortious conduct of A while A is carrying out the scope of the authority granted. It is not material whether the tortious act was in accordance to instructions, only whether it was done in the scope of authority granted.

An exception to these rules is found where injury is caused by the *fraud* of A. In the usual instance, P is not liable to T for lies, untruths, fraudulent statements, or deceitful acts of A—unless P in some manner acquiesced or encouraged such acts of A with T.

If A exceeds his or her authority, P has no obligation to discharge A upon the demand of T, but in many instances that is just what happens. Principals do not appreciate agents who do not follow instructions or who ignore house rules.

Duties of T to P

Generally, T has a duty to honor all contracts entered into with A on behalf of P. But, as mentioned, fraud, deceit, or other such acts of A would impair the right of P to claim the benefit of a contract that arose out of such acts. These acts would provide T with a legal defense against A—and thus would provide a legal defense against P, as we have just stated.

NOTICE

An important part of agency law has grown up around the principle of "notice." P is bound by notice or knowledge that A receives while in the conduct of authority granted. *This is true whether it is passed on to P or not.* The notice or knowledge must bear, however, upon the scope of authority. Agents are expected to pass on relevant notice and knowledge acquired while carrying out their authority.

For example, an agent unloading a shipment of goods discovers that the goods are nonconforming. The agent fails to pass this along to P and an unreasonable amount of time elapses, so that P loses the right to reject. P is bound to pay the price for the goods—even though they are not what P ordered.

Principals must create a system of "notice routing" and train their agents in the use of this system.

TERMINATION OF THE RELATIONSHIP

If an agency is created to last until a specified time, or until a certain act is completed, it would end at that time. Other agencies are "agencies at will" and continue for indefinite time periods until P or A decides to end the relationship.

Must Give Notice of Termination

Once an agency is terminated, P must give notice to third parties to make certain that A's subsequent acts do not bind P. Direct notice, such as by letter, should be given to all those with whom A had transacted business on behalf of P. General notice should be given to all others. "We wish to invite the public to stop at our inn and meet our new innkeeper" would be general notice that the prior innkeeper is no longer on the job.

Turning from agency, let's briefly examine a relationship closely related to agency–yet different in its legal consequences.

INDEPENDENT CONTRACTORS

In many business situations, a principal (P) wants specific results to be accomplished but wants them carried out by one who is neither an agent nor employee. The laws of independent contractors (IC) covers this type of situation.

The test applied to determine if an independent contractor relationship exists is twofold:

1. Is the one doing the job being paid a fixed price or rate for a completed project?
2. Is there an absence of control over that person or firm by the principal?

If the answer is "yes" to both, an independent contractor situation is in existence. In determining if this relationship exists, as a general rule common, not statutory, law prevails. If the answer to one of these questions is "no," then in all probability an agency exists and the law of agency will be applied.

If, under a contract, one can dictate the result and direct the means by which it is reached, it *would not* be an independent contractor situation. But this does not mean that a principal cannot make periodic inspections in person or by agents and employees to make certain that the specifications are being met. This is permitted and expected. Yet one must keep in mind the distinction between mere inspection and active supervision. The latter may convert an independent-contractor relationship into an agency—something that the principal may not want to happen. If it does happen, the principal faces the risk of loss to third parties. This is the reason for creating the IC relationship in the first place.

Another test often applied by a court is whether or not the principal can terminate the services of the other at will. If so, it is usually a master-servant or principal-agent, not an IC relationship.

The method of payment is another test applied: Payment based upon time denotes a master-servant relationship; lump sum payment, a principal-independent contractor situation.

An innkeeper-principal contracts with an independent contractor to accomplish certain work at the inn. The IC then uses his or her agents to go about completing the work. Two possible legal results can emerge from this situation; Figure 8.6 illustrates them.

Losing the IC Protection

The most common way that this happens at the inn is for Innkeeper P to exercise day-by-day control of the activities of the IC. When this happens in practice, the courts, when called upon to decide where legal liability must fall, will invariably hold that the innkeeper had, in fact, become the principal of the IC and thus must face agency liability.

An exception to this, however, is found where a union hall sends workers to work a banquet at the inn. Here it is necessary for the innkeeper to exercise direct control over the union employees but, as a matter of law, the workers remain agents of the union hall and not the inn.

Liability of Principal

Normally, if a principal uses care in the selection of an IC, P is not liable for negligent, careless, or wrongful acts of the IC. However, if an IC brings into being a situation for which the principal has primary responsibility, P cannot use the IC relationship to escape that responsibility. For example, a hotel must make certain that fire exits are not blocked. If an IC, while doing repair work in the hotel, blocks an exit, the hotel will be responsible for injury or death caused by the blocked exit.

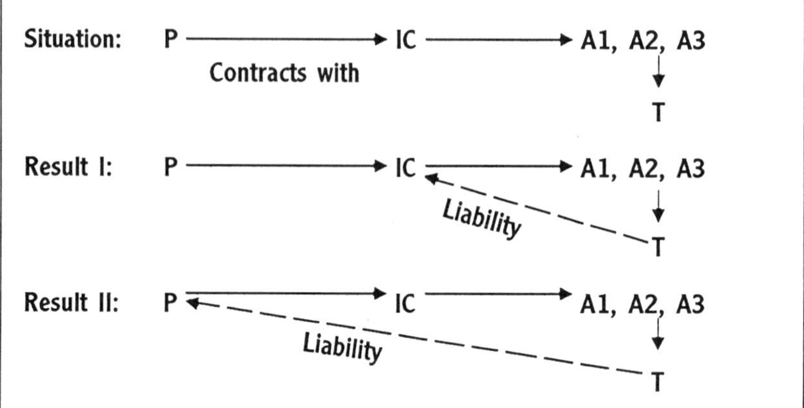

Result II was caused because, in some manner, Innkeeper P lost the benefit of the contract with the IC and was held by a court to be the principal of the IC. That is a result that must be avoided by the innkeeper.

Figure 8.6 Losing the IC protection.

In *Page v. Sloan*, Chapter 5, the innkeeper claimed that the person hired to make repairs to the water heater was an independent contractor. Thus the innkeeper was saying, "If this person repaired the water heater in a negligent manner, and if this negligence was the proximate cause of the death of the guest, then I am not responsible as a matter of law." The problem is, the courts hold that an innkeeper cannot delegate his or her innkeeping duties to third parties. In addition, if the innkeeper is negligent in hiring, employing, or selecting an independent contractor, *that* negligence is actionable.

Generally, a principal is not liable for injuries suffered by *servants and agents of the IC.* This presumes, of course, that such injuries arise while the injured party is in the services of the IC, and also assumes that the principal in no way contributes to the injury. As a commonsense rule, a principal should treat servants and agents of an IC just as any other third parties would be treated. Care and caution are always good business.

An IC is not an employee of the principal as defined in the workers' compensation laws, and therefore is not insurable under such laws. It is the responsibility of the IC to subscribe to these funds and to make certain all servants and agents of the IC are properly covered. Conversely, the IC is responsible for withholding, fringe benefits, and the like for its agents and employees. These

COURTHOUSE, Lincoln, Illinois.

are not the responsibility of P and represent one of the reasons for using the IC relationship. However, state law must be examined on this point.

In most states, the use of an independent contractor to carry out business projects relieves the one who has contracted for the services of the responsibility of carrying workers' compensation coverage on the employees and agents of the independent contractor.

Thus, when an innkeeper hires Zero Construction Company to repair the pool at the inn, the company and not the inn will be responsible for compensation coverage on its employees. This is to protect them in the event they are injured while on the job.

However, the State of Nevada has an unusual provision in its "Industrial Insurance Act" (the equivalent of workers' compensation coverage in other states). It is found in NRS 616.085 and reads as follows:

"Subcontractors and their employees shall be deemed to be employees of the principal contractor."

NRS 616.115, goes on:

"Subcontractors shall include independent contractors."

A literal reading of these two provisions from the Nevada Revised Statutes could lead one to the conclusion that one (such as an innkeeper) who contracts with an independent contractor would be responsible for compensation coverage for the workers of the independent contractor.

Liability of IC

An independent contractor is responsible to third parties, in contract and tort, for acts of its employees and agents carried out under authority granted. Since ICs must also act through servants and agents, principles of agency apply to them and their employees and agents.

The decision to use an IC and not an agent is one, of course, for management.

MECHANICS' AND LABORERS' LIENS

One risk confronted by owner-principals who contract for services from independent contractors is the danger of third-party suppliers and laborers gaining the right to file "mechanics'" and "laborers' liens." These are filed against the real estate of the owner-principal that is improved by materials supplied and labor performed.

All states have laws permitting such liens provided that they are filed promptly. Usual time periods are sixty or ninety days after the last material was supplied or the last labor performed. When properly filed, they become a lien against the real estate of the owner-principal. Thus an innkeeper who contracts with an IC to build a pool may wind up with liens against the inn for debts owed by the IC.

Guarding Against

One can guard against such liens by making certain that laborers and suppliers are paid out of proceeds due to the independent contractor. It is practice for principal-owners to require proof of payment before funds are distributed to the IC. Mechanics' liens are seldom used where materials are purchased by employees or agents, nor are laborers' liens used for work done by them. In these instances, the principal is liable for the materials and labor and must see that these obligations are met and the suppliers and laborers know this.

If a suing lawyer is able to convince a court that an alleged independent contractor is not in fact such, then agency law will be applied. This in turn makes the one who contracted for that person, or firm's services, responsible for any defects or defaults in such service that resulted in injury or loss to others.

SUMMARY

The independent contractor relationship can be used in many instances where specific results are to be achieved. The advantages of the relationship lie in the sharply reduced liability of the inn. Independent contractors have been used to build swimming pools, remodel motels into closed-dome recreation areas, pave parking lots, and build new motels and hotels from the ground up. The most obvious problems arise when an IC is chosen that does shoddy or undependable work, or fails to pay laborers or suppliers. Such persons and firms must be avoided in the first instance if possible. *Page v. Sloan* taught us that.

QUESTIONS

1. Distinguish an agency relationship from an independent contractor relationship by using the characteristics of each.
2. What is the distinction between agents, servants, and mere employees?
3. Give an example of an "agency by estoppel" in the motel business.
4. Distinguish between implied and ostensible authority.
5. True or False. An agent can ratify unauthorized acts of another agent, so long as the agents serve the same principal.
6. Give an example of a set-off that may arise in an undisclosed principal situation.
7. What is the effect on P, of fraud on the part of A to T, that P knows nothing about? Why?
8. What items would you want your salesperson-agents to place on their daily customer-call reports?
9. Name three reasons why an inn owner would want work to be done by an independent contractor and not by agents.
10. True or False. An IC will use agents to carry forth his or her work, and the rules of agency will apply to *that* relationship.

ENDNOTES

1. *International Trucking v. U.S. (Ct. Claims)*, 281 F.2d 457.
2. *Turner v. Zip*, 65 N.W. 2d 427.
3. *Morse v. Jones*, 223 La. 212, 65 So. 2d 317.
4. *Forrest v. Hawkins*, 169 Va. 470, 194 S.E. 721 (1938).
5. UCC 2-203.
6. *Chandler v. Kelley*, 149 Va. 221, 141 S.E. 389 (1928).
7. *Richmond Guano Co. v. E.I. Dupont*, 284 Fed. 803 (4th Cir. 1922).

9

HRI Employee-Agent Relations

I poured myself a mug of coffee and took it into my office. A place for rational analysis. Legal theory. Precedents, hoary old Latin terms, statutes and torts and contracts, all the good stuff that was evolved to enable attorneys to maintain an abstracted distance from the human pain and inequity the law is supposed to mediate. In one corner of my office, I have two shoulder-high file cabinets crammed with abstractions. Two shelves of weighty tomes full of more abstractions. Thousands of little legal pigeonholes, each with its unique shape, into which real flesh-and-blood people are supposed to be fitted.

The fit never seems perfect.

Those volumes and file cabinets are full of laws. But they're not the law. That's why they put people into offices like mine, along with the files and the books. Laws are like automobiles: They need lawyers to make them go.

The Vulgar Boatman, William G. Tapply

OVERVIEW

In this chapter, we want to take a look at the fundamental laws that come into play between HRI management and their agents and employees. This view is important because the laws that regulate the HRI/guest/traveler/patron relationship are often affected by the HRI management/staff relationship. When one goes bad, the other can suffer too.

There are various ways to view a modern business, and the outcome of the view often depends upon who is standing in what pair of shoes. A manager sees things one way—a guest at an inn almost always has a counterview. The employee or agent, in turn, tends to view both management and guests or patrons from a different, unique point of view. Sometimes the view of the agent/employee can be a detriment to the inn because it may have his or her own personal interests as its basis rather than the interests of the business.

In addition, the legal demands and commands of the law that originate with employees and agents can place financial burdens on the inn in issue. This is especially so when these legal requirements are not understood, are misinterpreted, or worse yet, are ignored. Thus we want to become exposed to enough of the more important laws of the HRI management/employee/agent relationship to be able to more effectively function as HRI managers. To that end, in this chapter we will examine the fundamental laws that regulate the employee-agent relationship with management. This will then be followed by an examination of the most important labor statutes in Chapter 10.

MANAGEMENT AND LAW

A diversity of laws, both common and statutory, are involved in the management of a hotel, restaurant, or other hospitality facility. Included are the laws of agency, estoppel, tort, those found in the Uniform Commercial Code, Civil Rights Act, the Consumer Credit Protection Act, to name a few, as well as principles of criminal law. These laws in turn have a direct effect upon the responsibilities of both employers and employees and, by necessity, control the relationship that exists between them. If these laws are violated by the employer, legal consequences may follow. Conversely, the same is true if they are ignored or violated by the employee. The result is a "legal balance" that must be achieved for the good of all concerned.

Maslow's hierarchy theory,[1] with its five stages that lead to "self-actualization," does not fare badly when analyzed from a strict legal point of view in relation to this legal balance. In addition, the theories of McGregor[2] contain points that match up reasonably well with legal realities. By combining features of both, one could arrive at what could be called "legal aspects of traditional motivational theories."

First, McGregor's theory X holds that employees do not like to work. In some instances this is probably closer to the realities of a work-a-day world than his theory Y. The latter holds that it is natural to work. There is truth in theory Y but people still prefer leisure to work. The ready acceptance of the shorter workweek and the increasing success of the hospitality-recreation industry are proof of this.

Thus, if it is true that employees do not like to work, even if it is natural to do so, it is also true that employers do not like to pay wages. The reasons are many: dissatisfaction with job performance, insufficient economic return to the employer for services performed, theft on the job by employees, misuse of company property, and resentment of unions and other outside pressures that have relegated the employer to a "partner status" with the employee.

Therein lies a legal factor of importance: The employer is contractually obligated to pay the wages agreed upon, provided the required services are performed—which they often are not. An employee can slow down on a job—and steal a steak or two from the inn kitchen and suffer no consequences—but the employer will be sued if the paycheck is not forthcoming. If the job default on the part of the employee is great, the employer would be justified in terminating the employment. As a matter of law, the employer has no legal obligation to make a job available to anyone. If a job *is* made available, and if someone is given that job, the legal obligations under contract law arise.

In addition, once the status of employer-employee arises, the laws of agency come into play, placing precise duties on both: the duty of loyalty, care, caution, productivity and others upon the employee; the duty to provide a safe place to work, the duty to compensate as agreed, and others, upon the employer.

Maslow's first level of "survival" is thus just as much the legal responsibility of the employee as it is of the employer.

The second level of "security and safety" is primarily the responsibility of management, but only insofar as it relates to the safety of the employee. As mentioned, management has no responsibility to make jobs available at all. Under the Occupational Safety and Health Act,[3] the employer must supply a safe place to work and keep it that way. In turn, the employees have a legal duty to make use of all safety devices supplied and to follow all safety instructions. Failure to do so can result in job termination.

Third, Maslow tells us that the worker needs to "belong." He or she must feel a part of the formal organization. It is said that informal organizations and company-supplied recreational programs can provide at least part of this need. But when management is called upon to provide recreational programs, the law of tort must be considered as a by-product of such programs. Will an employee be injured during such activities? If so, is this injury one obtained "on the job" so as to place it under workers' compensation coverage? Or will it be covered under traditional tort principles? What if a *third party* is injured by the employee during such activities, such as at an inn picnic? Tort principles are then solely in operation. (It can be argued that "play" is one of the goals that the employee is working for and should not be a responsibility of management and is thus completely outside the scope of the responsibility of management.)

"The ego need" can perhaps best be met through the simple expedient of a job well done by the employee. After all, this is a presumed obligation in all employment contracts. One can hardly successfully argue that an outstanding job is beyond what was expected at the time that the contract was entered into. Management should not accede to such an argument. It is true that superior job performance needs to be rewarded. But this is probably best provided by promotion rather than increased pay for something that the employee was legally obligated to provide at the outset. Poor job performance should be rewarded by demotion or dismissal for the reason that it is a breach of contract. While management can do much to promote superior job performance, it nevertheless remains the legal obligation of the employee to provide it. Even the dishwasher at the inn can satisfy the ego need by becoming the best—or equal to the best—dishwasher in that particular business.

Self-actualization naturally follows from the attainment of superior job performance and is also an extension of the contractual obligation. It is logically not a permanent status and the employee must constantly strive to maintain it.

In sum, there are serious legal overtones to the motivational aspects of HRI management, and we have merely touched upon the topic here. Rather than continue an abstract discussion of motivational factors and management here, it will be more useful to look to the laws that affect the HRI management-staff relationship.

The At-Will Doctrine

This phrase has been used for decades in the United States to describe what can be called the "traditional legal relationship between employers and employees." As a practical matter, it meant that the employee could leave the employment as she or he saw fit, but it actually meant that the employer could fire the employee for any reason, or for no reason at all. Only where there was a collective bargaining agreement or other contract in effect between the parties, was an exception found. The doctrine of "at-will employment" has been severely weakened by court decisions of the past few years.

North Dakota is an "at-will" employment state, provided the employee is hired for an indefinite term. This means that the employer or employee may end the employment at anytime. On the other hand, even in North Dakota, if other promises are made, such as those found in an employee handbook, the courts may refuse to apply the "at-will doctrine" and look to the other promises to resolve the situation.

Over forty states have modified the right of employers to fire "at-will" without cause being stated. This modification has given rise to numerous cases brought to protect fired employees. As a result, there now exists a Plaintiff's Employment Lawyer's Association.

The most common theories to support the right of fired employees to recover their jobs or damages are (1) the promises contained in the employee manual (if any), (2) implied contract, and (3) violations of public policy. Employee manuals, or "handbooks," will be discussed later in this chapter. In relation to the at-will doctrine, the Texas Supreme Court has called it "a relic that belongs in a museum and not in the law."

The next topic of interest is that of "job applications."

Job Applications

There exists in the HRI industry today a fear of lawsuits that may be brought in conjunction with job applications. Thus, it is a good legal idea to include in job applications a clause such as the following: "I agree that the inn shall have the right to contact my former employers, the persons whom I have given as references, and those involved in my education as set forth in this application for employment." Such a clause is a "legal waiver" and may be useful to the inn if the job application becomes an issue in court at a future date.

It is permissible to ask all applicants about criminal convictions and periods of incarceration. All relevant background information can be asked for with exceptions being made for age, sex, marital status, pregnancy, and disability. References must be provided by the applicant and no laws at the moment prohibit this. Details of education of the applicant can be requested as well as information about previous job activity.

Tracing Former Employees

Trial lawyers who represent inns often have difficulty in locating those who were employed at the time of the incident in question and were witnesses to it, but who have departed before litigation is started. This is due to the high turnover rate in the industry.

One way to offset this problem is to have employees who are filling out job applications include names and addresses of older members of their families. Such persons are more likely to remain in one location for longer periods of time. This would assist lawyers in tracing former hotel employees.

Background Checks

Contrary to a current popular misconception, there are no laws that prevent a potential employer from making background checks on job applicants. On the contrary, there are many laws, such as those covering sex offenders of the young, that require that thorough background investigations be made of all job applicants. Such investigations should be made as quickly as possible.

Laws created by the courts and some legislatures proscribe unreasonable intrusions into one's privacy. Such laws do not prevent reasonable inquiry for private business use. The Fourth Amendment, for example, gives a hotel guest the assurance that his or her hotel room will be free of "unreasonable searches and seizures." It does not give a job applicant with something to hide the right to demand that the potential employer be denied the right to uncover that past.

A practical problem that confronts one who carries out background checks is the "false resume."

The False Resume

The use of false information on job applications has been common in the past and seems to be on the increase at the present time. Studies have shown that about 30 percent of all job applications contain information that is not true.

In addition, facts disclosed on applications often contain information that is true but misleading. This creates practical problems for the HRI manager. There are laws that provide penalties for those who give false information on job applications, but these laws generally do not assist the employer when making hiring decisions.

To offset this problem, can employers make use of lie detector tests to uncover false resumes?

Polygraph Tests

A federal law,[4] effective December 27, 1988, bans the general use of polygraph lie detector tests by private employers. Over forty states had previously passed statutes that reached the same result. This law prohibits use of a psychological stress evaluator, or a voice stress analyzer, for preemployment or random testing of employees.

Some polygraph tests are permitted, but their use is limited to matters of economic loss or injury to the employer's business and a great many requirements must be met by the employer prior to their use.

This federal law is enforced by the U.S. Department of Labor, Wage and Hour Division, and requires all employers to post a sign alerting employees to the ban on polygraph testing in the workplace.

Once the background check is completed, hiring decisions must now be made and these decisions are influenced by a variety of legal matters.

Employees and Releases

It is a good business practice to include a clause in all employment contracts to the effect that, if an applicant has given false information on the job application, such falsification is grounds for immediate dismissal. This is a form of legal "release."

Another variation of this "release" is to use a clause in the contract which allows the employer to have access to all criminal records of the new employee, whether misdemeanor or felony records. If such criminal records are uncovered, and they materially affect the business, the employer then has the right to terminate the employment.

Another hiring matter concerns "foreign nationals" and "aliens."

Immigrant Employees

The Immigration Reform and Control Act of 1986 lays down rules that must be followed when hiring immigrants. The basic rule is that a form called "1-9" must be completed for each such employee and maintained as provided in the act. Substantial penalties are provided for those who fail to comply, in the form of fines of up to $3,000 for each unauthorized employee plus possible criminal sentences of up to five years in jail.

HRI employers must make certain that Form 1-9 is filled out completely and accurately. It is clear that the U.S. Department of Justice, Immigration and Naturalization looks closely at the HRI industry in this regard because it is this industry which attracts and has utilized illegal aliens in unusually large numbers.

Also, as discussed in Chapter 10, the Civil Rights Act of 1964/72 prohibits discrimination in hiring on the grounds of "national origin." For this reason, *all* employees should be handled the same in regard to Form 1-9. Potential employees should never be turned away, or existing employees fired, because of "foreign appearance" or foreign language.

When an HRI manager files the papers to allow an alien to remain in the United States, the employer is the "petitioner" and the employee in question is the "beneficiary." The petitioner can revoke the petition at any time and for any reason.

Associated with the hiring of employees is the doctrine of "business necessity."

"Business Necessity" in Employment

Business reasons for which management decisions are made at HRI operations are usually accepted by American judges. But such decisions should be documented in in-house records. This is important if it should become necessary to justify the decisions in court at a later time.

As an example, a hotel located near the United Nations might well decide to hire a desk clerk who speaks four languages, rather than a more highly trained person who speaks only one language.

Those in charge of the inn's personnel offices must be able to give reasons for hiring certain employees. These reasons generally must *not* be based upon race, color, religion, national origin, sex, age, or physical handicap. If they are based upon solid business reasons, then any claim of discrimination will usually fail in a court action brought by one denied employment.[5]

When one hires an employee, that person is taken on the condition that he or she is actually in good health at the time. If an employee falls on the job because he is clumsy, it would be no legal defense for the employer to claim that other workers are agile and would not have fallen under the same conditions. This rule of law makes it mandatory that as much as possible be learned of the physical and mental ability of those being considered for employment.

Discrimination in Hiring

Refusing to hire applicants who have criminal records, where time has been served for those offenses, may lead to charges of discrimination against the inn. On the other hand, if there is a good *business reason* for such refusal, that refusal may pass legal muster. An example might be refusing to hire a convicted car thief to handle valet parking.

The EEOC, which has jurisdiction over such matters, suggests that employers faced with such circumstances consider the following:

1. The time that has passed since the criminal conviction.
2. The nature of the job in question.
3. The seriousness of the offense which led to the conviction.

Discrimination against handicapped persons is prohibited by the Americans with Disabilities Act unless a reasonable accommodation of that person cannot be made in the employment.[6] The following illustrates what a failure to uncover a criminal background can mean in court.

> Hotels aren't like other businesses. Hotel employees have easy access to guests and their property, and given that access, hotels must check employee backgrounds. That takes time and money, but avoiding just one negligent hiring lawsuit will be repayment 1,000 times over.
>
> One Arizona case saw $6 million ($1 million in actual damages and $5 million in punitive damages) awarded to the husband of a woman murdered by a new employee. During the trial it became apparent the hotel had done practically nothing to verify the background of the assailant-employee. The husband's lawyer argued it would have been easy to discover the employee had a history of violence with only a minimum background check.
>
> The jury decided the inn was reckless and grossly negligent in failing to conduct a sufficient background check. That check would have disclosed a history of violence, aggravated assault and attempted rape.[7]

One final matter to be considered in relation to hiring employees at the inn is the use of probationary periods.

Probationary Periods

The constant need for employees in the HRI industry often mandates hiring before complete background checks can be carried out. A protective measure that the inn can take is to hire on a "probationary basis," reserving the right to terminate the employment if harmful information about the employee is subsequently discovered.

Once the inn/employee relationship becomes operational, other legal matters come to the front. The unionization of employees is one and the use of employee manuals, or "handbooks," is another.

Unions at Inns

Whether or not an inn becomes unionized is a matter of bargaining and decision making. However, recent hotel/union litigation has made it clear that in dealing with those who are seeking to unionize a particular hotel, care is in order as to what the hotel says or promises.[8]

One strong point for management emerges: One and only one person should be designated to handle union matters. All others must be instructed to pass on all union matters to that person. The designated person in turn must consult with counsel and be highly trained in the area of labor relations and union negotiation.

In turn, the attorney with whom that person consults must be chosen for his or her skill in the subject of unionization. It is a simple fact of legal life that not all American lawyers are expert in union legal matters. On the other hand, it is a legal truism that most union lawyers are labor-law experts. The danger inherent in these two facts is apparent. The inn which is confronted with unionization, or which may be dealing with an existing union, must make certain that its legal representation is equal to the legal talent on the other side.

Related to unions at the inn, often as a result of collective bargaining, are employee manuals or "handbooks."

Employee Handbooks

When such manuals are used, management must be careful about what they contain and understand how the courts view them.

These handbooks must include a provision that any falsification of job applications or resumes will be grounds for immediate termination. Also, it is a good legal idea to include a clause to the effect that all employees, as a condition of their hiring, agree to waive their right to sue any persons or business firms who may supply information about them. Such waivers, if given voluntarily and understood at the time that they are given, are most often upheld by the courts.

A disadvantage of such handbooks, is found in the way the courts view them. They can, under proper facts and circumstances, be used *against* the inn.

The well-intentioned innkeeper, in the absence of a union, usually does not intend for an employee "handbook" to be binding upon anyone. However, the courts almost always view such a document in a different light. The courts often hold that such handbooks did *not* arise from an agreement in the absence of union bargaining, and allow that fact to be used against the inn.

If such handbooks are given unilaterally to the employees, the courts will allow them to be introduced into evidence as part of the contract that exists between the inn and the employee. This is so because the courts view the handbook as a "unilateral contract"—one in which only one side made promises, but one in which the other side relied upon those promises.

Employee Handbook Example

Employee X is hired at No Show Motel and there is no written contract involved. The inn presents to Employee X an "employee handbook" that contains details on health, accident, and vacation benefits, and which also contains a statement that "no employee will be fired unless procedures are followed." Employee X is then fired for not doing her job. No formal procedures are followed. Many courts would hold the handbook to be a unilateral contract: The hotel makes a promise and the employee relies upon it. By not keeping its promise to "follow procedures," the firing was a breach of contract.

If something occurs that is not covered in the employee handbook, but is so unusual that it was not anticipated, the employee who commits the act may still be disciplined or terminated, and the courts will uphold that action.

A Wisconsin court in 1985 ruled that the terms found within the handbook given to an employee at the time of hiring were contractual and thus binding upon both the inn and the employee. Thus, when the employee was fired for violations of what the handbook contained, the Wisconsin court sustained the validity of the handbook.[9]

As stated previously, such handbooks can also be used against an inn, if the terms within them favor the fired employee.[10]

Employee Manuals and Inn Security

Having such manuals in use, especially when they relate to security, is not enough. It is necessary that employees and agents understand what these manuals say and be trained to carry out the mandates contained in them. Failure to do so may prompt a court to hold an inn responsible for an injurious incident in spite of the manual.[11] It thus follows that security and other measures set forth in employee/agent manuals be made the subject of employee training sessions.

States that have recognized employee handbooks as unilateral contracts include Idaho, Illinois, Massachusetts, Michigan, Minnesota, Nevada, New Jersey, and Washington.

On the other hand, North Dakota has refused to find a unilateral contract in an employee handbook where the handbook itself contained a conspicuous disclaimer that stated: "This Employee Handbook has been drafted as a guideline for our employees. It shall not be construed to form a contract between the company and its employees."[12]

Once the inn/employee/agent relationship becomes operational, a variety of other legal matters come into play, and a selection follows.

Employee Goals and Standards

Standards that employees are expected to meet must be clear and capable of being accurately measured. Goals established for employees must also be attainable. If either or both of these rules are violated, employees are penalized and thus tend to become frustrated in their job performance. This is legally dangerous for the inn because poor job performance may result in legal liability to the inn.

Employee "Value"

The courts are holding that an employee who stays on a job and who does not seek other employment is giving something of value to the employer. Thus remaining on the job, especially in the face of adversity, such as poor or unsafe working conditions, may well provide sufficient contract "consideration" to support promises, direct or indirect, which may have been made by an innkeeper or which may be implied from the employment relationship.

Employees and Security

It is good inn practice to instruct all employees and agents to keep a close watch for any activities or conditions at the inn that appear out of the ordinary. If such are observed, a report must be made to that employee's superior immediately. That superior, in turn, must see to it that the information is relayed to the proper personnel and acted upon as quickly as possible.

Employees and Luggage Keys

In the HRI industry, many employees handle countless items of luggage of guests. It is known that theft-inclined employees will arm themselves with a variety of keys that can be used to enter luggage. It is essential that management take reasonable steps to locate and fire those who have such keys.

As part of the security involving keys, luggage, and guests, periodic checks should be made of the employees' lockers. Such checks are generally permissible and especially so if this is provided for in the employee handbook.

Concessions to Employees

Supervisory personnel must be cautioned that making exceptions to one employee may prompt a court to use that concession against the inn when another employee is disciplined for the same infraction. For example, if Employee X is habitually late for work but is routinely forgiven by his or her supervisor, it could well cause legal problems if Employee Y is later disciplined for being late for work. Supervisory personnel must be trained to avoid such differential treatment.

Defamation of Inn Employees

At law, "defamation" is an offense which, when proven, can lead to damages against the offending person. It can take one of two forms: "libel," the use of the printed word, or "slander," the use of the spoken word. For either to be actionable, a two-part legal test must be met:

1. A false statement about the employee in question must be knowingly made.
2. That false statement must be "published": brought to the minds of one or more other persons.

It should be house policy never to discuss with others in-house what an employee did, or failed to do or is suspected of doing.

A topic of growing concern to the innkeeper is that of drug testing of employees and agents.

A Drug-Free Workplace

In drug testing at the inn, it is not wise to single out groups for testing such as hourly employees, or those who work from "midnight until eight A.M." Such a policy gives lawyers a reason to challenge the testing when employees are fired because of it. If a testing program looks as though it might have discriminatory overtones, it need not be eliminated but it should be rethought and redesigned to cancel that impression.

Unions and Drug Testing

It is important for the inn to insert a clause in the union contract that allows the testing of employees for drugs and alcohol under reasonable circumstances. This can also be repeated in employee handbooks.

Random testing will not pass court muster so testing must be based on objective symptoms, such as physical behavioral signs, or be carried out at times agreeable to both union and management. Even so, tests based on "reasonable" factors involve problems of their own.

If public safety is involved, the courts may approve random testing such as the testing of gun-carrying guards, lifeguards at swimming pools, and the like.

Harrah's Hotel in Reno, Nevada, issued an order requiring all employees to wear a ribbon at work that said that they were "drug free." Several employees refused to comply and they were suspended without pay. A court upheld the suspensions. In Las Vegas, the refusal of an employee to take a drug or alcohol test after the employee's discharge was held to be conclusive evidence that the termination was proper.[13]

The courts tend to uphold drug-testing programs at inns if they are fairly and impartially carried out.

Posting of Employee Legal Information

Inns that are covered by federal law must post four employee notices at each business location. Three of these are covered in Chapter 10 and the fourth was discussed previously in this chapter.

1. The Williams-Steiger Occupational Safety and Health Act of 1970.
2. Title VII of the Civil Rights Act of 1964.
3. Fair Labor Standards Act.
4. The Employee Polygraph Protection Act of 1988.

Over thirty states have fair employment statutes which require additional posting, and California, District of Columbia, Idaho, Iowa, Kansas, Maryland, Michigan, Nevada, and Pennsylvania require that state fair employment laws be posted in Spanish and English.

The final topic of the chapter concerns the firing of employees at the inn, an activity that often leads to litigation.

Firing Employees at the Inn

Contrary to the "at-will" employment doctrine, the firing of minority employees, older employees, pregnant employees, female employees, and others has led to many lawsuits in recent years. Many employees, because of federal and state laws, have become members of "protected classes."

On the other hand, if it is determined that there is sufficient reason to fire an employee, the termination should be carried out promptly. To delay the firing could lead to problems if the delay should result in injury or loss to a guest at the inn.

Such a delay can also cause another problem. Assume that an undesirable employee is allowed to continue working but is then fired later when he or she becomes ill. The delay may prompt a jury to find the firing to be illegal. For a case in which the fired employee recovered over $80,000 in back pay and over $80,000 in future pay plus benefits, see *Folz v. Marriott Corp.*, 594 F. Supp. 1007 (Missouri 1984).

Firing Employees in an At-Will State

While over 80 percent of our states have modified the "at-will employment doctrine," Hawaii still remains an "at-will" state. However, it too has modified this doctrine to protect employees from being fired where "public policy" or "freedom of speech" are involved. Do these exceptions apply to an employee for getting drunk and swearing at an employee picnic, who after a proper disciplinary hearing, was fired? A 1988 Hawaii decision has answered the question in the negative, thus upholding the firing.[14]

James Getty's Hotel, Gettysburgh, Pennslyvania.

The Quoted Salary at Firing Time

If the innkeeper had quoted an employee a yearly salary at the time of hiring, such as "$30,000" a year, the courts generally take the position that the innkeeper has guaranteed the employee one year's salary and will use that standard in deciding severance pay.

On the other hand, if a weekly or monthly wage was agreed upon, this wage will usually be accepted by the courts at the time that the employee is fired.

Inn Employees Called for Jury Duty

To fire an inn employee because he or she is called for federal jury duty and serves would place the employer in criminal contempt. State laws reach a similar result where inn employees are fired for serving on state juries.

The best policy to follow is to allow time off the job to employees called for federal or state jury duty. They should be replaced temporarily. To this end, it is good management policy to make up the difference in what the court pays them and what they would have earned if they had remained on the job at the inn. To see what can happen if an opposite policy is adopted, see *Piergg v. Poulos*, 542 So. 2D 377 (Florida, 1989).

An adjunct to the firing of employees is the use of termination conferences. Such conferences can be of benefit to the inn as well as the fired employee. However, they can lead to legal difficulty if not carried out properly.

Termination Conference

Though disagreeable to both the employer and the employee who is being terminated, such conferences can still be beneficial to both sides. On the other hand, they can lead to litigation if the employee being fired feels that an injustice has occurred in the handling of the meeting.

The decision to fire an employee must be based upon substantial evidence and company procedures must be properly followed. Studies have shown that such conferences should be held early in the week rather than on weekends.

A written record should be made of the conference. In addition, the now-fired employee should be informed of all benefits that are available to her or him. An agreement should be reached as to a letter of recommendation that will be written to future employers and what it will contain.

Regardless of the actions of the fired employee while on the job, the innkeeper must release all control over that person in the future. Nothing must be done to actively prevent the fired employee from obtaining employment elsewhere. On the other hand, it must be made clear that the innkeeper has a duty to report all facts if specific inquiry is made by others in the future, especially if the acts of the fired employee were criminal in nature.

QUESTIONS

1. True or False. The "at-will doctrine," as it is seen in employment law situations, is now on the decline in the majority of our states because its rationale no longer reflects the realities of the workplace of the 1990s.
2. True or False. The courts tend to treat employee handbooks as being unilateral contracts. This means that the terms contained within them are promises made by the innkeeper.
3. True or False. It is important to know what questions should *not* be included in job applications used at the inn.
4. True or False. The privacy laws, both federal and state, prohibit detailed inquiry into the lives of potential inn employees.

5. True or False. Constitutional prohibitions do not apply to public employers.
6. What type of questions should not be used on the job application form used at the inn?
7. What type of questions should the innkeeper include on the job application form used at the inn?
8. List three items that the innkeeper should place into the handbook given to newly hired employees at the inn.
9. List three items that the innkeeper should *not* place into the handbook given to newly hired employees at the inn.
10. Why must considerable thought be given to an "exit interview" of an employee, and what kind of legal dangers does the innkeeper face at such sessions?

ENDNOTES

1. Maslow, Abraham Arnold (U.S. psychologist, 1908–70).
2. McGregor, Douglas Murray (U.S. College President, 1906–64).
3. USCA, Title 29, Ch. 15.
4. 29 USC 2001 *et seq.*
5. *Becker v. Wenco,* 638 F. Supp. 650 (New York 1986).
6. *Davidsons v. Shoney's Big Boy Restaurant,* 380 S.E. 2D 232 (West Virginia 1989).
7. *Hospitality Law,* Volume 5, Number 4, April 1990, p. 1, speaking of *Gilmore v. Best Western International, Inc.,* Polls County, Florida, 1989, no citation available.
8. *Georgetown Hotel v. N.L.R.B.,* 835 F.2D 1467 (D.C. 1987).
9. *Ferraro v. Kolesch,* 368 N.W. 2D 666 (Wisconsin 1985).
10. *Thompson v. American Motors Inns,* 623 F. Supp. 409 (Virginia 1985).
11. *MacQuarrie v. Howard Johnson Co.,* 877 F. 2D 126 (Delaware 1989).
12. *Bailey v. Perkins Restaurants,* 398 N.W. 2D 120 (North Dakota 1986).
13. *Fremont Hotel v. Esposito,* 760 P.2D 122 (Nevada 1988).
14. *Pagdilao v. Maui Hotel,* 703 F. Supp. 863 (Hawaii 1988).

10

Statutory Laws of HRI Employment

Whenever I hear someone speak of the Industrial Revolution as something that occurred in the past, I am tempted to revise his sense of history. The Industrial Revolution is in full swing today. Indeed, it is constantly being accelerated. The only thing that has changed is the character of its leadership. Whereas it was said two generations ago that industry was being led into new fields by the oil barons, the bankers, the railroad builders, and other "captains of industry," in this decade the leadership of the industrial revolution has fallen largely to enterprising scientists and engineers. They are developing products undreamed of a few years ago, and it is they who now seek new worlds to conquer.

My Years with Xerox, John H. Dessauer

OVERVIEW

In this chapter we will examine the principal statutory laws that apply to HRI operations and see what legal duties they impose upon hotels, motels, restaurants, bars, and related businesses. Look for the ways in which these statutes influence management decisions.

In Chapter 9, a variety of laws that relate to employee-agent relations with management were examined. Many of the rules and policies discussed there have their basis in both federal and state statutes. It is necessary to learn more about those statutes in order to better understand what the law expects of those who manage HRI operations. Included in these statutes are the Fair Labor Standards Act and its amendments, wage attachment provisions of the

Consumer Credit Protection Act, workers' compensation acts, unemployment compensation laws, the Civil Rights Act of 1964 and its amendments, the Americans with Disabilities Act, and the Occupational Safety and Health Act. We will then close this chapter with a discussion of "restrictive covenants" and how they can be used in employment situations at the HRI operation.

A good law with which to begin is the Fair Labor Standards Act of 1938, as amended.

FAIR LABOR STANDARDS ACT

One of the primary and most often consulted laws at any HRI operation is the federal Fair Labor Standards Act. Enacted in 1938,[1] it has been amended several times to keep it in step with the development of business over the last half century. As originally enacted, this law restricted the use of child labor; set a minimum wage of 25 cents per hour; set the standard work week at forty-four hours; provided for time and one-half pay for all hours over the standard work week, and set down recordkeeping requirements. The latter was provided so that the Department of Labor could monitor compliance with the law. The coverage of the law is essentially the same today but changes have been made in its terms and new sections have been added.

While the FLSA was challenged early on as being unconstitutional, it was upheld by the U.S. Supreme Court as a lawful extension of the commerce power of the U.S. Constitution. Today, in modified and expanded form, it represents one of the key HRI employee-agent laws.

WHAT IS REQUIRED TODAY?

Today[2] the minimum wage that must be paid in covered businesses is $4.25 per hour and the standard work week is forty hours. While over 60 percent of the states have similar laws and though some of their minimum wage requirements are less than $4.25 per hour, most HRI operations will fall under the federal coverage. This is true because most HRI businesses are in interstate commerce or affect interstate commerce. Overtime pay is required for all work over forty hours in one week at a rate of 1½ times the regular rate of pay per each overtime hour, although an exception is found for restaurant employees.

These provisions for overtime apply whether an employee is paid on a flat, hourly, or contingent basis such as a percent of sales. Hours for two consecutive weeks cannot be averaged to avoid the overtime. The test is whether or not there was overtime in one week. If there was, it must be paid—or the employee must be given compensation for it in some other form—at the time-and-one-half rate.

If the employee agrees to accept time off for the overtime worked, it must be taken off during the work period in which the overtime accrued. It cannot be taken during a different work period. The purpose of the law is first to provide for overtime pay and, second, to make certain that the employee enjoys the direct benefit of it in money or time off during that pay period.[3]

Flat Pay

Care must be used in paying nonsupervisory or other exempt persons with a flat rate. Even though the employee agrees to the flat-rate pay, if that person works overtime, the additional pay must be provided as overtime. Before flat-pay agreements are entered into, advice is needed so that overtime hours will be reflected in the actual sums paid. The flat pay has to become an adjusted rate.

Other Wage Rules

If employees or agents attend seminars, conferences, or go on "familiarization trips," care must again be exercised. The general rule is that, if the attendance is mandatory, the hours spent, including travel, must be considered in the calculation of overtime pay. If such attendance is voluntary and the employee has a true option of attending or not, the hours need not be counted. Again, advice is needed.

Who Is Not Covered by the FLSA?

Outside of intrastate businesses, exemptions to the coverage of the law are provided for professionals, supervisors, managers, restaurant employees, and some outside sales personnel. The legal problem, however, is in the determination of whether or not an employee-agent is in fact exempt. Having the title of "manager" or "supervisor" is not enough. The law provides legal tests that must be met and once again it becomes a one-on-one question that needs legal attention.

Special certificates can be obtained from the Administrator of the Wage and Hour Division of the Department of Labor to exempt full-time students from coverage, as well as the handicapped, learners, and others. This exemption provision can be useful in HRI operations and provides a means of cutting costs for regular and special events at hotels, restaurants, and at other HRI facilities.

Also exempt from coverage are businesses that have a gross annual income of less than $500,000.[4] The law does not require sick, severance, vacation, or holiday pay. There are no limits placed on the number of hours that can be worked in any week by those over the age of sixteen years. There are limits, however, on the *type* of work that those under eighteen years can engage in.

Child Labor Rules

The FLSA sets standards for the employment of those under the age of eighteen years. In hazardous work, one must be eighteen or older. In nonhazardous occupations, the norm is sixteen or older. Those who are fourteen and fifteen can be employed in sales and clerical work, for short hours, outside of normal school hours.

Many other provisions are found in the FLSA and many of them place burdens on HRI operations.[5] Some examples include provisions for tip pooling and tip credit, meals and meal credits, uniform allowances and maintenance, and the use of full-time students at reduced wages.

Minimum Wage Law

A person being paid $3.35 in 1988 was, in fact, receiving $2.56 per hour in 1981 dollars. The same ratio is true today with the $4.25 per hour wage. About 15 million American workers earn the minimum wage and such persons traditionally fall victim to inflation when the minimum wage is not increased.

Who are the "Low Paid"?

The "low paid" include the dishwasher, the bus boy (or girl), guest room attendants and other housekeeping personnel, parking lot attendants, short-order cooks, and others who do menial work at the inn. The prior $362,500 gross-annual-income exemption provided in the federal minimum wage law allowed the states to set lower limits for those businesses that grossed less than the federal minimum. Many states, including Nevada, took advantage of that exception. In 1987, Nevada decided to forgo the exemption and came into compliance with the federal law.

Two of our states have consistently required that the minimum wage of those employed within them be higher than the federal minimum wage law. Those states are Alaska and California. Effective July 1, 1988, California raised the state minimum wage law to $4.25 per hour. Excluded from the coverage were public employees and those earning $60 a month or more in tips. Also currently before the California courts is the issue of "subminimum wages" for those who are receiving tips that supplement their income. Tips have been the subject matter of substantial federal legislation.

Tip Income

The 1982 federal tax act required that restaurants and bars at inns report income received by employees from tips. Regulations of a temporary nature to implement the federal statute were then created. These rules became effective in January 1983. They required restaurants and bars to report gross receipts from sales, the total charge receipts, the tips shown on these receipts, and service charges made. The purpose of the federal law was to get a "tax handle" on tip income that had otherwise been slipping through the IRS net.

Tip Income, 1985

By 1985, the federal law required each restaurant operator to file IRS form 8027, "The Employer's Annual Information Return for Tip Income and Allocated Tips." While the IRS expected over 120,000 food-service operators to file the form, less than one-third complied. The modest penalties for failure to comply, $50 in most instances, provides a reason for the noncompliance.

The federal tax law that went into effect on January 1, 1988, requires restaurants to pay taxes on tips received by foodservers–a far cry from what the tip laws required in the beginning. If foodservers falsely report tip earnings, the IRS can now hold the restaurant liable for unreported income.

The status of the tip laws can relegate the innkeeper to a "co-conspirator" status when foodservers do not report total income.

Tip Income as a Social Issue

Many persons want the decision of whether or not to leave tips to be left solely to the patron. In Chicago, two women have formed an organization to that effect: WAIT: "Waitresses Against Involuntary Tipping." At the heart of the WAIT concept are two ideas: restaurants do not understand the needs of their employees, and, if tip income is to be eliminated, the foodservers should be provided other benefits.

On the other hand, many foodservers believe they would come out ahead with a service charge in lieu of tips. The argument for a European-type service charge at the inn restaurant to replace the traditional tip is countered by pointing out that foodservers who know they will receive an automatic 15 percent service charge will tend to lose motivation, will pay less attention to customers, and will generally deliver a reduced quality of service, claims Arnie Morton, the owner of a popular restaurant in Chicago known as "Arnies's."

Under the FLSA, "tipped employees" are those who customarily receive more than $30 per month in tips.

Working for Tips Only

In such an instance, does the fact that the worker receives no salary remove that person from coverage under workers' compensation if injured on the job? If that person has a work schedule, must wear a uniform, or meet other requirements as those who are in fact on salary, the courts will hold him or her to be an employee even in the absence of a salary and thus extend compensation coverage to them, *Sunshine Lounge v. Commissioner*, 720 P.2D 81 (Arizona, 1986).

Training Wage

This is a rate of pay that is sharply under the minimum wage for those who are in training for a job that will pay the minimum wage or higher. The FLSA, as amended, provides for such a wage for a period not to exceed 180 days. Many legitimate uses can be found for this provision in the HRI industry.

Covered in the FLSA amendments are provisions for the handling of "tips" received by employees and "allocation" of these tips.

Tips and Tip Allocation

The Tax Equity and Fiscal Responsibility Act of 1982 laid down the following rules relating to tips and allocation of tips at HRI operations:

1. If a business has ten or more employees on a typical business day, the food and beverage operations there are covered.
2. If a business has twenty-five or more employees, allocation of tips must be based on individual sales.
3. All tips must be reported to the IRS by the employees.
4. If reported tips fall below 8 percent of sales, management must allocate tips to employees who fail to report that amount or less.

To avoid audit and fines, all tips must be reported. Failure to do so will result in underpayment of FICA taxes to the detriment of the employees. The criminal penalties are apparent also.

In July 1989, a judge in the Federal District Court in the District of Columbia sentenced eight waiters to jail each night for three months for failing to fully report their tips to the IRS. They were further fined $1,000 each and had to pay tax on unreported tips of $145,000, plus interest and penalties.

A Change in Tip Laws

The Tax Act of 1986 made a change in tip allocation for larger employers. Starting in January 1987, those with twenty-five or more employees had to allocate tips based on the employees' share of the gross receipts. Smaller employers could allocate tips based on gross receipts or on the ratio of hours worked to all hours worked as totalled.

The FLSA also contains provisions for "tip credits."

Tip Credits

Effective April 1, 1991, the minimum wage was raised to $4.25 per hour and the tip credit was increased from 40 percent to 50 percent. What this does for the HRI employer is to lessen the effect of the raise in the minimum wage. Thus from this date forward, tipped employees will receive $2.13 per hour plus tips, resulting in an actual increase in wages of twelve cents per hour over the old rate of $3.35 per hour that ended on April 1, 1990.

Can All Tips Be Kept by Management?

In a restaurant case in Seattle, Washington, management kept all tips and then used these funds, and others, to pay wages to valet parking employees. The Supreme Court of Washington held this to be illegal, stating: ". . . the valets were 'tipped employees' under

[FLSA]. [FLSA] mandates that tipped employees are to keep all of their tips before an employer can deduct even 40 percent of their minimum wage obligations [now 50 percent]. Therefore, an arrangement where the employer takes all of an employee's tips and uses this money to fulfill apparently all of his minimum wage obligation–and help to pay other expenses as well–cannot be legal under the present law. . . ."[6]

Leaving tips and tip allocations, it is next useful to become acquainted with a 1963 amendment to the FLSA, and it too had to do with wages.

Equal Pay Act

The FLSA was amended in 1963 to provide equal pay for men and women who perform similar or like jobs at the work site. Under this amendment, employers cannot discriminate on the basis of sex for equal work. This amendment *does* apply to local and state governments. Thus, whether a job applicant has children or not is of no concern to the hiring business. If it is made a concern, it could be discrimination on the grounds of sex. If male and female front-desk clerks do the same work, they must be paid the same pay. Seniority and superior job performance would be exceptions to the rule but the basic rule is firm. In addition, a male cannot have his wages reduced to make a female's wages the same as his. This too would be discrimination on the grounds of sex and thus a federal violation.

The Equal Employment Opportunity Commission has the authority to enforce the Equal Pay Act.[7] This federal law was designed to assist in meeting the mandates of the Fair Labor Standards Act.

Equal Pay Act and "Comparable Worth"

In 1981, the U.S. Supreme Court endorsed the idea that men and women should be paid the same amount when they do different jobs but where the jobs require equal responsibility and training. However, in June 1985, the Equal Employment Opportunity Commission rejected the use of "comparable worth" as a means of deciding whether or not job discrimination existed in any particular case. The Commission held that "comparable worth" is not recognized under Title VII of the Civil Rights Act of 1964. In this particular case, the Service Employees International Union alleged that "the words of the EEOC carry a ring of hypocrisy for the 49 million working women in the United States." The following, while not an inn case, illustrates the view of the courts:

> Female licensed practical nurse, who specialized in ophthalmic surgery, brought action charging hospital with violating Equal Pay Act. The United States District Court for the District of Minnesota, Donald R. Ross, Circuit Judge, sitting by designation, rendered judgment for the nurse, and the hospital appealed. The Court of Appeals, Henley, Circuit Judge, held that: (1) finding that actual work performed by plaintiff was substantially equal to actual work performed by a male employee, who had been hired as a urological assistant, was not clearly erroneous and (2) although unlawful sex discrimination was established when the male's base salary was raised above that of plaintiff, it was error to award plaintiff damages for the period between the date of the male's hiring and date of the salary increase where additional payments over and above the increase were not designed to compensate the male for work he had done during such period but to compensate him for his loss resulting from the unavailability of the extra work that had been promised him on commencement of his employment.[8]

Related to the payment of wages is the problem for management that is created by another federal law, found in Title III of the Consumer Credit Protection Act.[9] The unusual feature of this law, as it relates to wages, is that it places obligations upon the employer for defaults that have occurred with creditors of the employee or agent. This law regulates the "attachment" or "garnishment" of the wages of employees or agents who are covered by the FLSA.

WAGE ATTACHMENTS

The attachment of wages of judgment debtors by judgment creditors is a popular method of collecting debts. The fact that more than 100,000 attachments are made each year bears witness to this. Under the federal Consumer Credit Protection Act, "wage attachments" are called "garnishments."

A "garnishment" means "any legal or equitable procedure through which the earnings of any individual are required to be withheld for payment of any debt."

While garnishment is popular with those who are collecting debts, what about from the point of view of a hotel-motel operator? Doesn't garnishment require extra bookwork for payroll personnel?

Isn't it, in reality, a first-class nuisance? The answer to these questions is an emphatic "yes."

So, why not fire the garnished employee and save all the worry and work? Only one problem with this: If you fire an employee for one garnishment, you have violated the CCPA. You have also violated the Fair Labor Standards Act as well because the direct result of the firing would be to deny the employee the minimum wage.

An employer who willfully violates the CCPA (not to mention the FLSA) is subject to a fine of not more than $1,000 or a prison sentence of not more than one year—or both.

Since the CCPA prohibits firing for one garnishment, can we fire the employee who has *two* garnishments? One court has held that you can't even do that *until the first is paid off.*[10]

What Do We Do at the Inn?

First, we must determine that the garnishment order is from a court in which judgment has been taken against the debtor. Never begin a wage attachment on the mere word of anyone. Insist upon an exemplified (certified) copy of the court order.

Next, we must then determine what, if any, portion of the employee's wages may be deducted each pay period.

What Does the State Law Say?

State laws that are in substantial compliance with the CCPA may prevail if the state has been granted an exemption. Kentucky is an example. In addition, any state law *that is more favorable to the debtor* will control the percentage that can be deducted from the wages of the employee. In New York the limit is 10 percent, while under the CCPA it is 25 percent. So in New York the limit is 10 percent.

Third, with the above in mind, we can begin calculations for purposes of deductions. In doing this, we must look to the statutory formula. (In the following example, we are assuming that we are in a state that follows the 25 percent rule of the CCPA and that the employee is paid weekly.)

Formula

When a wage earner has wages subjected to garnishment, the amount that can be taken from those wages must not exceed 25 percent of the "disposable earnings" for the period, or the amount ". . . by which disposal earnings exceed 30 times the federal minimum hourly wage prescribed by section 6 (a) of the Fair Labor Standards Act of 1938 in effect at the time the earnings are payable."[11]

To Translate

The minimum wage, as of April 1, 1991, is $4.25 per hour. Thirty times $4.25 equals $127.50. If a worker has a weekly wage of $152.00, and has deductions of $24.50 for Social Security, income tax, and fringe benefits, his "disposable earnings" would be $127.50 *and this sum is exempt from garnishment!* If one cent is withheld, the penalty provisions mentioned above become operative.

Caution Is in Order

The innkeeper receives a call from a member of the local bar who informs the innkeeper that a garnishment order is in the mail and that 25 percent of the debtor-employee's wages can be withheld starting next payday. The employee is earning the $152.00 per week mentioned. See the danger? The employer can make *no* deductions at all for that week, or the next, or the next after that.

Change the Facts

The debtor-employee is earning $175.00 per week. Deductions total $30.00, leaving $145.00 in disposable earnings. The employer can deduct only the sum above $127.50 or $17.50 for that week. This sum does not exceed 25 percent of the disposable earnings.

Raise the wage to $300.00 per week with deductions of $50.00. This leaves $250.00. So now we can take out $122.50, right? No, wrong. The 25 percent provision now controls and this applies to "disposable earnings," which now total $250.00. Twenty-five percent of this is $62.50. This is the limit that can be deducted for this week, leaving the employee $187.50 free to take home. If the state limit is 10 percent, then the deduction would be reduced accordingly.

Policy Reasons

Two policies are reflected in this tricky federal law: (1) to ensure each worker the unrestricted use of the minimum wage and (2) to set outside limits, by percent, to prevent the wholesale removal of large chunks of a wage-earner's salary when that person is earning a fairly substantial wage.

Summary

The garnishment law is one that the inn must be aware of and comply with strictly. Care must be used in computations and distribution of the withheld funds. These must be paid as directed by the court. While there are exceptions to the above rules, let the court spell these out. In the vast majority of garnishments today, the above rules will apply. Failure to comply with these rules can be a serious mistake.

WORKERS' COMPENSATION

These laws are designed to provide benefits for those employees or agents who are injured while "on the job" as those words have come to be defined by law. The benefits paid for those found eligible are based on a percentage of the employee's wages and applicable state tables. The laws of each state must be looked to in this area. The benefits paid are not taxable to the employee.

Covered workers cannot sue their employers because workers' compensation is the sole remedy. But if the worker is injured on the job by the negligence of third parties, then an independent tort action may be brought against that third party. Any recovery must first be used to repay any state funds received under the "collateral source" rule.

The first workers' compensation laws were passed by the English Parliament and placed strict liability upon the employers. That policy has come down to us today and remains in effect. However, if an employee deliberately injures himself or herself on the job, the employer is excused from liability upon proof of the self-inflicted injury.

Today, injuries to an employee while on duty are considered a cost of operations. The policy of the law is to spread this loss over those who will benefit from the labor, and not force the employee to suffer the loss alone. Today the compensation laws are recognized as being remedial in nature–they were created to remedy a specific social problem. Thus, under the rules of statutory construction, the courts will construe these statutes liberally and not strictly. (Statutes that are in derogation of common law, on the other hand, must be construed strictly.) Translated, this means that any doubt will be resolved by the courts in *favor of the injured person.* In that manner, the purpose of such laws will be achieved. Examine Figure 10.1.

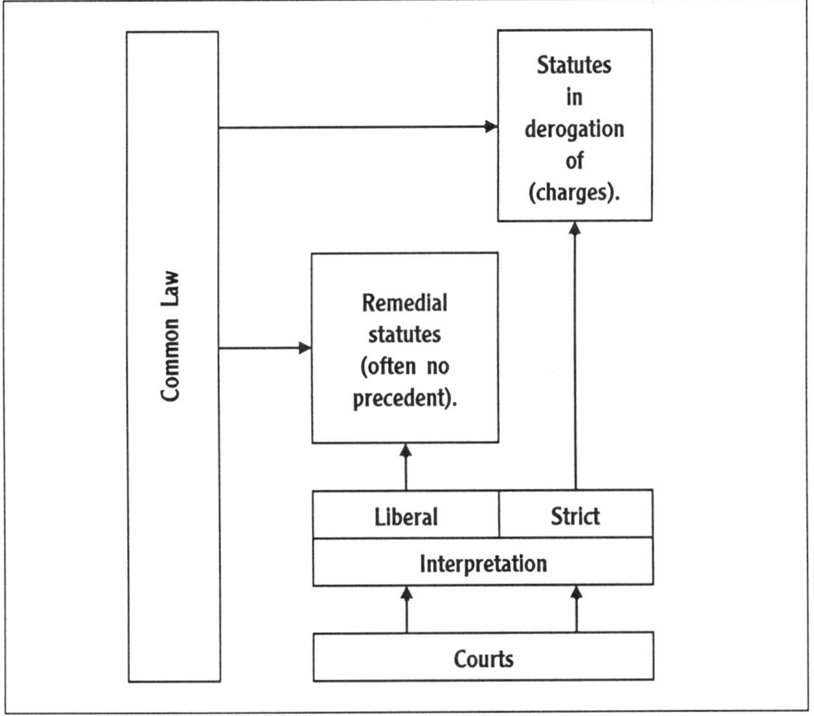

FIGURE 10.1 Interpretation of statutes.

When workers' compensation cases work their way into the courts, some unusual results are often seen.

Are Nonsalaried Persons Covered?

Shelly Johns was a lounge dancer at the Dancing Sunshines Lounge in Arizona where she performed for tips only. After slipping on a wet floor, she applied for workers' compensation. The lounge argued that she was an independent contractor and thus not eligible for compensation. The court found that she had a posted work schedule and had to wear a specific uniform. The court used these facts to hold her to be an employee for compensation purposes.[12]

How About a Degenerative Bone Disease?

Beverly Morgan quit her job as a masseuse at the Desert Inn Hotel and Casino in Las Vegas. Under directions of an agent of the

Desert Inn, she filed her claim too late. Desert Inn contested both the type of injury and the late filing.

The Supreme Court of Nevada granted full benefits, holding: "The evidence supports that Morgan's degenerative joint disease qualifies as an occupational disease which arose out of and in the course of her employment as a masseuse for Desert Inn. She first began to have problems with her hands while employed as a masseuse for Desert Inn. Her job as a masseuse involved inordinate use of her hands. As she continued her employment, her problems worsened. She was diagnosed as having a disease 'aggravated by overuse' in the performance of her job . . . there is a direct causal connection between her work conditions and the aggravation of the disease, the disease worsened as a natural incident of her continued work, and her work can be 'fairly traced' as the proximate cause of her worsened condition." The court pointed out that "Although Morgan's is an occupational disease claim, she erroneously filed a claim for an industrial accident at Gibbens' direction. Because its own agent gave Morgan the wrong information, Desert Inn cannot now benefit from Morgan's failure to strictly comply with the statute. . . ."[13]

When Is an Accident Compensable?

In answering this question, the courts have developed two applicable tests. First, was the employee "on the job" when placed at risk and then injured? This is called a "positional risk"—that is, the employee was in a position to be injured by reason of being at work. Second, was the employee in the scope of his or her employment when the injury occurred? This is called "actual risk"—that is, the injury arose in the scope of employment and "as a result of the employment." If one or both tests are met, the injury is compensable. Applying these two tests in court is not always clear, however.

To illustrate, Fay Jones worked at the King's Arms Tavern, where she prepared salads, cut pies, dipped ice cream, and made coffee and tea. While arriving at work one morning, she took trash from her car to deposit in the tavern waste area and fell while doing so. This happened before she had entered the tavern itself. Was she at "actual risk" when injured?

The Virginia Court of Appeals stated that when an employee chooses to go to a dangerous place outside of her place of employment, any injury sustained there is not compensable. But in this case, the court held that: "Mrs. Jones did not choose to go to a dangerous place where her employment did not necessarily carry her. She went to what was an appropriate place provided by the employer for employees to dispose of trash. The mere fact that she stepped over to a trash receptacle for a personal need does not take the accident out of the course of her employment or cause the accident to become one not arising out of her employment. Accidents which arise out of the conditions of the workplace should be compensable if the activity which gave rise to the accident is of a nature reasonably to be expected by the employer and occurred at a place and time where an employee might reasonably be expected to be."[14]

As a general rule, if an inn maintains workers' compensation coverage, that is the sole source of recovery for injuries sustained by employees while "on the job." This includes extreme situations such as the housekeeper raped in a hotel room while trying to perform her maintenance duties, *Twin City v. Home*, 650 F. Supp. 785 (Pennsylvania, 1986). There are exceptions to this rule, however.

"Personal Animosity" Rule

In many states, the courts recognize a "personal animosity" rule and treat it as an exception to the general rule that an employer is obligated to pay compensation to a worker injured "on the job." Thus if inn employee X is injured by the fall of a wall-mounted television set while cleaning a guest room, employee X is entitled to receive workers' compensation as provided by law. On the other hand, if employee X is assaulted by employee Y because of a personal dispute unrelated to the business of the inn, in most states employee X would not qualify for benefits. The reason is that, while the injury occurred at the job site, it in fact had nothing to do with the work being carried out there.

By statute, in some states such as Texas, after maximum payment is collected under workers' compensation, suit can then be brought against an employer if the employer had been guilty of gross negligence. To illustrate, a San Antonio Holiday Inn had to pay almost $200,000 extra to the widow of a security guard slain by a burglar at the inn. It was a house rule that security guards could not carry firearms and that was the basis of the widow's successful claim. She argued that her husband should have been allowed to be armed.

In Maryland, a court rule has developed that allows direct suit to be brought, after workers' compensation claims have been settled, for emotional distress caused by delayed payment of the claim.

Both the Texas statute and the Maryland court decision represent intrusions into the common principle that, if workers' compensation is in effect it bars all further claims against the inn.

Leaving the topic of workers' compensation, it is useful to learn something about a companion law not concerned with injury, but rather with the loss of wages.

UNEMPLOYMENT COMPENSATION

All of our states have programs designed to compensate qualified employees who become unemployed under specified conditions. The costs of the administration of these programs are mostly paid for by the federal government, while the funds for the benefits come from payroll taxes levied by each state.

Denial of Benefits

Benefits to an employee will be denied under the following conditions: the employee is fired for misconduct on the job, is voluntarily taking part in a labor dispute, has not been off the job for the prescribed time period (one week is typical), has refused another job for which he or she is fitted by prior training and experience, refuses to actively seek other work, or has resigned without cause.

In most other instances of unemployment, payments based upon state scales and salary level will be paid to the employee without concern about need.

While there are many court decisions that are concerned with the unemployment compensation laws, just one will be mentioned for purposes of illustration.

An employer who breaches an employment contract, which leads the employee to resign, gives cause to the employee to recover unemployment compensation in spite of the fact that the employee resigned voluntarily. Such resignations must be for "good cause attributable to the employer." Breaching an employment contract meets that test.[15]

One of the more important areas of concern to the HRI manager is found in the civil rights acts, both federal and state. In many instances the federal act has served as a "model" for the laws that have been adopted by state legislatures. That happened in Nevada. It is to that federal law that we now turn.[16]

CIVIL RIGHTS ACT OF 1964

The Civil Rights Act of 1964, as amended in 1972, imposes two primary legal duties upon an innkeeper. First, the innkeeper is covered when employees are hired to work at the inn. There must not be discrimination in this hiring on the grounds of race, color, creed, national origin, sex, or age. Title VII covers the hiring of employees.

Second, Title II of the act prohibits discrimination at "places of public accommodation" and inns fall into that classification. It is interesting to note that Title VII prohibits discrimination on the grounds of sex—while Title II does not. Thus sex discrimination is not covered at places of public accommodation, but other laws reach that result.

Title II thus creates a duty to receive which is independent of, and in addition to, the common-law duty to receive.

Before the federal civil rights laws become operative, however, there must be federal power over the business in question. This power can be triggered in two ways. First, the operation of the business must have some effect upon interstate commerce. Most inns would be swept in under this provision because most of the persons served are travelers who are crossing state lines in their travels. It can come about in another way and that is when discrimination at a hotel or motel or inn is "supported by state action."[17] An example of this, out of the recent past, were state laws that prohibited members of certain races from occupying rooms at hotels and motels in a state. The constitutionality of the Civil Rights Act of 1964 was upheld by the United States Supreme Court in *Heart of Atlanta Motel v. United States,* 379 U.S. 241 (1964).

Equal Employment Opportunity Act

The Civil Rights Act of 1964 contained an obvious weakness: It did not give the Equal Employment Opportunity Commission (EEOC) the power to issue "cease-and-desist" orders in the federal courts. Attempts were made to give the EEOC this power but they failed.

Instead of asking for cease-and-desist powers, the Nixon Administration suggested that the EEOC be given the power to file suits in federal court and to represent those who had meritorious employment-discrimination claims. The commission could file suit, however, only after all steps had been taken to conciliate the matter without court action. This seemed to satisfy the federal lawmakers.

In 1972, the House acted first, with the Senate strengthening the bill. President Nixon signed it into law on March 27, 1972, and it became effective at once. This law was an amendment of Title VII of the Civil Rights Act of 1964. We will examine briefly the changes in the coverage of Title VII.

Changes in Title VII

State and Local Government

Under the original act, employees of state and local government were excluded from coverage. They are now covered, subject to the exemptions set forth below.

Federal Employees

These employees are not within the power of EEOC, but the 1972 amendment makes it clear that the federal government shall not discriminate in personnel matters by reasons of race, color, sex, religion, or national origin. The Office of Employment Opportunity and not the EEOC, has power to hear federal employment discrimination matters.

Number of Employees

Title VII originally applied to employers with twenty-five or more employees. This was reduced to fifteen. This change became effective March 24, 1973.

Joint Labor-Management

Apprenticeship training and retraining programs are now covered. These programs were administered in the past by joint committees of labor and management. Discrimination cannot now be practiced in admission to, or administration of, these training programs.

Exemptions

Teachers and religious corporations or organizations, originally exempt from the 1964 Act, are now covered. However, a church, for example, can still discriminate on the basis of religion in hiring an employee, but not on the basis of race, color, sex, or national origin. As to coverage to state and local governments, *elected* officials are exempt, as well as their assistants.

Use of the Courts

If the EEOC is unable to reach a conciliation with the employer, union, employment agency, or joint labor-management committee within 30 days after a charge is filed, the federal courts can be used by the Commission. If the Commission fails to act, or if the complaining party is not satisfied with the actions taken by the Commission, that person has direct access to the federal courts. If a state or local government is involved, the Attorney General can bring the court action. Once a suit is brought and the complaining party has set up its defense, the judge has two alternatives: hear the case promptly or appoint a "master" within 120 days to hear the case. These deadlines were written into the law to prevent procrastination by the EEOC or the courts—or both.

Employer's Obligations

An employer cannot discriminate against a job applicant, or against one who is already an employee, on the grounds set forth above. This extends to compensation, pay raises, and promotions. Likewise, employees cannot be segregated, classified, or deprived of employment opportunities on the stated grounds. For example, any test used in hiring or promotion cannot be a general intelligence test; it must relate to the job in question. A cook cannot be required to pass the same test as a cashier at the front desk of an inn.[17]

Exceptions

Members of the Communist Party, or a party-front organization, can be discriminated against on that ground. Religious societies can discriminate on the basis of religion, as mentioned. If a government program requires security clearance, then one who does not have that clearance can be discriminated against. A motel operating on an Indian reservation can show preference toward Indians in its hiring practices. If an inn has a bona fide seniority system in operation, or a merit-award system based on quality of work, then different compensation can be paid under those conditions. These must be "good faith" programs.

The question of employee "imbalance" is something that the courts are beginning to clarify. It is clear from the Act that imbalances existing as of the date of passage of the law are not affected. The *continuation* of previous imbalances must be guarded against. "Affirmative-action plans" (plans to eradicate prior discrimination) for government construction and manufacturing by private contractors have been upheld.[18]

The inn should create and be able to demonstrate that there is in operation an affirmative-action program that complies with these laws. Many businesses hire or appoint someone to carry out this function. In the small business, it can be a part-time job.

When confronted with a charge of violations of the EEOA, one should do the following: seek legal advice; reply at once on Form 131, which will be provided the employer within 10 days of the charge; conduct an independent investigation; and finally, draft and maintain a detailed written report of the incident that gave rise to the charge of discrimination. Such a report can be used in negotiations with the commission, or in court if one intends to fight the accusation. The filing of an EEOA complaint or charge is just an accusation. Proof must still be forthcoming from the one claiming the discrimination.[19]

Notices and Recordkeeping

Notices created by the EEOC must be posted as required and records kept as prescribed. However, if an employer is covered by state fair-employment practices law, one set of records can meet both requirements. If an inn feels that the recordkeeping requirements will present an undue hardship, an application for an exemption must be made directly to the EEOC, not to a court as was permitted in the 1964 law. If the request is denied, one can then look to the courts for recordkeeping relief if there is good cause for it.

How About a Hotel with a Casino?

If a hotel which is under the coverage of the Civil Rights Act also has a casino, the casino would be subject to the terms of the CRA.[20] In Nevada, a casino is specifically listed as a place of "public accommodation" and thus not only would the federal CRA apply, but the state law as well.[21]

What Relief Is Available for Violations?

As to relief available for violations of the federal law, injunctive relief can be sought against HRI violators. Declaratory relief can also be sought–but there are no direct provisions for money recovery for the complainant. (Many *state* civil rights acts *do* permit money recoveries.)

On the other hand, violations of the federal law could in some instances trigger other federal laws which could lead to money damages. There are no criminal penalties available under the law.

Normally one who complains of civil rights violations is expected to seek injunctive relief at his or her own expense against the offending establishment. If successful, the prevailing party may be awarded attorney fees and costs by the court.

What About "Private Clubs"?

Bars and taverns that serve drinks only and do not use musical devices and electronic and other games are not covered.[22] Private clubs that are not open to the public are not covered. In determining if an establishment is in fact a "private club," the courts will look for "selectivity" through a true-management organization with formal rules for determining membership. The "key clubs" found in many Eastern inns in states that have bottle-liquor laws would *not* meet the test of a private club since they admit strangers. Thus, they cannot discriminate in such clubs on civil rights grounds. As one court said: "Selectivity is the essence of a private club."[23] The key clubs could not meet this test. Yet if a club is truly private, it is exempt from the law and can engage in discrimination. "Private discrimination does not give rise to a violation."[24] The burden of establishing whether or not a club is private would be upon management and not the one complaining of discrimination.[25]

When looking at the impact of the federal Civil Rights Act as amended, one must also take into consideration the fact that the states have such laws. This tends to compound the possible penalties for violations.

The Nevada Example:

Nevada Revised Statutes define a "place of public accommodation." (See Chapter 5.)

This is then followed by a one-sentence statute:

> All persons are entitled to the full and equal enjoyment of the goods, services, facilities, privileges, advantages, and accommodations of any place of public accommodation, without discrimination or segregation on the ground of race, color, religion, national origin, or physical or visual handicap.

Not all states created such statutes, however, and the federal law fills this void. Other than voting acts, this was the first federal civil rights act in the United States for ninety years.

Through court cases and interpretation, other matters are now associated with the Act. A few of these follow.

Akin to the Common-Law Duty to Receive

Centuries ago, the English courts created the duty to receive that we have discussed before. In effect, this also created a common-law duty not to discriminate against members of the traveling public. As an 1794 court said, innkeepers "cannot refuse to receive guests, so neither can they impose unreasonable terms upon them."[26]

An American court in 1874 spoke of the duty of carriers, whose duties are analogous to innkeepers, in this way:

> A service for the public necessarily implies equal treatment in its performance when the right to serve is common. Because the institution, so to speak, is public, every member of the community stands on an equality as to the right to its benefit, and therefore, the carrier cannot discriminate between individuals for whom he will render the service. In the very nature, then, of his duty and of the public right, his conduct should be equal and just to all.[27]

Exactly Who Is Covered?

While all HRI properties, other than private clubs, are covered, what about a YMCA, trailer parks, RV parks, campgrounds, cottages at beach resorts, and places that serve transient guests by the week rather than the day? All such places would be covered if they seek out-of-state patrons.

A small inn of five or fewer rooms which is occupied by the owner, even though that person seeks transient guests, is *not* covered because such a business is specifically excluded.

Legal Discrimination

If a good-faith employment qualification requires it, such as male attendants in the male restroom at the inn, employers may legally discriminate on the basis of sex in that instance. The same is true in relation to national origin or religion. In HRI management situations, decisions should be made on the basis of *business needs* and not sex, race, color, religion, or other proscribed areas.

In almost all instances, employers who have claimed that sex (male) is a bona fide employment qualification have failed in court. Thus a claim that laws that require that a baseball umpire, a hunting guide, a walk-way supervisor, a stenographer, a casino card dealer, a race car driver, a lifeguard, a flight attendant, and many more, must be of one sex or another, have failed in court. For example, it would violate the sex law of Title VII to insist that only men could be lifeguards since they must clean the men's restrooms. The courts point out, "Who is to clean the women's rooms?"

Inconsistent treatment of employees will always be looked at with suspicion by the courts. If a house rule states, for example, that employees shall not drink on the job, and a white employee drinks but is not fired while a black employee drinks and is fired, a *prima facie* case of a civil rights violation has arisen.

Racial Discrimination Is Covered: Or Is It?

"Race may well involve more than mere skin pigment," ruled the U.S. Supreme Court in 1987. Justice Byron R. White, writing for the court, said that "Congress intended to protect from discrimination identifiable classes of persons who are subjected to intentional discrimination solely because of their ancestry or ethnic characteristics." Thus members of the Jewish or Muslim faiths are also covered by the civil rights laws even though they are considered to be members of the Caucasian race. The coverage of the law is *not* restricted to African Americans.

In June 1989, the U.S. Supreme Court held that a simple comparison of minority and white workers is not in itself, in the absence of something further, enough to prove racial discrimination. The ruling was heralded as "a major step to the rear for civil rights." The decision said that it is not the comparison of black and white, but rather a comparison between the racial composition of the labor market and the job to be filled. The ruling was sharply against numerical quotas in the workplace. A Kansas case will illustrate a related matter.

A member of a minority race was being interviewed for a job at a Kansas City hotel. After the interview, it was determined by management that the applicant was too "dominant" in his thinking and had an employment background that indicated that he would not be a "team player" at the hotel. He was not hired.

His suit for discrimination under Title VII was dismissed. The court ruled that the reasons for not hiring that person were legitimate business reasons and that race had not entered into the decision not to hire. *Clay v. Hyatt Regency Hotel*, 724 F. 2D 721 (1984).

In 1988, in an opinion written by Justice William Brennan, the U.S. Supreme Court ruled that it was all right for a public employer to favor a woman for a particular job over a man who was better qualified in training, experience, and test scoring. It was a strong advance for the concept of "reverse discrimination," which has the practical effect of inverting Title VII. To say it another way, a woman cannot be denied a job solely on the basis of her sex, but there is no harm in favoring a woman.

A male employee at an airport inn was terminated and replaced by a female bartender. The letter given to the fired male said "Your termination was caused by a policy decision; uniforms were purchased for an all-female bar." The court found for the fired bartender, awarding back pay and attorney's fees, *Airport Inn, Inc. v. Nebraska EEOC and Michael Sump*, 353 N.W. 2D 727 (Nebraska, 1984).

Sexual Harassment

These claims fall under Title VII and can result in injunctions that require rehiring of employees plus attorneys' fees. Payment of back wages may also be ordered by the court. It is clear that males may also be the victims of sexual harassment.

Sexual Harassment and Insurance Coverage

An insurance policy issued to an inn provides, among other things, that the insurance company will pay all sums that the inn may become obligated to pay "because of bodily injury or property damages caused by an occurrence."

The policy contained definitions of "bodily injury" and "occurrence." These definitions allowed the insurance company to avoid paying the judgment against the inn. The judgment had arisen out of sexual harassment by executives of the inn against employees and thus did not involve "bodily injury," *Presidential Hotel v. Canal Insurance Co.*, 373 S.E. 2D 671 (Georgia, 1988).

Constructive Discharge and Civil Rights

When an employee voluntarily quits a job, is it still possible for a successful claim of discrimination to be brought against an employer? The answer is "yes" if the employee is forced from the job because of conditions there. This happened to Elizabeth Levendos at a restaurant where she worked. Here is what the court had to say: "While we can imagine a maitre d' who might not object to exclusion from management meetings, denial of authority to order supplies, false accusations of stealing from and drinking on the job, and who might not be disturbed by rumors and remarks that she would be replaced by a male, her employer's refusal to talk with her and to find wine bottles in her locker, we find that these events are clearly not trivial. It is of course plausible that a jury could decide ultimately that a reasonable person would tolerate some or even all of these occurrences without being forced to quit. It is equally plausible, however, that a jury would come to the opposite conclusion. . . . Thus we hold that Levendos . . . presented sufficient evidence to raise a genuine issue of material fact regarding whether she was constructively discharged from her position."[28]

Use of "VIP" Cards

Can the use of such cards at HRI operations, where some are sold and others given away free, and which are designed to allow immediate access to a restaurant or bar while others must wait, violate the discrimination laws? A federal district judge sitting in Kentucky has said "yes."

The court issued an injunction not to "Engage in any act or practice which is intended to limit or discourage black persons from patronizing the Glass Menagerie, including but not limited to using pretexts such as the requirement of a 'VIP Card' for admission in order to limit the number of blacks in the Glass Menagerie, and providing any priority in admission to the Glass Menagerie to present holders of 'VIP Cards.'"[29]

How About Dealers in Casinos?

Can a gambler who prefers white males to black dealers force a casino to substitute a dealer on this basis? Caesar's Hotel and Casino at Atlantic City did just that. A New Jersey administrative law judge ruled that this was both race and sex discrimination and fined Caesar's $15,600, the amount lost by the gambler. The state gaming regulators then raised the fine to $250,000.

Other Dangers of Harassment

Where such conduct is carried out at an inn with the knowledge of management, suits are certain to follow. As asked previously, will the insurance policies of the inn that provide coverage for "bodily injury" apply and give protection to the hotel? A Georgia court has also said "no" since harassment in the form that it was carried out at the inn in question resulted in "mental damages" and not bodily injury. The policy in question provided no coverage for mental injury.[30]

Do Hotels Always Lose?

For a case in which a court action brought by the EEOC against a hotel on the grounds of religious discrimination failed, see *EEOC v. Caribe Hilton International,* 821 F.2D 74 (Puerto Rico, 1987). The evidence showed that the hotel had "bent over backwards" to accommodate a Seventh Day Adventist whose religious beliefs prevented him from working from sundown Friday to sundown Saturday. The court found that the employee had been totally uncooperative with the hotel.

California Civil Rights Act

The Mayan nightclub opened in early 1990, on South Hill Street in Los Angeles, California. Four persons tried to attain admission but were turned away arbitrarily because of an alleged violation of a "dress code." However, no such dress code in fact existed. The four sought an award under the California Unruh Civil Rights Act of 1959, and were awarded $250 each.

The 1866 Civil Rights Law

This law, found in section 1981 of the Federal Code, was enacted by Congress to allow the newly freed slaves to negotiate and enforce contracts. Can this civil rights law of the last century be used to press claims of racial harassment on the job? In a June 1989 decision, the U.S. Supreme Court ruled in the negative.

AGE DISCRIMINATION IN EMPLOYMENT ACT

The 1967 ADEA prohibits discrimination because of age for those employees between the ages of 40 and 65. The law is limited, however, to employers of twenty-five or more persons. (These basic provisions have been changed as will be discussed below.) The statute can be found in 29 USC 621, *et. seq.* In 1977, the age limit was raised to 70.

In October 1986, Congress passed legislation designed to give the elderly "new hope, new courage and a new feeling of meaningfulness." The 1986 amendment does away with any age limit except for sensitive jobs such as CIA, FBI agents, and air controllers. There are no exemptions that would seem to apply to HRI operations. Congress estimated that this law would add about 200,000 persons to the nation's work force and would generate about $3 billion in revenue.

This law applies to any employer who has twenty or more employees for 20 weeks of each calendar year. The law is administered by the Equal Employment Opportunity Commission.

There are four times when termination because of age is permissible: (1) When a seniority system requires certain persons to step down; (2) when facts *other than age* demand that the older person be let go; (3) where age is a bona fide qualification of employment at a particular business; and (4) the discipline or discharge of an employee is for a good cause such as stealing or dishonesty. Where discharge does not fall under the above criteria, that person is entitled to back pay and commissions, and if the discharge was wilful, the damages are to be doubled. This feature came about by an amendment to the 1967 statute.

Certain procedural matters are attached to this law. The complaining person must notify the EEOC within 180 days of the alleged unlawful employment practice. The EEOC then has 60 days to attempt to settle the dispute. If no resolution follows, the one making the complaint can then go to the courts. That person is then entitled to a jury trial.

When Congress enacted the ADEA, it incorporated the enforcement provisions of the FLSA (Fair Labor Standards Act) into it.

A most striking age (and sex) discrimination case involved the Las Vegas Hilton where thirty-seven white, male workers, thirty-two of whom were over forty years of age, were replaced by twenty-four females and thirteen males, all but one of whom were under forty years of age. The jury that heard the case "found age discrimination was involved" and awarded the thirty-seven plaintiffs sums ranging from $7,000 to $106,000 for lost wages, $200,000 for emotional distress, and $30 million for punitive damages.

The judge also found that sex discrimination was involved and added $1.6 million to the verdict. (Sex discrimination under the 1964 Act is reserved to the court.)

Added to those sums were prejudgment interest and attorneys' fees, boosting the total award upward of $50 million. All in all not a good day for Hilton Hotels, *Brooks v. Hilton Casinos,* 714 F. Supp. 1115 (Nevada, 1989).

Turning from age discrimination, another little-known federal statute that applies to the inn is the Employment Retirement Income Security Act, ERISA.

In *Folz v. Marriott Corp.* 594 F, Supp. 1007 (Missouri, 1984), a hotel employee brought action against the hotel for violation of the provision of ERISA that provides: "It shall be unlawful . . . to discharge, fine, suspend, expel, discipline, or discriminate against a participant or beneficiary for exercising any right to which he is entitled under the provisions of an employee benefit plan . . . or for the purpose of interfering with the attainment of any right to which such participant may become entitled under the plan. . . ."

The court found in favor of Folz and awarded back pay of $88,677; future pay of $88,443; and ordered that all life insurance, sick leave, medical benefits, stock options, and other benefits be reinstated. It is necessary now to return to the Civil Rights Act in order to see what was enacted in 1978.

A 1978 amendment to the 1964 Civil Rights Act expanded sex discrimination to include pregnancy and this too is of concern to the inn in hiring, as well as in firing, employees. Title VII of the Civil Rights Act of 1964 prohibits a covered employer from discharging or otherwise discriminating against any individual "with respect to compensation, terms, conditions, or privileges of employment because of such individual's sex." The 1978 Amendment makes it clear that "because of sex" includes pregnancy, childbirth, or related medical problems and the amendment so provides.

An example of the upshot of the 1978 amendment is that an employer cannot allow women to continue to work and then fire them because they become pregnant. That is sex discrimination and violates the 1978 Act. An adverse inn decision such as this entitles the pregnant employee to all lost back pay, all lost benefits (such as vacation, health, and retirement), plus court costs and reasonable attorney fees.[31]

When hiring, do not ask applicants if they are pregnant, do not fire employees who become pregnant for that reason alone, do not refuse to rehire employees who were pregnant but who are able to return to their jobs. Here are the main words of this federal statute:

> The terms 'because of sex' or 'on the basis of sex' include but are not limited to because of or on the basis of pregnancy, childbirth, or related medical conditions; and women affected by pregnancy, childbirth, or related medical conditions shall be treated the same for all employment-related purposes, including receipt of benefits under fringe benefit programs, as other persons not so affected but similar in their ability or inability to work. . . .

It is not wise to inquire of female applicants about their potential plans to have children. In addition, pregnancy cannot be given as a reason to deny promotion, or to deny employment in the first instance. For an example of how the 1978 pregnancy amendment to Title VII is applied in court, see *Ensor v. Painter,* 661 F. Supp. 21 (Tennessee, 1987). In this case, two pregnant workers were fired because they "were pregnant and could not perform their duties." Those words graphically illustrate the problem that the amendment was designed to prevent.

An odd twist of these laws is found in the fact that, if employees' insurance plans cover pregnant employees, such plans must also cover *pregnant wives of employees.* This is not so strange perhaps when one considers that if this were *not* the law, it would amount to discrimination against the male employee who has a pregnant wife.

In addition to the federal pregnancy law, the states have also taken action.

Pregnancy Laws in the States

California law requires employers to grant leave to a pregnant employee, not to exceed four months. The California law also requires that, upon returning, such employees must be reinstated to their former jobs. If such jobs are no longer available because of "business necessity," the employer must then make a reasonable good-faith effort to place that employee in a similar job elsewhere. A challenge to the California law reached the U.S. Supreme Court, where the law was upheld, *California Federal v. Guerra,* 107 S. Ct. 683 (California, 1987).

Maternity Leave in the States

More and more states are passing statutes that require employers to treat pregnant workers exactly as they treat employees who are sick or disabled. If certain benefits are extended to a cook injured in an inn kitchen, those same benefits must also be given to the front-desk clerk who becomes pregnant.

Turning from the topic of sex/pregnancy discrimination, it is necessary to learn something about the most recent amendment of the 1964 Civil Rights Act. This is the Americans With Disabilities Act, ADA.

AMERICANS WITH DISABILITIES ACT

The ADA had its beginnings in the Vocational Rehabilitation Act of 1973. This federal law controlled federal contractors and those who were receiving federal funds where structures were involved which the handicapped would be using.

This new addition to the law has an impact upon the HRI industry in both design and use of hospitality facilities. At the design stage of a new inn, for example, failure to learn what this law requires, and failure to implement those requirements, could result in serious losses. These losses could come from adverse jury verdicts and from the costs of redoing physical facilities at hotels, motels, and inns under court order. This law was signed into effect on July 26, 1990, by President George Bush. The Act makes it clear that nothing in ADA is to be interpreted so as to reduce coverage under the Act. In addition, if state law provides *greater care* for the disabled, such laws are to be given preference.

Who Are the "Disabled"?

These persons are defined under the ADA as being those with:

1. Mental impairment.
2. Physical impairment.
3. Any condition that limits "major life activities."

What Is Not Covered by ADA?

The following are not covered:

1. Sexual behavior disorders.
2. Transvestism.
3. Transsexualism.

HOTEL, SAN DIEGO BAY, San Diego, California.

4. Psychoactive substance-induced organic mental disorders (drug-induced psychosis).
5. Compulsive gambling.
6. Kleptomania (compulsion to steal).
7. Pyromania (compulsion to set fires).
8. Current alcohol and drug abuse.

Which Employers Are Covered?

The ADA, as originally enacted, included only those businesses with twenty-five or more employees. This was true for the first two years after the passage of the law. That number has now been decreased to "fifteen or more employees." This figure is to be calculated "on a daily basis."

ADA makes it illegal to discriminate against a qualified, disabled individual in job application procedures, hiring, firing, compensation, advancement, job training, or other conditions and privileges of employment.

The ADA is neutral on drug testing. Under the law, drug testing is not considered to be a "medical examination."

This Act has been called the "world's first declaration of equality" for the disabled. It must be remembered that the law also applies to guests at the inn, not only the employees there.

To close out the chapter, brief mention will be made of contracts designed to control employees after they leave their jobs at the inn. Such contracts are known as "restrictive covenants."

RESTRICTIVE COVENANTS

One matter of concern for the inn is the loss of personnel who may take to competitors skills, knowledge, and even business "secrets" developed with the original employer. To prevent this, it is common to place into the employment contract a paragraph stating that, upon termination of employment, the employee agrees not to engage in a like or similar business or trade within a prescribed radius for a given number of months or years. Such provisions are commonly referred to as "restrictive employment clauses."

If these are reasonable in time and distance, the courts will uphold them as a legitimate subject of contract. If unreasonable, the courts may reduce the time and distance in part or refuse to honor them at all. If an innkeeper agrees in the employment contract never to work as an innkeeper if he or she leaves that employment, that promise is void as being against public policy and a court would refuse to enforce it.

A travel-agent employee signed a restrictive employment contract in which he agreed not to work in the travel-agency business in two named towns or within a radius of sixty miles after termination of employment. The court held the restriction to be unreasonable and thus unenforceable.[32]

QUESTIONS

1. True or False. Many federal employment laws, as they relate to inns, have been enacted since 1960.
2. Give one probable reason why the number of "jurisdictional employees" was reduced from twenty-five to fifteen persons under EEOA.
3. What was the weakness in the 1964 Civil Rights Act as it related to employment?
4. Give one probable reason why teachers were exempted from the 1964 Act, and one reason why they are included now.
5. Give one example of when it would be lawful to discriminate in employment at an inn.

6. Why can't the same employment test be used for all applicants for employment at a motel?
7. What is an "affirmative action" plan?
8. Why are private clubs exempt from civil rights laws coverage?
9. List three unlawful business HRI employment practices.
10. How do Title VII rules differ from workers' compensation laws?

ENDNOTES

1. 29 USC 201, et seq.
2. As of April 1, 1991.
3. *Brock v. Claridge Hotel and Casino,* 711 F. Supp. 779 (New Jersey, 1989).
4. As of April 1, 1991.
5. *Wirtz v. Healy,* 227 F. Supp. 123 (1964).
6. *Winans v. W.A.S. Inc.,* 772 P.2D 1001 (Washington, 1989).
7. 29 USC sec. 213 (b) (8) (A).
8. *Ridgeway v. United States,* 563 F. Supp. 123 (1964).
9. *P.L.* 90-321, 82 *Stat.* 146 et seq. Act of May 29, 1968.
10. *Brennan v. Kroger Co.,* No. 79-1726 (7th Cir., April 9, 1975).
11. Title III, Section 303 (a) (2).
12. *Dancing Sunshines Lounge v. Industrial Commissioner,* 720 P. 2D 81 (Arizona, 1986).
13. *Desert Inn Casino & Hotel v. Morgan,* 792 P.2D 400 (Nevada, 1990).
14. *Jones v. Colonial Williamsburg Found,* 392 S.E. 2D 848 (Virginia, 1990).
15. *Baker v. Fanny Farmer,* 394 N.W. 2D 564 (Minnesota, 1986).
16. 42 USC sec. 2000 e -2000 (15).
17. Civil Rights Act, 1964, Title II, sec. 201 (b).
18. *Griggs v. Duke Power Co.,* U.S. Sup. Ct., 3 FEP Cases 175 (1971).
19. *Contractors Ass'n. of Eastern Pa. v. Hodgson,* 3rd Cir. 1971 3 FEP Cases 395, cert. denied, U.S. Sup. Ct., 3 FEP Cases 1030 (1971).
20. *Rosado v. Maysonet v. Solis,* 400 F. Supp. 576 (DPR 1975).
21. Nevada Revised Statutes, 651.050.
22. *Selden v. Topaza,* 447 F. 2D 165 (Fifth Circuit, 1971).

23. *Bell v. Denwood,* 312 F. Supp. 251 (D. Maryland, 1970).
24. *Moose Lodge v. Irvis,* 407 U.S. 163, 92 S. Ct. 1965 (1972).
25. *U.S. v. Richberg,* 398 F.2D 523 (Fifth Circuit, 1968).
26. *Kirkman v. Shawcross,* 6 East. 519, 101 Eng. Rep. 410, 412 (King's Bench, 1794).
27. *Messenger v. Pennsylvania R.R.*, 37 Nv. 531, 534 (1874).
28. *Levendos v. Stern Entertainment, Inc.*, 860 F.2D 1227 (Pennsylvania, 1988).
29. *U.S. v. Glass Menagerie, Inc.,* 702 F. Supp. 139 (Kentucky, 1988).
30. *Presidential Hotel v. Canal Insurance Co.,* 373 S.E. 2D 671 (Georgia, 1988).
31. *EEOC v. Newton Inn Association,* 647 F. Supp. 957 (Virginia, 1986).
32. *United Travel Service, Inc. v. Weber,* 108 Ill. App. 2D 353, 247 N.E. 2D 801 (1969).

11

Credit Cards, Debit Cards, and Electronic Money at HRI Operations

He was an easy touch for old buddies; some of his employees were cheating him; he was betting huge sums on losing football teams; and his free-wheeling life-style was prohibitively expensive. So he did what he could to economize. He rented his stores and delivery trucks for extra cash to a hijacking gang and he began using hot credit cards when he went out at night.

The hot credit cards, obtained by Weinberg from his underworld friends, rarely caused problems. "I'd go to joints owned by wise guys [mobsters]," said Weinberg. "As soon as I started drinkin', I'd tell the bartenders that I had a hot card and I'd tell them to put $30 or $40 on the card for themselves. They loved me." The cards, obtained by the underworld from muggers and burglars, were discarded every few weeks and replaced with freshly stolen ones.

Robert W. Greene,
The Sting Man

OVERVIEW

In this chapter we want to examine the law as it relates to the use of credit cards, debit cards, and electronic money. A high percentage of the income at the inn comes from these sources of funds.

Credit cards are widely accepted at most HRI facilities across the United States and around the world. The law which controls their use is, in some ways, associated with the laws of commercial (money) paper. Yet credit-card charge slips are *not* commercial

Palace Hotel, Fulton, Missouri, about two blocks from the church where Winston Churchill made his "Iron Curtain" speech in 1947.

paper. They do represent a way of transferring funds and are thus another form of credit money.

These cards represent a revolution that struck the credit industry following World War II. While credit cards had been issued by oil companies prior to that time, such as Amoco with the first oil card in 1914, the movement did not gain momentum until American Express, Diner's Club, and Carte Blanche entered the picture. By 1969, there was about $2.5 billion outstanding on credit-card accounts. By 1980, the sum had reached $120 billion and today the annual charge amounts to more than $120 billion. That sum does not include another $85 billion in sales made on "in-house" cards such as those issued by some hotels and charges on a multitude of oil company cards.

The fact that credit cards are usually acceptable at HRI operations is common knowledge. What is not so widely known are the rules of law that control their use. It is true that the typical inn has a credit-card manual which guides the employees in the use of credit cards. Yet such a manual falls far short of what one must know to gain a legal understanding of the nature of credit cards and their use. It is the purpose of this chapter to examine the most important of those laws because, as will be seen, credit cards can be a profit-making device–or they can become an instrument of loss. To begin with, it is necessary to distinguish credit cards from "debit cards" for they are not the same.

DEBIT CARDS

While credit cards are used to create credit and to charge purchases, debit cards are designed to *deliver money* that is already in existence. Examples would be the cards used at bank terminals to make cash withdrawals. On the other hand, the credit card creates credit where none existed before the charge was made. Legally, the card charge slip is a promise to pay for the credit extended at an agreed point in the future. Yet it is more than that.

While the credit created by the credit card is often used to pay for services at HRI facilities, the cash from the debit card seldom is–although it may be on occasion. The reason for this is that the debit-card user is most often a local, while the credit-card holder is the traveler.

Associated with credit and debit cards, yet distinct from them, are *transfers of funds* carried out by electronic means. Here no cards are involved.

ELECTRONIC MONEY

For some time, the hardware has been in place nationally for the payment of bills and debts without the use of cards–and without the use of checks or other paper. It had been predicted a few years ago that this new concept would make banking and credit cards obsolete by this decade. This did not come to pass, however, because the average person is quite concerned–and cautious–about any system that can strip him or her instantly of personal funds.

In spite of this wariness, many banks are using the system, including Mellon Bank in Pittsburgh, Bank of Delaware in Wilmington, and the First National City Bank of New York, to mention a few. Many banks have actively marketed the system and have developed measures to assure customers of the safety of this means of "paying the bills." Widespread acceptance has not yet come, but it is most likely that it will.[1]

The use of electronic money is important because, at HRI operations where terminals are installed, guests who are arriving or leaving can transfer funds for services to the HRI unit or directly to its account. Such transfers could mean vast savings on credit-card charges and interest on the "float" time of checks–and even cash–that is being used to pay the bills. Cash accepted at the inn in the evening loses interest before it can be deposited in the morning. This is not so with electronic transfers.

Congress is aware of the potential and has enacted the Electronics Fund Transfer Act. This act creates a national commission on electronic transfers and sets down rules for the operations of "EFTs." The Board of Governors of the Federal Reserve System has created regulations to implement this law, which is part of Title II of the Consumer Credit Protection Act. The possible uses of EFTs in HRI operations are numerous and should be examined by the HRI manager. Examples of transfers include telephone transfer of funds, payment of bills by preauthorized debits, direct deposit of funds to accounts, and others. Debit cards and EFTs are two methods by which bills may be paid. This brings us to the third method–credit cards.

CREDIT CARDS

In light of the EFTs and increasing use of the computer, the credit card system is beginning to show its age. It is cumbersome in many ways, can be an actual inconvenience at the front desk or to the restaurant cashier, and results in delays in final payment. When a knowledgeable person sees some of the legal characteristics of credit cards and looks at them realistically, it becomes apparent that they are not the final solution at all. Let's look at a couple of their legal features.

First, the credit-card system operates on offer and acceptance. Next, while these cards are often used to buy items of personal property or "goods," the law of Article 2 of the UCC does *not* apply to them because the credit extended by their use is a *service* and not a sale. Third, credit-card systems can exist on a two-contract basis–and a three-contract basis as well. It is useful to understand the difference between these contract systems.

Three-Contract System

Most credit-card companies operate on a three-contract, and thus a three-party, system.

The First Contract

The first contract arises between the applicant for the card and the card issuer. In the terms and conditions of issuance of the card, it is customary for the issuer to make written terms a part of the contract between the issuer and the cardholder. Figure 11.1 is an example of the credit terms of Union Oil Company of California.

Through this offer-and-acceptance process, the cardholder becomes bound by the terms of the agreement, if the card is used. There is no obligation to use it, however. The face or back of the cards also often contain contractual terms such as "This card remains the property of the issuer and must be surrendered upon demand," "The issuer reserves the right to cancel this card at any time," and similar provisions.

The Second Contract

The second contract has its beginning when the cardholder offers the card at an HRI facility in lieu of cash or other payment, for

NEW TERMS

UNION 76 REVOLVING CREDIT PLAN*

Terms: Cardholder agrees to pay Union Oil Co. of Calif., 425 First St., San Francisco, CA 94105 within 25 days of your monthly Closing Date either of the following, as shown on your monthly statement:

1. The New Balance, or
2. An amount not less than the Minimum Due. Payment of less than the New Balance will result in the addition of a **FINANCE CHARGE**

Calculation of Minimum Due:

I. If your New Balance is less than $500, the Minimum Due is:
   1. The full amount of the New Balance if under $25, or
   2. 10% of the New Balance or $25, whichever is greater, plus
   3. Any unpaid portion of the previous statement's Minimum Due.

II. If your New Balance is more than $500, the Minimum Due is:
   1. $50, plus
   2. Any unpaid portion of the previous statement's Minimum Due, plus
   3. Any amount of the New Balance that is more than the total of (a) $500, and (b) the unpaid portion of the previous statement's Minimum Due.

FINANCE CHARGE Calculations: If the Previous Balance shown on your monthly statement is more than the total of Payments and Credits received prior to your Closing Date, a **FINANCE CHARGE** will be computed by applying the Periodic Rate of 1½%. **ANNUAL PERCENTAGE RATE** 18% (Exceptions listed below) to the "Balance

FIGURE 11.1 *(Continued)*

on Which **FINANCE CHARGE** Computed" as printed on your monthly statement. The "Balance on Which **FINANCE CHARGE** Computed" is your average daily balance calculated by dividing the "Which **FINANCE CHARGE** Computed" is your average daily balance calculated by dividing the number of days in your billing period into the total of amounts owing from your previous statement on each day of the billing period after first deducting credits, unpaid Insurance Premiums, unpaid **FINANCE CHARGES,** and Payments when received and adding current charges on the date they are posted to your account. Current month charges are not included for customers in Arizona, Massachusetts, Minnesota, Mississippi, Montana, Nebraska, New Mexico, and Rhode Island. Any calculated **FINANCE CHARGE** will be adjusted to a minimum of 50 cents (where permitted by state law).

EXCEPTION RATES	PERIODIC RATE	ANNUAL PERCENTAGE RATE
AR	.83%	10%
Total Bal: WA		
Bal. over $250: CT		
Bal. over $500: DC, DE, MA, MD, MO, NY, TX	1.00%	12%
Bal. over $700: NJ		
Bal. over $750: WV		
Bal. over $1,000: AK, CA, SC		
Bal. over $800: MS		
Bal. over $300: KS	1.16%	14%
Total Bal: PA		
Bal. to $250: CT	1.25%	15%
Bal. over $500: IA, VT		
Bal. over $1,000: WI		
Total Bal: MN	1.33%	16%
Bal. over $500: NM		
Total Bal: MI, SD	1.70%	20%
Total Bal: NV		
Bal. to $300: KS	1.75%	21%
Bal. to $500: NE		

Revolving privileges may be withdrawn at any time. Total amount owing may be declared immediately due and payable, for failure to pay at least the Minimum Due each month. (Cardholders residing outside the state of purchase will be assessed a **FINANCE CHARGE** rate determined by the laws of their state of residence).

*These terms apply notwithstanding any conflicting terms that may appear on the delivery ticket received at time of purchase.

Figure 11.1

services and food and drink received. It is now necessary for the HRI component to accept the offer or reject it. In most instances, use of the card has been invited and it will be accepted after verifying its validity.

However, some HRI operations will not accept credit cards and there is no law that says they must do so. An exception would be in those instances in which cards appear to be accepted and a guest or patron relies upon that representation. Refusal to accept a card under those conditions might lead to an actionable complaint, especially if the cardholder suffered embarrassment or other discomfort as a result of the refusal.

Otherwise, there is no common-law duty to accept credit cards for they were not known at common law. If they are accepted, the third contract arises and becomes operational.

The Third Contract

The third contract comes into being when the charge slip is tendered to the issuer—or an independent issuer—and is accepted for payment. This acceptance creates two contractual obligations within the third contract. The issuer is now obligated to pay (in part) the charge slip to the one tendering it, and the cardholder is obligated to repay the issuer the full amount charged to the card.

The profit to the issuer comes by the deduction of "points" from the amount of the original charge. These points range from 3 to 10 percent. The cardholder remits the full amount, giving the issuer thc profit from the difference. In the usual situations, the system works well and everyone, in theory at least, benefits from the transaction. The cardholder gets the benefit of the extension of credit; the one accepting the charge gets the profits from the sale, less the points; the issuer profits from the points deducted. Examine Figure 11.2.

The charge slips made by the impression from the credit card have some characteristics of checks. For example, it is not unusual for those who have accepted the charges to use them to pay *their* bills. This is common at service stations and other HRI locations that have a high volume of credit-card business. This generally will work, however, only where a "two-contract system" is in operation.

Two-Contract System

It is not unusual for large companies to issue credit cards designed to be accepted at captive outlets. Service station credit cards are

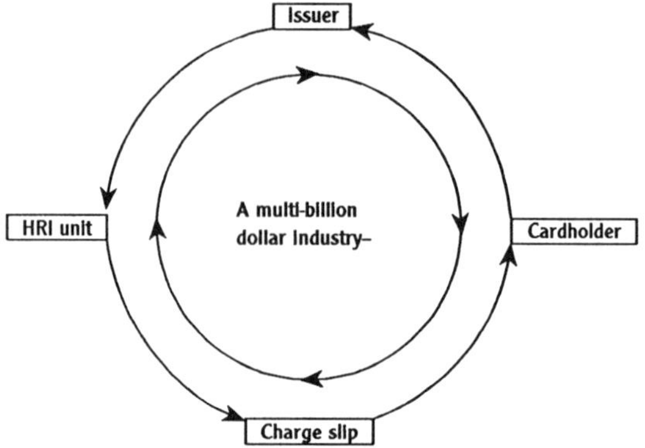

FIGURE 11.2 Credit cards—the three contracts in operation.

the best example, although department stores do this and so do some HRI facilities. The charges made on these cards are billed directly to the cardholder, who pays directly to the home company. There are no third parties involved. This is essentially an accounts-receivable system and is quite profitable for many companies. Such in-house credit-card systems can be used by the HRI industry, and some hotel and motel chains do just that.

Since the charge slips are often used in the two-contract system much like money, such as when a service station operator pays for the new delivery of gas with charge slips, there is some question as to whether these slips have taken on aspects of money. That is, might these charge slips be negotiable so as to meet the requirements of "negotiability"?

Credit-Card Charge Slips—Are They Commercial Paper?

We can answer the question by asking a second one. Do these charge slips meet the requirements of negotiability? If so, they would be commercial paper. If not, they would not be. Let's test a Visa charge receipt against the five requirements of negotiable paper.

First, it is signed. Second, since it contains the words "I promise to pay," it meets test number two. Third, it is for a sum certain if the charge, tip, and tax are filled in and totaled. Fourth, it would be payable at a definite time because of the terms of the cardholder's contract, "payable in full upon receipt of invoice."

It fails the test of negotiability, however, on the fifth requirement, since it is not payable "to the order" of anyone.

Payable to the Order of?

These words on commercial paper mean that the person to whom the paper is transferred *has the right to order the sum of money on it paid to someone else.* Clearly this right is not found on a credit-card charge slip. If it were, it could cause legal problems. Assume that X charges his motel room to his American Express card and an impression is made on a completed charge slip. The front-desk clerk keeps the top copy and gives X his copy. If it were negotiable, the motel would have the right to indorse the charge slip and order the sum of money represented by it paid to someone else. That is, the motel could use the charge slip to pay its bills. (This is done in two-party credit-card arrangements.) That right is not there nor does the credit-card company want it to be. Thus the fifth requirement of negotiability is missing and for good business reasons. If the slips could be ordered paid to others, the parent card company would never know at any moment what charges had been made or the standing of any credit limit of the cardholders.

Thus the charge slip is surrendered to the parent card company, which will in turn issue its check for the charges made, less the "points." The check issued can then be used by the motel to pay its bills to third parties—but the charge slip cannot. When we issue a check, it is an "order to pay" funds that are already in existence. When a cardholder signs a credit charge slip, there are no funds behind it. It is simply the creation of a credit obligation.

In addition to the regular card companies, there are also "independents."

Independent Card Companies

Independent credit-card companies will purchase charge slips at a discount and then collect them directly from the persons who made the charges. The disadvantage of this is that the value decreases the more hands the charge slips go through.

In the HRI Industry

HRI managers should examine the credit-card systems in use at each facility closely, for a change in procedures might result in substantial savings. Alternatives are available to credit-card use and these should be looked at.

Lost Credit Cards

Cards that are lost by holders must be reported at once to the issuer under the terms of the first contract. If this is done, then, under federal law, the responsibility of the cardholder for unauthorized charges made before notice is given is $50. If unauthorized charges are made after notice, there is no liability to the cardholder as to those charges. There is great protection here for the cardholder.

Business Credit Cards

Many companies subscribe to large numbers of credit cards for use by their employees in the field. The $50 limit is in effect for each card so issued. Any losses to the company cannot be passed back to the employee who lost the card. An issuer of ten or more cards to one company can negotiate with that company to raise the limit of loss higher than $50 per card.

The burden of proof is on the issuer to show that the use was authorized–not on the cardholder to show that it was not. Under regulations which became effective May 10, 1980, if a *debit* card is lost or stolen and the bank involved is given notice within two working days, the limit on liability for unauthorized use is $50. If the cardholder waits more than two days but less than sixty, the limit increases to $500. If more than sixty days goes by without notice being given, the cardholder has open-ended liability and this could mean the complete loss of the personal funds which can be withdrawn with the debit card.

Cancellation of a Credit Card

Normally the decision of a card company to cancel a credit card is an internal matter for the issuer and of no concern to the HRI manager. What is of concern is that care must be exercised so that canceled, expired, lost, or stolen cards are not accepted for charges. Normal authorization procedures will take care of most of these problems.

Yet cancellation by the company may still lead to litigation. In *Miller v. American Express Co.*,[2] a card was revoked upon the death of the card-holding husband. When the wife tendered it for an automobile rental charge, the charge was refused. Suit was brought for humiliation and inconvenience, basing the cause of action upon the Equal Credit Opportunity Act, which is the 1972 amendment to the Civil Rights Act of 1964. The case was settled pending remand for trial for the amount of $23,484 actual damages, $10,000 punitive damages, and $16,516 attorney fees.

Credit Cards and the Civil Rights Act.

The Civil Rights Act of 1964, with its subsequent amendments, has found application in the credit-card industry. Soon after the CRA became effective, the Federal Trade Commission began an investigation to see if the credit practices of the issuers discriminated against card applicants.

Amoco Oil Company was targeted and charged with discrimination in the issuance of their oil company cards. They were caught in a unique manner: They were using the ZIP codes of applicants to make it difficult for minorities in designated areas to obtain credit cards. In a consent decree, Amoco agreed to settle the charges for $200,000.[3]

Credit Cards and Criminal Law

Evidence may be introduced in a criminal trial of the "illegitimate value" of credit cards so as to give them a value for prosecution for theft purposes. In one case, the person accused of theft argued that by stealing a credit card, he had stolen nothing of value until a charge was made with it. This he had not done. The court held that evidence could be offered to show the street value of stolen credit cards ranges from $25 to $500, depending upon the locale in which they are offered for sale. Thus the card *itself* has value.

Two matters of importance remain for discussion. Both are directly involved in all HRI operations that accept credit cards. The first has to do with Truth-in-Lending and the Fair Credit Reporting Act, and the second with the payment of rewards for picking up "bandit" credit cards from guests and patrons.

"TRUTH-IN-LENDING" AT THE FRONT DESK

The Consumer Credit Protection Act, [4] was enacted by Congress to provide assistance to consumers in areas involving credit. The law has been amended to add additional titles (including the Electronic Fund Transfer Act) and was originally intended to control the professional credit-reporting industry that is found throughout the nation. Yet it also applies to any business that becomes involved in "consumer-credit reporting." This is where the HRI enters the picture.

What Does the FCRA Say?

The law has two primary features. First, if credit information *furnished by others* is passed on, the person or firm giving out that information becomes a credit-reporting agency under the act, which means that the rules and regulations of the law must be followed. This makes it important that care be used at any HRI facility when passing along second-hand credit information about employees, agents, guests, and patrons.

Second, if credit is denied, the consumer must be told who supplied the information upon which the credit refusal was made. This will be explored in a moment.

A Distinguishing Feature

It is now necessary to distinguish two points in order to better understand the FCRA. First, as just stated, it applies only to those persons or firms who pass on credit information *supplied by others.* That activity makes one a credit-reporting agency. Second, it does not apply to information gained from personal experience. Thus, if a guest causes damage at a motel or refuses to pay, that information can be given to another motel who inquires about it. But the inquiring motel *cannot give that information to others* for it is not based on *its* experience. This distinction is important.

What this means in practice is that care must be exercised in credit information situations. Not only does the FCRA require this so do the privacy laws. Personnel must be carefully trained not to give out credit information except under legal advice. The dangers are apparent and silence is very much in order.

Credit Is Denied, What Now?

If consumer credit is denied, the consumer must be given the name and address of the person or firm that supplied the information upon which the refusal was based. There is no requirement that the consumer be told *why* because, once the consumer has the name and address of the reporting agency, he or she has specific rights in reference to getting full information from that source.

So when a would-be guest, on a nonbusiness trip, tenders an American Express card at a hotel front desk and the card charge is refused, the Act is in effect. The hotel now has a legal obligation to tell the consumer the source of the information upon which the denial was based.

This information, of course, should be given to the consumer in a quiet, private manner so as not to cause unnecessary embarrassment. It would also be well to do it on a written form. A carbon can be made with the copy being retained by the hotel. Figure 11.3 is a suggested form. The original can be given to the consumer without comment, making sure that the consumer can read English. Alternate arrangements can then be made for payment.

This is a developing area of HRI law and the suggestions made here may have to be modified as the case law develops. But caution is in order in all credit denials and use of the form might keep the HRI facility out of litigation that may arise later because of the denial of consumer credit.

A serious HRI problem can arise when major credit-card companies offer rewards for the recapture of canceled or "bandit" credit cards.

_____ 19___

Your Card Company has refused to accept any charge on your account

____

This information was given to us by:

____

____

____

We would be pleased to accept another form of payment.

____

Clerk
Zero Motel
100 Zero Road
Zero, USA

FIGURE 11.3

CREDIT-CARD REWARDS

The card companies are willing to pay rewards to HRI employees who recapture credit cards that have been canceled, lost, or stolen. These rewards are usually $25 or $50. Figure 11.4 is a reward check paid to a student at the College of Hotel Administration, University of Nevada, Las Vegas, for picking up a card. There is nothing inherently wrong in card companies requesting that their bandit cards be returned to them. The danger lies in HRI personnel becoming more interested in the reward than in customer relations.

If cards are taken from cardholders publicly, with resulting embarrassment and humiliation, legal problems may follow. The Wood case that follows involves that type of situation and raises serious warnings to HRI managers.

The case involves a franchise holder of a Holiday Inn located in Phenix City, Alabama. The inn was owned by Interstate Inns, Inc., a South Carolina corporation, who held the franchise with the Holiday Inn, Inc., a corporation formed in Tennessee.

CROCKER BANK
Fremont Hub # 144
Fremont, CA 94538

11-8
1210

DEO 222051790

T.T.S. INC.
PAY EXACTLY 25 AND 00 CTS

PAY TO THE
ORDER OF

Jim Harris/ Front Desk
c/o Ambassador Inn
377 E Flamingo
Las Vegas, NV 89109

Tymshare Transaction Services, Inc.
P. O. BOX 5000
FREMONT, CALIFORNIA 94538

51790

		ACCOUNT	CENTER	AMOUNT	DESCRIPTION
		NET AMOUNT		$25.00	
					4320 057 006 056

THE ALERT AND RESPONSIVE MERCHANT IS ESSENTIAL IN THE EFFORT TO REDUCE FRAUD AND TO CONTROL THE MISUSE OF CREDIT CARDS.
Form MEO 18

WE APPRECIATE YOUR COOPERATION AND SUPPORT IN RECOVERING A BANK CHARGE CARD, AND ARE PLEASED TO PRESENT YOU WITH THIS REWARD.

FIGURE 11.4

At the time of this case (1975), Gulf Oil Corporation, a Pennsylvania corporation, had a credit-card arrangement with Holiday Inns, Inc., whereby Gulf credit cards could be used at Holiday Inns for room and other charges. (That arrangement has now been terminated.) One of the defendants in the case was the front-desk clerk, Goynes, an agent and employee of the South Carolina corporation.

The suit was filed in an Alabama federal court under "diversity jurisdiction" since the parties in the suit were from different states and the amount in controversy exceeded $10,000. If the parties had all been from one state, or if less than $10,000 had been involved, the suit would have been brought in an Alabama state court. What happened is set forth in the opinion of the court. (The $10,000 figure has now been raised to $50,000.)

WOOD V. HOLIDAY INNS, INC., ET AL.
508 F. 2d 167 (5th Cir. 1975)

On the evening before the morning in question, Plaintiff checked into the Inn at Phenix City and submitted his Gulf credit card for the purpose of having it imprinted on a credit memorandum of the motel. After the imprint was taken, the card was returned to him, and he retired. While the evidence was in conflict as to the transactions between the Plaintiff and the Defendant Goynes on the following morning, there was evidence from which the jury might have found, and apparently they did find, the following: That, at 5:00 A.M. the following morning the Defendant Goynes called the Plaintiff's room, awakened the Plaintiff from his repose, and informed him that he would like to obtain the Plaintiff's credit card for the purpose of making an imprint on a credit memorandum of the motel as the imprint made the night before was indistinct, and another imprint was needed; that after some conversation it was agreed that Goynes take the card, secure the imprint, and return it within a few minutes to the Plaintiff; that some thirty minutes later, Plaintiff, not having resecured his card and feeling that for some purpose someone had fraudulently secured his card, the Plaintiff dressed and went to the front desk and was informed by the Defendant Goynes that his credit had been revoked and that Goynes had telegraphic authority from National Data Processing, Inc., a computerizing service for Defendant Gulf Oil, to pick up Plaintiff's card and terminate his credit. It was conceded that Goynes obtained the credit card and asked Plaintiff to arrange to pay his bill in cash.

[At this point, other than the deception of the clerk, all seems to be in order.]

The credit manager of Gulf Oil testified that, on the previous day, he had reviewed the credit file of the Plaintiff; had found that the Plaintiff had been charging in ever-increasing amounts on his Gulf credit card; that he had during the current month paid to Gulf a substantial bill and charged to Gulf another bill which charges almost equaled the Plaintiff's total monthly income; that in the last three months the Plaintiff had paid his bill more than thirty days after the time the bill was sent to him; and that these facts caused him to suspect that the Plaintiff would soon be unable to pay his Gulf account. He, therefore, ordered the credit terminated and the card revoked or picked up.

The method for terminating the credit and picking up the card was that, on order of Gulf, National Data Processing sent out a communication to all Gulf agents and all desk clerks of Holiday Inns, in short, those most likely to come into contact with such credit cards, a list of all credit cards revoked and asked them to secure possession thereof for Gulf for a reward to be paid by Gulf. Suggestions as to how such cards might tactfully be repossessed had been sent out by Gulf, and there was no evidence that Gulf authorized use of rudeness or false pretenses in securing the credit cards.

After repossession of the card, the Defendant Goynes was paid by Gulf a reward for the same.

Wood's anger and frustration continued to build. Three days later, while he was relating the incident to a friend, he had a heart attack, precipitated apparently by the stress of the incidents surrounding the revocation of credit.

Wood sued the Gulf Oil Corporation, Holiday Inns, Inc., Interstate Inns, Inc. (the owner of the Phenix City Holiday Inn), and Jessie Goynes. Interstate and Goynes denied any negligence or wrongful conduct and asserted by way of cross-claim that they were acting under the direction of Gulf and were therefore entitled to indemnification by Gulf.

After trial, the jury returned a verdict in favor of Wood but apportioned damages in the amounts of $25,000 compensatory damages against Gulf, $25,000 punitive damages against Interstate and Goynes, and $10,000 punitive damages against Holiday Inns. The court then granted the motions of Gulf and Holiday Inns, Inc., for judgments notwithstanding the verdict and granted the motion of Interstate and Goynes for a new trial.

[These motions, made in writing and usually argued orally to the court, fix the right of appeal.]

Findings

Wood's primary claim against Gulf is based upon the Fair Credit Reporting Act, 15 U.S.C. §§1681-1681a(f) (1974). The Act charges "consumer reporting agencies" and users of "consumer credit reports" with various responsibilities. Gulf argues that it was not a consumer reporting agency as defined in 15 U.S.C. §1681a(f), and the district court so held, apparently as a matter of law.

The Act defines a consumer reporting agency as: " [A]ny person which, for monetary fees, dues, or on a cooperative nonprofit basis, regularly engages in whole or in part in the practice of assembling or evaluating consumer credit information or other information on consumers for the purpose of furnishing consumer reports to third parties. . . . 15 U.S.C. §1681a(f)."

Much of the confusion in this case stems from the multifaceted position of the Phenix City facility, the recipient of Gulf's communication. The Phenix City Holiday Inn accepted the Gulf credit card and was therefore Gulf's representative in facilitating the extension of Gulf's credit. But the Phenix City facility also honored a number of major credit cards, and, in fact, nothing prevented the Phenix City Inn from extending credit on its own account.

The communication by Gulf to the Phenix City Inn was made to a separate business entity. However, the credit to be extended was Gulf's, and the Phenix City facility was merely acting as Gulf's representative in extending the credit. Hence, the communication was not "for the purpose of furnishing consumer reports to third parties." It was merely directed from Gulf to its local representative, made for the purpose of protecting Gulf rather than for the purpose of influencing the Phenix City Inn's own credit decision.

[It can be seen at this point how important it is for the inn to comply with the FCRA.]

Wood next maintained that Gulf is liable under 15 U.S.C. §1681m(a) as a user of a credit report. This section provides:

"Whenever credit or insurance for personal, family, or household purposes, or employment involving a consumer is denied or the charge for such credit or insurance is increased either wholly or partly because of information contained in a consumer report from a consumer reporting agency, the user of the consumer report shall so advise the consumer against whom such adverse action has been taken and supply the name and address of the consumer reporting agency making the report."

The district court held that there was no evidence that Wood was damaged by Gulf's failure to report the name and address of the reporting agency. Wood renews his argument on appeal, contending that if Gulf had informed him promptly of its decision to terminate his credit, the incident at the Holiday Inn would have been avoided.

Apparently, the only requirement placed upon a "user" of a credit report is the duty to disclose the name and address of the reporting agency when credit is denied. 15 U.S.C. §1681m. There is no evidence that the actions of Goynes or the reaction of Wood would have been any different if Wood had been told at the time his credit card was withdrawn that Gulf held an unfavorable credit report from the Tupelo reporting agency.

We need not base our decision upon the timing of the notification, however, for there is no indication that Gulf relied upon this report in making its decision to revoke Wood's credit. Gulf certainly had a credit report in its possession, but there is uncontradicted testimony that this report played no part in Gulf's decision.

There was simply nothing in the consumer report which could have caused Gulf to terminate Wood's credit. Not only was all of the information contained in the report already in Gulf's possession, but the only inference that one could draw from the report was favorable to Wood. Indeed the condition which caused the termination of credit–Wood's monthly income in relation to the charges on his account–was in no way conveyed by the report.

[Here we see evidence of negligence on the part of the credit reporting agency and Gulf as well.]

Hence, we feel that the district judge properly dismissed the cause of action based upon the "user" provision of the Fair Credit Reporting Act.

Wood's final theory of liability was based upon the notion that Goynes acted as Gulf's agent when he seized the credit card. The district court characterized Wood's complaint as an allegation that his injury had been caused by breach of the common law duty of the innkeeper to his guests. Since there was no evidence that Gulf had acted as an innkeeper in this case, the lower court absolved Gulf of any liability. Alternatively, the judge held that there was no substantial evidence that Goynes acted as the agent of Gulf when he seized the card.

Wood stipulated at the pre-trial hearing of October 4, 1973, that one of his allegations was based upon the breach of the innkeeper's duty. However, the pre-trial order indicates Wood also averred that he was subjected to "offensive, abusive and insulting conduct, action and language" by Goynes and that Gulf's liability is predicated "upon the actions of Jessie Goynes, if Goynes is determined to be the agent of Gulf Oil." Therefore, we do not believe that Wood's allegation against Gulf was based upon breach of the innkeeper's duty. Rather, we believe that Wood's alleged cause of action sounds in tort, at least as against Gulf, and it is therefore appropriate to consider the question of the agency relationship between Goynes and Gulf. . . .

[Here the court steps away from the question of the innkeeper's duty, a topic which we will examine in detail in Chapter 12, and which looks to tort liability under the law of agency.]

The existence and scope of a principal-agent relationship is generally for the jury to determine and the burden of proving agency rests upon the party asserting its existence. . . .

The relationship between Interstate and Goynes is a source of confusion in this case. Not only are both of these parties represented by the same attorney, but the other litigants in the case have consistently treated Interstate and Goynes as a single party, combined, for purposes of reference, under the rubric "Innkeeper." It is conceded by all parties that Goynes acted as the agent and servant of Interstate; Gulf and Holiday Inns, Inc. The culpability of Gulf and that of Holiday Inns, Inc., as principals is based upon the relationship between Goynes and each of the companies as well as the companies' positions vis-a-vis Interstate.

Gulf has argued throughout this appeal that when a local Holiday Inn extends credit on Gulf's credit card, it is extending Gulf's credit rather than its own. Indeed, the Gulf credit system allows the local Holiday Inn to extend up to $150 of Gulf's credit without even contacting a "higher authority" for certification. Moreover, Gulf's agreement with National Data provided that the latter was to supply credit information upon request to "dealers, employees, and agents" of Gulf. At trial Gulf acknowledged that these categories included the Phenix City Holiday Inn. In light of these facts, it would not seem unreasonable for a jury to conclude that the Phenix City Inn was Gulf's agent for the extension of Gulf's credit and the revocation of Gulf credit cards.

The district court focused almost entirely upon Goynes' seizure of Wood's credit card in evaluating the extent of Gulf's supervision and control over Goynes. But in the overall context of Gulf's credit network, Gulf's supervision over Goynes appears to be more detailed. By virtue of his employment, as a servant of Interstate, Goynes' duties included the general supervision and management of the Phenix City facility at night. In this capacity, he presumably had authority to extend up to $150 of Gulf's credit, without even contacting anyone.

Wood also asks us to review the district court's grant of a new trial to Interstate and Goynes. The lower court set aside the verdict against these defendants and granted a new trial because, *inter alia*, the form of the verdict indicated that the jury was obviously confused. It is settled law that a trial court's ruling on a motion for a new trial will not be reviewed in an appellate court in the absence of a clear abuse of discretion.

The grant of a new trial in this case was not an abuse of discretion, for the form of the verdict indicated confusion. For example, the jury awarded differing amounts of damages against Holiday Inns, Inc., and Interstate, in spite of the fact that the liability of both parties resulted proximately from the single act of Goynes. A plaintiff cannot ordinarily recover a judgment for different amounts against joint tortfeasors. . . .

Where verdicts in the same case are inconsistent on their faces indicating that the jury was confused, a new trial is certainly appropriate and may even be required. Therefore, we will not overturn the trial court's decision.

Finally, Wood appeals the district court's conclusion that there was no substantial evidence upon which a jury could reasonably decide that Goynes was the agent of Holiday Inns, Inc. The district court based its conclusion upon the finding that Interstate and Goynes were not operating the business of Holiday Inns, Inc., that Holiday Inns, Inc., owned no interest in the Phenix City facility, that Holiday Inns, Inc., maintained only a franchise agreement with Interstate, and that Holiday Inns, Inc., had no right of control over Goynes when he obtained the credit card.

In reaching its determination that Goynes was not the agent of Holiday Inns, Inc., the district court focused almost exclusively on the relationship between Interstate and Holiday Inns, Inc. In assessing the extent of Holiday Inns, Inc.'s liability for Goynes' actions, it is again appropriate to analyze Goynes' position in "subagency" terms. There is considerable evidence in the record indicating a high degree of control over Interstate by Holiday Inns, Inc. The license agreement between the two parties required Interstate to build and maintain the facility as specified by the parent company, and to observe strictly the "Rules of Operation" as promulgated by the Holiday Inns, Inc., board of directors. Interstate was also required to permit regular inspection of the Phenix City facility by Holiday Inn inspectors in order to insure compliance with the Rules of Operation. The agreement further provided that any substantial violation of its terms would give Holiday Inns, Inc., the right to cancel Interstate's license. It was implicit in the agreement that Interstate as a corporate entity would not maintain the Phenix City Inn, but would hire servants for this purpose.

We believe that this was sufficient evidence from which a jury could reasonably conclude that Holiday Inns, Inc., should be liable for Goynes' actions. However, we do not base our holding on the degree of control that Holiday Inns, Inc., maintained over Goynes. Rather we believe that Wood presented more than insubstantial evidence as to the liability of Holiday Inns, Inc., on a theory of apparent authority.

An agency relationship may arise from acts and appearances which lead others to believe that such a relationship has been created. . . . This concept of apparent authority is based upon manifestations by the alleged principal to third persons, and reasonable belief by those persons that the alleged agent is authorized to bind the principal. . . . "The manifestations of the principal may be made directly to the third person, or may be made to the community, by signs or advertising. . . ."

Questions of apparent authority are questions of fact, and are therefore for the jury to determine. The license agreement between Holiday Inns, Inc., and Interstate provided that the Phenix City facility should be constructed and operated so that it would be "readily recognizable by the public as part of the national system of 'Holiday Inns.'" Indeed, the Phenix City facility was required to use the same service marks and trademarks, and exterior and interior decor as the Holiday Inns owned by the parent company. A jury could therefore reasonably conclude that the license agreement required the Phenix City facility to be of such an appearance that travelers would believe it was owned by Holiday Inns, Inc.

The gravamen of Wood's complaint against Holiday Inns, Inc., is based upon the breach of the innkeeper's common-law duty to his guests. Although the innkeeper's duty was apparently delictual in origin, . . . breach of this duty in Alabama appears to sound in contract. When Wood contracted with the Phenix City Holiday Inn for lodging he contracted for proper treatment by the servants of the innkeeper. . . . However, there is virtually no way Wood could have known that the servants in the Phenix City facility were servants of Interstate, not of Holiday Inns, Inc. Indeed, the manifestations that Holiday Inns, Inc., required Interstate to make could only have served to convince Wood that Jessie Goynes was a servant of the parent company.

We believe that reasonable men could differ regarding Wood's evidence of apparent authority and that the issue should therefore be determined by the jury. . . . The district court charged the jury below that the relationship of agency between Goynes and Holiday Inns, Inc., could be implied if the jury found that Holiday Inns, Inc., through its advertising and control, held out to the general public that Interstate Inns in Phenix City, Alabama, was its agent. On the basis of these instructions, the jury held Holiday Inns, Inc., liable for Goynes' actions. However, the jury manifested its confusion as to the proper application of law to the facts by holding Holiday Inns, Inc., liable in an amount different from that of Interstate Inns, although the liability of both alleged principals was based upon the same act. Rather than merely reinstating the jury's verdict, then, we believe the interests of justice would be better served by remanding Wood's action against Holiday Inns, Inc., to the district court for retrial.

Cross-appellants Interstate and Goynes appeal the lower court's decision denying indemnification. We believe the district court was correct.

Under Alabama law, an agent is entitled to indemnification for any amounts he has been required to pay for his principal in the performance of his agency. . . . However, the principal is not required to indemnify the agent for harm resulting solely from the agent's negligence.

Hence, in the absence of agreements to the contrary, an agent has no right to indemnity for damages suffered by reason of his own fraud, misconduct or other tort, even if the wrong was committed within the scope of the agent's employment. . . .

Goynes and Interstate have introduced no substantial evidence upon which a reasonable jury could conclude that Gulf was negligent. The only relevant action undertaken by Gulf was its directive to pick up Wood's credit card. However, by virtue of a statement contained on the card, and in the credit card application signed by Wood, Gulf retained the contractual right to revoke the credit card without notice. Hence, Gulf's decision to terminate Wood's credit was not tortious, and Goynes and Interstate have shown no duty which Gulf is alleged to have breached.

The theory of Wood's case is based upon the harm he is alleged to have suffered because of the manner in which his card was revoked. Any harm to Wood must have resulted solely from the actions of Goynes, since Gulf has not been shown to have been negligent. We therefore believe no substantial evidence has been presented which would justify the indemnification of Goynes and Interstate.

For the reasons set forth above, we affirm in part, reverse in part, and remand for proceedings not inconsistent with this opinion.

QUESTIONS

1. EFTs have not caught on as had been anticipated. Name two reasons why this probably happened.
2. Why would Amoco voluntarily pay $200,000 rather than contest the charge of credit-card discrimination?
3. What house rules can be placed into effect to discourage the "credit-card reward" syndrome on the part of HRI employees? Why should this be done?
4. Why does the FCRA not require that the consumer be told why consumer credit is being denied?
5. True or False. The Federal CCPA applies to business credit transactions just the same as consumer credit transactions.
6. If innkeeper X tells innkeeper Y that guest Z did damage to his (X's) motel, has the FCRA been violated?
7. What is required to make one a "credit-reporting agency"?
8. Why do courts hold that a stolen credit card has a value even though it is never used to make an unauthorized charge?
9. Explain how American Express makes a profit from the charge slips that come to it from HRI operations.
10. Why is a credit-card charge slip not "commercial paper"?

ENDNOTES

1. *First National Bank v. Mularkey,* 385 N.Y.S. 2d 473 (Civ. Ct. Queens Co., 1976).
2. 26 ATLA L. Rep. 117, 688 F. 2d 1235 (9th Cir. 1982).
3. *U.S. News & World Report,* May 19, 1980.
4. P.L. 90.321: 82 *Stat.* 146 *et seq.*, act of May 29, 1968.

12

Legal Duties of Innkeepers and Guests

To enhance his studies and to earn pocket money as well, Bing got a part-time job working in the law offices of Colonel Charles S. Albert, who was a legal counsel for the Great Northern Railway. Bing's job was recording the garnishments brought against railroad employees and occasionally typing out briefs for the colonel and his assistant. It was pretty mundane stuff, and the only excitement Bing got out of it was when he'd find the name of an old high-school or neighborhood friend and would warn the friend to draw on his pay before the judgment was served.

Bing Crosby, the Hollow Man,
Donald Shepherd and Robert F. Slatzer

OVERVIEW

In this chapter, we will examine the HRI function of innkeeping, centering our attention on the legal duties of both innkeepers and guests. The duty of the innkeeper under English law is the same as the duty under the common law of our states: to use ordinary reasonable care in the operation of the inn, taking into consideration "foreseeability."

The business of innkeeping is public in nature and therefore duties arise on the part of the innkeeper that are influenced by the public need. These include the duty to receive guests and the property of guests; the duty to provide suitable accommodations; the duty to treat all guests with a reasonable standard of care and courtesy; the duty to care for the person as well as the property of guests; and the duty to comply with applicable health laws. Con-

MALBOROUGH BLENHEIM, during the glory days at Atlantic City, New Jersey.

versely, the guest has duties to the innkeeper, principally conducting oneself with reasonable decorum and paying for services received. These and other legal duties of the innkeeper, as well as the guest, will be examined in this chapter. Here's what a judge had to say about travel and innkeeping:

> In the past, many courts have viewed travel as a privilege and as a luxury. And until comparatively recently it was true that travel was for the rich and leisure classes. However, the last two decades have seen an extraordinary increase in the demand for travel services from all sectors and classes of our society. Travel by vacationers has become accepted as a necessity which can be and should be enjoyed by all citizens in this country. The concept of travel as a right is very old and is a fundamental part of our culture.
>
> A corollary principle is the right of all travelers to receive the quality of travel services contracted for and reasonably expected without deviation. Hotels should not be relieved of liability for the damages which they cause through breaches of contract, fraud, negligence, and illegality.[1]

Consequently, it becomes important to make certain that the expectations of travelers are met. In addition, it becomes necessary that the requirements of law (and equity) be met because mandates are found there as dictates of law. Failure to meet these mandates may lead to legal liability and losses may follow in court. A good place to begin is by an examination of the sources of the legal duties that are placed upon innkeepers. Examine Figure 12.1.

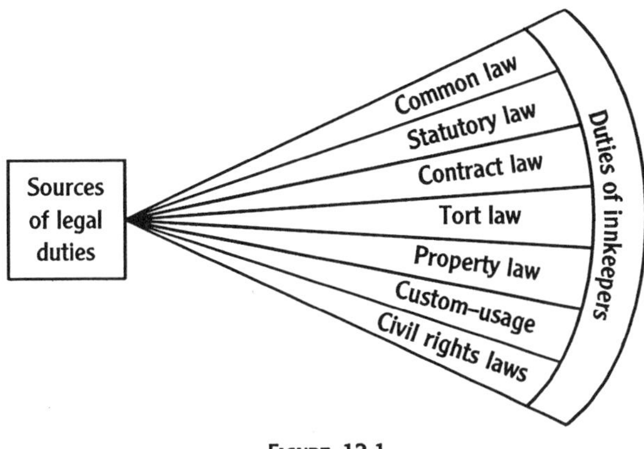

FIGURE 12.1

SOURCES OF LEGAL DUTIES OF INNKEEPERS

Legal duties of innkeepers can be traced to seven sources. First are those principles of law that developed through court rulings during the past ten centuries. This is the "common law" that we have encountered before. The second source of duties is found in statutes—although there are not too many of them, as we have seen. The following excerpt is from the Virginia Code. This appeared in 1849—over 142 years ago, making it one of the first state codes to deal with innkeeping by statute:

> Every person licensed to keep an ordinary, or house of public entertainment, shall constantly provide the same with lodging and diet for travellers and their servants, and, unless it be dispensed with as aforesaid, with stableage and provender, or pasturage and provender (as the season may require) for their horses. Any such person may, at the place of a muster or public sale, distant a mile or more from another ordinary, with the consent of the proprietor of such place, vend meat or drink as at his ordinary.[2]

Found in this partial quote of a much longer statute is a little of the color of another age.

A third source of duties is found in contract law, both conventional and sales. When an innkeeper becomes bound contractually, the legal duty arises to honor the terms of that contract. Fourth, the demands of the law of tort give rise to corresponding duties to see that torts are not committed against guests, employees, and third parties. "Tort" always involves an injury or other loss, usually due to negligence.

Property law enters the picture as the fifth source and will be developed as a duty, in detail, in Chapters 18 and 19. A sixth source is found in the federal and state civil rights laws. These laws raise the legal duty not to engage in discrimination in hiring, in receiving travelers at the inn, in serving patrons at other HRI facilities, and other matters as discussed in Chapter 10.

A final source is found in the ancient customs and usages of innkeeping. Many legal duties of innkeepers are based on the practices of inns across the centuries. The courts look to these practices to establish standards in modern cases. These standards are also modified and broadened through court decisions.

DUTIES OWED TO WHOM?

Innkeepers' duties are primarily owed to the traveler as he or she becomes a guest at the inn. Yet the law extends duties to other classes of persons, including invitees (other than guests), locals, trespassers–and even thieves. However, the *degree* of liability *decreases* as the legal standing of each class moves downward. To illustrate this principle, examine Figure 12.2. The degree of legal duty owed to one who is attempting to rob an inn is slight, yet the innkeeper could not cause unnecessary harm to that person for there is a legal duty not to do so. There is a growing minority of states that repudiate the old common-law doctrine equating liability, or the lack of it, to the status of the victim. Thus a trespasser is no longer automatically barred from recovering for injuries negligently inflicted by a landowner. Rather, one's status in relation

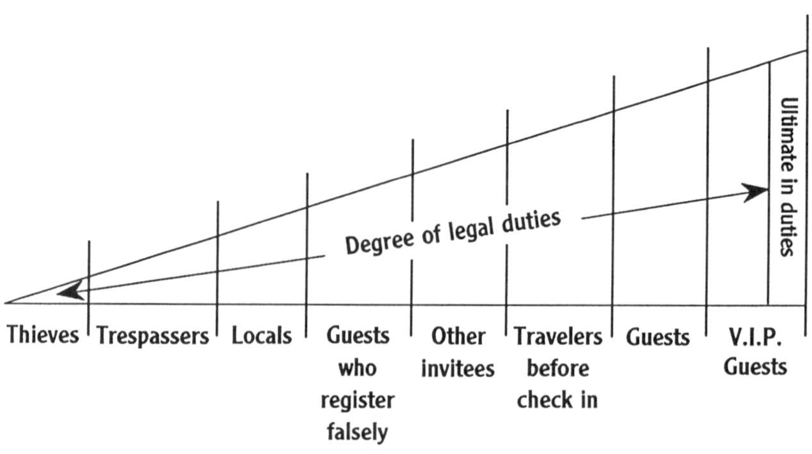

FIGURE 12.2

to liability is a jury question, not a question of law. The jury is not required to apply a decreasing standard of care based upon status in the states where this trend is evolving.

A combination of common law, statutory law, and custom, coupled with the public nature of inns, brings into play duties that are also public in nature. This is so because these duties are designed to protect the public in general.

PUBLIC DUTIES

It has long been recognized that when one enters the innkeeping business, duties of a public nature have been assumed. Thus, what may have been private property at the outset assumes a public character. If A inherits $500,000 from his grandfather, that money is private and can be controlled solely by A. If A invests the money in a small inn, the character of the money (property) has been changed in two ways: (1) personal property has been converted to real and (2) the property is now affected by the public interest, need, and control. One can withdraw such money and regain private control, but so long as the public use continues, the control is mandated by public need. Many of these publicly related duties arise out of the common law as well as custom—but many of them are statutory.

Public Health Duties

Each state, by statute, provides health requirements that must be met by those who serve the public in travel, lodging, and other hospitality functions, such as restaurant food service.

In most instances, these statutes are old, often having been adopted when our states were formed. While some of them appear quaint by modern standards, they make up an important part of the duties that fall upon innkeepers, restaurant operators, and others. The statutes that follow are from Nevada.[3] (They are old and only a small portion of them are set out.)

447.020 Cleanliness of bedding; wornout and unfit bedding.

1. All bedding, bedclothes or bed covering, including mattresses, quilts, blankets, sheets, pillows or comforters, used in any hotel in this state must be kept clean and free from all filth or dirt.

2. No bedding, bedclothes or bed covering, including mattresses, quilts, blankets, sheets, pillows or comforters, shall be used which is wornout or unsanitary for use by human beings according to the true intent and meaning of this chapter.

[2:136:1915; 1919 RL p. 2811; NCL §3338]

447.030 Extermination of vermin. Any room in any hotel in this state which is or shall be infested with vermin or bedbugs or similar things shall be thoroughly fumigated, disinfected and renovated until such vermin or bedbugs or other similar things are entirely exterminated.

[3:136:1915; 1919 RL p. 2811; NCL §3339]

447.080 Air space, floor area and ceiling height of rooms. No room for sleeping purposes shall have less than 500 cubic feet of air space for each occupant. The floor area of each sleeping room must be at least 80 square feet and at least 7 feet in width. All rooms must have a ceiling height of at least 8 feet.

[5b:136:1915; added 1945, 384; 1943 NCL §3341b]

447.090 Amount of bedding required; furnishing clean sheets and pillow slips; size of sheets.

1. Every bed kept or used in any hotel in this state for the accommodation of any person or guest must be provided with a sufficient supply of clean bedding.

2. Clean sheets and pillow slips shall be supplied for each bed in a hotel as often as the bed is assigned to a different person.

3. Sheets shall be at least 98 inches long and of sufficient width to cover the mattress and spring completely.

[6:136:1915; 1919 RL p. 2811; NCL §3342]

[*A statute such as this one can play a role when ordering goods for the inn.*]

447.100 Fumigation of room after occupation by person having contagious, infectious disease. Whenever any room in any hotel shall have been occupied by any person having a contagious or infectious disease, the room shall be thoroughly fumigated under the direction of the health authority, and all bedding therein thoroughly disinfected before the room shall be occupied by any other person. In any event, such room shall not be let to any person for at least 48 hours after such fumigation or disinfection.

[7:136:1915; 1919 RL p. 2811; NCL §3343]—(NRS A 1969, 1022)

447.110 Bathing facilities.

1. In every hotel in existence prior to October 1, 1945, at least one bathtub or shower shall be installed in a separate compartment on a public hallway or court for every 20, or fractional part of 20, guestrooms, on the same floor as the hallway or court which are not provided with private baths.

2. In every hotel built after October 1, 1945, at least one bathtub or shower provided with hot and cold water shall be installed

in a separate compartment on a public hallway or court for every 10, or fractional part of 10, guestrooms on the same floor as the hallway or court which are not provided with private baths.

[7a:136:1915; added 1945, 384; 1943 NCL §3343a]

447.120 Towels to be furnished.

1. Every hotel within this state having a public washstand or washbowl, where different persons gather to wash themselves, must keep a sufficient supply of clean, individual towels for the use of such persons within easy access of or to such persons and in plain sight and view.

These statutes are old—but typical. Many other points arise in the laws of inns, hotels, and motels.

While inns are associated with public need and are public houses, are they such in regard to statutes that prohibit solicitation of prostitution in "public places?" The answer may be "yes" in those instances where an innkeeper knows of the activity and allows it to continue. In such a case, the innkeeper could face loss of a bar license, restaurant license—and perhaps the license to operate the inn itself. The prostitute, at the same time, could be prosecuted under criminal law.[4]

By far the most important duty of the innkeeper is the "duty to receive." This duty comes to us out of the pages of time.

DUTY TO RECEIVE

It has long been recognized that, as a matter of law, those engaged in the public venture of innkeeping must receive all who seek accommodations, up to the limits of their capacity. The duty is almost, but not quite, absolute, for there are exceptions.

An important point, however, is that the duty extends to *travelers,* and does not necessarily extend to "locals" who may use services provided at the inn. However, a local *could* be a traveler and it has been so held.[5] The test applied to determine whether one is a "traveler" is the transient nature of the stay.

This classification is important because, as a general rule, an innkeeper does not owe special duties to those who are not "travelers." A lodger, boarder, or tenant at the inn would not be a traveler because the stay is not transient or temporary in nature. In addition, an innkeeper may *lose* legal protection in certain instances, especially if the person in question is not a traveler.

The duty to receive also extends to those who are normally unable to contract, such as those under eighteen years of age. An innkeeper would, however, have the right to determine if the minor is capable of paying for the services. There is no requirement that one furnish lodging to a minor for free. The minor would be liable for the reasonable value of necessities furnished and would not be able to disaffirm the contract later on the grounds of incompetency. The liability of the minor would be in *quasi-contract* (and not in true contract).

Time of Day or Night?

Must an innkeeper be prepared to receive guests twenty-four hours a day? In the *Rex v. Ivens* case that follows, Williams, a law clerk (called "prosecutor" in the case), tried to gain admission at the Bell Inn, at Chepstow, at a time when the husband and wife who operated the inn had retired for the night. What happened after that is spelled out in the court's opinion.

REX V. IVENS[6]

". . . With respect to the non-tender of the money by the prosecutor, it is now a custom so universal with innkeepers to trust that a person will pay before he leaves an inn, that it cannot be necessary for a guest to tender money before he goes into an inn; indeed, in the present case, no objection was made that Mr. Williams did not make a tender; and they did not even insinuate that they had any suspicion that he could not pay for whatever entertainment might be furnished to him. I think, therefore, that that cannot be set up as a defense. It however remains for me next to consider the case with respect to the hour of the night at which Mr. Williams applied for admission; and the opinion which I have formed is, that the lateness of the hour is no excuse to the defendant for refusing to receive the prosecutor into his inn. Why are inns established? For the reception of travellers, who are often very far distant from their own homes. Now, at what time is it most essential that travellers should not be denied admission into the inns? I should say when they are benighted, and when, from any casualty, or from the badness of the roads, they arrive at an inn at a very late hour. Indeed, in former times, when the roads were much worse, and were much infested with robbers, a late hour of the night was the time, of all others, at which the traveller most required to be received into an inn. I think therefore, that if the traveller conducts himself properly, the innkeeper is bound to admit him, at whatever hour of the night he may arrive. The only other question in this case is, whether the defendant's inn was full. There is no direct evidence on the part of the prosecution that it was not. But I think the conduct of the parties shows that the inn was not full; because, if it had been, there could have been no use in the landlady asking the prosecutor his name, and saying, that if he would tell it, she would ring for one of the servants."

The verdict under the misdemeanor (criminal) statute under which this case was brought was "guilty," thus pointing out the duty of an innkeeper to receive even in the "wee hours" of the morning—so long as space is available. This rule is firm in modern innkeeping law.

Today

It is the usual practice at inns that are located in high-crime areas to lock outside doors at designated times of the night. Yet admittance must be possible by the use of a bell or key or other device to alert those on duty. An innkeeper must readmit a guest who has left the inn and then returns—even if that return is at 3:00 A.M. The duty to receive remains regardless of the time of day or night and even more so if one has a reservation. In the latter instance, not only is there a common-law duty to receive, but a contractual one as well.

State Laws

Many states have criminal statutes which provide that an innkeeper who wrongfully refuses to receive can be indicted and brought to trial for violation of the statute. (*Rex v. Ivens* shows us the early English view.) Additionally, in most states an action may be brought in instances of refusal of admission for the civil wrong. This would be a tort action for breach of the common-law duty.

Refusing to receive one who has a seeing-eye dog would not be a valid refusal even if the inn does not have facilities for the animal. This is an area in which a solid knowledge of state law is in order. For example, Nevada has a statute that creates a legal duty to receive dogs under the stated circumstances. The statute follows:

1. It is unlawful for a place of public accommodation to:
   (a) Refuse service to a visually handicapped person because he is accompanied by a guide dog; or
   (b) Charge an additional fee for such guide dog.

2. A place of accommodation may require proof that a dog is a guide dog. Such requirement may be satisfied, by way of example and not of limitation, by exhibition of the identification card normally presented to a visually handicapped person upon his graduation from a guide dog school.

3. A guide dog shall not be presumed dangerous by reason of the fact it is not muzzled.

4. This section does not relieve a visually handicapped person from liability for damage which may be caused by his guide dog.

5. Visually handicapped persons accompanied by guide dogs shall be subject to the same conditions and limitations that apply to persons who are not so handicapped and accompanied.[7]

However, there are times when an innkeeper can refuse to receive—and indeed, in some instances *there is a duty not to receive.*

Excuses to the Duty to Receive

If all of the rooms of an inn are occupied, this is reason enough to refuse to receive. Yet, if the inn is full and one presents himself with a valid *reservation* for that night, the inn must still receive. If a potential guest appears in an intoxicated, filthy condition, this is a valid excuse not to receive. If one with a communicable disease attempts to register, that person *must* be refused. But in many instances, one seeking a lodging room may well be sick and in need of assistance. In such instances, the innkeeper may refuse to receive but should seek outside help for that person.

There are other reasons why one can refuse to receive; one is the absence of baggage. But, as a general rule, when rooms are available the innkeeper should receive, so long as it is determined that the would-be guest will be able to pay for services. It is no longer legal to refuse on the grounds of race, color, religion, or national origin—and it is unwise to refuse on the grounds of "lack of apparent stature." For example, a well-groomed traveler dressed in blue jeans should not be refused admittance at the resort hotel—even though this was common practice in the immediate past. A soldier should not be turned away because other soldiers had caused problems at the inn. Selective discrimination is unwise today–and unlawful as well, as we have seen in Chapter 10.

Absence of Baggage

In the modern motel as contrasted to hotel, the innkeeper is seldom concerned about guests traveling without baggage. In fact, to even make this determination would place an undue burden upon the staff of the inn. Yet if it is determined that a person, or a group of persons, is or are traveling without baggage, the innkeeper would have the right to make discreet inquiry, and perhaps refuse to admit on those grounds. In refusing on these grounds, care would still be in order, however. In the case of inns that have a check-in valet service, the absence of baggage would be more noticeable and easier to detect. Yet one must remember that even those of substance can travel with a minimum of personal effects and business travelers are often in that category.

Related to the duty to receive is the corresponding duty to receive normal "traveling goods" of the guest-to-be.

DUTY TO RECEIVE GOODS

Since an innkeeper has a duty to receive, it follows that the goods of a guest must also be received. This is a general statement and has limitations. For example, a guest must be permitted to bring into the inn baggage and other items customarily taken into inns. A more difficult question arises in reference to pets and excess goods, such as a truck load of sound equipment that a guest wants placed inside of the inn. The duty to receive goods might not extend to ordinary pets and equipment and those goods could be refused.

A traveler often brings property to the inn that he or she does not own. The innkeeper has no right to question ownership, for that is not his or her business. On the other hand, if suspected contraband is in a hotel room, then other rights of the innkeeper may become involved; they will be examined in the next chapter. But the general rule is that innkeepers are not policemen or policewomen or police agencies–and should not try to be.

Two of the more encompassing duties of the innkeeper are the duty to provide a safe place to work and the duty to provide a safe place to stay.

A SAFE PLACE TO WORK

Under tort (negligence) rules, it is mandatory that the inn be a safe place for those who work there. This is especially so under the provisions of the Occupational Safety and Health Act, known as OSHA. This law provides standards that must be complied with at each covered place of business.

In addition to this, the inn must also be a safe place for a guest to stay.

A SAFE PLACE TO STAY[8]

The innkeeper is not an insurer of the safety of the guest. The only duty is to use ordinary, reasonable care in providing a safe place to stay. "Owner or operator of motel is not insurer of customer who uses premises, but only owes duty to maintain premises in reasonable safe and suitable conditions," *(Buck v. Del City Apartments Inc.*, 431 P. 2d 360).

With this in mind, the innkeeper must act as a reasonable person would in the maintenance of his or her property. And in the absence of this reasonable care, the innkeeper could be held liable to the guest in the event of injury under the law of torts, "a violation of a duty imposed by general law," (*Blacks Law Dictionary,* 5th ed.)., or negligence, "the omission to do something which a reasonable man would do," (*Blacks Law Dictionary,* 5th ed.).

"A hotel proprietor is not an insurer of safety of customers, and is only liable for injuries resulting from his negligence and is bound to exercise reasonable care to keep premises in reasonable safe condition for customers and others invited expressly or impliedly to enter," *(Alsup v. Saratoga Hotel,* 229 P. 2d 985).

This brings us to the question of the relationship between the innkeeper and persons injured. There are three classes of persons who can be injured: invitees, licensees and trespassers. Invitees, which include the inn guest *(Wagner v. Coronet Hotel*, 458 P. 2d 390), are invited onto the premises for the advantage of the innkeeper. To this type of person the innkeeper owes the highest duty of care, and must inform these persons of any latent or known danger. Therefore, the innkeeper must use reasonable care "to discover actual conditions of premises and make them safe or warn business visitor of any dangerous condition" *(Silverton v. Marler,* 389 P. 2d 3).

The second type of person is a licensee, "any person who comes upon the land with a privilege arising from the consent of the possessor" (Prosser, *Law of Torts Hornbook*, 4th ed.). This type of person comes onto the land for the advantage of themselves and not the innkeeper. This could include guests of guests. For this person, too, the innkeeper must warn of dangers. But once a licensee becomes aware of dangerous conditions, does not adhere to such warnings and injury occurs, the inn may not be liable under the assumption of risk doctrine, "where plaintiff assumes consequences of injury occurring through fault of defendant" (*Blacks Law Dictionary*, 5th ed.), or under the doctrine of contributory negligence, "the act of omission amounting to want of ordinary care on part of complaining party" (*Blacks Law Dictionary*, 5th ed.).

In either case, the "proximate cause," "that which . . . produces the injury, and without which the result would not have happened" (*Blacks Law Dictionary*, 5th ed.), would be the deciding factor of liability (*Dempsey v. Alamo Hotel*, 418 P. 2d 58), and in most states this is decided by a jury (*Worth v. Reed*, 384 P. 2d 1017).

The third type of person is trespasser, "a person who enters or remains upon land in the possession of another without a privilege to do so" (Second Restatement of Torts, Sec. 329). This person is not a guest of the inn. In this case, the innkeeper is not obligated to warn the trespasser of dangers that might exist. The "duty of hotelkeeper to exercise ordinary and reasonable care [is] to keep in reasonable safe condition those parts of the hotel where guests are invited or expected to go" (*Balin v. Lysle, Rishel Post No. 68, American Legion, Hutchinson*, 280 P. 2d 623).

Not only must the innkeeper act as a reasonable person would and warn of dangerous conditions, the innkeeper must "foresee" what might happen if he does not correct dangerous conditions. "Proprietor of hotel has duty to warn invitee of latent dangers of which he knows or in exercise of reasonable care should have known and to take reasonable precautions to protect invitee from dangers which are foreseeable from arrangement or use of premises" (*Mickel v. Haines Enterprises, Inc.*, 400 P. 2d 518).

With these illustrations in mind, the best way for the innkeeper to limit his or her liability for injuries to the guest is to inspect the property for dangerous conditions in the guest areas, warn the guest and licensees of such dangerous conditions, foresee the consequences of such dangers, and, if appropriate, have those dangers corrected.

OTHER EXAMPLES OF INNKEEPERS' DUTIES

The duty of the innkeeper to keep the premises safe for business invitees (guests and patrons) has been held to be nondelegable.

Breach of this duty has been a constant source of court action including negligently building a front door at the inn that causes an injury;[9] spilling sulfuric acid on a dance floor, causing a patron to slip and suffer acid burns;[10] absence of a night manager, and no smoke alarms or sprinklers, resulting in harm to guests;[11] unsafe window latches, allowing a child to fall to its death;[12] failing to keep outside areas of the inn lighted, resulting in a fall of a guest;[13] and failing to provide door locks that cannot be opened from the outside,[14] to sketch a few.

On the other hand, an innkeeper does not have to guard against the abnormal or unusual; does not have to provide a fireproof hotel;[15] need not be a nurse for a child;[16] have screens in windows;[17] or be a banker, doctor, nurse, lawyer, or rescue team. The law does not expect perfection; it does expect ordinary, reasonable care, taking into consideration all of the facts and surrounding circumstances.

The law *does* expect the innkeeper to warn of known, concealed dangers[18] and to warn not only those who make ordinary use of facilities–such as a swimming pool–but to warn those who make customary use of a facility, which use is known to the innkeeper.[19] An example of this was observed at an inn near JFK International Airport, Long Island, New York, where the neighborhood kids climb the fence and swim in their clothes after the pool closes for the night. The duty to warn of hidden dangers would extend to them because the innkeeper there knows that the kids do this.

The State of Georgia has enacted a statute that requires that inns post exit instructions in all "sleeping rooms, meeting rooms and other rooms open to the public," Georgia Regulations, Section 120-3-3:05. These regulations specifically require that a warning notice be placed above each elevator button in hotels and motels in that state that says, "In the event of fire, do not use this elevator." The regulations then provide that "evacuation routes be shown" by arrows that disclose the nearest route to the exit.

When HRI operations provide parking facilities for their guests, or patrons, they must realistically take into consideration the surrounding facts and circumstances of that facility. Must those who park there walk through an unlighted area to get to the inn? Is there dangerous traffic on a street which must be crossed? Is the parking lot located in a high crime area? Are there other reasons why a person parking in the lot should be on the lookout for his or her personal safety? The common-law requirement that innkeepers exercise reasonable care comes to the front in such circumstances, *Warrington v. Bird*, 499 A.2d 1026 (New Jersey, 1985).

Does an innkeeper have a duty to warn guests after another guest has been robbed at gun point? What if no warning is given and the robber remains on the premises and then robs again fifteen minutes later? Does the second victim have a cause of action against the hotel in negligence for failing to warn? There is authority in Arizona that no such duty exists, but common sense dictates that until it is certain that the robber has departed, the innkeeper should assume that the robber is still on the premises and guests should be warned accordingly.

The courts tend to excuse innkeepers from the duty to warn of dangers where those dangers are so obvious as to alert guests to stay away from them. As a situation in point, a snow- and ice-covered hill is located behind a motel. A guest tries to climb that hill and then falls and is injured. Most courts would excuse the innkeeper from liability, *Graf v. State,* 498 N.Y.S. 2d 913 (New York, 1986).

When the inn wants to claim that a danger which resulted in an injury to a guest was "obvious," it must be remembered that if such danger was obvious to the guest, it should have also been obvious to the inn. In that regard, a court is likely to hold that the inn should have removed the danger. What is obvious to the innkeeper on the other hand, may not be so obvious to the guest who just arrived at the inn and who has never been there before.

Many lawsuits were brought against the former MGM Grand Hotel in Las Vegas as a result of a fire there in 1980 which left 87 dead and hundreds injured. A little-noted side issue of this disaster were the claims filed against the hotel alleging that there was a failure to provide fire warnings in Spanish. The complaint alleged that while MGM solicited foreign-speaking guests, it did not provide multilingual signs for fire drills or safety tips.

The dangerous character of chemicals and equipment used at the inn pool must be communicated in English, and other languages if appropriate, to users of that facility. Signs must be posted, and employees must be trained to provide such warnings. Failure to do so may well be held by a court to be negligence, *Tucker v. Dixon,* 144 Colo. 79, 355 P. 2d 79 (Colorado, 1960).

The duty to warn will vary with inns at different locations. Resort hotels and motels such as those found along more popular lakes and rivers in our states have a particular concern not found in inns located elsewhere. It has to do with the tendency of those who occupy guest rooms at such inns, and who have a boat or camp site in the area, to clean fish in the hotel rooms, to use camp cooking gear in the rooms, and to bring propane tanks into the room. Such activities create hazards and are of concern to management. The duty to warn all guests at such inns comes to the front at such locations, and monitoring by room maintenance personnel is very much in order.

Management of Sam's Town Hotel and Casino, located in Las Vegas, Nevada, and opened in 1978, came to realize that, although the property was popular and successful, they had a serious problem with room security. The hotel portion of the complex had been constructed in a giant "U" with the two open wings pointing away from the casino and the front-desk area. This design made it possible for those who were so inclined to have direct access to first-floor rooms from outside windows. Such persons would be completely out of sight of those in the front portions of the hotel.

Being knowledgeable businesspersons, and also being innkeepers who endeavor to use ordinary care in the operation of their business, management had steel bars installed across all first-floor windows to prevent entry from the outside. These bars are welded into squares to cover each window. But making that decision, which eliminated one legal danger, created a second one: Would those bars deny window exit to guests who may become trapped in their rooms due to smoke or fire? This problem was recognized and solved by the installation of a release device on each window that allowed the bars to swing outward, giving a clear exit to anyone in the room.

Thus, an initial legal problem was solved by the creation of a second problem which in turn also had to be resolved. As it turned out, the second problem led to yet another: What if occupants of the rooms were not aware of the release? Was it foreseeable that some guests in the rooms, confronted by fire or other emergency, might think that the bars on the windows would prevent them from ready exit to the outside? The management thought so and created signs made of brilliant red plastic material with white letters, measuring 7" by 13". Each first-floor room has such a sign located on the wall near the window with a large arrow pointing toward the release button. The sign says in large letters "In Case of Fire Push Button to Open Security Bar." In this manner the management at Sam's Town has completely met some of the legal duties imposed upon them by law: the duty to warn.

It is important to point out that these signs are not particularly attractive and may in fact cause concern to some persons who occupy these rooms. Management would have avoided their use if there had been an alternative. Unfortunately, there was no alternative; the facts and the duty to warn require that those signs not only be there, but, in case someone should decide to remove one for a souvenir that it be replaced promptly.

Duty to Warn: An Extreme Example

At an inn that is part of a national chain, located less than one mile from the international footbridge that separates El Paso, Texas, from Cuidad Juarez, Mexico, a sophisticated warning system is in operation. The parking areas contain large signs warning of the dangers of theft of property from autos. As one checks in at the front desk, the information and warning are given verbally of the high crime situation that faces the inn each day and night. As one enters the elevator, wall signs warn "to have the room key in hand when the elevator stops and to proceed quickly to the guest room and lock one's-self in." Upon entering the room, a warning from the El Paso Chief of Police about the crime situation is found on the dresser mirror. The management there is fully aware of the crime situation and has made it a strong point to share that information with guests.

As a general rule of the common law, the greater a danger at the inn, the greater is the duty to warn those who may become exposed to it. An example is to be found in the weight and exercise rooms that have become popular at inns in recent years. While such facilities will be routinely used by those who are experienced in their use, the unexperienced and minors who will invariably find their way into them can be injured by the equipment. Such facilities must be constantly supervised by competent personnel during the hours that they are open. Once closed, care must be exercised to make certain that after-hours entry is not possible.

Other examples of what must be reported to guests include warning that a fire, which could spread, has broken out at a remote area of the inn; warnings that the inn is in a high crime area and that previous crimes have occurred there; that the river below a water slide at the inn drops during certain months of the year, thus reducing the depth of the water; that seafoods offered in the restaurant may be toxic at certain times of the year; that no lifeguard is on duty at the pool; that parking lots are unattended; and many other such items that may cause the guest harm or loss if not reported. This discussion of warnings brings to the front an important point: Such warnings may in fact prevent costly lawsuits.

Lawsuit Prevention

The first consideration in the prevention of lawsuits against the HRI unit is to make every reasonable effort to remove the hazard. After that, when such efforts are not completely successful, another factor, which has to do directly with employees, enters the picture. It is common knowledge in the HRI industry that in many instances of lawsuits against an inn, there was a background of rude, poor, or insolent behavior on the part of an employee against the injured person. Thus constant training of employees, along with explanations of their expected behavior toward guests and others, is always in order. This is especially so since more and more persons are becoming aware of the possibility of receiving windfall income in cases of negligence or breach of contract, and are running to law offices to enquire about such income. To treat the simple legal fact casually can be a big mistake at the inn.

The duty to warn is complemented by the duty to supervise. And this duty in turn involves infants, the blind, and other disabled persons.

Duty to Supervise

This duty is an extension of the legal duty to warn. It is possible that once the duty to warn has been met, the duty to supervise has commenced. If the activity warned of concerns continuing danger, or if children or invalids are involved, the duty to supervise arises. The HRI unit must then send sufficient personnel to ensure that that duty is met. Thus, in some instances a new legal duty arises: the duty to supervise.

The duty to warn and supervise increases where small children who are mobile, and infants who are not, are guests at the inn, *Waugh v. Duke,* 248 F. Supp. 626 (North Carolina, 1960). A luxury that any inn does not have is the right to refuse to receive children of any age. This is true in spite of the fact that such persons cannot make binding contracts on their own behalf. Thus, the innkeeper is legally bound to receive minors who apply for admission as guests, as well as other infants accompanied by adults, *Watson v. Cross,* 63 KY 147 (1865). Minors who are unaccompanied become legally liable for necessities even though they cannot make binding contracts in their own names. Innkeepers have a duty to serve infants—a duty that is not found in any other business endeavor, Williston on Contracts, sections 241, 242 (1959 Edition).

When it becomes evident that there are numerous children present at the inn, the standard of care must be upgraded until that condition returns to normal levels. The duty to warn can come into sharper focus under such circumstances, and the innkeeper must react accordingly.

An excellent house rule to implement at the inn is that children who use game rooms or video rooms must be accompanied by an adult. A conspicuous sign to that effect should be posted at the entrance of the room or arcade, and the rule should be enforced. The obvious danger in not having such a rule is that an unattended child might be enticed away in one manner or another. Such events often lead to the death of the child and the inn would have to face the possibility of liability for the death if such an unfortunate event should occur.

In regard to the matter of infants or minors at the inn, various cities and states have enacted ordinances or state statutes that consider the minors at the inn both as guests and as employees. For example, some larger cities require that innkeepers report to the city police the presence of unaccompanied minor children at the inn. Nevada has two statutes that could impact inn operations in that state.

Nevada Revised Statutes, 609.210, 4, prohibits the use of those under the age of sixteen to act as ". . . a messenger for delivering letters, telegrams, packages or bundles to any house of prostitution or assignation . . ." or to "any dancehall . . . where alcoholic beverages are dispensed."

Nevada Revised Statutes 605.240, subsection 2, sets forth a provision that could cause some concern to hotel and casino operators. It reads as follows: "The presence of a child in any establishment during working hours shall constitute *prima facie* evidence of its employment therein."

Turning from the internal affairs of the inn, is there a duty to warn inn guests of dangers at properties that are adjacent or close to the inn but not owned or operated by the inn, or of dangerous undertow conditions at ocean-front properties?

At ocean-front HRI properties, dangerous undertow conditions are often experienced at certain times of each year. Management knows or should know of such conditions, and in turn must give proper warnings to guests of those conditions. Failure to give notice, or failure to give notice that is seen and understood by guests, can lead to legal liability of the property. For such a case involving severe waves that injured a guest, see *Tarshis v. Lahaina*, 480 F. 2d 1019 (9th Cir., 1973).

When considering the safety of guests arriving or departing, crime problems at the inn and its immediate surroundings must be taken into consideration. Failure to warn of known dangers at adjacent properties can well place liability upon the innkeeper, *Banks v. Hyatt*, 722 F. 2d 214 (Louisiana, 1984). For a case where a Holiday Inn in Star City, West Virginia, was held liable in the sum of $147,000 to a tennis player who fell down an embankment on property adjacent to the inn, see *Ventura v. Wingardner,* 357 S.E. 2d 764 (West Virginia, 1987).

Duty to Warn Employees

All employees must be warned of the potential danger in the use of cleaning compounds at the inn. For example, ammonia, chlorine, bromide, or fluoride, when mixed, will form a toxic gas. In addition, warnings must be made about the use of fertilizers, fumigants, and pesticides. Eye, hand, and skin protection are mandatory when employees make use of such substances at the inn as part of their job requirements.

Duty to Protect Guests from Employees

A primary duty of employees of the inn is to see that guests are not injured from any cause. Thus this duty rests squarely upon the innkeeper by virtue of both common law and agency law. If an employee negligently or deliberately injures a guest, tort liability falls on the employee. Liability may also fall upon the innkeeper as well. The liability on the innkeeper would be for the full extent of the loss and would be based upon *respondeat superior* or upon the contract theory of liability.

For this rule to work, the employee must be on duty and acting in the scope of his or her employment. Yet is has been held that an innkeeper was responsible for molestation of a 15-year-old guest by an employee who was *not* acting in the scope of his employment at the time but nevertheless was at the inn when the attack took place.[20] The responsibility of the innkeeper in this area is approaching strict liability and comes close to the duty the law places on common carriers for injuries caused to passengers by employees.

Conversely, the innkeeper has a duty to protect employees from guests and others as well.[21] This places the innkeeper in a position where he or she must protect guests from employees, other guests, and third parties; protect employees from guests and third parties; protect third parties on the inn premises from guests, third parties, and employees; and provide the security to see that all of this is done. It is an important area for consideration at all inns—and an expensive one.

To make the legal situation of the innkeeper even more interesting, guests often invite others to their rooms or to dinner at the inn's dining facility. This compounds the responsibilities of the innkeeper, especially when an employee injuries such guests of guests. Yet such persons are not "guests" within the innkeeping meaning since they have not been accepted by the innkeeper. Thus the law is not quite as strict in this area and provides some protection for the innkeeper.

Invited Nonguests

If a guest invites a nonguest to an inn, the innkeeper should use care and caution before excluding that person. While such a person would not be an inn guest, the duties of the innkeeper could well come into play. This is especially true if the innkeeper is aware of the facts. Care and diplomacy would be in order. If the invited nonguest is there for immoral or illegal purposes, or if the invited nonguest engages in obnoxious or undesirable conduct, the innkeeper could exclude on those grounds.

In the following case, an innkeeper wound up in court because of the refusal to admit the wife of a guest to the guest's room. The court spells out the law and the innkeeper prevailed in the end. But it might have been better to have admitted the wife after it had been determined that the husband was expecting her. Still, caution is in order. If the wife had been admitted and if she had removed property of the husband, the innkeeper might have been held responsible for that property. It should be observed that this case was decided in a "community property" state–Louisiana. Under community property law, husbands and wives are deemed to jointly own all property acquired during marriage. It makes no difference who pays for it. While community property rights are mentioned in the case, they have no effect on the outcome because of a Louisiana statute on contract rights.

CAMPBELL V. WOMACK[22]

EDWARDS, Judge.

This suit was brought by Elvin Campbell and his wife for damages resulting from breach of contract and embarrassment, humiliation and mental anguish, sustained by Mrs. Campbell as a result of the defendants' refusal to admit Mrs. Campbell to her husband's motel room. The defendants' motion for summary judgment was granted and the action was dismissed. From this dismissal, plaintiffs have appealed.

Plaintiff, Elvin Campbell, is engaged in the sand and gravel business. Since the nature of his business often requires his absence from his home in St. Francisville, Mr. Campbell generally obtains temporary accommodations in the area in which he is working. For this purpose, Mr. Campbell rented a double room on a month to month basis at the Rodeway Inn, in Morgan City, Louisiana. The room was registered in Mr. Campbell's name only.

From time to time, Mr. Campbell would share his room with certain of his employees; in fact he obtained additional keys for the convenience of these employees. It also appears that Mr. Campbell was joined by his wife on some weekends and holidays, and that they jointly occupied his room on those occasions. However, Mrs. Campbell was not given a key to the motel room. On one such weekend, Mrs. Campbell, arriving while her husband was not at the motel, attempted to obtain the key to her husband's room from the desk clerk, Barbara Womack. This request was denied, since the desk clerk found that Mrs. Campbell was neither a registered guest for that room nor had the registered guest, her husband, communicated to the motel management, his authorization to release his room key to Mrs. Campbell. Plaintiffs allege that this refusal was in a loud, rude, and abusive manner. After a second request and refusal, Mrs. Campbell became distressed, left the Rodeway Inn, and obtained a room at another motel. Shortly thereafter, suit was filed against the motel and the desk clerk, Barbara Womack.

Plaintiffs' main contention is that Mrs. Campbell was entitled to a key to her husband's room since she had acquired the status of a guest from her previous stays with her husband in the motel room. The leading pronouncement in Louisiana on the creation of a guest status is found in *Moody v. Kenny*, 153 La. 1007, 97 So. 21 (1923). There it is stated at page 22:

> ". . . a mere guest of the registered occupant of a room at a hotel, who shares such room with its occupant without the knowledge or consent of the hotel management, would not be a guest of the hotel, as there would be no contractual relations in such case between such third person and the hotel. . . ."

Plaintiffs would have us conclude from this statement that once the motel management gained knowledge on the previous occasions that Mrs. Campbell was sharing the motel room with the registered occupant, the motel was thereafter estopped to deny Mrs. Campbell the key to that room. The fallacy of this argument is apparent, since under it even a casual visitor to a hotel guest's room would be entitled to return at a later time and demand a key to the guest's room, so long as the hotel management had knowledge of the initial visit.

The motel clerk was under no duty to give Mrs. Campbell, a third party, the key to one of its guest's rooms. In fact, the motel had an affirmative duty, stemming from a guest's rights of privacy and peaceful possession, not to allow unregistered and unauthorized third parties to gain access to the rooms of its guest (cf. LSA–C.C. art. 2965-67).

The additional fact that Mrs. Campbell offered proof of her identity and her marital relation with the room's registered occupant does not alter her third-party status; nor does it lessen the duty owed by the motel to its guest. The mere fact of marriage does not imply that the wife has full authorization from her husband at all times and as to all matters, (LSA–C.C. art. 2404). Besides, how could Mrs. Campbell prove to the motel's satisfaction that the then present marital situation was amicable? This information is not susceptible of ready proof.

The plaintiffs further contend that since the rental contract was entered into during the existence of their marriage it was therefore a community asset, and that Mrs. Campbell was entitled to the use of the motel room based on her rights in the community. We need not reach the issue of Mrs. Campbell's community property rights in the motel room, since under the clear language of LSA–C.C. art. 2404, she had no right to enforce the rental contract.

Having found that Mrs. Campbell was not entitled to demand a key to the motel room, and further that no authorization to admit her was communicated to the motel by her husband, there was no breach of contract.

The affidavits submitted by each side demonstrate that the only issues in dispute are, did Mrs. Campbell share her husband's motel room, and did the motel have knowledge of this? Neither issue is material to this suit since regardless of how they are resolved, the plaintiffs cannot prevail. When the evidence submitted on the motion leaves no relevant, genuine issue of fact, and when reasonable minds must inevitably conclude that the mover is entitled to judgment on the facts before the court, the motion for summary judgment should be granted.

Accordingly, the trial court properly granted defendants' motion for summary judgment.

For the reasons assigned the judgment of the trial court is affirmed at appellants' cost.

AFFIRMED.

A variety of other duties arise in innkeeping and other HRI operations as well. The following are samples.

Suitable Accommodations

An innkeeper must furnish the kind of accommodations for lodging and food and other services that could reasonably be expected to be found at that particular inn. In addition, an innkeeper is held at law to have control of the rooms of the inn. Thus other ancillary duties are imposed, such as the duty to keep the rooms clean and toilets sanitized, to provide fire escapes and fire protection devices, and many others.

Courteous Treatment

A guest at an inn has the right to receive courteous treatment from the innkeeper, the employees, and agents of the inn. The duty of courteous treatment is as old as the law of innkeeping and will be implied from the inn-guest relationship itself. An innkeeper must school employees and agents on the need to be courteous to arriving and departing guests and while they are in, as well as outside, of the inn.

Phone Calls and Messages

A by-product of innkeeping is the flow of phone calls, telegrams, mail, and other messages for guests. Most inns handle such matters in a routine fashion and problems seldom arise. Telegrams, letters, and written messages can be maintained at the front desk. Phone messages for absent guests should be written and placed there also. This requires guests to check periodically at the front desk for such items.

Receipt of registered mail for a guest should be handled with more caution. The requirement of signing before delivery gives notice that the mail contains something of more than passing interest.

Are Telephones Necessary? A Texas Case

The Texas court had before it a case involving a claim by a woman who had been raped while a guest in the hotel, and the rape occurred as the result of the hotel failing to supply her with a room having a secure lock, whereby the rapist was able to gain entry into the room. The jury decided the woman had been raped because the lock was inadequate to provide the necessary security to protect her.

The property involved was one of the economy hotels operated by a nationwide chain. As an effort to keep down construction and operating costs, these hotels do not install telephones in the rooms. The jurors, in handing down their decision, admonished the hotel for failing to have telephones in the rooms so that people who were threatened would have a way to summon help.

> How much this lack of a telephone influenced the jury we will never know, but they did choose to single this shortcoming out.
>
> The award in this case was $188,275–$75,000 of which was punitive damages. Was this jury trying to tell the industry that a failure to have a telephone or some other means of summoning aid from the room amounts to a failure to provide security to the guest? And further, that such failure will result in monetary damages should the guest be injured as a result of an attack which may have been prevented or mitigated if aid could have been summoned?
>
> Are the courts and juries in the various jurisdictions throughout the country telling the innkeepers to shape up or pay out?[23]

Does an innkeeper, through his or her agents, have a duty to come to the rescue of a guest who has gotten into a life-threatening situation?

A Legal Duty to Rescue?

As a general legal principle, the common law does not place a duty upon the HRI industry to rescue those who may get into a position of peril at the inn unless the peril was caused by the innkeeper or its agents.[24] What the law does require is that the innkeeper exercise ordinary reasonable care, taking into consideration the principle of "foreseeability." If fire breaks out at the inn, professional help must be sought as quickly as possible and suitable warnings must be given to guests at the inn. There is, however, no duty on the innkeeper to attempt to enter a burning room and assist a guest out of it. That is the job of the professionals who have been timely summoned.

On the other hand, if rescue is attempted, as it might well be under certain circumstances, and if the rescue attempt is carried out carelessly, that could well give rise to a cause of action in tort for the negligent rescue attempt.

Because of the latter situation many of our states have enacted "good samaritan" laws designed to hold harmless one who steps forward in an attempt to rescue, but who perhaps does so in a careless manner. As a general legal rule, however, rescue is best left to the professionals. A judge had this to say about rescue:

> Whether a duty initially exists to come to the aid of another, it is clear that once the hotelkeeper does come to the aid of the guest or patron, he will be liable to the guest if through his negligence he puts him in a worse condition than that in which he found him or causes the guest to refrain from taking any

> steps for his protection by causing him to rely on the hotel-keeper's assistance.
>
> Because of the possibility of fraud occasioned by the above rule, a number of states have adopted "good samaritan" statutes which bar recovery against the rescuer in the absence of proof of willful or wantonly inflicted harm. The New York Education Law, section 6527, exempts from civil liability licensed physicians who gratuitously render first aid or treatment at the scene of an accident or other emergency to a person who is ill, unconscious, or injured except in the case of gross negligence. Section 6611 applies this exemption to dentists, and section 6908 applies it to registered nurses and licensed practical nurses.[25]

To close the chapter, let's briefly examine the duties owed to the inn by guests. Breach of these duties gives rise to the right of the innkeeper to remove such persons from the inn as well as to sue for any losses to the inn.

DUTIES OF GUESTS

The principal duty that a guest owes to an innkeeper is to conduct himself or herself in a courteous, reasonably dignified manner at all times. Guests should, but do not always, refrain from riding the tops of outside elevators; throwing furniture into pools; stealing towels; hanging from balconies; or running through the inn with abandon. Such conduct can be used as a defense against actions brought against the innkeeper for injuries that grew out of such activities.

In *Gore v. Whitemore Hotel Co.*,[26] the court held that the guests were under a duty to refrain from unlawful and disorderly conduct which endangered the safety of others; that a willful violation of that duty forfeited the right of a guest to possession of the room; and that when the innkeeper became aware of the disorderly conduct of the guest, the innkeeper had a duty to exercise reasonable care to abate or keep down the condition, and the right to remove the guest from the hotel.

Other duties of guests include the duty to pay for services and food and drink,[27] not burn down a hotel room, and not steal from the inn.

In the Fireman's case, a hotel in downtown Las Vegas brought a negligence action against former guests who had caused a fire at that hotel. The doctrine of *res ipsa loquitur* was involved, and the hotel was not successful in its suit. The reason the hotel lost the case is the point to look for.

FIREMAN'S FUND V. KNOBBE[28]

MOWBRAY, Justice:

The sole issue presented is whether the doctrine of *res ipsa loquitur* may be invoked to recover damages from a hotel's guests for a fire that originated in one of the guests' rooms. The district judge on a motion for summary judgment held that under the facts presented the doctrine was not applicable. We agree and affirm.

1. A fire was discovered in a hotel room in Las Vegas. The cause of the fire was determined to be a cigarette. On the night of the fire, the room was occupied by Respondents John and Marilyn Doherty. The Dohertys were traveling in the company of Respondents Andrew and Geraldine Knobbe, who occupied an adjoining, connecting room.

2. A complaint was filed by appellant insurance company against respondents, claiming subrogation to the rights of the hotel and alleging negligence predicated on a standard evidentiary negligence theory and on the doctrine of *res ipsa loquitur*. Respondents moved for summary judgment. The court denied the motion, on the ground that there was a conflict of material fact under the standard evidentiary theory; however, the court granted the motion as to the *res ipsa loquitur* theory of liability. Appellant then stipulated that there was insufficient evidence to establish negligence without the aid of *res ipsa loquitur*. This appeal followed.

3. In *Bialer v. St. Mary's Hosp.*, 83 Nev. 241, 243, 427 P.2d 957, 958 (1967), this court said:

> For the doctrine of *res ipsa loquitur* to apply, three conditions must be met: (1) the event must be of a kind which ordinarily does not occur in the absence of someone's negligence; (2) the event must be caused by an agency or instrumentality within the exclusive control of the defendant; and (3) the event must not have been due to any voluntary action or contribution on the part of the plaintiff.

Evidence was presented that the hotel had 18 keys to the room where the fire occurred. The staff was not questioned to determine whether anyone had entered the room after the four respondents had departed and before the discovery of the fire. Further, appellant failed to demonstrate that respondents had exclusive control or joint control of the instrumentality causing the damage. Taken in the light most favorable to the appellant, the evidence established that all four respondents were smoking in the room. While each had exclusive control of his or her own cigarette, there is no evidence as to which cigarette started the fire. Traditionally, such a failure defeats the plaintiff's case. There have been cases, however, in which *res ipsa loquitur* has been applied to multiple defendants, thereby shifting the burden to each individual defendant to present exculpating evidence. Appellant relies upon the leading case of *Ybarra v. Spangard*, 25 Cal.2d 486, 154 P.2d 687 (1944), in urging this theory in this case. In Ybarra, an appendectomy patient who awoke with a shoulder injury was permitted to invoke the doctrine of *res ipsa loquitur* in whose care he had been while unconscious. No showing had been made as to which defendant or what instrumentality had caused the injury. The court concluded this did not bar the doctrine, holding, however, that the ruling was limited to the fact situation presented.

The rule has also been applied, upon occasion, in a variety of other fact situations: *Smith v. Claude Neon Lights, Inc.*, 110 N.J.L. 326, 164 A. 423 (1933) (plaintiff injured by falling sign sued owner of building and light company which erected and maintained sign); *Schroeder v. City & County Sav. Bank*, 293 N.Y. 370, 57 N.E.2d 57 (1944) (plaintiff injured by collapse of construction barricade sued owner of building and two construction companies); *Bond v. Otis Elevator Co.*, 388 S.W.2d 681 (Tex. 1965) (plaintiff injured when elevator went into free fall sued owner of building and company which installed and maintained elevator); *Burr v. Sherwin-Williams Co.*, 258 P.2d 58 (Cal.App., 1953) (plaintiff whose cotton crop was damaged by insecticide spray sued manufacturer of spray, spraying company, and local cooperative which advised use of spray); *Raber v. Tumin*, 36 Cal.2d 654, 226 P.2d 574 (1951) (plaintiff injured by a falling ladder sued lessee of premises and carpenter doing repairs on premises). In the foregoing cases, the instrumentality causing the damage was known. While the plaintiff had not established which defendant had been negligent, he had established that each was at some time or to some extent responsible for that instrumentality. Only the cases involving unconscious patients lack direct evidence as to both the particular defendant and the particular instrumentality responsible, as does the instant case.

More commonly, it has been held that when any of several defendants wholly independent of each other may be responsible for plaintiff's injury, the doctrine of *res ipsa loquitur* cannot be applied. See, e.g., *Estes v. Estes*, 127 S.W.2d 78 (Mo.App. 1939); *Gerber v. Faber*, 54 Cal.App.2d 674, 129 P.2d 485 (1942); *Wolf v. American Tract Soc'y*, 164 N.Y. 30, 58 N.E. 31 (1900). In Wolf the plaintiff had been injured by a brick falling from a building under construction in which 19 independent contractors were at work. The court rejected the lower court's application of *res ipsa loquitur* to two of these contractors, which would have required them to come forward with proof of their innocence. It concluded, at 32, that:

Cases must occasionally happen where the person really responsible for a personal injury cannot be identified or pointed out by proof, as in this case; and then it is far better and more consistent with reason and law that the injury should go without redress, than that innocent persons should be held responsible, upon some strained construction of the law developed for the occasion.

Clearly, the doctrine has no application in this case, where there is lacking even a scintilla of evidence indicating which respondent had control of the cigarette that started the fire.

The order granting summary judgment is affirmed.

Larceny by Lodger

Most states have statutes such as the following that can lead to criminal prosecution of a guest:

> Any lodger who takes away, with intent to steal, embezzle, or purloin, any bedding, furniture, goods, or chattels which he is to use in or with his lodging, is guilty of grand or petit larceny, according to the value of the property so taken, and shall be punished accordingly.

QUESTIONS

1. Why is the "duty to receive" so strong in the lodging industry today?
2. Name three times when an innkeeper can lawfully refuse to receive.
3. Name two legal reasons why lodging facilities must be properly maintained.
4. What does "nondelegable" mean to an innkeeper?
5. Is it legally wise to operate an inn without room phones?
6. Why did the insurance company lose its case in *Fireman's Fund v. Knobbe*?
7. What does "res ipsa loquitur" mean as it was discussed in this chapter?
8. What is the primary legal duty of innkeepers?
9. Write a brief paragraph on what the policy will be at your inn in reference to minors.
10. True or False. It can be expected that other novel suits will arise in the future out of the innkeeper-guest relationship.

ENDNOTES

1. Thomas A. Dickerson, *Travel Law.* Law Journal Seminars Press, New York, sec. 106(1).
2. Virginia Code, William F. Ritchie, Richmond, Virginia, 1849. Title 28, Taverns, Travel and Highways and Patrols, sec. 4.
3. Nevada Revised Statutes, 447.020 to 447.210. Dates of passage or revisions follow each statute.
4. *Italiano v. N.Y.,* 59 A.D. 2d 820, 399 NYS. 2d 727 (1977).
5. *Walling v. Potter,* 35 Conn. 183, 185 (1868).
6. 7 *Car. & P.* 213, 173 *Eng. Rep.* 94 (1835).
7. Nevada Revised Statutes, 651.075.
8. By James O. Eiler, Esquire, writing in the *Hotel and Casino Law Letter.*
9. *Bardwell Motor Inn, Inc. v. Accavallo,* 381 A. 2d 1061 (Vt. 1977).
10. *Ott v. Faison,* 287 Ala. 700, 255 So. 2d 38 (1971).
11. *Mazer v. Sememza,* 177 So. 2d 880, 882 (Fla. App. 1965).
12. *Baker v. Dallas Hotel Co.,* 73 R 2d 825 (5th Cir. 1934).
13. *Withrow v. Woozencraft,* 90 N.M. 48, 559 P. 2d 425 (1976).
14. *Garzilli v. Howard Johnson's Motor Lodges, Inc.,* 419 F. Supp. 1201 (E.D. N.Y. 1976), the "Connie Francis" case.
15. 11 *supra.*
16. 12 *supra.*
17. 12 *supra.*
18. *Tarshis v. Lahaina Investment Corporation,* 480 F. 2d 1019 (9th Cir. 1973).
19. *First Arlington v. McQuire,* 311 So. 2d 146 (Fla. App. 1975).
20. *Tobin v. Slutsky,* 506 F. 2d 1097 (2d Cir. 1974).
21. *Sapp v. Holiday Inns, Inc.,* 348 So. 2d 363 (Fla. App. 1977).
22. 345 So. 2d 96 (La. App. 1977), No. 11120
23. Dr. Anthony G. Marshall and Dr. Elio C. Bellucci, "Innkeeper's Security: Quo Vadis." *Florida Hotel & Motel News,* March 1983.
24. *McLean v. University Club,* 97 N.E. 2d 194 (Mass. 1951).
25. Sherry, *supra.*
26. 229 Mo. App. 910, 83 S.W. 2d 114.
27. Morningstar.
28. 562 P. 2d 825 (Nv. 1977).

13

Legal Liability and HRI Management

My hotel philosophy agrees with that of Boswell as expressed in his Life of Dr. Johnson*: "There is nothing which as yet been contrived by man by which so much happiness is produced as by a good tavern or inn."*

Be My Guest, Conrad Hilton

OVERVIEW

In Chapter 12 we took a look at areas of responsibility that the law places on innkeepers. What we did not see was how those duties place legal obligations upon management to see that they are met. The breach of those duties–which often comes from negligent or misinformed management–can lead to legal liability.

In almost all cases of liability which led to litigation, what was done wrong at the inn might have been avoided. Most lawsuits that are filed could have been prevented by the change of some fact or circumstance. Such changes can come about by the use of sound management practices. Thus, management becomes closely tied to legal liability in that sense. If a disclaimer leads a guest to use more care, which avoids the loss of valuables at an inn, that use avoids liability because liability does not arise. If a sign at a pool warning that a lifeguard is not on duty causes a father to watch his children more carefully, which in turn prevents injury or death, then liability has again been avoided.

The responsibility for establishing proper legal practices falls squarely upon management. The law of agency makes this so and one cannot use as a defense that "My employee did it, not I." Also one cannot claim that "Since I delegated the repair of the elevator to Otis Company, look to them for the injuries caused by the fall of the elevator," because the rule is that innkeepers cannot delegate their basic duties to others so as to avoid liability for them. To facilitate our discussion, the material is divided into three parts: liability and the courts; management by agency, and legal management.

LIABILITY AND THE COURTS

To be "liable," as that word is used in law, means to be "bound or obligated in law or equity; responsible; chargeable; answerable; compellable to make satisfaction, compensation, or restitution."[1] It is the "condition of being bound to respond because a wrong has occurred."[2]

Thus liability is ". . . the state of being bound or obligated in law or justice to do, pay, or make good something; the state of one who is bound in law or justice to do something which may be enforced by action."[3]

The definitions break down into three parts: First, liability is involuntary as to the one who suffers it. Second, the condition is forced on the defaulting person or firm by court action. Third, the result of this court action can be enforced by "action." Translated into simple terms it means this: The inn has been sued even though it did not want to be; the action in court was forced upon it and ended in a judgment against it. The judgment can now be enforced by attachment or execution against the assets of the inn, even though the facility strongly objects to it. In short, it is an undesirable legal position to be in.

How Does Liability Arise?

Legal liability can come about in a variety of ways, including but not limited to the following:

1. Breach of contract, sales or conventional. (Contract liability.)
2. Negligence or carelessness. (Tort liability.)
3. Deliberate, willful acts that cause injury. (Tort and criminal liability.)
4. By acts of one's agents. (Contract and tort liability based on the law of agency.)
5. Breach of a bailment obligation. (Contract liability.)
6. Breach of warranty of food and beverages sold. (Contract liability.)

7. Statutory violations (negligence per se):
   a. Dram Shop Act violations.
   b. Fire, health, and building-code violations.
   c. By other statutes.
8. By fraud and misrepresentation:
   a. Overreaching.
   b. Puffing (promising too much).
9. Others, such as the rules of evidence, *res ipsa loquitur* (which raises an inference of negligence), and many others.

Examine Figure 13.1.

Liability can attach in three ways. First, it can be forced upon a person or business through a lawsuit, with the subsequent award of damages by court judgment. Second, the one at fault may admit liability, thus accepting legal responsibility. This happens more often than one might suppose and has the practical effect of avoiding lawyer and court costs as well as adverse publicity from the court action. Third, responsibility for an injury or loss may be accepted *without admitting liability*. The main reason for doing this is to maintain the goodwill of the person or persons who have suffered the loss while avoiding any admission of wrongdoing.

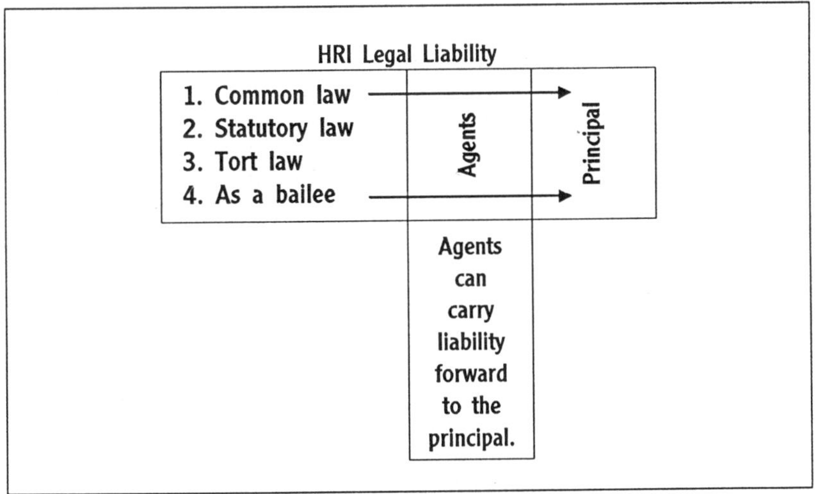

FIGURE 13.1 HRI legal liability.

Decisions Needed

HRI managers are often faced with the need to make decisions involving legal liability situations. For instance, a guest at an inn has been injured or has suffered some other loss. Should the liability be assumed or not? Should a lawyer be consulted at the outset? If suit is brought by the guest, other questions arise. Should the accusation of liability be defended? Should this lawyer be retained or that one? If the case goes bad in the lower court, should an appeal be undertaken? Are there reasons for the appeal other than financial, such as the desire to avoid an undesirable precedent if the case decision is allowed to stand? These and other decisions face the HRI manager and, while the advice of a lawyer should be sought, in most instances the final decisions are for management.

Limits on Legal Liability by Statute

Toward the end of the last century, both the federal and state governments began to enact laws to place limits upon the liability of HRI facilities. At the state level, the legislatures enacted statutes to limit the common-law liability of innkeepers for the loss of guests' money, property, and valuables. The policy reason for these laws was to lift some of the harshness of common-law liability.[4] Liability was limited in other areas also.

The State of Nevada provides a good example of such other statutes. First, the following was declared as the public policy of the state:

> The legislature declares that the purpose of this subsection is to effectuate the public policy of the State of Nevada by encouraging the recreational use of land, lakes, reservoirs and other waters owned or controlled by any public or quasi-municipal agency or corporation of this state, wherever such land or water may be situated.[5]

The statute then follows:

> 1. An award for damages in an action sounding in tort brought under NRS 41.031 may not exceed the sum of $50,000, exclusive of interest computed from the date of judgment, to or for the benefit of any claimant. An award may not include any amount as exemplary or punitive damages.
> 2. The limitations of subsection 1 upon the amount and nature of damages which may be awarded apply also to any action sounding in tort and arising from any recreational activity or recreational use of land or water.

In 1983, Nevada amended its civil rights statute to limit a recovery in court by a prevailing plaintiff to actual damages for economic loss and exemplary damages for an act ". . . such as intentional discrimination in an amount not to exceed $1,000." The law allows the plaintiff to recover costs and reasonable attorney fees.[6]

These statutes make it clear that Nevada gives considerable protection to its innkeepers and others in the HRI function. All states have such statutes, but in varying form.

The trend that started in the last century of placing limits on liability on HRI components saw a dramatic reversal with the deregulation of the airlines in 1978, effective 1983.[7] This deregulation lifts much of the protection that airlines could get through their tariffs. Airlines must now face common-law liability under traditional legal rules. There is no indication, however, that existing statutory protection of other HRI functions will be lifted in the near future.

Returning to innkeeping, *timing* often becomes involved in deciding what the liability of an innkeeper may be in a given situation. An example of this is found in the question, "When does the inn-guest relationship begin and when does it end?"

Inn-Guest Relationship: Starts When? Ends When?

For example, the question becomes particularly important in deciding the degree of liability for valuables lost at the inn. If the guest relationship is in effect, the loss-of-valuables statutes may limit the innkeeper's liability. If the relationship has ended, the matter may be controlled by the law of bailment. In the latter, there are no limits on liability for the innkeeper who breaches his or her duties as a bailee other than the value of the property itself.

A variety of cases are found in the case reports and some rules can be set forth out of them. If a guest settles the bill, although intending to return in a few days, the relationship has ended in Missouri.[8] Thus valuables left at the inn by the paid-up guest would be held by the innkeeper as a bailee. In a Tennessee case,[9] a guest left money with a clerk, settled the bill, and left, intending to return in a day or two. The former guest was delayed in returning for several weeks. The court held that the innkeeper was not liable for the money left with the clerk.

In an early case,[10] where a guest left the inn owing 25 cents —leaving property as security—intending to return shortly, the court distinguished "dead goods" left at the inn from "live goods" such as a horse. "The property lost was "dead goods"–and the same rules do not obtain as if it had been a horse. For in the latter case, the host would have had "benefit by the continuance of the horse with him." In the former he would have "no benefit," and therefore the host would not be charged with a loss in the absence of the guest."

It is clear that the temporary absence of a guest during the day will not end the relationship.[11] Neither will eating meals elsewhere end it,[12] or going out "on the town."[13] If a guest pays early for the purpose of obtaining funds for the day, the relationship has not ended at that point.[14]

Conversely, if a guest pays a bill intending to avoid a charge for the day, even if intending to return that night, the relationship is at an end.[15] The court stated in the last case: "The expectation thereafter to become a guest did not continue the relationship and it terminated at his instance, and for his advantage, by settling his account for entertainment. An innkeeper is chargeable as such because of the profit derived from entertaining. *The right to charge is the criterion of the innkeeper's liability* [emphasis added]."

The obligations of a host to a guest may give way, under appropriate facts, to the rules that define the rights of bailors and bailees in mutual-benefit bailments. When this happens, the host may lose all or part of the protection given by the "loss of valuables" statutes. This is why it is so important to determine when the innkeeper-guest relationship ends. From that point on, the innkeeper must use extra caution when dealing with the property of the former guest.

Not only does timing become involved in legal liability, so does the *extent* of liability, for it can be great in some instances, moderate in others, and slight in still others.

Degree of Liability

The degree or extent of legal liability of an inn will depend upon the relationship that has been formed between the inn and the patron or guest. For example, in a bailment for hire, the bailee (HRI manager) must use ordinary care. In a gratuitous bailment, the care might be somewhat less than ordinary care. Figure 13.2 illustrates this concept.

There are different theories that the trial lawyer can look to in deciding whether to take a case involving HRI liability.

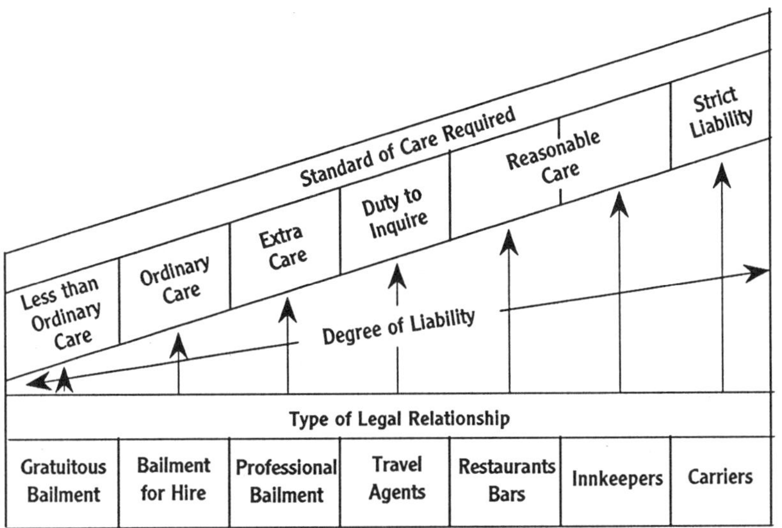

FIGURE 13.2

THEORIES OF LEGAL LIABILITY

Res Ipsa Loquitur

One theory of legal liability that is being called upon more and more in HRI litigation is that of *res ipsa loquitur*–"the thing speaks for itself" It has been used against guests as the Fireman's case in Chapter 12 tells us, and it has been used against inns as was seen in *Page v. Sloan,* in Chapter 5.

This theory of liability is actually a rule of evidence used in court under certain circumstances ". . . whereby negligence of the alleged wrongdoer may be inferred from the mere fact an accident happened provided the character of the accident and the circumstances attending it lead reasonably to the belief that in the absence of negligence it would not have occurred and that the thing which caused the injury is shown to have been under the management and control of alleged wrongdoer."[16]

The rule had its beginning in *Byrne v. Boadle.*[17] In that case, Chief Judge Pollack had this to say:

> The learned counsel was quite right in saying that there are many accidents from which no presumption of negligence can arise, but I think it would be wrong to lay down as a rule that in no case can presumption of negligence arise from the fact of an accident. The present case upon the evidence comes to this, a man is pass-

> ing in front of the premises of a dealer in flour, and there falls down upon him a barrel of flour. I think it apparent that the barrel was in the custody of the defendant who occupied the premises, and who is responsible for the acts of his servants who had the control of it; and in my opinion the fact of its falling is *prima facie* evidence of negligence, and the plaintiff who was injured by it is not bound to show that it could not fall without negligence, but if there are any facts inconsistent with negligence it is for the defendant to prove them.

The legal effect of the RIL doctrine is that it takes from the injured plaintiff the burden of proving the cause of the injury. This is the rule in normal cases, but, if this rule were universal, it would force an injured person to explain, for example, why an elevator fell in a hotel. The plaintiff would have to prove facts that may be impossible to determine after the injury occurs. The plaintiff knows nothing of the construction of the hotel and the installation of the elevator. Thus the rule of RIL says that, if the elevator was under the care and control of the innkeeper and if the injury would not have happened in the absence of negligence, the burden shifts to the innkeeper to show that the injury was caused by some other means than his or her negligence.

The doctrine of RIL has been applied in a fall of a mirror from a wall case[18] to a suit brought for injuries in a hotel elevator[19] and other cases, as we have seen. Another theory of legal liability is that of "third-party beneficiary."

Third-Party Beneficiary

Travelers are often injured or caused loss in foreign nations and find it difficult to bring suits there because of the problems of distance and expense of foreign counsel. It thus becomes desirable, if possible, to shift that liability to inns or others at the place of residence of the injured traveler. One theory of law under which this is being done is that of "third-party beneficiary." If a traveler is sold a travel package by a local inn, for example, and injury occurs elsewhere, the inn can possibly be sued since it benefitted from the contract and was thus a third-party beneficiary. The leading case on this point is the Klakis case, discussed later.[20]

Breach of the Standard of Care

The standard that is being applied today in the courts is that of a "reasonable innkeeper" who possesses that standard of skill and knowledge that could be expected of one who occupies that position at that particular location. Factors that the courts take into consideration when deciding if the standard was met include not only the location of the inn but the quality of the inn as claimed in its ads and brochures, the room rates charged, the history of the inn, and the training and experience of the innkeeper.

If what an innkeeper did does not measure up to this standard, liability may attach. The forerunner of this was the "reasonable person" standard, a reliable unit of measure that can be used in court in a variety of legal situations.

THE "REASONABLE MAN"

One of the most flexible legal rules is that of the "reasonable person." Under this doctrine, what one did in the operation of a business in which another suffered a loss is tested against what the reasonable businessperson would have or would not have done under like or similar circumstances. If a jury should find that the standard of the reasonable person was met by the business person in question, then that person may be excused from legal liability. On the other hand, if this standard is not met, then the jury may find fault. If the jury then finds that this fault was the proximate (actual) cause of the loss, they can assess damages (money) against the defaulting person or firm. A. P. Herbert, writing in *Misleading Cases in the Common Law,*[21] had this to say about the "reasonable man."

> The Common Law of England has been laboriously built about a mythical figure—the figure of "The Reasonable Man."
>
> It is impossible to travel anywhere or to travel for long in that confusing forest of learned judgments which constitutes the Common Law of England without encountering the Reasonable Man. He is at every turn, an ever-present help in time of trouble, and his apparitions make the road to equity and right. There never has been a problem, however difficult, which His Majesty's judges have not in the end been able to resolve by asking themselves the simple question, "Was this or was it not the conduct of a reasonable man?" and leaving that question to be answered by the jury.
>
> This noble creature . . . is one who invariably looks where he is going, and is careful to examine the immediate foreground before he executes a leap or bound; who neither star-gazes nor is lost in meditation when approaching trap-doors or the margin of a dock; who records in every case upon the counterfoils of cheques such ample details as are desirable, scrupulously substitutes the word "Order" for the word "Bearer," crosses the instrument "a/c Payee only," and registers the package in which it is

> dispatched; who never mounts a moving omnibus and does not alight from any car while the train is in motion; who investigates exhaustively the bona fides of every mendicant before distributing alms, and will inform himself of the history and habits of a dog before administering a caress; who believes no gossip, nor repeats it, without firm basis for believing it to be true; who never drives his ball till those in front of him have definitely vacated the putting-green which is his own objective; who never from the year's end to another makes an excessive demand upon his wife, his neighbors, his servants, his ox, or his ass; who in the way of business looks only for that narrow margin of profit which twelve men such as himself would reckon to be "fair," and contemplates his fellow-merchants, their agents, and their goods, with that degree of suspicion and distrust which the law deems admirable; who never swears, gambles, or loses his temper; who uses nothing except in moderation, and even while he flogs his child is meditating only on the golden mean. Devoid, in short, of any human weakness, with not one single saving vice, sans prejudice, procrastination, ill-nature, avarice, and absence of mind, as careful for his own safety as he is for that of others, this excellent but odious character stands like a monument in our Courts of Justice, vainly appealing to his fellow-citizens to order their lives after his own example. . . .

Substitute Standard

In many of the health and safety laws, standards are set forth that must be met by those covered by the laws. The courts may adopt these standards and use them to determine if there is liability. However, before a court will do this, criteria must be met as are set forth in Restatement of Torts (Second), section 286 (1965):

> The court may adopt as the standard of conduct of a reasonable man the requirements of a legislative enactment or an administrative regulation whose purpose is found to be exclusively or in part
>
> "(a) to protect a class of persons which includes the one whose interest is invaded, and
>
> "(b) to protect the particular interest which is invaded, and
>
> "(c) to protect that interest against the kind of harm which has resulted, and
>
> "(d) to protect that interest against the particular hazard from which the harm results.

Before legal liability can result in a judgment, there must first be court action. What follows is a brief sketch of the procedures that are found in court actions.

PROCEDURES

First an incident must arise that involves some alleged violation of a legal duty. As an example, guest Hayward is assaulted while staying at a Holiday Inn in Virginia, and claims that there is responsibility on the part of the inn. The inn claims that the injury was due to the carelessness of Hayward and is thus not their responsibility.[22] The parties have each taken a position; one claims there is liability, the other denies that there is.

Former Guest Files Suit

Suit is then filed in a federal court in the Eastern District of Virginia. The theory of the case is that, by advertising that its inns were a "safe place to stay," Holiday Inn made an express warranty. So, when the guest was assaulted this was a breach of that warranty and the inn was responsible.

A suit is started by the preparation and filing in court of a "complaint," within which the theory of the case is set forth. This complaint is then served (handed to or other notice given) on the defendant–the one who is being sued. Under rules of procedures of the federal courts, and most states, the defendant has twenty days in which to respond and admit or deny the allegations of the complaint. This response is called the "answer."

Discovery Stage

The complaint-and-answer stage moves quickly. The next step takes more time and is known as the "discovery stage." Here the parties have alternatives available which are designed to allow them to uncover as much information as possible about each other's case. The plaintiff may want to examine records of the defendant. The defendant may want the plaintiff to submit to a physical examination by a doctor of defendants's choosing.

Other matters take place at this stage, including the taking of depositions and the use of interrogatories.

Case Matures

In time–about one or two years in federal courts in Virginia–the case will be given a trial date and thus it has "matured."

Trial

At the time of the trial, the burden of proof is on the plaintiff.

The plaintiff must prove in court, by a preponderance of the evidence, the following:

1. That a national ad had been used by the defendant in which it promised that its inns were safe places to stay.
2. That on the strength of this warranty plaintiff entered into a contract with the defendant by becoming a guest at the inn.
3. That this warranty was breached, which breach was the proximate cause of the losses suffered.
4. That money losses were suffered by the plaintiff as the proximate result of the breach.

If the plaintiff can produce evidence to establish the above, he has made out a *prima facie* (on the face of it) case. It now becomes the burden of the defendant to rebut this *prima facie* case. Examine Figure 13.3.

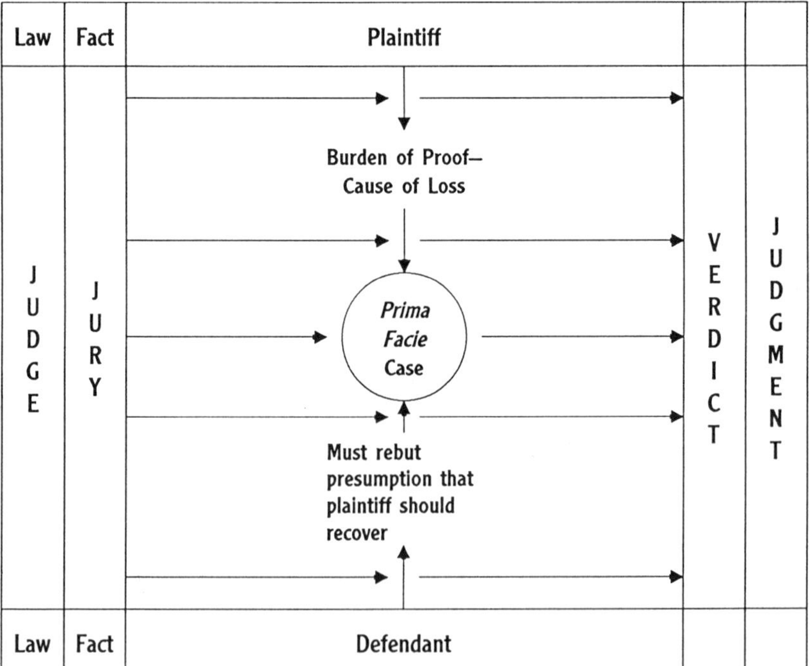

FIGURE 13.3 Proof process in court.

The Defense

The burden has now shifted to the defendant, who must come forward with evidence to rebut the presumption raised by the plaintiff's case. If the defendant cannot do this, the court will direct a verdict for the plaintiff and set a hearing on damages. In most cases, HRI lawsuits are vigorously defended and adequate defenses are presented and thus the court will not direct a verdict.

At common law, an innkeeper has three defenses that relieve him or her from liability to a guest: an act of God, an act of the public enemy, and negligence on the part of the guest. The latter was the defense raised in the above situation.

The Hayward case went to the jury upon a charge (called "instructions" in state courts) from the federal judge which told the jury the controlling principles of law. (See Chapters 15, 20, and 21 for examples.)

Since the plaintiff had proven his losses, the verdict was returned for him in the sum that the jury felt he should recover.

It is by this process, sketched briefly here, that enforceable liability arises. Other factors become involved in finding legal liability or its absence, and a few of them will be mentioned.

Other Defenses Available

Other legal defenses include comparative negligence, contributory negligence, statutory protection, and others.

Comparative Negligence

Over half of our states have now adopted, by statute or court ruling, the doctrine of comparative negligence. Under this rule of law, if an HRI facility, through its agents, causes a loss to Guest B, but Guest B contributed to that loss, the guest must pay for the portion of the loss that can be attributed to him or her. This determination becomes a question of fact for a jury to be arrived at under instructions (or charge) from the judge.

If, after trial, the jury awards Guest B $100,000 and finds that the percent of negligence of B was 40 percent, then B has the right to be paid $60,000 by the defendant. In this manner, the guest has paid for her or his portion of the loss. Some states follow the "50 percent rule" and apply it in comparative negligence cases. Here, if the finding of the jury is 50 percent liability on each party, or more than 50 percent on the plaintiff's behalf, no recovery is allowed. A more complete discussion of this topic will follow in Chapter 14 along with a discussion of the older doctrine of contributory negligence. A brief discussion of the latter follows.

Contributory Negligence

Less than one-half of our states still follow the old doctrine of contributory negligence. This harsh rule of law had its beginning in the case of *Butterfield v. Forrestor*,[23] a case that involved a tipsy horseman who rode into a pole leaning across the road and was injured. The rule that came out of that case was that, if one contributes to his or her own injury due to negligence, even though slight, this bars that person from recovery. Figure 13.4 provides further illustration of contributory negligence.

It is useful to examine negligence in more detail in order to understand how the courts treat it.

Negligence as a Cause of Action and a Defense—The Court View

> Negligent conduct may be active or passive. Active negligent conduct is the commission of an act resulting in injury to another, in breach of a legal duty owed to such other, and falling below the standard of the reasonably prudent person under the circumstances. Passive negligent conduct is the failure to act, in violation of the actor's legal duty under the circumstances, resulting in injury to another.
>
> The innkeeper owes his guests or others similarly situated the legal duty to provide reasonably safe premises. The interest the law seeks to compensate is that of protecting a guest or other person against the infliction of unintentional harm.[24]

The negligence rules force the inn into a standard of conduct that is of the same or higher level accepted in the industry, taking into consideration the factors mentioned previously. Proving negligence is the burden of the plaintiff.

Proving Negligence

"We have said many times that the law does not require every fact and circumstance which make up a case of negligence to be proved by direct and positive evidence or by the testimony of eyewitnesses, and that circumstantial evidence alone may authorize a finding of

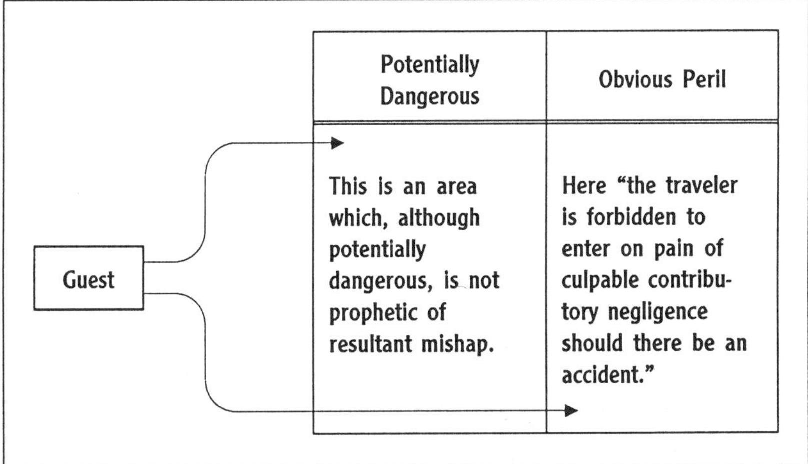

FIGURE 13.4 Contributory negligence—the closeness of the two areas. Source: *Morris v. Atlantic and Pacific Tea Company*, 384 Pa. 464, 469, 121 A. 2d 135 (1956).

negligence. Negligence may be inferred from all of the facts plus the surrounding circumstances, and where the evidence of such facts and circumstances are such as to take the case out of the realm of conjecture, and into the realm of the field of legitimate inference from established facts, a prima facie case has been made."[25]

Not only must the plaintiff prove negligence, the burden is on the plaintiff to prove, by clear and convincing proof, the amount of the losses suffered.

Proof of Damages

In civil cases it is necessary for the plaintiff to prove the loss by enough evidence to convince a jury that the loss should be compensated. In court this is spoken of as a "proof of damages." There are four types of damages that can be sought, depending upon the nature of the case.

Types of Damages

The types are (1) actual damages, (2) consequential or resulting damages, (3) punitive or exemplary damages, and (4) nominal damages.

1. Actual damages are those that result from out-of-pocket losses. If A is turned away from Motel X because of overbooking,

and goes to Motel Y next door but has to pay $10 more, the actual loss to A is $10, provided the rooms are comparable.

2. Consequential or resulting damages are those that flow as a consequence of the acts of the defendant. Here other factors come into consideration. The courts have allowed recovery if default and its extent can be proven with reasonable certainty. The *fact* of the loss must be proven with certainty–the *amount* does not have to be. Thus, in breach of contract cases actual and consequential damages can be recovered if the proof is clear, precise, and with no guessing involved.

3. The third type are punitive or exemplary damages and can be recovered in some cases involving a tort. Such damages are designed to sting or punish the one who committed outrageous and unnecessary torts. Verdicts have been awarded into the millions for punitive damages. In a breach of contract case, however, punitive damages normally cannot be awarded. Yet if the breach of contract is accompanied by a tort, they can be, but only if the act was deliberate, willful, and of such a nature as to shock one's conscience. Mere negligent acts will not lead to punitive damages in tort cases. Lawyers refer to such as "whammy damages."

4. The fourth type are those where the plaintiff proves liability to the satisfaction of a jury, but does not convince them of the losses. These are called "nominal damages" and usually take this form: "We the jury find for the plaintiff and assess his loss at $1.00." Such a verdict has the effect of placing the costs of the lawsuit upon the defendant.

As the courts go about the business of deciding liability issues and guiding juries in reaching verdicts on damages, other rules of law become involved. One of the more important is found in court interpretation of statutes.

Statutory Interpretation

In applying safety, health, and other HRI statutes, the courts must have guidelines to assist them in adapting the statutes to the situations before them. Two rules have developed.

Rule One: If a statute is in "derogation" (against) the common-law rule, the statute must be construed strictly by the court. In other words, the courts do not favor statutes that change the common law. On the other hand, if the statute is specific and plain on its face, then the statute will be applied. If it is vague or abstract, the court must interpret it in favor of the common law. Thus youth bows to age.

Rule Two: Legislation (statutes) can be "remedial" in nature. That is, the statute was brought into being to solve some contemporary social problem. Such legislation does not change the common law and must be interpreted liberally by the courts to assist the legislatures in solving the problem that is the subject of the statute. To say it another way, the courts will interpret remedial legislation so as to advance its purposes. An example is found in the workers' compensation laws.

The two rules can be summed up like this: To change the common law, there must be clear, unambiguous legislation. To remedy a social ill, the courts must assist in the process. Examine Figure 13.5.

Turning from the matter of the nature of legal liability, let's take a look at management principles and the law of agency which can create liability. We will then close the chapter by looking at other legal areas that have an influence upon management. It must be emphasized once again that good management techniques can prevent or minimize legal liability.

MANAGEMENT BY AGENCY

The law of agency, as we know it today, is relatively new when compared with the laws of contract, property, tort, and other legal

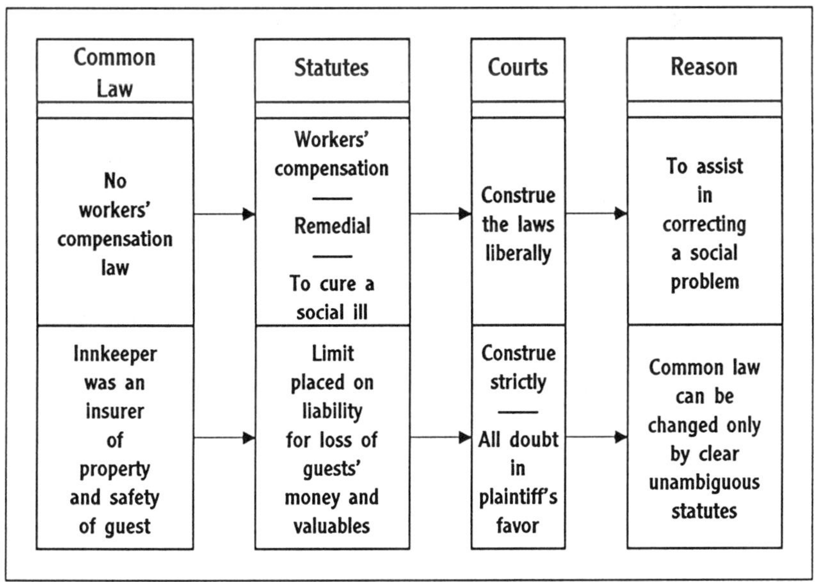

FIGURE 13.5 Court interpretation.

areas. This is true because the *need* for such a law did not exist until the coming of the Industrial Revolution. At that time and thereafter, due to expanding manufacturing of goods and perpetually increasing markets, it was no longer possible for one person or one family to carry on commerce as it had been practiced over prior centuries. It became necessary for those in business to operate through others in order to carry on the manufacture, sale, and distribution of goods and to provide other services.

When this began to happen, a body of law was needed to regulate these new business activities. As it happened, there had been in existence principles of law that were destined to form the basis of the laws of agency. These had grown out of the laws of slavery.

Historically, a slave was "chattel" or personal property. Having no legal rights, the slave depended upon the master to provide the necessities of life. Thus the master contracted as needed to maintain the slave and otherwise cared for and supported him or her.

If it should happen that the slave caused injury to another's person or property, it was a corresponding duty of the master to stand good for the damages. As the common-law judges said, "*respondeat superior*"—"let the master respond." It was not that the master had committed an offense. It was simply that the master had the *responsibility* for the damage done. Thus it was liability without fault.

Today, this principle forms the basis of the law of agency and "*qui facit per alium, facit per se,*" "who acts through another, acts himself," has become a frequently repeated statement in court and the law books.

Today the laws of agency form the environment or "surroundings" within which management principles must be carried out. Failure to recognize this may lead one to believe that the law of agency is a detached subject that comes into play only at prescribed times. The opposite is the truth and agency law provides an overlay within which management principles must function. Indeed, the law of agency often determines the *form* that management principles must take. It is a case of one controlling the other.

To facilitate an understanding of this law, it is helpful to look at some principles of management and compare them with rules of agency. By doing this, one can see how one influences the development of the other and the role played by legal liability at the inn.

Inn Organizations

Two organizations are recognized within the inn: the informal and the formal organization. The former is created by the employees

PULLMAN INN, near the Brigham Young University campus. Provo, Utah.

and operates on a "word-of-mouth" or "grapevine" basis. Thus, this organization is made up of agents and employees of the inn. In turn, the smart manager will make use of this informal organization to relay information; to permit the employee-agents to engage in self-regulation, and to permit natural leaders to play a role in running the business. Conversely, this organization must be watched carefully to make certain it is not being used in ways that may be harmful. In the latter event, movement of personnel and perhaps firings would be in order. Thus management must be certain that its members (the informal organization) are functioning for the good of the business.

The formal inn organization is something else. It is created by management and usually has five to fifteen departments. These departments are broken into such classes as line, staff, front and back of the house, and centralized and decentralized. The principles of delegation come to the front in the line departments. When one delegates, the law of agency says that what the other does is the act of the person doing the delegation. Thus legal responsibility flows with the delegation and this flow is upward.

Staff departments are classed as advisory and functional. The former may be "pure staff" and have no authority over line departments. Yet the functions they perform will form the pattern that will be followed by others, who in turn bind the main organization by agency law.

Functional staff may, in turn, have some control over line and thus be in the same position as one who delegates and thus be bound accordingly.

The principle of "unity of command" tells us that each employee should have but one boss. This is essential under agency law in order to prevent an agent from being faced with conflicting orders. If this happens and loss results to third parties, management is responsible. It would not be a good legal defense to claim that a second boss had issued a valid order that, if followed, would have prevented the loss.

The principle of "span of control" dictates that four to seven persons should report to one superior. Again, this is essential under agency law to make certain that proper supervision of agents is carried out. One person can be in only so many places in a given time period and can adequately supervise only so many persons.

Finally, the principles of division of responsibility and internal correlation of data will go a long way in avoiding the theft of goods and embezzlement of funds. One must remember that theft of company funds, even by forged checks, almost always remains the responsibility of the inn. The Uniform Commercial Code and the laws of agency make it so.

Thus, in this brief discussion we have seen that the law of agency does play a part in the pattern by which an inn is managed. While many management principles have been arrived at by scientific study, others have developed out of the need to comply with agency law.

To close the chapter, we will examine some situations in which the law lays down guidelines for the practices and procedures which must be created and then implemented by management at the inn in order to avoid, or at least decrease, legal liability there. Most of these topics will be examined in further detail in Chapter 14.

Legal Management

The management practices adopted in business must be geared to the law because of the dangers that can arise if they are not. We will look at six specific examples.

Remodeling

Remodeling seems like an innocent enough activity, yet legal matters can have an influence upon it. Consider *Rosier v. Gainesville Inn Assoc. Ltd.*,[26] which is summarized as follows:

Of Lock and Keys

In this case as in general, room keys and locks have been a constant source of problems for innkeepers from both a practical and legal point of view. What kind of legal problems arise from the use of lock and keys—especially when each room is furnished with a chain lock by which the room can be secured from the inside?

At Zero Motel

In this case, the motel is located in a well-visited tourist area in Florida. The room tower proved to be too small for the overflow visitors so an addition was built. Each of these rooms has a chain lock by which each door can be secured from the inside. All of the rooms in the new addition have locks with built-in deadbolts.

It is a practice at Zero Motel to issue only one key per guest. A second one will be issued if requested and proper identification is given. In this event, a colored card is placed in the rack to indicate that a second key is out. If a *third* key is requested, management sends a clerk to the room to open it. The passkey used by the maids is kept on a leather band and is carried around the neck of the maid or other service personnel who may have to enter the room. This key is accounted for each evening and placed under lock and key itself. A nice key policy—so what can go wrong?

First

There is the problem of the older locks. Is it negligence not to replace them? Perhaps not in itself, but what about after it is learned that someone has been entering rooms in the old wing without permission? This fact may constitute notice that something is wrong.

Second

There is the fact that the older doors contain chain locks on the inside only. Can the innkeeper be certain that the guests will use them?

Third

If a guest fails to use the chain lock, whose fault is an entry *when the guest is in the room?* Whose fault is it if the guest is *not* in the room? A chain lock or deadbolt cannot secure an empty room. So—back to the keys again.

Husband and Wife Check In

As they retire for the night, neither of them thinks to fasten the chain lock.

During the night the husband awakens to find an intruder at the foot of the bed. A struggle ensues; the guest is injured; the intruder flees, leaving a passkey on a leather neck band lying on the floor. Just as the wife tries to close the door, the intruder re-enters, grabs the passkey, and disappears. In the morning all passkeys are in their proper location.

Liability on the Innkeeper?

The judge before whom the case is brought believes not and directs a verdict in favor of the innkeeper. On appeal the upper court holds that "evidence on issues whether motel's failure to use [deadbolt] locks was proximate cause of guest's injuries and whether motel could reasonably foresee such injuries where [the innkeeper] had knowledge of prior [entries] carried out in similar manner was for the jury."

"For the Jury"

Expensive words. They mean that the case must go to trial for a hearing on the merits. What about the failure of the guest to use the chain lock that was provided? Isn't that contributory negligence and thus a good defense? Possibly so, but that is also a question of fact to be decided by a jury. All in all, an expensive matter now faces the innkeeper: waiting for trial, time in court, attorney fees, bad publicity, and all because of old locks.

Summary

Replacing old locks in an old wing is an expensive item. But compared with the expense of a new series of rooms, the cost of new locks will at least appear to be relatively minor. So, if faced with such a situation, why not include upgrading of the old locks as part of the contract for building the new addition? The cost might turn out to be a good liability insurance.

New Construction

Before new construction is started at an inn, a "legal-requirement opinion" should be sought. There will be statutes that require sewage to be kept free from effluvia arising from any sewer, drain, or other source under the control of the inn; provisions for room ventilation will be set forth; size of rooms in cubic feet will be specified and must be met in the construction; provisions will be found for ventilation, screening, bathing facilities, garbage disposal, and countless other points that must be met including the Americans with Disability Act.

Thus, in new construction as well as in remodeling, close attention is in order to see that the laws are met. Failure to do so could be negligence per se and could lead to liability.

Many HRI operations use brochures and national advertisements as part of their marketing programs. The law has something to say about such use.

Brochures and National Ads

Representations made in brochures and ads are often held by the courts to be warranties. Breach of these warranties could be a breach of contract and might lead to liability. Suits being brought in such instances are usually based on negligence, breach of contract, and fraudulent misrepresentation.[27]

Generally, an inn is not responsible for the acts of an independent contractor who operates a shop at the inn. Yet if an inn brochure or ad leads guests to believe the shop belongs to the inn, liability can attach to the inn for defaults of the shop owner.[28]

A travel brochure showed a hotel by the sea on the "north shore of Jamaica." It was in fact five miles from the sea and had only a narrow beach covered with tar. Recovery was permitted in a class action by over 200 tourists for breach of the contract of warranty.[29]

Trial lawyers want to get brochures into evidence because they establish the standards by which what was actually received can be measured.

Brochures cannot be used to avoid race, color, or creed. A brochure that reads "serving Christian interests since 1914" would violate the civil rights laws. These and other factors must be taken into consideration when deciding to use brochures and ads and in deciding the form that they should take.

Disclaimers

From early times, disclaimers have been used in contracts with guests and patrons. Indeed, disclaimers *should* be used today even in those states where they will not be upheld in the courts because they provide warnings which often prevent some harmful event.

If it becomes necessary to ask a court to enforce them where they are normally honored, the courts may still refuse to uphold them for three reasons. First, they may be held to violate public policy. Second, they were not called to the attention of the person against whom they were supposed to limit liability. Third, they were not conspicuous; that is, printed in bold type so as to assist in bringing them to the attention of other persons.

Contract disclaimers usually cannot relieve one of his or her own negligence or fraud. So they can be circumvented on these grounds by the plaintiff's lawyers rather than on the grounds of breach of contract. If the breach is so material that the traveler in fact received nothing, the courts will hold the disclaimer void as a matter of law. One cannot contract to provide something, give nothing, and then avoid liability because of a disclaimer.[30] Disclaimers must be brought to a traveler's attention and must be clear.[31]

In *Klakis v. Nationwide Leisure Corp.*,[32] the court held that, while the disclaimer contained in the brochure of the travel agent would work to cover incidental delays in air transportation, ". . . it is not a defense to delay of sufficient magnitude to vitiate [impair] the contract for the simple reason that such delay strikes at the heart of the performance bargained for. . . ." The carrier had failed to provide the flight and the passengers sued both the carrier and the travel agent.

Disclaimers on cruise ship tickets require notice of claims of loss to be filed within a certain time frame. An early case held that three days was too short but that fifteen days was not. Congress, by specific act,[33] set the time period at not less than six months to file such claims.

Exceedingly fine print has led the courts to refuse to uphold air-flight disclaimers.[34] The travel-trial lawyers are looking at the marketing methods of the HRI components to see how the travel service was sold. By going into the details, it is possible to circumvent the disclaimers and even use them to shift liability to others.

To the HRI manager, this means that thought must be given to the form of disclaimers. They must be in conspicuous language, they should be simple in content, and they should be brought to the attention of the traveler.

Pricing at the Inn

During the reign of King Edward III of England, Parliament enacted a statute to compel inn and tavern keepers to charge reasonable prices to those who traveled in the realm. The courts apply this rule[35] and it is very much a part of HRI operations today.

The courts recognize variations, of course. For example, inn rates that favor residents of a particular state over those who travel to that state are not unlawful and do not violate the law.[36] The *quality* of the inn is often looked at by the courts in determining if there is legal liability. An inn does not have to advertise itself as "five star" to be held to the standards of a five-star inn. The price charged may well play a role in this determination.[37] Likewise, the courts hold that the "cost of security is built into the rate." The more the room rate, the higher the security that a court may say must be offered to protect the guests while on the premises. Examine Figure 13.6.

While price is one determinant of guest and patron security, it is not correct to infer that courts view *very low* room rates as permitting the inn to have low security standards. Minimum standards apply at law irrespective of price, size, and quality of the inn.

Thus the inn has legal guidelines to take into consideration when establishing not only room rates but rates for food, drink, and other services as well.

House rules are guidelines that are created unilaterally at HRI facilities and placed into use to set certain standards that guests, patrons, invitees, and employees are expected to follow.

Price of Room per Night	Nature of Inn	Location	View of Court
$3,000.00	Caesar's Palace top suite	Las Vegas	Don't let *anything* go wrong
$200.00	Deluxe	Atlantic City	Things had better go smoothly
$125.00	Extra nice	Center of Golden Triangle, Pittsburgh	Be nice and careful
$60.00	National chain	Interstate	Use reasonable care
$28.00	No frills	Small town	Clean linen
$8.00	Low quality	Skid row	?

FIGURE 13.6 The thermometer of room rates.

House Rules

Once an innkeeper places a house rule into operation, it is important that notice be given to the class to be covered by it. Once notice is given, the rule must be applied evenly and equally to all who are covered by it.

By the use of house rules, we can limit liability for injury at a pool, it being a house rule, properly posted, of course, that guests swim at their own risk. We can limit our liability for loss of hat and coat in a restaurant by the rule that we do not accept responsibility.

In Chapter 14, "Inn Premises Liability," we will examine house rules in more detail, along with contributory negligence, comparative negligence, negligence per se, assumption of the risk, and other topics identified in this chapter.

QUESTIONS

1. Explain what "liability" means and the concern it creates at HRI operations.
2. Why does the degree of legal liability depend upon the relationship of the parties involved?
3. What was, and still is, the unfair feature of the doctrine of contributory negligence?
4. What were the three common-law defenses? Are they still in use or have they been modified?
5. What is the rule of statutory construction that is applied to remedial statutes?
6. Name two factors that should be taken into consideration when deciding whether or not to use brochures at an inn.
7. Name three reasons why disclaimers may not be honored by a court.
8. True or False. The deregulation of the airlines may be the forerunner of a movement to place stronger liability on the HRI industry.
9. Under what conditions may punitive damages be awarded?
10. Name a rational reason for limiting the liability of innkeepers for loss of money, valuables, and property of guests.

ENDNOTES

1. *Homan v. Employers,* 345 Mo. 650, 136 S.W 2d 289, 298.
2. *Pacific v. Murdock,* 193 Ark. 327, 99 S.W 2d 233, 235.
3. *Fidelity v. Diamond,* 310 Ill. App. 387, 34 N.E. 2d 123.
4. Nevada Revised Statutes, 651.050 as amended in 1979.
5. Nevada Revised Statutes, 41.035.
6. Nevada Revised Statutes, 651.050 as amended January 1983.
7. Federal Aviation Act of 1958, amended October 24, 1978, 92 Stat. 1705.
8. *McKeever v. Kramer,* 203 Mo. App. 269, 218 S.W. 403 (1918).
9. *Whitmore v. Haroldson,* 2 Lea. (Tenn.) 312 (1879).
10. *Hays v. Turner,* 23 Iowa 214 (1867).
11. *Drope v. Theyar* (1650) Popham, 178, 79 Eng. Reprint 1274; *White's Case* (1553), 2 Dyer 158B, 73 Eng. Reprint, 343.
12. *McDaniels v. Robinson,* 26 Vt. 316, 52 Am. Dec. 574 (1854).
13. *McDonald v. Edgerton,* 5 Barb 562, N.Y. (1849).
14. *Brown Hotel Co. v. Burckhart,* 13 Colo. App. 59, 56, P. 188 (1899).
15. *Miller v. Peeples,* 60 Miss. 819, 45 Am. Rep 23 (1883) (Emphasis added).
16. *Hillen v. Hooker,* 484 S.W 2d 111, 115 (Tex. App.).
17. *Byrne v. Boadle,* 2 Hurl. & Colt. 722 (1863).
18. *Deming Hotel v. Prox.,* 142 Ind. App. 603, 236 N.E. 2d 613 (1968).
19. *Notice v. Regent,* 429 N.Y.S. 2d 437 (1980).
20. *Klakis v. Nationwide Leisure Corp.,* 73 A.D. 2d 521, N.Y.S. 2d 407 (1979).
21. 9-13 (6th Ed, 1931).
22. *Hayward v. Holiday Inns, Inc.,* 459 F. Supp. 634 (ED Va. 1978).
23. *Butterfield v. Forrestor,* 11 East 60, 103 Eng. Rep. 926 (1809).
24. Sherry, *supra.*
25. *Connolly v. Nicollet Hotel,* 254 Minn. 373, 95 N.W. 2d 657 (1959).
26. 347 So. 2d 1100 (Fla. App. No. DD-199) (July 1977).
27. *Simon v. Cunard,* 75 A.D. 2d 283, 428 N.Y.S. 2d 52 (1980).
28. *Stevenson v. Four Winds,* 462 F. 2d 899 (5th Cir. 1972).
29. *Guadagno v. Diamond,* 89 Misc. 2d 697, 423 N.Y.S. 2d 783 (1976).
30. Klakis, *supra.*

31. *Gross v. Sweet,* 49 N.Y. 2d 102, 424 N.Y.S. 2d 365, 400 N.E. 2d 306 (1979).
32. Klakis, *supra.*
33. 46 USC 183 b.
34. *Owens v. Ilatalia,* 70 Misc. 2d 719, 334 N.Y.S. 2d 789 (1972).
35. *Kirkman v. Shaw Cross,* 101 Eng. Rep. 410, 6 East 519 (King's Bench (1794).
36. *Archibald v. Cinerama Hotel,* 73 Cal. App. 3d 152, 140 Cal. Rptr. 599 (1977).
37. *McKee v. Sheraton,* 269 F. 2d 669 (2d Cir. 1959).

14

Inn Premises Liability

A large-eyed woman wearing a full skirt and silver New Balance running shoes opened a file folder and told me that in fact Robert Rambeaux was registered at Julliard. He was taking a course in composition with a practicum in woodwinds.

"What's his address?" I said. "He still living on First Street?"

"I'm sorry, sir, it's against our policy to give out that sort of information."

"Quite right," I said. "People drive you crazy if they know where you live. A person has a right to privacy."

She smiled at me and nodded. Her hair was pulled back behind her ears and fell to her shoulders. She didn't look very old, but there were gray streaks in her hair. Premature. Probably from worrying about the rights of privacy.

Taming a Sea-Horse, Robert B. Parker

OVERVIEW

In Chapter 13 we became acquainted with legal liability at the inn and saw how legal requirements and standards can place responsibility upon inn management. In this chapter we want to expand on the topics of Chapter 13 and find out how the principles discussed there apply in specific inn situations. The cases that have gone to court because of injury and loss have been of a remarkable variety as well as quantity.

"Throughout the hospitality industry, litigation continues to mount. Although owners and managers do all they can to prevent occurrences which create lawsuits, and constantly attempt to purchase sufficient insurance to cover themselves, this is not always possible and sometimes, if possible, is too expensive," reports *Lodging Hospitality,* March 1988, p. 24.

Jury Verdict Research, Inc., an organization located at Solon, Ohio, that collects, analyzes, and reports jury verdicts throughout the nation, provides some sobering statistics about verdicts against hotels, motels, inns, and bed-and-breakfast operations. For example, over 50 percent of the verdicts obtained by plaintiffs against inns exceed $100,000. Those who sue for assaults and security violations recover 69 percent of the time. The most frequent claims arise out of slip-and-fall incidents, sexual assaults, and fires. The slip-and-fall plaintiffs are successful 56 percent of the time. Three percent of inn plaintiffs obtain verdicts of over $1 million. All in all, not a rosy liability picture for the innkeeper.

It is a simple fact of inn life that the innkeeper cannot monitor everything that all guests are doing at the inn at any given time. Perhaps it is true today that service to guests is being reduced in the industry. While the requirement of service is stressed, at least on the surface, so many other factors seem to sidetrack it. Such factors include increasing size of inns, turnover of management and employees, and staff transfers to other inns. Add to this the fact that "good service" is also "labor-intensive" and one can begin to gain some insight into why service is being reduced for guests rather than being increased. The typical manager concludes that she or he cannot support increasing service on a sound economic basis. In all of this lies a legal problem because the primary concern of the innkeeper must be guest protection.

"Because inns are places of public accommodation and are obligated by law to accept virtually everyone who presents himself or herself and asks for a room, there is no opportunity to check out the guests as to their honesty or whether they are bent on committing a crime. Therefore, the hotel has to proceed as if every guest needed protection from every other guest as well as from invitees, trespassers, and hotel employees, and then provide security accordingly.

"The occupants of an inn and those who use the facility must rely upon the innkeeper to supply their protection because they cannot avail themselves of the unusual security provided by a municipality through its police department; and the failure of the inn to meet this responsibility could render it liable in damages," *Florida Hotel & Motel News,* March, 1983, p. 26.

"While second-guessing every outcome of a legal question is impossible, maintaining a basic awareness of trends is required for effective inn management. Keeping abreast of legal issues used to be a good idea for hoteliers. Now it's essential for survival," says Sheila E. Murphy, Ph.D., Vice President, Reservations, Ramada, Inc.

Liability for Crimes at a Hotel

As a general legal rule, an innkeeper is not held liable for crimes committed by third paries which could not be anticipated. An armed robbery at the front desk which results in injury to a guest is an example. But liability may follow in the manner in which the innkeeper responds to the crime. For example, failing to respond promptly to a call for help from a guest who was raped in her room, and though bound managed to summon help on the phone, resulted in a verdict of almost $100,000. While front-desk personnel had promptly called the police, no effort was made to enter the room and assist the victim. Instead, inn personnel remained outside the room until the police arrived, listening to the cries for help from the guest within, *Boles v. La Quinta Motor Inns*, 680 F. 2d 1077 (Texas, 1982).

Connie Francis Case

In this case, an assault on the singer in her motel room resulted in a verdict against the Howard Johnson chain in the sum of $2.5 million for Connie Francis and $25,000 for her husband. The original award to the husband had been higher but was reduced on appeal, *Garzilli v. Howard Johnson's*, 419 F. Supp. 1210 (E.D.N.Y., 1976).

Promises of the Innkeeper

If a guest or patron is injured at the inn, a tort situation has arisen. If the innkeeper promises to pay medical bills, a contract situation has arisen. As a basic rule, it is best to withhold contract promises until there has been some determination of fault. Making contract promises before such determination may result in an inn paying for injuries that it otherwise had no legal obligation to pay. That is not usually good business.

Guest Complaints

All complaints made by guests, patrons, invitees, and others at the inn must be responded to. If it is necessary to send someone to a guest room upon receipt of a complaint, it is best to have that person accompanied by another. After the complaint is resolved, a written report must be prepared and retained by management.

Screening Daily Reports

An important daily function of the inn manager is to learn what went on at the inn in each 24-hour period. The obvious way to do this is to examine and analyze the accident reports, theft complaints, cash receipt summaries, front-desk records, and all documents that create a word picture of the preceding hours. Any item of an unusual nature or anything that raises a suspicion in the mind of the manager must be followed up at once.

Another technique used by careful innkeepers is to walk portions of the inn each day. In making daily rounds of an inn, a particular item that deserves scrutiny are railings and balconies at the property. Are the railings secure? Are they high enough? Are the spaces between upright bars large enough for an infant to crawl through?

Another important item to look for are lighting problems. Since these can be observed at night only, the walking routine must be carried out by the innkeeper at periodic times at night—or by agents who do the same thing and report the results to the innkeeper. It is a simple fact that an unreplaced burned-out bulb in a dangerous area of the inn is exactly the same as a dangerous area of the inn at which no light bulb is installed in the first instance.

The faulty areas which are observed, or those matters that might cause legal problems in the future, must be relayed to the proper persons so that corrective or preventative action may be taken promptly.

That is not enough, however, from a legal point of view since it may later become impossible in court to prove that what was in fact ordered had actually been done. An answer to this is for the innkeeper to supplement the "walking routine" with a daily "walking log" in which the facts are recorded. It need not be a treatise but should contain dates, times, items observed, orders given, and the time of completion of corrections, and it should be maintained as a permanent record.

An adjunct to walking inspections of the inn premises is an idea that has sound basis in psychology. It has to do with learning the names of as many employees as possible and greeting them by name on the walking tours. The morale lift of a room-attendant supervisor, who is having a difficult morning, is easy to understand when the passing innkeeper greets her by name. It is a management technique worth considering and it has legal overtones that give it substance. For example, knowing names would assist in convincing a jury that the innkeeper did use reasonable care at the inn.

Outside Inspections

In addition to the innkeeper's walking routine, it would be wise to ask a member of the local police force to go along on such a walk. That person should be asked for recommendations which in turn should be documented and then acted on.

Inspection by Others

While the innkeepers's duty to make continuing inspection of the inn premises is widely recognized, an extension of that basic premise is developing. It has to do with inspections by others independent of the innkeeper, such as fire inspectors, health inspectors, insurance experts, and others. While such "invited inspections" can be expensive, they may uncover potential problems at the property in question. Records should be made of these inspections, and all potentially dangerous matters related to them must be timely corrected. Calling in a professional inspection firm to check elevators, safety at the pool, security at the inn generally, and security at the front desk can lead to the reduction of guest losses in the areas inspected.

On the other hand, it must always be remembered that inspections by outsiders will not change the basic "delegation" rule of innkeeping law.

INABILITY OF INNS TO DELEGATE LEGAL RESPONSIBILITY FOR LOSSES

While it is well established that inns cannot escape legal responsibility by claiming delegation to others, such as Otis Company to care for elevators, or Westinghouse to care for escalators, there is another safeguard available. The technique is to require such companies to agree to carry indemnity insurance to cover the inn should it be held liable for injury, losses, or death.

Leaving our discussion of innkeeper's practices, it becomes necessary to expand on topics introduced in Chapter 13. These include negligence, gross negligence, *prima facie* negligence, negligence per se, assumption of the risk, contributory negligence, comparative negligence, house rules, disclaimers, waivers, and releases. After our examination of these topics, we will then look to specific items as they relate to liability at the inn.

Negligence

The concept of negligence developed in the courts over many centuries. Today it forms the principal ground for recovery under the legal doctrine of "tort." Its most common form is found in the failure of the offending person to use ordinary, reasonable care, taking into consideration foreseeability.

As it is found in our courts, negligence can assume many forms. It can be "active"–doing something that one should not have done; "passive"–failing to do something that one should have done; "gross"–carelessness that is severe; "slight"–something of lesser impact; "*prima facie*"–enough carelessness to require one to explain; "per se"–an act that is identified by a court as being negligence in itself; "contributory"–carelessness that feeds off of carelessness; and "comparative"–negligence that is weighed against other carelessness.

In addition, the doctrines of "assumption of the risk" and "proximate cause" also enter the picture where they are applicable and can affect or even cancel out the above types, classes, or forms of negligence.

Prima Facie Rule of Negligence

Under this doctrine, the injury to a guest or the loss of a guest's property raises only a presumption of negligence. Presumptions can be rebutted (contested) in court and if this happens they are thus destroyed if the evidence is sufficient. This leaves the innkeeper free of legal liability. The doctrine of *prima facie* negligence has been adopted by court decision in some states, *Asseltyne v. Fat Hotel*, 222 Minn. 91, 23 N.W. 2d 357 (1946), and by statutes in others, *Faucett v. Nichols*, 64 N.Y. 377 (1876). In both court decisions and statutes, the reason advanced for the use of the doctrine is that it reduces the harshness of the ancient insurer's liability of innkeepers, and the harshness of the more recent (1809) doctrine of contributory negligence.

As the example of the adoption of this doctrine by court action early in this century, the state of Indiana rejected the common-law concept of insurer's liability and substituted in its place that of "*prima facie* liability." Under this doctrine, the innkeeper has the opportunity to convince the jury that the loss was not due to fault of the inn, *Treichlinger v. French Lick Springs Hotel*, 196 Mo. 686, 102 S.W. 101 (1917).

When a state adopts the "*prima facie* rule," as did Indiana, it also has an effect on "contributory negligence."

Contributory Negligence

As mentioned previously, this doctrine had its birth in the rather infamous case of *Butterfield v. Forrester,* 11 East 60, 103 Eng. Rep. 926 (1809). A more recent example appears in a case where a guest in a Nebraska inn, who had been there three days, stopped at the front desk. Close to the front desk was a double set of glass doors which the guest walked into, breaking the glass door and causing injury to his nose. This happened because one of the double doors would open but the other was kept locked. The court that heard the case agreed that the inn was negligent in locating the glass doors so close to the front desk. Yet the court held that the contributory negligence of the guest was a complete bar and the inn was exonerated from liability, *Karna v. Byron Reed,* 374 F. Supp. 687 (Nebraska, 1974).

This legal doctrine has now been refined in many states by that of comparative negligence. Under this doctrine, the jury is allowed to determine the percent of negligence that should be attributed to the plaintiff and the innkeeper.

To Illustrate

Guest X is injured at the inn and the jury finds as part of its verdict that the injury should be compensated by the payment of $100,000. The jury further finds that the negligence was 70 percent the innkeeper's and 30 percent the guest's. Examine Figure 14.1. The innkeeper thus has a defense as to $30,000 but is obligated by the verdict to pay $70,000. (Under the 1809 rule of contributory negligence, the guest would have been completely barred from recovery.)

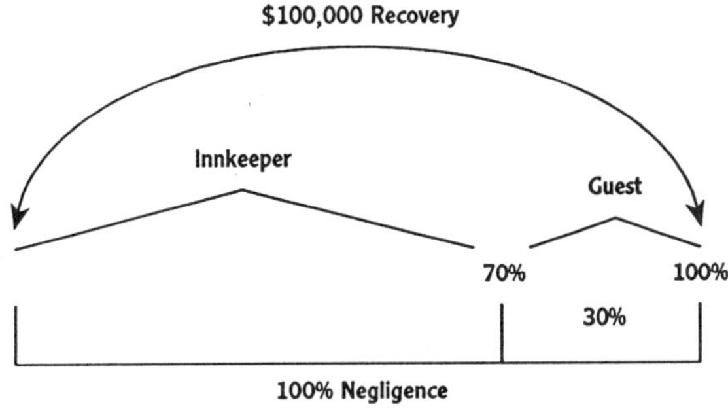

FIGURE 14.1

Comparative Negligence

As in illustration of comparative negligence in action in New Mexico, see the slip-and-fall case in which a delivery man at a restaurant was held to be 25 percent negligent, his employer 5 percent negligent, and the restaurant 70 percent negligent. The award was $1.5 million, which meant that the restaurant had to pay 70 percent of that sum, *Wilkins v. Truck Stop of America*, U.S. District Court (New Mexico, 1986).

There are two variations of the comparative negligence doctrine. The first is the "pure form" which is illustrated by the New Mexico case above as well as Figure 14.1. Other states that follow the pure form include California, Florida, and New York to mention a few. The second variation is the "50–50" form.

"Fifty Percent Form"

Here, if the jury finds that the negligence is equal, or finds that the negligence of the plaintiff exceeds that of the defendant, no recovery is allowed to the plaintiff. Oregon follows this rule, *Dutch Properties, Inc. v. Pac-Sam, Inc.*, 778 P. 2D 969 (Oregon, 1989), as does Idaho and Illinois. In Idaho, a non-party to a lawsuit may be included in a jury verdict for purposes of the percentages, but that party will not have to pay any portion of the judgment.

A specialized form of negligence which reaches a result different than contributory and comparative negligence, is "negligence per se." What this legal doctrine does is establish standards that must be met by the innkeeper under penalty of legal liability if such standards are not met.

Negligence Per Se

If a state statute requires an inn manager to do a certain act or acts, then failure to do so could be negligence per se. In addition, the HRI industry may have industry standards that also place demands on inns in the same areas covered by the statute. Failure to meet industry standards would be held by a court to be negligence—but not negligence per se. Thus, the inn manager faces a possible two-edged sword of legal liability: negligence per se on one edge and ordinary negligence on the other. If either becomes the proximate cause of loss to a guest, responsibility will follow.

The use of negligence per se in practice means that only the noncompliance of the statute must be proven by the plaintiff. There is no need for the plaintiff to prove that there was also further negligence. Thus the two-edged sword can cut on both edges—or it may cut only on one.

Illustrating the acceptance of statutory regulations as the legal standard to be applied is a Florida situation which was eventually settled out of court. A building code required that uprights on hotel balconies be no more than eight inches apart. The hotel had been constructed with balcony upright distances over eight inches but less than nine inches. A child fell through one of the spaces and the hotel settled for over $1.7 million, the claim being that there was negligence per se on behalf of the inn. The case had been tried before a jury, but was settled before a verdict was returned, *Carranna v. Eades,* 466 So. 2d 259 (Florida, 1985).

Once an HRI unit has violated a statute that applies to it, overcoming the presumption that the violation caused the loss or injury that resulted is extremely difficult. That presumption will be upheld unless heavy evidence is introduced to overcome it. In the Florida balcony case, the inn felt that it could not overcome this presumption and chose to settle out of court.

The doctrine can arise in not one, but two ways:

1. The action taken at the inn violates a statute or ordinance.
2. The action taken was so removed from what an ordinary reasonable person would have expected, that there is no question that a prudent person would not have acted that way.

This makes it a matter of law for the judge, *Whitehead v. Ramada,* 529 S.W. 2d. 366 (Kentucky 1975).

One instance when a court may not allow the doctrine of negligence per se to come into operation is when a satisfactory explanation is given that explains why the statute in question was not followed. In that instance, assuming the explanation is accepted by the court, the doctrine will not be applied. In the absence of such explanation, it will be.

A few locales in the United States do not yet require that smoke detectors be placed in each inn room, and thus the failure to provide them would not give rise to negligence per se. Yet it is an industry standard today to install them and failure to do so would be negligence. This double legal trap is difficult to overcome. The best way to avoid it, of course, is compliance not only with statutes and ordinances, but with industry standards as well.

If state or local laws provide for steps that must be taken in regard to lighting, failure to meet these requirements could be held by a court to be negligence per se.

If a statute says that a lifeguard must be provided at inn pools, failure to provide one would be negligence per se.

Negligence per se is encountered in other areas of law, such as at hospitals. The *National Law Journal*, October 28, 1985, reported the following: "A court can find negligence as a matter of law for an obvious violation of the standard of care required, the Supreme Court of Montana held Sept. 12."

> In *Rudeck v. Wright*, 84-84, Alfred Rudeck died as a result of complications arising from a length of surgical gauze left in his abdomen after a hernia operation. The trial court found that the doctor was negligent as a matter of law. Observing that if a foreign body is mistakenly left in a patient's body it takes no expert medical testimony to establish that the surgeon was negligent, [thus,] the high court adopted the negligence per se rule and held that there was no error.

Related to the law of negligence is the old common-law defense of assumption of the risk. The name of this doctrine describes what its office has been for centuries. It is now in its period of demise, however.

Assumption of the Risk

In more and more jurisdictions, with Louisiana serving as an example, the common-law doctrine of "assumption of the risk" is being replaced with the comparative negligence doctrine. This change replaces a complete bar to recovery for an injured person with a more humane principle that says "compare the fault of both parties and require them to pay their share in the loss." In Louisiana, the assumption of the risk rule has now been eliminated, *Murray v. Ramada*, 521 So. 2d 1123 (Louisiana, 1988).

Assumption of the risk and contributory negligence, which are solid legal defenses in many cases, are not available when children are injured at the inn. Also, one cannot assume a risk that one is not aware of, *Hooks v. Sheraton*, 578 F. 2d 313 (District of Columbia, 1977).

A final legal doctrine becomes involved in inn premises liability cases.

Proximate Cause

"Proximate cause" has been defined as " . . . that cause, which is natural and continuous sequence, unbroken by an intervening cause, [that] produces an injury that would not otherwise have occurred." It must be established by the plaintiff in premises liability cases and its absence will be a bar to the plaintiff's case. Examine Figure 14.2.

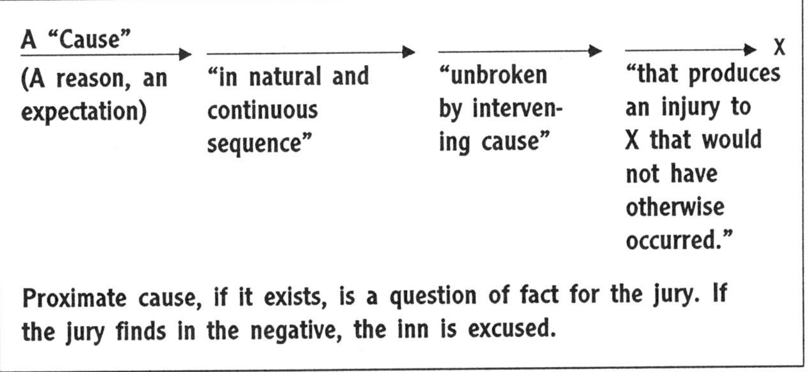

FIGURE 14.2

With this background of the law of negligence and common-law defenses and doctrines, it next becomes useful to see how the law plays such an active role in all aspects of inn operations. Numerous facilities are available at an inn, such as guest rooms, parking garages, swimming pools, game rooms, exercise rooms, restaurants, bars, and other facilities. The traveler who has become a guest will assume that everything offered to her or him is safe to use, of good quality, and will not cause harm.

A place to begin is with balconies. These have been popular in inn construction in the recent past but a look at current inn construction will disclose that they have fallen into disfavor.

Balconies

In a Mississippi case, a woman conventioneer became intoxicated at an inn and fell over the rail of a balcony, resulting in severe injuries. Since it was established at trial that the railing was eight inches lower than called for by the building code, the inn settled the part of the case that was based on the low rail. The Mississippi Supreme Court pointed out that had this railing been the proper height, the conventioneer would have recovered nothing.

Five inn balcony fall deaths occurred in Florida in 1986, and prompted the legislature of that state to enact a "balcony bill."

Florida's "Balcony Bill"

During certain times of the year, many inns in Florida experience a rash of disorderly conduct by visitors to that state. Such has resulted in many falls, elevator related injuries, and death. This legislation allows innkeepers who believe that disorderly conduct could lead to death or injury, to take the offending person into custody and hold him or her for "a reasonable time" until the police arrive. The "disorderly conduct" includes corruption of morals, disturbance of peace and quiet, and acts that may "outrage public decency." Jail penalties are provided, and innkeepers and police are provided immunity from liability for acting under the bill.

Elevators and Escalators

If elevators and escalators are maintained by the companies that install them, can the innkeeper escape liability for death or injury caused by their use? The U.S. Court of Appeals for the Fifth Circuit has answered that question in the negative. The escalator in question connected the third floor of the inn with the lobby. At trial it was determined that the escalator created an "unreasonable risk of injury to others." The judge who wrote the opinion said ". . . a hotel keeper who draws a benefit from escalators, and has custody for purposes of strict liability, cannot escape liability when things go wrong by delegation of responsibility," *Blansit v. Hyatt Corp.*, 874 F. 2d 1015 (Louisiana, 1989).

While the hotel cannot escape liability by delegation, it nevertheless should have had an agreement with Westinghouse, the company that installed and maintained the escalator, to hold the hotel harmless for injuries resulting from use of the escalator. In New York state, the law allows inns to use such a contract clause with those who maintain elevators and escalators. In a case in Manhattan where a woman fell while departing an elevator that was not level with the floor, a jury found the inn 80 percent negligent, the maintenance company 20 percent negligent, and awarded the sum of $250,000. While New York state recognizes that the innkeeper's duty as to elevators is nondelegable, the above clause allowed the inn to recover $50,000 from the maintenance company.

Entertainment at the Inn

At Harrah's Hotel in Reno, Nevada, singer Paul Revere closed his show by throwing paper hats to the audience. While reaching for a hat, a spectator on an upper level fell and injured a woman below. Her suit against the hotel, for more than $450,000, resulted in a jury verdict in favor of the guest and her husband. The theory was that by allowing items to be thrown to an audience, a dangerous and negligent situation had been created.

At a Massachusetts club, a rock band placed dishes of flash powder, which were ignited as part of their performance, along the edge of the stage. An audience member thought these dishes were ash trays and while attempting to put out a cigarette before the show caused the powder to explode, burning his face. Not hearing anything from the injured person, the club failed to notify its insurance company. About six months later, the injured person filed suit and the insurance company denied coverage because it had not been told of the injury ". . . as soon as practical," as required by the policy. The Massachusetts Court of Appeals upheld the dismissal of the insurance company, leaving the inn to face liability alone, *Powell v. Fireman's Fund*, 529 N.E. 2d 1228 (Massachusetts, 1988).

Hotel Basketball Courts

A small amount of sand on the hotel basketball court caused a guest to fall, with resulting injuries. A verdict of $55,000 was overturned on appeal because the hotel had been able to show that it exercised reasonable care in maintaining the surface of the court. If the proof had not been offered, the verdict would have been upheld, *Ginsberg v. Levbourne Realty*, 298 N.Y.S. 2d 80 (New York, 1969). The courts will hold the inn to the duty of using reasonable care when the inn supplies courts and equipment for use by its guests and invitees. Such duty is greater if children use the facilities, *Dillon v. Keatington Racketball Club*, 390 N.W. 2d 212 (Michigan, 1986).

Part of the entertainment furnished to guests and invitees at many inns across the nation includes weight and exercise rooms. If such are to be offered, adequate supervision must be provided; instructions in the use of equipment must be given; regular inspections must be carried out; and the instructions of the manufacturers of the equipment must be strictly followed. These guidelines were laid down in *Burkhardt v. Health & Tennis Corp.*, 730 S.W. 2d 367 (Texas, 1987).

Fire Laws

Perhaps the strictest fire code ever adopted has now been enacted in Clark County, Nevada, where the former MGM Grand Hotel is located. This code provides that in all buildings that rise higher than 55 feet above the lowest fire department access, automatic sprinkler systems must be installed in all exit corridors, and each guest room must be protected by at least one sprinkler head. It also provides for the installation of automatic sprinklers in the building's basement if the entire floor area exceeds 1,500 square feet or any portion of the basement which is more than 75 feet from an opening.

This code also provides more stringent standards regarding the air supply to guest rooms. Supplying air to guests' rooms from the exit corridors is prohibited, and openings between guests' rooms and exit corridors must be sealed unless: (1) approved smoke detectors are installed at specified spacing, fire dampers are installed in the air vents, and the activation of the corridor smoke detectors automatically causes the air supply system for the corridors to stop and the fire dampers to close; or (2) an approved smoke and fire damper is installed in an approved manner in the corridor; or (3) the entire building has an automatic sprinkler system.

In addition, the code states that there must be a voice communication system that is at least a one-way communications system to the guest rooms, public assembly areas, exit corridors, and stairways. There are also standards on emergency lighting, exit illumination, fire alarm systems without manual delays, and self-closing devices on doors. Other provisions include certain posting requirements with which hotels must strictly comply.

All fire liability insurance policies provide a time period within which the carrier must be notified before the liability of the carrier becomes fixed. In law, such a provision is known as a "condition precedent." If the insured meets the condition, the obligation of the insurance company becomes fixed. If the condition is not met, all contractual obligations of the insurance company cease and the policyholder is thus uninsured as to that occurrence. Some policies set a specific time period, such as "30 days." Others are more general with notice being required "as soon as practical."

In purchasing inn insurance, it is essential to distinguish "actual loss" from "replacement cost." A dishwasher in the restaurant destroyed by a short-circuit fire may have an actual value of $2,000 as of the day of the fire. The replacement cost may in fact be $5,000. The importance of the choice of words in the insurance policy is obvious.

In Michigan, if an inn guest negligently causes a fire loss, that person cannot be charged with the amount of the loss. The reasoning of the courts there is that the sum charged for the room includes some proportional part of the fire insurance policy. Thus the guest is covered for his or her negligent act in setting the fire, just as if the fire policy had been issued in his or her name, *Wausau v. Underwriter's Ins. Co. v. Crook,* 455 N.W. 2d 309 (Michigan, 1990). "Attention is called to *Faucett v. Nichols* 64 N.Y. 377 (1876), involving the application of a statute absolving an innkeeper for the loss of a guest's property by reason of an incendiary fire, wherein the court stated that a negligent act which preceded and facilitated the crime of incendiarism was as much within the statute as a negligent failure to remove and protect the property of a guest after the fire had started."

The federal fire code is called the Federal Fire Prevention and Control Act of 1974, and is found in 15 USC, section 2201, *et seq.* It is administered by the U.S. Fire Administration.

Related to the legal duty to use reasonable care in the operation of the inn is the duty to make certain that the physical surroundings are safe for use. Thus, even though an innkeeper uses reasonable care in the operation of the inn, and even though the innkeeper warns of known dangers as well as those that may arise, there is another area of law that may make the innkeeper liable. It is known as the "implied warranty," and is often seen in furniture liability cases.

Furniture

To illustrate: The inn provides chairs for use at the side of the inn swimming pool. Management was careful in the purchase of the chairs and asked professional advice in purchasing them. Once the chairs arrived at the inn, and after they were placed in use, management made it a point to check them from time to time. The ones that needed it were repaired and those chairs that could not be repaired were replaced.

A guest at the inn sat down on a chair which fell apart, causing severe injuries to the guest. A lawsuit followed. The court which heard the case admitted that there was no negligence on the part of the innkeeper which could have caused the injury. Thus, there was no tort liability.

On the other hand, the court said that a guest at an inn should not be held to the duty of inspecting a chair upon which he or she was about to sit. The court held that there was a breach of the "implied warranty" that the chair was suitable to use. Thus, there was contract liability even though there was no tort liability, *Schnitzer v. Nixon and Heath, d/b/a/Cavalier Manor Motel,* 439 F. 2d 940 (Virginia, 1971).

In a Georgia case, a restaurant patron sat down in a chair and the wicker covering of the chair gave way, causing the guest to fall into the chair itself. The court held the restaurant liable on the grounds that an inspection would have disclosed the deterioration of the wicker, *Gary Hotel Courts, Inc. v. Perry,* 2515 E. 2d 37 (Georgia, 1978).

Care must be exercised to make certain furniture purchased for the inn is flameproof, solidly constructed, and otherwise acceptable to be used by guests who obtain the inn room for the night. A special reason for this is that the courts will allow advertisements of inns to be shown to the jury to assist them in determining what standard of quality and care was offered by the inn to potential guests. Such ads almost always show rooms and furniture. That displayed quality would then become a standard to be used in measuring the loss caused by the injury that resulted, *Tobin v. Slutsky*, 506 F. 2d 1097 (2d Cir. 1974).

From time to time, chairs do collapse in restaurants and tumble patrons to the floor. If the chair was in the restaurants' custody (easy enough to prove), if the chair had a defect (easy enough to prove), and if the defect caused injury to the patron, the restaurant is going to have to pay, *Perkins v. Rick's*, 514 So. 2d 180 (Louisiana, 1987).

Glass

In a Missouri case, a small boy slipped on wet tile and fell through the plate glass in the sliding door in the inn room. The jury allocated the fault at 40 percent to Howard Johnson Company and 60 percent to the franchisee. The youth was given $600,000, the mother $100,000, and the awards were upheld on appeal. Evidence was used at the trial to show that when the inn had been built in the 1960s, it was known in the industry that the use of plate glass instead of safety glass was unreasonably dangerous, *Jenkins v. McLean Hotels, Inc.*, 859 F. 2d 598 (Missouri, 1988). Related to the plate glass problem is a new doctrine of law known as the "open space illusion."

Open expanses of glass raise a legal problem in that guests and others may walk into them and be injured. Children have run into such expanses of glass and have been injured severely or killed. Consideration should be given to the installation of safety glass instead of plate glass. The latter breaks upon contact while the former does not. A second point is that such open expanses of glass could have wooden bars placed across them to break the open space illusion. A third idea is that such glass areas could have decals placed on them to alert guests to the fact that the glass is there. Another possibility is to arrange furniture so as to turn foot traffic away from the glass. A statute in Minnesota requires that open expanses of glass be marked in some manner to prevent persons from walking into them, *Peterson v. Haule, d/b/a/ Chisholm Dairy Queen*, 230 N.W. 2d 51 (Minnesota, 1975).

In the absence of a statute such as Minnesota's, an injured guest can still proceed on the common-law theory of negligence for allowing the open space illusion to exist in the first instance, *Waugh v. Duke,* 248 F. Supp. 626 (1960). Glass panels should never be located in places where guests and patrons are likely to turn into them. Such a space becomes a dangerous area in the inn, *Karna v. Reed,* 374 F. Supp. 687 (1974).

Lights

Lights of proper intensity must be in place and kept operable at all times of darkness. Many interior stairs at the inn should be kept lighted 24 hours a day, and it is almost always a good idea to keep the front-desk area constantly lighted. Room corridors should be lit with high-efficiency fluorescent bulbs; public areas should be in a warm white fluorescent; stairwells in cool white; and baths in high-quality fluorescent white. Using improper lighting may lead to the claim that the insufficient lighting caused some loss that can be tied to it.

Or, worse yet, failure to replace lights which becomes the proximate cause of injuries can lead to even greater losses. The Rappaport case in Chapter 1 is an example. In this case it must be remembered that the injured guest was attempting to reach her "temporary home-away-from home" at the time that the injury occurred. She had every right to have been making the attempt because, as the judge who wrote the opinion observed, "her only alternative was to stay in her car until daylight before attempting to proceed to her room." The judge did not feel that this alternative was consistent with the circumstances. Thus the failure to adequately light and keep lit the access way from the parking lot to her room comes into sharp focus. Was this failure the proximate cause of her injury? A jury is likely to think so at trial.

The jury must also determine if Mrs. Rappaport was guilty of contributory negligence provided the case is tried in a contributory negligence state. This factor could bar her from recovery. If the case is tried in a comparative negligence state, then the percentage of Mrs. Rappaport's negligence, if any, would be decided by the jury and her dollar award reduced accordingly.

In a Myrtle Beach, South Carolina, case, a guest returned to the inn after dark and no lights were on in the area where his room was located. After using his car lights to allow access to his family, he started toward the room and fell over a rock. The summary judgment granted by the trial court was reversed on appeal, the court holding that there was a breach of the duty of the inn to ". . . provide sufficient illumination to enable a guest to use the walkway in safety," *Bowling v. Lewis*, 261 F. 2d 311 (South Carolina, 1958).

If adequate lighting is in place but is not turned on, liability can still follow. A restaurant patron entered a room marked "rest rooms" in which she found herself in darkness. As she felt for a light switch, she fell down a flight of stairs. The trial court dismissed the case because of her contributory negligence. On appeal, the Pennsylvania Supreme Court reversed that decision and sent the matter back for a jury trial holding that "Those entering a dark toilet room to which they are invited cannot be adjudged negligent as a matter of law," *McNally v. Liebowitz*, 445 A 2d 716 (Pennsylvania, 1982).

The duties to provide adequate lighting can extend off the premises in some cases. An example of this is where the parking lot requires that a public road be crossed to leave the parking lot and return to it. In a New Jersey case, liability attached to a restaurant where two invitees were struck by an auto while crossing the road, killing one and severely injuring the other. The inadequate lighting was held to be the cause of the death and injuries, *Warrington v. Bird*, 499 A 2d 1026 (New Jersey, 1985).

Pests and Vermin

Bees in a hotel room that caused a guest to slip and fall in the shower resulted in a $48,000 verdict against the inn, *Brasseaux v. Stand-By Corp.*, 402 So. 2d 140 (Louisiana, 1981). To see how certain inns in Kentucky warn guests of pest and vermin problems, see Figure 14.3.

When purchasing an inn, it is essential that the buyer include a provision in the purchase contract that will make the eradication of pests and vermin the responsibility of the seller. Otherwise, the buyer may find himself or herself facing the liability that would go with a pest and vermin infested inn.

Phones

While there are no existing laws that require that inns provide guest room telephones, it is still good inn policy to have them available in the lobby, in the public rooms, in each guest room,

Dear Guest,

Due to the fact that this Inn is situated in a rural setting, we occasionally have hard shell beetles fly in from outside, and also have grasshoppers.

They are completely harmless, and although similar in appearance, they are not cockroaches.

We service this Inn on a regular basis, for your comfort and peace of mind.

Thank you for understanding.

Lynn Jacobs
Southern Exterminators

FIGURE 14.3

and perhaps in the elevators as well. Such phones should be accompanied by decals giving a reminder of the 911 emergency number. The installation of such phones would be evidence of reasonable care, just as their absence might be looked at as a lack of reasonable care.

Two phone-related legal problems follow: One has to do with guests making calls to others outside of the inn, and the other has to do with outsiders who are calling to talk to guests at the inn. In the first situation, the privacy laws apply to records of calls made from the inn by guests. Such records should not be released except upon a court order or a search warrant. Guests have the protection of the Fourth Amendment while staying at the inn.

The privacy laws and the Fourth Amendment also apply to the second situation and that has to do with the location of the guest at the inn. Care must be utilized to protect the privacy of that location. For example, a call that requests the room number of Guest X should be replied to with a refusal to grant that request. On the other hand, a phone inquiry about whether or not Guest X is at the inn should be answered in the affirmative. To deny that a guest is present might lead to other legal problems since it would be a falsehood.

An incoming call that requests that a specific room number be called can be responded to safely, as would an incoming call which says "Guest X is staying at your inn. Would you please ring his room." But in the last two instances, the room number should be protected. Let the guests give out their room numbers if they choose to do so–the innkeeper must not be the one to do it.

Records

The publication *Hospitality Law* offered the following advice in reference to the time periods during which inn records should be maintained: "A night auditor, wondering about possible tax problems, recently asked *Hospitality Law* how long it was necessary to keep business records because they had become a storage problem.

"The Internal Revenue Service (IRS) is allowed to go back three years, unless the organization alleges returns are fraudulent. In that case the IRS can go back as far as it wants to. The latter situation is going to be very unusual, the Helmsley case being the exception.

"Several accountants told *Hospitality Law* that it largely depends on how cautious the innkeeper is. For some reason, many corporations retain records for seven years. A number of accountants acknowledged that custom but indicated that four years is probably sufficient. In many instances records are recapped in other records, and in many instances the recap is sufficient. Call the hotel's accountant or lawyer when particular factors may create an unusual situation."

Slip-and-Fall

As the statistics provided by Jury Verdict Research, Inc. tell us (see page 290), one of the most common causes of liability at the inn is the "slip-and-fall" or some variation of it. Such variations include the "trip-and-fall," the "step-up-and-fall-backward," the "step-forward, fall-downward," and "the abrupt-fall-off."

More than 3 million Americans are victims of falls each year. Of these, more than 12,000 die from the injuries sustained in the falls. Many of these occur at inns on floors that have some slippery substance on them. It is not the presence of such substances that gives rise to legal liability but the negligence in allowing such substances to remain. If there is grease on a stairwell and it is allowed to remain there until someone slips on it and falls, the inn must pay for the injuries that result, *Ashley v. Oclean*, 518 So. 2d 943 (Florida, 1987).

In inn bars, the most common fall injuries are caused by slip-and-fall or step-out-and-fall-down cases. Poor lighting often contributes to this, as well as unremoved slippery substances and even the failure to turn on lights.

There are areas at the inn where spills or leaks result in slippery floors. Such a condition is aggravated if the floor is made of tile. A solution is to post someone to watch over such areas. If the posted employee sees that a dangerous situation has occurred, such as the fall of butter from a room-service tray, that person must respond immediately, *McGinnis v. Sunbelt*, 326 S.E. 2d 3 (Georgia, 1985).

In some slip-trip cases, the guest or patron involved does not in fact fall, but catches him or herself in such a violent manner that injury still results. The legal consequences to the inn could well be the same as if the fall had in fact been concluded.

What if a nondefective product, such as soap sold by Georgia Pacific to the inn, leaks onto the floor, is not cleaned up, and slip-and-fall results? Is the inn liable? Is the inn entitled to contribution from Georgia Pacific? In a Florida case, the court said "yes" to the first question and "no" to the second, leaving the inn responsible for a verdict of over $1 million, *Georgia Pacific Corp. v. Reid*, 501 So. 2d 653 (Florida, 1990).

In humid parts of the nation, fallen leaves that become wet may result in liability for a slip-and-fall caused by them, *Luxen v. Holiday Inn, Inc.*, 566 F. Supp. 1484 (Missouri, 1983).

Once a slippery condition, such as leaking water from an ice machine, or food dropped from room-service trays, comes into being on stairs, a common-law duty arises to correct that situation at once. If maintenance personnel leave work on Friday and do not come back until Monday and a slip-and-fall occurs in between, the inn is going to be held liable, *Lorio v. San Antonio Inn*, 454 So. 2d 864 (Louisiana, 1984).

A variety of other substances and conditions often result in liability, including wet stairs, *Lorio v. San Antonio Inn, supra;* drippings from a grill, *Wilkins v. Truck Stops of America*, United States District Court, New Mexico (1986); butter spilled from a plate of sauteed mushrooms, *McGinnis v. Sunbelt*, 326 S.E. 2d 3 (Georgia, 1985); accumulation of water and sand around a beach shower in front of the inn, *Taylor v. Tolbert*, 439 So. 2d 991 (Florida, 1983), and many other situations.

Once a fall occurs at the inn, care must be exercised as to what is said or promised to the injured person. A patron leaving a restaurant in a Georgia town tripped, fell, and suffered serious injuries. The restaurant manager told her at the scene "to get medical care and we will pay the costs." The medical bills reached $3,000 and the restaurant refused to pay, claiming that the promise was "naked": unsupported by consideration and thus unenforceable.

The Georgia Appeals Court felt otherwise, holding that the restaurant gained a benefit from the promise in the form of good will and that the question of liability was for a jury to decide, *Folk's Inc. v. Dobbs*, 352 S.E. 2d 212 (Georgia, 1986). In the Folk's, Inc., case, what started out as a tort matter also wound up as a breach of contract. That gives the injured person two ways to seek recovery.

A legal defense in trip-and-fall cases is that of "trivial defects." In a California Tort Claims Act case the court dismissed the suit on the grounds that the claim was "trivial" and not covered by the California statute, *Ursino v. Big Boy*, 237 Cal. Rptr. 413 (California, 1987). The California law permits a court (judge) to decide if what caused an injury was "trivial" or "substantial," thus making it a matter of law and not one of fact for a jury.

Snow and Ice

Special inn policies must be developed to be used in inclement weather. Conversely, it is essential that such policies be implemented with precision and authority when the inclement weather arrives. To have a policy, but not place it into effective use, is an actionable form of negligence.

Subtle variations of legal rules find their way into inn operations. Examples are those situations in which an innkeeper recognizes a legal obligation, takes action to correct the problem, and then discontinues that action before the situation is resolved. For example, during a heavy snowfall, an inn had personnel shovel snow and ice from the walkways from the time that the snow started until 10:00 P.M. At that time the employees were told to go home.

After the snow and ice removal was discontinued, a guest slipped and fell and was severely injured. The court ruled that the discontinuance was negligence. The jury found that the negligence was the proximate cause of the injury to the guest, and the inn had to pay for the losses sustained, *Robinson v. Paul*, 248 F. Supp. 632 (District of Columbia, 1965).

In an Indiana case involving a slip-and-fall on ice and snow at a restaurant, the judge read the following instruction to the jury on behalf of the plaintiff: "The duty of the owner or operator of a business that is open to the public is to exercise reasonable care in keeping that part of the sidewalk in proper condition for the passage of customers rightfully using it." This instruction was challenged by the defendant but was upheld on appeal, *Poe v. Tate*, 315 N.E. 2d 392 (Indiana, 1974).

Illinois is one of a very few states that absolve an innkeeper from liability for slip-and-falls due to a "natural accumulation of snow and ice." On the other hand, in that state if some *other* condition accompanied the slip-and-fall, such as lack of adequate lighting, the courts will allow a jury to determine the proximate cause of the fall, *Weber v. Chen Enterprises, Inc.*, 540 N.E. 2d 957 (Illinois, 1989).

Resort hotels that maintain ski areas have also had their share of liability cases. A 1978 Vermont case involved a resort that advertised its ski runs as being "fairway-like trails." The resort was held liable for over $1 million for injuries sustained by a skier who hit an obstruction on a ski run and became a quadriplegic, *Sundday v. Stratton*, 390 A. 2d 398 (Vermont, 1978). Some states responded to the Sunday case by enacting laws to relieve ski operators of ski liability.

Inns in ski areas have been held liable for failing to maintain sidewalks high enough to keep toboggans away from obstructions on a toboggan run, *Bazzdlo v. Placid March Co.*, 422 F. 2d 842 (New York, 1970); for failing to properly operate a ski lift, *Trigg v. City and County of Denver*, 784 F. 2d 1058 (Colorado, 1986); and for allowing sharp roots to protrude through the snow on a ski run, *Brewer v. Ski Lift, Inc.*, 762 P. 2d 226 (Montana, 1988).

Stairs and Handrails

A Kentucky Ramada Inn had three stairs leading to an outside door. A guest slipped on a substance at the top step, reached for a guard rail only to find that none existed, and was injured. The Kentucky Court of Appeals held that the Lexington Building Code required handrails on "stairs." The court held that the inn did not comply with the code, thus the new trial was ordered to be held under the doctrine of negligence per se, *Whitehead v. Ramada Inns, Inc.*, 529 S.W. 2d 366 (Kentucky, 1975).

Oregon law holds that three stairs or less do not have to have handrails. In a fall case at a restaurant at Corvallis, a patron descended four steps to a landing, which then had two steps leading downward in a different direction. It was at the two steps that she fell. The Uniform Building of Corvallis requires handrails for stairways but exempts stairways that have less than four risers. The court viewed the double set of stairs as being separate, thus finding for the restaurant, *McNamara v. The Night Deposit, Inc.*, 659 P. 2d 440 (Oregon, 1983).

Swimming Pools

Hospitality surveys disclose that about 85 percent of the traveling public expect the inn to have a swimming pool. The same studies disclose the fact that less than 20 percent of those surveyed actually use the pool at the inn at which they stay. In addition, in cases against inns for pool-related injuries, the costs for attorney fees for the inn may be two or three times the recovery by the plaintiff. For example, a jury award of $25,000 in a pool injury case may cost the inn $75,000 to defend.

In addition to the economics, the courts tend to favor injured pool plaintiffs. The reason is that, since the pool was provided, it is natural for guests to use it. Thus one who pays to become a guest at an inn which provides a pool will not allow the inn to claim that the guest using the pool was a trespasser, *Sweet v. Clare-Mar.*, 526 N.E. 2d 74 (Ohio, 1988); nor will a court hold that diving into a pool without checking the depth of the water is "recklessness as a matter of law," *Porter v. City of Peekskill*, 555 N.Y.S. 2d 146 (New York, 1990); a court will also not say that a swimmer should have seen a "no diving" sign located on a pool equipment door which, when closed, conceals the sign.

In the not-too-distant past, swimming pools were "deep diving" affairs but that is no longer true. Today, pools are essentially shallow places where diving is best avoided, or at least restricted. One idea is to paint the various depths in the pool different colors. The shallow end can be painted in red, the intermediate area yellow, and the balance of the pool green.

Parents may well be guilty of failure to adequately watch their children who are using the inn pool. However, that does not relieve the inn of legal liability if the negligence of the inn was the proximate cause of the injury or death. When negligent conditions at the inn are allowed to continue, that fact is relevant and the judge will allow the jury to consider it. In addition, it is a psychological fact that guests at the inn's pool tend to relax and thus become less safety-conscious.

When placing depth markers in a pool, it is essential that the symbol for feet, or the word "feet" be used. In a San Diego inn pool case, the four-foot depth was marked "4" in block numbers. A Mexican national read that "4" as "meters" and suffered severe head injuries while diving into the four-foot depth. The case against the inn was settled out of court for a substantial sum.

Self-contained breathing units and masks must be made available for use in chlorine treatment. OSHA requires that the masks be fitted for the individual worker. In addition, rubber gloves and aprons must also be used. When hypochlorite is used, it must be remembered that it is an unstable product, and water or oil which comes in contact with it can cause a chemical fire. While most states do not require lifeguards at inn pools, such as the Louisiana Sanitary Code does, more and more cities have such a requirement by ordinance. Under these local laws, not only must glass containers be prohibited at inn pools, but plastic containers as well. Only soft plastic containers should be permitted at pool side.

A television comedian once told the story of the swimming pool that had a 12 foot killer shark in it. The lifeguard said it was okay to swim in the pool since the shark was complacent. The legal question is not, however, whether the shark is in fact complacent. The legal question is whether or not the shark should be in the pool in the first place.

Water Temperature at the Inn

The courts are in agreement that water temperature at the inn should not exceed 102 degrees. Some state health departments raise that limit to 104 degrees, but that may be too high. Sediment buildup in water heaters that prevent thermostats from functioning can cause water temperatures to rise dramatically. That, in turn, can result in scalding and burns. Sediment can also close up cold water lines, resulting in a slower flow of cold water at points where it should mix with hot water to cool it. Anti-scald devices are available for inn bath and shower tub facilities. These are single-mixer control valves. What they do is ensure that the water temperature never exceeds a designated temperature.

Miscellaneous Liability Matters at the Inn

A variety of other legal matters have led to liability at the inn, including power failures that result in a fall, *Shute v. Prom Motor Hotels, Inc., supra*—although one court has ruled for the inn on that score, *Ottimo v. Posadas de Puerto Rico Associates, Inc.*, 721 F. Supp. 1499 (Puerto Rico, 1989); a bright glare off tile that obstructs the view of a guest, *Sherman v. Arno (Flamingo Hotel)*, 383 P. 2d 741 (Arizona, 1963); an unguarded drain, *Benandi v. Shoney's, Inc.*, 526 So. 2d 338 (Louisiana, 1988); an elevator fall, *Scott v. Churchill*, 15 Misc. 80 (1895); an attack on a guest while in a guestroom, *Kiefel v. Las Vegas Hacienda, Inc.*, 404 F. 2d 1163 (7th Cir.), see also *Orlando Executive Park, Inc. v. P.D.R.*, 402 So. 2d 442 (5th Cir., 1981); and injuries to a guest caused by an unsupervised revolving door, *Schubert v. Hotel Astor, Inc.*, 168 Misc. 431, 5 N.Y.S. 2d 203 (Sup. Ct., 1938).

QUESTIONS

1. Jury Verdict Research, Inc., reports that plaintiffs in slip-and-fall cases are successful over 50 percent of the time. What reasons might be suggested for this fact and what message do these reasons carry to the innkeeper?

2. The "innkeepers' delegation" rule is well established in American inn law. How would you describe this rule to someone who has no knowledge about it, using a brief example?
3. What is the legal danger to be found in making promises to those who have just suffered some injury or loss at the inn?
4. In many of the inn liability situations discussed in this chapter, the courts seem to favor the injured plaintiffs. The courts seem to be saying that ". . . it is your inn and the guest is only a temporary visitor so let's resolve legal doubts in favor of the guest." Might there be developing a new "public policy" in reference to the operation of American inns?
5. What are the dangers inherent in the use of plate glass at the inn?
6. The Illinois rule on the removal of snow and ice clearly favors the innkeeper. What reason might have prompted the courts there to have assumed this legal position? (Would the courts in Florida ever have occasion to do the same thing?)
7. What is the unfairness found in the California "trivial defects" rule where a guest at an inn suffers substantial injury because of such a trivial defect?
8. Why does the Fourth Amendment apply to a guest at an inn?
9. Can you see a similarity between painting portions of the inn pool different colors and using different-intensity light bulbs at various locations at the inn?
10. Are the court decisions discussed in this chapter pointing toward inn standards that may, in time, identify the "ideal inn"?

ENDNOTES

In this chapter, citations were left within the text itself directly following the quotes. This was done in order to allow readers to identify readily the state and the decision year of cases and better understand the newness of what is discussed.

15

Legal Rights of Innkeepers and Guests

After a while you learn to translate the vacation-folder jargon. When you read "conducive to complete relaxation," it means the place is dead. "A charming atmosphere of rustic simplicity" means no inside plumbing. "Twenty-fifth season under the same owner/management" means they haven't been able to sell the place. "Bathing nearby" means the hotel has no swimming pool. "Spacious grounds–350 acres" means you've got to walk two miles from your cottage to the dining room.

–Part Pups

OVERVIEW

The purpose of this chapter is to become acquainted with the legal rights that the law extends to innkeepers. These create a latitude within which innkeepers can operate. In addition, the law extends privileges to guests and that too will be examined.

Adjunct to HRI liability, as we discussed it in the last two chapters, are those areas of HRI management in which the law extends certain rights and privileges to the HRI manager and innkeeper.

As these rights are exercised, liability seldom flows from them because the law recognizes them as a grace or special privilege. They represent a "head room" or operating space and provide a latitude in management. They remove the worry of liability from the picture, at least in the areas covered.

At the same time, such rights often run headlong into rights enjoyed by guests and patrons. The innkeeper has the right to clean the room in the morning–and the guest has the right to occupy the room until check-out time. If the rights of one are enforced, the rights of the other are disturbed. This is understood, of course, and in practice a certain blending or balancing is expected. The careful innkeeper will see to this and avoid as much conflict as possible.

A helpful place at which to begin is with the rooms of the inn because here the legal rights of innkeepers find full measure.

DIRECT AND CONTINUING CONTROL

An innkeeper, as distinguished from a landlord, is in direct and continued control of his or her guest rooms.[1] Each room in an inn is considered to be a private room in the sole charge of the innkeeper, even while occupied by the guest. The innkeeper will defer to the privacy and comfort of the guest, of course, as a matter of good innkeeping, but the legal control and continuing possession remain in the innkeeper at all times. The room in the inn is regarded as part of the "house of the innkeeper."[2]

A tenant, for example, gains a property interest in the rooms or apartments that he or she rents from the landlord. This is not true, however, in innkeeping law since the guest obtains only a "revocable license" or privilege to occupy the room for the period of the stay.

The license can be revoked for failure to pay the room charges, for disorderly conduct at the inn, for immoral conduct on the premises, and other such reasons. In sum, the guest does not gain a property interest in the room at the inn.

Guests' Rights to the Rooms

A guest at an inn has a mere personal contract to the room assigned. There is no property interest in the real estate nor does the innkeeper want there to be.

Since all contracts contain implied rights and duties on both sides, any deviation of these on the part of the guest would justify the innkeeper in treating the contract as being at an end.

Once a guest has been received and is registered, legal rights of the innkeeper come to the front. They include the right to move a guest to a new room, the right to enter the room under certain conditions, the right to take extreme actions in the event of emergencies, the right to eject guests under certain conditions, and others. After an examination of these rights of the innkeepers, we will examine the rights of guests.

ASSIGNING NEW ROOMS

An innkeeper retains the right to move a guest from one room to another. This should be done only, however, upon a showing of good cause. It would be a duty of the guest to cooperate in the change. The innkeeper should provide assistance to minimize inconvenience to the guest.

While an innkeeper has the right to change the rooms of a guest, the actual move must be done carefully, using due care with the guest's goods and valuables. If the guest's room is changed in his or her absence, and baggage and other effects are lost during the transfer due to carelessness, the guest will have a right to recover the full value of those items.[3]

Entry of Rooms

Once a guest is assigned a room, the legal status of the guest is as described previously. As a practical matter, however, the innkeeper will defer to the guest and step back so as to allow privacy which is consistent with good inn practices. This of course must be qualified by the need to clean the room, the right to reassign a new room, and others.

An innkeeper has a right to enter an inn room to turn down a loud radio, and indeed has a legal duty to do so if it is disturbing others.[4]

Effect of Emergencies

In the event of an emergency, such as a fire or escaping gas from a derailed train, or a broken water line in the room itself, the innkeeper is given wide latitude. It then becomes a matter of acting as a reasonable innkeeper would act under like or similar circumstances. The innkeeper can, and must, enter to warn of outside dangers. Further, his or her agents can enter to stop further damage. Common sense controls.

One of the rights of the innkeeper that is given recognition by the courts is the right to eject guests for nonpayment of rooms and services.

Ejection for Nonpayment

If a guest does not pay for entertainment (including the room and other service), or if it is determined that he or she will not be able to pay, the innkeeper can exclude that person. This can be done by a request to leave or by the use of a lockout.

After the lockout, the innkeeper can claim his or her rights under the "rights of the innkeepers lien" as found in many statute books, and in the common law as well. These liens apply to property of the guest that had been brought into the "confines of the inn."

When an innkeeper revokes the room license of a guest by ejecting that person, the former guest is now a nonguest. One legal implication of this fact is that it is possible that statutes that provide protection to the innkeeper for the loss of a guest's property may no longer apply. To illustrate, assume that a guest in Nevada has declared valuables at the front desk at an inn. The liability of the innkeeper for such valuables is limited by statute to $750 unless the innkeeper agrees to assume a higher obligation and does so in writing. If the valuables are destroyed by fire while in the safe, and if there is no gross negligence on the part of the innkeeper, the limitation applies. But, assume for a moment that, before the goods are destroyed by fire, the innkeeper ejects the guest. The goods are *then* lost by fire. Does the statute limit liability or has the protection been lost since the former guest is now a nonguest? In ejecting a guest, consideration must be given to the property and money and valuables of the guest at the same time.

There are other grounds for ejection of guests.

Misconduct of a Guest

Misconduct of a guest at an inn, such as taking part in an illegal or immoral activity, is grounds for ejection of that person. Such is tantamount to a breach of contract on the part of the guest. If there is misconduct by the guest, but the misconduct ends and the guest is not ejected, then the courts recognize that there is a waiver, or forgiveness, and the inn-guest relationship continues.[5]

Holdover Guests

"The guest who overstays the agreed time limit may be required to leave. If he (she) refuses, he may be evicted in a reasonable manner, not inflicting unnecessary injury or undue humiliation upon the guest. The usual method is to remove the guest's luggage from his room during his absence and to double-lock the door so as to deny entry."[6]

In New York, on the other hand, it is not legal to evict a holdover, even if this causes a breach of contract with an arriving guest. In Connecticut, a holdover can be removed only by the use of a landlord-tenant-like process. In Hawaii, a holdover is treated as a trespasser and, in Puerto Rico, the police can be called in to remove holdovers at the request of the innkeeper. The rule is thus not uniform on this point.

Disorderly House

An innkeeper must not allow the inn to become disorderly or to be used for immoral purposes. The inn was not created for such purposes, and the innkeeper must use care to avoid being prosecuted for running a "house of ill fame." For a case in which an innkeeper was so prosecuted, see *People v. McCarthy*,[7] 119 N.Y.S. 2d 435, 204 Misc. 460 (Magis. Ct., 1953).

Prostitutes can be legally excluded from inns,[8] so that activity is not such a great problem so long as it is controlled properly. The disorderly house statutes of the states make it so and must be obeyed. An example follows:

> Keeping disorderly house. Any person who shall keep any disorderly house, or any house or public resort, by which the peace, comfort or decency of the immediate neighborhood, or of any family thereof, is habitually disturbed, or who shall keep any inn in a disorderly manner, is guilty of a misdemeanor.[9]

Lockouts

While there are many times when an innkeeper has the right to eject guests, what happens when a guest resists ejection? Can physical violence be resorted to? In cases of outrageous conduct on the part of a guest, such as physical violence, the answer may well be "yes." But in the normal situation, the answer would be "no." Nonviolent resistance of ejection cannot be met with violence because the courts will not permit it. Therefore what can the innkeeper do?

One technique being used in innkeeping is the use of the lockout. This is carried out by double-locking the guest's room or by use of a "clam device" that slips over door knobs. This is done of course while the guest is absent from the room. Lockouts are effective because they separate the guest from his or her belongings. They usually result in settlement at the front desk in exchange for release of the goods and the departure of the guest.

Search of Rooms

If an inn room is being used for illegal purposes, such as drug sales or prostitution, the innkeeper and his or her agents and employees have a legal right to enter that room as part of the innkeeping function. Incriminating items found may be admitted in court against the defendants.[10]

So long as an innkeeper remains in the innkeeper function—doing what is reasonably necessary to run the inn properly and efficiently—the courts hold that any criminal arrests by police which might follow are valid.

If the innkeeper remains in the innkeeping role, such as checking to see if a room is vacant, even though in the company of a police officer, and if the guest is caught in a criminal act, the courts hold that the rights of the guest have not been violated. Thus, when an innkeeper opened an inn room door after check-out hour to see if the room was vacated, the innkeeper was in the innkeeping role. The arrests by the police officer who then observed robbery suspects in the room was held to be valid. The Sumdum case illustrates this point.

RICK SUMDUM, APPELLANT, V. STATE OF ALASKA
612 P. 2d 1018 (1980).

Before RABINOWITZ, C. J., and CONNOR, BOOCHEVER, BURKE and MATTHEWS, JJ.

MATTHEWS, Justice.

The defendant, Rick Sumdum, contends that the police entry into his motel room was the product of an illegal search, and that the evidence of stolen goods found on his person pursuant to that entry should be suppressed. The superior court denied the motion to suppress[11] and we affirm.

At 5:30 A.M., May 7, 1978, Pete Heger was awakened by an intruder in his motel room at the Driftwood Lodge in Juneau. Later that morning, Heger's roommate, Roy Claxton, discovered that his watch, cash, and marijuana were missing. The Driftwood's manager, Leona Gran, was notified of the theft, and the police were summoned. In the presence of the police, Heger described the burglar to other lodgers, one of whom pointed to room 38 and said Rick Sumdum was the one they wanted.

This identification was made at approximately 12:30 P.M., some one and one-half hours after the Driftwood's posted checkout time of 11:00 A.M. Gran informed the police that room 38 was registered in the name of one K. Brown, and that neither the registered guest nor anyone else had yet reregistered.

At the suppression hearing Gran testified that it was her responsibility to ascertain whether guests who had failed to appear by 11:00 A.M. were "skips,"[12] and if they were not, whether they intended to vacate their room or reregister. Her customary procedure was to telephone the occupants of the room, knock on their door, and enter their room, in that order, if such steps were necessary for the determination she was required to make. Though she had not yet done so when room 38 was suggested as the suspected burglar's quarters, the manager testified that she intended to and certainly would have followed her customary procedures even if the police had not been present.

On her own initiative, Gran telephoned room 38 and received no answer. Thereupon, Gran, Pete Heger, Dave Heger, Roy Claxton, and two police officers, walked over to room 38. Gran knocked on the door, received no response, and retrieved the key from her office. She then opened the door. From the doorway, the two men could be seen, both apparently asleep. Also clearly visible, on the outstretched wrist of the man on the cot closest to the door, was a distinctive watch[13] which Claxton immediately identified as his own. In addition, the clothing worn by the man fit the description given earlier by Heger.[14] The police officers then entered the motel room and arrested and handcuffed the suspect, Rick Sumdum. They searched his person, finding sixty dollars in cash, and searched under his cot, finding a buckknife. At the station house, a bag of marijuana was found strapped to Sumdum's leg.

The door of a home, even if open, presents a firm constitutional barrier to police searches unless conducted pursuant to a warrant or within an exception to the warrant requirement. *State v. Spietz,* 531 P.2d 521, 525 (Alaska, 1975). See also, *Erickson v. State,* 507 P.2d 508, 515 (Alaska, 1973). But there has been no showing that the officers opened Sumdum's door or intended to do so in order to search.

Once Gran opened the door to Sumdum's room and the police officers saw a man fitting the description of the burglary suspect, wearing a watch identified as stolen in the burglary, they had probable cause to arrest.[15] The officers entered in order to effectuate an arrest. The exigent circumstances presented by the sudden confrontation with the possibility of an armed and apt to flee felony suspect authorized the officers' immediate entry into the room. See generally, *Finch v. State,* 592 P.2d 1196, 1198 (Alaska, 1979); *State v. Spietz,* 531 P.2d 521, 523-25 (Alaska, 1975). See also *State v. War-*

ness, 26 Ariz.App. 359, 548 P.2d 853, 855-56 (1976). As a minimum the police officers could conduct a search incident to that arrest of Sumdum's person and seize evidence of the burglary. See, e.g., *Weltin v. State,* 574 P.2d 816, 818-19 (Alaska, 1978); *McCoy v. State,* 491 P.2d 127, 132-33 (Alaska, 1971); *Merrill v. State,* 423 P.2d 686, 699-700 (Alaska), *cert. denied,* 386 U.S. 1040, 87 S.Ct. 1497, 18 L.Ed.2d 607 (1967). Therefore, if the officers' view of the room was validly obtained, Sumdum's contention that the entry was illegal and that any evidence seized must be suppressed as the product of an illegal search is without merit.

A guest in a motel has a constitutionally protected right to privacy in his motel room and motel personnel cannot consent to a search of the guest's room. *Stoner v. California,* 376 U.S. 483, 490, 84 S.Ct. 889, 893, 11 L.Ed.2d 856, 861, *rehearing denied,* 377 U.S. 940, 84 S.Ct. 1330, 12 L.Ed.2d 303 (1964); *Finch v. State,* 592 P.2d 1196, 1197 n. 3 (Alaska, 1979); *Robinson v. State,* 578 P.2d 141, 142 (Alaska, 1978). But after the rental period has terminated, a guest's reasonable expectations of privacy are greatly diminished with respect to the right of motel management to enter. See *United States v. Jackson,* 585 F.2d 653, 658 (4th Cir. 1978); *United States v. Akin,* 562 F.2d 459, 464 (7th Cir. 1977), *cert. denied,* 435 U.S. 933, 98 S.Ct. 1509, 55 L.Ed.2d 531 (1978); *United States v. Parizo,* 514 F.2d 52, 54-55 (2d Cir. 1975); *United States v. Croft,* 429 F.2d 884, 887 (10th Cir. 1970); *State v. Mascarenas,* 86 N.M. 692, 526 P.2d 1285, 1286 (App. 1974); *State v. Taggart,* 14 Or.App. 408, 512 P.2d 1359, 1364 (1973), *cert. denied,* 419 U.S. 877, 95 S.Ct. 141, 42 L.Ed.2d 117 (1974); *State v. Roff,* 70 Wash.2d 606, 424 P.2d 643, 646-47 (1976). See also *People v. Van* Eyk, 56 Cal.2d 471, 15 Cal.Rptr. 150, 154, 364 P.2d 326, 330 (1961), *cert. denied,* 369 U.S. 824, 82 S.Ct. 838, 7 L.Ed.2d 788 (1962); *People v. Crayton,* 174 Cal.App.2d 267, 344 P.2d 627, 629 (1959); *State v. Chiles,* 595 P.2d 1130, 1136 (Kan., 1979). Gran testified that motel guests frequently left without paying their bill. After check-out time, she tried to contact Sumdum by phoning his room and by knocking at his door, but there was no response. Gran then opened the door to his room in order to determine whether he had vacated. Her authority to do so, at the time she would normally have done so,[16] in accordance with her customary procedure, was not altered by the presence of the police.[17] Assuming the police were in a location which did not violate Sumdum's rights before the door was opened, Gran's opening of the door for a legitimate private purpose did not constitute an illegal search merely because the police were present.

It is beyond dispute that the police officers were entitled to walk up to Sumdum's door in order to investigate the burglary. See *Pistro v. State,* 590 P.2d 884, 886-87 (Alaska, 1979).[18] The fact that they did not avert their eyes when Gran opened the door, does not convert their view of the room from a common passageway into an illegal search.

Sumdum contends that the police officers' observation of him through the open door was not inadvertent and, therefore, does not come within the "plain view" exception to the requirement that no search or seizure can be made without a warrant. Inadvertence is a precondition to a valid seizure of evidence under the plain view exception. *Coolidge v. New Hampshire,* 403 U.S. 443, 470, 91 S.Ct. 2022, 2040, 29 L.Ed.2d 564, 585 (1971); *Reeves v. State,* 599 P.2d 727, 739 (Alaska, 1979). But the kind of plain view to which the inadvertence requirement applies only takes place after there has been an initial search or intrusion.

[P]lain view does not occur until a search is in progress. In each case, this initial intrusion is justified by a warrant or by an exception such as "hot pursuit" or search incident to a lawful arrest, or by an extraneous valid reason for the officer's presence. *Coolidge v. New Hampshire,* 403 U.S. at 467, 91 S.Ct. at 2039, 29 L.Ed.2d at 584. The inadvertence requirement of the plain view doctrine has never been thought to apply where the observation precedes the intrusion. It does not prevent police officers who are lawfully positioned in a public area from intentionally looking for suspects or incriminating evidence freely visible within the confines of a constitutionally protected area. 1 W. La Fave, Search and Seizure 2.2, at 242-43 (1978).

Finally, Sumdum contends that seizure of the buckknife from under his mattress was the product of an unlawful search. Since the knife is but one of three allegedly stolen and identifiable items found in Sumdum's possession, however, we do not see how our discussion of this point will have any effect on the plea of nolo contendere already entered by the defendant.

The judgment of the superior court is AFFIRMED.

One of the rights of an innkeeper is the right to claim a lien upon the property of guests for the room and other charges. This right existed at common law but today is provided by statute in most states. These statutes set forth the procedures that must be followed to enforce the lien.

Innkeepers' Lien

At common law, the innkeeper was given a lien (claim) against the property of each guest if the guest did not pay for the services and goods received at the inn. This meant that the inn had the right to hold property of the guest and sell it if necessary, in order to obtain payment.

This rule is the law of all states today. The constitutionality of the lien, however, where the property is sold without notice, has been successfully challenged in California, Florida, Nebraska, and New York. In these states, notice must be given before the sale can be carried out.

Nature of the Lien

The lien covers all charges owed by the guest, including loans that may have been made by the innkeeper. The lien can be enforced only during the current inn-guest relationship. A debt unpaid from last year by a guest cannot form the basis of a lien this year.

An innkeeper does not have to receive into the inn excess goods carried by a guest but, if they are received, the lien attaches to them.

The lien is effective against property that might otherwise be protected by the bankruptcy laws.

If a guest brings property to an inn that is owned by others, the lien attaches to the detriment of the third-party owner. With stolen goods, the prevailing view is that the lien does *not* attach and the true owner can have possession of the goods.

If the lien attaches and the goods are then sold to others by the guest, the lien is not defeated. Once the lien attaches and the innkeeper takes possession of the goods, other rules control.

Care and Caution

An innkeeper must use the same care and caution with liened goods as he or she would use with his or her own. If the property is placed to use, credit must be given for the value of that use. An innkeeper who has a lien upon corporate stock of a guest that had been declared at a front desk would have to exercise the care and caution that would be expected if the innkeeper owned the stock. The same would be true if pets were liened: they would have to be fed, watered, and properly maintained.

End of Lien

The lien can end by payment by the goods being returned to the owner, or by the conversion of the property by the innkeeper. That of course would be an illegal act. It can also be waived as mentioned previously. While four states have held the lien to be unconstitutional in the absence of notice and a hearing, Illinois, Minnesota, and other states have upheld the lien.

The procedural steps that must be followed in enforcing the lien will vary from state to state and legal advice must be sought and followed. The typical lien statute requires that notice be given, that sale be held at public auction, and that proceeds be accounted for. The statutes provide for the balance to be paid to the former guest if his or her address is known, which it often is not. In that event, excess funds usually forfeit to the state.

Leaving the rights of innkeepers, let's take a look at some of the rights of guests that have not already been mentioned. The chapter will then be closed with a look at cases that illustrate the principals discussed here.

RIGHTS OF GUESTS

The word "right" is a noun and, taken in an abstract sense, refers to ". . . justice, ethical correctness, or consonance with the rules of law or the principles of morals." In this signification it answers to one meaning of the Latin "jus," and serves to indicate law in the abstract, considered as the foundation of all rights or the complex of underlying moral principles which impart the character of justice to all positive law, or give it an ethical content."[19]

Taken in a concrete sense, a right is ". . . a power, privilege, facility, or demand, inherent in one person and incident upon another."[20]

Constitutional law provides us with four basic rights. These can be classified as personal, natural, political, and civil. One of our primary concerns, of course, is with civil rights.

Civil Rights

These are rights ". . . as belong to every citizen of the state or country, or, in a wider sense, to all its inhabitants, and are not connected with the organization or administration of government. They include the rights of property, marriage, protection of laws, freedom of contract, trial by jury . . . ," and others.[21] Or, as otherwise defined, civil rights are rights appertaining to a person in virtue of his citizenship in a state or community. Rights capable of being enforced or redressed in a civil action. Also a term applied to certain rights secured to citizens of the United States by the thirteenth and fourteenth amendments to the constitution, and by various acts of congress made in pursuance thereof.[22]

Following is section 201, Title II[23] of the Civil Rights Act of 1964:

Section 201. *Establishments Covered*

(a) All persons shall be entitled to the full and equal enjoyment of the goods, services, facilities, privileges, advantages, and accommodations of any place of public accommodation, as defined in this section, without discrimination or segregation on the ground of race, color, religion, or national origin.

(b) Each of the following establishments which serves the public is a place of public accommodation within the meaning of this title if its operations affect commerce, or if discrimination or segregation by it is supported by State action:

(1) any inn, hotel, motel, or other establishment which provides lodging to transient guests, other than an establishment located within a building which contains not more than five rooms for rent or hire and which is actually occupied by the proprietor of such establishment as his residence;

(2) any restaurant, cafeteria, lunchroom, lunch counter, soda fountain, or other facility principally engaged in selling food for consumption on the premises, including, but not limited to, any such facility located on the premises of any retail establishment; or any gasoline station;

(3) any motion picture house, theater, concert hall, sports arena, stadium or other place of exhibition or entertainment; and

(4) any establishment (A) (i) which is physically located within the premises of any establishment otherwise covered by this subsection, or (ii) within the premises of which is physically located any such covered establishment, and (B) which holds itself out as serving patrons of such covered establishment.

(c) The operations of an establishment affect commerce within the meaning of this title if (1) it is one of the establishments described in paragraph (1) of subsection (b); (2) in the case of an establishment described in paragraph (2) of subsection (b), it serves or offers to serve interstate travellers, or a substantial portion of the food which it serves, or gasoline or other products which it sells, has moved in commerce; (3) in the case of an establishment described in paragraph (3) of subsection (b), it customarily presents films, performances, athletic teams, exhibitions, or other sources of entertainment which move in commerce; and (4) in the case of an establishment described in paragraph (4) of subsection (b), it is physically located within the premises of, or there is physically located within its premises, an establishment the operations of which affect commerce within the meaning of this subsection. For the purposes of this section, "commerce" means travel, trade, traffic, commerce, transportation, or communication among the several States, or between the District of Columbia and any State, or between any foreign country or any territory or possession and any State or the District of Columbia, or between points in the same State but through any other State or the District of Columbia or a foreign country.

(d) Discrimination or segregation by an establishment is supported by State action within the meaning of this title if such discrimination or segregation (1) is carried on under color of any law, statute, ordinance, or regulation; or (2) is carried on under color of any custom or usage required or enforced by officials of the State or political subdivision thereof; or (3) is required by action of the State or political subdivision thereof.

(e) The provisions of this title shall not apply to private clubs or other establishment not in fact open to the public, except to the extent that the facilities of such establishment are made available to the customers or patrons of an establishment within the scope of subsection (b).

Thus the civil rights acts, both federal and state, comprise an important legal right of travelers and guests and especially so when it comes time to receive them. The first federal civil rights act involving inns had been enacted in 1875. In a case interpreting that law in 1883, it was held that inn facilities had to be separate but equal for the members of the colored race. The decision went on to say, however, that if there were no separate facilities, minorities had to do without. This remained the rule for all practical purposes until 1964.

Another right of a guest is that of privacy.

Privacy

It has been held that an inn does not have a legal right to disclose to the police phone calls made by a guest without proper legal process.[23]

Yet if it is suspected that a room is being used for illegal purposes, the innkeeper has a legal right to reassert control to the extent necessary to determine if illegal activities are in fact being carried out,[24] but for purposes of the inn only.

"A guest in a motel has a constitutionally protected right to privacy in his motel room and motel personnel cannot consent to a search (by the police) of the guest's room."[25]

This protected right ends of course when the inn-guest relationship ends. At that time, the innkeeper can enter freely, and can seek police help for that purpose if the need is felt. Any discoveries by the police at that time would be admissible in court against the former guest as seen in the Sumdum case.

One of the legal rights that an innkeeper has is to eject guests—as well as nonguests—who engage in disorderly, undesirable, or other unacceptable conduct at the inn. Most states have statutes similar to the following:

> **Eviction of disorderly persons.** Every owner or keeper of any hotel, inn, motel, motor court, or boardinghouse or lodginghouse in this state shall have the right to evict from such premises anyone who acts in a disorderly manner, or who destroys the property of any such owner or keeper, or who causes a public disturbance in or upon such premises.[26]

In the absence of a statute, the common-law right to so evict remains. In exercising one's rights under these laws, common or statutory, discretion and care would always be in order.

The McHugh case that follows illustrates the principle that an innkeeper has the right to exclude a guest who acts in a disorderly manner. The case goes on, however, and demonstrates the pitfalls that may arise when a guest is in fact ill and not intoxicated, as was suspected.

Mrs. McHugh has brought suit against the hotel, claiming that the act of excluding her husband from the hotel was done negligently and carelessly, resulting in or contributing to his death. The case tells the legal story and there are points to be learned from it.

MCHUGH V. SCHLOSSER ET AL.
292 A. 291 (S. Ct. Penna., 1894).

WILLIAMS, J. The defendants are hotel keepers in the city of Pittsburgh. McHugh was their guest, and died in an alley appurtenant to the hotel on the 2d day of February, 1891. Mary McHugh, the plaintiff, is his widow, and she seeks to recover damages for the loss of her husband, alleging that it was caused by the improper conduct of the defendants and their employees. An examination of the testimony shows that McHugh came to the Hotel Schlosser late on Friday night, January 30th, registered, was assigned to, and paid for, a room for the night, and retired. On Saturday and Sunday he complained of being ill, and remained most of both days in bed. A physician was sent for at his request, who prescribed for him. He also asked for and obtained several drinks during the same time, and an empty bottle or bottles remained in his room after he left it. During the forenoon of Monday he seemed bewildered, and wandered about the hall on the floor on which his room was. About the middle of the day the housekeeper reported to Schlosser that he was out of his room, and sitting half dressed on the side of the bed in another room. Schlosser and his porter both started in search of McHugh, and Schlosser seems to have exhibited some excitement or anger. He was found, and the porter led him to his room. While this was being done Schlosser said to him, "You can't stay here any longer;" to which McHugh replied, "I'll git." The porter, on reaching his room, put his coat, hat, and shoes on him, and at once led him to the freight elevator, put him on it, and had him let down to the ground floor. He then took him through a door, used for freight, out into an alley some four or five feet wide, that led to Penn Avenue. Rain was falling, and the day was cold. A stream of rain water and dissolving snow was running down the alley. McHugh was without overshoes, overcoat, or wraps of any description. When the porter had gotten him part way down the alley he fell to the pavement. While he was lying in the water, and the porter standing near him, a lady passed along the sidewalk on Penn Avenue and saw him. She walked a square, found Officer White, and reported to him what she had seen. He went to the alley to investigate, and when he arrived McHugh had been gotten to his feet, but was leaning heavily against the wall of the hotel, apparently unable to step. The porter was behind him with his hands upon him, apparently urging him forward. What followed will be best told in the officer's own words. He says: "I asked, 'What's the matter with this man Mr. Powers?' He says, 'He's sick.' I says 'He ought to have something done for him', and at that time he fell right in the alley on his back. He had his coat open, no vest, and his shoes were untied. He had strings in his shoes, but not tied." The officer was asked if the man spoke after he reached the place where he was, and he replied thus: "He spoke to me. Somebody said he was drunk. He rolled his eyes up, and says: 'Officer, I am not drunk. I am sick. I wish you would get an ambulance and have me taken to the hospital.' Then I ran to the patrol box." It required about 20 minutes to get an ambulance on the ground. During all this time the man continued to lie on the pavement in the alley. At length, after an exposure of about half an hour in the storm, and on the pavement, the ambulance came. He was placed on a stretcher, lifted into the ambulance, and taken to police headquarters, and thence to the hospital; but all signs of life had disappeared when he was laid on the hospital floor. The post-mortem examination disclosed the fact that the immediate cause of death was valvular disease of the heart. The theory of the plaintiff was that the shock from exposure to wet and cold in the alley had, in his feeble and unprotected condition, brought on the heart failure from which he died; and, as the exposure resulted from the conduct or directions of the defendants, they were responsible for his death. Three principal questions were thus raised: First. What duty does an innkeeper owe to his guest? Second. What connection was there between the defendants' disregard of their duty, if they did disregard it in any particular, and the death of Mr. McHugh? Third. If the plaintiff be entitled to recover, what is the measure of her damages?

FIRST QUESTION

The attention of the court was drawn to the first of these questions by the defendants' third point, in which the learned judge was asked to instruct the jury, in substance, that if the deceased was troublesome to the defendants, and annoying to their guests, they might rightfully put him out of their house, if they used no unnecessary force or violence. This point was refused as framed, but the learned judge proceeded to state the rule thus: "If the annoying acts were willful, the defendants could remove decedent in the manner stated in point. If, however, they were the result of sickness, although they might, under certain circumstances, remove him, such removal must be in a manner suited to his condition." This was saying that if McHugh was intoxicated, and the disturbances made by him were due to his intoxication, he might be treated as a drunken man; but if he was sick, and the disturbances caused by him were due to his sickness, he must be treated with the consideration due to a sick man. This is a correct statement of the rule. In the delirium of a fever a sick man may become very troublesome to a hotel keeper, and his groans and cries may be annoying to the occupants of rooms near him; but this would not justify turning him forcibly from his bed into the street during a winter storm. What the condition of the decedent really was went properly to the jury for determination. If they found the fact to be that he was suffering from sickness, then the learned judge properly said that, if his removal was to be undertaken, it should be conducted in a manner suited to one in his condition.

SECOND QUESTION

The second question was raised by the defendants' fourth point, which was as follows: "If McHugh died of heart disease, and defendants had no reason to believe that he was so sick that his removal from the house would cause his death, they cannot be held responsible in this action, even though the mere incident of his removal from the house may have in some degree contributed to bring it on at that time." This was refused. It could not have been affirmed without qualification; but its refusal, without more, left the jury without any rule whatever upon the subject. The question which the defendants were bound to consider before putting the decedent out in the storm was not whether such exposure would surely cause death, but what was it reasonable to suppose might follow such a sudden exposure of the decedent in the condition in which he then was. What were the probable consequences of pushing a sick man, in the condition the decedent was in, out into the storm, without adequate covering, and, when he fell, from inability to stand on his feet, leaving him to lie in the stream of melting ice and snow that ran over the pavement of the alley for about a half hour in all, in the condition in which Officer White found him?

THIRD QUESTION

The third question was raised by the defendants' first point. No evidence was given tending to show the earning powers or the habits of industry and thrift of the deceased. For this reason the court was asked to instruct the jury that "nothing more than nominal damages can be recovered in this action." This was refused, and the jury was told in the general charge that, as the evidence fixed his age, and gave information about his health and habits, they might from this data estimate his earning capacity, and the pecuniary loss of the plaintiff. Now, it is true, as said in *Railroad Co. v. Keller,* 67 Pa. St. 300, that since the acts of 1851 and 1855 life has a value which the law will recognize, and which the survivors who are entitled to sue may recover at law. It is true that this value is to be fixed by the jury in view of all the circumstances, and it is not necessarily limited to what is known as "nominal damages." But it is also true that when the probable earnings of the deceased are to be taken into account in fixing the damages it is the duty of the plaintiff to show the earning power of the deceased, or give such evidence in regard to his business, business habits, and past earnings, as may afford some basis from which earning capacity may be fairly estimated. The true measure of damages is the pecuniary loss suffered, without any solatium for mental suffering or grief; and the pecuniary loss is what the deceased would probably have earned by his labor, physical or intellectual, in his business or profession, if the injury that caused death had not befallen him, and which would have gone to the support of his family. In fixing this amount consideration should be given to the age of the deceased, his health, his ability and disposition to labor, his habits of living, and his expenditures. It is very clear that the refusal of the first and fourth points without explanation left the jury without any adequate instruction on the important questions to which these points related. The consequence was a verdict based on earning power of the deceased, which the learned judge felt constrained to reduce, and without some evidence from which the calculation of the pecuniary loss of the plaintiff may be made. The judgment is reversed, and a *venire facias de novo* awarded.

This means that the case must now go back for a second jury trial. At this new trial, the plaintiff must produce evidence of the earning power of the decedent under the guidelines set down by the upper court. The trial judge must also instruct the jury on the points set out by the upper court.

A guest who refuses to pay for services—or who will not be able to pay for services when due—may be ejected on those grounds. But again, care is in order. The Morningstar case has been around since 1914 and is recognized as a leading case on point.

MORNINGSTAR V. LAFAYETTE HOTEL
211 N.Y. 465, 105 N.E. 656 (1914).

CARDOZO, J. The plaintiff was a guest at the Lafayette Hotel in the city of Buffalo. He seems to have wearied of the hotel fare, and his yearning for variety has provoked this lawsuit. He went forth and purchased some spare-ribs, which he presented to the hotel chef with a request that they be cooked for him and brought to his room. This was done, but with the welcome viands there came the unwelcome addition of a bill or check for $1, which he was asked to sign. He refused to do so, claiming that the charge was excessive. That evening he dined at the cafe, and was again asked to sign for the extra service, and again declined. The following morning, Sunday, when he presented himself at the breakfast table, he was told that he would not be served. This announcement was made publicly, in the hearing of other guests. He remained at the hotel till Tuesday, taking his meals elsewhere, and he then left. The trial judge left it to the jury to say whether the charge of $1.00 was a reasonable one, instructing them that, if it was, the defendant had a right to refuse to serve the plaintiff further, and that, if it was not, the refusal was wrongful. In this, there was no error. An innkeeper is not required to entertain a guest who has refused to pay a lawful charge. Whether the charge in controversy was excessive was a question for the jury.

[Note: This states the rule. What happened at trial varied from the rule and the court discusses that next.]

The plaintiff says, however, that there was error in the admission of evidence which vitiates the verdict. In this we think that he is right. He alleged in his complaint that the defendant's conduct had injured his reputation. He offered no proof on that point but the defendant took advantage of the averment to prove what the plaintiff's reputation was. A number of hotel proprietors were called as witnesses by the defendant and under objection were allowed to prove that, in their respective hotels, the plaintiffs reputation was that of a chronic faultfinder. Some of them were permitted to say that the plaintiff was known as a "kicker." Others were permitted to say that his reputation was bad, not in respect of any moral qualities, but as the guest of a hotel. The trial judge charged the jury that they must find for the defendant if they concluded that the plaintiff had suffered no damage, and this evidence was received to show that he had suffered none. It is impossible to justify the ruling. The plaintiff, if wrongfully ejected from the cafe, was entitled to recover damages for injury to his feelings as a result of the humiliation; but his reputation as a faultfinder was certainly not at issue. The damages recoverable for such a wrong were no less because the occupants of other hotels were of the opinion that he complained too freely. In substance, it has been held that the plaintiff might be refused damages for the insult of being put out of a public dining room because other innkeepers considered him an undesirable guest.

It is no concern of ours that the controversy at the root of this lawsuit may seem to be trivial. That fact supplies, indeed, the greater reason why the jury should not have been misled into the belief that justice might therefore be denied to the suitor. To enforce one's rights when they are violated is never a legal wrong, and may often be a moral duty. It happens in many instances that the violation passes with no effort to redress it—sometimes from praiseworthy forbearance, sometimes from weakness, sometimes from mere inertia. But the law, which creates a right, can certainly not concede that an insistence upon its enforcement is evidence of a wrong. A great jurist, Rudolf von Ihering, in his "Struggle for Law," ascribes the development of law itself to the persistence in human nature of the impulse to resent aggression, and maintains the thesis that the individual owes the duty to himself and to society never to permit a legal right to be wantonly infringed. There has been criticism of Ihering's view, due largely, it may be, to the failure to take note of the limitations that accompany it; but it has at least its germ of truth. The plaintiff chose to resist a wrong which, if it may seem trivial to some, must have seemed substantial to him; and his readiness to stand upon his rights should not have been proved to his disparagement.

The judgment must be reversed, and a new trial granted, with costs to abide the event.

WILLARD BARTLETT, C. J., and WERNER, HISCOCK, CHASE, CUDDEBACK, and MILLER, JJ., concur.

Judgment reversed, etc.

In the Raider case, the innkeeper took charge of the room of a guest based upon the negative reputation of that person. The court was not shocked by that action at all.

RAIDER V. DIXIE INN
248 S.W. 229 (Kentucky, 1923)

SAMPSON, C.J. Appellant, Thelma Raider, applied to the Dixie Inn, at Richmond, for entertainment, and paid her board and lodging for a week in advance, saying that her home was in Estill county and she had come to Richmond, at the expense of her mother, to take treatments from a physician. At the end of the week she paid in advance for another week, and so on until the end of a month, when she went down town, and on returning was informed by the proprietor and his wife, who are appellees in this case, that she no longer had a room at that hotel, and remarked to her that no explanation was due her as to why they had requested or forced her removal. Alleging that she was mortified and humiliated by the words and conduct of the proprietors of the hotel, appellant, Raider, brought this action to recover damages in the sum of $5,000. Appellees answered, and denied the averments of the petition in so far as such averments set forth harsh or improper conduct on the part of the proprietors of the hotel, but admitted that they had required appellant to vacate her room and to leave the hotel, and gave as their reason for so doing that she was a woman of bad character, recently an inmate of a house of prostitution in the city of Richmond, and had been such for many years next before she came to the Inn, and was in said city a notoriously immoral character, but that appellees did not know her when she applied for entertainment at their hotel, but immediately upon learning who she was and her manner of life had moved her belongings out of the room into the lobby of the hotel, and kindly, quietly, and respectfully asked her to leave: that they had in their hotel several ladies of good reputation who were embarrassed by the presence of appellant in the hotel and who declined to associate with her and were about to withdraw from the hotel if she continued to lodge there; that appellant had not been of good behavior since she had become a patron of the hotel. Appellant moved to strike certain of the affirmative averments from the answer, but, without waiving this motion, filed an amended petition in which she set forth substantially the same facts which she had in her original petition, adding the following paragraph:

"Plaintiff says that she is advised that these defendants (the Dixie Inn) had a legal right to remove her, and that she does not question that right, but that she was removed as a guest for hire from said Dixie Inn at a time that was improper and in a manner that was unduly disrespectful and insulting, and that she was greatly mortified and humiliated thereby, and suffered indignity because of the wrongful manner in which she was removed from said Dixie Inn as herein set out and complained of." The court dismissed her petition and she appealed.

As a general rule a guest who has been admitted to an inn may afterwards be excluded therefrom by the innkeeper if the guest refuses to pay his bill, or if he becomes obnoxious to the guests by his own fault, is a person of general bad reputation, or has ceased to be a traveler by becoming a resident.

It appears, therefore, fully settled that an innkeeper may lawfully refuse to entertain objectionable characters, if to do so is calculated to injure his business or to place himself, business, or guests in a hazardous, uncomfortable, or dangerous situation. The innkeeper need not accept any one as a guest who is calculated to and will injure his business. *State v. Steele,* 106 N.C. 766, 11 S.E. 478, 8 L. R. A. 516, 19 Am. St. Rep. 573. A prize fighter who has been guilty of law breaking may be excluded. *Nelson v. Boldt* (C.

C.) 180 Fed. 779. Neither is an innkeeper required to entertain a card shark *(Watkins v. Cope,* 84 N. J. Law, 143, 86 Atl. 545); a thief *(Markham v. Brown,* 8 N. H. 523, 31 Am. Dec. 209); persons of bad reputation or those who are under suspicion *(Goodenow v. Travis,* 3 Johns, [N. Y.] 427; *State v. Steele, supra*); drunken and disorderly persons *(Atwater v. Sawyer,* 76 Me. 539, 49 Am. Rep. 634); one who commits a trespass by breaking in the door *(Goodenow v. Travis, supra)*; one who is filthy or who subjects the guests to annoyance *(Pidgeon v. Legge,* 5 Week. Rep. 649; see *Morningstar v. Hotel Co.,* 211 N. Y. 465, 105 N.E. 656, 52 L. R. A. [N. S.] 740, and the notes thereto attached).

It therefore appears that the managers of the Dixie Inn had the right to exclude appellant from their hotel upon several grounds without becoming liable therefor, unless the means employed to remove her were unlawful. The petition admits as much by its averment saying:

"She [appellant] is advised that these defendants [appellees] had a legal right to remove her, and that she did not question that right."

It being conceded that appellees had the right to remove appellant from the hotel, the only remaining question is: Did they do so in a proper manner, or did they employ unlawful means to exclude her? The averments of the petition show she was not present at the time they took charge of her room and placed her belongings in the lobby of the hotel, where they were easily accessible to her; that when she came in they quietly told her that they had taken charge of her room, but gave no reason for doing so. We must believe from the averments of the petition that very little was said, and that the whole proceeding was very quiet and orderly. As they had a right to exclude her from the hotel, they were guilty of no wrong in telling her so, even though there were other persons present in the lobby at the time they gave her such information, which is denied.

The averments of the petition as amended "that appellees removed appellant from the hotel in an improper manner and were unduly disrespectful and insulting" are mere conclusions of the pleader, and are not supported by the statement of facts found elsewhere in the petition.

The petition as amended did not state a cause of action in favor of appellant against appellees, and the trial court properly sustained a general demurrer thereto.

Judgment affirmed.

Nonguest Females

What are the rights of an innkeeper, through security personnel, to question both male and female nonguests who are using the public rooms of an inn but have no intention of becoming guests? The Jenkins case illustrates one modern view and discloses the attitude of the judge as he speaks of the situation. There is no inn-guest relationship and the opinion reflects the weight that the court places on that fact.

EJECTION OF NONGUESTS

JENKINS V. KENTUCKY HOTEL
261 Ky. 419, 87 S.W. 2d 951 (1935).

STITES, Justice.

Appellant, Ellen Jenkins, brought this action against the appellee, Kentucky Hotel, Inc., to recover damages for an alleged assault claimed to have arisen from a request of the house detective, about 9 o'clock in the evening of June 21, 1934, that she leave the lobby of the hotel. Upon the trial of the case, the court peremptorily instructed the jury to find a verdict for the appellee at the close of the testimony for the appellant. On the night in question, appellant says that she went to the Kentucky Hotel for the purpose of meeting her brother and sister-in-law, who were attending a meeting then in progress on the fourth floor of the hotel. She inquired of the clerk if the meeting was still going on, and, on being told that it was, she took a seat in the lobby, at a place near the elevators, where she could see who came down. While thus seated, the house detective approached her and asked what she was doing there. She told him the object and purpose of her visit, and she says that the detective told her, in a rude and insulting manner, that no such meeting as she claimed was being held in the hotel, and ordered her to leave the premises. She says that his manner and demeanor were so menacing and threatening that she believed that unless she followed his instructions he would use force bodily to evict her. Rather than be subjected to physical force, she says she left the premises and went out into the rain, where she remained for some minutes, and later came back into the hotel and went up to the meeting on the fourth floor, where she joined her brother and sister-in-law.

It is admitted that appellant was at most a mere licensee, and that if she had been requested in a proper manner to leave the lobby and had failed to do so, reasonable force could lawfully have been used to eject her. It is contended, however, that the rude and insulting manner accompanying the request to leave was an assault. With this we cannot agree. Howsoever culpable may have been the words or attitude of the detective, there was no unlawful offer of injury by force, and nothing, so far as the evidence discloses, from which a reasonable person might anticipate the exercise of more force than the law permitted. This court has approved the following definition: "An assault is an unlawful offer of corporeal injury to another by force, or force unlawfully directed toward the person of another, under such circumstances as create a well-founded fear of immediate peril," *Smith v. Gowdy,* 196 Ky. 281, 244 S. W. 678, 679, 29 A. L. R. 1353. The words used by the detective, as recited by appellant, contained no offer of force whatever, either lawful or unlawful. While his manner, according to appellant, was rude and highly objectionable, it was nothing more. He had the right to eject appellant if she refused to leave as requested. Bad manners are not actionable. However unfortunate this affair may have been, from the standpoint of both appellant and appellee, there was nothing in the acts or conduct complained of that constituted an assault. There was no breach of any legal duty owed to appellant.

Judgment affirmed.

QUESTIONS

1. What practical matters should be considered in deciding to move a guest to a new room?
2. Name three instances in which an innkeeper can lawfully enter the room of a guest without notice.
3. In the McHugh case, might the inn personnel have been acting in good faith? Was there any negligence on the part of the police officer?
4. Under what conditions would the "lockout" be considered?
5. What are the rights of innkeepers in keeping nonguests out of lobbies?
6. What is the "innkeepers lien"?
7. Define "civil rights."
8. True or False. Civil rights were ignored by our courts for a relatively long period of time or at least it seems so from the dates on leading cases.
9. Does the Civil Rights Act of 1964 apply to private clubs? Why?
10. What might be one explanation for the length and detail of the McHugh case?

ENDNOTES

1. *Flax v. Monticello Realty Co.*, 185 Va. 474 (Sp. Ct. Va., 1946).
2. *Kane v. Ten Eyck Co., Inc.*, 175 N.Y.S. 2d 88, 92 (1943).
3. *Milner Hotels, Inc. v. Lyon,* 302 Ky. 717, 196 S.W. 2d 364 (1946).
4. *People v. Henning,* 96 Cal. Rptr. 294 (Cal. App. 3d 872, 1971).
5. *Lucas v. Omel,* 61 N.Y.S. 659 (1900).
6. Sherry, *supra* at p. 115.
7. *People v. McCarthy,* 119 N.Y.S. 2d 435 (1953).
8. *Kelly v. United States*, 248 A. 2d 884 (D.C. App. 1975).
9. Nevada Revised Statutes, 201.420.
10. *People v. Sales,* 136 Cal. Rptr. 328, 68 Cal. App. 3d 418 (1977).
11. Sumdum subsequently entered a plea of *nolo contendere* while preserving his right to appeal the issues raised in his motion to suppress.
12. Gran indicated that guests frequently abandoned their rooms without paying. See note 17 *infra.*
13. The watchband was silver and was inlaid with a large turquoise stone.
14. Heger had been able to observe that the intruder had Indian features, wore his hair in a ponytail, and was wearing overalls and a striped shirt.
15. At that time AS 12.25.030 provided:

    A private person or a peace officer without a warrant may arrest a person:

    1. For a crime committed or attempted in his presence.
    2. When the person has committed a felony, although not in his presence.
    3. When a felony has in fact been committed, and he has reasonable cause for believing the person to have committed it.
16. Gran testified:

    Q. But for the presence of the officer would you at that time have gone up and knocked on the door?

    A. Oh, yes, definitely.

    Q. At that very time?

    A. Maybe not at that specific moment but within a very short time. I certainly would have because it was already after 12:00 o'clock [check-out time].

17. We do not conclude that the police instigated Gran's investigation or that she was an agent of the police. However, we note that the question is a close one. She was acting in conjunction with the police and perhaps at the direction of the police. She testified:

    [W]hen nobody will answer the door or the phone, many times they are what we call a skip, they've left, and so we go up and check the room to see if there's anything in it. And so I went up and rapped on the door and nobody answered, so I asked them [the police officers] if they would like me to get a key and went up and opened the door. . . . This occurred after Gran informed the police that she was going up to room 38 to determine if anyone was inside and gave them permission to accompany her. If police presence results in actions that would not normally have occurred in the time frame in question, the court will look carefully at the circumstances to determine whether independent private purposes are merely a sham for warrantless police searches.
18. At the least, Gran had the authority to consent to their entering the motel hallway to do so, since such authority derives from "mutual use of the property by persons generally having joint access or control for most purposes. . . ." *United States v. Matlock,* 415 U.S. 164, 171 n. 7, 94 S.Ct. 988, 993 n. 7, 39 L.Ed.2d 242, 250 n. 7 (1974).
19. *Black's Law Dictionary,* 4th Edition.
20. *Ibid.*
21. *Winnett v. Adams,* 71 Neb. 817, 99 N.W. 681.
22. *State v. Powers,* 51 N.L. 432, 17 A. 969.
23. *People v. Blair,* 25 Cal. 3d 640, 602 P. 2d 738 (1979).
24. *People v. Minervini,* 20 Cal. App. 3d 832, 98 Cal. Rptr. 107 (1971).
25. *Stoner v. California, supra* in Sumdum case.
26. Nevada Revised Statutes, 651.020.

16

Inn-Made Law, Practices and Policies

"The door?" the Chief asked.

"Here's where it gets cute," Boone said. "No keyhole showing on the outside."

He explained how the new electric locks worked. The door was opened by the insertion of a coded magnetic card into an outside slot. When closed, the door locked automatically. It was even necessary to insert the card into an inside slot when exiting from the room.

"A good security system," he told Delaney. "It's cut way down on hotel B-and-E's. They don't care if you don't turn in the card when you leave because the magnetic code for the lock is changed when a guest checks out, and a new card issued. No way for a locksmith to duplicate the code."

"There must be a passcard for all the rooms," the Chief said.

"Oh sure. Held by the Security Section. The chambermaids have cards only for the rooms on the floor they service."

"Well," Delaney said grudgingly, "it sounds good, but sooner or later some wise-ass will figure out how to beat it. But the important thing is that the killer couldn't have left Wolheim's room without putting the card in the slot on the inside of the door. Have I got that right?"

The Third Deadly Sin, Lawrence Sanders

OVERVIEW

In the last chapter we saw how the law grants a significant leeway or latitude to the innkeeper in the operation of the inn. In this chapter, we want to expand on the rights that the law provides because, if such rights are used intelligently, the likelihood of legal liability can be sharply reduced and the quality of the inn will be upgraded.

Looking backward for a moment, we find that twelfth-century England had no constitution. The inns which flourished in those times were not under constitutional law. Yet there existed the foundation upon which a sophisticated government would, in time, evolve. Privilege was the order of the day and it came from the crown, from the lawmakers, and from status itself. It was a system of "feudal hierarchy." In those days it was a refined political theory, much more subtle than mere allegiance, and all of this influenced inn law as it developed.

The Magna Carta was a product of war and it came into being at the time of the emergence of the day-to-day practices of English inns. The Magna Carta itself was not unique. In 1183, Emperor Frederick Barbarossa, in the Treaty of Constance, granted liberties to towns in Northern Italy. Others followed with such grants, including King Alphonso VIII in 1188, Emperor Frederick II in 1220, and King Andrew II of Hungary in 1222. All of this had a direct effect upon the development of the laws of innkeeping, because the latter was in the making along with the former. Along with the Magna Carta, other factors influenced the development of inn law, including practical and regal matters.

A sample of a practical factor is a simple historical fact that persons had to travel from their homes to the marketplaces. Thus "the lodging industry was born, thousands of years ago, to facilitate commerce. Ancient tribesmen moved down from the hills to Mediterranean shores to barter their wares. They were housed–transiently–in huts and dugouts by the side of the sea. They paid the hairy innkeepers of ancient times in barter: They exchanged polished flints, horn and bone. They were exchanging goods. That has always been the key purpose of lodging: to extend the boundaries of the world wherein men and women in commerce exchange goods–and, in more civilized societies, services." (*Lodging*, May, 1982, p. 2.)

A sample of a "regal" factor was the rule of St. Edward the Confessor: The "Awn Hinde" proclamation. Under the old *awn hinde* rule, the traveler who held over for three days became a "domestic" and thus became a member of the innkeeper's family for legal purposes. If that person then became injured or lost property, the insurer status of the innkeeper did not apply. On the other hand, this old English rule placed obligations upon the innkeeper for acts of that person while at the inn. This "regal" fact encouraged innkeepers to get travelers back onto the road in no more than three days so as to reduce the legal responsibility of the innkeeper.

Leaving this brief historical discussion, it is useful to examine the premise upon which this chapter is based.

PREMISE OF CHAPTER

While the workings of early English kings, the Magna Carta, early decisions of English courts, and practical factors shaped innkeeping law, there has always been the opportunity, limited in early centuries but almost unlimited now, for the innkeeper to create his or her own system of "law." This is especially so today and will grow in importance in the future. This "making of law at the inn" has found approval in cases where the issue has been before modern courts. There is every reason to expect that this will be true in the future since it makes the inn self-regulating. This in turn tends to reduce the workload of the courts.

The opportunity to create "inn-made" laws and policies arises in a variety of ways. Included are the manner in which travelers are handled; the endless ways in which the quality of the inn can be upgraded; the continued development of inn policies around the world; care being utilized in planning and construction of the forthcoming inn; house rules; disclaimers; waivers; releases and other in-house activities. The premise of the chapter then, is that a major portion of the law which regulates the inn can, and should, come from the inn itself. A good starting point is in the way travelers are handled at the inn. Examine Figure 16.1.

TRAVELERS AND THE WAY THEY ARE TREATED

The purpose of innkeeping is to facilitate travel and to accommodate travelers to that end. The function of the laws of innkeeping is to lay guidelines and provide the standards by which innkeeping is to be carried out, and to lay the basis by which disputes that arise can be resolved. The former exists because of the need to facilitate a system of travel; the latter, to ensure that the goal of the former is realized. It is a simple fact of inn life that 60 percent of the innkeeper's time is spent undoing mistakes that are made at the inn, and this simply should not be so. The problems begin as travelers arrive at the inn and seek to become guests there. What is their legal right to do so?

Inn-Made Law, Policies, and Practices, Contrasted to the Courts	
The Inn	**The Courts**
Quality standards	Common law
House policies	Statutory law
Treatment of travelers	Case precedents
Care in design and construction	Rules
World inn trends and their legal implications	*Stare decisis*
	Custom
Contracting away liability:	Trade usage
Disclaimers	History
Waivers/Releases	Constitutions
Releases after the injury	Contracts
House rules	Tort
Trade usage	Property law
Inn customs	Administrative regulations
Foreseeability	Employment law
Attitude of innkeeper	

FIGURE 16.1

Right to Seek Admittance

It is a general rule that ". . . an innkeeper gives a general license to all persons to enter his house. Consequently, it is not a trespass to enter an inn without a previous actual invitation but, where persons enter an inn, not as guests, but intent on pleasure or profit to be derived from intercourse with its inmates, they are there, not of right, but under an implied license that the landlord [innkeeper] may revoke at any time. The respondent did not enter the inn as a guest or with the intention of becoming one and it was his duty to leave peaceably when ordered to do so, and in case of his refusal to leave on request appellant was entitled to use such force as was reasonably necessary to remove him," *Hopp v. Thompson,* 72 S.D. 574, 38 N.W. 2d 133, 135 (1949). The right of the traveler to enter, when seeking to become a guest, must be honored by house policy and nothing must be done that runs counter to it. Further, it must be house policy to treat the traveler, once accepted as a guest, as a temporary member of the household, for the law for centuries has said just that.

Travelers who use the services of inns are almost always strangers there. Of course, repeat travelers will be familiar with the premises but this is certainly not true of all guests. Thus the law has never expected the traveling stranger to search out unknown dangers at the inn. The converse is true and it is a duty that is placed upon the innkeeper to give warning of dangers. This is a positive duty and requires positive action by the innkeeper.

The legal responsibilities of the inn can take on different implications as one tries to form new conceptual approaches to inn management. Not all innkeepers will operate the same way nor are they expected to. The courts have long recognized that innkeeping is, after all, a business. Thus, profits are allowed, but at the same time, the needs of the traveler must be recognized and protected. The courts do not require perfection of innkeepers, only that they conduct themselves in a reasonable manner.

The conduct of the innkeeper, acting through agents, requires that many house policies be adopted and enforced. Unprofessional comments are always out of order because they tend to distract the traveler or guest, which in turn could cause a loss or injury. Solo female travelers should be offered an escort to their rooms, which in turn should be promptly provided if the new guest accepts the offer. At the room, the door should be knocked upon first with sufficient time being allowed for a reply before the female guest enters the room.

As adjunct to the solo female traveler, they should never be assigned to an obscure or hard-to-reach room. The house policy should be that they are assigned to rooms on lower floors and close to house phones and elevators. The mere arrival of the solo female traveler at the front desk should be a signal to personnel there. When such a guest checks out, an offer of an escort is always in order.

Those who know how to operate equipment and amenities at the inn, which in turn will be used by guests, should be in charge of such equipment and amenities. Included would be ice machines, elevators, escalators, equipment in fitness rooms, and equipment at the pool.

Nurses who are sent to rooms upon request, instead of a doctor, must be qualified and licensed, *Stahlin v. Hilton Hotels Corp.*, 484 F. 2d 580 (Illinois, 1974). Many other "traveler-oriented" house policies are desirable and arise in practice. Failure to implement such policies can well result in lawyers entering the picture later. Consider what Roy M. Cohn, in *How to Stand up for Your Rights and Win!*, p. 177, had to say:

> I know a family whose vacation was an abomination. Everyone was in a terrible mood until they began to plan the lawsuit during the

vacation. They vied with each other to see who could come up with the best and most creative evidence for a future lawsuit. This turned into a family sport, and they began to root for everything to go wrong so they could document it. They even suffered a sense of disappointment at the few things that were delivered as promised. They returned home armed to the teeth and the travel agent gave them most of their money back, for a "ruined" vacation, which in retrospect was one of their most successful and fun-filled.

Turning from the techniques of handling travelers at the inn, a related topic is that of "quality standards" as contrasted to "legal standards." These areas are not the same, yet meeting quality standards can satisfy other requirements of law.

QUALITY STANDARDS AND LEGAL STANDARDS

First, as examples of legal standards, consider the following quotes, one from a court and the other from a legal treatise. Considered together, they provide the standards that an inn must measure up to as a matter of law. The court quote is from *Page v. Sloan*, 281 N.C. 697, 190 S.E. 2d 189 (North Carolina, 1972). The case is found in Chapter 5.

HUSKINS, J.: "What standard of care is required of innkeepers with respect to their guests?

"An innkeeper is not an insurer of the personal safety of his guests. He is required to exercise due care to keep his premises in a reasonably safe condition and to warn his guests of any hidden peril. [Citation omitted.] The duties thus imposed upon an innkeeper for the protection of his guests are nondelegable, and liability cannot be avoided on the ground that their performance was entrusted to an independent contractor. 40 *Am. Jur.* 2d, *Hotels, Motels and Restaurants Sec. 81.*"

The statement from the legal treatise is Section 341 of the Restatement of Torts, 2nd ed.:

Sec. 341. Activities Dangerous to Licensees

A possessor of land is subject to his licensees for physical harm caused to them by his failure to carry on his activities with reasonable care for their safety, if, but only if,

(a) he should expect that they will not discover or realize the danger, and

(b) they do not know or have reason to know of the possessor's activities and of the risk involved.

Now, compare these legal standards with quality standards so as to distinguish them. Standards of quality at the inn involve the policies and practices that are carried out there as a matter of good inn management. It is the state of mind of the innkeeper reflected through the attitudes, actions, and even emotions of the employees, agents, and others at the inn. It refers to doing things, not so much because the law requires it, but rather because management desires it. It is the actions and attitudes that are designed to please and provide comfort for the guest and promote the confidence of the guest.

Standards include many legal duties, of course, such as the duty to warn, the duty to receive travelers, and the duty to protect guests, but it goes beyond those legal duties. It is a condition at the inn that will satisfy legal requirements, but will do more than that. That is what makes "quality" something that is created by the inn and not by law. It represents standards that are basically the same—no higher, no lower. It is thus a constant condition.

Franchise agreements of most national inn chains require that quality standards be maintained even though the law does not make that demand. Quality can thus be a matter of contract between a franchisor and franchisee. If a guest at one component of an inn chain has a bad experience, or forms a bad impression of the inn, it will reflect upon and affect all of the other components of the chain.

Many national chains use a system of unannounced inspections at the inns. Days Inns, Holiday Inns, and Howard Johnson's Motor Lodges see the inspection as a "communication tool," a public relations opportunity, and a means of control.

Chris Roush, a business writer for the *Sarasota & Herald-Tribune,* made this report in May 1990:

> "It's a good communication tool," said Ron Thomas, general manager of the Howard Johnson's Motor Lodge in Punta Gorda.
>
> "The inspector not only serves as an inspector, but he also explains new standards. It's an opportunity for the inspector to get out on the property and talk to the individual operator," Thomas said.
>
> The New Jersey-based Howard Johnson's inspects its 450 hotels twice a year, sending executives from its regional offices to spend a day at each hotel.
>
> "They want, basically, the standards to be the same," said Thomas, whose hotel ranked fourth overall nationwide and first in the Southeast after the most-recent inspections.
>
> "One of the most important inspections," Thomas said, "is where all guests spend most of their time on the hotel property—their room."

> Howard Johnson's inspectors randomly select 10 percent of the rooms at a hotel, preventing local managers from handpicking what rooms are examined.
>
> "He basically does a pretty thorough inspection," Thomas said.
>
> Garling said that the Days Inn inspector selects 20 rooms at each property to give the white-glove treatment. Those also are selected without prior knowledge, Garling said.
>
> [John] Anderson said that Holiday Inn inspections depend on how well the property did in the last one. Prior to the March 9 inspection, the Holiday Inn-Longboat Key had not done as well, but $1 million worth of renovations cured the problems.
>
> Inspections are a vital part of the hospitality industry, Anderson said. If a guest has a bad stay at one Holiday Inn, he will assume the worst about the entire chain.
>
> "They blame every Holiday Inn in the whole wide world," Anderson said. "That's the way they look at it."

In a Citicorp Diners Club study report titled "Quest for Quality," sponsored by the American Hotel and Motel Association and funded by Citicorp Diners Club, "quality" at the inn was discussed in the following manner (p. 3):

> "Quality" is something that almost every person and every organization thinks they have—and yet very few people can define what it means! Most people try to define "quality" by saying that it is "the best" or "the finest," or the "most outstanding." "Quality food," they will say, "is food that is excellent." "A quality car" is the "best" car made.
>
> Another problem in using superlatives in defining "quality" is that we tend to equate "best," "finest," "most outstanding" with cost. We tend to think that things that cost more must be better and, therefore, higher quality. If this were the case, it would be impossible to run a "quality" hotel or motel that charged average rates and catered to the average American. And, the vast majority of Americans would be unable to afford "quality." This, of course, is not true at all. Quality is not a function of how much something costs but, rather, how well it meets the expectations of those who purchase it. The person who stays at the budget motel does not expect valet parking, an expensive lobby, extra-large guest rooms, room service, same-day laundry service and so forth. They do expect a place to park, a friendly, efficient room clerk, a clean, comfortable room, safety and security. If those expectations are met, the budget motel can be said to have delivered a quality product and service. On the other hand, the guest who wants more service and more lavish accommodations, and is willing to pay for them, would not feel that quality had been delivered if the room was dirty, the shower didn't work correctly, and the employees were not friendly.

> Regardless of the type of accommodations, a guest stays there with certain expectations. When these expectations are met, he has received quality. When his expectations are not met, quality is absent. Now we have a definition of "quality" that we can use.
>
> Quality means everyone doing their job correctly each and every time. Quality is consistency of performance. People always return where the performance is consistent. We want our expectations met every time without surprises. When it doesn't happen—that is, when we have to argue and hassle to get what we expect, we simply do business with someone else the next time. Such is the case with the hotel and motel guest.
>
> Many people believe that "standards" are desired levels of performance. When a standard is set, it becomes a requirement and should be met each and every time the job is performed. To do otherwise is to render the standard useless. If we have a standard to provide our guests with a clean guest room, then, each and every time we room a guest, the room must be clean. Otherwise, the standard means nothing.

Figure 16.2 is a recap from the Citicorp Diners Club study showing how guests react to hospitality error (p. 10).

Thus, quality standards are of importance to the inn, represent good inn practices, and almost always exceed the legal standards.

The search for quality often parallels marketing efforts and the latter can create legal difficulties in some situations. Inns around the world are constantly involved in new ventures and a summary of some current situations can contribute to our discussion.

INN ACTIVITIES AROUND THE WORLD

At Kissimmee, Florida, Days Suites offers a "price-is-right" package that allows a family of four to spend an entire week visiting Disney World for "about $1,000." It is both a marketing ploy and a part of the quality image that they project.

In Paris, overlooking the Place de la Concorde, the Hotel de Crillion, billed as the "Palace on the Place," is the epitome of French elegance and impeccable taste. With a restored Ancient Regime splendor, its staff is considered to be razor-sharp in the inn service world. The Crillion has become a symbol of classical French taste and culture. Its facade, facing the Egyptian obelisk that marks the spot where a guillotine stood during the French Revolution, was built in 1758 by Louis XV's architect. Out of respect for the building's history, its owners (the Taitinger family) have restored the original Bourbon decor with faultless taste.

OCCURRENCE FREQUENCY AND DISCONTINUANCE RATE
(by sex)

	MALE		FEMALE	
	FREQ	DISC RATE	FREQ	DISC RATE
Unsatisfactory food service	19%	20%	13%	18%
Tired facility–poor maintenance	18	27	13	35
Slow check-in, check-out	18	15	18	31
Employees not friendly	12	32	9	48
Room not ready upon arrival	10	11	13	15
Poor overall service	9	48	10	58
Requested room type N/A	7	14	7	16
Morning wake up call not made	5	14	3	19
No record of reservation	4	31	5	27
Overbooked–guest walked	2	59	1	81
Overall:				
Frequency rate per trip	1.035		.909	
Discontinuance rate	24%		31%	
Trip per discontinuance	4.0		3.5	

FIGURE 16.2

Quality at this hotel represents the ultimate and far exceeds the legal requirements for hotels in France–or any other nation of the world for that matter. Such an extreme level of physical surroundings and service might be used *against* the hotel when a deviation from the quality standards results in an injury or a loss. The French courts might well adopt the quality standards of the hotel as the ones to be applied in court, thus making them legal standards. In this regard, the exquisiteness of that particular hotel makes this an unusual situation.

Services in other fashions abound at inns around the world. The Metro Richmond (Virginia) Hotel and Motel Association offers free inn rooms for cancer patients being treated in that city. At the Opryland Hotel in Nashville, Tennessee, from October 14, 1990 to January 20, 1991, guests were charged $145 per person, double occupancy for two nights, which included admission to "Masterworks"–an exhibit of 60 original paintings by Picasso, Renoir, Van Gogh, and other masters; a most unusual amenity for a hotel.

Hospitals have entered the world-inn picture. The Barnes Hospital in St. Louis operates a 20-room lodge for its patients and visitors and charges according to income. In Minneapolis, the Abbot North-western Hospital runs a 48-room hotel, and the Good Samaritan Hospital in Phoenix, Arizona, operates 9 inn rooms at the hospital. This represents a new movement in innkeeping and will undoubtedly open a new era of inn law.

Days Inns of Atlanta has targeted India for an extension of its American-based chain. India has strict laws on foreign business operations and especially on the movement of profits and equity investments out of that nation. Days Inn is thus increasing their legal burden by this expansion.

A unique form of inn is found in "rolling hotels"–inns operated on trains. There are three in Europe: The Al Andaluz, the Royal Scotsman, and the Orient Express, and one in the United States: the American European Express which runs from Chicago to Washington D.C. The legal and quality standards in such train operations are unique, as are the logistical needs.

Other unique inns include the Seattle, Washington, "M.V. Challenger," a 96-foot tugboat which offers seven guest rooms, four with baths. At Bardstown, Kentucky, a former jail now is operated as a five-room inn. Unique inns are found in a lighthouse at Amelia Island, Florida; a stone mansion of 1760, listed in the National Register and located at Middleway, West Virginia; and a ghost town in Virgelle, Montana, a town with just one resident.

The *Successful Hotel Marketer,* volume 3, no. 19, p. 2, gave suggestions on how an inn in a crowded market–or a unique market–can set itself off from the pack.

> The Omni San Diego Hotel stresses service, and as a result ranks fifth in service among the 43 Omni Hotel properties.
>
> One service program used by the hotel is the "Omni Service Tradition Program," which strives to involve employees in the hotel's future by making them more aware of the product and encouraging them to create good guest experiences. Ambassadors are elected to advise hotel management on how to improve services, facilities, and the working environment.

HUMANITARIAN TRENDS

> A special motel is offered by the National Institutes of Health at Bethesda, Maryland. It is called the "Children's Inn" and is a place where the family can walk down the hill to one of two spacious 24-hour kitchens and make its own sandwiches–with food the parents brought themselves and stored earlier in a refrigerator.
>
> If it has been a tough day, and you need someone to talk to, there is almost certainly another parent nearby who has been going through a similar ordeal and who can provide some emotional support. And there are two playrooms full of toys.
>
> "It makes me think of home," Christina said during her last visit.

> The opening of the Children's Inn in June was the culmination of a longtime dream of institutes' staffers. Located on the institutes' campus, the facility is a kind of halfway house for children who are being treated at the institutes' clinical center and their families.
>
> Here, parents can cook and care for their children much as they do at home. The two sunlit playrooms make it easy for parents to keep an eye on their kids. One even has special glass that filters out ultraviolet rays (chemotherapy often makes skin sensitive to sunlight).
>
> *Las Vegas Review Journal,*
> September 16, 1990, p. 10B.

Humanitarian standards set by the Children's Inn may be reflected in laws directed toward inns for the benefit of the homeless or low-income renters.

On October 24, 1986, the *New York Times* reported that two New York City motels were ordered to rent rooms to homeless families. The motels had had empty rooms but had turned the homeless families away in Bulls Head, S.I., and Sheepshead Bay in Brooklyn.

The New York Civil Rights Law prohibits inns from refusing to accept persons without good cause. This was the basis of the suit brought by the affirmative-litigation division of the city's Law Department. The suit was brought in equity and a restraining order was sought and issued by the court. The court also pointed out that the common law required innkeepers to receive all who were able to pay.

It should be remembered that while there is a civil rights and a common-law duty to receive, the homeless families could not claim the right to remain in the motels for an indefinite period. The duty to receive only applies to *travelers* and the families would be expected to resume their travels in a relatively short period of time.

At least one national chain decided to do something about the homeless by hiring homeless people to work at their inns. The program was started in 1988 and, as of 1990, the chain had hired 35 homeless persons. That chain is Days Inns of America and, as Richard A. Smith, vice president of human resources says, "Traditional hiring practices are dying." The program of Days Inns includes the hiring of the elderly and the handicapped in addition to the homeless. Today, they accept referrals from shelters, pay up to $7.00 per hour, and provide rooms at the inn for such persons for a small daily charge. On the inn-law side of this dramatic program is the development of a covenant that sets forth specific rules that must be followed by those persons in the use of the inn rooms. Of the first 35 homeless that were hired, 16 remained on the job and proceeded in the direction of obtaining their own homes.

In Bangkok, Thailand, the Oriental, one of the most elegant hotels there, has started to purchase fruits and vegetables for use at the hotel from the hill tribes of that nation. Meo and Karen Tribesmen grow a vast variety of fruit and vegetables on the former opium farms. Cold-climate flowers are grown on Mount Inthanon which rises to over 8,400 feet. The hotel purchases these flowers for decorating. These new farms have become tourist attractions in themselves and the association of the hotel with them forms a national tourist combination.

In Pasadena, California, the owners of the historic Huntington Hotel uncovered beautiful antique stained-glass windows. Measuring 4 feet high and 2 feet wide, the windows contain green, gold, and clay-colored designs. At some time in the past, these windows had been sealed over and forgotten. It is believed that they were installed when the eight-story hotel was constructed in 1906. The potential legal danger here is that the windows may not be structurally sound although it is believed that they are.

An Unusual Discount

The Highcliffe Hotel in Bournemouth, England, offers a 40 percent discount for newly married couples if the new bride brings her mother with them. The mother receives a bottle of gin and flowers in her room. If the groom brings his father, the discount is increased to 50 percent. The logic behind offering the discounts is clear; it increases occupancy. What legal problems may lurk within this discount plan is yet to be seen.

An Unusual Location

One of the most unusual locations for an inn in the United States is the one found at Cloudcraft, in the Sacramento Mountains in southeastern New Mexico. The town itself has a population of only a little over 500 persons, so The Lodge, which was built in 1899 for railroad employees and opened to the public in 1906, is the town's largest employer. The Lodge is a Bavarian-style structure painted in burgundy and gray tones, with stained-glass windows and an imposing onion dome made of copper. From the front porch one can see two nations and three U.S. states at this 9000-foot elevation.

Conrad Hilton lived there in the 1930s; Judy Garland and Clark Gable arrived together in 1940. Garland carved her name in the observatory tower under a rainbow. Pancho Villa stayed there in

1911, and the mahogany bar in the main lounge supposedly came from the home of Al Capone. A most unusual legal situation arose there in the recent past. A bear cub got onto the hotel roof and management coaxed it off, hoping not to arouse the ire of the mother who was somewhere in the vicinity.

The hotel mascot is a former chambermaid who vanished from the hotel years ago without trace. Various paintings of her are located about the inn and even a stained-glass window has been dedicated to her—an unusual situation.

The closest that a major hotel may ever come to flying is the Primadonna Hotel and Casino, located in Stateline, Nevada. The theme there is "carnival" and features a hot-air balloon, a World War I German fighter plane, a hang glider, a merry-go-round, a Ferris wheel, and many pictures of circus figures. It is a playful design and was created by the Primm family.

Before leaving our brief view of practices, policies, and laws of inns in the United States and elsewhere, mention will be made of hotel codes in two nations. Although these nations are quite small, it is surprising to learn of the concern that they express about the operations of their inns. It is an example for other nations to consider.

Some national laws regulate the activities of hotel managers. For example, in the Ethiopia Civil Code of 1960 is found a fully developed set of rules that set forth the legal parameters of the relationship between a hotel manager and his or her guests. This is the only nation, at the present time, that has a set of rules in a civil code in such a complete fashion.

The hotelkeeper's duty to safeguard his or her guests is firmly fixed in the common law of England and the United States. The rule is part of the Hotel Proprietor's Act of Ireland, 1963, Section 4.

Returning to our chapter premise that the inn can solve many of its legal problems through internal practices and policies, brief mention must be made of the importance of design and new construction. There is an opportunity here not only to comply with existing laws, but to provide for contingencies that older inns will not be able to avoid.

Existing statutory and ordinance requirements must be met in order to avoid a later charge of negligence per se as was seen in the Hook's case in Chapter 14. Plate glass must be avoided in all new inn construction. Safety factors must be taken into consideration at the time of the design of the inn so as to avoid "dead spaces" where crimes could be committed unobserved. Inn design must be a team effort calling upon the expertise of inn associations, insurance carriers, and even local police departments. While only brief mention of it is made here, this should not be thought of as an attempt to minimize the importance of inn design and construction as a way to reduce legal liability.

One of the more far-reaching ways that inn-made law can be brought into being is by the creation and implementation of house rules, disclaimers, waivers, and releases.

IMPLEMENTATION OF INN-MADE LAW

House Rules

While the early common law placed a heavy legal burden upon the innkeeper by making her or him an "insurer," and while modern inn law creates a variety of pressures on the operator of the inn, the law nevertheless recognizes that the innkeeper has a right to create certain "rules of the house" and consequently to expect that those rules will be followed by guests and others. The courts tend to uphold such rules if reasonable, if proper notice is given of them, and if they are uniformly applied, without discrimination. The basis of this concept is found in the early case of *Rogers v. People*, 86 N.Y. 360, in which the court said "The room in the inn is regarded as part of the 'house of the innkeeper.'" While the law lays heavy duties on the shoulders of the innkeeper, the house is not that of the guest. Consequently, reasonable house rules are in order.

House Rules and Religion

Most inns provide Bibles in guest rooms as a practice or unwritten rule of the house. A group in Madison, Wisconsin, known as "Freedom from Religion," was unable to force innkeepers there to remove Bibles from inn rooms. On the other hand, can a house rule be enforced which prohibits in-house, room-to-room solicitation by religious groups? In *People v. Thorpe,* 101 N.Y.S. 2d 986 (New York, 1950), the court held that "The hotel manager, in stopping (their) preaching activities and in requesting them to leave the hotel, infringed no rights of the defendants since the Constitution does not guarantee them any right to go freely onto private property for such purposes."

House Rules Limiting Access

If there are areas of the inn which are to be off-limits to employees, guests, invitees, and others, conspicuous notice must be given of that fact. In the case of workers' compensation coverage, the courts tend to hold that an employee is "on the job" for purposes of coverage if he or she is on the premises of the inn and has a right to be there. Failure to give notice of "off-limit" areas can be tantamount to inn approval for employees to be there.

Check-In Identification House Rules

Many inns have a rule that two items of identification must be produced at check-in time, especially at inns which are located in high crime areas. Some inns use the rule as a means of controlling the use of the inn by locals. Prostitution, drug dealing, and other criminal acts are often carried out by locals at inns that will admit them. A few states have a double-identification rule by statute, usually called "true-name registration" laws. A house rule to the same effect accomplishes the same purpose and will be upheld by the courts if uniformly applied.

Check-In, Check-Out House Rules

For many decades it was an almost universal rule of the house for the check-in and check-out hour to be 12:00 noon. It really made little difference at the inns and smaller hotels that dotted the nation. However, the coming of the "megahotels" in New York City, Los Angeles, Las Vegas, and elsewhere, changed all that. Could the innkeepers make the check-in time 2:00 in the afternoon and the check-out time 11:00 in the morning? As it turned out, the common law never defined what a "room for the night" meant in actual hours, and it is now common practice industry wide, to use the variable-hour pattern. It is of great assistance to room personnel and it results in a more smoothly running house for all concerned.

House Rules Regarding Infants

It is a good house rule to provide that children under certain ages, such as eight, are not to take part in hazardous recreational activities at the inn such as horseback riding, water skiing, or other such activities. For this rule to be held enforceable in court, direct notice of the rule must be given to the parents of the child. Failure of the parents to comply where injury or death to a child results will be looked at as contributory negligence, or at least as providing mitigating circumstances.

House Rules in Snow Country

At inns located in areas where snow falls heavily each year, it is essential that house rules be established and implemented in regard to that situation. These rules should establish who will begin the snow and ice removal; how soon that activity will start after a heavy snowfall; what follow-up procedures will be taken afterwards, such as the spreading of salt on the swept areas. Such house rules on snow removal should also be spelled out specifically in employee manuals. Records should be made of the actions that were taken under these rules. This will be most helpful in court when a guest who falls on snow or ice at the inn claims that the innkeeper was not exercising reasonable care in the snow and ice removal.

Dress Codes for Guests and Invitees

Dress codes tend to be upheld in court if they are reasonable; if notice is given; if they are uniformly applied; and if they do not discriminate on the basis of sex, age, color, or other civil rights grounds. In *Moolemaar v. Atlas Motor Inns, Inc.*, 616 F. 2d 87 (Virgin Islands, 1980), the court said that: ". . . Dress codes of varying degrees of formality are common at restaurants and nightclubs and insistence upon them by proprietors is not unusual, extreme or outrageous."

Dress Codes for Employees

It is generally agreed that there is a "standard look" for members of the various professions, and that there should be such a look for the employee and management levels in the HRI industry. One practical way to handle the matter is to require all employees to comply with a "uniform" requirement. In the inn industry, these uniforms are sometimes referred to as "costumes" because, in fact, they often turn out to be just that. It amounts to an industry "dress-code house rule" for employees.

Not all such house rules are accepted without complaint, especially in inns which are unionized. A major hotel in Las Vegas attempted to implement a house rule that set forth standards of dress and appearance of employees. The house rule was a "spruce-up regulation" and touched on points of employee neatness in regard to perfume, make-up, jewelry, hair style, fingernail care, and related items. The rule also required that employees maintained a body weight that was "proportionate to their height and body structure." The union representing the largest number of employees affected by the rule mounted a successful attack against it. The union argued that the house rule was too extreme.

House Rules on Employee Parking

A reasonable house rule would be one that requires employees to park their autos in specific parking areas. Whether such areas are attended or not might raise legal problems should an employee's auto be stolen, but if the rule is a reasonable one in all likelihood it will be upheld in court.

House Rules on Employee Dating

A rule found at many inns is that supervisory personnel shall not date employees in lower worker classifications. A challenge to such a rule has been overruled by a federal court. The court found that such a rule has legitimate business reasons in that it will tend to prevent sexual harassment, especially when the upper employee has the power to grant or deny raises or promotions to the lower echelon employee, *Sears v. Ryder,* 596 F. Supp. 1001 (Maine, 1984).

The creation and implementation of employee-related house rules should always be reviewed by counsel because they may lead to claims of a tort for the invasion of privacy, or a breach of fair dealing and good faith. The latter two are implied in all employment contracts. Such rules may also violate the civil rights laws if there is a "dissimilarity in treatment between the sexes," *Zentiska v. Pooler Motel, LTD.*, 708 F. Supp. 1321 (Georgia, 1989).

Can Guests Create Their Own Rules?

There are court cases in which inn guests have created their own "rules of the game," and then have sued the inn where injury or loss resulted because the inn did not enforce the guest-made rules. The courts almost always refuse to give credence to such claims and tend to dismiss such suits. It does not seem reasonable to require innkeepers to enforce unilateral rules, created by guests, which are not known to the innkeeper. As one court said, such a rule would be "onerous and patronizing," and refused to uphold it, *Dillon v. Keatington,* 390 S.W. 2d 212 (Michigan, 1986).

House rules may be written and they may be unwritten. The question is, will the courts give legal effect to one or the other, or both? A lot will depend upon the facts and circumstances in individual cases, but some unwritten house rules have become so well established in the inn industry that they have become standards through trade usage. Thus, the courts may uphold unwritten rules in some instances just as they will written ones.

On the other hand, reliance upon so-called "unwritten rules" can be avoided simply by placing them in writing, giving proper notice of them, and enforcing them at the inn. This is true whether they are posted in guest rooms, posted on bulletin boards, or handed out at guest registration time.

Rules at Campgrounds

Rules of the type that we have been discussing are also used at public recreation areas–local, state, and federal. An example is found in the camping permits issued at the Lake Mead National Recreation Area in southern Nevada. See Figure 16.3.

A final in-house way to limit or eliminate liability at the inn is the use of "contracts to limit liability." These will be covered under the headings of "disclaimers," "waivers," and "releases." Disclaimers and waivers become entwined in both practice and in the courts as was discussed previously. They are often hard to distinguish. In addition, releases are of two types: those that waive a legal right and thus are waivers, and those that surrender an accrued legal right upon payment of money and are thus releases. To solve this dilemma, the topics will be treated together, and an attempt will be made here to distinguish them.

Disclaimers/Waivers/Releases

Because of the potential danger of a court ruling that an employee handbook is in fact a unilateral contract, many inns are using disclaimers in such handbooks, as was mentioned previously. A typical disclaimer states that "The handbook shall not be treated as a contract between the inn and the employer. Rather it only represents the policies and practice of the inn *in re*, the philosophy of the inn." In *Bailey v. Perkins,* the North Dakota court upheld the disclaimer, which was conspicuous, to the detriment of the employees there, 398 N.W. 2d 120 (North Dakota, 1986).

A source of considerable litigation at inns are the health and fitness areas that have become popular in recent years. Providing such amenities raises the question, "Who is to be responsible for injuries that occur there?" Lack of supervision is an issue in many of these cases.

CAMPING REGULATIONS

1. Camp in designated sites only.
2. Do not drain water on ground.
3. Quiet hours are 10:00 P.M. to 6:00 A.M.
4. Pets must be leashed or under physical control.
5. No bathing, cleaning food or utensils at water spigots.
6. Additional information and regulations are posted on bulletin boards.

MAXIMUM OCCUPANCY PER SITE

1. One (1) vehicle plus any towed vehicles or (4) motorcycles.
2. Eight (8) persons.

FIGURE 16.3

There is a legal difference between supervising such facilities and providing instruction at them. Providing instruction is no defense to the claim of lack of supervision. One technique is to limit the number of users at the facility by use of a house rule. This may anger some guests at the inn, but the courts will uphold it if proper notice is given and the rule is uniformly applied. It is a house rule that will facilitate supervision, which in turn will reduce injuries. Also, disclaimers and waivers can be prepared and used at such facilities.

Jogging trails are another popular amenity that lead to court claims. Inns in major cities are even allowing jogging on their roofs. The cases abound with instances of falls, robberies, rapes, and other crimes against joggers for which claims are being filed against the inns. Thus, if such activity is permitted by the inn, disclaimers and warnings must be given to potential users of these facilities. It must be made clear that the inn cannot guarantee safety for those who engage in use of the facilities. Rules should specify that joggers use the trails at their own risk and that the inn assumes no responsibility for use. If a minor is involved a waiver should be signed by a parent or guardian and if such are not present, the minor should be denied use of the facilities.

The legal effectiveness of such waivers is not uniform from state to state. Many courts reject them on public policy grounds as being an unfair form of bargaining. Other courts will reject them if they are not clear or if the guest did not in fact know of them. In an Arizona case, horseback riding was available for guests. When signing up for the rides, a disclaimer-waiver-release was inserted inside the receipts given to each guest upon payment. After a guest was killed by a horse, the court held the waiver to be ineffective since the guest had never, in fact, seen the disclaimer, *DiMaria v. Coordinated,* 526 N.Y.S. 2d 19 (New York, 1988). New York law prohibits the owner or operator of a "recreational facility" from using disclaimers to absolve the owner of liability for injury or other loss to those who use the facilities in question. Not all states have such laws. On the other hand, if the innkeeper has a signed waiver or disclaimer or release, and if the judge allows it to be considered by a jury, it will usually have an effect on the outcome of the trial in favor of the innkeeper. It will show the jury that the injured guest was aware of the dangers before the injury or loss occurred.

Using disclaimers, waivers, and releases involves paperwork, time, and care, but almost always represents a good inn practice and assists in the creation of inn-made law. These are the ideas that this chapter was created to convey. A few final points about disclaimers will close the chapter.

A disclaimer folded into a receipt given to an inn guest who buys a bus tour in the city, which is not called to the attention of the guest or not actually seen by the guest, will receive no legal recognition in court, just as the horse case in Arizona.

Another situation in which disclaimers will not be upheld by the courts is where they attempt to transfer all risk to the guest. The reason for this is that, as a matter of public policy, the law does not allow one to contract away all responsibilities for one's acts. Thus, the disclaimer must contract away normal risks and not all risks. Needless to say, the drafting of a good disclaimer, whether for the parking lot, the fitness room, or other recreational facilities at the inn, must be done by counsel.

Disclaimers in Employee Manuals

Do disclaimers work when placed in employee manuals? For example, in an "at-will" employment state, will a statement in the employee manual to the effect that "the parties hereto agree that nothing contained in this manual shall negate the 'at-will' right of both parties under the laws of the state," supersede the promises in the employee manual? In North Dakota the answer is "yes," *Bailey v. Perkins' Restaurants,* 398, N.W. 2d 120 (North Dakota, 1986).

In Georgia, the courts have ruled that disclaimers fairly entered into by both parties who understand their nature are binding contracts. Thus, "It is the paramount policy of this state that courts will not lightly interfere with the freedom of the parties to contract," *My Fair Lady v. Harris,* 364 S.E. 2d 580 (Georgia, 1988).

QUESTIONS

1. What does the phrase "inn-made law" suggest to you? How would you describe the phrase?
2. What is the main difference between a legal standard and a quality standard?
3. In this chapter, activities of various inns in the United States and elsewhere were identified. Can you think of one new legal issue that may arise in the future from the activities described here?
4. If a particular inn has extraordinary in-house standards, such as the Mirage in Las Vegas or the Crillion in Paris, why might an American or French court decide to use those standards to measure the conduct of those inns where guests suffered a loss? Would this, in your opinion, tend to discourage the creation and implementation of quality standards at other inns?
5. What is the legal danger in trying to rely upon an unwritten house rule in a court case against the inn?
6. What is the legal logic of using disclaimers in the handbooks given to inn employees?
7. It is obvious that hospitals are entering the innkeeping picture in a positive manner. What possible legal consequence might result from this? Could the spreading of diseases from the hospital to guests at the inn become an issue? How about AIDS?
8. Sketch an instance in which the careless use of a disclaimer at the inn could result in a court holding that the disclaimer was ineffective.
9. True or False. The fact that the courts hold that the inn is the house of the innkeeper subjects the inn to constitutional control because of that fact alone.
10. Is it likely that in the future the desire to assist the homeless and low-income families will play a larger role in inn law? Provide one pro and one con thought on this issue.

ENDNOTES

In this chapter, citations were left within the text itself, directly following the quotes. This was done in order to allow readers to identify readily the state and the decision year of cases and better understand the newness of what is discussed.

17

Reservations, Rates, and Registration

It is generally conceded that the first modern-type hotel was the Tremont House in Boston. It opened October 16, 1829, with an elaborate dinner. With 170 rooms, the rate was $2 per day which included four meals. One could rent a single room and each room had a separate key, a washbowl, a free cake of soap for each guest, gas lights, and a pitcher, with eight bathrooms in the basement with ample water.

The first hotel for strict hotel purposes in the United States was the City Hotel on Broadway below Wall Street in New York City, which opened in 1794. It had 70 rooms.

John R. Goodwin

OVERVIEW

In this chapter we will examine some of the legal basics that become involved in the making of reservations, as well as in check-in procedures at inns. Emphasis will be placed upon the creation of the inn-guest relationship, pricing, and overbooking. This discussion will then be followed by appropriate case examples with emphasis on the landmark Rainbow case.

FORMING THE INN-GUEST RELATIONSHIP

The relationship that comes into being between the innkeeper and the traveler who becomes a guest has long been recognized as being "special." The courts give stronger attention to "special relationships" than they do to the more ordinary kind. The point of

Pony Express Station, Gothenburg, Nebraska.

time at which the relationship becomes operational is of legal importance and it is not always the time of actual registration. While that act is *prima facie* evidence that the relationship has come into being, it can arise before that point in time. This is so because it is based upon consent and not contract in all instances. It *may* be based on contract and the consent almost always results in a contract, but that is not the legal test.

The intent of the traveler to become a guest must be coupled with the agreement of the innkeeper to accept that person. Thus if X, who is registered, gives his key to Y, who does not register, and the innkeeper knows of the exchange of the key and does not object, Y is also a guest at law. The innkeeper, of course, faced with this situation, should make it clear that the acceptance of Y is subject to proper registration.[1] Making a reservation is different from registration. Examine Figure 17.1

There must always be an opportunity for the innkeeper to accept or reject the traveler. One can never become a guest at the inn by unilateral action. The consent of the inn usually comes through actions of agents and most frequently arises by registration. There is no need for a formal contract, although there usually will be one because the law will imply the contract if the consent of the inn is given. The consent can be evidenced by the furnishing of a room key, by the providing of food and drink, or the extending of other inn services to the traveler. Meeting a traveler at the entrance to the inn and providing assistance with his or her luggage can supply the consent. No lapse of time is required. If the consent is given, the relationship begins immediately.

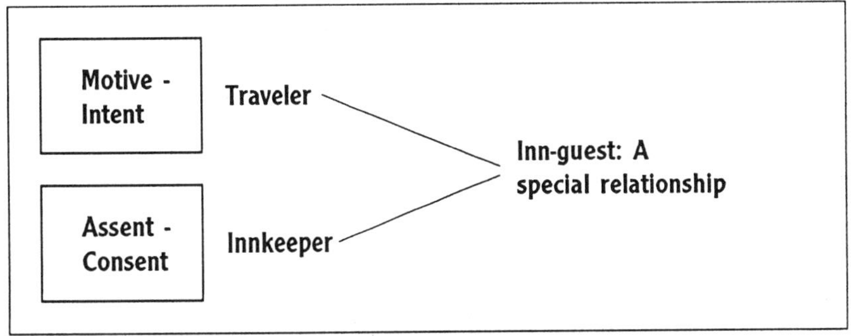

FIGURE 17.1 Formation of the inn-guest relationship.

The law has placed reliance upon consent for so long that if the refusal to grant the consent is wrongful or even illegal, the courts still find that there is no inn-guest relationship, *Bird v. Bird,* 123 Eng. Rep. 47, 337 (C.P., 1558).

One can become a guest without ever intending to take a room and it was so held in *Overstreet v. Moser,* 88 Mo. Ct. App. 72 (Missouri, 1901). On the other hand, in a 1409 case, a traveler asked to be accepted but was wrongfully turned away because that person was to serve on a jury the next morning. While he was furnished a key, the agreement was that he was to look out for himself. The court held that there was no inn-guest relationship, *Y-B Anon,* 11 Hen. 4 (England, 1409).

The key of course, where a traveler does not take a room but may be held to be a guest, is that the traveler is in the course of a journey and the inn is used temporarily to further the journey. Resorting to the inn for drink only created the relationship, *McDonald v. Edgerton,* 5 Barb. 560 (Sup. Ct. New York, 1849), as did remaining in a public room while waiting for a train, *Overstreet v. Moser,* 88 Mo. Ct. App. 72 (Missouri, 1901). The act of leaving goods at the inn with the intent of returning for them later also created the relationship, *Bennett v. Mellor,* 101 Eng. Rep. 154 (King's Bench, 1793).

Where the head of a household registers at the inn and does so for his family, all become guests although only one registered, *Holland v. Pack,* 7 Tenn. 151 (Tennessee, 1823). A business luncheon at the inn, attended by locals, does not make those who attend its guests. They are not in the "course of a journey." Conversely, if a local is received with intent for him or her to be a guest, that person is then a guest, *Walling v. Potter,* 35 Conn. 183 (Connecticut, 1868). Many inns refuse to rent rooms to locals, and the common law recognizes the right to do so since they are not in the class that inn law was designed to protect in the beginning.

The next topic for consideration is making a reservation. This is an activity in which the legal aspects have not been uniform in the minds of inn-law text authors. The 1990 case of *Rainbow v. Hilton Hotel Corporation* found in this chapter will help solidify legal thinking on the subject in the future.

MAKING A RESERVATION

"Making a reservation" is the act of contacting a lodging facility in advance of arrival and gaining in return the assurance that accommodations will be available on the date and at the time requested. The making of reservations has become routine and reliable. Yet, problems often arise. In many instances the problems are legal in nature. To illustrate, does a phone reservation for a motel room, not accompanied by an advanced payment, create a binding contract on the part of the innkeeper to hold that room as promised? Conversely, does there even have to be a binding contract to hold either of the parties to their promises: the one to hold the room and the other to occupy it as promised? Problems arise in practice and it is our purpose in this chapter to examine some of these problems and see how the courts have handled them. This will give us a working insight into how they will be handled in the future in light of the Rainbow case.

A good way to begin is by equating the six requirements of a conventional contract with the steps that take place in making reservations both with and without deposits.

The Reservation Contract

The contractual elements of a reservation would appear to be as follows:

1. Offer–Made by the traveler. "I will need a room on August 3, 4, 5, 19–, double beds, down and out." (It is communicated, made in good faith, and is definite.)
2. Acceptance–The agreement of the inn to provide and hold the room upon payment of a one-day deposit in advance.
3. Consideration–The payment of the deposit, or the exchange of the promises.
4. Mutuality–Apparent.

5. Legal purpose–Presumed. (If not, the contract would fail. An example would be a room reservation made for the purpose of engaging in immoral activity.)
6. Competent parties–An innkeeper has a duty to receive infants as well as adults, so this seldom causes legal problems in practice.

Now assume that the reservation is by teletype in the morning for a 6:00 P.M. guaranteed arrival, given with an American Express Card number. Is there *now* a contract?

1. Offer–Made by the traveler.
2. Acceptance–An indication of the willingness of the inn to be bound. If the traveler is told "Sorry, we are full," the matter ends there.
3. Consideration–The traveler has promised to take the room and the inn has promised to provide it. These mutual promises would provide the consideration–"quid pro quo."
4. Mutuality–Apparent.
5. Legal purpose–Presumed.
6. Competent parties–No problems, as indicated previously.

In both instances, it appears that a binding contract has resulted. Sales principles would *not* apply because a *service* is involved.

If the room is not available when the guest arrives, there would be a breach of contract by the inn. If the traveler does not cancel by 6:00 P.M. and does not show, that would be a breach of contract by the traveler.

Contract Counterpart

Thus the *common-law duty* that innkeepers must receive all guests has a counterpart in the law of contract where, under the facts, there is a *contractual duty* to receive. In the latter, the innkeeper cannot use the normal excuses *not* to receive because to do so would breach the contract. In the case of the common-law duty to receive, the usual excuses, such as a full house, would be valid.

The distinction between the common-law duty and the contractual duty was recognized by a leading author on the subject of contracts: "The obligations of an innkeeper arising from the common-law relation of innkeeper and guest are imposed by law irrespective of contract, and may arise when no contract is or can be made. There is, nevertheless, frequently a contract between the parties fixing the terms of their relation within the limit which the law allows."[2]

Excuses for Nonperformance

Under contract rules, once a contract is in being, there are few excuses for nonperformance that will be accepted by a court. A "mutual mistake" might be one excuse. Another might be "impossibility." What is impossible at law, however, is not the same as an impossibility in the normal sense. If an inn is full, it would be "impossible," in the normal sense of that word, to grant a room to a late arrival who has a reservation. Yet this would not be a *legal impossibility* and could not be used as an excuse for nonperformance. The sealing off of an inn by police agencies because of poisonous gas leakage from a train derailment would provide an excuse at law. So would the destruction of a lodging unit by fire.

If there is a breach of a contractual relationship, the guest must allege and prove the existence of the contract. A complaint that fails to allege a contract would be defective. The guest would also have the burden of proving the damages (losses), if any, that were suffered. In an increasingly large number of inn cases being decided each year, it is becoming evident that two facts are emerging: Guests are more willing than ever to sue, and they are succeeding in carrying the burden of proof in court.

It is important that the terms of a reservation contract be clear because the law requires certainty. In a California case, a travel business made a reservation at the inn for 250 rooms. An exchange of letters was made and the travel business changed what they had first called a "tentative reservation" to one they confirmed in their letter. The 250 rooms were not used by the travel business as agreed. In the lawsuit by the inn, the court found that there had been a contract and that it had been breached, and awarded the inn $15,300 in damages, *Hotel Del Coronado v. Quip Systems*, 186 N.R.L. Journ. (New York, 1981).

In *Freeman v. Kiamesha Concord Inn*, 76 Misc. 2d 915, 351 N.Y.S. 2d 541 (New York, 1974), the court held that: "The solicitation of a reservation, the making of a reservation by the transmittal of a deposit and the acceptance of the deposit constituted a binding contract in accordance with traditional contract principles of offer and acceptance."

In addition to the requirement of contract certainty, the courts will not allow the plain terms of a contract to be changed by custom or trade usage.

> The court did not err by charging that plaintiff's liability evidence was not ambiguous–what the court charged was that the purpose of the evidence concerning custom and usage was to help under-

stand what the parties intended and understood *if* there was uncertainty or ambiguity. The court said that the plain terms of the contract prevail over a trade usage or custom, that evidence of custom or usage cannot be considered to destroy a contract, or to make the rights and liabilities of the parties to a contract other than those created by the contract terms. The court also said that custom and usage evidence cannot create an ambiguity where none exists and that where the terms of an express contract are clear and unambiguous, they cannot be varied or contradicted because they differ from those usually found in a particular trade or business. Whether or not there was ambiguity was left to the jury, *King of Prussia Enterprises, Inc. v. Greyhound Lines, Inc.*, 457 F. Supp. 2d 56 (E.D. Pa. 1978), affirmed 595 F. 2d 1212 (3rd Circuit, 1979).

Making a binding reservation contract does not create the inn-guest relationship. To illustrate, if a traveler in Los Angeles makes a reservation by phone at an inn in Las Vegas, that person would not be a guest at the inn until he or she arrives and is accepted there. Any other rule would subject the innkeeper to unnecessary and unneeded responsibilities. The traveler now arrives at the inn and is turned away. There has simply been a breach of contract by the inn. In this instance the inn-guest relationship did not come into being.

The reservation and check-in process brings into focus the rates that will be charged at the inn. What does the law have to say about what prices may be charged to the traveler who is soon to become a guest?

ROOM RATES

In the matter of rates charged for a room at the inn, the law makes a distinction between rates which are quoted when one makes a reservation, and the rates that are charged to the arriving traveler who has no reservation. The reason for the difference is subtle, but legally important. When one calls for a reservation, the matter of rates quoted is simply a matter of agreement (contract). Even if the rate quoted should be exorbitant, no harm comes to the traveler since the room is not going to be used until a later date. The inquiring traveler can simply refuse to agree to the rate and seek accommodations elsewhere.

On the other hand, when the traveler arrives at the inn after a hard day's travel and is in need of the room for the night, the quoting of an exorbitant rate would have the practical effect of forcing the traveler to pay the price or seek another inn. It is these situations that the law has long sought to prevent. Thus, the law has long held that the price quoted the traveler must be "reasonable." If the law were otherwise, the unreasonable rate would be a form of extortion and at the same time would tend to hinder travel. Since the law mandates that an innkeeper make "reasonable charges" for rooms, services, and food and drink furnished to travelers, it becomes a logical question to ask, "Just what price is that?"

The answer to the question will be determined as an accounting function in many instances where an inn is alleged to have made unreasonable charges. Or a court may look to rates charged at like or similar inns. Where the accounting approach is used, the court, acting through a "master"—an accountant appointed by the court—will determine overhead costs at the inn for the previous year. Factored in would be part-time help, utility costs, thefts by guests, percent of no-shows, and the like. A sum for a reasonable profit will be added. Once a total is reached, the master will look at the occupancy rate, taking into consideration the break-even point and the seasonal-occupancy variance. It will then become a matter of determining what rates for rooms, food and drink, and other services must be charged to equal the total sum. If these figures come close to the charges that are actually required at the inn, courts would find that those rates are "reasonable."

Another factor that could be considered in such calculations would be the "amenity creep" that may have occurred at the inn in the year under investigation. This is a new inn phrase that describes the upgrading of services and the adding of new facilities which in turn may justify the charging of higher rates. The courts could be expected to make an allowance for more than just the costs of such upgrading because what may have started as an economy-oriented operation may now be classified as a mid-class operation. Natural growth can be expected at the inn, but that is not what we are talking about. It is something more.

"Amenity creep" is an economic principle that logically drives room rates higher and increases the legal duties of innkeepers as well. The "creep" creates a void as the inn is upgraded. It is thus dynamic in impact on room rates and should be explained to the court if an inn is ever accused of charging unreasonable rates.

Today it is unusual to find the amount charged by innkeepers to be challenged in court, but in light of the Rainbow case, that may change in the future. In an early King's Bench case, the court said that the charge made by the innkeeper would be upheld if it were not extravagant; "a person residing at an inn cannot live so cheaply as at his own house," *Proctor v. Nicholson,* 173 Eng. Rep. 30, 31 (King's Bench, 1835). The question of the extravagance of a restaurant charge was an issue in the Morningstar case.

"The requirement that the compensation should be reasonable is a necessary corollary of the requirement that the guest should be received, for if it were open to the innkeeper to charge what he pleased he might exclude such applicants as he did not care to entertain by the mere device of demanding from them an unreasonable payment. They [innkeepers] do not deal upon *contracts* as others do, they only make bills, in which they cannot set unreasonable rates; if they do, they are indictable for extortion. . . ," *Newton v. Trigg*, 89 Eng. Rep. 566 (K. B., 1691) (emphasis in original).

Room Rates and Statutes

The legislatures of the states have enacted a variety of statutes that are concerned with room rates. Most of these require that the rates be posted in each guest room showing prices per day for one person, two persons, and more. None of these statutes observed to date tell the innkeeper what the rates charged must be. The common law plays that role, as we have seen. The innkeeper is thus free to set the rate, so long as it is reasonable, and to vary the rate during different seasons of the year or during local events where that becomes prudent.

It has been observed, in many inns, that the highest seasonal rate is posted in each room, but lower rates are charged during the slow periods of business. It is often a statutory requirement that the maximum charge be posted. No legal harm seems to be involved in such a practice. On the other hand charging more than the posted rate could cause legal problems. It would certainly not be appreciated by guests who take notice that this has happened. Following is a sample of a posting statute:

> 651.030 Posting of rates; liability for overcharge.
>
> 1. Every keeper of any hotel, inn, motel or motor court in this state shall post, in a conspicuous place in the office and in every bedroom of such establishment, a printed copy of NRS 651.010 to 651.030, inclusive, and a statement of charge or rate of charges by the day for lodging.
> 2. No charge or sum shall be collected for any greater or other sum than he is entitled to by the general rules and regulations of such establishment.
> 3. For any violation of this section, or any provision herein contained, the offender shall forfeit to the injured party 3 times the amount of the sum charged in excess of what he is entitled to charge. [3:256:1953]

The statutes of some states such as California, Florida, and Nevada prohibit the advertising of hotel, motel, and inn-room rates on outdoor signs. This statute does not prohibit advertising of Nevada inn rates outside of the state and such advertising is seen in California, Arizona, Utah, Idaho, and near the borders of Nevada for Nevada inns. The statute does not prohibit television, newspaper, and radio ads about inn rates and these are seen and heard in great abundance throughout the state and near the borders.

As an adjunct to the Nevada prohibition on advertising room rates, as one drives south on Interstate 15 about 35 miles north of Las Vegas, a series of billboards are encountered that advertise room rates for inns on The Strip and in "Glitter Gulch." Do these outdoor signs violate the Nevada statute? As it turns out the answer is "no," because these billboards are on land owned by the Moapa Indian Reservation and this land is not subject to Nevada state law. This represents an opportunity for the Native Americans or tribe to profit from a law that denies such a use to other landowners in the state.

The Florida Advertising Statute

The sign statute in Florida says: "No person shall display or cause to be displayed any sign which may be seen from a public highway or street, which sign includes a statement or numbers relating to the rates charged at a public lodging establishment renting by the day or week, unless such sign includes in letters and figures of similar size and prominence the following additional information: the number of rental units in the establishment and the rates charged for each, whether the rates quoted are for single or multiple occupancy if such fact affects the rate charged, and the dates during which such rates are in effect. . . ."

Motel 6 wanted to erect two types of signs in that state. One was to read "Motel 6, $20.95 single, all rooms, all year." The other was to say "Motel 6, $20.95 single." The Florida Department of Business Regulation and the Division of Hotels and Restaurants of that state both ruled that these proposed signs violated the above statute. These agencies based their decision upon the fact that the signs were misleading, since higher rates would be charged at the inns depending upon the circumstances, and "all rooms" did not cover dates in which the rates would be in effect. On appeal, this holding was upheld, *Motel 6 v. Dept. of Business Regulation*, 560 So. 2d 1322 (Florida, 1990). This decision resulted in the removal of price signs at many of the Motel 6 units across the nation. In Las Vegas, the room-price sign was replaced by one that now says "We will leave the light on for you."

Turning from the statutes that apply to rates charged at the inn, a look back at a former time can provide some insight into rates that are charged at modern inns. This quote comes from *English Wayfaring in the Middle Ages,* J. Jusserand, 4th ed., 1961:

> Inns were intended for the middle class merchants, small landowners, itinerant packmen, etc. A certain number of beds were placed in one room. . . . Each man bought separately what he wished to eat, chiefly bread, a little meat, and some beer. Complaints as to the excessive prices were not much less frequent then than now. . . . The people petitioned Parliament and the King interfered accordingly with his accustomed useless goodwill. Edward III promulgated, in the twenty-third year of his reign (1350), a statute to constrain "hostelers et herbergers" to sell food at reasonable prices; and again, four years later, tried to put an end to the "great and outrageous cost" of victuals kept up in all the realm by innkeepers and other retailers of victuals, to the great detriment of the people traveling through the realm.

Preferred-Rate Contracts at the Inn

Preferred-rate contracts are contracts negotiated with the inn at the time that reservations are made. These contracts usually result in a lower room price being agreed upon than will be charged to the solo traveler who seeks a room for the night. The courts see no problem with this so long as the granting of a preferred rate is available on a uniform basis. Such rates are frequently granted to businesses who wish to use the inn for business reasons and the preferred rate tends to attract this business.

Advance Payment

If an inn requests that the reservation be paid in advance, the other party has a duty to comply. This is true for the simple reason that there never was any common-law duty *to make a reservation.* Thus, when an inn requests a down payment or places some condition upon the reservation, it becomes a matter of contract and contract law will apply. If the guest-to-be fails to meet the condition, then no contract results. Examine Figure 17.2.

In addition, it is the practice for front-desk personnel to require the credit card that will be used for payment to be tendered at check-in so that an imprint may be made of it on a charge slip. Upon checking out, the guest is asked to sign after the charge amount has been added. If the guest should leave without checking

Express Conditions:

1. "Payment for one day in advance."
2. "Payment for three days in advance."
3. "Minimum stay required."
4. "Must arrive by 6:00 P.M."
5. "Two-nights only on weekends."
6. Others such as in group bookings.

Implied Conditions:

1. Must be in acceptable condition.
2. Must make satisfactory arrangement for payment.
3. Will not overstay.
4. Others.

FIGURE 17.2 Placing conditions on reservations.

out, the inn would, at law, have implied permission to enter the charges, adding the guest's name to the charge slip. By taking the credit card impression in advance, the inn has ample time to determine if the charge will be accepted by the card company, or if the card has been canceled or stolen.

A problem associated with taking credit-card numbers or impressions as assurance of payment is the possibility that the person using the card will call the credit-card company and demand that the company not honor the charge. Most major credit-card companies, and notably American Express, refuse to honor such requests. In addition, the right to stop payment of checks under the Uniform Commercial Code does not apply to contracts involving credit cards.

Refunding Deposits

When advance deposits are made by cash or check, and the one who made the deposit does not show at the inn as agreed, should the deposit be returned? The rules of contract law become involved in answering this question. First, one who has a contract breached by the other party must "mitigate"–keep down–the losses of the one who breached the contract. In the case of a room reservation, this means selling the room or rooms to others if possible. If this is done and the inn fills up, there has been no loss so the deposit should be refunded, less any handling costs.

On the other hand, if the inn does not fill up, then it would appear that the inn has lost the profits that would have been made if the promise to occupy the room or rooms had been kept. In that event, the deposit can be retained as part of the damages suffered by the inn because of the breach. If the deposit was for more than a routine sum, however, it is best to consult legal counsel about whether or not to retain the full amount.

In many instance, such as when the inn agrees to hold large numbers of rooms for conventions, sports teams, and the like, advance deposits are requested. If such a request is not met, the pending contract fails and the inn is free to sell the rooms to others. When deposits are made and the contract arises, a concern of the innkeeper is that the balance be paid as agreed. Another legal technique is to require a guarantee from another to cover the contingency of the contracting party failing to pay the balance.

Guarantees of Payment

Such guarantees can be of one of two forms:

1. Guarantee of payment.
2. Guarantee of collectibility.

The first guarantee is the best, of course, because the one guaranteeing payment can be looked to as soon as it becomes certain that the primary party is not going to pay. In the second situation, the inn must exhaust all efforts to collect before the guaranteeing party can be looked to for payment. The form to be used for a guarantee of payment should be prepared by counsel.

REGISTRATION (CHECK-IN)

A variety of legal matters arise as the traveler is greeted at the front desk and the registration or check-in process begins. This is so whether the traveler has a reservation or is seeking to be admitted under his or her common-law right to be received. Included in this process are the keeping of guest registers, the matter of false registration, true name registration, protecting the privacy of those who are checking in, and related topics. There are excellent books on the market that set forth the variety of computer systems and front-desk techniques that have been developed and which are constantly evolving. Our only concern here is to examine the legal aspects of the procedure. To begin with, must we use some form of "guest register"?

Guest Registers

At common law, there was no requirement that such a register be kept and that rule prevails in many states today. As a business practice, however, such records have traditionally been kept. On display at the Del Coronado Hotel in San Diego is the register used there over 100 years ago. The names, addresses, rates charged, and other data concerned with those long-departed guests can be seen in beautiful script penmanship.

Other states, such as Nevada and New York, have statutes that require the keeping of "receipts" or registers. New York has two statutes addressing the subject.

> The owner, lessee, proprietor or manager of any hotel, motel, tourist cabins, camp, resort, tavern, inn, boarding or lodging house shall keep for a period of three years a register which shall show the name, residence, date of arrival and departure of his guests. Such record may be kept within the meaning of this section when reproduced on any photographic, photostatic, microfilm, microcard, miniature photographic or other process which actually reproduced the original record, Section 204 of the New York General Business Law.
>
> Every keeper of a hotel, lodging house, boarding house or rooming house in a town or city, shall cause to be kept for a period of one year a record showing the name and residence and the date of arrival and departure of his guests or lodgers and the room, rooms or bed occupied by them, which record shall have a space in which each guest or lodger shall sign his name. The keeping of but one person as a guest or lodger in any building shall not constitute such building either a boarding house or a rooming house within the meaning of this section, Section 61 (1) of the New York Election Law.

The registration rule prevailing in Louisiana, a civil law state, is that a guest may be accepted at an inn there without any registration at all. A register does not have to be signed to prove the contract between the parties. The inn-guest contracts in that state are matters of oral assent and no further formality is needed to make them legal. This rule is essentially that of the common law even though Louisiana is a civil law state.

A related question is whether a guest register is open to police inspection without a search warrant. While the U.S. Supreme Court has held that a guest's room is entitled to the protection of the Fourth Amendment, *Stoner v. California,* 376 U.S. 483, 490, *rehearing denied,* 377 U.S. 940 (U.S. Supreme Court, 1964), it is not clear if the same rule applies to the register. In a Massachusetts case, in which there is a statute requiring that a register be kept and made available for ". . . the inspection of the licensing authorities, their agents and police," it was held that the Fourth Amendment prohibition against unlawful searches and seizures did not apply to the register, *Commonwealth v. Blinn,* 503 N.E. 2d 25 (Massachusetts, 1987). A fine legal point here is that the police only wanted to know if Blinn was at the inn. If a criminal investigation had been going on, that might have made a difference in the ruling of the court.

Privacy and Protection of Registered Guests

First, the courts will not allow a division of duties between the innkeeper and the registered guest. "The hotel's duty [to the registered guest] was singular and it certainly was not divided with [the guest]," *Kane v. Ten Eyck Co., Inc.*, 175 N.Y.S. 2d 88, 92 (New York, 1943).

In some inns there are persons who frequent inn lobbies trying to spot unaccompanied female travelers. Once spotted, they attempt to discover the location of the room being assigned to that person. Front-desk personnel must never announce the number of the room key being handed to a solo female traveler and, as a matter of caution, should not do so with *any* traveler at registration.

Preregistration

More and more inns, especially the larger ones, are going to systems in which the registration is done before the traveler arrives at the front desk. Two variations are seen today. At the Las Vegas Hilton, for example, travelers in the check-in line are contacted by an automated radio check-in system in which their room needs and other data are obtained and recorded before the traveler actually reaches the desk. In the second variation, the registration is completed before the traveler arrives at the inn. The legal concern in such systems is in regard to the actual time that the inn-guest relationship begins.

Another legal registration matter has to do with people who register falsely at the inn.

False Registration

It is not uncommon for persons to register at inns under false names. Show personalities and others do it as a matter of course, and in such cases no legal problems are encountered since management takes part in the false registration. A better question arises when someone using an inn for an immoral purpose, for example, registers falsely and is then injured at the inn.

Over the years the courts have come to agree that even though a guest may register falsely in order to carry out an illegal or immoral purpose at the inn, this in itself does not excuse the innkeeper of the duty to use ordinary care in reference to that person. In short, the false registration, standing alone, is not a defense to a negligent injury of the guest caused by the innkeeper. The Rapee case in this chapter illustrates this view, which seems to be the majority view.[3]

There is, however, a minority view in the courts that holds just the opposite.[4] In spite of the view of the courts in any given state, the innkeeper is well advised to use ordinary care in dealing with all guests—whether they may be falsely registered or not, for it is not always possible to know.

True-Name Registration

The legislatures have at times expressed concern about false registration at inns. It is a means of taking up spurious residence for fraudulent voting purposes; it is a means of skipping out on the support of families; it is a means of avoiding obligations due to creditors. This concern has found expression in statutes that place a burden upon innkeepers to prohibit those checking in from using false identities.

These laws are designed to aid law-enforcement agencies in tracing criminals, "skips," and others. Arkansas, Massachusetts, New Hampshire, North Carolina, Ohio, and Vermont have such laws. Positive identification is required in those states at inn registration time—and it is a good idea in other states as well. This procedure tends to reduce the likelihood of adverse acts being committed by the person who has been positively identified.

Acceptable Condition of Traveler

Even though a traveler may have a contract with an inn, that person would still have the duty to present himself or herself in a presentable condition. If not, that person could be denied admittance in spite of the contract. This would be tantamount to a breach of contract on the part of the traveler. If the inn cannot sell the room for that night to another, there would be liability on the part of the traveler to make up that loss. The advance deposit could be applied to this loss. However, once confronted with such a situation, upon denial of admittance because of drunkenness, disorderly conduct, or the like, management might do well to return the advance deposit in order to encourage the traveler to seek accommodations elsewhere.

Late Arrivals

The duty to receive extends to late arrivals, especially if there is a contract. There have been cases where courts have prosecuted innkeepers for breach of this duty (see *Rex v. Ivens,* in Chapter 12). But today, late arrivals with proper reservations present few problems. If facilities are available for the late arrival who does not have a reservation, then the common-law duty to receive requires that a room be provided regardless of the hour.

Breach by the Traveler

Nonshowing travelers is a day-to-day matter and one for handling by desk personnel. But what if a reservation is for a block of rooms to accommodate a football team or an orchestra? In that event, an innkeeper should treat the matter with greater formality.

First, it would be well to have prepared in advance a form contract to cover large bookings. This contract should provide for the contingency of cancellation at a date too late to re-let to others, setting forth how damages will be measured. Next, the contract should be signed by someone of the traveling party who has the authority to do so, and perhaps guaranteed by a third party.

By taking these steps, collection of losses due to breach by travelers would be minimized when group booking is involved.

A topic that is related to guest registration is "overbooking" and it almost always involves the making of reservations.

OVERBOOKING

"Economic necessity" in the case of airlines may justify overbooking so long as alternative service is available. However, it is not so clear that the same should be true in inn reservations and registration.

In airline travel, the traveler is renting *transportation on personal property.* The purpose is to achieve movement from one point to another. In the case of lodging, one is *renting space inside of real property*—something that by necessity cannot be moved. In the latter, substitution of other accommodations may be unacceptable, undesirable, or both.

Yet, due to the problem of "no-shows," management tends to compensate by "overbooking." While it is true that a no-show guest will be liable for a room that remains empty, as a practical matter little can be done about enforcing the collection. The use of "in-chain" VIP cards or taking the numbers of major credit cards as part of the reservation tend to ensure that notice of cancellation will be received from no-shows.

Yet, the contract obligation remains to hold the room if the traveler arrives at the last minute—or even later. Thus a problem exists and the legal solution to it is not clear. Examine Figure 17.3.

Courts tend to frown upon overbooking for a simple legal reason: It is usually a breach of contract. If there were no contract, there could never be overbooking. When such breach occurs, the law must give the offended person a legal remedy should that person ask for it in court. It must be understood, of course, that the remedy given may not always result in measurable damages. Yet the constant danger in overbooking situations is that it may.

The courts are not in a position to say, "We will entertain breach of contract cases in our courts except in cases of overbooking." It would take a specific act of a legislature to permit such a result and the legislatures have not so acted. Courts cannot make exceptions to the laws that they have sworn to uphold.

It is essential in overbooking situations for inn personnel to use caution in talking with would-be guests who are now being "walked."

How It Happened	Damages Faced
1. Mistake	Actual
2. Negligence	Actual
3. Misunderstanding	Actual
4. Deliberate Act	Punitive
5. Bait and Switch	Punitive
6. Fraud	Punitive

FIGURE 17.3 Overbooking.

It would be unwise, for example, for a front-desk person to admit the overbooking. If this is done, it may be held by a court to be an admission that can be used as evidence against the innkeeper. Such admission would then be proof of the breach of the reservation contract. It would be much better for personnel to take all reasonable steps to place the bumped person elsewhere, saying nothing at all or as little as possible about why the walking became necessary.

If an inn carelessly overbooks, that act gives rise to a cause of action for the negligent wrong. If an HRI unit overbooks, *knowing in advance that it cannot honor the reservations,* that is fraud. Punitive damages can be sought in fraud cases.

Overbooking and Industry Standards

Industry standards may not in fact be "reasonable conduct" and the courts may thus refuse to accept such standards as a legal defense. A prime example in the HRI industry is the widespread practice of overbooking. Thus, circumstances may require that the innkeeper not only meet the requirements of industry standards, but exceed them on occasion and that is true in overbooking.

While some courts recognize that mere overbooking which is not carried out by design and results from an unexpected cause is a breach of contract, the circumstances may be considered by the jury when awarding damages, *Wells v. Holiday Inn,* 522 F. Supp. 1023 (Missouri, 1981). In the Wells case there was expert testimony that there is an average overbooking rate nationwide of one-half of 1 percent, and the walk rate at the Holiday Inn in question was much lower. While the plaintiff recovered, the damages were limited.

Florida specifically prohibits overbooking by regulation. If overbooking does occur, the inn must make "every effort to find comparable accommodations." If the traveler does not accept the substitute, all deposits must be returned. Rules have been written in that state to enforce the regulation and a fine of up to $500 can be levied, while the travelers are free to pursue their legal remedies for the breach of contract.

Overbooking often arises from a deliberate "bait-and-switch" effort and that seems to have been the motive in *Dold v. Outrigger Hotel,* 501 P. 2d 368 (S. Ct. Hawaii, 1972). First, the travelers were baited in their reservations with a promise of ocean-front rooms. Upon arrival, the switch was made to an inn off the beach. The hotel was receiving money for each referral to the inn. The court allowed recovery to the travelers who refused to accept the substituted premises. This is a poor practice to allow agents and employees to engage in–and it is completely out of line for management to pursue it as a business policy.

Causes of Overbooking

Overbooking occurs when too many reservation contracts are made. It can also be unintentional when caused by unplanned overstays, room damage, severe weather conditions, storm warnings that prevent travelers from moving on, and other causes. Such situations will not lead to the same results as deliberate overbooking.

An interesting sidelight on this subject arose at the University of Nevada, Las Vegas. First, in 1983 Nevada set a limit of $1,000 for punitive or exemplary damages for violations of the state's civil rights laws.

This statute amends Nevada Revised Statutes 651.050 to 651.110. This section allows a person who is discriminated against to sue for economic loss and actual damages. He or she can also collect costs and reasonable attorney's fees. But it limits the exemplary damages for intentional discrimination to not more than $1,000.

A student in a graduate class of Dr. Jerome J. Vallen was working with this statute[5] and came to an interesting conclusion in reference to it. He said that if his inn was being sued for overbooking, and if the damages looked high, he would claim that he was not overbooked but *that he was discriminating against that person!* Examine Figure 17.4. A final registration matter also has to do with reservations.

Minimum-Period Reservation Contracts

It is the custom of resort and many other lodging facilities to require that reservations be made for minimum time periods, such as three days, even if only a one-day advance payment is required. This is true in Florida during certain months and at lodging facilities close to major racing events. What is the contractual obligation of a guest who checks out before the minimum time period has expired? If the accommodations cannot be rented, which is often the case, the former guest would have a contractual obligation to make up the loss.[6]

Thus we see that the reservation contractual obligation rests on *both* parties and either can be looked to for breach of that contract.

In *Cardinal Consulting Company v. Circo Resorts, Inc.* (Circus-Circus in Las Vegas), 297 N.W. 2d 260 (Minn., 1980), the plaintiff

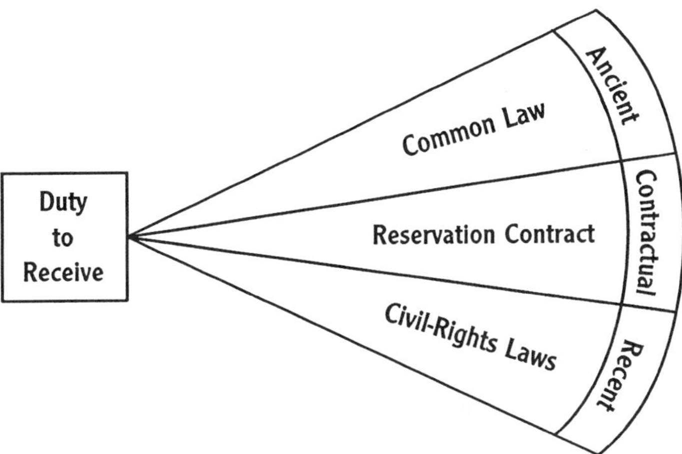

FIGURE 17.4 Increased legal duties to receive.

was awarded $71,500 in damages for loss of profits resulting from the defendant's breach of reservations.

With the above discussion of reservations, check-in, rates, and related topics in mind, it is useful to examine cases on those topics. In such cases one can see the reasoning of the courts as they apply the law in an attempt to reach just conclusions. In these cases the courts not only set forth the facts, but provide sufficient legal information to make these cases useful to students and lawyers alike.

Case Number One

In this first case, a guest registered falsely at an inn. The guest was then injured due to a failure of the innkeeper to use due care in the maintenance of an elevator. The inn also failed in its duty to warn the injured guest of the hazard of the elevator door. Can the false registration of the guest be used as a defense against the tort action that the guest brought for the resulting injuries?

RAPPEE V. BEACON HOTEL CORPORATION
293 N.Y.S. 196, 56 N.E. 2d 548 (1944).

LOUGHRAN, Judge.

Plaintiff and his fiancee registered at the defendant's hotel as husband and wife under an assumed name and then went out for the evening. On their return at an early hour the next morning, there was no response to his repeated ringing of the elevator bell at the ground floor, because the elevators were not operated below the mezzanine at that time of day. Eventually, the plaintiff leaned against the shaft door of an elevator to listen more closely for what seemed to be the sound of an approaching car. His weight caused the door to slide open and he fell into a pit below. A judgment for his damages has been affirmed and is now challenged by the defendant in this court.

[The Judge Instructs (Charges) the Jury]

In his charge the Trial Judge said to the jury: "It was the duty of the defendant to see that the elevator doors were properly closed. The gates or doors leading to the shafts of the elevator were required to be locked or bolted or securely fastened on the shaft side, that is, from the inside. . . . The duty which I have charged you the law imposes upon the defendant in the maintenance and operation of passenger elevators is not diminished by the fact that the plaintiff may have intended to occupy a room with a female not his wife or that he imposed upon the hotel authorities by misrepresenting some person to be his wife, or by making use of an assumed name. I charge you that for the purposes of your consideration of this case the plaintiff was a guest of the hotel and that the obligation of due care as I have charged it to you was applicable to this plaintiff in the same manner as to other guests and to other persons lawfully on the premises." To these instructions counsel for the defendant took the following exception: "I respectfully except to that part of your Honor's charge in which you stated that the plaintiff was a guest of the hotel and the same duty which was owing to any guest of the hotel was due and owing to him."

On the strength of this exception, the defendant argues that the plaintiff's fraudulent misrepresentation of his personality made him a trespasser on the hotel premises. We cannot assent to that argument. The misstatement of their names and status by the plaintiff and his companion certainly did not prove that the defendant's one and only purpose in their case was to treat with other particular individuals who were not present at the time. Foremost on the defendant's part was an intention to contract with the man and the woman who had put signatures on the register and, that being so, the plaintiff became a guest of the hotel, though the defendant may perhaps have been deceived as to his identity.

Whether the plaintiff's trickery was nevertheless enough to disable him from maintaining this action was an additional question. (See *Beale on Innkeepers and Hotels*, 136.) The defendant insists there was error in the negative answer that was given thereto in the passage we have quoted from the charge of the Trial Judge. But so much of that excerpt as asserted the plaintiff's position as a guest was sound,—or so we have said; and a general exception to an instruction that is correct in part cannot be sustained. For that reason, the defendant's exception to the charge is of no avail at this point. The defendant did not in its answer set up the plaintiff's imposture as a defense. More than that, the motion for dismissal of the complaint made by the defendant at the close of the case did not mention that matter at all. Thus there is no formal warrant in this record for the defendant's demand that the plaintiff forfeit his recovery for his misconduct.

The defendant invokes the statute against keeping houses of ill-fame, Penal Law, §1146, Consol. Laws, c. 40. The provisions thereof have not persuaded us that we should dismiss this complaint on some theory of public policy.

The judgment should be affirmed, with costs.

LEHMAN, C. J., RIPPEY, LEWIS, CONWAY, DESMOND, and THACHER, JJ., concur.

Judgment affirmed.

Case Number Two

The Rainbow case that follows is a landmark decision and one that will set standards for overbooking cases in the future. The court in this case finds that not only was the overbooking damaging to the goodwill of the plaintiff, but that it was also fraud because of the manner in which it was carried out. Curiously enough, the court does not allow damages for breach of the reservation contract, but that finding must be examined carefully. What the court was saying was that, since damages were allowed for injury to goodwill, double damages cannot be recovered for breach of contract.

The court repeatedly finds in the case that the reservation was a contract, that it was breached, and that jurisdiction of the court was proper, and thus upheld the damages as a result of the breach of contract. This decision comes as close as any court has in holding that a reservation at the inn is a binding contract and that breach of it will allow a jury to award damages. The frightening aspect of the case is the finding of fraud by Hilton Hotels Corporation.

Since the practice of overbooking reported in this case was so blatant that even the bus driver who took walked travelers elsewhere was part of it, and since such activity tends to frustrate interstate commerce, might Congress enter the picture with a federal law to prevent such activity? Also, might prosecuting attorneys decide to begin to prosecute innkeepers for such fraud? After all, fraud is not only a matter of civil-law concern, it is also a crime. It must be remembered that *Rex v. Ivens*, in Chapter 12, was a criminal prosecution in England for refusing to accept a traveler at the inn. This case contains many important legal points.

OVERBOOKING-BREACH OF CONTRACT AND FRAUD DAMAGES

BY JAMES O. EILER, ESQ.

A Federal Court of Appeals recently affirmed a federal trial court jury verdict which awarded a travel agency $37,500.00 for loss to its goodwill for the misrepresentations made by employees of the Fontainbleau Hilton Hotel.

In *Rainbow Travel Service, Inc. v. Hilton Hotels Corp.*, 896 F.2d 1233 (10th Cir., 1990), the Court of Appeals agreed with the trial court judgment that sufficient evidence existed that the Hilton Hotel misrepresented the hotel's room availability when it confirmed the reservations of the travel agency for its tour block of rooms.

A. A Hotel Reservation Is a Legally Enforceable Contract:

Hotel reservation contracts can be in writing (see *Rainbow Travel Service, Inc. v. Hilton Hotels Corp., supra*) or, oral (see *Dold v. Outrigger Hotel and Hawaii Hotels Operating Co.*, 54 Haw. 18; 501 P.2d 368 (1972), and will be valid and enforceable. If the hotel fails to comply with the terms of the reservation, the hotel can be sued for breach of contract.

B. Damages for Breach of the Reservation Contract:

In California, the measure of damages for breach of a contract "is the amount which will compensate the party aggrieved for all detriment proximately caused thereby, or which, in the ordinary course of things, would likely to result therefrom," (California Civil Code, section 3300.)

Generally, the party who breaches the contract must put the nonbreaching party in as good a position as the nonbreaching party would have been in if the contract had not been breached. This measure of damages could include, but is not limited to, refunding any money paid by the nonbreaching party, paying the nonbreaching party any money it expended to obtain alternative or substituted compliance, and any costs associated with enforcing its contractual rights which may include attorney fees.

C. Overbooking and Fraud Damages – The Rainbow Travel Case:

According to the decision, the Rainbow Tour Service had entered into a contract for room reservation with the Fontainbleau Hilton Hotel in Miami Beach, Florida, for several rooms. The tour agent is a tour operator in Oklahoma and contacted the hotel because of advertisements the hotel had sent to Oklahoma. The hotel had sent contracts which called for the hotel to reserve 105 rooms for the tour operator for one weekend, and a second contract which required the hotel to reserve 45 rooms during the same weekend. The tour operator signed the contracts and returned them to the hotel. Several months before the arrival dates, the hotel confirmed the tour operator's reservations by mail and requested prepayment for one night for the rooms. The tour operator sent a payment of over $6,000.00. The hotel sent another confirmation a few months before the arrival and requested the remainder of the first night's payment. The tour operator then sent a final customer list and the remainder of the down payment.

The president of the tour operator went to Miami a few days before the arrival of his group to make sure all the arrangements had been made. The first group arrived and was accommodated as planned. The tour operator's president met with the hotel tour representative four times within a three-day period to make sure all had been properly arranged for his group's arrival. Each time he was told everything was fine, and all the rooms would be available. When the second group arrived at the hotel the next day, they were told by the Hilton representatives that no rooms were available. The hotel made arrangements for the group to stay at another hotel ten blocks away from the Hilton. The tour operator sued the hotel, alleging breach of contract and fraud.

The jury found in favor of the tour operator and awarded $37,500.00 in damages for loss of goodwill. The jury believed there was sufficient evidence to find that the hotel had committed fraud when it confirmed that everything was fine and that all rooms were available. The evidence submitted by the tour operator was that the hotel had a departure figure and should have known that a substantial number of people would overstay their announced departure date. It also showed that the hotel gave a block of rooms on that same day to another group that had not reserved any rooms. The hotel did not inform the tour operator of its practice of overbooking and was not told there was a possibility that "guaranteed" reservations might be dishonored.

The hotel argued that the overbooking situation was due to facts beyond its control such as guests extending their stay at the hotel, and rooms being out of order for repairs. However, the tour operator offered into evidence the hotel's own policy manual which indicated that the hotel never told a guest that they were "overbooked" and that if such a situation arose, that they were to inform the guest that something occurred outside the control of the hotel such as:

1. Scheduled departures do not vacate their rooms.
2. Engineering problems with the room (pipe bursted, thus water leaks, air conditioning, heating out of commission, broken glass, etc.)

The hotel also argued that its reservations agent could not have known about the lack of rooms without performing some series of complicated calculations. The court was of the opinion that if this were true, the hotel may have made assertions regarding the availability of rooms without knowledge of the truth.

Evidence was also offered that the hotel was extremely busy during the week of the tour operator's group's visit, and that for several days before the arrival, the hotel was sold out and had to dishonor other reservations.

The hotel had argued that it needed to sell 115 percent capacity of the hotel based on a 15 percent no-show factor. The night clerk's summary for the night before the intended arrival date of the group indicated that the hotel would be short of rooms even if the 15 percent no-show factor was taken into account, and all 15 percent failed to show.

Finally, the court was under the opinion that the hotel's explanation concerning its treatment of the tour group's reservations lacked candor in that the hotel had indicated that it had not become aware of the shortage of rooms until after the president of the tour operator went to the airport to pick up the tour, even though when the group arrived they already had assigned specific rooms at the hotel to which they had been relocated.

The court took all of the evidence into consideration and held that there was sufficient evidence for the jury to find that the hotel committed a fraud, and thus, the award for the loss to the goodwill of the tour operator was justified. The appellate court was of the opinion that a reasonable juror could find that the hotel recklessly made statements without knowledge of their truth, and that the hotel did so with the intention that the tour group rely upon those representations and that in fact that the tour group did rely on them to their detriment.

The tour operator offered evidence that he had lost business as a result of the breach by the hotel of the reservation contracts because most of his business was done by word of mouth. He offered evidence of his booking reservations, reputation in the community for providing good services, that witnesses had stated that they were dissatisfied with the tour operator because of the hotel incident, and such witnesses probably would not choose the tour operator again as a travel agent.

D. The Hotel Can Also Sue for Breach:

Hotels can also sue for breach of contract when the guest does not show up or the tour operator cancels the reservation after the hotel had reserved rooms for the group. In *King of Prussia Enterprises, Inc. v. Greyhound Lines, Inc.*, 457 F.2d 56 (E.D. Penn., 1978), a hotel sued a travel agent when the travel agent breached a room block contract at the hotel. The hotel was located near Philadelphia during the 1976 Bicentennial time period and also during the 41st International Eucaristic Congress. The tour operator had contracted directly with the hotel for all of the hotel's 200 rooms instead of going through the Housing Bureau for the Eucaristic Congress. A deposit of $10,000.00 was sent to the hotel, indicating that it was a deposit for 200 rooms. When the hotel requested the balances due on the deposits for the rooms several times, the hotel was informed that the checks were forthcoming. Approximately one month before the arrival of the group, the group operator informed the hotel that it was canceling its reservations and asked for a refund of all deposits made. The jury believed there was an enforceable contract between the parties and awarded the hotel $58,900.00

for damages. The tour operator's motion for new trial was denied as the appellate court was of the opinion that there was sufficient evidence for the jury to conclude that there was a contract and that it had been breached. See also, *Hotel Del Cordono Corporation v. Food Service Equipment Distributor Association*, 783 F.2d 1323 (9th Cir., 1986).

E. Conclusion

Every time a reservation is made for a room in a hotel, a reservation contract exists that is legally enforceable even if the contract is made orally or in writing. If the hotel breaches that contract, the hotel can be subject to normal contract damages which would include out-of-pocket expenses to the potential guest, any damages to the guest to put them into the position they would have been if the contract had been complied with, and loss of profits as long as the loss of profits are not speculative and uncertain. If the hotel misrepresents its room availability, the hotel could be subject to damages for fraud which could include punitive damages.

If hotels continue the practice of overbooking rooms, hotels can expect some federal regulation much like the airlines industry had undergone in the early 1970s. It is therefore suggested that all hotel operators reevaluate their position on overbooking based on an imaginary no-show factor, considering the costly effects of not doing so in today's litigious society.

Case Number Three

In the Thomas case that follows, we see an older breach-of-reservation case (1955). Here a would-be guest was turned away because of his race. This happened at a time when the guest-to-be also had a valid reservation contract. In addition, the hotel was not full; thus, the hotel had a common-law duty to receive this traveler without regard to the reservation or his race.

This is a situation where a man attempting to check in at a front desk was turned away when the hotel had *three* duties to receive that person. Mr. Thomas waited over two years to bring his lawsuit against the hotel so the statute of limitations became involved.

Two of his three causes of action were barred by the statute of limitations. The first of these alleged that the innkeeper breached his common-law duty to receive. If true, this would be a tort and was barred in Kansas courts after two years. Second was the allegation that by turning him away because of his color, the Kansas Civil Rights Act was violated. This cause of action was also barred.

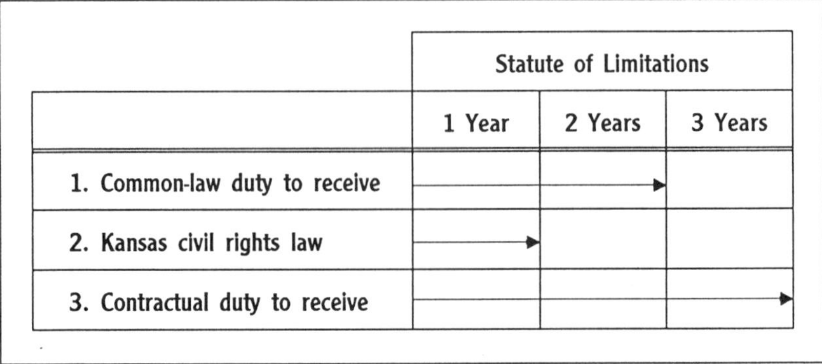

FIGURE 17.5 Causes of action in Kansas.

His third cause of action alleged a breach of a reservation contract. Here, the statute of limitations in Kansas was three years and the court held that he could go to trial on this cause of action. Examine Figure 17.5.

At trial the burden of proof will be on Mr. Thomas to prove the following:

1. That there was a binding reservation contract between himself and the hotel.
2. That the hotel, acting through its lawful agents, broke this contract.

If Mr. Thomas carries the burden on these two points, he will then have to prove what he lost because of the breach.

THOMAS V. PICK HOTELS CORPORATION
244 F. 2d 664 (US Ct. App. 10th Cir. 1955).

MURRAH, Circuit Judge.

Earl D. Thomas, a Negro, sued The Pick Hotels Corporation and others for damages resulting from a denial of hotel accommodations.

The trial court sustained a motion to dismiss the amended complaint on the grounds that the action against the appellee was barred by the Kansas two-year statute of limitations, Kansas G.S.1949, 60-306(3), as one "for injury to the rights of another, not arising on contract. . . ."

As we understand appellant's contentions on appeal, they are to the effect that his claim is governed by the Kansas three-year statute of limitations, Kansas G.S.1949, 60-306(2), as (1) one upon a contract, express or implied, or (2) one based upon the common-law duty of an innkeeper to provide nondiscriminatory accommodations to all, or (3) as one upon a claim, the liability for which is created by the Kansas Civil Rights Statute, Kansas G.S.1949, 21-2424.

The second section of the Kansas statute of limitations provides that "an action upon contract, not in writing, express or implied; an action upon a liability created by statute, other than a forfeiture or penalty" can only be brought within three years after accrual. Kansas G.S. 1949, 60-306(2).

[How the Case Got Into Federal Court]

The action against this appellee hotel corporation based on *diversity of citizenship* and requisite amount in controversy, was commenced within three years from the accrual of the asserted claim. And if by a liberal interpretation of the pleadings, they can be said to state a claim or claims upon which relief, not barred by the three-year statute of limitations, can be granted, it is our duty to so construe them, although they may be alternatively or inconsistently stated.

But there is nothing in the common law or the statute to preclude the parties from entering into a valid and enforceable contract for hotel accommodations. Certainly a contract of this kind is not against public policy of the State of Kansas. Indeed the statute and the common law sanction the contract by forbidding the innkeeper from making any distinction on account of race or color.

The complaint pleads a written contract to provide hotel accommodations on a given date subsequently modified by a telephone conversation, and it pleads an arbitrary refusal to provide such accommodations. The prayer is for damages, compensatory and punitive. But if the demand or prayer is for relief in tort, it in no way affects the right to recover on the contract, for the dimensions of a lawsuit are measured by what is pleaded and proven, not what is demanded.

We conclude that the complaint states a claim on an express contract to provide hotel accommodations and a breach of that contract. The claim is therefore governed by the Kansas three-year statute of limitations as one arising under a contract express or implied.

The judgment is accordingly reversed.

QUESTIONS

1. Do you know why mutual promises provide "consideration"? If not, ask.
2. What legal problems does the inn face in overbooking?

3. Why did the court refuse to allow the false registration in the Rapee case to be used as a reason to deny recovery?
4. What was the main point that the court wanted to make in the Rainbow case?
5. Set out the difference between "consequential" and "punitive" damages.
6. Why does the law refuse to allow punitive damages in contract cases?
7. Explain how a breach of contract could develop into a tort situation, using an example.
8. True or False. Group bookings at an inn should be handled with the same informality as customary bookings.
9. Discuss one implication of a federal law on overbooking.
10. Can you think of a legal problem that may arise when taking an unsigned impression of a guest's credit card at check-in?

ENDNOTES

1. *Moody v. Kenny,* 153 La. 1007, 97 So. 21 (1923).
2. *Williston on Contracts,* Vol. 5 sec. 1070.
3. See also *Cramer v. Tarr,* 165 F. Supp. 130 (Maine, 1958).
4. *Jones v. Bland,* 182 N.C. 70, 108 S.E. 344 (1921).
5. Ronald Terrell, Spring 1983.
6. *Freeman v. Kiamesha Concord, Inc.*, 351 N.Y.S. 2d 541 (1974).

18

Property of Guests: An Introduction

Henry's jump-off point of St. Joseph was the most raucous of the frontier outfitting towns. Hotels, saloons, gambling houses, streets, and even churches were thronged from late March on. The din was incessant, a mixture of hissing and clanking steamboats, lowing cows, braying mules, shouting men, and the tinny tones of organ-grinders. Most of the gathering argonauts pitched tents on the undulating prairie around the little town, creating a canvas village which came alive at night with campfires, music, and laughter. The few who were able to get rooms at $1 a day at such hotels as the Edgar House complained of meager meals and filthy sheets.[1]

Gold Dust,
Donald Dale Jackson

OVERVIEW

The property that guests bring to the inn is classified by the court cases into three categories:

1. Goods.
2. Transportation.
3. Money and valuables.

In this chapter we will become acquainted with the law in reference to all three categories in a general way. In Chapter 19, we will examine the statutes that limit inn liability for loss of property.

At any given moment at the inn, the amount of cash, jewelry, clothing, goods, automobiles, and other property belonging to guests will represent a substantial value. At the Mirage in Las Vegas, for example, such value will reach into the multimillions of dollars regardless of the time of day or night. At smaller inns, the value may not be so great, yet it will always be substantial. The innkeeper must keep this fact in mind because of the constant danger of loss, theft, or damage to such property. This is particularly true since it was the marketing efforts of the inn that brought about this accumulation of wealth and value. In addition, this accumulation has been done for the benefit of the inn and the law has always said that when one benefits in business, one must also carry certain burdens that may result. This principle is subject to exceptions, yet the basic rule remains.

This means that innkeeping creates a high-risk situation and the law quite early directed its attention to this matter. The question was, who has the legal liability for the loss of goods, autos, and valuables of guests? The question is important in practice because, in every loss of a guest's property, *someone* has to bear that loss. It is the job of the courts to make this determination or to lay down rules that will guide the parties in settling the matter out of court. If a defaulting innkeeper knows that he or she will lose in court, it makes good sense to cover the loss and avoid the litigation.

On the other hand, it is often difficult for courts to make this determination because the law is not clear in every case. In such situations it often becomes a matter for a jury to decide. If there are statutes that limit the liability of the innkeeper, or if a disclaimer (waiver of liability) is involved, then the words of the statute or the terms of the disclaimer will play a role in the determination of who shall bear that loss.

To make it more complex, the *nature* of the lost property becomes involved, as does the *location* of the loss at the inn. Add the other facts and circumstances of the loss and one encounters a complicated legal situation. To assist in understanding the problem, it is helpful to look first at some legal classifications.

PROPERTY OF GUESTS: SOME CLASSIFICATIONS

One who takes a course in business law quickly learns to distinguish "real property," "mixed property," and "personal property." The first is the earth and everything permanently attached to it. The second consists of property that has the characteristics of both real and personal property. An example would be bricks that are being laid in cement or mortar in the walls of a new inn. The latter consists of "movables" such as rings, suitcases, clothes, cash, automobiles, cameras, binoculars, and thousands of other items that guests bring into inns. We can eliminate real and mixed property from our discussion since guests are not normally involved with such property at the inn. (It *could* happen, however, where a guest buys into the property or a contractor is staying at the inn while building an addition to it.)

Thus, what a guest usually brings into the confines of the inn, including automobiles, would be personal property. The word "personal" has to do with the type of action that is brought in court when such property is lost through theft or other loss. This personal property category must now be subdivided.

Classes of Personal Property

The personal property that guests bring into inns is subdivided into three categories.

1. Goods

This is a catch-all category and means all general property of guests brought into an inn, but does *not* include automobiles or money and valuables.

2. A Guest's Means of Transportation

An automobile, while being personal property, has not been treated the same as money and valuables and "goods." The legal reason for this will be explored later in this chapter.

3. Money and Valuables

In this category we encounter rings, watches, jewelry of all types, ornaments, money, and other items of more than casual value. The category has been held to include business papers and the work product of professionals. This subclassification must now be further divided into valuables that a guest *uses* while at the inn and valuables that are *in excess* and not necessarily used during the guest's stay. Valuable jewels often fall into both categories. When the guest wears them, they are "in use." When the use ends, they are "in excess."

Valuables in excess can be further divided into valuables that are "hidden" and valuables that are "not hidden." An example of the former would be an heirloom watch carried in the guest's luggage of which the innkeeper takes custody. If the luggage is lost, the innkeeper may be responsible for the luggage but probably not the watch. If the innkeeper knew the watch was there, then liability for it might follow.

When determining liability for loss of a guest's property, the *location* of the loss, as well as its *cause*, will have a bearing upon the outcome.

Classification by Location and Cause of Loss

The location where property is lost at an inn can have a legal bearing upon the responsibility for the loss. For example, a suitcase left in a hallway and stolen is different legally than a suitcase left on the back seat of the guest's automobile, which is valet-parked at an inn.

In addition, the *cause* of the loss becomes important. If a guest leaves a room unlocked and goods are stolen, that is one thing. If an innkeeper fails to have electrical wiring repaired and this causes a fire that destroys a guest's goods, that is another.

In addition to these factors, the courts have classed property by what the guest *did* with that property. These can be called "classifications of intent."

Classifications of Intent

Mislaid Property

This is property that the guest placed at a particular location, such as a drawer in an inn room, and then forgot where he or she put it. In this situation, there was no intention on the part of the guest to give up the property.

Lost Property

This is property that has left the possession of the guest through carelessness or inadvertence and the location of which is not known to the guest. There was no intention to lose the property, yet it happened.

Abandoned Property

Here title and ownership are intentionally given up by the guest. This happens frequently in innkeeping as guests check out leaving partially filled whiskey or soft-drink bottles in the room or tossing a broken umbrella into a garbage can.

Treasure Trove

In this situation, money or valuables (or both) of unknown ownership are found. This happens in innkeeping and in such cases the courts usually hold that there was no intention on the part of the true owner to give up the goods.

In the case of *Jackson v. Steinberg*,[2] while cleaning a guest room a chambermaid found eight $100 bills under the lining of a dresser drawer. She delivered them to the innkeeper. The owner of the money could not be found and the maid sued the innkeeper for the money. After the maid received a verdict in the lower court, the innkeeper appealed. The upper court had this to say:

"From the manner in which the bills in the instant case were carefully concealed beneath the paper lining of the drawer, it must be presumed that the concealment was affected intentionally and deliberately. The bills, therefore, cannot be regarded as abandoned property.

"With regard to plaintiff's contention that the bills constituted treasure trove, it has been held that the law of treasure trove has been merged with that of lost goods generally, at least so far as respects the rights of the finder. Treasure trove, it is said, may, in our commercial age, include the paper representatives of gold and silver.

"The natural assumption is that the person who concealed the bills in the case at bar was a guest of the hotel. Their considerable value, and the manner of their concealment, indicate that the person who concealed them did so for the purposes of security, and with the intention of reclaiming them. They were, therefore, to be classified not as lost, but as misplaced or forgotten property and the defendant, as occupier of the premises where they were found, had the right and duty to take them into his possession and to hold them as a gratuitous bailee for the true owner.

It would seem that, as to articles voluntarily concealed by a guest, the very act of concealment would indicate that such articles have not been placed "in the protection of the house" and so, while the articles remain concealed, the innkeeper ordinarily would not have the responsibility of a bailee therefore. Upon their discovery by the innkeeper or his servant, however, the innkeeper's responsibility and duty as bailee for the owner becomes fixed. [Thus the maid lost the case. The innkeeper must find the owner or surrender the money to the state.]

Turning from our examination of the classifications of property, it becomes important to go back and find out how this law developed. To permit an orderly discussion, we will look at two time spans. The first is the "common-law period" which spanned the last ten centuries. The second ran from about the thirteenth century to 1890, and will be called the "transition period."

THE COMMON-LAW PERIOD

History tells us that a thousand years ago innkeeping flourished throughout the world. In England in particular there was a desire to make travel possible throughout the King's realm and a corresponding effort was made to promote that travel.

Not only was it necessary for private persons to travel for business and other purposes, there was also a need for the king or queen and his or her entourage to move about in the island kingdom to hold court, collect taxes, and bring the power of the crown directly to the people. It was a way of binding the people into a nation both actually and in spirit.

To facilitate this travel, it was necessary to encourage the development of inns and taverns at appropriate places, because the travelers had to be accommodated. As the early inns and taverns developed, legal problems arose in their operations. One of these was the loss of property of guests who were staying at an inn. It became necessary for the courts of England to hear and decide such cases where the parties involved could not reach settlement.

As these decisions were handed down, they began to form a body of law that could be used as guides by innkeepers. As we have seen, this body of law is known today as the "common law" because the rulings were "in common" to all of the subjects of the realm. When the American Colonies began to be formed, the common law was adopted in each of them as it suited the needs of the courts there. This law was in turn passed on to the American states following Independence.

It was in this manner that the common-law rules came down to us today. The rules that developed at common law were based upon the realities of those early years and were designed to be fair to the traveler. One traveling on horseback or by coach over long distances was in constant peril. Travelers were looked upon as victims not only by highway bandits, but by unscrupulous innkeepers as well. If one on such a journey lost his or her clothing, valuables, or means of transportation, that person was literally stranded.

Thus the rule developed that an innkeeper was responsible for the loss of goods, transportation, and valuables of a guest, once those items were brought within the confines of the inn. The innkeeper, much like a common carrier today, became an insurer of the goods and valuables of each person who became a guest at the inn.

As with so many rules of law, the English courts recognized three exceptions. First, if the loss was due to the traveler's carelessness, the innkeeper was excused from liability. Second, if the loss was due to "an Act of God," the innkeeper was also excused. Finally, if the loss was caused by "the public enemy" the innkeeper was again excused.

An act of God was defined as an accident "which could not have been occasioned by human agency but proceeded from physical causes alone."[3]

The "public enemy" meant armed persons from an invading force originating outside of England. The term was not broad enough to include an armed robber and the courts so hold today.

Out of this process came the principle of *infra hospitium.*

Infra Hospitium

It became necessary for the courts to decide at what point in time the liability of the innkeeper arose and at what point in time it came to an end. Thus came into being the rule of *infra hospitium* (pronounced "infra hospish-e-em"). This rule marked the beginning as that point in time when the traveler and the traveler's baggage came within the confines of the inn. At that time, as a matter of law, the baggage was in the care and custody of the innkeeper and the duty to safeguard it arose. Conversely the burden ended when the guest and the baggage left the confines of the inn.[4]

Through interpretation over the years, the courts have extended the "confines of the inn" rule to include adjacent fields where horses of a traveler were placed and then lost[5] and parking garages detached from a hotel where goods were stolen from guests' automobiles parked there for the convenience of the innkeeper.[6] Thus the confines of the inn at law may, depending upon the facts of the case, include real estate that is not part of the inn or even close to it. It is the *use* of the real estate by the innkeeper that controls the result.

As part of the common law of innkeeping, the courts began to apply the law of bailment to the property of guests. For example, if a guest left baggage at the inn for safekeeping after checking out, the rule of liability could not be that of *infra hospitium* since the traveler had ceased to be a guest. This was true even though the baggage was still within the confines of the inn. The liability of the innkeeper was now based upon the law of bailment. This law required that the innkeeper exercise ordinary care for the baggage until reclaimed by the traveler. If the baggage was then lost due to the negligence of the innkeeper, liability attached for its full value. If the loss was due to causes beyond the control of the innkeeper, such as a fire started by lightning, there was no liability at all.

It is helpful to examine bailment law at this point because the modern innkeeper often finds himself or herself in the position of a bailee.

Bailment Law as Applied to Innkeeping

A bailment is a legal relationship in which personal property is delivered by the bailor to the bailee–the one who receives the property. The bailee is then to accomplish a purpose (such as storage of the goods) after which the goods are to be returned to the bailor. In some bailments, the goods are to be improved by the bailee.[7] An example would be leaving a suit at the cleaners to be cleaned and pressed. See Figure 18.1.

An Example

A guest leaves a suitcase in an inn room while checking out. The room maid takes the suitcase to the front desk. A bailment as to the suitcase arises between the guest and the innkeeper at the moment of possession by the maid. The innkeeper must safeguard the suitcase and return it to the bailor-guest. It should be observed that the "delivery" was not actual and that the bailment was not agreed upon. Thus a bailment can arise by a voluntary agreement–or it can arise involuntarily by "constructive delivery." The legal effect is the same.

Summary

Legal points in a bailment are as follows:

1. There is delivery (actual or constructive) of goods to the bailee.
2. Title to the goods *does not* pass to the bailee.
3. The true owner of the goods may be a third party and not the bailor.
4. The bailee must use reasonable care with the goods and store them or improve them as agreed.

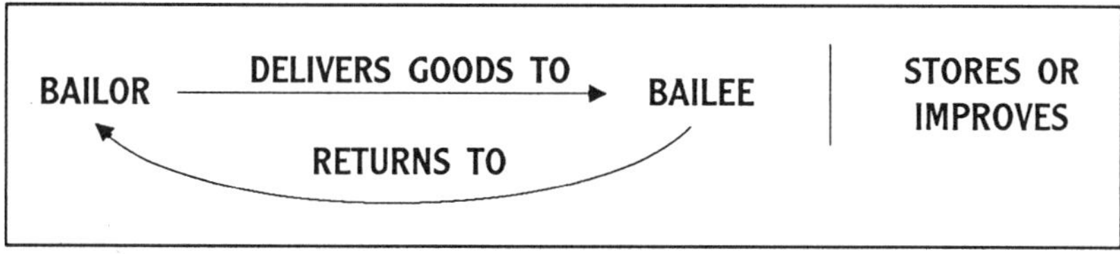

FIGURE 18.1

5. The bailee must, at some point in time, return the goods (or improved goods) to the bailor.

The key to a bailment is the giving up of control of the goods by the owner or the one who possesses them, and the assumption of that control by the bailee or the bailee's agent. In the previous example, once the maid found the suitcase, the innkeeper assumed control under the law of agency.

Distinguish this from a situation where a passerby sees an object lying on the ground but does not pick it up. There would be no bailment since possession was not taken. Also, the passerby had no control of the *location* where the object was seen.

Burden of Proof

In a bailment lawsuit, proof of (1) a contract of bailment, (2) delivery of the item to the innkeeper, (3) demand for the return of the item, and (4) failure of the innkeeper to redeliver the item, makes a *prima facie* case for the plaintiff.[8]

The burden then shifts to the innkeeper, who must show that he or she exercised reasonable care for the property that was lost.[9] If the innkeeper does not carry this burden, the innkeeper can be held responsible for the full value of the lost property.

When the courts made the innkeepers insurers, the innkeepers naturally began to look for ways to cut down on the harshness of the common-law rule. This led to what we referred to earlier as the "transition stage." It is to that period of time that we now direct our attention.

TRANSITION STAGE

When inns were scattered throughout the English countryside and there were fewer travelers, the innkeepers were able to control their inns and in turn care for the property of guests as mandated by the common law. The innkeeper would often greet incoming guests personally and see to the safety of their horses, coaches, and baggage.

In addition, the innkeeper often dined with the guests, which gave him or her an opportunity to learn of the wishes or complaints of each guest. This gave the innkeeper the control that a parent exercises over a family. This personal attention went about as far as possible toward meeting the requirements of the common law. The law said that the host had to care for the guests and their property and the innkeepers did just that. It was the golden age of innkeeping—but it was not to last.

The Desire to Limit Liability

As inns began to grow in number and size, the personal control enjoyed by early innkeepers began to fade. With more rooms and with guests arriving in increasing numbers both day and night, the innkeepers began to lose control. It was no longer possible for them to keep their entire operation in view. They were forced to use employees and agents to do what they had previously been able to do themselves. When this happened, the incidence of loss of property of guests began to rise. It was thus natural for innkeepers to look for ways to reduce the common-law liability because of the heavy burden that it placed upon them. This search led to "house rules," as we discussed them in Chapter 17, as well as "disclaimers."

House Rules

Innkeepers began to use "rules of the house" that affected both travelers and employees. Such use was in fact an attempt to reassert some control over what the courts had declared to be a "public house." If the rules were not obeyed, it was reasonable to expect the courts to pass some of the blame or loss along to those who did not obey them.

Before the courts would allow recovery to be barred for this reason, however, two tests had to be met. First the rule had to be reasonable and, second, the guest had to know of it. If an innkeeper tried to use house rules to avoid the duty to receive, or the duty not to negligently cause loss of property or injury to a guest, the courts would refuse to honor them and this is true today.

Innkeepers did not stop in their quest for limits on liability with house rules, however. They began to use the contract in an attempt to further limit their liability. Today such contracts or agreements are known as disclaimers or "exculpatory clauses." The latter phrase means ". . . clearing or tending to clear from alleged fault or guilt."[10]

Disclaimers to Limit Liability

While the courts have accepted reasonable house rules as a way for an innkeeper to limit his or her liability, they have frowned upon contract disclaimers in many instances. Thus some courts have held that ". . . contracts that limit liability are void as being contrary to public policy."[11] In other jurisdictions the courts become disturbed with them when they are used to take unfair advantage, that is, when guests have no choice but to agree to them.

On the other hand, if disclaimers are used in a reasonable manner and if proper notice of them is given, the courts will generally allow them to be used as a defense. When a guest is given a disclaimer, it has the practical effect of alerting that person to the limit on liability. This, in turn, encourages the guest to exercise more care and caution with property while it is on those premises. Thus disclaimers serve two purposes: They may give the innkeeper a defense and they may *prevent loss in the first place.*

Some Sample Disclaimers

The parking ticket in Figure 18.2, is from the parking lot of a hotel in Las Vegas, Nevada.

It contains forty-nine words, four periods, two commas, and one dash. Translating the legal words into common English, here is what it has to say:

"You are hereby notified that this piece of paper is legally binding upon you under provisions of American contract law and if you fail to read it, you will be bound by what it says nevertheless. We are landlords, not bailees and we are leasing to you an eight by twenty foot space in our parking lot. We do not care what you choose to place on that space during your lease, but whatever you do place there, is done so at your own risk and we accept absolutely no responsibility if what you place there is damaged or lost. This ticket cannot be used by any other person and is good on this day only. This is a short-term lease. You have no right to leave this space and return on this day. If you do leave, this lease is at an end at that point of time."

The disclaimer in Figure 18.3 is self-explanatory.

The disclaimer in Figure 18.4 was taken from one of the leading theme parks in the United States. This ticket is given when

NOTICE

THIS CONTRACT LIMITS OUR LIABILITY—READ IT

WE RENT SPACE ONLY.
No bailment is created and we are not responsible for loss of, or damage to, car or contents. This ticket is not transferable.

PLACE OTHER SIDE UP
Ticket covers only day purchased.

NO IN AND OUT PRIVILEGES

FIGURE 18.2

paying for admission to the parking lot. The same terms are also painted on large signs located at the driver's eye level at each of the entrance ticket booths. These signs have in large letters across the top, "PLEASE READ THIS CONTRACT." The combination of notices makes it hard for a patron who suffered a loss of property

Mission San Juan Capistrano

FOUNDED NOV. 1st, 1775

CALIFORNIA

THE PERSON USING THIS TICKET ASSUMES ALL RISK OF PERSONAL INJURY AND LOSS OF PROPERTY. MANAGEMENT RESERVES THE RIGHT TO REVOKE THE LICENSE GRANTED BY THIS TICKET.

VAYA CON DIOS

FIGURE 18.3

THIS CONTRACT LIMITS OUR LIABILITY—READ IT

This ticket LICENSES the holder to park ONE VEHICLE as directed. The management hereby declares itself NOT RESPONSIBLE for and assumes no liability arising from fire, theft, damage to or loss of the vehicle or any article left therein. ONLY A LICENSE OF SPACE IS GRANTED HEREBY AND NO BAILMENT IS CREATED. Acceptance of this ticket constitutes acknowledgment by holder that he or she has read and agrees to the provisions of the foregoing contract.

FIGURE 18.4

there to say that he or she did not know of the disclaimer. In the state where this double disclaimer is used—California—a state statute requires the double use.

Disclaimer Cases

In an Oklahoma case, a guest checked baggage at a hotel checkroom and was given a receipt. On the reverse of the receipt were the following words:

> In consideration of the receipt and free storage . . . for which this check is issued, it is agreed . . . that the hotel shall not be liable for loss or damage to said property unless caused by the negligence of the hotel in which event only the hotel shall be liable for a sum not to exceed $25.00. The hotel shall not in any event be liable for loss or damage to said property by fire, theft or moth, whether caused by its own negligence or otherwise.

Following a loss of a guest's goods, the guest sued and won in the lower trial court. The hotel then appealed to the appellate court. The upper court held that ". . . such alleged contractual limitations are contrary to public policy and void."[12]

In a more recent case, the bailee of a fur coat was allowed recovery in spite of a $100 limitation on liability found on the storage papers.[13]

In a 1957 hotel parking lot case,[14] a guest had baggage and other property stolen from his automobile which had been parked by a hotel attendant upon a detached parking lot. The lot was not a part of the hotel property and the hotel simply leased parking space there for overflow business. The case was decided in favor of the guest on the grounds of *infra hospitium*, negligence of the innkeeper, and bailment for hire. This happened even though the guest had been given a disclaimer at the time the auto was surrendered to be parked. Here is what the court had to say when it refused to give legal effect to the disclaimer:

> We therefore . . . remand the case for a determination of the reasonable value of the lost property and the costs of repairs to the automobile, and for entry of judgment for the appellant [plaintiff] in such sum against the hotel. In so doing, we are mindful that the court has many times ruled that the printed notice of limitation of liability on the claim check is not binding *unless the terms are known to the bailor (guest).*[15] The complete absence of testimony as to the knowledge of the limitation and agreement to it makes any contention of limited liability untenable. Reversed with instructions. [Emphasis added].

This case tells us two things: First, we must have our employees specifically call attention to our disclaimers and, second, if we ever go to trial on such matters, we must put testimony into the record to show that the attention of the guest had been called to the terms of the disclaimers.

RESPONSIBILITY FOR LOSS OF ONE'S OWN PROPERTY

There are times when a guest has the sole responsibility for the loss of his or her property at an inn; four examples will illustrate.

Instructions Given by the Guest

The guest gives particular instructions which are then followed by the innkeeper through his or her employees or agents. The directions are followed and the car is stolen. A court would in all probability place the responsibility on the guest–unless the innkeeper knew of some danger in the situation and failed to warn the guest of it.

Loss Caused by Roommate

A guest's roommate steals from the guest. The loss would have to be carried by the guest since the guest, not the innkeeper, selected the roommate and brought him or her into the inn. In those rare instances where guests are doubled up by the innkeeper, the result could be different.

Guest Uses Outsider

A guest authorizes someone from outside of the inn to handle his or her goods and that person damages or steals or loses them. There would be no liability on the innkeeper since the outside party would be the agent of the guest. Of course, the guest would have legal recourse against such agent.

A guest can incur personal liability through contributory negligence.

Contributory Negligence

Negligence has been defined as ". . . the failure to use such reasonable care and caution as would be expected of a reasonable man."[16] Negligence may result in liability to the innkeeper for loss of a guest's property but not if the guest has been guilty of contributory negligence.

Contributory Negligence Revisited

Contributory negligence is ". . . the act or omission amounting to want of ordinary care on part of complaining party which, concurring with [the innkeeper's] negligence, is the proximate cause of [the loss]. . . ."[17] When goods of a guest are lost, contributory negligence will bar recovery from the innkeeper. It has been traditional to allow a jury to determine if contributory negligence was present. It would be a question of fact—not law.

Contributory negligence is distinguished from "comparative negligence." In the states where this rule is in effect, the guest shares the responsibility for loss when both the innkeeper and the guest have been negligent, as was discussed in Chapter 14.

Comparative Negligence

Many states have adopted the rule of comparative negligence to replace the older and harsher rule of contributory negligence. Some states have passed statutes to adopt this rule and others have done so by rulings of the state courts. So one may find comparative negligence in one state by legislative act and in another by "doctrine" or the common law of that state.[18]

Leaving our general discussion of property, let's look at how the laws of property are applied to the transportation that guests bring to the inn.

GUESTS' AUTOS AND CONTENTS

> Another point raised is that the court erred in refusing to give defendant's offered instruction 'D,' which limited to $200 the amount of damages which the jury might award. This was offered under the theory that the loss came under 419,010, RSMo 1959, V.A.M.S., which limits innkeepers' liability for certain losses to $200. The statute relates to the loss of any money, jewelry, wearing apparel, baggage or other property of a guest. It is contended that the words 'or other property' includes a guest's automobile.
>
> Under the rule or maxim of construction known as *ejusdem generis,* general words following the enumeration of particular classes of things will be construed as applying to things of the same general nature or class of those enumerated. Applying that rule to the statute in question, the words 'or other property' obviously applied to things carried into the hotel by the guest. It would not include the guest's automobile.[19]

The innkeeper has traditionally been held to strict liability for the loss of a guest's means of transportation, once such transportation has been brought within the confines of the inn–*infra hospitium.* The old cases were concerned with saddle horses, drays, and other carriages with their teams.[20] The early cases extended the "confines of the inn" to include not only in-house parking or storage areas, but adjacent areas that were used by the inn's guests. In an early case, a field near an inn was held by the court to be within the confines, when the innkeeper placed the saddle horse of a traveler there to pasture and the horse subsequently vanished.[21]

THEORIES OF LIABILITY FOR AUTOS AND CONTENTS

In determining the liability for the loss of a guest's means of transportation (hereinafter called "auto"), the courts proceed on one of three theories:

1. Negligence of the innkeeper.
2. Breach of bailment responsibility where the auto is held in a bailment.
3. Strict liability under the common-law doctrine of *infra hospitium.*

Negligence

If the innkeeper has (1) taken control of the auto; (2) has been careless with it; and (3) this carelessness has been the proximate cause of the loss, then the courts have little hesitation in placing liability upon the innkeeper. In this three-part requirement, we see the absence of ordinary care.

In Bidlake,[22] the plaintiff upon driving up to the hotel, preparatory to registering at the hotel, was asked by the doorman if he wished his car parked. It was the practice of the hotel to have a doorman or night porter at the entrance to the hotel. Among other things, the doorman or night porter was authorized to arrange to have a guest's vehicle driven to a nearby garage for parking if the guest so desired. Plaintiff did wish to have his car parked and gave the doorman the auto keys. The doorman, instead of making the necessary arrangements for parking, took the car on a frolic of his own in the course of which he looted the glove compartment of the car and damaged the car.

Plaintiff sued the hotel for damage to his car and the value of the articles taken from the glove compartment on a theory of negligence. After a trial to the court, judgment was entered for the defendant. Plaintiff appealed.

On appeal, the Supreme Court of Colorado held defendant liable and reversed the judgment.

Bailment Theory

In the typical auto bailment, the keys are taken and a receipt issued for later reclamation. In bailment situations, one who suffered the loss must first prove that there was a contract of bailment and then must prove the value of what was lost. If a stolen item has a fair market value, that is what the court will allow as a recovery. On the other hand, if a stolen item has sentimental value only, such as a photo of a deceased child, the court will allow a jury to decide value.

The burden of proof then shifts to the bailee, who must prove that she or he did exercise ordinary care during the bailment. If the bailee can so convince a jury, then legal liability can be avoided for the loss.

Contents of Autos

An off-shoot of the problems caused by loss or damage to a guest's means of transportation is found in the theft of goods from *within* those vehicles. An innkeeper's responsibility for the goods of a guest brought into an inn is quite different than that for goods left in a vehicle. If an innkeeper does not know that diamonds are in the vehicle, there would probably be no innkeeper's or bailee's liability as to the diamonds. While the car may be within the confines of the inn, a court may hold that the diamonds are not. If the vehicle is accepted by an attendant, parked, and the keys retained, liability for auto loss may attach. If the guest self-parks the vehicle, it probably would not. If the damage or loss is caused by an agent or employee of the inn, then liability would attach to the inn. The same would be true when the inn uses the services of a parking facility owned by others. The agency relationship with the third party would perpetuate the liability of the inn to the same degree as if the parking lot had been operated by an employee of the inn.

Some courts hold that notice or knowledge of the contents of autos is required of the innkeeper before liability can attach to him or her. In the Hallman case in this chapter, the court said, however, that there was no need for specific notice. Thus it seems to be a case-by-case matter.

For example, in Park-O-Tell in this chapter, the court held that there was a bailment of the auto itself. The court then further held that there was also a bailment as to those items customarily carried in the auto even if the innkeeper had no actual notice of them. Thus there would be a bailment of the spare tire, the jack, and tire chains. The reasoning of the court was that these items can be expected to be there and the guest is not expected to take them to the guest room.

To complicate matters, the courts make a further distinction between "ordinary" bailees and those who are "professional" bailees. The standard of care is much higher for the latter.

> The courts, while recognizing that an ordinary bailee may contract to exempt himself from liability for loss of or damage to the goods, occasioned by his own negligence or that of his employee, exhibit a strong tendency to hold contracts of this character, when entered into by bailees in the course of general dealing with the public to be violative of public policy and this tendency becomes more pronounced in the more recent decisions. These bailees, who are termed "professional," as distinguished from "ordinary," bailees, are those who make it their principal business to act as bailees and who deal with the public on a uniform and not an individual basis, such as owners or proprietors of parcel checkrooms, garages, parking stations, and parking lots, carriers, innkeepers, and warehousemen. The basis for denying the right of such bailees to limit their liability for their own negligence is that the public, in dealing with them, lacks practical equality of bargain-

> ing power, since it must either accede to the conditions sought to be imposed or else forego the desired service. It is said that a bailee who is performing services for which the public has a substantial need should not be permitted to use this circumstance to coerce the members of the public into contracts of this kind. . . .[23]

Innkeepers who regularly take custody of the autos of guests fall into the professional category. Because of this bailment liability, many hotels and, in particular, motels, forego all contact with guests' autos, making it clear that they are accepting no liability for the safety of the autos or their contents.

There is a natural interest in limiting liability for autos and contents and there are some ways that it can be done. Some possibilities include the use of disclaimers, getting autos under the protection of the property statutes, and having the states pass special statutes to cover autos and contents.

Limiting Liability by Disclaimers

As discussed in this chapter, in the absence of statutes that limit liability an innkeeper *cannot* limit liabilities that arise out of his or her various duties. Due to the public nature of this calling, it would be against public policy to allow the innkeeper to do so. But as to the automobile of a guest, the innkeeper is generally a bailee. In the absence of a statute to the contrary, a bailee can limit liability if it is done properly.

Disclaimers used at inns often take the form seen in Figures 18.2 and 18.4. The bailment is specifically disclaimed. In addition, the ticket says that space only is rented. Such provisions have been upheld on the grounds that, because the words are on the ticket, there is just a *lease of land.*[24] There is a vast legal difference between taking custody and control of an auto, and allowing a guest to park an auto on land that is leased to the guests. It must be remembered, however, that the disclaimer will not work if it is not brought to the attention of the owner of the auto—and some courts will not uphold them as being against public policy.

Are Autos and Contents "Money and Valuables"?

Do the statutes that limit liability for money and valuables apply to autos and their contents? Under Missouri Revised Statutes,[25] the statute limits liability for "any money, jewelry, wearing apparel, baggage, or other property of a guest." In *Phoenix v. Royale,*[26] the innkeeper's lawyer argued that "other property of a guest" included the auto and contents and thus the innkeeper's liability was limited to $200 under the Missouri statute.

The court applied the rule of *ejusdem generis*: a rule of court interpretation. Under this rule, where general words follow an enumeration of specific items, the general words are to be held to apply to the class of items specifically listed.[27] It works like this. The statute lists:

1. Money.
2. Jewelry.
3. Wearing apparel.
4. Baggage.
5. Other property of a guest.

By applying this rule of statutory construction, the court must read number 5 as meaning watches, coats, shoes, ornaments, cash, coins, rings, brief cases, and other such items that are carried into the inn. Autos would *not* be included and the protection of the statute is lost. Examine Figure 18.5. Thus, money and valuables statutes are generally held not to apply to the auto.

"Under a statute relieving an innkeeper of liability for loss of personal baggage other than valuables, when a guest failed to deposit such baggage in a checkroom or other convenient place for storage provided by the innkeeper, a guest whose automobile was stolen from the hotel garage was, in *Savoy Hotel Corp. v. Sparks,*[28]

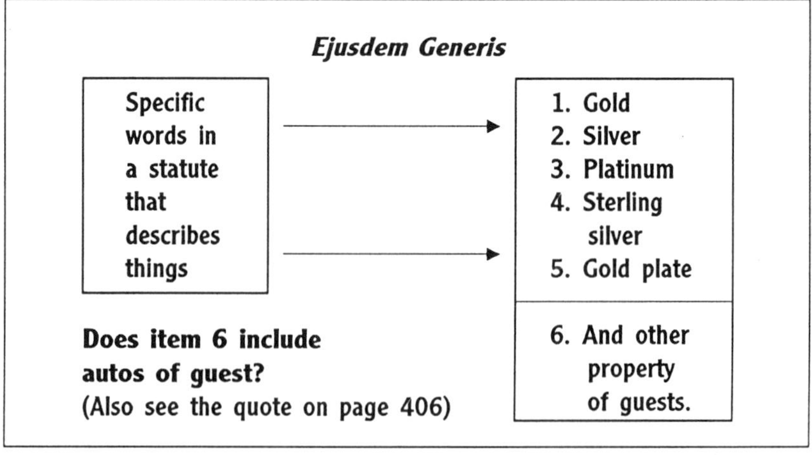

FIGURE 18.5

precluded from any recovery for certain articles of personal baggage which he had left in the automobile, since the garage was not an authorized agent for the storing of any personal property other than cars. Stating that the statute did not apply to the hotel's derivative liability for damage to the automobile, the court reduced the judgment against the hotel to the stipulated amount of such damage."

By far the best inn protection for liability of autos of guests and patrons and the contents thereof come from statutes that specifically cover such items. Unfortunately, at the present time, very few jurisdictions have enacted such laws.

Statutory Limits on Loss of Autos and Contents

On August 2, 1956, "by the Queen's most Excellent Majesty, by and with the advice and consent of the Lords, Spiritual and Temporal, and Commons," the Nova Scotia Parliament enacted the following statute:

> Without prejudice to any other liability or right of his with respect thereto the proprietor of a hotel shall not as an innkeeper be liable to make good to any guest of his any loss of or damage to, or have any lien on, any vehicle or any property left therein, or any horse or other live animal or its harness or other equipment. Hotel Proprietors Act, 1956, 26 & 27 Vict. c.41 (2), repealing the Innkeepers Liability Act of 1863.

The statute of Puerto Rico provides as follows:

> No innkeeper shall be liable to any guest, or other person, for any loss sustained by reason of theft of, or damage done to, any motor vehicle or other conveyance while parked in any free parking lot maintained by such innkeeper, or for any loss sustained by reason of the theft of, or damage done to any personal property left in such vehicle or other conveyance while so parked; provided, however, that nothing contained in this section shall be construed as to relieve any person of liability for his own willful act.[29]

The Puerto Rico statute goes on to state that, if free parking is provided, the regular services of the inn will not make the relationship one for hire or mutual benefit. Thus the statute strikes down the common-law position on this point.[30]

In Iowa, the following statute is found:[31]

> No keeper or owner of any hotel, inn or eating house shall be liable by reason of his innkeeper's liability or his responsibility as innkeeper to any guest for the loss of or damage to the automobile

> or other conveyance of such guest left in any garage not personally owned and operated by such hotel, inn or eating house or the owner or keeper thereof.

The Iowa statute makes it clear that innkeepers and restaurant operators who operate parking areas are bailees for hire, but liability is limited to the sum of $50 for the auto and contents. Under this statute, the guest can gain additional protection by listing and placing a value on specific items.[32]

Another possibility for limiting liability for autos is by the use of closed lots with "ticket spitters" and check-out lanes to collect fees. These spitters, however, became the subject of a blistering legal opinion in 1980 in the Buffalo City Court, in *Carlock v. Multiple Parking Services, Inc.*[33] Selected portions of what the court had to say about the theft of an auto there provide guidelines for considering the use of such automated devices at parking lots:

In our society today, the use of the automobile as the main mode of transportation is irrefutably established (with the possible exception of the City of New York). A person does not really choose where to park; he parks as close to his destination as possible. The fee he pays depends more on the distance he must then walk to the main business district or other specific area of attraction, rather than the perceived amount of security offered by supposedly competing operators.

What the developing line of precedent has created, is the absurd situation where, the less an operator spends, the less likely he will be found liable for damage or loss of a vehicle. Thus, even though he may be charging (in the Buffalo-Erie County metro area today) up to three dollars per day, per car, for long-term parking, or fifty cents per hour, per car (with an average of ten cars per space, per day) in a short-term lot, we are not holding him responsible for the care of the property left with him. Therefore, he saves money by putting on a "ticket spitter" instead of an attendant; or posts disclaimer notices which some courts have found significant as evidence of a supposed implied contractual understanding; or by not fencing his lot; or by not providing adequate lighting; or by not providing a guard for security; or by any combination of these factors. The net result is that he saves further sums because he is not found liable for damage or loss to vehicles. This last conclusion may not be entirely true, today in the City of Buffalo, as we shall soon see.

All of this exploration and analysis leads this Court to one conclusion: the "bailment theory" as a basis for recovery in parking lot cases is no longer appropriate. We assume this was the state of mind and conclusion reached by the Court of Appeals in 1976, in regard to the archaic distinctions between the status of persons on real property, and the consequent duty of care owed them.[34]

The new standard to be followed . . . was to be ". . . reasonable care under the circumstances whereby foreseeability shall be a measure of liability."[35]

Therefore, this Court need not decide whether a bailment was created in the instant case. The measure we will apply is that of "reasonable care under the circumstances whereby foreseeability shall be a measure of liability."

The Court further finds that the attendant's failure to observe the acts of vandalism–which, by nature of the damage caused, had to be overt and observable–was also negligence, attributable to the defendant. This is true, whether the attendant was officially on duty or not, since the defendant cannot establish when the damage took place. Even though the plaintiff has the burden of proof, since he wasn't present and the defendant's employee was, the burden of coming forward with those facts shifts to the defendant.

The plaintiff's burden is met by his showing that the defendant failed to exercise ". . . reasonable care under the circumstances, whereby foreseeability shall be a measure of liability."

Will the use of free parking lots or parking spaces solve the problem?

Free Parking Lots and Spaces

It has been held that a free parking lot furnished by an innkeeper *is an invitation to park there.* When a guest accepts that invitation, this brings the auto *infra hospitium* with the attending liability.[36] Other courts have held just the opposite, letting the case be decided on negligence or bailment grounds.[37]

Other inns enter into contracts with independent contractors to operate parking lots in an attempt to escape innkeeper liability for autos and contents. This arrangement has been held, however, not to change the inn-guest obligations and the courts generally hold the private garage to be the agent of the innkeeper.

On the other hand, if there is in fact no inn-guest relationship, then the *infra hospitium* rule would not be applied at all. A plaintiff who was attending a banquet at a hotel was held not to be a guest.[38]

The apparent authority of agents who take custody of autos at inns is usually said by the courts to be enough to bind the inn as to the safety of both the auto and its contents.[39] The guest-to-be does not "have to search behind the uniform of the valet" for actual authority to accept the auto on behalf of the innkeeper.

Under the pending international treaty, Hotelkeeper's Contract, autos and contents can be excluded from liability coverage by any adopting nation that may decide to do so. This would be the ultimate protection for innkeepers in the adopting nations, but it would apply only to the autos, and their contents, of international travelers. On the other hand, international travelers' autos and contents should be subject to the innkeepers' lien, giving a double benefit to innkeepers in the adopting nations, Section 24, Hotelkeeper's Contract. It is not known at the present time whether the United States will become an adopting nation.

In the Park-O-Tell case that follows, the court held that all that was necessary was that the auto and its contents:

1. Be brought into the inn in the usual manner.
2. Not be under the exclusive control of the guest.
3. Be under the control of the innkeeper, expressly or implied.

PARK-O-TELL V. ROSKAMP
203 Okla. 493, 223 P. 2d 375 (1950).

JOHNSON, Justice.

The parties herein occupied reverse positions in the trial court, and they will hereafter be referred to as plaintiff and defendant.

The plaintiff alleged in his petition that he and his wife registered as guests at the defendant's hotel, known as Park-O-Tell in Oklahoma City on October 15, 1946; that in consideration of the room rent paid defendant furnished a garage in which to park the plaintiff's automobile; that on the afternoon of said day, after registering at the hotel, he turned the custody of his car over to an attendant of the defendant; that plaintiff saw the attendant drive his automobile into the garage and park it; that at the time he turned the car over to the attendant it contained numerous personal belongings of the plaintiff and his wife, a list of which plaintiff attached to his petition; that on October 16 he asked for his car, but defendant failed to deliver the same to plaintiff; that after making search of the garage defendant advised him that the car had been stolen; that the car was of the value of $1,700.00; that the personal property of plaintiff and wife was left in the car placed in custody of defendant was of the value of $935.40; that by reason of the theft of his vehicle he expended $191.00 railroad fare to return home; and prayed judgment for $2,826.40.

Defendant answered denying generally the allegations of the plaintiff's petition, and specifically alleged that it made no charge for parking purposes for the use of said garage and that it makes none to any of its guests; that it took no possession, custody or control of the plaintiff's automobile or any of its contents; that the automobile was not placed in its care or custody; and that it takes no custody of any of the automobiles of its guests, either by servants, agents, employees or otherwise. Defendant further alleged that plaintiff left his keys in his automobile, and was thereby guilty of negligence and that his loss was due to lack of care of plaintiff; and that plaintiff assumed full responsibility of any and all losses.

Upon the issues thus joined, trial was had to a jury. The court instructed the jury that under the facts in the case the defendant was liable to plaintiff and submitted to the jury only the question of the reasonable cash value of the automobile and contents. Verdict was for the plaintiff for $2,500.00, upon which the court rendered judgment accordingly. From this judgment the defendant appeals.

Defendant presents error under two propositions: First, "The innkeepers law does not apply to the automobile or its contents." Second "The question of liability, under proper instructions, should have been submitted to the jury."

It is asserted under proposition one that neither the law of innkeepers nor the law of bailments applies, and that the only liability, if any, rests upon the law of reasonable care and negligence.

The trial court submitted this case to the jury on the theory that it came within the innkeepers statute, 15 O.S.1941 §501, which provides:

> An innkeeper or keeper of a boarding house is liable for all losses of or injuries to, personal property placed by his guests or boarders under his care, unless occasioned by an irresistible superhuman cause, by a public enemy, by the negligence of the owner, or by the act of someone whom he brought into the inn or boarding house.

The defendant admits that the Park-O-Tell is a place with a wide, sweeping drive into the center of the hotel, with parking space in the hotel and also space at the back of the hotel, which is enclosed where, when needed, cars of guests are parked; that the parking facilities are advertised as a part of the accommodations furnished to the guests without extra charge. Defendant insists, however, that the hotel did not take possession of the guests' automobiles, but it is undisputed that attendants did take guests' automobiles at the entrance of the hotel, drive them into the hotel and park them, usually leaving the keys in them; that if driven into the hotel by the guest, the guest was instructed where to park; that often it was necessary for the attendants to move the cars from one place to another in the hotel. Defendant to sustain its contention that it did not take or have possession of plaintiff's car suggests that plaintiff retained the right to go and get his automobile or the contents thereof at any time he desired; that plaintiff went into the hotel where his car was parked and took from it some personal items and returned to his room; that by doing so he knew that the keys were left in his car, and when he failed to lock the car and take the keys he was thereby guilty of negligence.

A review of the evidence convinces us that the evidence that plaintiff placed his automobile and its contents under defendant's care and that the plaintiff was without negligence is so conclusive that the trial court in the exercise of sound judicial discretion would have been compelled to set aside a verdict for the defendant. Under these circumstances the court was justified in its instruction taking from the jury the question of liability and leaving to it the question of damages.

Under the common-law rule an innkeeper, although not negligent, was liable for loss of property of a guest unless the guest was guilty of negligence or the loss was occasioned by an act of God or the public enemy.

This court in *Abercrombie v. Edwards,* 62 Okl. 54, 161 P. 1084, with reference to the innkeepers statute of Oklahoma, sec. 501, *supra,* in the fourth syllabus said: "The provision of this statute that the innkeeper is liable for goods of his guests, 'placed under his care,' is declaratory of the common law, not restrictive thereof. Under such provisions it is not necessary, in order to render the innkeeper liable for their loss, that the goods be placed under his special care, or that notice be given of their arrival. It is sufficient if they are brought into the inn in the usual and ordinary way and are not retained under the exclusive control of the guest, but are under the general and implied control of the innkeeper."

The term "property" as used in this statute, it being declaratory of the common law, is broad enough to cover an automobile and its contents. 43 C.J.S., Innkeepers, §16.

The trial court in overruling motion for a new trial appropriately stated the issues and law in this case as follows:

"The legal question presented on the trial and on the motion is novel and no case in point on the facts has been found.

"The material facts were undisputed, the Court instructed the jury to find for the plaintiff under the innkeeper statute (O.S. 1941, 15-501), instructed them on the measure of damages (O.S. 1941, 12-590), and a verdict was returned for the value of the car, and personal property left in it at the time it was parked with the defendant.

"The defendant contends that its liability, if any, is that of bailee as to the car, and in no event is defendant liable under the facts, for its contents.

"The defendant was an innkeeper and the plaintiff was a guest, when the loss occurred. All the facts and circumstances, including defendant's name, point to the fact that it was an inn having, and holding itself out to the public as providing the facilities peculiar to an inn catering to transients traveling in private automobiles with their baggage and other accessories of travel. The conveniences offered to such travelers by an inn of this nature are well known. Emphasis is placed, as shown by the evidence, on the 'parking' feature, that is, the guest is relieved as a primary part of the services offered, of the burden and necessity of securing a safe parking, that is storage, place for his car and its contents. That latter are not usually all necessary for the enjoyment of the food and lodging provided for a temporary stay in an inn and the storing of the car with contents in it is a decided convenience, and one which was furnished by the defendant.

"The offer of the defendant made to the public was accepted by the plaintiff. It was the intent of the parties that the defendant was furnishing and the plaintiff paying for the above mentioned service. The car and its contents, therefore, were personal property placed under the care of the defendant under the innkeeper statute."

Defendant's proposition two that the question of liability, under proper instructions, should have been submitted to the jury is without merit.

The material facts being undisputed, the loss of plaintiff's property, and the relationship of innkeeper and guest as between defendant and the plaintiff being established, and there being no evidence of negligence of plaintiff, the question of legal liability under the innkeepers law was properly determined by the court and it was not error under the facts in this case to instruct the jury to return a verdict for the plaintiff.

In view of what has been said, we deem further discussion unnecessary. The judgment is affirmed.

WELCH, CORN, LUTTRELL and HALLEY, JJ., concur.

GIBSON and O'NEAL, JJ., dissent.

The Ross case that follows illustrates the confines of the inn rule once again. In states that do not follow this rule, liability would have to be based upon negligence or bailment liability.

The plaintiffs planned a wedding and reception at the hotel and thus were not guests in the inn-guest sense, but were nonguests or third parties. After goods were stolen from their auto, the innkeeper asked the court to provide the protection of the "$100 value-not-stated" statute of the state in question. The court rejected this, however, holding that a bailment had arisen between the innkeeper and the nonguest. The innkeeper-bailee had been negligent through its agent; thus liability attached for the full value.

It should be observed that a disclaimer had been used at the time the keys to the auto were taken but the court refused to give it legal effect because the plaintiff's attention had not been called to it.

ROSS V. KIRKEBY HOTELS
160 N.Y.S. 2d 978 (1957)

HOFSTADTER, Justice.

The plaintiffs, husband and wife, recovered below against the defendant, the operator of the Hotel Warwick, in the City of New York, the full value of their luggage and wearing apparel stolen from the husband's automobile. The plaintiffs were to be married at the Warwick on the day of the theft, the arrangements for the ceremony and the reception to follow at the hotel having been made by the bride's mother. The husband, accompanied by his brother, arrived at the hotel in his car the morning of his wedding day.

The trial court was justified in finding that the car was placed in the care of the hotel doorman, with specific instructions to park it in the hotel garage, so that nothing would go wrong; that the doorman undertook to do so, and told the plaintiff husband to leave the keys in the ignition switch. As the husband entered the hotel with his brother, he saw the doorman drive the automobile away. At the time the value of the car and its contents was not stated, nor was a written receipt of any kind issued by the defendant. Later in the day, when the husband came out of the hotel to arrange for the delivery of his car, he found it in the street and discovered that it had been broken into and that all its contents were missing. The doorman admitted that he had not placed the car in a garage, but had parked it across the street from the hotel.

It is undisputed that the plaintiffs did not register as guests of the hotel, that no room was assigned to them, and that the sole purpose of their visit was to participate in the wedding ceremony and reception.

The delivery of the car to the defendant's doorman to be placed in a garage, in the circumstances stated, constituted a bailment, *Galowitz v. Magner,* 208 App.Div. 6, 203 N.Y.S. 421, and parking the car on the street instead was a violation of the terms of the bailment, which of itself imposed liability on the defendant irrespective of negligence, *Mortimer v. Otto,* 206 N.Y. 89, 99 N.E. 189. Leaving the car containing the plaintiffs' wardrobe in the street, especially after the explicit instructions that it be placed in a garage, likewise warranted a finding of negligence, because of the defendant's failure to exercise the care imposed on it by law as a bailee.

The defendant urges, however, that the bailment was an incident of the relation of hotel keeper and guest between it and the plaintiffs and that, because of this relation, it is entitled to the limitation of liability prescribed by section 201 of the General Business Law. This section, so far as here material, provides:

"No hotel keeper except as provided in the foregoing section shall be liable for damage to or loss of wearing apparel or other personal property in the room or rooms assigned to a guest for any sum exceeding the sum of five hundred dollars, unless it shall appear that such loss occurred through the fault or negligence of such keeper, nor shall he be liable in any sum exceeding the sum of one hundred dollars for the loss of or damage to any such property when delivered to such keeper for storage or safe keeping in the store room, baggage room or other place elsewhere than in the room or rooms assigned to such guest, unless at the time of delivering the same for storage or safe keeping such value in excess of one hundred dollars shall be stated and a written receipt, stating such value, shall be issued by such keeper, but in no event shall such keeper be liable beyond five hundred dollars, unless it shall appear that such loss occurred through his fault or negligence. . . ."

Though the plaintiffs' loss is found to have occurred through the defendant's fault or negligence, the impact of the section must nevertheless be considered, for when, as here, no value is stated at the time of the guest's delivery of the property to the hotel keeper, the statutory limitation becomes applicable, notwithstanding the hotel keeper's negligence, *Honig v. Riley,* 244 N.Y. 105, 155 N.E. 65; *Adler v. Savoy Plaza, Inc.*, 279 App. Div. 110, 115, 117, 108 N.Y.S.2d 80, 84, 86. It, therefore, becomes necessary to determine whether the plaintiffs were guests of the hotel within the purview of section 201.

It is to be noted that section 201 refers at several points to "the room or rooms assigned" to the guest. Thus, the assignment of a room to be occupied is stressed as an element of the relation. The court is aware of the cases relied on by the appellant, in which the relation of hotel keeper and guest has been held to arise before the actual assignment of a room, *Adler v. Savoy Plaza, Inc.*, 279 App.Div. 110, 108 N.Y.S.2d 80 or to carry over the limitation after the guest no longer occupies his room, *Dilkes v. Hotel Sheraton, Inc.*, 282 App.Div. 488, 125 N.Y.S.2d 38. In those cases, however, the occupancy of a room was in definite contemplation or had already occurred, so that the acceptance of the plaintiffs property for safekeeping could fairly be treated as something done in the course of the usual relation between hotel and guest.

This vital element of the relation is totally absent in the case at bar. The plaintiffs did not seek or receive lodging at the defendant's hotel. As stated, they came solely to attend the marriage function. They did not request that a room be assigned to them and neither they nor the defendant at any time had in mind their occupancy of a room. Their presence in the hotel for a purpose other than that of becoming guests did not make them guests within the language or intent of section 201 of the General Business Law, dealing with the relation of hotel keeper and guest in its traditional sense. It follows that the defendant is not entitled to the benefit of the limitation of liability and that the plaintiffs were correctly permitted to recover the full value of their property.

Judgment affirmed.

STEUER and AURELIO, JJ., concur.

In the Hallman case the auto was taken by a valet to a detached parking lot and the valet saw the goods in the auto. Notice to the agent was thus imputed by law to the innkeeper. While a disclaimer was used, it was not called to the attention of the guest and the court refused to uphold it.

Three things should have been done in this case by the innkeeper acting through his or her agent:

1. The guest should have been informed that the auto was to be parked on a detached lot.
2. The guest should have been warned not to leave goods in the auto.
3. The disclaimer should have been called to the attention of the guest.

Had these things been done, the guest would probably have protected the contents and thus prevented the loss.

HALLMAN V. FEDERAL PARKING SERVICES
134 A. 2d 382 (1957)

From an adverse ruling in the trial court appellant brings this appeal to recover the value of personal property removed from his (hotel guest) automobile by theft while he was a guest at the New Colonial Hotel.

The facts as developed by the evidence disclosed that on the evening of November 8, 1956, appellant with his wife and daughter stopped for a night's lodging at the hotel, in the course of their journey to Florida. When registering with the desk clerk, appellant asked if the hotel had parking facilities and was assured that the vehicle would be taken care of by the bellboy. The desk clerk testified that it was normal procedure in the hotel for the bellboy to ask an arriving guest if he wanted his car parked. The bellboy would then get a claim check from the hotel, supplied it by appellee parking lot, if the guest desired this service.

The baggage necessary for the use of the parties during their brief stay was transferred to appellant's room and the automobile was delivered for the night by the bellboy to an open parking lot independently managed and controlled by appellee Federal Parking Services, Incorporated. There the automobile was turned over to an attendant who locked it and retained the keys. At the time the vehicle was taken to the lot, it contained pieces of luggage on the rear seat and floor, wearing apparel hung on racks, and the usual items of traveling paraphernalia, some of which had been placed under a seat. On the bellboy's return to the hotel, he gave appellant a claim check bearing the name of the parking lot and the stamped name "New Colonial." The claim check contained a printed notice limiting liability which provided that the parking lot was not responsible for loss due to theft and articles in vehicles were left at the owner's risk.

The following morning when appellant arrived at the lot for his automobile, he discovered the side window broken. The glove compartment had been forced open and emptied and personal property, including that placed under the seat, valued at approximately $557 had been removed.

From these facts the court concluded as a matter of law (1) that there was no contract of bailment between the hotel and appellant; (2) that the doctrine of *infra hospitium* was inapplicable; and (3) that while a contract of bailment existed between the parking lot and appellant, there was no showing that it failed to exercise the degree of care required. We are unable to agree with these conclusions in whole.

We need not resolve the arrangement between the hotel and the parking lot as to whether the hotel was the agent of the parking lot or vice versa as the paucity of evidence on this point would permit a purely conjectural solution at most. We pass then to a consideration of the relationship existing between appellant and both the hotel and the parking lot and the degrees of liability, if any, to be imposed.

Appellant argues that once the property of a guest is taken into the custody and control of the innkeeper the goods are considered *infra hospitium* and the liability for loss or destruction of the goods imposed is that of an insurer, unless the property is lost or destroyed by an act of God, the public enemy, or by fault of the guest. This is undoubtedly the rule of common law having its source in the ancient case of Calye which dealt with the innkeeper's liability for the loss of a guest's horse put to pasture. The common-law rule is of force in this jurisdiction. The doctrine of *infra hospitium* has been applied in cases where a car or its contents are lost while in the exclusive care and custody of a hotel. However, where the hotel takes custody of the vehicle, as here, and delivers it to a lot or garage not an integral part of the hotel and thereafter a loss of the property occurs, the better rule imposes the liability of a bailee for hire on the hotel. As such, it is required to exercise an ordinary degree of care to protect and return the property of which it assumes custody.

We conclude that when the bellboy, with actual authority of the hotel to deliver automobiles to the lot, took possession of the keys and the vehicle, both the vehicle and the contents of the automobile were accepted by the hotel into its custody. It had physical control and the intent to control the property; a bailment relationship was therefore created. Accordingly, the trial court's conclusion that there was no contract of bailment between the hotel and appellant was erroneous. That payment for parking was made to the lot and not the hotel is immaterial for the service was incident to this type of a business and a hotel, particularly in a metropolitan area, derives indirect benefits and profits by providing such facilities.

Turning to the hotel's acceptance of the property in the vehicle, appellant and his family were in transit stopping only for the night. They could reasonably be expected to leave luggage, wearing apparel, and other personal belongings in the car not necessary for their night's lodging. Courts have uniformly held that the liability of a bailee for hire for the loss of property in an automobile depends on notice or knowledge of the contents. The notice need not be actual or express; constructive or implied notice may be inferred. Clearly the hotel was put on notice that appellant was a traveler and the apparel hanging from racks was in plain view. Upon entering the car the luggage on the floor and rear seats could easily be seen, and common knowledge and experience could anticipate that the car might contain in its interior other articles normally carried by travelers.

In substance the evidence in this case simply disclosed that the hotel held itself out to appellant as providing parking facilities for his car. In reliance on the information of the desk clerk the car with most of its contents in plain view was entrusted to the hotel for safekeeping. The vehicle with its property was accepted by the hotel through its bellboy, who by actual authority and hotel practice was empowered to accept it. While the claim check given appellant contained both the names of the hotel and lot, appellant could have reasonably inferred that his car with its contents was still in the care and custody of the hotel.

The bulk of the defense evidence consisted of an attempt to show appellant's contributory negligence in leaving the property in the car and an attempt to show that the lot had exercised due care. We have previously discussed and disposed of the first point. A review of the evidence reveals that no explanation or justification is offered by the hotel for its failure to redeliver the property other than the fact of theft. Some evidence other than the mere allegation of theft is necessary before the burden of proving the bailee's negligence is shifted back to the bailor. The hotel has neither offered proof sufficient in weight and quality to show the loss was not connected with the lack of proper care on its part, nor has it offered any affirmative proof that it exercised the ordinary degree of care required in order to refute the inference of the *prima facie* case and prevent recovery.

We therefore reverse the judgment of the lower court and remand the case for a determination of the reasonable value of the lost property and the costs of repairs to the automobile, and for entry of judgment for the appellant in such sum against the hotel. In so doing, we are mindful that the court has many times ruled that the printed notice of limitation of liability on the claim check is not binding unless the terms are known to the bailor. The complete absence of testimony as to knowledge of the limitation and agreement to it makes any contention of limited liability untenable.

Reversed with instructions.

QUESTIONS

1. What policy reason prompted the courts to hold early innkeepers responsible for the loss of transportation of guests?
2. Might the "confines of an inn" include a distant parking lot? Under what circumstances?
3. How would you define "reasonable care"? How would this standard be applied in a court?
4. What effect does the negligence of a guest have upon the innkeeper's liability for loss of the guest's auto?
5. Why would an innkeeper try to claim the status of bailee if an auto is stolen from the inn when in fact there may be no bailment?
6. Explain briefly how the "confines of the inn" rule could be used by a court to include real estate that is in fact not a part of the inn. When courts make such rulings, might they be in the process of developing a new phase in innkeeping law?
7. Give examples of "real property," "mixed property," and "personal property" at an inn. Why is it important legally to be able to distinguish them?
8. If a guest accidentally loses a watch that she is wearing and there was no fault on the innkeeper, should the innkeeper be held responsible under modern law? Why?
9. What is the legal difference between mislaid and abandoned property? What effect might this difference have in a case where a guest is suing for the value of lost property?
10. Regarding the case of *Jackson v. Steinberg*, several years have gone by and no one has claimed the eight $100 bills. What happens to the money now? Should the innkeeper have kept the money in an interest-drawing account? Why?

ENDNOTES

1. Donald Dale Jackson, *Gold Dust*. Alfred A. Knopf, New York, 1980; p. 146.
2. *Jackson v. Steinberg*, 186 Or. 129, 200 P. 2d 376 (1948).
3. *Middough v. U.S.*, 293 F. Supp. 977, 980 (D.C. Wyo.).

4. *Davidson v. Madison Corporation,* App. Div. 421, 247 N.Y.S. 789, 795 (New York, 1931).
5. *Cayle's Case,* 8 Co. Rep. 32a, 77 Eng. Rep. 529 (K.B., 1584).
6. *Park-O-Tell v. Roskamp,* 203 Okl. 493, 233 P. 2d 375.
7. *Story on Bailments,* 9th ed. at page 27.
8. *Right Way Laundry v. Davis,* 98 Okl. 264, 255 P. 345.
9. *Smith v. Maher,* 84 Okl. 49, 202 P. 321, 23 A.L.R. 270.
10. *Baird v. State,* 246 S.W. 2d 192, 195.
11. *Scott Auto & Supply v. McQueen,* 111 Okl. 107, 226 P. 372, *Oklahoma City Hotel Co. v. Levine,* 189 Okl. 331, 116 P. 2d 997, 999 (1941).
12. *Oklahoma City Hotel Co. v. Levine, supra.*
13. *Carter v. Reichlin Furriers,* 21 U.C.C. Rep. (Conn. Supp., June, 1977), applying U.C.C. 7-204 (2).
14. *Hallman v. Federal Parking Services,* 134 A. 2d 382 (1957).
15. *Manning v. Lamb,* D.C. Mun. App., 89 A. 2d 882, *Palace Laundry Dry Cleaning Co. v. Cole,* D.C. Mun. App., 41 A. 2d 231.
16. *Hamrick v. McCutcheon,* 101 W. Va. 485,133 S.E. 127, 129.
17. *Honaker v. Critchfield,* 247 Ky. 495, 57 S.W. 2d 502.
18. See *NY CPLR* 1411 (McKinney Supp. 1975).
19. *Phoenix Assurance Co. v. Royale Investment Co.,* 393 S.W. 2d 43 (No. Ct. App., 1965).
20. *Hulett v. Swift,* 33 N.Y. 571, 88 Am. Dec. 405 (1865).
21. *Cayle's Case,* 8 Co. Rep. 32a., 77 Eng. Rep. 529 (K.B., 1584).
22. *Bidlake v. Shirley Hotel,* 133 Colo. 160, 292 P. 2d 749 (1950).
23. *8 Am. Jur. 2d,* para. 131, page 1026.
24. *Wall v. Airport,* 40 Ill. 2d 506, 244 N.E. 2d 190 (1969).
25. 419.010.
26. 393 S.W. 2d 43 (Mo. Ct. App., 1965).
27. *U.S. v. La Brecque,* D.C. N.J., 419 R. Supp. 430, 432, *Aleksich v. Indus.,* 116 Mont. 127, 151 P. 2d 1016, 1021.
28. 57 *Tenn App.* 537, 421 S.W. 2d 98 (1967).
29. Ch. 35, sec. 715.
30. Sec. 711 (e).
31. Nonliability for Conveyance, sec. 105.7.
32. Sec. 105.8.
33. 103 Misc. 2d 943, 427 N.Y.S. 2d 670 (Buffalo City Ct. 1980).
34. *Basso v. Miller,* 40 N.Y. 2d 233, 386 N.Y.S. 2d 564, 352 N.E. 2d 868 (1976).

35. *Basso v. Miller,* 40 N.Y. 2d 233, 352 N.E. 2d 868, 872.
36. *William v. Linnitt,* 1 K.B. 565 (C.A., 1950).
37. *Lader v. Warsher,* 165 Misc. 559, 1 N.Y.S. 2d 160 (Columbia Co., 1937).
38. *Edwards Hotel v. Terry,* 185 Misc. 824, 187 So. 519 (1939), *Ross v. Kirkeby,* in this chapter.
39. Bidlake, *supra.*

19

Property of Guests: The Statutory View

The imposition of strict liability on the innkeeper found its origin in the conditions existing in England in the fourteenth and fifteenth centuries. Inadequate means of travel, the sparsely settled country and the constant exposure to robbers left the traveler with the inn practically his only hope for protection. Innkeepers themselves, and their servants, were often as dishonest as the highwaymen roaming the countryside and were not beyond joining forces with the outlaws to relieve travelers and guests, by connivance or force, of their valuables and goods. Under such conditions it was purely a matter of necessity and policy for the law to require the innkeeper to exert his utmost efforts to protect his guests' property and to assure results by imposing legal liability for loss without regard to fault.

Minnesota Fire and Marine v. Matson,
44 Haw. 59, 61, 352 P. 2d 337 (1960)

OVERVIEW

In the last chapter, we took a close look at the common-law liability of innkeepers for the loss of property and autos of guests. In addition, we examined steps taken historically by innkeepers to reduce that liability. In this chapter, we will look at another way to limit liability—the most effective of them all. This came in the form of statutory protections.

In the last century, American innkeeping began to spread from coast to coast, and it became a process that has not ceased. The expansion of inns at that time almost always paralleled the construction of the telegraph and railway systems. During that century the legislatures of the existing, and later the forming states, began to enact statutes to place limits upon the liability of innkeepers for the loss of property of guests. New York state took the lead with its statute of 1855. Many reasons prompted this. First, the realities of earlier centuries were fading in a more modern America. The travelers of the 1800s simply did not need the protection that travelers had needed 500 years before. The *American Law Reports (ALR)* expressed it this way:

> The statutes defining the limits of an innkeeper's liability for loss of or injury to his guest's property represent a legislative intent to soften what has been termed an unduly harsh common-law rule.
>
> In former times, there were a number of sound reasons to justify the public policy of imposing a strict rule of liability on innkeepers. And so, at common law, the innkeeper was an insurer of property brought by a guest to his inn and he was relieved of liability for the loss of such property only where the loss occurred through an act of God, through an act of a public enemy, or through the fault of the guest himself.
>
> Since the passing of years has erased much of the need for such absolute liability, the modern innkeeper is often permitted by statute to lessen his responsibility to certain limits, if he provides suitable locks on his guests' rooms, provides a safe for the protection of their valuables, and provides adequate notice of the presence of that safe and in some cases, of his limited liability.[1]

Such statutes have a practical effect: They force some of the care for the goods and valuables of the guest upon the guest himself or herself. This in turn "protects the inn against unrestricted liability for articles of value belonging to a guest that can be conveniently stored in a safe or some similar secure receptacle where the hotel may not even know that the guest has such valuables. The liability is limited provided that the inn makes available such a secure facility and posts notice to that effect. If the guest chooses not to avail himself or herself of that secure facility, having notice thereof, it is surely not an unreasonable legislative decision to exculpate the inn from any liability if the guest thereafter sustains the loss of or damage to those valuable articles."[2]

Public policy becomes involved in these laws. As one judge wrote, speaking of guests: "Those who carry with them large amounts of money or jewelry must take other measures for their protection. The added costs to the hotelkeeper of providing such protection, even as against the willful act or negligence of an employee, is in the last analysis one of his costs of operation reflected in the rates charged to all. Why should those guests who do not need such protection pay for the cost of those who do?"[3]

Since 1872, California has provided for limited liability in those instances where the inn provided a fireproof safe for use by guests and were notified of the availability of the safe.[4]

Since 1895, in the same state, a limit on liability has been provided for innkeepers for other losses to personal property of guests:

> The liability of an innkeeper, hotel keeper, operator of a licensed hospital, rest home or sanitarium, furnished apartment house keeper, furnished bungalow court keeper, boarding house or lodging house keeper, for losses of or injuries to personal property, is that of a depositary for hire; provided, however, that in no case shall such liability exceed the sum of one hundred dollars ($100) for each trunk and its contents, fifty dollars ($50) for each valise or traveling bag and contents, ten dollars ($10) for each box, bundle or package and contents, and two hundred fifty dollars ($250) for all other personal property of any kind, unless he shall have consented in writing with the owner thereof to assume a greater liability.[5]

The willingness of the state legislatures to limit liability that had been so well established for centuries is the important point. If this change had not taken place, it would have taken the courts another 100 years to have achieved the same result by court rulings.

These laws usually take one of three forms. First are those statutes that limit liability for fire loss. Next are those statutes that limit liability for loss of goods as they are being transported to the inn. Finally, there are those that limit liability for loss of money and valuables. We are most concerned about the latter category and will devote most of the chapter to that topic. The others will be examined briefly first. Many inn property statutes are of the "minimum-maximum" variety.

Minimum-Maximum Statutes

In the states that have enacted such statutes, they usually take a "minimum-maximum" form with two value levels. The first is the "no-value-stated" level and represents the minimum liability for loss. The second is the "value-stated" level and represents the maximum liability of the innkeeper. Examine Figure 19.1.

If a guest's goods are accepted by the innkeeper and no value is set, the minimum amount of the statute, such as $75 or $100, sets the top limit of the liability of the innkeeper should such goods be lost, destroyed by fire, or lost while in transit.

If a value is stated, and if the innkeeper accepts this value, the upper limit of the statute, such as $500, controls and this becomes the limit of liability.

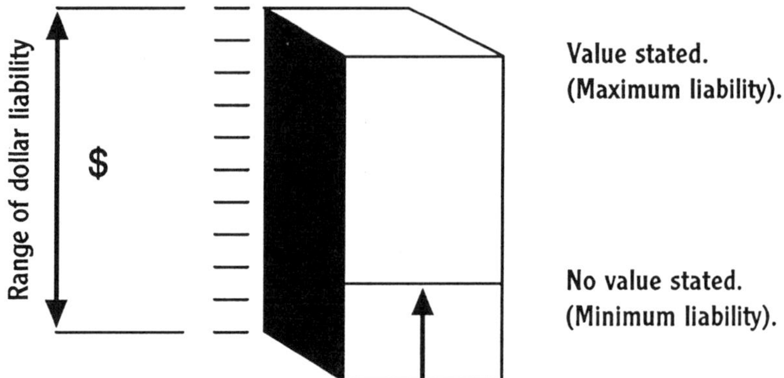

FIGURE 19.1 Legal effect of minimum-maximum statutes.

Under the typical statute, the innkeeper can refuse to accept liability for more than the maximum amount, although he or she may choose to do so. If the innkeeper refuses the higher amount, this forces the guest to accept that limit, or to make other arrangements for the safety of the goods or other items. This takes the innkeeper out of the storage and banking business which, after all, is not the primary purpose of the inn in the first place.

Under some state laws, if the innkeeper is negligent while custodian of the goods or other items, the limits do not apply and the guest is entitled to recover the full value. The burden is on the guest to prove the value of the items lost.

Loss by Fire

The statutes that limit liability for loss by fire, or loss by other means, are similar. A limit is placed on liability unless it appears that the loss was caused by the fault or negligence of the innkeeper. In the case of stored baggage, a double limit on liability is often encountered. If a guest who checks baggage with the innkeeper fails to state a value, the limit on liability is set by statute, such as $100. If a value is declared, the limit on liability is set at another figure, such as $500.

Loss of Goods in Transit to the Inn

The statutes that limit liability for the loss of property of a guest while in transit follow the minimum value declared–maximum pattern, much as stored baggage provisions.

The statutes presuppose that the loss was *not* caused by the negligence of the innkeeper. If it was, the liability would be the full value of the goods and not the statutory limitation. This is so since the negligence would be the cause of the loss and the innkeeper would lose the protection of the statute.

Check-Room Statutes

In New York, state statutes limit checkroom liability to $200 if no charge is made. If a value is stated on the claim receipt, the limit on liability is increased, but this is a ceiling. The ceiling is lost if the innkeeper or his or her agents are negligent in handling the property in question.

In each state, it is important for the innkeeper to seek a legal opinion on what statutes are available to limit liability for property of guests at the inn. As part of the legal opinion of counsel, it should be spelled out specifically what must be done to gain the protection of the limits on liability under those statutes. It must be remembered that, if one fails to gain such protection, perhaps through inadvertence or maybe simple ignorance of the law, then the common law controls.

Some Sample State Statutes

The statute that limits liability in Nevada reads as follows:

> 1. No owner or keeper of any hotel, inn, motel, motor court, boardinghouse or lodginghouse in this state is civilly liable for the theft, loss, damage or destruction of any property left in the room of any guest of such an establishment because of theft, burglary, fire or otherwise, in the absence of gross neglect by the owner or keeper.
> 2. If an owner or keeper of any hotel, inn, motel, motor court, boardinghouse or lodginghouse in this state provides a fireproof safe or vault in which guests may deposit property for safekeeping, and notice of this service is personally given to a guest or posted in the office and the guest's room, the owner or keeper is not liable for the theft, loss, damage or destruction of any property which is not offered for deposit in the safe or vault by a guest unless the owner or keeper is grossly negligent. An owner or keeper is not obligated to receive property to deposit for safekeeping which exceeds $750 in value or is of a size which cannot easily fit within the safe or vault.
> 3. The liability of the owner or keeper under this section does not exceed the sum of $750 for any property of an individual guest,

> unless the owner or keeper receives the property for deposit for safekeeping and consents to assume a liability greater than $750 for its theft, loss, damage, or destruction in a written agreement in which the guest specifies the value of the property.[6]

Virginia and West Virginia

In Virginia, no innkeeper is liable for loss of baggage or personal property in excess of $300. And no innkeeper shall be liable for the loss of jewelry or other valuables if notice is given that they must be deposited in the inn safe, nor is the innkeeper obliged to accept valuables in excess of $500.[7] If locks are provided and notice is given, no liability shall attach if the guest fails to lock the room.[8] Liability in case of fire is limited to $250 per guest.[9]

In West Virginia, the statute provides that the liability for loss of property shall be limited to $250. And no liability shall attach to the loss of jewelry or other valuables if notice requiring that such valuables be deposited in the inn safe is given, unless such valuables are lost after being deposited.[10] The fact that the guest was intoxicated and was careless with his money, exhibiting it freely and refusing to give it to the innkeeper, or that his door was unlocked, does not establish negligence on the part of the guest so as to relieve the innkeeper from liability for loss caused by theft by one of his employees.[11] When merchandise was stolen from an automobile in a parking lot it was held that the use of a parking lot by guests was included in the room rental, and when the innkeeper knew that a guest had left valuables stored in his automobile the innkeeper was liable for such loss.[12]

If a guest of an inn has notice of a requirement that he or she should deposit money and valuables at the office or be personally responsible for its safety, failure to make such a deposit is negligence, barring a recovery for a loss of such property by theft from a room.[13] But such deposit made on several previous occasions, and the presence of a printed notice of such requirement not shown to have been brought to one's attention, are not conclusive evidence of such knowledge. A finding of a jury against a hotel cannot generally be disturbed by the court.[14]

Colorado

Under Colorado statutes, an inn that provides a safe and posts notice is not liable for loss of money and valuables unless they are placed in the safe by the guests. If they are so placed and then lost, recovery is limited to the actual value of the items up to a maximum of $5,000. Inns in Colorado can accept higher value, in writing, but they do not have to do so. Thus an innkeeper there who is asked to place $100,000 in the inn safe cannot refuse to do so, but has the right to refuse *liability* above $5,000.

Under Colorado law, if an inn does not provide a safe for storage of guests' valuables or if personal property is of such a nature that it cannot be stored in a safe, the inn is not liable for loss or damage caused by fire, unforeseen causes, or unavoidable accident, unless loss or damage occurs on account of the negligence of the inn. In that event, recovery would be limited only by the amount of loss or damage suffered. But if damage or loss is occasioned by foreseeable cause and other than by fire or unavoidable accident, the inn is liable for the full amount of the loss or damage.[15]

Kansas

The lodging law of Kansas, provides in part, as follows:

> Sec. 2 (a) No hotel or motel keeper in this state shall be liable for the loss of, or damage to, any baggage, luggage, wearing apparel, personal effects or other like property of a guest, lodger or boarder in an amount in excess to two hundred fifty dollars ($250), unless the same has actually been delivered by such guest, lodger or boarder, to such hotel or motel keeper, or his authorized agent or clerk in the registration office of such hotel, or motel for safekeeping, in which event a receipt for each such article shall thereupon issue or in lieu thereof such hotel or motel keeper shall assume liability in a larger amount with reference to such property.[16]

Maryland

A money and valuables notice taken from a Maryland inn says:

> 1. This hotel will not be responsible for money, jewelry, securities, and plate belonging to guests unless deposited in the safe or other depositary provided by the hotel and, in the event of such deposit, shall not be responsible for the loss thereof in excess of $300 unless the article deposited shall, at the time of deposit, be exhibited to the management and the value thereof declared by the depositor. In no event shall the hotel be required to accept for safekeeping any such property having a declared value in excess of $1000, nor be liable in excess of that amount.
> 2. The liability of the hotel with respect to property of guests left

> in the baggage room or in the guest rooms of the hotel (other than money, jewelry, securities and plate) shall not exceed $300.
>
> In accordance with the above section, the management has provided an iron safe for the safe keeping of the money, jewelry and plate belonging to guests, and they are requested to deposit the same at the hotel office, otherwise the management will not be responsible for the loss of any such articles except as provided by law.
>
> Guests are requested to lock their rooms, and to chain all doors when retiring for the night to prevent intrusion either by design or mistake, also to lock their doors when leaving the room.[17]

Observe that the Maryland notice mentions "plate," referring to dinnerware.

Missouri

This notice offers another variation:

> Sec. 419.010. Innkeeper Liable, when—
>
> Sec. 419.010. No hotel or innkeeper in this state is liable for the loss of any money, jewelry, wearing apparel, baggage or other property of a guest in a total sum greater than two hundred dollars, unless the hotel keeper or innkeeper by an agreement in writing individually, or by the authorized agent or clerk in charge of the office of the hotel or inn, voluntarily assumes a greater liability with reference to such property. As regards money, jewelry or baggage, an hotel keeper or innkeeper is not liable in any event for the loss thereof or damage thereto, unless the same was actually delivered by the guest to him or his authorized agent, or clerk, in the office of the hotel or inn, and the receipt thereof acknowledged by the delivery to the guest of a claim check of the hotel keeper or innkeeper, unless the loss or damage occurs through the willful negligence or wrongdoing of the hotel keeper or innkeeper, his servants or employees. This section shall be posted in the office of every hotel and inn and in every guest room thereof, and unless so posted the same does not apply in the case of hotel keepers failing to post same.[18]

Florida

> Section 509.111, LIABILITY FOR PROPERTY OF GUESTS AND TENANTS: (1) The proprietor or manager of a hotel, apartment house, rooming house, motor court, trailer court or boarding house in this State shall, in no event, be liable or responsible for any loss of any moneys, securities, jewelry or precious stones of any kind whatever belonging to any lodger, boarder, guest, tenant or occupant of or in said hotel, apartment, rooming house, board-

ing house, motor court or trailer court, unless the owner thereof shall make a special deposit of said property and take a receipt in writing therefor from the proprietor or manager or a clerk in the office of said establishment, which receipt shall set forth the value of said property; provided, however, that no proprietor or manager or clerk in the office of a hotel, apartment house, rooming house, motor court, trailer court or boarding house in this state shall be obliged to receive from any one lodger, boarder, guest, tenant or occupant of or in said hotel, apartment house, rooming house, motor court, trailer court or boarding house, a deposit of any money, securities, jewelry or precious stones of any kind whatever, exceeding a combined total value of One Thousand Dollars ($1,000.00) or shall he be liable in damages in a sum in excess thereof unless such proprietor, manager, or clerk accept voluntarily such chattels for safekeeping, having a combined total value in excess of One Thousand Dollars ($1,000.00), then and in such event he shall be liable in damages in a sum equal to the damage sustained by such lodger, boarder, guest, tenant or occupant.[19]

California

Section 1859. Liability of innkeepers, etc.: Limitations as to amount: Assumption of greater liability. The liability of an innkeeper, hotelkeeper, operator of a licensed hospital, rest home or sanitarium, furnished apartment house keeper, furnished bungalow court keeper, boardinghouse or lodginghouse keeper, for losses of or injuries to personal property, is that of a depositary for hire; provided, however, that in no case shall such liability exceed the sum of one thousand dollars ($1,000) in the aggregate. In no case shall liability exceed, for each item of described property, the respective sums of five hundred dollars ($500) for each trunk and its contents, two hundred fifty ($250) for each valise or traveling bag and its contents, two hundred fifty dollars ($250) for each box, bundle or package and its contents, and two hundred fifty dollars ($250) for all other personal property of any kind, unless he shall have consented in writing with the owner thereof to assume a greater liability. (Enacted 1872; Stats.1895, c. 47, p. 49, §1; Stats.1957, c. 1251, p. 2557, §1; Stats.1979, c. 705, §1.)[20]

Turning from this sampling of the statutes, it is important to look at the nature of these laws because important points arise in their use.

The Statutes in Use

The "loss-of-valuables" statutes almost uniformly contain the following requirements that must be met by the innkeeper:

1. The innkeeper must provide a safe for valuables.
2. The guest must be given notice in a prescribed manner that the safe is available and must be told the liability limit in dollars.
3. The guest must be given notice that failure to declare valuables at the front desk may relieve the innkeeper of liability if such valuables are lost.
4. A statutory limit is set beyond which the innkeeper will not be liable for loss of declared valuables.
5. The innkeeper may accept liability for valuables beyond the statutory limit but does not have to do so.

In addition, in most states, the declaration must be made in writing. In some states such as Nevada, an innkeeper does not have to receive valuables if ". . . [they are] of a size which cannot easily fit within the safe or vault."[21]

Also, some but not all states allow the statutory limit to apply, ". . . unless the owner or keeper is grossly negligent."[22] In states that have such provisions, the benefit of the statutory limit may be lost if the keeper is grossly negligent. In some states' statutes, the word "grossly" is left out. In those states, protection of the statutes may be lost if the keeper is negligent, but not grossly so.

If the statute does not have the negligence exception, what then? Some states allow the protection of the statutory limitation if the keeper is negligent. See *Lazare Kaplan & Sons, Inc. v. Pensacola Hotel Co.*,[23] applying Florida law. Other cases hold that if there is negligence on the part of the host, the protection is lost. This means that the host may be held liable for the proven value of lost valuables.[24]

Under 15 Oklahoma Statutes Annotated, section 503a, the guest must ". . . advise such person [host] of the actual value of . . ." the property being declared, and this is true regardless of the cause of the loss. Thus, if a guest signs an instrument stating the maximum value of goods as $1,500, even though the goods may consist of over one quarter million dollars in cash, the host's liability is limited to $1,500. This also precludes federal jurisdiction since the amount in controversy must exceed $50,000.[25]

In many jurisdictions a negligent host is held liable for the full value of lost valuables. But even in those jurisdictions, if the guest fails to carry the burden of proof, the statutory limit on liability will be applied.[26] If the guest does not wish to be limited on liability, the guest must make arrangements to safeguard the valuables elsewhere, such as at a bank. This is the reason for the statutes in the first place.

Yet problems arise anyway and it is useful to look at some of them. To illustrate, A leaves a valuable watch at a front desk. The watch is sealed in an envelope and locked in a safety deposit drawer. A fire breaks out at the inn and the innkeeper removes the watch, intending to protect it from the fire, but then negligently loses it. The liability extends to the full value of the watch. If the watch had remained in the safe and had been destroyed, the statutory limitation would have applied.

Another distinction is found when deposited property is stolen by the innkeeper or by an employee. In the former, liability for the full value would attach. In the latter, the statutory limitation would control. In these illustrations, we are assuming that the value of the deposited property had not been declared at a higher value. If it had been, the innkeeper had the right to refuse the risk. But if the risk had been accepted, the statutory limitation would not apply.

The next question is this: can an innkeeper disclaim liability for all property of guests and forget about these laws?

Disclaiming All Innkeeper Liability

Can all liability on the part of an innkeeper be disclaimed? A motel owner in southern California tried to do just that. The registration card at the front desk included the clause: "We are not responsible

Bed and Breakfast, Rapid City, South Dakota.

for money, valuables, or goods of any type that may be brought onto the motel premises, in a car, or into the guest room."

Can the California motel owner ignore the California statute and create his own law to cover the lost property situation? The answer is "No." By attempting to disclaim liability, the innkeeper has common-law liability and is an insurer of the goods of the guests.

It is wise to create protective laws for use in the inn *only* if a state law does not preempt a given area. If such a law exists, it is foolish not to follow it. Examine Figure 19.2.

Losing the Protection of the Statutes

In New York, failure to comply with the statutory limitations on liability revives the common-law rule and the innkeeper has become an insurer once again.[27] An innkeeper who chooses not to take advantage of the statutes that limit liability waives the protection of those statutes.[28]

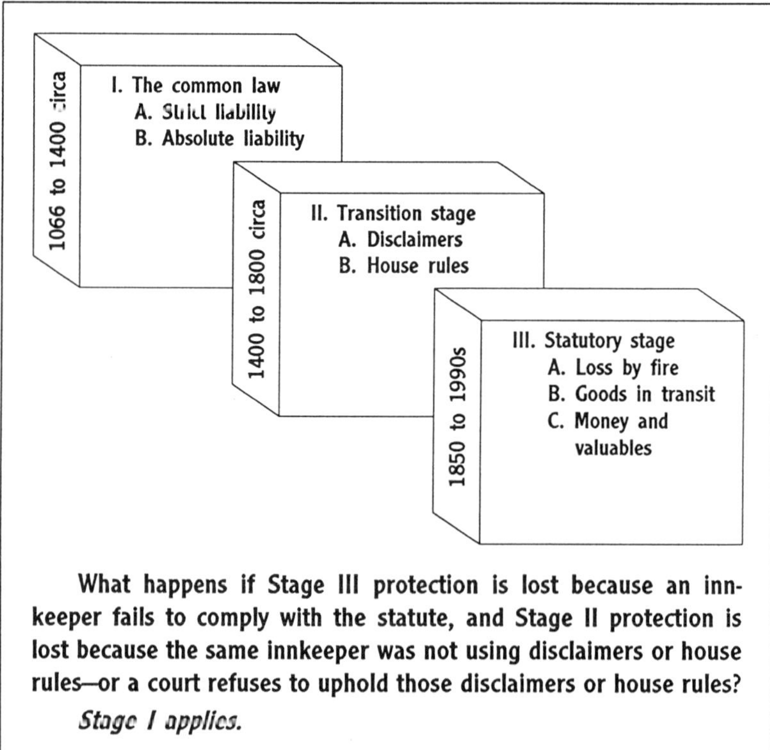

What happens if Stage III protection is lost because an innkeeper fails to comply with the statute, and Stage II protection is lost because the same innkeeper was not using disclaimers or house rules—or a court refuses to uphold those disclaimers or house rules?

Stage I applies.

FIGURE 19.2

In the operation of these statutes, the declaration of excess value often becomes an issue in court.

Declaration of Excess Value

The burden is on the guest to declare excess value of goods brought to the front desk for safekeeping. It is not the responsibility of the innkeeper to see that such declaration is made. The innkeeper is not in a position to know if excess value *should* be declared so the law makes it the burden of the guest.[29] If a dispute arises later as to whether excess value had in fact been declared and accepted by the innkeeper, the burden of proof is again upon the guest.

An innkeeper can accept excess value when it is declared by the guest—or he or she has the right in most states to refuse to accept excess value. If the excess value is accepted, most states require that it be done in writing by the innkeeper.

Accepting Excess Value

If an innkeeper should decide to accept excess value to accommodate a guest, then a form such as suggested in Figure 19.3 should be used. If a form is not used, there should still be something placed in writing because the statutes require this. The writing should state the amount in dollars for which the innkeeper is willing to accept responsibility.

To illustrate, Innkeeper Smith accepts a diamond ring from Guest X, thinking the ring is worth $2,000, and agrees in writing to waive the protection of the money and valuables statute. The ring is then lost by the innkeeper. The guest refuses $2,000 and sues for the value of the ring. The proof in court is that the ring is worth $100,000. The innkeeper may be held to that amount, having waived the protection of the statute. This could have been avoided if a writing had been used "accepting liability not to exceed $2,000." The guest should sign or initial the writing and be given a copy.

Before these statutes can become operative, guests must be given proper notice of them.

Notice of Limits on Liability

It becomes important in practice to read the statute of the state in question to see how notice is to be given. In reading the previous

ZERO MOTEL

Declaration of Valuables

Under the provisions of (state statute), I hereby declare the following for safekeeping:

1.

2.

3.

I declare the value of the above to be $ ____________________ total.

I have read this form and understand it and agree to be bound by it.

____
Guest

____
Date

____
Room Number

- -

I, Innkeeper of Zero Motel, accept the above items and I DO—I DO NOT (circle one) accept the evaluation of them.

____
Innkeeper, Zero Motel

____
Date

FIGURE 19.3

samples offered, it can be seen that the notice requirements are not uniform. It is one area in which the HRI manager should not improvise.

How About Notice on Room Mirrors?

One court has held that placing notices on the mirrors in inn rooms met the requirements of the statute of the state in question.[30] On the other hand, another court has held that placing the notice under the glass of inn dressers made the matter a jury question as to whether notice had been adequately given. In both of these cases, the innkeepers had been challenged on the adequacy of the notice. If notice had been given as prescribed by the applicable statutes, neither case would have been brought in the first place.

These notices should be made by separate, distinct writing, in large enough type to be easily read. They should not be combined with information about the location of the ice machine and the fire escapes. Those notices are important, of course, but should be kept separate from the money and valuable notices.[31]

Quantity of Posting

The Arkansas and Pennsylvania valuables statutes both require that notice of the limit on liability, $300 in both states, be posted in ". . . no less than ten conspicuous places" at the inn. A copy of the statute of each state is to be mounted by suitable fastenings and kept posted constantly. In an Arkansas case where a dealer had coins and jewelry worth $100,000 or more stolen from his room, the $300 limit worked at the first trial. There was evidence at that trial, however, that there were not ten conspicuous notices posted at the inn as required by the statute. The appeals court sent the case back for a second trial holding that if there were in fact no posting at ten conspicuous locations at the inn, the $300 limit does not apply, *Grimes M.H. Motel*, 776 S.W. 2d 336 (Arkansas, 1989).

In a Pennsylvania case, a coin dealer had a coin collection stolen and there were no notices posted at ten conspicuous places as required by the valuables statute. The notice was on the registration form and while that is a good inn practice, it does not comply with Pennsylvania law. There was also evidence that the room keys were not marked "Do not duplicate" and evidence that the inn had a poor key control system. The jury found for the coin dealer in the sum of over $34,000, but found him to have been 49 percent negligent, reducing his recovery to a little less than $18,000. To this the judge added over $7,700 in "delay damages," giving the coin dealer a recovery of over $25,000. If the ten signs had been posted, the recovery would have been $300.

Notices Inside Room Closets

At a major hotel and casino in Las Vegas, it was observed that a notice form was in each guest room, but was placed inside the room alcove that served as a closet. Once clothes were placed on hangers, the notice could no longer be seen. In a 1990 Florida case, those exact conditions existed and the judge said ". . . it is doubtful whether the subject statute was posted 'in a prominent place' when it was placed on the inside of the open closet" in the guest's room, *Fennema v. Howard Johnson's*, 559 So. 2d 1231 (Florida, 1990). Needless to say, the hotel and casino in Las Vegas now have their notices in frames on the inside of each guest room, at normal eye level.

In a similar Pennsylvania case, where postings are required at at least ten prominent locations, the notice posted at the wall beside the front desk was obscured by a potted plant. The guests who lost valuables at the inn claimed that they never saw the notice when they checked in. A motion for summary judgment of $300 for the defendant was denied. The court held that whether or not the notice had been seen was a question of fact for a jury to decide. If the plaintiffs can convince the jury that they had not seen the sign, they will be able to recover the full value of their loss, *Latini v. Loew's Corp.*, 657 F. Supp. 475 (1987).

The innkeeper must always remember that if the notices required by the statutes are posted conspicuously and properly, the courts will consistently hold that the statutory limits apply, *O'Rourke v. Hilton Hotels Corp.*, 560 So. 2d 76 (Louisiana, 1990).

Limiting Hours That Safe Is Available

What if hours are placed upon the availability of the safe such as "Safe available for money and valuables declaration from 8:00 A.M. to 5:00 P.M."? It has been held that during the hours when the safe is not available, *the statutory protection is lost.* The innkeeper then becomes an insurer of the safety of all money and valuables of the guests until the safe becomes available again.[32]

At the Concord Hotel in New York, a house rule made the front-desk safe available from 8 A.M. to 11 P.M. When guests lost valuables from their rooms during the night, the court held that the statutory limitation did not apply. The judge said that nowhere in the statute does it suggest that ". . . an innkeeper may provide a safe part of the time and yet gain the benefit of the exemption all of the time," *Zaldin v. Concord Hotel*, 421 N.Y.S. 2d 858 (New York, 1979). Thus the maintenance of a proper safe, the giving of correct and conspicuous notice of its availability, and in fact having it available at all times is essential in inns in all of our states. This is one aspect of inn law that no innkeeper wants to come up short on. Related to the availability of the safe is the inn safe that is full.

The Inn Safe Is Full

This is an unusual occurrence at the inn, but it could happen. What if a guest wants to deposit money and valuables but is turned away because the safe is full? While there is no case in point at the moment, a court may well hold that there was no safe available so the protection of the statute would be lost if that particular guest had that property stolen at the inn. If an innkeeper should be caught in such a situation, it would be a wise management decision to take extraordinary care and see that the valuables are protected in some reasonable manner. If an inn safe fills up repeatedly, new safe facilities must be promptly acquired. The movement that began a few years back to place individual safes in each guest room has cut down on the use of front-desk safes, but has in turn created new legal problems at the inn.

IN-ROOM SAFES

Over the past several years, different companies have begun to manufacture and market a variety of safes designed to be placed in each guest room so that the guest may have private access to them. While a charge is made for the use, they are popular with guests. The movement to install such safes in older inns started off slowly, but their use in remodeled inns and in new construction has become almost an industry standard. Figure 19.4 contains some details about one brand of these safes.

A microprocessor-controlled keyless safe for use in hotels, motels and condos in Las Vegas and throughout the United States, "Elsafe," is now being distributed through a growing chain of local affiliates, including Elsafe Nevada at 900 E. Karen Ave., C-202 (369-9415).

Used in 37 countries and with nearly 6,000 in use in Hawaiian hotels, Elsafe consists of a full-size steel safe that enables guests to select their own combination by depressing numbers on a telephone-type keyboard. A microprocessor stores the combination and allows the safe to be opened only when that combination is entered.

Each new combination is displayed on a digital readout panel for 14 seconds to help the guest remember the combination. A million combinations are possible.

If the wrong combination is tried, the digital panel flashes to tell the user to try again. As a safeguard against outsiders trying to arrive at the combination through trial and error, the safe mechanism refuses to function for 30 minutes after the wrong combination is tried three times.

Interior of the safe measures 18.5 gallons (70 liters)—enough to store brief cases, large purses, cameras and cassette players. Walls are ⅕-inch thick steel. Doors are ⅓-inch thick and designed to prevent jimmying. The safe is bolted to the floor from the inside to prevent removal.

Las Vegas Sun, "Monday Morning Briefs"
August 8, 1983, p. 6A.

FIGURE 19.4

The legal problem is this: Are they "safes" within the meaning of the money and valuables statutes that limit liability if a "safe" is provided and proper notice is given? This question has not yet been before a court, but there is a legal reason why a judge will probably answer that question "no." Almost without exception, the money and valuables statutes in our states were enacted before the first in-room safes appeared on the market. Faced with that fact, a court will almost always rule that something which was not developed until after the statutes were enacted could not have been in the contemplation of the lawmakers who wrote and enacted the statutes. The court would look to trade usage as of the time of the enactment of the statutes and what they would find would be the traditional front-desk safe. That is to say, of course, that there is an absence of a statute specially written to extend inn protection to the in-room safes.

Hawaii's In-Room Safe Statute

Since Hawaiian inns were the first big users of in-room safes, it seems fitting that that state would be the first one to amend its "valuables" statute to make it clear that the statutory limit on the liability of the inn extends to these special safes. Until such laws are enacted in the other states, the innkeeper who decides to install such safes has a legal problem. Legal advice should be sought when deciding to install such safes. Some form of notice, or perhaps a waiver, would be in order to make it clear that the in-room safe is for the mere convenience of the guest and that the inn still maintains the traditional safe and stands on its limit on liability.

Another problem might be found in the making of charges for their use.

Charging for the Safe

If in-room safes are used by guests, a charge such as three dollars per day is often made for that use. This sum is added to the guest's daily bill for as long as the use continues. This procedure is at variance with prior inn practices where no charge was made to use the front-desk safe. Might the fact that a charge was made for the in-room safe influence the court that may have to decide the question of liability for stolen property?

It would be unwise, for example, to make a charge for the use of the traditional front-desk safe. The reason for this is that guests may claim they did not use the front-desk safe because they objected to the charge. It must be remembered that these statutes are a "grace" extended to the innkeepers by the legislatures. The latter granted the limit on liability on the basis of the trade-off that the inn would provide the safe and give notice of it. A court may well hold that if a charge is made at the front desk, the inn did not "provide" the safe! It is a subtle legal point but one that a careful lawyer would pick up on quickly. So the charge for the in-room safe could well cause problems in the future.

The plus side of the in-room safe picture, of course, is that there has been very little loss by guests who make use of such safes. Another legal plus is that the very act of providing such safes must be looked at by the courts as proof that the innkeepers are demonstrating a form of care when providing these safes. "Gross negligence" has been defined as "the failure to provide any care." Providing the in-room safes would protect the innkeeper from a charge of gross negligence in that regard.

How About a Blanket Charge for In-Room Safes?

A 116-room inn in midtown Manhattan provided in-room safes and placed a daily charge of $1.50 on the bill of each guest, keeping no record of whether the safes were in fact used. This is a very unwise practice, because it violates Section 206 of the New York General Business Law which states, "No charge or sum shall be collected or received by any such hotel keeper or innkeeper for any service not actually rendered. . . . For any violation of this section the offender shall forfeit to the injured party three times the amount so charged, and shall not be entitled to receive any money for meals, services or time charged." A hotel student, Rama Kalminou, from the University of Nevada, Las Vegas, brought that practice to a stop at that inn.

If in-room safes are of an inferior quality and if that quality becomes a factor in the loss of a guest's property, the courts will probably allow the loss to be recovered. Also, if such safes are not inspected on a regular basis and properly maintained, the courts will use those facts against the innkeeper. Safes cannot be placed in guest rooms and then ignored.

The biggest legal mistake that could be made in reference to in-room safes would be to try to substitute them for the traditional front-desk safe. The courts would never buy that one in the absence of a specific statute permitting it to be done.

Does the Front-Desk Safe Have to Be Fireproof?

Some states, such as Nevada and Oklahoma, specifically say that the safe must be fireproof. It has been held that, otherwise, if there is no statutory requirement that it be fireproof, it does not have to be, and the notice does not have to say that it is.[33]

This brings us to a final question about safes: Just what is a "safe"?

What Is a "Safe"?

In a New York case, two salesmen deposited $2 million in jewelry at the front desk of the Mayfair Regent and all appeared to be in order; that is until the safe was broken into and the jewelry was stolen. Since the hotel had provided a safe, notice had been given that the safe was available, and the jewelry had been deposited as required by the statute, it seemed clear to the trial court that the liability of the hotel was limited to the statutory amount of $500 per person. Upon appeal the upper court reversed, however, holding that there was evidence that the safe deposit boxes were in an unguarded room; that there was public access to that room; that a list of those who had valuables on deposit was available at the hotel; and that the walls of the safe-deposit room were made of mere plasterboard. The upper court in New York sent the case back for a determination of the security measures in effect at the hotel. The case was then settled without retrial.[34]

In New York and Elsewhere

In New York, if a guest fails to deposit valuables, the innkeeper has no responsibility even if loss is caused by theft by the employees of the inn, or by the negligence of the innkeeper. If goods are declared, the liability is limited to $500 unless a higher value is declared. If loss now results from theft by employees or negligence of the innkeeper, the liability is not limited to $500. If, on the other hand, the valuables or goods are stolen from the innkeeper by unknown persons, the liability is still limited.[35] It thus becomes a matter of "role playing" on both sides.

In the absence of such statutory protection in New York, once the goods and valuables of a guest are brought *infra hospitium*, the innkeeper is an insurer of the safety of those goods and money and valuables to their full value.[36] Thus the innkeeper wants the protection of the statutes and must do all that is necessary to obtain that protection. If a question arises as to whether there was compliance with the statutes, the burden is on the innkeeper and not the guest to prove that there was.[37]

For the statutes to apply, it is not necessary that the money and valuables or goods be brought to the inn by the guest. The statutes apply where property was delivered to an inn from an airline where it had been lost and then found. The property was then placed upon a bellhop stand from which it vanished. The $1,000 limit on liability of the New Mexico statute was held to apply.[38]

The New York statute has been held to apply even if the inn fails to place the declared valuables in the safe.[39] This was a harsh decision, since it did not take into consideration the negligence on the part of the innkeeper. Yet the decision shows how strong these statutes are when applied in court.

However, for negligence of the innkeeper to defeat the protection of the statutes, a distinction must be made between active and passive negligence. It has been held that to hold an innkeeper liable for negligence there must be some active "misfeasance." Nonfeasance, on the other hand, such as failure to have additional security on hand, is not enough. As one court said it, "Nonfeasance has not made the situation worse." Active misfeasance does make the situation worse and is needed to hold the innkeeper liable. In its absence, the courts will dismiss such suits.[40]

By interpretation, the courts have included certain items under the coverage of the statutes and excluded others. It has been held that a watch, chain, and rosary, each being an article of use and not worn as ornaments, are not "jewels or ornaments" within the meaning of the statute.[41] The same has been held for silver tableforks, a silver soup ladle, and an heirloom watch,[42] and for a gold pen and pencil in a case[43] and a silver-mounted set on a traveling bag.[44]

In addition to such exclusions by court decisions, many of the statutes have provisions that set limits for the loss of merchant samples at an inn. Such samples have posed problems for the state courts that do not have such specific coverage in the statutes. Under certain conditions, nonnegotiable paper may be held by a court to be a valuable within the meaning of that word. An example might be a dissertation prepared by a Ph.D. candidate after years of research and study and which is lost at an inn. The statutes would probably extend to that item and the innkeeper's liability would be limited for its loss.

Do these money and valuables statutes represent a "taking of property" as prohibited by the Fourteenth Amendment? They have been so challenged in California and Colorado but have been upheld in those states.[45]

In a Georgia case, a bag containing $9,000 was left in a room by a guest. The money was then turned in to a supervisor by a room maid and was subsequently stolen by another employee. The Days Inn in question provided a safe and gave notice of its availability. The court dismissed the case, holding that the Georgia property statute makes no exceptions even for the negligence of the innkeeper. The court said, "Thus, if the innkeeper posts notice of the availability of the safe pursuant to the statute, it is not liable for articles stolen from a guest's room even if its negligence contributed to the loss," *Gooden v. Days Inn*, 395 S.E. 2d 876 (Georgia, 1990). The unusual aspect of this case was the fact that the money had not been stolen from the guest's room. It had been stolen elsewhere, yet the statute gave the innkeeper perfect protection as to the loss.

Why Don't All Inns Comply?

It is reported fact in the HRI industry that many inn owners simply do not bother with meeting the terms of these statutes. The reasoning apparently is that "nothing is going to get lost or stolen very often, and if it does, it will not amount to much." That reasoning is sound perhaps in a Mom-and-Pop inn that caters to low-income persons. That reasoning is seriously flawed, however, at most other inns. It is like driving without insurance on the assumption that an accident is not likely to happen. It was reported in *Hospitality Law,* volume 5, no. 12, December 1990, that ". . . At least half of the [inns] in the country do not 'trouble themselves' enough to comply. They are courting trouble that is easily avoided."

The Statutes in Nevada

The Nevada property statute provides that protection of the coverage is lost if the innkeeper is "grossly negligent." Thus, a Nevada innkeeper can be negligent in the loss of a guest's money and valuables and the $750 limit still applies. (Review the Nevada statute on page 433.)

The Nevada statute uses the words "any individual," so if more than one person occupies a guest room the statute would be applicable to all of them. The statute also covers boardinghouses, lodginghouses, and motor courts, but RV parks are not mentioned.

Thus, if a guest should become a permanent resident at a Nevada inn, the limit on liability would still apply to that person even though he or she has become a tenant.

In the "Silver State" (Nevada), large items that cannot fit in the inn safe can be refused. This seems to be a reasonable provision, but there is a legal danger lurking in the background. What if a briefcase or suitcase is refused and it contains money and valuables that could have been separated and placed in the safe? Might a court hold that the protection of the statute was lost? There is no case in point at the time, but it would seem that a good house rule would be that anytime an item is turned down because of its size, the guest should be told that smaller parcels from inside the bigger one will be accepted for deposit.

If a guest wants a large sum of money accepted, or perhaps an 18K Rolex watch, it would probably be best in Nevada to accept the money or watch, making it clear that the limit on liability is not being waived. In that regard, nothing should be placed in writing that could be construed by the court as a waiver of the limit on liability. If the innkeeper decides to waive the limit, then a form such as that shown in Figure 19.3 could be used.

In a 1986 case brought in federal court in California, the court was called upon to construe the Nevada statute and found that it had "awkward language." Figure 19.5 is a summary of what the statute says including the ruling of the court. The U.S. Court of Appeals for the Fifth Circuit found that this statute has an additional meaning.

The case involved a trip to the Tropicana Hotel by Robert Kahn, a part-time jewelry broker. While checking out of the hotel, a bellman negligently allowed Mr. Kahn's brief case, containing over $50,000 in jewelry, to come up missing. It was never determined who stole it or how, but the empty case was found later on the hotel's golf course. The court held that the $750 limit applied "even when the innkeeper was grossly negligent" in spite of the fact that the statute says the limit shall not apply if the innkeeper is grossly negligent. The reason for this decision is that the Nevada statute is divided into three numbered paragraphs. The "gross negligence" phrase is found in paragraph 2. Paragraph 3 says in effect that "in all other instances of the loss of a guest's money and valuables, the limit shall be $750." There is no mention of gross negligence in paragraph 3. The result of this ruling is that the Nevada statute has been enlarged by court interpretation.

Two final matters that relate to the property, money, and valuables of guests, and the statutes that limit liability for them, need to be considered. The first has to do with property, money, and

	Facts	Innkeeper Is Negligent	Innkeeper Is Grossly Negligent
1.	Property is left in room and it is stolen.	No liability	$750 liability
2.	Notice is given and property is deposited in the front-desk safe.	$750 liability	?
3.	Notice given, property not placed in safe.	No liability	$750 liability
4.	No notice given and no safe provided.	$750 liability under Kahn	$750 liability under Kahn
5.	In-room safes provided but no front-desk safe.	$750 under Kahn	$750 under Kahn

FIGURE 19.5

valuables inadvertently left at an inn by the departing guest. The other has to do with property, money, and valuables lost or stolen during the check-out process.

PROPERTY LEFT AT INN AFTER CHECK-OUT

Most property left by travelers is lost or misplaced and not abandoned. Most states have statutes that control the situation. For example, the Nevada statute states, "All baggage or property of whatever description left at a hotel, inn, motor court, boardinghouse, or lodginghouse for the period of 60 days may be sold at public auction by the proprietor or proprietors thereof . . ."[46] under the following conditions:

1. Notice must be given as provided by NRS 108.500, 2, 3, and 4.
2. The sale must be carried out by public auction.

3. The proceeds of the sale shall be distributed as follows:
    a. Storage costs.
    b. Costs of sale.
    c. Balance to county treasurer.

After the funds are received by the county treasurer, they are paid into the county school district fund, subject to the right of the true owner to reclaim the balance within six months.

In some states, such as New York, the property may be retained by the innkeeper for ten days, during which time an effort must be made to find the owner. If the owner is not located, the property must be surrendered to the police.

Under the Nevada and New York laws, it can be seen that it is mandatory that all property, money, and valuables left at an inn be promptly delivered to management. The innkeeper then holds the property as a bailee and must use ordinary care in its security. The money and valuables statutes no longer apply since they apply only to guests—not departed guests.

Some inns make it a house rule that, after a period of time such as ninety days, unclaimed property is given to the employee who found it. Before such a rule can be placed in effect, it must be determined what the law of that state has to say about "property left at the inn."

The final topic of our discussion of the money and valuables statutes involves those unusual situations, where money and valuables are lost or stolen from a guest who is in the check-out process. The case that follows concerns that situation.

FREDDI SALISBURY V. ST. REGIS-SHERATON HOTEL CORP. 490 F. Supp. 449 (S.D. N.Y. 1980)

LASKER, District Judge.

On the morning of November 22, 1978, Mr. and Mrs. Roger Salisbury concluded a three day stay at the St. Regis-Sheraton Hotel in New York. While Mr. Salisbury paid the bill and surrendered their room key, Mrs. Salisbury checked their luggage with a bellhop in the lobby. The couple was to spend the day in town and return for the luggage that afternoon. Mrs. Salisbury did not inform the hotel, when she checked the luggage, that one of their pieces, a cosmetics case, contained jewelry and cosmetics worth over $60,000, and did not ask that the case be kept in the hotel's safe. Nor did she inform the hotel that the value of the case and its contents exceeded $100.

When the Salisburys returned to the hotel to retrieve their luggage at about 4:30 that afternoon, the cosmetics case containing the jewelry was missing. Mrs. Salisbury sued to recover the value of the case and its contents.

It is undisputed that posted conspicuously in the public areas of the hotel was a notice informing guests that the hotel provided a safe for the safekeeping of their valuables, and notifying them of the provisions of Sections 200 and 201 of the New York General Business Law, which provide:

"Whenever the proprietor or manager of any hotel, motel, inn or steamboat shall provide a safe in the office of such hotel, motel or steamboat, or other convenient place for the safe keeping of any money, jewels, ornaments, bank notes, bonds, negotiable securities or precious stones, belonging to the guests of or travelers in such hotel, motel, inn or steamboat, and shall notify the guests or travelers thereof by posting a notice stating the fact that such safe is provided, in which such property may be deposited, in a public and conspicuous place and manner in the office and public rooms, and in the public parlors of such hotel, motel, or inn, or saloon of such steamboat; and if such guest or traveler shall neglect to deliver such property, to the person in charge of such office for deposit in such safe, the proprietor or manager of such hotel, motel, or steamboat shall not be liable for any loss of such property, sustained by such guest or traveler by theft or otherwise; . . ."(§200)

"No hotel or motel keeper except as provided in the foregoing section shall be liable for damage to or loss of wearing apparel or other personal property in the lobby, hallways or in the room or rooms assigned to a guest for any sum exceeding the sum of five hundred dollars, unless it shall appear that such loss occurred through the fault or negligence of such keeper, nor shall he be liable in any sum exceeding the sum of one hundred dollars for the loss of or damage to any such property when delivered to such keeper for storage or safe keeping in the store room, baggage room or other place elsewhere than in the room or rooms assigned to such guest, unless at the time of delivering the same for storage or safe keeping such value in excess of one hundred dollars shall be stated and a written receipt, stating such value, shall be issued by such keeper, but in no event shall such keeper be liable beyond five hundred dollars, unless it shall appear that such loss occurred through his fault or negligence, . . ." (§201) [emphasis supplied]. Relying on these provisions, the hotel moves for summary judgment on the grounds that the undisputed facts establish that its liability cannot exceed $100, and therefore federal subject matter jurisdiction is lacking. Mrs. Salisbury cross-moves for summary judgment, asserting that sections 200 and 201 are inapplicable here because she was no longer a "guest" of the hotel at the time the loss occurred.

The question, then, is whether Mrs. Salisbury ceased to be a "guest" within the meaning of sections 200 and 201 when she checked out of the hotel, even though she arranged to have the hotel hold her luggage for the day. The two cases on which Mrs. Salisbury relies are clearly distinguishable.

In one, *Crosby v. Fifth Ave. Hotel Co.*, 173 Misc. 595, 20 N.Y.S.2d 227 (N.Y.C. Mun.Ct. 1939), modified, 173 Misc. 604, 17 N.Y.S.2d 498 (App.T. 1st Dept. 1940), a departing guest stored two trunks with the defendant hotel, and returned to reclaim them several years later only to discover that the hotel had sold them. The court concluded that the relationship involved was not that of innkeeper and guest, but rather that of bailee and bailor. Here, however, the lost luggage was not stored with the hotel for a lengthy period, but simply held for the day as an accommodation to departing guests. In the other case relied on by Mrs. Salisbury, *Ticehurst v. Beinbrink*, 72 Misc. 365, 129 N.Y.S. 838 (App.T.1911), the plaintiff arranged to leave his horse at an inn while he continued his journey by train. The court held that the plaintiff, who simply sought to board his horse, was not a "guest,"–"a transient person who resorts to or is received at an inn for the purpose of obtaining the accommodations which it purports to offer." This definition, however, applies quite well to the Salisburys.

It is not uncommon for a hotel to hold luggage for a few hours after guests check out as an accommodation to them. This would appear to be one of the services which a hotel performs for its guests in the normal course of its business, and there is no reason why it should be deemed to alter the otherwise existing legal relationship between them. Accordingly, we conclude that sections 200 and 201 are fully applicable in the circumstances of this case, and precludes any recovery against the hotel for the loss of Mrs. Salisbury's jewelry, and limits any recovery for the loss of the case and its other contents to $100. *Adler v. Savoy Plaza Inc.*, 279 App.Div. 110, 108 N.Y.S.2d 80 (1st Dept.1951).[47]

While we thus conclude that the hotel has an absolute defense to Mrs. Salisbury's suit for the value of her jewelry, we note that even if the relationship involved here were deemed a gratuitous bailment, as Mrs. Salisbury contends it should be, the hotel's liability would be limited to the value of articles ordinarily found in a cosmetics case, even if Mrs. Salisbury could establish that the hotel was grossly negligent in caring for her case. *Stephens v. Katz Parking System*, 75 Misc.2d 690, 692, 348 N.Y. S.2d 492, 495 (N.Y.C. Civ.Ct.1973); *Waters v. Beau Site Co.*, 114 Misc. 65, 186 N.Y. Supp. 731 (N.Y.C. Civ.Ct.1920). Even under her own view of the law, Mrs. Salisbury could not recover the value of her lost jewelry.

Since the most that could be recovered in this action is $100, it is evident that the amount in controversy does not exceed $10,000, and therefore federal subject matter jurisdiction is lacking. Accordingly, the defendant's motion for summary judgment dismissing the complaint is granted, and the plaintiff's cross motion for summary judgment is denied. [Federal jurisdiction now requires $50,000.]

It is so ordered.

In *Spiller v. Barclay Hotel*,[48] a guest who had completed check-out gave a bellhop her bags to take to her car, which was still on the hotel premises. One bag came up missing and the court held the hotel liable for the entire value of the bag and its contents. The court said that the money and valuables protection was lost as of the time that check-out was completed, thus creating a counterview to the Salisbury case above.

QUESTIONS

1. True or False. One must use care in placing into effect house rules that allow property left at an inn to become the property of the one who finds it.
2. What might be the reasoning of the lawyers who brought the lawsuits that challenged the money and valuables statutes as being unconstitutional?
3. What economic realities prompted our state legislatures to enact laws to limit the age-old liability of innkeepers as to the property of guests?
4. What happens in a minimum-maximum situation where no value has been stated on a guest's lost property?
5. What happens in a New York checkroom if a charge is made for the service?
6. Name one time when a legal opinion should be sought by the HRI manager on a question of liability for the property of guests.
7. Most of the statutory limits for money and valuables are under $1,000. Can you think of a historical reason why the limit in Colorado is $5,000?
8. What are the rights of an innkeeper in Nevada when property too large for the safe is tendered at the front desk?
9. What is the legal effect of failing to give proper notice as required by the money and valuables statutes?
10. What is the legal problem with in-room safes?

ENDNOTES

1. 37 *A.L.R.* 3d 1276, 1279-80 (1971).
2. *Diamond v. Super*, 149 *Cal. Rptr.* 813, 85 *Cal. App.* 3d 885 (1978).

3. *Levesque v. Columbia Hotel,* 141 Me. 398, 44 A. 2d 730.
4. Cal. Civil Code, sec. 1860 (1872).
5. Cal. Civil Code, sec. 1859 (1895).
6. Nevada Revised Statutes, A 1979, 651.010.
7. Sec. 1602, Michie's Va. Code (1942); sec. 35-10, Code of Virginia (1950).
8. Sec. 1603, Michie's Va. Code (1942); sec. 35-11. Code of Virginia (1950).
9. Sec. 1604, Michie's Va. Code (1942); sec. 35-12, Code of Virginia (1950).
10. Sec. 1366, Michie's W Va. Code (1943).
11. *Cunningham v. Bucky,* 42 W. Va. 671, 26 S.E. 442, 57 Am. St. Rep. 876, 35 *L.R.A.* 850.
12. *Weisman v. Holley Hotel Co.*, 128 W. Va. 476, 37 S.E. 2d 94.
13. *Nesben v. Jackson,* 89 W. Va. 470, 109 S.E. 489.
14. *Nesben v. Jackson, supra.*
15. C.R.S. '63, 68-1-5, 68-1-6, 68-1-11 [C.R.S. '73, 12-44-105, 12-44-106, 12-44-111].
16. Lodging Law of Kansas, Sections 1 through 4.
17. Public General Laws of Maryland, Chapter 24, Acts of 1939, sections 1 and 2.
18. Missouri Hotel Law, Sections 419.010 to 419.030.
19. Laws of Florida, 1955, Chapter 509, Chapter 85.
20. California Hotel and Motel Law, Sections 1850 to 1860.
21. Nevada Revised Statutes, 651.010 (2).
22. Nevada Revised Statutes, 651.010 (2).
23. 153 F. Supp. 31, *affd.* 253 F. 2d 410 (D.C. Fl. 1957).
24. *Edwards House v. Davis,* 124 Miss. 485, 86 So. 849 (1921). *Elcox v. Hill,* 98 U.S. 218, 25 L. Ed. 103 (1878, applying Illinois law).
25. *Kalpakian v. Oklahoma Sheraton,* 398 F. 2d 243, 37 A.L.R. 3d 1268 (1968).
26. *De Panfield v. Hilton,* 33 Misc. 2d 967, 231 N.Y.S. 2d 906 (1962).
27. *Insurance Company of North America, Inc. v. Holiday Inns, Inc.*, 337 N.Y.S. 2d 68 (Sup. Ct. Saratoga Co. 1972).
28. *Friedman v. Breslin,* 51 A.D. 268, 65 N.Y.S. 5 (2d Dept. 1900).
29. *Sagman v. Richmond Hotel,* 139 F. Supp. 407 (E.D. Va. 1956).
30. *Terry v. Linscott Hotel Corporation,* 617 P. 2d 56 (Ariz. App. 1980).

31. *North River v. Tish,* 64 N.J. Super. 357, 166 A. 2d 169 (1960).
32. *Modell et al. v. Kiamesh Concord, Inc.*, 421 N.Y.S. 2d 858.
33. Terry, *supra.*
34. *Gonalves v. Regent International Hotel Ltd.*, 406 N.Y.S. 2d 750 (1982).
35. *Milthiser v. Beau Site Co.,* 251 N.Y. 290, 167 N.E. 447 (1929).
36. *Zaldin v. Concord Hotel,* 48 N.Y. 2d 107, 421 N.Y.S. 2d 859 (1979).
37. Insurance Company of North America, *supra.*
38. *Albuquerque Hilton v. Haley,* 565 P. 2d 1027 (1977).
39. *Carlton v. Beacon Hotel,* 3 A.D. 228, 157 N.Y.S. 2d 774 (1st Dep. 1956).
40. Terry, *supra.*
41. *Jones v. Hotel Latham Co.*, 62 Misc. 620, 115 N.Y.S. 1084.
42. *Hoorise Waters & Co. v. Gerard,* 189 N.Y. 302, 82 N.E. 143, 24 L.R.A. N.S. 958.
43. *Briggs v. Todd,* 28 Misc. 208, 59 N.Y.S. 23.
44. *Rosenplaenter v. Rorssle,* 54 N.Y. 262.
45. Diamond, *supra.*
46. Nevada Revised Statutes 108.490.
47. In addition, the hotel asserts in its Rule 9(g) statement that the value of the contents of the case other than jewelry did not exceed $300. This statement is said to be based on a representation made by Mrs. Salisbury's attorney. Mrs. Salisbury does not contend to the contrary, and has not submitted a Rule 9(g) statement of her own. Thus, she may be deemed to have admitted the truth of the assertion, Rule 9(g), General Rules of the United States District Courts for the Southern and Eastern Districts of New York, which further establishes that the amount in controversy here is not sufficient to sustain federal subject matter jurisdiction.
48. 68 Misc. 2d 400, 327 N.Y.S. 2d 426 (Civ. Ct. N.Y. 1972).

20

Guests and Third Parties: Injury to; Ejection of the Unruly; Those Who are Disturbed; Defamation; Crisis Planning; and the "Sally Board" Principle

COCHRANE, J.: "The primary and fundamental function of an inn seems clearly to have been to furnish entertainment and lodging for the traveler on his journey. This at all times seems to have been its distinguishing feature. This idea has been expressed in the literature of ages, in history, sacred and profane, in fiction and in poetry. So true is this that the term 'inn' seems always to have been used in connection with the corresponding notion of travelers seeking the accommodation and protection of the inn. Thus the Christian era dawned on a Judean scene, where travelers away from home who had gone up to be taxed pursuant to the decree of the Roman emperor, sought refuge in a manger 'because there was no room for them in the inn.' Sir Walter Scott characterizes the inn of the old days of Merry England as 'the free rendezvous of all travelers' of which the bonny Black Bear of Cumnor village, not conducted merely, but 'ruled by Giles Gosling, a man of a goodly person.' as landlord, was a typical instance. And so the most illustrious bard of England says, referring to the time of approaching twilight, with the west glimmering with streaks of day, 'now spurs the lated traveler apace to gain the timely inn.'"

Crapo v. Rockwell
48 Misc. 1, 94 N.Y.S. 1122 (Sup. Ct. 1905)

What we are interested in now are the dangers that face the weary traveler who gains the timely inn.

OVERVIEW

In Chapter 12, we became acquainted with the basic legal duties of innkeepers and guests. In Chapter 13 we explored the fundamentals of legal liability at the inn. This was followed by Chapter 14 in which we examined danger areas of the inn and in Chapter 16, we looked at some ways to avoid legal liability through "inn-made law" and practices. Much of what we examined there was based on tort law, but a considerable amount of it included contract principles too. It now becomes necessary to center our attention on injury to guests and third parties. There are countless ways that injuries can occur at the inn and we need some ideas about how to deal with them when they arise, and also how to minimize them.

Some of the topics discussed here have been introduced in previous chapters. A few of them have not been, however, such as ejecting unruly guests, handling guests who are disturbed or who are acting suspiciously, "The Sally Board" principle, and crisis planning, to name a few. Thus, in this chapter we are examining an area of law that is concerned with tort law. Criminal law is occasionally touched upon but contract law is only incidental to our discussion here.

Up to this point, our emphasis has been upon general inn duties and rights as well as responsibility for loss of goods, money and valuables, and autos of guests and others. Here the emphasis will change and the focus will be upon injury. In this chapter we will examine the principles that become involved when a guest is injured in his or her person, reputation, or mind as contrasted to the injury to that person's goods. While the law often limits the liability of an innkeeper for the loss or injury to *goods* of a guest, here we encounter an area in which there are usually no statutory limits. Recovery for injuries to one's person, reputation, or mind is controlled (1) by the skill of defense counsel and (2) reluctance that a jury may have in assessing damages at too high a figure. These are intangibles and one cannot afford to assume that the inn's counsel will do a good defense job, or that a jury may be restrained when arriving at a verdict. The opposite is often true.

We must keep in mind as we proceed that the principles of Chapter 13 are also applied in injury cases and, to that end, it is useful to review the contents of that chapter. Proof of loss, burden of proof, defenses available, and the types of damages that can be sought are the same in injury cases as they are in contract and other loss cases.

In all inns the premises that are made available to guests, patrons, and other invitees must be maintained in a safe, clean, habitable condition. If they are not, injury often follows and litigation results. Examine Figure 20.1.

LEGAL LIABILITY OF THE INNKEEPER

Liability can come into existence at several levels and the following is a listing of the types of injury liability:

1. **Strict liability.** This was the standard at common law and is still recognized when an inherently dangerous item is used at the inn.
2. **Ordinary negligence.** This basis of liability arises when the innkeeper fails to use ordinary care.
3. **Gross negligence.** This happens when the innkeeper is overtly careless in the operation of the inn.
4. **Negligence per se.** This status arises when the innkeeper fails to meet the requirements of state statutes or city ordinances and the court adopts those laws as the standards to measure the case at hand.

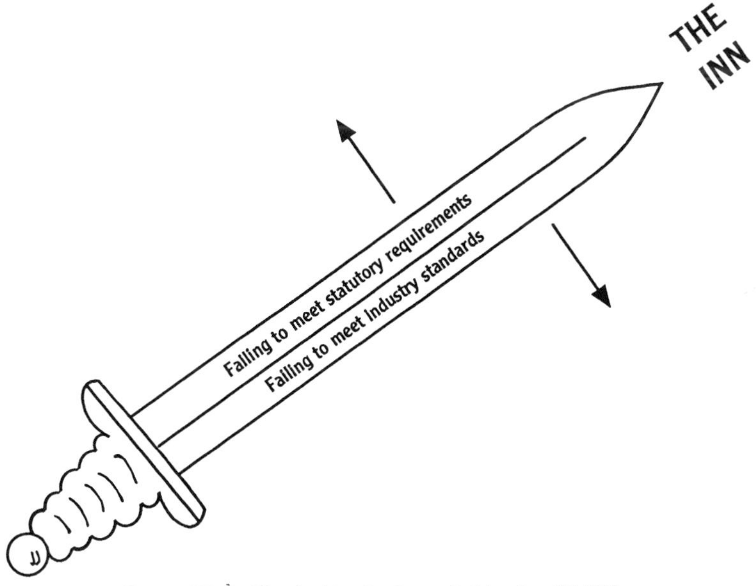

FIGURE 20.1 The double-edged sword of inn legal liability.

These four items create tort liability. There is a fifth liability item and it is based on contract:

5. **Breach of implied warranties.** This arises at the inn when standards that are ordinarily expected, such as service of merchantable food, does not in fact arise. Serving contaminated food would be an example and so would providing unsafe furniture for guest use.

Modern innkeeping law represents a set of boundaries within which the inn must operate. These boundaries will include what should be done, what can be anticipated there, what a court is going to say should have been done, and what in fact does happen. The innkeeper is faced with a myriad of situations that represent a flow of happenings that require perpetual decisions to handle them properly. Is this decision better than that one? Is a report required of that particular incident? If this is done, what is likely to be the legal consequences? What might be the consequences if it isn't done?

These "boundaries of the law" are often tested in court where the rules of substantive and procedural law predominate. All facts, inferences, and impressions will be considered by the jury in an inn case. In addition, the fact that a national chain is doing business in a particular state gives the courts of that state jurisdiction, *Wronikowski v. General,* 716 F. Supp. 5 (Minnesota, 1989). As to the degree of proof, the "preponderance of the evidence" rule will apply in almost all inn injury cases. Examine Figure 20.2.

Burden of Proof

In most inn injury cases, the burden is on the plaintiff to prove proximate cause and negligence. In some instances, however, the burden is shifted to the inn. An example would be in a case in which a wall-mounted television falls, injuring a guest. Here, the thing that caused the injury was in the control of the inn. Second, such an event usually does not happen. When this two-part test is met, the burden shifts to the inn to convince the jury that the injury was not due to the negligence of the inn. This is the doctrine of *res ipsa loquitur,* "the thing speaks for itself," *Deming Hotel Co. v. Prox,* 142 Ind. App. 603, 236 N.E. 2d 613 (Indiana, 1968). See also *Page v. Sloan* in Chapter 5. For tort liability to attach to the inn, something must connect the negligence of the inn with the injury that results to a guest or third party. That legal connection is supplied by the presence of "proximate cause," and this is part of the burden of proof that the law places on the plaintiff. In the

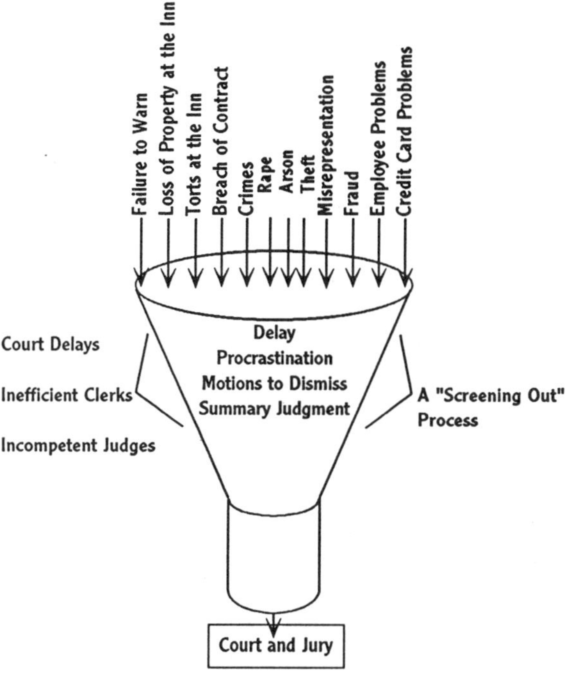

The "Funnel Concept."
What Actually Gets to a Court and Jury?

FIGURE 20.2

falling television case, it would be quite easy for the plaintiff to carry the burden of proving proximate cause.

Every favorable inference that can be drawn from the evidence will be given to the plaintiff. This is a right that American courts traditionally extend to those who bring injury cases to the courts. What it means is that disputed questions will be given to the jury to decide. If judges in the lower courts dismiss injury cases where there were such disputed questions, the upper courts will almost always send the cases back for trial by jury. Perhaps the most constant source of inn injury cases is the failure of the inn to provide safe premises.

SAFE PREMISES

Innkeepers have a legal duty to maintain safe premises at all times, not only for guests and patrons but employees as well. Floors, stairways, and walkways must be kept clean and free of slippery substances;[1] stairwells and outside areas must be kept well lighted at night;[2] elevators must be kept in good repair because responsibility for them cannot be delegated to third parties;[3] window screens, where they are used, must be adequately fastened to prevent children from falling from windows;[4] and large plate-glass spans must be closed off with protective railings or furniture to prevent guests from walking into them. Rooms and furnishings must be inspected constantly to prevent unsafe conditions from occurring, such as loose legs on chairs, unsafe wall television mounts,[5] and defective shower or tub fittings that may lead to scald burns.[6] Rollaway beds and child beds must be offered in a safe, sanitary form and proper vermin control must be utilized.

It is common knowledge in the industry that certain locations at the inn are more likely to produce injuries or crimes than others. Balconies and stairways are two examples. In addition, repeated occurrences such as elevator robberies create a "track record" that requires a response by the inn. Assume that an inn had sixteen reported cases of nonviolent crimes on the premises during the past four years. Since there were no reported instances of violent crimes, the inn had taken no steps to prevent them. If a violent crime now occurs, can the series of nonviolent crimes be used to show that a violent crime could reasonably have been foreseen? A Delaware court has answered that question in the affirmative, *MacQuarrie v. Howard Johnson*, 877 F. 2d 126 (Delaware, 1989).

When Injuries Occur to Children

When injuries do occur at the inn, the immediate actions that are taken may have a bearing upon what the outcome may be if the matter winds up in court. For example, injuries involving children must be given immediate, detailed attention. Reports must be written up, witnesses must be identified and addresses recorded, photos must be taken if relevant, and diagrams must be made of the accident. Thus, children are always of concern, and innkeepers are required to receive them at the inn. The mere fact of infancy does not justify the refusal to admit them, especially when they are traveling alone, 2. S. *Williston on Contracts*, section 241-242 (3rd ed. 1959). The doctrine of *res ipsa loquitur* applies when children are injured at the inn. The injury raises an inference that what happened to the minor would not have occurred in the absence of negligence on the part of the inn, *Zimmer v. Celebrities*, 615 P. 2d 76 (Colorado, 1980). One who deals with minors must exercise more care than when dealing with adults. Thus, when an innkeeper sees that more than the usual number of minors are present at the inn, more caution is in order. The acts of minors are always unpredictable, so "child proofing" is in order to make danger areas at the inn safe for minors. Some city ordinances, such as in San Francisco, require innkeepers to notify the police immediately when unaccompanied minors show up at the inn. Laws of this type assist in reducing injuries to minors. If minors are locals, the inn may, and probably should, refuse to receive them, especially if it is expected that the intent of the stay is for partying purposes. Almost all city inns have a house rule in this regard.

When injuries occur to any person, minor or adult, the innkeeper should always ask an immediate question and find and record the answer to it: "Why was the injured person at that particular location at the inn when injured?" The answer could well provide a strong legal defense later. To illustrate, "Why was a guest using the iced stairs when the elevator was at hand?" Or, "Why was the guest walking through the kitchen when the accident took place?" Or, "Why was the guest in an area of the inn that had been closed for the night?" In addition, the entire area surrounding the location of the injury should be scrutinized immediately by someone assigned to that inspection. Anything out of the ordinary should be observed and recorded such as a tipped-over suitcase 10 feet away, or a broken branch on a nearby potted plant.

Many other things occur at the inn that may cause the premises to be unsafe and which can lead to injury to guests and others. Unruly persons are an example.

UNRULY PERSONS AT THE INN

If guests become intoxicated and abusive to others, those persons' right to remain at the inn may come to an end if the innkeeper decides to call the forfeiture. If such a person is allowed to remain at the inn and if that person should assault another, the failure to remove may be held to be the proximate cause of the injuries that resulted.

Failing to Eject Such Persons

The law creates a rather impressive list of things that innkeepers have a right to do in carrying out their business operations. On the other hand, the law has a way of "reversing its tracks." An example of this is to be found in the failure to do something that one in fact had a legal right to do in the first instance. To illustrate, an innkeeper has a right to eject those persons who are creating a disturbance, or who conduct themselves in such a manner as to make their continued presence undesirable. But what might be the legal consequences if an innkeeper fails or simply overlooks the right to eject and does nothing when the circumstances indicate that the offending person should be removed from the inn? A 1970 Kansas case provides some insights.

To begin with, the judge stated that the general rule of the common law is as follows: "A proprietor [sic] of an inn . . . is liable for an assault upon a guest . . . by another person . . . where he [she] has reason to anticipate such assault, and fails to exercise reasonable care under the circumstances to prevent the assault or interfere with its execution . . .", *Kimple v. Foster,* 469 P. 2d 281 (Kansas, 1970). In this case the court was satisfied that the bar operator (called "proprietor" above), acting through agents, had more than ample notice that trouble was brewing and that ejection of the offending parties was needed to prevent it. The failure to exercise the right to eject resulted in liability for failing to act. Thus what started out as a legal right ended up as a violation of a legal duty.

A related question is, "What happens if the unruly person is lawfully removed from the inn and then causes injury or death to outsiders?" Might the ejection of that person be held by a court to be the proximate cause of what happened to the outsiders? When an ejected friend of a guest killed a third party four miles from the inn, a court ruled that "In this case, no duty of the [inn] can be found . . . to supervise the activities of the [inn] guest's visitor after he left the premises. The [inn] had fulfilled any duty it had to passersby to keep the premises reasonably safe. It has no further duty . . ." to outside third parties, *Upthergrove v. Myers,* 299 N.W. 2d 29 (Minnesota, 1981).

On the other hand, a Louisiana case in which a person was killed just four feet from the front door of the inn complex provides some further insight into the matter. While the case did not involve an ejected guest, it indicates that proximity might make a difference in the legal results when unruly guests are ejected and then cause injury to others. Four miles is far different than four feet. The judge in the Louisiana case said that "Dr. Banks did not make it through the entrance doors to the complex. We refuse to transform those doors into an impregnable legal wall of immunity. . . ," *Banks v. Hyatt Corporation,* 722 F. 2d 214 (Louisiana, 1984). A wise house policy when ejecting an unruly guest would be to have a security guard escort that person to his or her automobile, provided he or she is in a condition to drive, and see to it that he or she exits the inn premises. That should satisfy a court. Ejecting a person who is too intoxicated to drive, however, is going to require police assistance and the police should be called for that purpose.

Related to the problem of unruly guests are those who are disturbed, distressed, angry, or who may be acting suspiciously while at the inn.

Disturbed or Suspicious Persons at the Inn

Inn personnel must be trained to watch for those who are disturbed, irritated, angry, or who are acting in a suspicious manner. When such characteristics are observed, immediate reports must be made so that someone with authority may enter the picture. It may amount to nothing more than a few words of inquiry, but it may also defuse a potentially dangerous situation. If persons are seen at places in the inn where they should not be, that gives rise to a suspicion and so does a guest who is angry or irritated.

In inn situations where large numbers of people gather, such conditions must not be allowed to pass without attention being paid to them. It is a matter of continuing to assert control over the inn because the law allows this. Traditionally, inn personnel, such as room maids, have been reluctant to say anything to such persons out of fear of offending a guest. This is understandable, yet a superior must be notified when unusual behavior or activity is observed at the inn. The superior in turn must approach the person and ask if assistance can be given. In the case of persons who are acting suspiciously, identification can be asked for. While some guests may be offended by this, it must be remembered that the law recognizes that the house is that of the innkeeper and has long said that the innkeeper has the right, and indeed the duty, to take all reasonable steps to maintain the sanctity and security of the inn. A court will not fault an innkeeper for doing that. It amounts to little more than using reasonable care and that is what the law requires. As a court said, it is necessary for the innkeeper, at all reasonable times, to ". . . have control over every part of the (inn), even though separate parts thereof may be occupied by guests for hire," *People v. Thorpe,* 101 N.Y.S. 2d 986 (New York, 1950).

Nonguests: Suspicious or Undesirable Persons

Those who enter an inn who are not guests or are not patrons of the restaurant or bar have no legal standing to be there. At most, they can claim an implied license, but that can be revoked at any time by the innkeeper or her or his agents, *Kelly v. U.S.*, 348 A. 2d 864 (District of Columbia, 1975).

Another concern of innkeepers are those persons who are intent on taking their own lives. Does the innkeeper have responsibilities in that regard?

The Potential Suicide

If notice of such a possibility is received at the inn, immediate notice must be given to the police, security, and management at the inn. In a 1975 Georgia case it was alleged in court that the inn had been warned that a guest had threatened to commit suicide and had failed to take action to avert that possibility. The evidence at trial, however, failed to convince the jury that those claims were true and the inn was exonerated. The legal point is, of course, if the jury had been convinced of the allegations, the inn could well have been held responsible for the death.

OTHER INN INJURY MATTERS

Louisiana Revised Statutes, Section 40:1580 (1981), requires inns to post, on the inside of the entry door to each guest room, a map that sets out the routes to follow from each room to the fire exits. New York state has a similar law: N.Y. Labor Law, section 473-a, (McKinney, 1981).

Effective January 1, 1982, the New York legislature added the following to section 204 of the New York General Business Law: "204-a. Safety chain latches required. Every person, firm or corporation engaged in the business of furnishing public lodging accommodations in hotels, motels or motor courts shall install and maintain, on the inside of each entrance door to every rental unit for which there is a duplicate or master key which would afford entry to said unit by one other than the occupant, a safety chain latch."

A 1989 change in federal law is going to have an impact on inn injury cases.

A Change in Federal Law

For many years, before an injured guest could bring a lawsuit in federal court in that person's home state, a two-part test had to be met:

1. The inn and the injured person had to be "diverse" to each other; that is, they had to be from different states.
2. The amount in controversy had to be $10,000 or more.

If the two tests were met, the injured person could bring the lawsuit in a federal district court where that person lived. This often placed the inn in court hundreds or even thousands of miles from where the inn was located. Effective May 18, 1989, the jurisdictional amount was raised to $50,000. This means that inn injury cases of less than $50,000 will have to be brought in the county courts where the injury occurred.

Injury to Professional Persons

Inn injury cases where professionals are involved, and especially where death results, are always given closer scrutiny by the courts than cases that involve ordinary persons. Thus if it becomes known that a person checking in is a medical doctor, it would be good inn practice to alert personnel to that fact and to greet that person by his or her title. It is a situation much like that where minors are present at the inn. The law increases standards where minors are present at the inn and seems to do that where professional persons are also present.

Later in this chapter, the matter of rats being present at the inn is discussed. Such vermin can cause injury to guests at the inn. Failure to control their presence can cause the premises to be unsafe in the eyes of the courts. Examine Figure 20.3.

Vermin Control[7]

An innkeeper is not an insurer of the safety of the guest.[8] However, the innkeeper must meet certain requirements such as providing a safe and clean inn, especially one free of insects.[9]

State laws impose duties on innkeepers to provide a sanitary inn[10] and impose penalties[11] if these requirements are not met.

It is a misdemeanor in Nevada not to comply with the sanitary regulations imposed by law. An innkeeper must keep the inn premises free of "vermin or bedbugs or similar things."[12] And if such "things" are found or known to be found on the property, especially guest rooms, the innkeeper must "thoroughly fumigate, disinfect and renovate until such vermin or bedbugs . . . are entirely exterminated."[13]

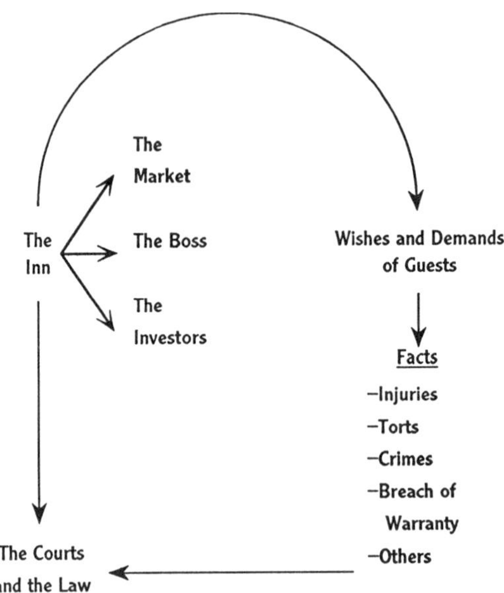

FIGURE 20.3 The inn picture injury-wise.

When the weather changes, so do the habits of insects and vermin. Las Vegas, unfortunately, sometimes becomes home to bedbugs and beetles. When this happens, innkeepers must combat the problem to comply with state law. But what exactly does "fumigate, disinfect, and renovate" mean? To fumigate means "the act of smoking or applying smoke or gas, as in disinfecting . . . apartments; disinfection"[14]; disinfected means "made free from *injurious* or contagious diseases; immunization"[15] (emphasis added); and to renovate means "to renew, make over, or repair, or to restore to freshness, purity, a sound state, or newness of appearance."

If such a condition exists and the innkeeper does not remove it, or at least warn the guest of its existence and the actions for correcting it, a foreseeable action in negligence could occur. A Michigan court awarded an injured guest $25,000 for being bitten by a rat.[16] The court decided that the Michigan housing law (like Nevada law 447.030 with respect to inns and public accommodations) did not impose "absolute liability on hotelkeeper for failure to keep premises free from rats but *rather imposes liability only if he knew or should have known of such dangerous conditions*" (emphasis added).[17] It is this foreseeability about which the innkeeper must worry. If an innkeeper has had problems with insects in the past, or if a whole town is infected, the innkeeper must correct the problem and warn the guest or be party to a negligence suit.

Other Considerations

An innkeeper cannot escape liability for a falling elevator that causes injury to a guest, even though the innkeeper employs experts to keep the elevator in safe condition. This duty and others like it cannot be delegated.[18] Liability was attached for sending a "nurse" to examine an injured guest, when the person sent was not in fact a nurse, had no qualifications, and did not properly diagnose the injury, to the detriment of the guest.[19] Again even the suicide of a guest can give rise to legal liability in cases where the inn had notice of suicidal tendencies of a guest and did not react properly to this information.[20] There are literally hundreds of cases where innkeepers have been held responsible for attacks on guests while in their rooms,[21] and even for the murder of a guest during a robbery attempt.[22]

Confines of the Inn

Walkways must be kept free of ice and debris. Railings must be provided at elevated portions of walkways and alongside pools and recreation areas. Parking lots must be well lighted and, if autos are handled by agents of the inn, the lot should be fenced and adequate security provided for the safety of guests and patrons and their autos.

An injured guest or patron may be barred from recovery, of course, if that person in some manner contributed to his or her injury, the same as contributory negligence will bar recovery for loss or damage to goods. Also, as more and more states adopt the doctrine of comparative negligence, this too will become a factor to be considered. Some states, such as West Virginia, have adopted the doctrine by court decision; others, such as New York and Minnesota, have enacted specific statutes.[23]

If the proximate cause[24] of the injury is the negligence of the innkeeper or an agent or employee, even if there was contributory negligence, the innkeeper may be held liable for the loss sustained. The secret in avoiding liability for injury is to avoid being careless in the operation of the inn. An area in which this is especially true is in the operation and maintenance of swimming pools.

Swimming Pools

If one were to devise a way in which guests could be injured in a perpetual fashion, it would be difficult to improve upon the swimming pool. Guests are constantly falling, diving into partly filled pools after dark, falling from diving boards, colliding with one another in the water when diving, and, in general, injuring themselves and others.

One should consider a pool as a high-risk area and treat it accordingly. If it is beneficial to maintain a pool, then it is mandatory that enough funds be allocated for proper maintenance. For example, what might be the liability of an innkeeper who permits a pool to become unsanitary, resulting in serious sickness to those who use it? In addition, many states have health laws that do regulate swimming pools and so do most larger cities. One must comply with these laws.

Lawsuits arising out of pool injuries are not always successful to the plaintiff, but many are. Lawsuit losses often result for the following reasons:

1. Defective design of the pool.
2. Failure to maintain the pool properly.
3. Failure to erect suitable fences.
4. Failure to post signs stating that lifeguards are not on duty.
5. Failure to adequately supervise the pool.

1. Defective Design

The traditional inn pool has a shallow end, a middle-depth area, and a deep end, which usually includes a diving board. The shape of the pool is often dictated by the effect desired by the architect, and the edges of the pool are rounded, molded concrete or ceramic tile.

The *use* of the pool must always be kept in mind during the design. Does a fancy curve in a pool project into an area where one would dive? Is the diving board too strong for the size of the pool? Does the shallow portion of the pool extend too closely to the diving board? Is the lifeguard tower likely to be used as a diving area if unattended? Are the safety rope and floats located too far beyond the shallow zone? Does the material on the surface around the pool become slippery when wet?

These questions have been drawn from cases in which inns were found liable. In one case, a new diving board was installed which was too long for the pool. As a result, a diver was injured, resulting in paraplegia. The inn was found liable for $5 million.[25]

2. Improper Maintenance

Loose tile or concrete edges may result in tort liability for failure to make repairs. In one case, a man was found dead in a pool and the evidence disclosed the concrete rim was loose. It was theorized the fall had been caused by the loose tile. A recovery for the death was allowed under the doctrine of *res ipsa loquitur*. Failure to immediately clean up broken glass or hard plastic, or to remove slippery substances has also led to legal liability. Proper and consistent pool maintenance is mandatory. If it is economically important to have a pool, proper maintenance is legally necessary.[26]

3. Failure to Erect Fences

Suitable fences are essential to prevent small children, intoxicated guests, and others from entering the pool area. All states and most cities have statutes and ordinances that require such fences, and they must be included in the design of the inn pool and properly maintained.

4. Failure to Post Signs

Swimming pools are recognized by legislatures as well as the courts as high-risk areas, but having lifeguards on duty at all times is not mandatory. Some states, such as California, leave the decision to the pool operator. However, if a lifeguard is not on duty, a sign must be posted to warn the users. Failure to post a sign can result in liability in the event of injury. In locales where many foreign visitors use the pools, the warning signs should be printed in both English and the appropriate foreign language. For example, in Orange County, California, the home of Disneyland and Knott's Berry Farm, such warning signs could be printed in Japanese and Spanish as well as English. Examine Figure 20.4.

5. Failure to Provide Adequate Supervision

The failure to adequately supervise a pool, even when a lifeguard is not on duty, could result in a tort action. A system of inspection must be consistently enforced to demonstrate adequate supervision to the courts if it should become necessary later.

Leaving swimming pools, there are other injury matters that are of concern to the innkeeper.

Protection from Employees

Innkeepers have a duty to protect guests and patrons from acts of employees that may cause harm to the guest. The duty to protect

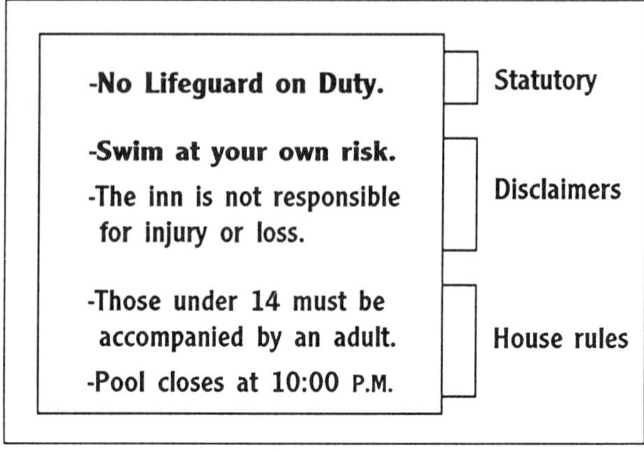

FIGURE 20.4

the guest is strong at law and requires that employees be schooled in the necessity of maintaining courteous, safe conduct toward guests and patrons at all times.

Some statutes and case decisions exonerate innkeepers from liability for willful acts of employees or agents toward guests while *off* duty.

Protection from Third Parties

Innkeepers have a duty to protect guests and patrons from injurious acts of third parties. Liability has attached where a third party became intoxicated and injured a guest;[27] where boisterous banquet patrons knocked down guests while running in the lobby; where by the spinning of revolving doors left unattended, a guest is injured. Failure to provide adequate security to prevent such injuries can lead to liability. Indeed, providing security that is adequate *and then reducing it for economy reasons,* could lead to the same result. In the Wisconsin case of *Weihert v. Piccione*,[28] the court had this to say:

> . . . [t]he proprietor of a place of business who holds it out to the public for entry for his business purposes is liable to members of the public while on the premises for such purpose for harm caused by the accidental negligence or intentional acts of third persons, if the proprietor by the exercise of reasonable care could have discovered that such acts were being done and could have protected the members of the public by controlling the conduct of the third persons, or by giving a warning adequate to enable them to avoid harm.

The rule of this case is now in Wisconsin Jury Instruction 1027.5. This instruction reads in part as follows:

> When one assembles a crowd or a large number of people upon his property for purposes of financial gain to himself, he assumes the responsibility of using ordinary care to protect the individuals from injury from causes reasonably to be anticipated. In the exercise of this duty, it is incumbent upon him to furnish a sufficient number of guards or attendants and to take other necessary precautions to control the actions of the crowd.

Liability has attached to a bar for the failure of the bartender to call the police after a fight broke out;[29] by having patio doors on inn rooms that can be entered from the outside, leading to an attack on a guest;[30] by permitting sex deviates and known criminals to wander around an inn;[31] and in many other ways.

The innkeeper must use reasonable care to control or avoid things that could go wrong even though, at best, this can be a difficult job. But it must be remembered that the law does not expect miracles; only that one act as a reasonable person would act under like or similar circumstances. Yet the things that can happen at inns cannot always be anticipated. The following news item illustrates:

> CHATTANOOGA, Tenn. A federal court jury has awarded $25,000 to a man who said he suffered a serious neck injury when he walked into a motel room occupied by a "skimpily clad" woman.
>
> James L. Hardy Jr. of Needville, Texas, claimed in a federal court lawsuit that a clerk at a Days Inn motel gave him the wrong key during a family vacation trip in July 1981, [and injured his neck while taking a second look].[32]

Before turning to cases to illustrate the principles discussed in this chapter, three topics will be sketched: defamation, crisis planning, and the "Sally Board" Principle. In all three, injuries to guests at the inn comes into focus.

DEFAMATION

This is a legal term that includes both "libel" and "slander." The former involves printed/written words while the latter involves spoken words. There are three elements that must be proven in court to allow one to gain a civil recovery on the claim of defamation. First, the printed/written or spoken words must have been untrue. Second, those words must have been "published" or communicated to another person or more than one person. Third, the published untruth must have caused injury to the person in question. If a jury hearing such a case finds that this three-part test has been met, appropriate damages can be awarded. The Moricoli case later in this chapter is an example of what the law of defamation can mean at the inn. While that case involved an entertainer, the principles apply to guests as well as employees. The following employee items illustrate.

Employers have a qualified privilege in Nevada to discuss employees as established by prior court decisions in that state. When a corporate officer discusses actions of an employee with another corporate officer, there has been no "publication" or communication, *Jones v. Golden Spike*, 623 P. 2d 970 (Nevada, 1981). In the Jones case, the claim that bartenders had been stealing was addressed to all of the bartenders in question. The court held that since all of those persons who heard the accusation were also the accused, there had been no "publication." If the accusation had been directed toward a particular person in the group, and had been false, a cause of action would have existed. Also, if an accusation against all of the bartenders was heard by an outside party, the entire group might have a valid claim of defamation except those in fact guilty of stealing.

Another example of defamation at an inn is found in *Columbia Sussex Corporation, Inc. v. Hay*, 627 S.W. 2d 270 (Kentucky, 1982). In that case a Best Western Hotel at Richwood, Kentucky, was robbed by a person who seemed to have inside information about the alarm system that was attached to the cash register. The president of the corporation which owned the inn demanded that the manager, Hay, take a lie detector test. He said to her if front of others words to the effect that "You will be surprised to find out who gave the robber the information," hinting that Hay was a suspect. It was later established that there was no connection between any employee and the robbery. Hay was fired shortly thereafter and brought a successful defamation suit against the hotel. While the appeals court sent the case back for retrial, the circumstances indicate that care must be used at the inn when discussing employees and guests in front of others. The confidential privilege that employers have with employees will work to the advantage of the employer as it did in the Hay case on appeal, but it will never work where guests are concerned. The policy of the house must always be to avoid defamation. Its avoidance is certainly part of the sanctity to be enjoyed by guests and employees as well.

The Moricoli case is a vivid illustration of how defamation can arise at an inn if an innkeeper is not careful. It could also arise if an inn provides false credit information to others about former guests or former employees. That would also be a violation of the Fair Credit Reporting Act. Truth at the inn is very much in order under modern laws.

Might a claim of defamation also arise in this situation: An inn in Billings, Montana, has a large picture frame on the wall beside the front desk. Inside this frame are dozens of checks that have been returned to the inn marked "insufficient funds." Included are many checks upon which stop-payment orders had been made. Apparently the innkeeper feels some compulsion to let others see these "return items" and has thus placed them on display. The legal problem with this is that the insufficient funds checks may have been made good in some other manner and the stop-payment checks may have been carried out legally under the Uniform Commercial Code. Since these checks have names and addresses on them, might some of them form the basis of a defamation case against the inn? It would seem that displaying these checks is not a wise inn decision. A better rule to adopt would be a "no check" or no display policy.

Turning from defamation, a matter that requires consideration is that of preparing for a crisis that may or may not happen at the inn.

CRISIS PLANNING AT THE INN

Inn personnel will not respond properly to a crisis unless they are trained for that contingency. It is important that the inn provide that training and there should be an inn crisis plan in effect. This plan should include phone numbers to be called, which doors are to be used when ambulances arrive, who is to be at those doors to direct police and ambulances to the location of the crisis, and other applicable matters. A crisis is something that no inn needs, but it is going to strike some of them. Perhaps the most dramatic example was the collapse of two walkways at the Hyatt Regency in Kansas City. See Figure 20.5 for a news report on that catastrophe. One way to alert inn personnel to what must be done if such a crisis strikes the inn is through clauses in the employee handbook. Other methods include bulletin board postings, group training sessions, and person-to-person instruction. Crisis planning is not a subject to dwell upon, but it is wise to make contingency plans.

One final matter deserves mention and it has to do with that period of time just after an injury has occurred. Does the inn have any legal matters to consider at that point in time? Many years ago, one of the authors had a client by the name of Sally Board

The death toll rose to 111 in the Hyatt Regency Hotel accident today, as officials began trying to determine what caused the collapse of two walkways suspended above the hotel lobby.

Late this afternoon, officials said only 12 bodies remained to be identified.

Public safety officials here said that the final toll was certain to rise when an accurate count was made of victims who subsequently died at area hospitals as a result of injuries they suffered in the accident.

Firefighters and police officials today were attempting to reconstruct what happened just after 7 o'clock last night when, without warning, two of three concrete walkways that spanned the width of the hotel lobby plunged to the floor where a dance was under way. Officials of the hotel, the city and the Governor's office promised investigations into the cause of the accident, in which 188 persons were injured.

Normally the 75-yard-long walkways are used by guests moving from the side of the building containing living quarters to meeting rooms on lower floors across the lobby. But at the weekly social event called the Tea Dance, participants were reportedly allowed to dance on the 10-to-12-foot-wide walks as well as in the lobby below.

New York Times
July 19, 1981, p. 1.

Figure 20.5

who resided in an inn near the university where she taught English. She was severely injured at the inn when an old-fashioned, brass door closer fell, striking her on the head. She filed suit against the inn for her injuries and recovered over a quarter of a million dollars. She told the author later that she would not have filed the suit if someone from the inn had taken a few moments to visit her at the hospital and express their condolences. No one from the inn had seen fit to do that.

THE "SALLY BOARD" PRINCIPLE

The inn must not insult injured guests by ignoring them, regardless of where the fault may lie. Steps must be taken to assure the injured person that the inn is concerned about him or her. This is not to say that a representative of the inn should confess liability. That should never be done. Concern can be expressed without making promises and that is what must be done.

Attorney William English of Oakton, Virginia, says that "What occurs after an accident (at the inn) is sometimes of great importance too. . . . People are looking for justice; sometimes just being

Los Altos Hotel and Apartments,
Long Beach, California, near the Queen Mary and the Spruce Goose on display there.

sympathetic will avoid a lawsuit." *Hospitality Law,* volume 5, no. 7, July 1990, p. 4, said it this way: "Injured guests are particularly vulnerable and quick to anger when they perceive (correctly or incorrectly) a 'don't give a damn' attitude on the part of the (inn) and its staff."

Leaving our discussion of injuries to guests and third parties, it is useful to examine some cases in which the matters discussed became involved in live situations. In these opinions, one gets an opportunity to see what the courts have to say about injuries at the inn.

The Mizenis case illustrates the danger where the cause of the slip-and-fall is the failure of the innkeeper to keep stairways free from ice and snow. In this case, the lower court granted summary judgment for the inn. This meant that the injured guest's case had been dismissed without trial. The Ohio Appellate court is now reviewing that dismissal.

MIZENIS V. SANDS MOTEL, INC.,
50 Ohio App. 2d 226, 362 N.E. 2d 661 (1975).

CLIFFORD F. BROWN, Presiding Judge.

This is an appeal from a summary judgment in favor of defendant Balconi and Smith, Inc., operators of the Sands Motel, arising out of an action by the plaintiff, a motel guest, who fell while descending an exterior stairway from a second floor motel room. The stairway was in a slippery and dangerous condition as the result of a natural accumulation of ice and snow.

The stipulation of facts by the parties considered in reaching a summary judgment, contained, *inter alia*, the following facts:

"1. The only means of ingress and egress to plaintiff's motel unit consisted of two exterior stairways, of metal construction, located at opposite ends of the motel unit.

"2. Both exterior stairways were in a slippery and dangerous condition due to a failure on the part of the motel to remove snow and ice that accumulated thereon. This slippery and dangerous condition had existed for three or more days prior to plaintiff's being assigned to his room. The accumulated ice and snow on these exterior stairways was made dangerous and slippery by virtue of the fact that it had been subjected to traffic by other persons and the surface had become packed and hard.

"3. Plaintiff became aware of the dangerous and slippery condition upon first ascending the stairs to enter the motel room which had been assigned to him. Plaintiff immediately phoned the motel desk and complained of the dangerous condition of the stairs and asked that it be remedied.

"4. Plaintiff considered all other possible means of egress but there were none other than the two exterior stairways. Using great care, on the morning of January 22, 1970, plaintiff descended the stairway. Plaintiff again complained to the motel desk clerk of the condition of the stairways.

"5. It was on the fifth trip on the same stairs on January 22, 1970, that plaintiff fell.

"6. On all occasions on which the plaintiff used the stairway, plaintiff used great care for his own safety, on all occasions using the hand rails, moving very slowly and watching very carefully where he was going. On his last descent from his motel unit, plaintiff's foot slipped from underneath him, causing him to fall and to sustain an injury to his leg. At the time plaintiff fell, he had hands on both hand rails, was moving cautiously, and was carefully watching where he was going.

"7. Plaintiff had been a guest of the motel on several other previous occasions during the winter months. On all these prior occasions the motel had removed ice and snow from the stairways."

The plaintiff-appellant sets forth two assignments of error as follows:

"1. The trial court erred in finding that there is no duty upon a motel operator to remove natural accumulations of snow within a reasonable time from the exterior stairways providing the only means of ingress and egress to the second floor occupants of the motel.

"2. The trial court erred in finding that the occupant of a second story motel who uses the only means of ingress and egress to his motel room, knowing that said means of ingress and egress is slippery, is charged with assuming the risk as a matter of law."

By granting summary judgment for defendants-appellees, the trial court, by implication, concluded that as a matter of law plaintiff was not entitled to recover for one or both of two reasons, namely: that reasonable minds could come to but one conclusion (1) that there was no duty owing by defendant to plaintiff concerning the accumulation of ice and snow on the exterior metal stairway where plaintiff fell and was injured, and, therefore, no negligence of defendant arose, and (2) plaintiff voluntarily assumed the risk of snowy and icy conditions of the exterior metal stairway which precipitated plaintiff's fall and consequent injuries.

Stated another way, the trial court, by rendering a summary judgment for defendant, determined that pursuant to Civ.R.56(C) there was no genuine issue as to any material fact concerning defendant's negligence–there being no negligence–or concerning plaintiff's assumption of the risk with regard to the snowy and icy condition of the exterior metal stairway–that as a matter of law plaintiff voluntarily assumed the risk and, therefore, defendant was entitled to a judgment in his favor.

A resolution of the question of whether there was a genuine issue of fact concerning defendant's negligence and the existence of plaintiff's voluntary assumption of the risk requires an analysis of the controlling judicial precedents applicable to this case.

Debie v. Cochran Pharmacy-Berwick, Inc. (1967), 11 Ohio St.2d. 38, 227 NE.2d 603, and *Sidle v. Humphrey* (1968), 13 Ohio St.2d 45, 233 N.E.2d 589, upon which defendants rely, define the obligations of an occupier of premises to a business invitee and stand for the following legal propositions:

1. Where the owner or occupier of business premises is not shown to have notice, actual or implied, that the natural accumulation of snow and ice on his premises has created a condition substantially more dangerous to his business invitees than they should have anticipated by reason of their knowledge of conditions prevailing generally in the area, there is a failure of proof of actionable negligence.

2. The mere fact standing alone that the owner or occupier has failed to remove natural accumulations of snow and ice from private walks on his business premises for an unreasonable time does not give rise to an action by a business invitee who claims damages for injuries occasioned by a fall thereon.

3. An occupier of premises is under no duty to protect a business invitee against dangers which are known to such invitee or are so obvious and apparent to such invitee that he may reasonably be expected to discover them and *protect himself against them.*

4. The dangers from natural accumulations of ice and snow are ordinarily so obvious and apparent that an occupier of premises may reasonably expect that a business invitee on his premises will discover those dangers and *protect himself against them,* and such occupier has no duty to his business invitee to remove natural accumulations of snow and ice from private walks and steps of his premises.

Even if, for the sake of argument, plaintiff is placed in the same status as the plaintiffs in *Debie* and *Sidle* cases, the first two legal propositions set out above are not applicable. In the present case, unlike *Debie* and *Sidle,* defendants did have actual notice that the ice and snow on the stairway created a condition substantially more dangerous to plaintiff than plaintiff should have anticipated by reason of his knowledge of conditions prevailing generally. Moreover, the failure of defendants as occupiers to remove the natural accumulations of snow and ice does not stand alone.

The third and fourth numbered propositions of law stated above, extracted from the *Sidle* case, raise genuine issues when applied to the record in this case, for these reasons. The obvious and apparent danger of the snowy, icy stairway to plaintiff, as a business invitee, was not, as a matter of law, a danger that he might "reasonably be expected to protect himself against," because the exterior stairways *were the only means of ingress and egress from his motel room.* Plaintiff sought protection by asking the motel manager to remedy the icy condition. Plaintiff's only other alternative for protecting himself, too absurd to suggest as a practical remedy, was to stay in his motel room until the spring thaws melted the snow and ice. As a minimum, reasonable minds should determine whether or not plaintiff should have protected himself in this or some other way. Therefore, summary judgment cannot be predicated upon the legal propositions contained in the *Debie* and *Sidle* cases.

Further, both *Debie* and *Sidle* distinguish and explain with approval *Oswald v. Jeraj* (1946), 146 Ohio St. 676, 67 N.E.2d 779, as a case which involves a landlord-tenant situation. *Oswald* is more closely akin to the factual situation and legal relationship of plaintiff as a motel guest of the defendants.

The obligation of an innkeeper to his guests, to keep stairways, entrances and hallways in a reasonably safe condition, does not arise expressly from the contract between the innkeeper and guest, but is implied because the use of stairways is necessary to gain access to the premises or to the guest's room, for which he contracted. It is stated in 29 Ohio Jurisprudence 2d 494, Inns & Restaurants, Section 20, that:

"Concerning the duty imposed by law upon an innkeeper to furnish safe premises to his guests and patrons . . . the innkeeper, who is not an insurer, must exercise reasonable care under the circumstances, his liability resting upon the same principles applicable in other cases where persons enter upon premises at the invitation of the owner or occupant and are injured in consequence of the dangerous condition of the premises."

Prosser, Torts (4th ed. 1971), page 407; annotation 49 A.L.R.3d 387, 394; Degraff, *Snow and Ice,* 21 Cornell L.Q. 436, 447-453 (1936); *cf Roth v. Trakas* (1930), 36 Ohio App. 136, 172 N.E. 847 and *Beaney v. Carlson* (1963), 174 Ohio St. 409, 411, 189 N.E.2d 880 (*Shopping Centers*); 29 Ohio Jurisprudence 2d, *supra.*

The Restatement of the Law 2d Torts, Para. 496E, has a comment on the necessity of voluntary assumption. The headnote reads:

"1. A plaintiff does not assume a risk of harm unless he voluntarily accepts the risk.

"2. The plaintiff's acceptance of a risk is not voluntary if the defendant's tortious conduct has left him no reasonable alternative course of conduct in order to (a) advert harm to himself or another, or (b) exercise or protect the right or privilege of which the defendant has no right to deprive him."

A motel guest's acceptance of a risk is not to be regarded as voluntary where the innkeeper's tortious conduct has forced upon him a choice of courses of conduct which leaves him no reasonable alternative to taking his chances. An innkeeper who, by his own wrong, has constrained the motel guest to choose between two evils cannot be permitted to say that the guest is barred from recovery because he made the wrong choice. The same is also true where the guest is compelled to accept the risk in order to exercise or protect a right or a privilege. A motel guest does not assume the risk of his innkeeper's negligence in maintaining a common passageway when it is the only exit from the premises.

In some cases the course of danger may be so extreme as to be out of all proportion to the value of the interest to be protected and the plaintiff may be charged with contributory negligence in his own unreasonable conduct. Prosser, *supra* at 452.

A basic element in assumption of the risk is venturousness. In the present case, we cannot conclude that merely because plaintiff Charles Mizenis was going back and forth on the icy stairway to his motel room that he was being venturous. However, there may be an element of contributory negligence in his conduct upon which reasonable minds could differ, and thus a jury question of contributory negligence exists. This also raises a jury question as to whether or not defendant, as an innkeeper, acted in a way a reasonably prudent person would have acted; thus, a jury issue of negligence of the defendant arises.

Accordingly, both assignments of error are well taken and the judgment of the Court of Common Pleas is reversed and this cause is remanded.

A way in which injury can be caused to another is by defamation.

Words of general abuse, or mere "insulting words" are usually held to be nonactionable. Yet some states have insulting-word statutes. Words that tend to cause violence toward another, even when the words are not published, become actionable under such laws.[33]

Publication, as it is used in defamation, refers to the communication of the words, written or spoken, to third parties. But, as just stated, publication is not required in the insulting-word statutes. The latter are intended to supplement the defamation laws and not to replace them.[34]

Some states, such as Illinois, apply what is called the "innocent-construction test" when deciding if defamation has occurred. This principle and others are discussed in the Moricoli case that follows. The importance of this case to the innkeeper is obvious.

MORICOLI V. SCHWARTZ
361 N.E. 2d 74 (1977)

STAMOS, Justice.

Plaintiff, Thomas Lane Moricoli, brought an action to recover damages for slanderous defamation of his character allegedly resulting from certain statements uttered by defendant, James L. Schwartz, and republished by defendant, Barbara T. Reid. Count I of the complaint contained an allegation of slander. Count II prayed for damages allegedly arising from a tortious interference with prospective economic advantage. Count III sought damages allegedly arising from a breach of contract. Plaintiff appeals from that part of an order of the Circuit Court of Cook County, dated August 8, 1975, that granted defendants' motion to dismiss Count I of plaintiffs complaint for failure to state facts upon which a cause of action may be predicated. The trial court found that the alleged defamatory words upon which the action was predicated are subject to being innocently construed and hence not actionable.

Plaintiff's complaint alleged *inter alia* that plaintiff is a singer and nightclub entertainer using the name of Tommy Lane for his performances; that he auditioned and contracted with defendant Reid, on behalf of defendant P&S Management, Inc., to appear at two of that corporation's hotels; that on September 16, 1974 at a meeting of the corporation's officers and staff and in the presence of defendant Reid and others, defendant Schwartz maliciously spoke of and concerning plaintiff in the following false and defamatory words: "Tommy Lane is a fag and we don't want any fag working for us."; that defendant Reid, on September 17, 1974, in the presence of plaintiff and others republished the statement of defendant Schwartz in the following false and defamatory words: "The contract is being canceled because Mr. Schwartz says Tommy Lane is a fag"; and that thereafter the contract was canceled. Plaintiff alleges that the aforementioned statements are slanderous per se inasmuch as they allege that plaintiff is a homosexual.

According to *Webster's Third International Dictionary of the English Language* (unabridged ed. 1966), the word "fag" admits of four commonly used meanings:

1. *fag / n* -s [ME *fagge* flap, knot in cloth] 1: FAG END 2: CIGARETTE;

2. *fag / vb* [obs E *fag* to droop] *vi* 1: to become weary: TIRE, FAG: 2: to work to exhaustion: DRUDGE, TOIL 3a: to be a fag: serve as a fag *(fagging* for older boys during his first year) b: to serve as a fag in the field in British school games; *vt* 1: to compel to serve as a fag 2: to exhaust by toil, drudgery or sustained heavy activity—often used with *out* 3: to make (the end of a rope) frayed or untwisted

3. *fag / n* -s 1: *chiefly British; a fatiguing task; DRUDGERY 2: an English public-school boy who acts as a servant to another boy in a higher form b: MENIAL, DRUDGE, SERVITOR.*

4. *fag* or *fag-got / n* -s [origin unknown] slang: HOMOSEXUAL.

In construing the meaning of the word "fag," we note that Illinois follows the innocent-construction rule. That rule holds that the statements in question are to be read as a whole and the words given their natural and obvious meaning, and requires that allegedly defamatory words which are capable of being read innocently must be so read and declared nonactionable as a matter of law. Such words will be given an innocent construction if they are reasonably susceptible of such construction or if the allegedly defamatory matter is ambiguous. Whether language is susceptible of an innocent construction is a question of law for the court, to be resolved by reading the language stripped of innuendo. This doctrine has been held to be applicable to both libel and slander actions.

When the words of the statements uttered in the instant case are given their obvious and natural meaning, we do not see how these words can be given an innocent construction. Although characterized as "slang," the aforementioned published authority indicates that the sole occasion upon which the word "fag" is commonly used in the United States, in the form of a noun and to connote an adult-human being, is with reference to a homosexual.

Moreover, defendants' reference to plaintiff as "fag" in conjunction with the assertion that this status served as ground for terminating plaintiff's term of employment may not be characterized as mere objectionable but nonactionable name-calling. At common law, words of abuse do not give an action for slander. However, where such words serve to mark their peculiar target as an object of scorn and reproach, they cannot be dismissed as mere terms of general abuse. We conclude that the trial court erred in finding that the statements in question are non-actionable as a matter of law upon application of the innocent-construction doctrine. Therefore, the judgment of the circuit court in this regard must be reversed.

This decision means that the plaintiff must go back to the lower court for trial and prove the losses suffered because of the defamation. If successful, the inn is facing a substantial loss in the way of damages. This case did not reappear in the appellate records and was perhaps settled before or during the retrial.

In the Hooks case that follows, we have the opportunity to see what can happen when the dictates of a statute were not followed in the construction of a swimming pool at an inn. We also have a chance to see how the courts use testimony of economists to assist in setting the amount of damages that should be awarded to injured persons. It is important to read the footnotes with the case because they contain key information about this situation.

HOOKS V. WASHINGTON SHERATON
578 F. 2d 313 (1977), No. 76-1958, decided December 22, 1977.

ROBB, Circuit Judge:

This diversity case arose out of the injuries suffered by 18-year old Thomas Hooks when he dove from the three-meter diving board at the Sheraton Park Hotel in Washington, D.C., in June 1971. The pool was equipped with a high performance aluminum "Duraflex" board that propelled Hooks, who was not an experienced diver, into shallow water where he struck his head on the bottom. As a result Hooks is a quadriplegic. Hooks and his parents sued the operator of the pool, the Washington Sheraton Corporation (hereafter Sheraton) and its parent, ITT, alleging negligence in the construction and operation of the pool.[35] Specifically, plaintiffs alleged that the depth of the water in the diving area of the pool did not comply with applicable District of Columbia regulations and that it was too shallow for a three-meter Duraflex diving board.

The District Court held a bifurcated (separated) trial on the issues of liability and damages. The jury found Sheraton liable to the plaintiffs and awarded $6,000,000 to Thomas Hooks and $1,000,000 to his parents. On motion by Sheraton the District Court ordered a new trial on the issue of damages unless plaintiffs filed remittiturs of the amounts exceeding $4,500,000 and $180,000 respectively. Plaintiffs filed the remittiturs.

In its appeal from the finding of liability Sheraton contends that the District Court improperly instructed the jury on the standard of care owed by hotelkeepers to their guests, and on the issue of negligence *per se*. Sheraton also contends that the damages awarded to Thomas Hooks are grossly excessive for three reasons: (1) the inclusion of evidence of the effect of inflation on Hooks' future expenses; (2) the exclusion of evidence of the impact of income taxes upon Hooks' future earnings; and (3) the closing argument by plaintiffs' counsel, which Sheraton says was inflammatory.

We conclude that only one of Sheraton's complaints is valid: the evidence concerning income taxes should have been received. Nevertheless, for reasons hereinafter stated, we affirm the judgment.

I. Liability–Instructions

Sheraton contends that the District Court improperly instructed the jury on a hotelkeeper's duty of care, that contrary to the law of the District of Columbia the instruction required Sheraton to give what Sheraton calls an "absolute warranty of safety" to its guests. Sheraton cites *Bellevue v. Haslup,* 80 U.S.App.D.C. 181, 182, 150 F.2d 160, 161 (1945) (*Per Curiam*); *Picking v. Carbonaro,* 178 A.2d 428, 429 (D.C.C.A. 1962). Appellees argue that the doctrine of implied warranty is now the law of the District of Columbia. Whether the *Bellevue* decision remains the law of the District of Columbia is an issue we need not reach because read in context the instruction here is not a warranty charge.

The District Court began its instructions on the issue of negligence by properly instructing the jury that . . . the owner of a hotel is liable for failure to use reasonable care to keep safe such parts of the premises as he may retain under his control either for his own use of for the common use of the guests or tenants of the hotel.

It is the duty of the tenants or guests to exercise ordinary care for their own safety. In other words, the owner of a hotel is not an insurer of the safety of his guests, but he does owe to them the duty to exercise reasonable care for their safety.

[Emphasis added]

The court then proceeded to instruct the jury on the general law of negligence, negligence *per se,* contributory negligence, and assumption of risk. The court's reference to warranty came in the context of the instruction on assumption of risk.

Before this rule [assumption of risk] is applied to defeat the plaintiff's claim, however, you must be satisfied by a preponderance of the evidence that the danger or hazard which caused the injuries of the plaintiff was open and apparent, that he was aware of it, or that in the exercise of reasonable care should have been aware of it, and that he voluntarily exposed or subjected himself to whatever hazard or danger might reasonably have been involved.

You are instructed that the owner or the operator of a hotel warrants to its patrons that the facilities of said hotel are safe for the use by its patrons, free from defects and dangerous designs, and that such facilities can be used in the use and manner for which they were intended without danger or risk of injury and that such facilities are reasonably fit and suitable for their intended use.

When a patron of such a hotel uses such facilities in the manner and method they were intended to be used, he does not assume the risk of injury and is not chargeable with contributory negligence if he sustains an injury in so doing. [Emphasis added]. It is apparent from the language before and after the sentence relating to warranty that in this sentence the court was explaining to the jury that when using the defendant's pool in the manner for which it was intended, Thomas Hooks did not assume the risk of injury from defects or dangerous design, of which he was not aware, and that he was entitled to rely on the hotel's representation that there were no such hidden perils. We think the jury could not have understood the one sentence, delivered in the course of seven pages dealing with negligence, to mean that the hotel owed an "absolute warranty of safety" to its guests. This we think is plain in light of the clear statement at the outset, that the hotel is not an insurer and that it owes its guests a duty of reasonable care. Accordingly we reject the argument that the instruction improperly imposed upon Sheraton a duty to give its guests an absolute warranty of safety.

Sheraton also contends that the District Court erred in instructing the jury on the issue of negligence *per se* because Sheraton had explained that any possible violations of the applicable District of Columbia regulations were consistent with due care. At trial Hooks offered evidence from which the jury could conclude that the pool failed to meet District of Columbia regulations concerning the depth of water required to be directly under as well as extending out from the end of the three-meter diving board.

Padlock, the third party defendant, introduced evidence on the dimensions of the pool, which showed that there might have been minor violations of the regulations.[36] In an effort to explain any violations, Sheraton called Mr. Brink, the chief of the District of Columbia Bureau of Air and Water Quality, to testify that the plans for the pool had been approved by his Bureau.

In *H.R.H. Construction Corp. v. Conroy,* 134 U.S.App.D.C. 7, 411 F.2d 722 (1969), this court drew a distinction between cases in which the defendant offers no explanation of a violation of a statute or regulation[37] and those in which the defendant introduces evidence tending to show that its failure to comply with the statute or regulation is consistent with the exercise of due care.[38] The instruction on negligence *per se* is proper only when no explanation is made, 134 U.S.App.D.C. at 9, 411 F.2d at 724. Sheraton urges us to hold that its evidence of the approval of the plans, the custom of inspection during construction, and the issuance of the operating license for the pool was enough to negative the inference of negligence *per se.* We disagree.

Mr. Brink testified that he personally approved the plans for the pool in 1960. He also testified that it is the custom for inspectors to check compliance during construction, and that a license to operate the pool would not have issued unless the pool had been built according to the plans. Mr. Brink did not testify from personal knowledge that the pool was so constructed, nor did anyone else. As it turned out, the pool was not so constructed. The approved plans called for a wooden diving board. In 1968 Sheraton replaced the original board with a high performance aluminum "Duraflex" board. Several experts, including the 1976 U.S. Olympic diving coach, testified that this type of board at the three-meter height is unsafe for the inexperienced divers likely to use a hotel pool. A college diving coach said that a Duraflex board "has a great deal more of elasticity and projects people higher in the air. . . . [I]f a person's balance is forward at the time [he leaves] that board, it's going to send him a lot farther out." Moreover, the aluminum board extended five inches farther into the pool than the original wooden board. This seems at first a small modification, but it is of particular importance to the question whether the pool depths violated District of Columbia regulations. The regulations require ten feet of water directly under the board and extending out from it for twelve feet. Thereafter the bottom may incline toward the surface at a rate of one foot of depth for every three feet of distance from the board. Obviously as the board extends farther over the water, the distance from the end of the board to the point where the bottom inclines toward the surface is reduced. The area where the bottom slopes up is where the injury occurred. Finally, plaintiffs introduced evidence that on the day of the accident, the pool's water level was several inches low. This too would reduce the depth of the water under and out from the diving board. There was no showing that the District of Columbia approved these deviations from the plans approved by Mr. Brink in 1960.[39] We conclude, therefore, that the negligence *per se* instruction given here was proper under the circumstances.

II. Damages

On the question of damages Sheraton contends that the jury award was so grossly excessive that it indicates a "runaway" jury motivated by passion and prejudice. The remittiturs, argues Sheraton, were insufficient to remedy the problem. Specifically, Sheraton objects to the admission of evidence of estimated future inflation, to an allegedly inflammatory closing argument, and to the exclusion of evidence of the effect of income taxes upon Thomas Hooks' future earnings.

We note at the outset that the District Court has broad discretion to order a remittitur in lieu of a new trial and we find no abuse of that discretion here. *See H.R.H. Construction Corp. v. Conroy, supra,* 134 U.S.App.D.C. 7, 8, & n.1, 411 F.2d 722, 723, & n.1 (1969). With respect to Sheraton's specific allegations of error, two are not properly before this court. Appellants conceded at oral argument that the issue of inflation had not been raised in the District Court; therefore it will not be considered here. Similarly, the objection to counsel's closing argument is not properly before us. Sheraton first raised this objection in its motion for a new trial, too late to preserve the point. We have reviewed the arguments in question and find no basis for treating them as plain error.

Sheraton's third contention with respect to damages is more troublesome. The District Court permitted Sheraton to cross examine plaintiffs' expert economist and statistician on the effect of income taxes upon Thomas Hooks' lost future earnings. In a subsequent ruling on plaintiffs' objection to this line of questioning, however, the court ordered the testimony stricken and admonished the jury to disregard it.

In *Runyon v. District* of *Columbia,* 150 U.S.App.D.C. 228, 231, 463 F.2d 1319, 1322 (1972), we held that in determining a decedent's projected future earnings probable income taxes are to be deducted. Hooks attempts to distinguish the *Runyon* case upon the ground that it was a death case in which the jury could award only the amount available to the estate after deducting taxes and the costs of maintenance of the decedent and his dependents. We are unable to perceive any distinction between death cases and personal injury cases in computing lost future earnings. In both situations the compensation is for future earnings lost as a result of a defendant's tortious act. That the estate in a death case receives only a net amount after taxes and expenses are deducted whereas the personal injury plaintiff is himself being compensated for his lost future earnings is a distinction without legal significance. "The primary aim in measuring damages is compensation, and this contemplates that the damages for a tort should place the injured person as nearly as possible in the condition he would have occupied if the wrong had not occurred . . . " C. McCormick, Law of Damages 560 (1935).

Both sides rely on the Second Circuit's *en banc* decision in *McWeeney v. New York,* N. H. & H. R. R., 282 F.2d 34 (2d Cir.), *cert. denied,* 364 U.S. 870, 81 S.Ct. 115, 5 L.Ed.2d 93 (1960). In the *McWeeney* case the Second Circuit concluded that juries should not be instructed to consider the effect of income taxes in determining awards for middle to low income plaintiffs.[40] The court reasoned that determination of future tax liability would be too speculative and confusing to the jury, and that countervailing factors of inflation and attorneys' fees reduce the recovery and offset the failure to consider taxes. 282 F.2d at 36-38. We are not persuaded by these reasons.

The existence of income taxes is hardly more speculative than is the assumption, indulged here, that Thomas Hooks would attain his dream of being a Boy Scout executive and that he would continue in that employment for forty years at ever increasing salaries. See n.[41] *infra.* To allow a plaintiff to attempt to prove what he would have earned yet to shut off as too speculative the defendant's attempt to show what he would have been taxed is in our opinion unjust. The second factor cited by the Second Circuit, jury confusion, is a more weighty consideration; but we think expert testimony, presented under the watchful eye of the experienced trial court, see Fed. R. Evid. 403, can reduce confusion to a minimum. Moreover, expert testimony will avoid the possibility of a tax-conscious jury attempting to include in its award its own uninformed allowance for income taxes. The third consideration, that excluding evidence of taxes offsets the effects of inflation and attorneys' fees, has no application here. Hooks presented extensive evidence of the effects of future inflation. As for attorneys' fees, they are typically borne by the parties. If we are to depart from this rule, it should be a step taken consciously by the legislature, not one blended into a judicial opinion under the guise of excluding tax evidence to offset plaintiffs need to compensate his attorney.

We are told by plaintiffs that in holding that income taxes should be considered we part company with the considered opinions of the vast majority of jurisdictions which have followed the *McWeeney* case. We question whether this is so, for Thomas Hooks would probably qualify as a high income plaintiff under the *McWeeney* rule. We note too that support for the *McWeeney* rule has begun to erode. See *Burlington Northern, Inc. v. Boxberger,* 529 F.2d 284, 288-94 (9th Cir. 1975), applying the "high income" exception; *Felder v. United States,* 543 F.2d 657, 665 (9th Cir. 1976).

We conclude that evidence of probable income taxes on lost future earnings should have been admitted.

The question remains whether a new trial on the issue of damages is required by our holding. For the reasons set forth below, we believe that the remittitur already filed by Thomas Hooks in the amount of $1,500,000 more than compensates for any error in excluding evidence of the effect of income taxes.

Plaintiffs' expert on economics and statistics, Dr. Miller, testified as to Thomas Hooks' potential future earnings. Using alternative career patterns, Dr. Miller estimated Thomas Hooks' potential lifetime earnings, assuming a 40-year work life and a salary growth rate of 4.5 percent. These totals were discounted to present value assuming investment at seven percent. Sheraton did not offer any testimony on Hooks' probable earnings. Sheraton did however cross examine Dr. Miller on the effects of income taxes on the various lifetime earnings that he had projected. Dr. Miller computed the taxes on the witness stand, assuming that with a standard deduction and one personal exemption Thomas Hooks would pay 20 percent of his gross income in taxes. The estimate of taxes ranges from $70,000 to $225,000.[41]

Sheraton points out, correctly, that for some of his hypothetical careers Thomas Hooks would be in a much higher tax bracket than the 20 percent used by Dr. Miller. With a general verdict we cannot know which potential income the jury decided Hooks would have realized. But a new trial is unnecessary because the trial court has already required and Hooks has accepted a $1,500,000 remittitur. Treating every variable most favorably to Sheraton, we assume that the jury believed Hooks would have had a career as a $40,000 Boy Scout executive and we further assume that Sheraton could have demonstrated conclusively that the tax rate would have been 40 percent. This would result in only $450,000 in taxes, less than one third of the amount already remitted by Thomas Hooks.

We have no doubt that we have the power to order a further remittitur as a condition of affirmance, but we are persuaded that the remittitur below is sufficient. It reduced the jury verdict by 25 percent and was more than three times the maximum amount assignable to the trial court's error. The District Court arrived at an amount of recovery which it found in conformity with the interests of justice. We are not inclined to upset that conclusion.

The Judgment is Affirmed.

QUESTIONS

1. State three reasons why an innkeeper must learn to be "liability-conscious" where injuries are involved.
2. What role does contributory negligence play in some injury cases in some states?
3. What was the legal issue in the Moricoli case?
4. What role did "asusmption of the risk" play in the Mizenis case?
5. Why is the duty to keep stairways in safe condition *implied* in law?
6. Why does assumption of the risk require "venturousness"?
7. What suggestions might you make about how a convention in a hotel can be controlled so as to prevent unnecessary injuries?
8. Why does the law place duties on innkeepers to protect those who are not guests?
9. List three areas of danger at an inn that has a swimming pool.
10. Draft a notice that may limit liability at a swimming pool that has no lifeguard on duty.

ENDNOTES

1. *Mizenis v. Sands Motel, supra.*
2. *Jenkins v. Missouri State Life Ins. Co.*, 334 Mo. 941, 69 S.W. 2d 666 (1934).
3. *Trulock v. Willey,* 187 F. 956 (8th Cir. 1911).
4. *Baker v. Dallas Hotel,* 162 Wash. 289, 298 P. 465 (1931).
5. *Lyttle v. Denney,* 222 Pa. 395, 71 A. 841 (1909).
6. *Parson v. Dwightstate Co.*, 301 Mass. 324, 17 N.E. 2d 197 (1938).
7. *DeLuce v. Fort Wayne Hotel,* 311 F. 2d 853 (6th Cir. 1962).

The following endnotes and the article to which they refer were taken from the *Hotel and Casino Law Letter,* Volume 2-1, November, 1983, by James O. Eiler.

8. See *Buck v. Del City Apartments, Inc.*, 431 P. 20.360. See also, *Hotel and Casino Law Letter, UNLV* Innkeeper's Duty to Provide A Safe Place to Stay. vol. 2-1, p. 26.

9. For statutory requirements as to keeping a clean and sanitary hotel, see *NRS* 447, *et seq.*
10. See *NRS* 447.030 with respect to "extermination of vermin."
11. See *NRS* 447.210.
12. *NRS* 447.030.
13. *Ibid.*
14. *Webster's New Twentieth Century Dictionary,* 1952.
15. *Black's Law Dictionary,* 5th edition, 1979.
16. *Words and Phrases,* vol. 36A. See also, *Harvey v. Switzerland General Insurance Co.,* Mo. App., 260 S.W. 2d 342, 344.
17. *Deluce v. Fort Wayne Hotel,* 311 F. 2d, 853 (1962).
18. *Scott v. Churchill,* 15 Misc. 80 (1895), 36 N.Y.S. 476, *affd.,* 157 N.Y. 692, 51 N.E. 1094 (1898).
19. *Stahlin v. Hilton Hotels Corporation,* 484 F.2d 580 (7th Cir. 1973).
20. *Sneider v. Hyatt Corporation,* 390 F. Supp. 976 (N.D. Ga., 1975).
21. In *Kiefel v. Las Vegas Hacienda, Inc.,* 404 F.2d 1163 (7th Cir.), *cert. denied,* 395 U.S. 908, *reh. denied,* 395 U.S. 987. *Garzilli* v. *Howard Johnson's Motor Lodges, Inc.,* 419 F. Supp 1210 (E.D.N.Y., 1976).
22. *Banks v. Hyatt Hotel Corp.,* (Docket No. 81-3377, 5th Cir. Court of Appeals).
23. N.Y.C.P.L.R., 1411 (McKinney Supp. 1975), Minn. State. Ann., sec. 604.01 (1969).
24. That which, in a natural and continuous sequence, unbroken by any efficient intervening cause, produces the injury, and without which the result would not have occurred. *Swayne v. Connecticut,* 86 Conn. 439, 85 A. 634, 635.
25. *Hooks v. Washington Sheraton Corp.,* 578 F.2d 313 (1977), *supra.*
26. *Brown v. Southern Venture Corp.,* 331 So.2d 207 (La. App. 1976), *cert. denied,* 334 So. 2d 211 (1976).
27. *Reibolt v. Bedient,* in Chapter 22.
28. 273 Wis. 448, 78 N.W. 2d 757 (1956).
29. *Kowalczuk v. Potter,* 63 Wis. 2d 511, 217 N.W. 2d 332 (1974).
30. *Garzilli v. Howard Johnson, supra.*
31. *Kiefely v. Las Vegas Hacienda, Inc.,* 39 F.R.D. 529 (ND Ill. 1966).
32. *Las Vegas Sun,* 4-7-83.
33. 361 N.E. 2D 74 (Illinois, 1977).
34. *Manuch v. City of Martinsville,* No. 14888, WV., July 7, 1981.

35. The builder of the pool, Paddock Corporation, was joined as a third-party defendant by Sheraton but the jury absolved Paddock of any responsibility for the accident.

36.

Distance from End of Diving Board	Depth (Paddock)	Depth (Hooks)	Depth (D.C. Regulation)
0′	10′ 5"	–	10′ 0"
12′	9′ 10$\frac{1}{2}$"	9′ 7$\frac{3}{16}$"	10′ 0"
14′	9′ 3$\frac{7}{8}$"	9′ 0"	9′ 4"
15′	9′ 0"	8′ 8$\frac{3}{16}$"	9′ 0"
17′	8′ 5"	8′ 1$\frac{3}{16}$"	8′ 3$\frac{5}{8}$"

(Sheraton Brief at 5)

37. See, e.g., *Ross v. Hartman*, 78 U.S.App.D.C. 217, 139 F.2d 14 (1943), *cert. denied*, 321 U.S. 790, 64 S.Ct. 790, 88 L.Ed. 1080 (1944); *Richardson v. Gregory*, 108 U.S.App.D.C. 263, 281 F.2d 626 (1960).

38. See, e.g., *Hecht Co. v. McLaughlin*, 93 U.S. App.D.C. 382, 214 F.2d 212 (1954); *Karlow v. Fitzgerald*, 110 U.S.App.D.C. 9, 288 F.2d 411 (1961).

39. Sheraton contends that semiannual inspections were carried out after the operating license was issued and after the board had been changed. However, these inspections appear to have been limited to testing water quality and could not explain any violation resulting from the change in the diving board.

40. The court suggested that income taxes might be considered properly in cases of high-income plaintiffs. 282 F.2d at 38. Subsequent decisions have followed this suggestion. *LeRoy v. Sabena Belgian World Airways*, 344 F.2d 266, 276 (2d Cir.), *cert. denied*, 382 U.S. 878, 86 S.Ct. 161, 15 L.Ed.2d 119 (1965); see *Petition of Marina Mercante Nicaraguense S. A.*, 364 F.2d 118, 126 (2d Cir. 1966), *cert. denied*, 385 U.S. 1005, 87 S.Ct. 710, 17 L.Ed.2d 544 (1967).

41.

Hypothetical Career	Present Value of Life Earnings	Tax (20%)
High School Graduate	$ 352,000	$ 70,000
Two Years College	402,000	81,000
College Graduate	536,844	107,844
Boy Scout executive ($25,000 yr.)	700,000	140,000
Boy Scout executive ($40,000/yr.)	1,125,348	[225,000]

Tr. 53, 87-88, 90, 104 (5/22/75). The $225,000 was not testified to by Dr. Miller but represents 20 percent of the $1,125,348 earnings for a Boy Scout executive averaging $40,000 per year over his lifetime.

21

Restaurants at the Inn: The Legal View

Stoodley's, when we entered, was doing a roaring business. It was the most fashionable of all the Portsmouth inns–so fashionable in fact, that from the profits of its nightly sales of lobsters and liquor, Stoodley, only two years later, built his Earl of Halifax Tavern, which for the comfort of its beds, the coziness of its tap-room and the quality of its food and drink, has no superior in Pennsylvania, Maryland, or even Virginia.

The tap-room at Stoodley's was long, wainscoted, and ceiled with first-growth pine the color of maple syrup; and at its far end was a bar with a sort of Dutch oven behind it. A bed of coals burned nightly in this open oven, even in hot weather, for broiling the small lobsters, fresh from the Piscataqua, for which Stoodley's is famous. In summer, the hinged roof above the oven was drawn up, allowing the heat to escape and the room to remain cool. In winter, with the roof closed, the oven radiated a rosy glow; and no matter how wildly the wind howled from the Isles of Shoals, or how high the drifts were piled in the streets without, Stoodley's tap-room was a delight. Young bloods, and old ones too, dropped in after an evening of business or pleasure for a glass of buttered rum while waiting for their lobsters to broil; then washed down the lobsters with a quart or two of Stoodley's ale.[1]

Northwest Passage, Kenneth Roberts

OVERVIEW

In this chapter, we will take a look at a sampling of the state and federal statutes, court decisions, administrative-law rulings, and other legal matters that become involved in the operation of restaurants at the inn today.

FOOD SERVICE AT COMMON LAW

The early common rule was that the inn had to furnish food and drink in addition to shelter and protection. This rule still prevails in New York and a majority of the states. There is a trend growing in the courts, however, toward removing food and drink as a requirement of innkeeping. It's also possible in those states which do have food and beverage requirements, to satisfy the requirements with soda pop and snack machines.

One of the first laws enacted in the American Colonies had to do with food and drink. In the year 1646, the General Court of the Massachusetts Bay Colony set forth by decree just how much bread a person should receive for a penny. The first general food law was enacted in Massachusetts on March 8, 1785. This law prohibited the sale of "diseased, corrupted, contagious, and unwholesome . . ." food and drink and provided penalties including ". . . fine and imprisonment, standing in the pillory . . ." or "some or all of these penalties."

In the late 1800s, chemical analysis of both food and drink, by Peter Collier of the U.S. Department of Agriculture, shocked the nation with disclosures of adulteration in alcoholic beverages, butter, oleo, margarine, and other food and drink products. The Bureau of Animal Industry was likewise concerned about the unsanitary conditions that were known to exist in the meat and other food packing operations. It took a book to bring the whole situation into focus.

It was *The Jungle*, by Upton Sinclair, published in February, 1906, that horrified the nation by what it disclosed was taking place at the Chicago slaughter and packing plants. President Theodore Roosevelt appointed a three-person commission whose report and recommendations resulted in the Pure Food and Drug Act of 1906. This law required that enforcement be carried out at all levels of processing and packing of food and drink. If the laws were to be meaningful, they had to apply across the board and so they do today. There are more than twenty federal food laws, and it is beyond the scope of this chapter to examine them here. The importance of these laws is that they ensure that the food and drink ultimately purchased by consumers is wholesome and free from dangerous defects.

TODAY

Today, producers and packers of food and drink, both retail and wholesale, are part of what is one of the most regulated industries in the world. This massive regulation carries over in some ways, but not all, to the serving of food and drink at restaurants and has an indirect effect at those operations. The bulk of legal control at the restaurant, however, comes from general law. In this chapter we want to become acquainted with some of these laws because the pure food and drug laws do not always ensure that the quality maintained at the packing stage will be found at the restaurant. First, as a matter of law, what is a "restaurant"?

WHAT IS A RESTAURANT?

A restaurant is a place of public accommodation where food is prepared, sold, and consumed on the premises or in carry-out form. The term is broad enough to include cafeterias, fast-food shops, grills, coffeehouses, cafes, and others, but does *not* include eating places at private clubs. The latter do not have the public features of a restaurant and thus are not "places of public accommodation."

While private clubs will be able to escape the strictures of the civil rights laws, they are still subject to other applicable statutory restaurant law and the common law as well.

There are duties, liabilities, and rights of restaurant operators (restaurateurs) that are distinct and separate from those of innkeepers. This is also true of bar operators, as we shall see in Chapter 22. Of course we must recognize that an innkeeper may also keep a restaurant and a bar simultaneously with the inn. In that event, multiple legal rights and responsibilities arise and this distinction is made in the cases. The innkeeper in such instances wears more than one legal hat, so to speak.

It is helpful to see how a court has defined the word "restaurant" and then see how it has been defined by a legislature.

Definition by a Court

"A restaurant is an establishment where meals and refreshments are served."[2] This court definition is short but serves its legal purpose. The definitions found in court cases will vary but this one is typical. Some definitions will address themselves to the public nature of restaurants.

Definition by Statute

The West Virginia Code, Michie, 1966,[3] defines a restaurant in this manner: "Every place where food without lodging is usually furnished to patrons and payment required therefore shall be deemed a restaurant. The provisions of this article shall not apply to temporary food sales, not exceeding two weeks in length, by religious, educational, charitable, or nonprofit organizations."

In this definition we see additional points. First, it is a place "without lodging." Next, the food furnished is to "patrons." Third, payment is required; thus one's home would not be a restaurant by this definition. Finally, the exemptions exclude temporary food sales not exceeding two weeks in length, by religious, educational, charitable, or nonprofit organizations. This has one unfortunate legal side effect: It makes the provisions of the West Virginia food service sanitation regulations inapplicable to such organizations. This would be true when such sales are conducted by the exempt organization in connection with carnivals, church activities, banquets, and fairs which involve the public.[4] This is an illustration of how an exception in a statute can destroy the reason for a law in the first place.

Definitions of restaurants by statute are also found in the Civil Rights Act of 1964 as amended in 1972, as well as in state civil rights laws. The Nevada Revised Statutes[5] provides: "Unless the context otherwise requires, 'place of public accommodation' means: 1. Any inn, hotel, motel, or other establishment which provides lodging to transient guests, except an establishment located within a building which contains not more than five rooms for rent or hire and which is actually occupied by the proprietor of such establishment as his residence; 2. any restaurant, cafeteria, lunchroom, lunch counter, soda fountain, casino, or any facility where spiritous or malt liquors are sold, including any such facility located on the premises of any retail establishment. . . ." This part of the statute makes it clear that hotels, restaurants, and taverns are places of public accommodation.

The Nevada statute then provides: "All persons are entitled to the full and equal enjoyment of the goods, services, facilities, privileges, advantages, and accommodations of any place of public accommodation, without discrimination or segregation on the ground of race, color, religion, national origin, or physical or visual handicap."

Thus in this state's civil rights laws we see another definition of what a restaurant is. Turning from definitions, it is necessary to notice an important legal distinction.

A Distinction

Some restaurants are constructed and operated as separate units from the inns they adjoin. This is especially so with the fast-food chains and many local as well as higher-quality restaurants. On the other hand, almost all inns have restaurants as part of the premises. It should be observed that the law does not have a separate body of rules for "attached" or "detached" restaurants. An innkeeper must keep this in mind for it would be a legal mistake to assume that laws that protect the innkeeper would also protect the innkeeper as a restaurateur. This is not so.

Turning from these preliminary matters, it is important to begin an examination of the legal duties of those who operate restaurants. To facilitate the discussion, we will separate the material and look first at the restaurant. The next chapter will be concerned with the laws of bars.

DUTIES OF RESTAURATEURS

To begin with, does a restaurateur have a common-law duty to receive all those persons who present themselves in presentable condition and able to pay for the services that they may request?

Duty to Receive?

Contrary to the common-law innkeeper rule, a restaurant operator does *not* have to receive all who seek services there. The early courts did not equate the need for food and drink by nontravelers in the same light as they did the need of the protection of the inn for the traveler. The nontraveler could go home for supper. Once the traveler was received at the inn, it was necessary to provide food and drink as part of the services of the inn. Indeed, in the early inns in the American West, the room was $1.00 for the night—but the food and drink were free. Thus the duty to receive applied to the inn—not to the restaurant.

The fact that the common law developed in this way gives the modern restaurant operator leeway in establishing house rules, setting dress codes, establishing opening and closing hours, and allows the operator to close the restaurant for a day or a week should that be the business decision. The law affords wide latitude in the operation of restaurants—even though it does not do so in receiving travelers at inns.

The following discusses how the restaurant and bar are operated at the inn in question. These practices in no way violate any common-law duty. (The inn under discussion is the one furthest north in the world.)

> This was the new Top of the World. It had opened in June, replacing the old Top of the World, which had been closed by the state

board of health, and which, subsequently, had burned down. The Top of the World was not, strictly speaking, a motel. For a motel you needed motorists, and there wasn't a motorist—or even a highway that was open to the public—within five hundred miles of the Top of the World.

A young white woman, sleepy and sullen, was behind the desk. She said yes they had rooms. Sixty-one eighty for a single, pay in advance.

She locked the money in a box inside a safe. Then she told us there was no running water. There had not been running water for three days. The water was obtained from a freshwater lake and was delivered to the motel in a truck. The truck engine had been broken for three days, she said, and the only mechanic in town had been too drunk to fix it, and he was still drunk, and was acting as if he planned to stay drunk until spring. There would not be water until someone could be found to fix the truck. This might mean flying a mechanic up from Fairbanks. If the ice fog in Fairbanks should ever lift.

She gave us more bad news when we asked how to get to the bar. The bar had been shut down since August, closed by the state police. Too many fistfights and knifings. The Eskimos of Barrow, apparently, did not handle their liquor very well.

We asked how to get to the restaurant.

The restaurant, she told us, was closed for the night.

"But it's only ten after six."

"That's right. The restaurant closes at six."

"Closes at six? What do you mean, closes at six? Who ever heard of a restaurant closing at six?"

She shrugged. "Mike wants it closed. Too much of a hassle keeping it open.[6]

While restaurants do not have to remain open twenty-four hours each day and there is no common-law duty for them to receive, there are times when the operator has a duty to receive on other legal grounds. Examples include the civil rights laws, both federal[7] and state,[8] and the duty to receive based upon contract.

Duty to Receive Under the Civil Rights Laws

These laws make it clear that a restaurateur cannot refuse to receive on the grounds of race, color, creed, national origin, sex, and, visual or other handicap. The legal effect of these laws is that, so long as the restaurant remains a place of public accommodation, these laws must not be violated. Thus there is a "civil rights duty to receive." Yet this duty would apply only while the restaurant is open.

These antidiscrimination laws, however, apply only to public as contrasted to private places. A true private club can establish its own qualifications for membership and set whatever standards it may choose without fear of a civil rights violation. To be a "private club," there must be an internal organization for the election of officers who have the power to control the organization. A public inn could not legally circumvent the civil rights laws by claiming its restaurant is private and available only to "members."

It is unwise business policy at restaurants to use a so-called dress code to keep minorities out while allowing others to enter who do not conform to that "code," to require minorities to stand in a line while others are admitted without hesitation, or to place a cover charge on minorities while no charge is made to others. The Red Onion chain of Mexican food restaurants had such facts brought to their attention in 1980, in a lawsuit against them. The restaurants in question would turn away minorities by claiming that they did not meet the standards of a "dress code" that in fact did not exist. The Carson, California, restaurant had to pay twenty-three persons $15,000 each for following this line of conduct. That comes to $345,000 and it takes a lot of taco sales to generate that kind of revenue.

Attorney Clyde L. Griffith, then legal counsel for the National Restaurant Association, was asked this question a few years back: "If a prospective customer appears at your restaurant in an objectionable manner—drunk, disorderly, barefoot, in improper dress . . . can you [legally] refuse to serve him [or her] . . . ?" His answer, as reported in the *Weekly Newsletter, Motel/Hotel Insider,* May 19, 1980, was "yes." Yet it is clear that such refusal of service must not be based on race, color, religion, national origin, age, sex, or physical handicap.

Duty to Receive by Contract

If one has a valid reservation contract at a restaurant and is refused service, that is another matter. There has now been a breach of the *contractual duty* to receive. The following case illustrates how the courts view this type of breach. This particular court is deciding whether or not the complaint filed in this case stated a cause of action.

HARDER V. AUBERGE DES FOUGERES[9]

PER CURIAM.

This is an appeal from an order of the Supreme Court at Special Term, entered March 7, 1972 in Albany County, which granted defendants' motion to dismiss the complaint for failure to state a cause of action.

The first cause of action alleged by appellant states, in part, that respondent "unlawfully, willfully, deliberately, and without just cause, refused to admit or seat plaintiff and his guests for dinner service even though plaintiff and his guests (a) had made a bona fide reservation, (b) requested service, and (c) were ready, willing and able to pay any reasonable charges imposed by defendants for such meal." And further that, "By reason of defendants' actions and failure to furnish plaintiff and his guests with appropriate accommodations in this restaurant, plaintiff and his guests were subjected to great inconvenience, humiliation, and insult and were exposed to public ridicule in the presence of a number of people in such restaurant. As a result of the activities of defendants, its officers, agents, representatives or employees, plaintiff and his guests, were forced to leave this restaurant and proceed to another place for their meals. Because of the commotion caused by defendants, plaintiff was injured in his good name and reputation which was absolutely uncalled for and unwarranted. . . ."

The complaint must be viewed in the framework of our liberal rules of pleading, and if what is stated is a cause of action cognizable by the courts of this State, the pleading must be sustained.

At common law, a person engaged in a public calling, such as an innkeeper or common carrier, was held to be under a duty to the general public and was obligated to serve, without discrimination, all who sought service. On the other hand, proprietors of private enterprises, such as places of amusement, were under no such obligation, enjoying an absolute power to serve whom they pleased.

In our view, a restaurant proprietor should be under the same duty as an innkeeper to receive all patrons who present themselves "in a fit condition," unless reasonable cause exists for a refusal to do so.

Blackstone stated that a cause of action would lie against "an innkeeper, or other victualler" who refused to admit a traveler without cause (3 *Blackstone's Comm.*, Sharswood ed., p. 166), and Judge Cardozo found that a "plaintiff, if wrongfully ejected from . . . [a] cafe, was entitled to recover damages for injury to his feelings as a result of the humiliation."

Furthermore, a proprietor of an inn or similar establishment, is under a duty to protect his patrons from injury, annoyance, or mistreatment through the acts of his servants or employees. The law imposes an obligation upon him to see that his agents and employees extend courteous and decent treatment to his guests, and holds himself liable in violation of this obligation by the use of insulting and abusive language. For these reasons we conclude that the allegations of the first cause of action adequately plead an intentional tort.

The order should be modified, on the law and the facts, so as to deny the motion to dismiss the first cause of action, and, as so modified, affirmed, without costs.

The next duty of restaurant keepers has to do with the property of patrons.

Duty to Protect Property of Patrons

The liability of a restaurateur for the loss of the property of patrons is usually based upon one of two legal theories: actual bailment or constructive bailment. In a fast-food carry-out restaurant, there would seldom be a bailment because patrons never stay long enough to consider checking a coat or handbag. Yet such property might be left there by accident, thus bringing into play the constructive legal theory of bailment. On the other hand, in the better-quality establishments, checkrooms are made available.

If loss of property of the patron does occur, the burden of proof is on the patron to prove the bailment and to prove failure to redeliver the goods. The burden then shifts to the operator to prove that he or she exercised ordinary care as a bailee. If this burden is not carried by the bailee then the loss will fall on the restaurant operator. Because of these rules, it is essential that the property of patrons be handled with care when acting as a bailee, and also when property left by a patron is found by employees or agents. There must be a firm house rule that such property must be taken at once to the person in charge. That person must in turn take reasonable steps to safeguard the property until the patron can reclaim it. Failure to take such steps can lead to legal liability if the property is lost before it can be reclaimed.

It should be remembered that, except in New York, the statutory limits on liability that protect innkeepers for the loss of money and valuables of a guest, *do not* apply to restaurants for they are not "hotels or motels." This is true even if they are *within* a hotel or motel.

Duty to Protect Patrons

It has long been a rule of restaurant law that those who are given service have the right to be safe and secure in their property as well as in their persons while obtaining this service. They are entitled to a reasonably calm atmosphere and safe surroundings that would be expected in that particular establishment. The bustle of a fast-food outlet would be legally unacceptable in a higher quality restaurant, for example.

Duty to Protect Patrons from Patrons

If X becomes unruly and threatens to injure Y, then a legal duty falls upon management to prevent that injury. The duty to protect extends also to third parties, and, in some instances, those who are not patrons at the property. A news item from the *Las Vegas Review Journal,* April 26,1983, illustrates what the duty to protect patrons can mean in practice.

> **Man wins $2.9 million judgment in shooting**
>
> Associated Press
>
> LOS ANGELES, Calif.–A jury awarded $2.9 million Monday to a man who was shot in the head as he chased a teen-age bandit from a Jack-in-the-Box restaurant, an attorney said.
>
> Keith Forrand, who was 24 years old at the time of the incident 5½ years ago, sued the fast-food chain for negligence for failing to protect its patrons, said his lawyer, Larry Grassini.
>
> Tim Bradford, attorney for Jack-in-the-Box, said his client "has to sit down and analyze the verdict" before deciding whether to appeal. But he added, "They probably will."
>
> Grassini said his client had stopped by a Glendale Jack-in-the-Box for a cup of coffee on his way to work at 7 a.m. on Nov. 17, 1977, when a 15-year-old walked up to the drive-through window and robbed it.
>
> Forrand, a regular patron, said a clerk yelled, "Stop him!" and Forrand jumped in his car and chased the boy, believing he had run off without paying for his food, Grassini said.

Duty to Protect Patrons from Employees

The duty to protect patrons extends to the employees and agents of the establishment. The courts make this doubly so since it was the place of business that hired the agent or employees in the first instance. The courts view that fact as placing additional duties of care on the one doing the hiring.

Management must use care and caution when screening applicants for jobs at HRI facilities. When employees cause injury to guests and patrons, the law places additional responsibility on management for the failure to screen out such employees. When a room-service clerk started a fire at the Las Vegas Hilton in 1982 that resulted in eight deaths and many injuries, civil suits resulted against management for their negligence in hiring that particular employee. (The employee was found guilty of murder.)

When employees cause injury to restaurant patrons, problems can also arise with insurance coverage. In a Pennsylvania case, an employee of a restaurant assaulted a patron, ". . . striking her with fists, and with great force and violence repeatedly shook, cast and threw the patron to the ground." The court ruled that this was a deliberate attack (tort). Since the insurance policy covered accidents only, the insurance company was excused from payment for the tort, *Gene's Restaurant v. Nationwide,* 548 A. 2d 246 (Pennsylvania, 1988).

At a Hardee's Restaurant in Independence, Missouri, off-duty police officers were hired as security guards and were instructed to control the loitering of teenagers. A guard arrested three persons without having just cause to do so, and the loitering charges were dismissed. The three persons then brought a civil action against the restaurant for false arrest. One settled out of court for $10,000 and the jury awarded the other two $7,500 each. The court ordered the restaurant to pay attorney fees of over $11,000, *Woodward v. Hardee's,* 643 F. Supp. 691 (Missouri, 1986).

Duty to Protect Employees from Patrons and Third Parties

The duty to protect does not stop with patrons and third parties, but extends to the employees and agents of the business itself. Thus there is a legal duty to protect employees who are being threatened or injured by patrons or third parties.

One of the major duties of the restaurant has to do with the quality of food and drink.

Duty to Provide Merchantable Food and Drink

To understand this legal duty, it is necessary to examine some features of the law of warranties as found in the Uniform Commercial Code, Article 2, Sales.

Warranties

A "warranty" at law, in the simplest sense, is a *promise.* We are concerned with the warranties found in the retail sale of food and drink. At common law, the serving of food and drink was held by the courts to be a *service* and not a *sale.* It has been a rule of law for centuries that warranties arise only with a sale. At common law, serving food and drink carried no legal warranties with it. This may have been a satisfactory rule in earlier centuries but it would be unsuitable in modern times. Thus, when patron X was served a meal at an early inn, he was buying the service and not the food.

The food and drink not consumed remained the property of the inn. In short, at common law there were no "doggy bags."

This has been changed and today the Uniform Commercial Code, Section 2-314(1) makes it clear that the sale of food and drink is just that, a sale and thus contractual. Since it is a sale, the sale carries with it promises (warranties) which become part of the contract.

The warranties can be "express" or they can be "implied." When the Code was drafted and its provisions went into operation as state after state adopted it, there was legal controversy over whether an *implied warranty of wholesomeness* attached between a restaurant operator and patrons who sought service there. Some courts held that the sale of food was a service and thus *no* warranties attached. This became the minority view, for the majority view was that the service of food and drink was a sale because of 2-314(1) of the UCC, and that is the modern view.

As a Virginia court said, "He [the patron] depends upon the experience and trade wisdom of the dispenser [of the food] in selecting the articles or ingredients of the food, and upon his skill in the preparation and service thereof. The customer has no effective opportunity to inspect or select so far as wholesomeness is concerned."

Thus today the serving of food and drink in a restaurant is a sale under the Uniform Commercial Code and carries an implied warranty that the food is wholesome and fit for human consumption. If it is not, there would be a breach of this implied promise and the one who served the unfit item or items would be liable under contract principles for damages.

The "Merchant" Requirement

For the implied warranty provisions of the UCC to apply, the one serving the food and drink must be a "merchant" within the legal meaning of that word. It is clear that a restaurant operator is a merchant and is expected to have the skill and ability of one in that type of business. Absence of that skill and ability is in itself a breach of an implied warranty. The second type of warranties are "express warranties."

Express Warranties

Express warranties arise because the operator of a restaurant specifically makes them. They can be made by the use of words—"we serve the world's finest beef"—and they can be made by pictures on menus. It is important in restaurant keeping, just as in any other business, not to make unnecessary warranties. If the sale does not measure up, or if the product is inferior, there would be a breach of the express warranty. If this breach results in injury or loss to the patron, legal action can follow.

UCC 2-313(1) states that there is an express warranty (promise) that the goods will conform to photos in advertisements. In a New York case, it was held that an ad that showed a photo did not conform to what was sold; thus, there was a breach of warranty.[10] Examine Figure 21.1.

Other examples of express warranties include "boneless fish," "Sanka coffee," "hand-picked," "sugar-free," "100% hamburger," "home-cooked," "the best," "unsurpassed," "top quality," and "finest in town." Such statements become the standards by which a court will measure what in fact was served to the patrons. While such statements appear to be good marketing techniques, the legal aspects of using them must be considered when drafting advertisements and writing menus. A restaurant in Las Vegas advertised "Two eight-ounce lobsters—$9.95." What in fact was being served were two four-ounce

Woman sues pizza chain for unsatisfying sandwich

ROCKVILLE, Md.—A suburban Washington D.C. pizza chain's refusal to take back a sandwich that allegedly failed to meet its menu description could cost the restaurant $300,000, under a pending Maryland lawsuit.

The lawsuit was triggered by Pizza Oven's kitchen's refusal to meet the demands of a dissatisfied customer whose sandwich allegedly "did not appear to be the item described in the menu." Her waitress, who unsuccessfully tried to return the food, told the woman that the kitchen was giving her a "hard time," the customer charged.

The suit contends that when the woman refused to pay for her uneaten sandwich, the cashier told the customer she "had no right to judge whether the item she ordered was as described on the menu."

In addition, the cashier shouted "we know all about you," threatened to call the police and told the customer never to return to Pizza Oven again, the woman alleged. These "slanderous and malicious statements," among other things, suggested that the woman "had committed an illegal or improper act," the complaint said.

Consequently, the woman suffered "humiliation, embarrassment, injury to her reputation and public standing, mental anguish and other losses," the suit charged. The customer is seeking $150,000 in damages from both Pizza Oven and the employee.

FIGURE 21.1

lobsters for a total of eight ounces. This is an obvious breach of the express warranty and the practice was stopped there.

Disclaiming Implied Warranties

The Uniform Commercial Code allows a restaurant operator to disclaim implied warranties if it is done in the manner specified in Article 2. The disclaimer must be *conspicuous* and must mention "fitness" and "merchantability." It is a good idea to use such disclaimers on menus when serving seafood or exotic items that may have possible side effects associated with them. For example, at times in the Caribbean, certain fish contain toxins that cause problems to persons unused to them. Natives of that region are not affected by the toxins, but that is not necessarily so for the tourist from Kansas. Thus a warning in disclaimer form is in order.

The implied warranty rule under Article 2 does not apply (1) if there is no "sale" of the food and drink, (2) may not be applied by a court if a proper disclaimer is used, and (3) usually becomes of no legal consequence when adequate care is used in the preparation and serving of food and drink. On the other hand, if *express* warranties are made, there is very little at law that can be done to get rid of them. One cannot expressly warrant that food is "home-cooked" and then in small print, claim that it is not home-cooked and by doing so, escape the express warranty. The courts will not buy that.

Foreign Substances in Food

Objects that are foreign to food and drink served in a restaurant could give rise to a breach of the implied warranty of merchantability. A foreign object would be something not found in the food or drink in nature. Such objects could also lead to litigation in tort for the negligence in allowing them to get into the food or drink. Some examples include glass in a bowl of soup, a pebble in a spinach salad, caustic acid in a beer bottle, and a nail served in food. One has a positive duty not to serve food and drink that contains such foreign objects. Yet what if the object served is *natural* and causes injury? Examples would include an olive pit in a martini that causes a broken tooth,[11] a cherry stone in a slice of cherry pie,[12] a chicken bone in a chicken pot pie,[13] and a pearl in a can of processed oysters that resulted in broken teeth.[14] The courts are not so quick to place responsibility upon the restaurant in such instances. The one who consumes such items should exercise some care since he or she would be on notice that these items could be found. Yet in all of the cases mentioned, the injured patron was able to recover in court.

Fish bones in fish, chicken bones in fried chicken, or clam shells or fish bones in fish gumbo or clam chowder are clearer examples of the type of cases in which the courts place greater responsibility upon the one consuming the food. On the other hand, there are situations in which a patron could not be expected to be looking for a natural substance in a food. A cherry pit in cherry ice cream would be an example. While the pit was natural to the cherry, it should not have survived the processing of the ice cream. The question of whether the one who consumed the ice cream acted reasonably while eating it was held to be a jury question and the case that had been appealed was returned to the lower court for determination of that issue.[15]

Thus there are two tests applied by the courts. The first is the "natural test," and the second is the "reasonable-expectation test." The latter places a higher standard of care upon the patron. But regardless of the legal theories, they place upon the restaurant operator an increased duty of care.

The U.S. Department of Agriculture (USDA) defines a "natural product" as one that contains no artificial ingredients and was processed minimally.

Food-Borne Illness

Great stress must be placed on sanitation and health of food handlers. If food contains bacteria because of improper preparation or lack of sanitation and illness results to patrons, the restaurant is going to find itself in court and in the newspapers. Jury Verdict Research reports that the average recovery for such illness exceeds $70,000 per case. Such illness can come from food handlers who have an intestinal organism known as shigella. It is similar in effect to salmonella but its source is the human body and not food. When such suits are brought, the burden is on the plaintiff to show that the illness was carried by the food. It is not enough to claim that illness followed the consumption of the food: It must be proved that the food caused the illness. In the case of shigella poisoning, the evidence will almost always be devastating to the restaurant. For example, symptoms include diarrhea, nausea, abdominal pain, and vomiting, and the presence of the bacteria can be established by laboratory testing. The organisms can be carried in the body of the patron for weeks after the food consumption and can be passed on to others by physical contact. This increases the legal risk to the restaurant because others may gain the right to sue.

At a Southland Motor Inn in Tulsa, Oklahoma, a patron dined one evening, became violently ill the next day, and was admitted to a hospital. The diagnosis made (in error) was that he had colitis. In the meantime, the innkeeper was notified of an outbreak of food poisoning (food-borne illness) among guests. Tests made of the employee who had prepared the food showed that that person had shigella. The inn made no attempt to notify the patron and others of that fact.

After finding out later that he had been exposed, the patron sued and recovered $375,000 compensatory damages and $500,000 in punitive damages. Both awards were upheld on appeal. The court ruled that the evidence showed that the inn ". . . had repeatedly violated health department regulations by permitting unsanitary conditions to exist in the restaurant. . . ; there was also evidence that [the inn] took no steps to notify guests that they had been exposed to shigella, apparently because [the inn] feared that the publicity would hurt its business. We believe that this evidence justifies submitting the issue to the jury and that the jury could have found that [the inn] acted in reckless and conscious disregard for the rights of [the patron]," *Averitt v. Southland Motor Inn*, 720 F. 2d 1178 (Oklahoma, 1983).

Liability to Whom?

If A invites B to have dinner at Restaurant X, and B is injured by a foreign substance in the food, is Restaurant X responsible even though A intended to pay for the food? The courts tend to answer this question in the affirmative, holding that there is an implied warranty to furnish suitable food to *both* of them, even though the actual contract is with A alone.[16]

Duty to Comply with State and Federal Statutes

There are many other state and federal laws that must be complied with. Two examples of state statutes and one federal law will illustrate. Two have to do with food and food preparation. The third has to do with entertainment at the restaurant.

Microwave Ovens

The current wide usage of microwave ovens for food preparation has resulted in statutes to protect those who might suffer harm because of their use. The following is typical.

> Any restaurant, hotel, motel, dining room, hospital, snack bar or any food dispensing facility utilizing a microwave oven shall prominently display a public notice in the following words:
>
> "NOTICE TO PERSONS HAVING HEART PACEMAKERS: This Establishment Uses a Microwave Oven."
>
> The state director of health shall be responsible for administering this section. He may delegate the duties to any county boards of health or combined local boards of health.
>
> The state health department shall purchase such notices assuring a uniform size and color of the notices.
>
> Any person, firm or corporation who shall violate any provision of this section shall be guilty of a misdemeanor, and, upon conviction thereof, shall be fined not less than one hundred dollars nor more than five hundred dollars.

There is a desire in the states to make certain that the food and drink served to the buying public is of a proper quality. An example is found in a Los Angeles policy memorandum that creates what is known as "accuracy-in-menus."

Accuracy-in-Menus (Sometimes Called "Truth-in-Menus")

The Los Angeles memo first sets forth the goal of the policy: to guarantee that buyers of food and drink get what they are supposed to. This is followed by examples of violations and concludes with enforcement provisions. Some examples include adulteration of products, hamburger not meeting specifications, imitation hamburger being offered as real hamburger, dairy products not meeting specifications, and others. Other guidelines are provided and one will be mentioned. "If food is prepared in the restaurant kitchen from a recipe under conditions and with ingredients similar to those used at home, the food may be advertised as 'homestyle' or 'homemade style'." Consequently food that is not being so prepared cannot be advertised in that manner.

Some states and many other cities have such menu laws and they are being enforced. An Albany, New York, restaurant was fined because its "fresh brook trout" had in fact been refrigerated. A Long Island restaurant was caught serving "Long Island duckling" that had in fact come from Wisconsin. (In both of the above instances there would also be a breach of the express warranties.) When the issue of accuracy-in-menus came up in New Jersey, the state inn association published Accuracy-In-Menu (AIM) guidelines and suggested that members submit copies of their menus so that they could be screened to see if they were in compliance with AIM requirements. The National Restaurant Association also has an

AIM code. As part of this movement, it must be remembered that disclaimers and warnings on menus are not out of order. In addition to alerting patrons to possible dangers, such disclaimers also assist in accurately describing the food and drink being offered at the restaurant. That is what the AIM laws are all about.

Related to AIM is a trend to require restaurants to make information about ingredients and nutritional value of the food available to patrons. McDonald's Corporation began such a voluntary disclosure program in 1986 in New York. States that now have this requirement by statute include California, New Jersey, New York, Pennsylvania, and Texas.

Moving away from our discussion of food laws as they relate to the restaurant, let's find out what role 17 United States Code 101, as amended, plays when the restaurant operator wants to use recorded or live music for entertainment of patrons.

FEDERAL COPYRIGHT STATUTES

The federal copyright law can cause legal problems at the restaurant where music is played. Examine Figure 21.2. To understand the nature of this problem, it is necessary to learn something about the legal rights of composers, publishers, and performers of music.

First, it is clear that the copyright laws protect composers and publishers just as they protect authors, poets, and others who produce creative material. For a restaurant to have the legal right to use music in a "public performance for profit," royalties must be paid to the composers and publishers of the music.

Bogie's faces lawsuit

A New York music licensing organization has filed suit in U.S. District Court against Bogie's, 4375 Las Vegas Blvd. South, charging the Las Vegas nightclub with violation of federal copyright laws.

The suit filed by Broadcast Music Inc., alleges that BMI-copyrighted songs were performed at Bogie's without the company's authorization in violation of the U.S. Copyright Act.

The company is seeking statutory damages in addition to attorney's fees and court costs.

BMI is the largest music licensing organization in the world, representing more than 71,000 writers and publishers. The suit was filed in Las Vegas federal court on April 19.

Las Vegas Sun, 4-26-84, p. 8C

FIGURE 21.2

To facilitate the collection of these royalties, the composers and publishers belong to "performing arts societies," such as the American Society of Composers, Authors, and Publishers, and Broadcast Music, Incorporated. These organizations use the contract to grant the legal right to use the works of their members. In this way, the composers and publishers receive royalties from the vast network of radio and television stations and other organizations that play the music for profit, including inns.

The courts have held that playing music for the enjoyment of customers in a restaurant is a public performance for profit. This makes the restaurant operator liable for the payment of royalties. There are some choices available to meet this mandate of federal law, and we will look at four of them.

First, one may simply decide to forego music. Second, if it is desirable to provide the music, one way to proceed is to play only the music of one organization. In this manner, a contract can be entered into, bringing the matter into compliance with the law. A third possibility, favored by many restaurant operators, is to use a programmed system such as MUZAK. The operator of the restaurant will pay a fee to MUZAK or other system operator who in turn will pay the royalties to the national organizations. A fourth choice is to use "jukebox" or other systems which are exempt from the copyright laws. However, to gain this exemption these systems must be owned by someone other than the person who uses them.

In the case of *Twentieth Century Music Corp. et al. v. Aiken,* the U.S. Supreme Court held that some small restaurant operators (1055 square feet in the Aiken case) could use "homestyle" speakers to broadcast music without liability for royalties. On the other hand, if an elaborate system of speakers is used in restaurants, the courts will hold that this is a copyright infringement.

A two-part test is used to decide if there has been a violation of the federal law. First, there has to be a "transmission." If a restaurant operator buys an audio tape and plays it at home for her own entertainment, there would be no "transmission." If she plays the same audio at the restaurant for her patrons, there would be. Second, there must be a "performance for profit." In most restaurants no charge is made for the music, yet the courts hold that it is a "performance for profit" because of the charges made for the food and drink.

Turning from the playing of music at the restaurant, there are a few miscellaneous legal matters that are of concern to the restaurant operator. After examining these, we will close the chapter with a restaurant property-loss case.

HOUSE RULES AND OTHER LEGAL ITEMS

Since restaurants do not have a common-law duty to receive, they can create and place into use reasonable rules of conduct for patrons as well as employees. An example would be the "no shoes, no service" policy seen around the nation. On a higher level, one finds the dress codes laid down at better restaurants. If patrons fail to meet the requirements of these rules, they can be excluded and service refused. The courts enforce such in-house rules and do not extend to would-be patrons at restaurants the same privileges that they do to guests at inns.

California law requires that each restaurant post first-aid instructions on how a choking patron can be provided assistance. The statute does not require the restaurant to apply such aid, but the restaurant must, of course, promptly call for outside assistance. If that is done and even if no first aid is given and death results, the courts will exonerate the restaurant from liability, *Breaux v. Gino's*, 200 Cal. Rpt. 260 (California, 1984). There must be a firm rule as to whether or not first aid is to be attempted by restaurant personnel. Aside from the humanitarian aspects, legal advice is required when making this decision. If aid is provided, proper training must be given to ensure that the aid is carried out properly. If the aid is attempted and the patron dies, the restaurant has a major legal problem. The estate of the deceased will probably claim that the attempted aid was not properly carried out. If no aid is given but prompt assistance is sought, the restaurant will escape legal liability. This represents one of the quirks of the American legal system.

In the American Southwest, summer temperatures soar above 120 degrees at times and ground temperatures can approach 200 degrees. At restaurants that offer outside playground facilities, consideration must be given to possible burns of children caused by contact with the metal and plastic of the equipment. Such a case was brought against a Las Vegas McDonald's. It was alleged that a three-year-old child suffered extensive burns to the buttocks and thighs and that the restaurant had failed to post signs warning of the extreme temperature of the metal and plastic on the equipment. While the Nevada Supreme Court dismissed the claim, it must be remembered that such a claim may prevail in court in the future. In this particular case, the jury was not convinced that the three-year-old child climbed onto the equipment and then remained there until severely burned on the buttocks and thighs. Perhaps the failure of the plaintiff to recover can be attributed to insufficient proof offered by the plaintiff's lawyer. Anyone who has touched 200 degree metal knows that it only takes an instant to be severely burned.

Restaurant No-Shows

While inns have had to contend with no-show reservation holders for decades, the problem has not been so pronounced at restaurants, yet it happens. Restaurants who hold tables for those who do not show usually lose income. As a result, there is an increasing willingness to sue defaulting persons for the breach of contract. It would be wise for the restaurant to do one of two things:

1. Refuse to make restaurant reservations, leaving it on a first-come, first-served basis.
2. Create a house rule that says that those who breach their reservation contracts will be sued for the loss of profits.

One other example of the types of house rules that the inn might consider is whether or not the restaurant will hire illegal aliens as employees. In California, for example, more than 760,000 persons work in restaurants and bars. It is estimated that 35 percent of these persons are illegal aliens. It is common in that state for government agents to make unannounced searches in an attempt to catch such persons. If agents have a search warrant, they can proceed with the search. If the search is warrantless, under the Fourth Amendment the operator can refuse to allow the search to continue. If the operator consents to the search, that satisfies the Fourth Amendment. Searching for illegal aliens is a criminal matter and must be distinguished from an administrative search, such as a health inspection. In a criminal search, someone may ultimately go to jail or be deported. In an administrative search, the result is usually a reprimand or a civil fine. A warrant is required in the criminal search unless permission is given, but none is required in an administrative search.

Restaurant operators may at times want to assist certain illegal aliens in gaining a lawful status. In doing this, there could be a tax advantage.

A Tax Tip for Restaurant Owners Employing Illegal Aliens

The manager at "Ernie's Diner," located in the lobby of the "No Show Inn," decides to assist an illegal alien employee in getting her immigration visa. Although the costs for this process can be as much as $10,000 per person for court and attorney fees, this expenditure may be a plus in the long run. To encourage this process, an income tax deduction is allowed for ". . . ordinary and business expenses . . ."

for the restaurant, giving the operator a tax deduction. However, if these costs are paid directly to the alien with instructions to pay them over, the alien will have that money taxed as income. That in turn requires the restaurant operator to pay into the funds required by employee laws. Thus, such payments should be made directly when assisting aliens.

Taxable Privileges on Alcoholic Beverages

Tennessee levies a 15 percent "taxable privilege" on alcoholic beverages that are served for consumption on the premises of restaurants in that state. Do cooking wines used in food preparation fall under that taxation? A court has held that such wines are not subject to the tax, *Copper Cellar v. Jackson,* 762 S.W. 2d 560 (Tennessee, 1988).

Meals Furnished to Restaurant Employees

When the restaurant furnishes meals on a regular basis to employees during working hours, the value of such meals is not subject to social security, federal unemployment, and workers' compensation taxes. On the reverse side, this value is subject to the income tax law and must be reported on the tax returns of the restaurant employees.

How About Fast-Food Containers?

A legal problem has arisen in reference to the containers that are used at most fast-food restaurants. Almost all such restaurants have been using styrofoam, nonbiodegradable containers to serve their products to their customers. The environmentalists believe that these containers may last 1,000 years buried in land fills and feel that this is an undesirable thing to allow to happen. The possibility of a lawsuit of immense proportions is there. The trend is toward using paper wrappings instead of plastic.

A final topic in thinking about the restaurant is choosing a name for it. Can there by legal problems in doing that?

What's in a Name?

If your name is Sony Florendo, can you name your restaurant "Sony's"? Sony found the answer when the Japanese "Sony Corporation" brought a multi-million dollar suit against her. She settled the issue by changing the name of her restaurant to "Sony Florendo's." The Japanese firm agreed to relinquish its claim that her use of the name was ". . . unfair competition and that it diminished the value of the Japanese worldwide trademark. . . ." The McDonald's Corporation successfully stopped Ken McShea from naming his new restaurant "McBagels." The court ruled that the use of this name would be unfair as well as a trademark violation. To balance the matter the court approved the use of the name "McSheagels," *McDonald's v. McBagels, Inc.*, 649 F. Supp. 1268 (New York, 1986). (McDonald's also stopped Quality International from using the name "McSleep Inn." The name was changed to "Sleep Inn.")

In 1988, a Miami court held that Burger King has trademark rights to the name "Chicken Tenders." This ruling required Pilgrim's Pride of Texas to change the name of its supermarket products which had been named "Chicken Breast Tenders." Walt Disney World also had to discontinue its "Chicken Tenders" at the Adventureland Veranda.

To close the chapter, we will look at a loss-of-property case at a restaurant. The circumstances of this case were unusual.

SUMMER V. HYATT CORP.
153 Ga. App. 684 266 S.E. 2d 333 (1980)

SHULMAN, Judge.

Plaintiff brought this action to recover damages for loss or theft of valuables from her purse, contending that the loss or theft was due to the negligence of defendant or to the maintenance of a nuisance by defendant. The loss or theft occurred in the rotating Polaris restaurant, operated by defendant and located atop the Hyatt Regency hotel owned by defendant. While plaintiff was registered as a guest at the hotel, she went into the restaurant and took a seat on the rotating portion of the structure, placing her purse on the stationary portion of the structure. Plaintiff's seat rotated away from her purse. When the purse was recovered, valuables were missing from it.

Defendant moved for and received summary judgment on the basis of plaintiff's admitted noncompliance with the hotel's regulations concerning the safekeeping of guests' valuables. See Code Ann. Sec 52-108 *et seq.; Jones v. Savannah Hotel Co.*, 141 Ga. 530(2), 81 S.E. 874. Plaintiff contends in this appeal from the order granting summary judgment to defendant that her status as an invitee of the restaurant, rather than her status as a hotel guest, controls the rights and liabilities of the parties to this action.

Although this precise question has not been decided in Georgia (that is, whether an "inn" guest retains guest status when such guest avails herself of a restaurant facility located on the premises of the hotel structure), several cases imply that the relationship of guest-innkeeper would remain in effect during the guest's occupation of a hotel's restaurant and bar. (See *Alpaugh v. Wolverton,* 184 Va. 943(2), 36 S.E.2d 906). For example, in *Walpert v. Bohan,* 126 Ga. 532, 534, 55 S.E. 181, 182, it was stated that "[O]ne who keeps a public house may, not inconsistently, *carry on a restaurant, cater to a select company, serve liquors at a bar, keep a shaving saloon, or permit outside parties to get up a ball on his premises, [but] as to strangers who avail themselves of such extraneous service, he is no innkeeper at all."* (Emphasis supplied.)

What *Walpert* implies is that an innkeeper who provides the above service to a guest of the inn remains in the status of an innkeeper in regard to such guest. As to a stranger, however; that is, one who is not a guest of the inn, the fact that an innkeeper provides the above services does not establish a guest-innkeeper relationship. The duties normally flowing from the position of innkeeper, therefore, are not owed to a stranger, but they are owed to a guest.

Diplomat Restaurant v. Townsend, 118 Ga. App. 694, 165 S.E.2d 317, likewise implies that a guest retains his guest status while patronizing a hotel restaurant. In *Diplomat Restaurant,* this court refused to apply the innkeeper statutes to one who "merely operated a restaurant and a bar for serving liquors," impliedly holding that its decision would have been contrary had the defendant likewise operated an inn.

Moreover, this court has previously found the relationship of innkeeper-guest to exist despite the fact that the guest was availing himself of facilities other than those used solely for lodging [rooms] and integral connecting portions of the hotel (lobby, elevators, etc.). See in this regard *Traylor v. Hyatt Corp.,* 122 Ga. App. 633(1), 178 S.E.2d 289, wherein the court held the innkeeper statutes applicable to a guest's loss of property from his car parked (for a separate fee) in the hotel's parking lot. See also *Ellerman v. Atlanta American & Hotel Corp.,* 126 Ga. App. 194(2), 191 S.E.2d 295.

We do not hold that an innkeeper retains his status as an innkeeper towards guests of the inn in regard to all extraneous services provided by the innkeeper, of which hotel guests as well as the general public partake (such as "boats for rowing and sailing . . . a public race course or golf links or a baseball," *Walpert, supra,* 126 Ga. 535, 55 S.E., 182).

But, under the circumstances of the case at bar, in view of the fact that plaintiff was in defendant's restaurant within the hotel structure, we conclude that plaintiff retained her guest status, as a matter of law, and that defendant continued to owe plaintiff the duties of an innkeeper, and that plaintiff accordingly was bound by the regulations established under Code Ann. Ch. 52-1.

That being so, plaintiff, as a guest, was required to comply with the posted rules in regard to the safety deposit of her valuables in order to recover against the defendant. The failure to do so precludes her recovery from defendant on the claims asserted. See *Jones, supra,* 141 Ga. p. 534, 81 S.E. 874.

Judgment affirmed.

QUILLIAN, P. J., and CARLEY, J., concur.

QUESTIONS

1. Why does the common-law duty to receive at the inn not apply to restaurants?
2. What is required to make a restaurant dress code legal?
3. What is the legal difference between a "tort" and an "accident" in liability insurance language?
4. What is the problem where frozen food is advertised as being "fresh"? Isn't all frozen food fresh to begin with?
5. Does the federal copyright law apply to in-room video shows where royalties are not paid to the copyright holders and a fee is charged the viewer? If no fee is charged, might a court still find that the fee is included in the room rate and that royalties are due the copyright holder?
6. "Privity of contract" is defined as "that connection or relationship which exists between two or more contracting parties." *Black's Law Dictionary,* Fifth Edition, p. 1079. Under what circumstances does this old legal doctrine become involved in the operation of a restaurant?
7. The "duty to receive" at common law did not extend to restaurants. Would the operation of modern restaurants be different if it had? What major difference would we notice?
8. The courts in the United States are beginning to develop the idea that the common-law duty of innkeepers to receive should be extended to restaurants. What would be a benefit to travelers if this happened? What would be a detriment to restaurant keepers?
9. The legal standards that must be met when serving food and drinks for a price are set forth in Article 2 of the

UCC. Why did the drafters use so much detail in these laws? What problems were they trying to cure?

10. True or False. If a substance is natural to a particular food, such as a clam shell to clam chowder, injury caused by its presence is automatically excused as a matter of law.

ENDNOTES

1. Kenneth Roberts, *Northwest Passage,* p. 44.
2. *Alpaugh v. Wolverton,* 184 Va. 943, 36 S.E. 2d 906.
3. Chapter 16, Article 6, Section 3 (1966).
4. Opinion, West Virginia Attorney General, January 9, 1970.
5. 651.050, 651.060 and 651.070.
6. Joe McGinnis, *Going to Extremes.* The New American Library, Inc., New York, pp. 58-59.
7. Title II, Civil Rights Act of 1964, 42 U.S.C. 2000, as amended in 1972.
8. In New York, see *McKinney's Supp.* 1972, section 296(2); In Nevada, p. 512.
9. 46 App. Div. 2d 98, 338 N.Y.S. 2d 356 (Third Dept. 1972).
10. *Rinkmasters, Inc., v. City of Utica,* 348 N.Y.S. 2d 940, 13 UCC Rep. 797 (1973).
11. *Hochberg v. O'Donnell's Restaurant Inc.,* 272 A. 2d 846, (DC App. 1977).
12. *Musso v. Picadilly Cafeterias, Inc.,* 178 So. 2d 421 (La. App. 1965).
13. *Mix v. Ingersoll Candy Co.,* 6 Col. 2d 674, 59 P. 2d 144 (1936).
14. *O'Dell v. DeJeans Packing Co.,* 24 UCC Rep. 311 (Okl. App., July 1978).
15. *William v. Braum,* 543 P. 2d 799 (Okl.1974).
16. *Conklin v. Hotel Waldorf Astoria,* 5 Misc. 2d 496, 169 N.Y.S. 2d 205 (N.Y. City Ct. 1957).

22

Bars, Lounges, Taverns, Pubs, and Saloons: The Legal View

Leiter ordered two dry martinis. "Just watch," he said sourly.

The martinis arrived. Leiter took one look at them and told the waiter to send over the barman. When the barman came, looking resentful, Leiter said, "My friend, I asked for a martini and not a soused olive." He picked the olive out of the glass with the cocktail stick. The glass, that had been three-quarters full, was now half full. Leiter said mildly, "This was being done to me while the only drink you knew was milk. I'd learned the basic economics of your business by the time you'd graduated to Coca-Cola. One bottle of Gordon's gin contains sixteen true measures–double measures, that is, the only ones I drink. Cut the gin with three ounces of water and that makes it up to twenty-two. Have a jigger glass with a big steal in the bottom and a bottle of those fat olives and you've got around twenty-eight measures. Bottles of gin here cost only two dollars retail, let's say around a dollar sixty wholesale. You charge eighty cents for a martini, a dollar sixty for two. Same price as a whole bottle of gin. And with your twenty-eight measures to the bottle, you've still got twenty-six left. That's a clear profit on one bottle of gin of around twenty-one dollars. Give you a dollar for the olives and the drop of vermouth and you've still got twenty dollars in your pocket. Now, my friend, that's too much profit, and if I could be bothered to take this martini to the management and then to the Tourist Board, you'd be in trouble. Be a good chap and mix us two large dry martinis without olives and with some slices of lemon peel separate. Okay? Right, then we're friends again."

Thunderball, Ian Fleming

OVERVIEW

In this chapter, we want to expand on the legal principles of restaurants as covered in Chapter 21 because, in practice, they are almost always combined with bars or lounges at the inn. The legal topic that has emerged in recent years as being of most importance to bars and restaurants is that of liquor liability. The majority of the chapter will be devoted to that subject.

Historically, there were three classes of persons or businesses that sold alcoholic beverages to travelers and others. The first was the "taverner," the very early Jewish seller of wines. This ancient occupation gave us the word "tavern." Next was the "publican," the English and Greek brewer and seller of beer. From this we get the word "pub." This is ". . . the most compressed piece of shorthand in the world. The village pub is a drinking house, a parish parliament, and a club rolled into one," Timothy Finn, *The CAMRA Beer Guide.* The third was the "dram shop" where hard liquors were sold by measure. Modern courts have adopted this latter phrase to describe the statutes and case decisions that make bar operators liable for injuries, loss, or death caused by persons who have become intoxicated by illegal liquor sales.

The past 1,000 years in particular have been replete with colorful accounts of the sale and consumption of alcoholic beverages and the enactment of laws to control that consumption. The royal courts of earlier times, for example, were constantly on the move, traveling 20 to 35 kilometers per day. Hundreds and perhaps thousands of persons accompanied those rulers. In Annalista Saxo, it was reported that in the year 968, a royal court in Europe consumed "ten tuns of wine, and as many tuns of beer," and "one thousand pigs and sheep." In this year, it was said that "many an involuntary host saw his wine cellar depleted." There was a demand for drink and the taverner, publican, and dram shop provided it, voluntarily or involuntarily.

THE LAWS OF DRINKING

The laws regulating the operation of taverns, pubs, and dram shops go back many centuries and have been associated historically with the laws of merchants. The Magna Carta of 1215, for example, discloses the interest of the English in promoting the activities of merchants as they went about their business both within and outside of the island nation. They regulated the activities of those

OLD LONE PINE HOTEL, Lone Pine, California.

merchants and developed a system of courts (Lex Mercatoria) and enacted laws to make certain that value was given for value.

An example is found in "Cap. 35" (Chapter 35) of the Great Charter. "There shall be standard measures of wine, ale and corn [the London quarter], throughout the kingdom. There shall also be a standard width of dyed cloth, russet, and haberjet, namely two ells [yards] within the selvedges [the specially woven edges]. Weights are to be standardized similarly."

Here, one sees the forerunner of our modern weights and measures laws. The Magna Carta was reissued several times in that century and one reissue came in 1297. Only four copies of that reissue exist and, in 1984, H. Ross Perot of Dallas, Texas, paid $1.5 million for one of those copies, which he brought to the United States. The copy had been in the Brudenell family since 1297. They had ruled near Northhamptonshire since the reign of Edward I. Thus, an early and important law from those times has touched our lives today. The copy is now in the National Archives and rests there with our Constitution and Declaration of Independence. The only other copy of Magna Carta and its reissues, written in Latin on sheepskin, existing outside of England, is located in Australia.

When Columbus discovered America, there were more than 300 brewers of beer in the city of London. Regulations were enacted to ensure that casks of beer held the amount that they were supposed to. Casks at that time, or "barrels" as we know them today, were made by "coopers." It was known then as the "cooperage industry," and the laws required that the coopers place marks on the casks to identify who had made them. By 1500, this industry was in decline because of the introduction of glass bottles and the creation of machines that could create cask staves. (The coming of metal barrels in 1946 put a near end to the coopers and their apprentices and journeymen.)

An interesting historical fact in relation to casks is that they would last for over fifty years. Thus, there was a demand for coopers to care for those casks and, in some cases, to cut them down to smaller sizes. They also had to be repaired and thus many persons were provided jobs during those times. There are still a few working coopers in England. Their work is done with primitive tools and by hand.

In 1531, the English Parliament passed an act that prohibited brewers from making the casks in which their own beer and ale was sold. This act stated: "Whereas the ale brewers and beer brewers of this realm of England have used, and daily do use, for their own singular lucre, profit and gain, to making in their own houses, their barrels, kilderkins and firkins of much less quantity than they ought to be, to great hurt, prejudice and damage of the King, liege, people, and contrary to divers Acts, Statutes, Ancient Laws and customs heretofore, made, had, and used, and to the destruction of the poor craft and mystery of coopers," Charles E. Tresise, *Tavern Treasures,* Blandford Press, Link House, West Street, Poole, Dorset, BH 15 LL, p. 131. This was an early attempt to separate labor from management.

The legal quantity standard in those years for beer casks was 36 gallons, and ale casks, 32 gallons. Ale was much stronger than beer, which was hopped, and also sweeter. A character in Green's Tu Quoque, an Elizabethan comedy, Sir Lionel Rash, says: 'I have sent my daughter this morning as far as Pimlico to fetch a draught of Derby ale that it may fetch a colour into her cheeks.' Derby was noted for its brewers, but one wonders how, in those times, ale was transported from Derby and nearby Burton upon Trent to London.

In 1728, the English Parliament created an act that prohibited wine in ". . . flasks, bottles or small casks," to be imported. The purpose of this law was to prevent smuggling. The statute was repealed in 1802. At that time, wine bottles as we know them today were becoming popular and thus was born the corkscrew.

After the turn of the nineteenth century, the English laws were directed toward seals. An early 1900 law required that bottles of beer have a seal over the top. The alleged purpose was to keep children from taking a swig. Those early laws also were concerned with labels.

"The best known of all beer labels is, of course, the famous Bass red triangle for their pale ale. An executive of the brewery sat all night on the steps of the registrar's office when the first trade marks were being allocated and thus the Bass red triangle is, in fact, Trade Mark No. 1; their diamond trade mark was the second entry and became Trade Mark No. 2. The same famous trade mark achieved further fame when a bottle of Bass, showing the red triangle, was included in a painting dated 1821, entitled 'Bar at the Folies Bergere', by Edouard (Edward) Manet," *Tavern Treasures.*

The British Licensing Act of 1902 required something that is directly related to our modern dram-shop laws. For centuries the drinking places were used to post proclamations, advertising, and legal notices because they were the places where the local population gathered.

One of the notices that had to be posted under the 1902 law had to do with habitual drunkards. "At this time it was customary, when a person was convicted of being an habitual drunkard, to pin up a notice in the public house where he or she had been arrested and on this notice would be a front and side view picture rather like those photographs taken of prisoners today. This was posted as a warning that the person was banned from drinking in that pub and, in some cases, in any pub in the district for a period of up to three years. The recent new regulation (1982) known as the 'Ban the Thug' Act, endeavors to emulate the regulations of eighty years ago and one wonders why the earlier law was ever allowed to lapse," *Tavern Treasures,* p. 131.

Just after World War I, an alcoholic beverage known as "absinthe" was being sold. This was a very strong spirit marinated in wormwood. It could cause blindness, impotence, alcoholism, and death. In 1919, France banned its consumption.

This brief look at a long and colorful history of drinking and the creation of laws to regulate that activity has brought us to the years where the modern dram-shop laws were born. There was precedent for them in those earlier laws that required the posting of notices about those who had been arrested for habitual drunkenness, as well as administrative liquor laws which were often labeled "dram-shop laws."

DRAM-SHOP LAWS

At common law, a dram shop was an establishment in which liquors were drunk on the premises. The phrase in old English law was synonymous with saloon, bar, or tavern. These laws are also known today as "civil liability acts" and may give rise to a presumption of negligence by the sale of alcoholic drinks to an intoxicated or minor person. As one court said, "In view of the fact that the statute prohibiting furnishing drinks to an obviously intoxicated person was adopted to protect the general public from injuries resulting from the excessive use of intoxicating liquor, a presumption of negligence on the part of the bar keeper arises when the statute is violated."[1]

Under these laws, the seller of alcoholic beverages that causes or contributes to intoxication is held liable for injury to others by the intoxicated person. These laws protect against an assault by that person as well as injury or death from the use of an auto or other means. The laws also give a cause of action to the family of the injured or deceased person for lost income.

There is wide variation in the liability imposed in the states that have these laws. In some the liability is severe, in others less so. It is thus necessary for bar operators to learn the nature and extent of legal liability of their particular states. This is especially so because these laws play a direct role in establishing closing times and policies that will be followed in the day-to-day operation of the bar.

How Do These Laws Work?

If a tavern keeper allows a patron—minor or adult—to become intoxicated, or serves drinks to one who is already intoxicated, legal liability may arise if that person causes injury or death to another. The proximate cause of the injury or death would be the sale of the alcohol. If the intoxicated person had visited several bars, in some states the liability will be spread among those who sold alcoholic beverages to that person.

Suit can now be brought by the injured person for losses sustained or, if the person is killed, by his or her spouse or children. In some states, even an employer has a right to sue.

Some states place a limit on recovery, while others do not. This too is an important fact for the tavern keeper to know for insurance purposes. Most states, however, do not place limits on liability, leaving it as a matter of proof in court.

These laws are beneficial to society in the long run because they tend to force tavern keepers to train their bartenders to use caution and discretion when serving drinks. It is a situation in which a good bartender can sharply reduce legal liability.

Can the Drunk Person Sue If Injured?

Historically, the dram-shop laws did not provide protection for the one who becomes intoxicated and injuries himself or herself. The reasoning was that that person would have to shoulder some of the blame for the injury or loss. Thus the right to sue where an intoxicated person killed himself but no one else did not survive to the widow or children. This position of the common law is now being looked at by the courts and it appears that a change will be coming in the future.

The Court of Appeals of Michigan has held that a wrongful death complaint stated a common-law cause of action for gross negligence for willful, wanton, and intentional misconduct independent of the Michigan Dram-Shop Act, when it alleged that the death of plaintiff's decedent, which occurred when the deceased fell from a bridge while intoxicated, was caused by the actions of defendant tavern owner in selling alcohol to the deceased even though he had been warned that the deceased was a hopeless alcoholic and had agreed not to serve him alcohol. The Court noted that an action under the Dram Shop Act was not available to the deceased's executrix, since it would not have been available to the deceased himself had he survived; the *common-law action* approved by the court, however, would be available to the intoxicated person himself.[2]

A news item illustrates the change that may be in the making:

> **Injury lawsuit to trial**
>
> A $2 million negligence suit began Tuesday in U.S. District Court dealing with claims by a California woman who admits getting drunk before falling over a stool at the Hotel Nevada.
>
> Mary Yuzra, 37, of Santa Ana, injured herself when she fell against a video game, and she claims it is the hotel's fault.
>
> Hotel attorney David Barron said in opening statements that the resort is not liable because the woman fell after she was struck by her boyfriend during an argument, and that caused the injury.
>
> According to her attorney, Marc Vincent of Santa Ana, Yuzra and the boyfriend arrived on Sept. 5, 1981, about noon, and while waiting for their room to be cleaned, started gambling.
>
> As she gambled, she was provided free drinks.
>
> "The hotel knew she was thoroughly intoxicated at least four to five hours before the accident," Vincent argued. She fell about 9 P.M.
>
> The hotel has a policy of cutting off drinks, offering meals or escorting people deemed intoxicated to their room. In Yuzra's case, this did not happen and she was allowed to continue even thought she was staggering through the casino.
>
> When she fell, she injured the left side of her face and she has permanent numbness caused by nerve damage, according to Vincent.[3]

More than one-half of our states have adopted dram-shop laws by legislative acts or by court decisions and this trend can be expected to continue.

ALCOHOL ABUSE AND THE BAR— THE LEGAL BACKGROUND

The sale of alcoholic beverages is a multimillion dollar business and one that can be quite profitable for hotels, motels, and other hospitality units. Such sales, however, carry with them considerable legal responsibilities, and indeed, legal dangers. This is true for a number of reasons including common-law rules, acts of legislative bodies—as well as the pressures that are being exerted by groups around the United States who are expending massive efforts directed to the removal of the drunk driver from the American highways. This movement, which has been gaining momentum nationally, has had an effect upon state courts and legislatures as well. "In recent years, many states have made penalties against drunken drivers more harsh, and numerous organizations have been formed to make people aware of the drunk driving problem."[4]

Drunk drivers are killing over 20,000 persons per year in the United States, injuring over 600,000 more, and costing our society an estimated $20 billion per year in medical, burial, and other costs.

Some examples of the organizations that have been formed in an attempt to stem this carnage include MADD (Mothers Against Drunk Driving), SADD (Students Against Drunk Driving), and RID-USA (Remove Intoxicated Drivers).

Thus the first question that is of interest to us is: "Who has the legal power to regulate the sale of alcoholic beverages in the United States?"

Sales Controlled by the States

The power to control the sale of intoxicating liquors resides solely in each state. This came about as a result of the Eighteenth Amendment which prohibited "the manufacture, sale, or transportation of intoxicating liquors within, the importation thereof into, or the exportation thereof from the United States and all territory subject to the jurisdiction thereof for beverage purposes." Ratified in 1919 and effective in 1920, this amendment opened up a period of lawlessness in the nation. The ultimate result was its repeal in 1933 by the Twenty-First Amendment which states: "The transportation or importation into any State, Territory, or possession of the United States for delivery or use therein of intoxicating liquors, in violation of the laws thereof, is hereby prohibited." Thus the sale of alcoholic beverages became a privilege that had to be granted by the states. The selling of intoxicants involves a substance that is given to deleterious tendency. Thus the states may regulate or suppress such sale, and such regulation or suppression in no way interferes with any inherent rights of citizenship.[5]

The sale of alcoholic beverages is controlled by the states in a variety of ways and these are summarized as follows:

1. The rules embodied in the Uniform Commercial Code, Article 2, Sales.
2. The common-law rules of negligence.
3. The rules laid down by state statutes including alcohol beverage control laws, and "Dram Shop" laws, or such rules as established by state court decisions.

Uniform Commercial Code, Article 2, Sales

Under the UCC, in all fifty states, the "serving for value of food or drink to be consumed either on the premises or elsewhere is a sale."[6] Thus "unless excluded or modified, a warranty that the goods shall be merchantable is implied in a contract for their sale if the seller is a merchant with respect to goods of that kind. . . . Goods to be merchantable must be at least such as . . . are fit for the ordinary purposes for which such goods are used."[7]

All operators of taverns and bars and other sellers of intoxicating liquors in package or otherwise, are merchants under the Uniform Commercial Code. Since this law makes the serving of drink a "sale," warranties arise that must be met by the seller. In this manner, the law provides standards for such sales, and thus serves as a liquor-sales control measure.

The second way that liquor sales are controlled is by the rules of common-law negligence. This is an effective control in that the presence of such law forces liquor sellers to control their business in order to avoid the legal consequences that can follow in court if they do not.

THE COMMON-LAW RULES OF NEGLIGENCE

The theory of common-law negligence has been used in court successfully time and again to recover damages from the sellers of alcoholic beverages where the one who consumed the drink caused injury to himself or herself or to third parties. In a Michigan case, mentioned previously,[8] recovery was allowed against a bar that had served alcoholic beverages to an alcoholic who subsequently fell to his death from a bridge while attempting to return home. The operator of the bar knew that the man was an alcoholic and had agreed previously not to serve drinks to him. Thus by making the sales on the night of his death, the seller was negligent, or had willingly engaged in misconduct by making the sales. Either activity will give rise to a common-law action for the loss sustained and the court so held.

The New Jersey Supreme Court has recognized a common-law action for negligence where a tavern served alcoholic beverages to a minor who subsequently caused injury to a third party.[9] Thus it becomes important that we understand a little more about "negligence" and how it is proved in court.

How Negligence Is Proved

The "plaintiff" (the one bringing the action in court) must prove four elements in a negligence case:

1. That there was a duty owed to the person who was injured or killed.
2. That there was a failure to live up to that duty.
3. That the failure was the proximate (direct) cause of the injury that resulted.
4. That monetary damages resulted as a consequence.

Thus the courts have a way to test conduct to see if it is actionable or to see whether it is excusable.

Standard of Care

The test is whether a reasonably prudent person at the time and place where the act complained of occurred should have recognized an unreasonable risk or likelihood of harm to others. Thus the standard of care becomes the conduct of a reasonable person of ordinary prudence under the circumstances,[10] and is a question of fact to be answered by a jury under instructions of the judge.

Failure to Maintain the Standard of Care

Serving alcoholic beverages to a person who is visibly intoxicated or to someone who is a minor does not meet the standard. If a bartender serves such a person and if the bartender should have known that the patron was intoxicated or a minor, then that bartender has not met the standard of care. If a jury determines that a reasonably prudent bartender, in similar circumstances, would have refused service, then the bartender (and the bar) was negligent.[11]

Courts have found liability when it was felt that a bartender should have known that a person was intoxicated or a minor.[12] Thus the standard of care has become very strict. "When alcoholic beverages are sold by a tavern keeper to a minor or to an intoxicated person, the unreasonable risk of harm not only to the minor or the intoxicated person but also to members of the traveling public may readily be recognized and foreseen; this is particularly evident in current times when traveling by a car to and from the tavern is so commonplace and accidents resulting from drinking are so frequent."[13]

To Compound the Problem

Liability has even been found in instances where drinks were refused but the intoxicated person was handled in such a manner that injury resulted. For example, if a bartender refuses drinks and puts that person out of the bar and thus back on the road in such a manner as to increase the peril of that person or others, liability may follow. As an illustration of this concept, a would-be drinker was refused service at a bar because of his intoxicated condition. After the refusal, the would-be patron asked if he could use the phone. There was an unlighted stairway on the way to the location of the phone and the bartender should have realized that there was danger of the person falling down the stairs. No assistance was offered, however. The drunk fell down the stairs, and the jury gave him $25,000 in damages in a subsequent court action.

The presence of negligence ". . . is tested by whether the reasonably prudent person at the time and place should recognize and foresee an unreasonable risk or likelihood of harm or danger to others. And correspondingly, the standard of care is the conduct of the reasonable person of ordinary prudence under the circumstances."[14]

Negligence standing alone, however, cannot form the basis of recovery in court. Something else is required.

Proximate Cause

The negligent act complained of, and not some other act must be the direct or actual (proximate) cause of the injury.[15]

Many cases have held that the sale of alcoholic beverages to an intoxicated person or to a minor was the proximate cause of injury to such persons, or others injured by them.[16] The latter situation forms the basis for legal liability under what are commonly known as "dram-shop laws," which in turn constitute a powerful legal control over those who sell alcoholic beverages.

Some states have such laws by legislative act; other states have them by court ruling, and some, such as Nevada, do not have either. Yet even in a non-dram shop state, an understanding of these laws is essential since many adjunct legal problems flow from their absence.

The concept of the dram-shop laws can be traced to an earlier England. The original purpose of such laws was to require tavern operators to support the families of those the operator allowed to become addicted to the consumption of alcoholic beverages. These laws, at first, did not permit recovery against the sellers by outside parties who were injured by the intoxicated person, and there was a legal reason for this.

At early common law, if an intoxicated person caused injury to another, the proximate cause of the injury (so the courts said) was the *consumption* of the alcohol and not the *sale* of it. The theory of this early rule was that each person who drank should be able to hold his or her liquor and was thus personally responsible to others that they may injure if they could not do so. This rule has now been changed in over one-half of our states by court decisions or by legislative acts. The first such legislative act in the United States came a little over 117 years ago.

"At the time of the enactment of the Dram Shop Act of 1873, the automobile had not been invented and modern highway traffic was a figment of the imagination. The rural inn and small town tavern were patronized by the local citizenry or by travelers in horse-drawn vehicles. Today, the hazards of travel by automobiles on modern highways has become a national problem. The drunken driver is a threat to the safety of many. The responsibility of the tavern keeper for contributing to the intoxication of a patron has long been regulated by statute. It is understandable that early cases did not recognize any duty of the innkeeper to the traveling public because a serious hazard did not exist. Through lack of necessity, this phase of negligence liability did not develop. However, there did exist general common-law rules of negligence liability based on foreseeability and proximate cause. It is a well-established, sound principle of legal philosophy that the common law is not static. Under the skillful interpretation of our courts, it has been adapted to changing times and conditions of our civilization."[17]

Violations of the dram-shop laws are treated by the courts as negligence per se. That is, the violation of the statute is itself negligence without need for anything further. An example of such a law illustrates the nature of this principle.

The New York General Obligation Law[18] provides: ". . . any person who shall be injured in person, property, means of support or otherwise by any intoxicated person, or by reason of the intoxication of any person against any person who shall, by unlawfully selling to or unlawfully assisting in procuring liquor for such intoxicated person, have caused or contributed to such intoxication," . . . has the right to sue the seller of the intoxicants and nothing further need be proven in order to recover.

Normally, the dram-shop laws do not give a cause of action against the seller where injury results to the one who consumed the drinks and not a third party. Yet such suits have been brought, as the Mitchell case illustrates.

Drunk Passengers—Who Is Responsible for Them?

Miss Mitchell became intoxicated at a tavern along with her escort. After passing out, she was helped to the auto of her companion who then proceeded to run the auto into a wall. The court allowed recovery against the seller of the intoxicants and in favor of Miss Mitchell. If Miss Mitchell had bought the intoxicants for her companion, the result might have been different but this was not the case. (In Michigan and Illinois, the result of this case would have been different.[19])

Suits brought under the dram-shop laws are separate from wrongful-death actions and do not replace those laws. To say it another way, if a tavern operator is sued under the dram-shop laws for the death of a third party caused by the serving of drinks to a minor or an intoxicated person, that operator can still be prosecuted by the state for the wrongful death, which is a criminal offense.

The legal liability faced by the sellers of alcoholic beverages will vary from state to state because there is presently no uniformity in the laws. This may change in the future, of course, particularly if the federal government should enter the picture, such as it did on the matter of the legal drinking age.

In some states, only the injured party or his or her immediate family can sue. In others, suit may be brought by parents of the injured or deceased person, and even employers of that person. Thus in some states the legal liability, and thus legal danger, is less than in others. Suits by parents to recover for the loss of services of a child can be brought only if the minor could have brought such a suit had he or she survived. Such suits by parents are thus "derivative"—that is, they come from the right of the child to sue had he or she survived.

Some states, by statute, limit the amount of recovery under the dram-shop laws. Connecticut is an example. In almost all other states, there is no limit on recovery, however, other than the value of the life lost, or the cost of the injuries sustained.

A constant problem is alcohol sales arises when one person purchases intoxicants and then passes them on to another who causes injury to a third person.

Delivery of Alcoholic Beverages to Others

The sale of alcoholic beverages to a minor, which is unlawful in itself, where the minor gives the drinks to another minor, raises legal problems. If a third party is injured by the second minor, is the seller liable to that third party? A Nevada court had this matter before it and ruled that even though it is unlawful to serve a minor, a bar cannot be held liable if that minor gives the liquor to a third party and that third party injures another.[20] Thus the seller won—but only because of the particular facts.

It is generally held in the courts that the dram-shop laws impose strict liability upon the sellers or servers of alcoholic beverages, and thus the defense of contributory negligence of the drinker is not available to the seller.

A few states, such as Virginia, have no dram-shop laws or ABC liability laws. No licensee to date has been held liable in that state for injury to third persons caused by an intoxicated person.

Missouri, like Virginia, does not have a dram-shop law, yet has allowed recovery by an injured third party against the seller of alcoholic beverages. This came about by court decision so the mere absence of a formal dram-shop law in itself is not sure-fire protection.

Repeal of Dram-Shop Laws

A few of our states have repealed their dram-shop laws, including Nebraska in 1935, Nevada in 1969, North Carolina in 1971, Oklahoma in 1959, and California in 1978. In most instances of repeal, the reasons for the action could be traced to unpopular court decisions which in turn promoted the repeal. The laws are not popular with everyone.

"In all too many states, Dram Shop liability has become outrageously unfair, exposing licensees to extraordinary hazard. It is a problem that must be addressed by state legislators. One logical way is a reasonable but firm cap on awards that juries may make. Meanwhile, licensees must make their personnel keenly aware of this hazard and institute cautions to minimize the likelihood of suit."[21] One fine legal control is found in "ABC" laws.

Alcoholic Beverage Control Laws

In the states that permit the wholesale, retail, and pouring sales of alcoholic beverages, one will find liquor-control administrative agencies. These agencies are charged with the regulation of such sales, and the administration of these laws is carried out by county-control boards. The primary control mechanism is the requirement of a license before alcoholic beverages can be legally sold.

In this manner the issuance of a license initially, and the retention of it, are subject to investigation, supervision, and subsequent investigation by the licensing authorities. Transgressions of the control laws can result in the loss of or suspension of such license, plus fines.

Liquor-control laws have a variety of requirements that must be met by each license applicant and licensee, including the posting of required notices at the place of sales,[22] the reporting of changes in ownership and management, rules that prohibit the employment of minors, and the training of employees in alcohol-awareness programs.

Such state and other legal regulations must be strictly complied with or one may face the loss of the privilege to engage in the legal sales of alcoholic beverages. These drinking laws are beginning to form a firm set of standards that must be measured up to. In addition, the application of these laws, both legislative and court-made, is creating a further body of bar laws. Some examples of what is happening in the courts follow.

Intoxicated persons pose a threat at the bar and inn not only to themselves, but to guests and third parties as well. Protecting them from their own actions is not the same as protecting others, *Mayo v. Hyatt,* 898 F. 2D 47 (Louisiana, 1990). Since 1969, Louisiana has had a rule that one who becomes voluntarily intoxicated must use the same degree of care for his or her own safety as one who is sober, *Guss v. Jack Tar*, 407 F. 2d 859 (Louisiana, 1969). But that rule still does not solve the third-party problems. In Idaho, if a bar operator knows of the propensity of a patron to cause harm to others and gives no warning, it becomes a question of fact for a jury as to whether or not the operator, acting through agents, should be held liable for injuries caused by that person to others while on or near the bar premises, *McGill v. Frasure,* 790 P. 2d (Idaho, 1990). In 1989, the Supreme Court of South Dakota ruled that when a dispute arises as to the proximate cause in an alcohol-related case, it becomes a question of fact and law for the courts and juries and not the legislatures. The statute there says that "the consumption of alcohol rather than the serving of it is the proximate cause of losses to third parties." Thus the Supreme Court of South Dakota overrode the South Dakota legislature on this legal point.

Third-party liability under the dram-shop laws customarily involves injuries or deaths caused by intoxicated auto drivers. Does such liability also apply where an intoxicated person commits a sexual assault upon a third party where no vehicle was involved? The bar argued that dram-shop liability applied only to those who were driving "vehicles." The appeals court rejected this argument and held that the dram-shop laws apply to the general public and not just those who are driving vehicles. Bar operators thus owe a duty not to serve alcoholic beverages to minors and those who are intoxicated, *S&A Beverage v. De Roune*, 753 S.W. 2d 507 (Texas, 1988).

Do Lawyers Personally Sue Restaurants and Bars?

At the "Bit of England," located at Burlingame, California, a lawyer had been refused bar service because of excessive consumption of alcoholic beverages. In being shown to the door, he claimed that such conduct ". . . caused injury to his law practice." The outcome of this situation is not known at the present, but it seems reasonable to conclude that a court will eventually uphold the right to refuse service to such an intoxicated lawyer, and indeed find that there is a duty to refuse further service.

At a New York bar, a young man was served drinks after it was obvious that he was intoxicated. He was ejected and then sustained injuries that resulted in his death. Upon appeal by the bar of the license revocation, the appellate court made two points: (1) By selling him drinks after he was intoxicated, the bar had participated in the disturbance that he caused, and (2) if the police had been called to eject him rather than having a bar employee do it, he would not have been allowed to drive, *Chestnut Tree v. Duffy*, 528, N.Y. 2d 723 (New York, 1988). Also in New York, a 52-day suspension of an on-premises liquor license and the forfeiture of a $1,000 bond for selling alcohol to minors was upheld, *Rumors Disco v. State Liquor Authority*, 524 N.Y.S. 2d 257 (New York, 1988).

Backing Up Alcohol Servers

If an alcohol server at a bar decides that a patron should not be furnished further drinks because of apparent intoxication, it is important for the manager to back up the bartender, not the patron. In a Pennsylvania case, a bartender refused to serve further drinks to a patron. The manager ordered further drinks to be served, but the bartender still refused and was fired. The bartender then sued for wrongful discharge. Being successful in her primary suit, the question then arose as to whether she can also get punitive damages if she can prove that the discharge was done ". . . with a reckless indifference to the interest of the employee, or for a bad motive." Many states had said "yes" to this question, but Pennsylvania had not. This federal court ruled that a federal judge could predict how a state court would rule if confronted by such a situation. The award of punitive damages was allowed to stand because the federal court felt that a state court would do likewise in this case. So, failing to back up the alcohol server became very expensive indeed for the bar, *Woodman v. AMF Leisureland*, 842 F. 2d 699 (Pennsylvania, 1988).

Bar House Rule

Employees at the Casa Del Torero were permitted to have drinks at the inn bar after their shifts ended. If such an employee then becomes intoxicated and injures himself or herself, is the bar relieved of liability? The court in Oregon said "no," effectively bringing an end to that house rule, *Dutch v. Pac-Sam, Inc.*, 778 P. 2d 969 (Oregon, 1989). In a Texas case, a cocktail waitress became severely intoxicated at the end of her shift and died in a one-car crash on the way home. The Texas court said that ". . . the duty is the same whether the foreseeable injury involves the drunkard himself [or herself] or a third party who may be in a place of peril because of that person's condition." In remanding this case for retrial, the Texas appeals court decision made it clear that it did not absolve the dead employee from responsibility. At retrial the jury would have to determine the percentages of negligence to be charged to the bar and the employee, *Pastor v. Champs,* 750 S.W. 2d 335 (Texas, 1988). Texas is in the ranks of the comparative negligence states.

A few other suggestions can be made about effective bar management based upon other court rulings. In inns that have more than one bar, a good management policy is to rotate bartenders at designated time periods. This will reduce opportunities for collusion with cocktail waitresses, failing to collect for drinks, working with prostitutes, gambling, and other detrimental things that can take place at bars. While such a policy may be resisted by bartenders, especially if they know that one bar is more profitable to them than another, the rotation policy has sound legal basis and should be considered by management.

The inn often serves as the entertainment center for the community in which it is located. This in turn means that persons of all ages can be expected to turn up there on a typical evening and often do. This makes it important, as a legal matter, that under-age persons be kept away from bars. Techniques that are becoming popular are the "color coded" wrist bracelets issued at the time that admission fees are paid, or the use of wrist stamps. Red gets you into the bar, black gets you to the game room with the other kids.

Dram-Shop Proportionate Liability

When more than one bar becomes involved in dram-shop payouts, a wise provision to include in the agreement between the bars is that each bar reserves the right to litigate its proportionate liability. In this manner, the plaintiff is removed from the picture. Then if evidence arises that the sharing had not been correct, it can be litigated as a separate matter between the bars.

Insurance Coverage

In third-party liability cases, it may well be that insurance coverage will not apply. In *Shefield's Insurance v. Lighthouse,* 763 P. 2d 669 (Montana, 1988), the court said ". . . we hold that coverage is specifically excluded by the language of the policy." That means that the bar is going to have to pay the damages out of assets of the bar without being able to look to their insurance carrier. As we saw in Chapter 21, this can come about because of the distinction between an attack (a criminal act) and a tort (a civil wrong). Legal scrutiny of insurance policies being purchased for the bar is always in order. Yet in practice, it is difficult for managers and even lawyers to understand what insurance policies say. A suggested technique is to ask the one selling the insurance a question such as, "Will this policy cover us in the event of a tort as well as a criminal act?" If the agent says that it will, it would be well to reduce that representation to writing and to attach it to the policy. In a later court dispute over what is or what is not covered by the policy, that letter might be nice to have. Many agents carry malpractice insurance on themselves. In the event their representations may later prove to be wrong and the insurance does not cover the occurrence, an action will then remain against the agent.

Leaving our brief review of rules and management guidelines, mention of recent legislative actions on third-party liability, both pro and con, will provide some insights and close the subject as well.

LEGISLATURES AND DRAM-SHOP LAWS

The blood-alcohol percentage used by the police in our various states was fairly well established at 0.10 percent. In a 175-pound person, this would require about one dram of 80 proof alcohol in the blood stream. Most state statutes have followed this percentage, but that is changing. In 1989, the Vermont senate reduced their level to 0.05, requiring one-half less drinking to be legally intoxicated. The Illinois legislature has banned "ladies' nights" and "happy hours." The Illinois Dram Shop Act also permits those who are injured by drunks to sue those who caused the intoxication. In that state, however, there is an exception. If the injured person is "guilty of complicity" in the intoxication, that person is barred from recovery. This is known as the "doctrine of complicity," *Steremberg v. SirLoin, Inc.*, 539 N.E. 2d 294 (Illinois, 1989).

The Missouri statute requires that the alcohol server first be convicted of selling to minors, or obviously intoxicated persons, before civil liability can attach to the server. This law leaves open the question of the right of injured third parties to have access to the court. The law is probably unconstitutional.

In 1988, the California legislature made an attempt to reintroduce dram-shop liability in that state. It had been stricken by previous court decisions. The effort came in the form of Assembly Bill 2495 and it failed to pass. An attempt by the New Mexico legislature at Santa Fe to set a limit of $50,000 in dram-shop cases was struck down by the New Mexico Supreme Court. The court felt that such limits lacked constitutional validity because they worked to the disadvantage of those injured or killed by persons who were illegally intoxicated. To say it another way, the court was saying that one injured by an unintoxicated driver could get a full recovery, while one injured by a drunk driver would be limited to $50,000. That would not be equal protection and the ruling makes good legal sense.

Leaving third-party liability, other lesser legal matters are involved in the operation of bars but they too affect management decisions.

Number of Bars

Many cities in the United States, such as Henderson, Nevada, limit the number of bars that can be located within the city limits. The city ordinance there limits bars to one for every 3,500 residents. With a 1991 population of 55,000, that works out to about 15 bars. Under this law, if the population reaches 150,000, and it is predicted that it might do just that by the year 2000, there will still be a limit of forty-three bar licenses issued. Bars there must also be at least 1500 feet from churches and schools. The previous city ordinance had specified 500 feet. Additionally, this law requires that bars that have 200 or more slot machines must also have 120 inn rooms or more.

In Chapter 21, we encountered the name situation with restaurants. The same problem exists at bars.

The Name Problem Applies to Bars

Two persons in Albany, New York, by the names of Mickey Colarusso and Mickey Vish, decided to use their first names on the sign outside of their bar. They had a sign created with a mouse on it dressed in a jacket and top hot, and called it "Mickey's Mousetrap." Walt Disney Productions, Inc., brought an injunction suit against them. The two Mickeys then added sunglasses and a moustache to their mouse but it did not satisfy the Disney lawyers or the court. An Alabama case involving an inn and its bars illustrates just how serious the name problem can be in court.

Trademark infringement damages are measured by determining the actual loss and then multiplying that figure by three. In this case, where an inn had continued to use the Ramada Inn name after the franchise had been terminated, the court allowed $15,000 to "restore Ramada's reputation"; $23,000 in lost franchise fees during the period in which the inn continued to use the Ramada name; interest of over $3,000; $5,000 to develop a new franchise in the area; all multiplied by three, which came to over $140,000 for the trademark infringement, *Ramada Inn, Inc. v. Cadsen Motel*, 804 F. 2d 1562 (Alabama, 1986).

A final example of how the bar can get into expensive legal difficulty is illustrated by what happened at the MGM Grand Hotel, at Reno Nevada. The following Associated Press news item tells the story.

> Associated Press
>
> RENO—Three people have filed objections to a proposed settlement of a lawsuit charging the MGM Grand Hotel with serving watered-down drinks and recycling leftover liquor.
>
> "The proposed settlement is not punitive," Cynthia and Dave Koepp complained in a written objection filed with Washoe District Judge Grant Bowen. "This settlement is ludicrous."
>
> Bowen has scheduled a hearing Friday to decide whether to approve the settlement. Under its terms, anyone who was served a drink at the Reno MGM between August 1978 and September 1979 is eligible to receive two free drinks at the hotel, or to attend a cocktail show for half-price.
>
> According to the lawsuit, filed by six disgruntled customers, bartenders at the Grand served certain fancy drinks without any alcohol, served cheaper brands of alcohol in place of more expensive brands, and saved unfinished drinks so the liquor could be served again.
>
> An estimated 1.8 million customers are believed to have purchased drinks during the one-year period covered by the suit.
>
> The Koepps, of Ventura, Calif., and Paul Hoydic of Whittier, Calif., were the only customers to file objections to the proposed settlement. Copies of the agreement were published in newspapers so that hotel customers could respond to the proposal.
>
> The Koepps and Hoydic apparently wrote their letters in conjunction with each other. Their letters were written in the same typeface, and said almost precisely the same thing.
>
> The three customers complained that it was unfair to require them to travel to the hotel to collect their compensation, and also said that not enough of an award was being offered by the hotel.
>
> They said the two-drink offer being made in the settlement was no greater than free drink offers made by many casinos to attract customers. "It is typical of all casinos to offer such 'come ons' to get people inside their doors," Hoydic wrote.
>
> The letters also complained that there was no assurance the MGM had mended its ways since the drink scandal. The hotel paid a $125,000 civil penalty to the federal Bureau of Alcohol, Tobacco and Firearms in January 1980 after admitting it had refilled and altered the contents of liquor bottles.

Of major importance at any bar is knowing how the law describes a "minor," and then determining who those persons are when they seek admittance to the bar. At the beginning of the 1980s, state law was varied in regard to age of majority, with ages running from 18 to 21, plus related rules that made exceptions for those who were married and the like. As could happen in other areas of inn law, it took action by Congress to get all of these states laws into a uniform position. This is how it happened.

Federal Drinking Law

In 1983 and the first part of 1984, leaders of the HRI industry and Congress were engaged in a fierce argument on the pros and cons of the enactment of a proposed federal drinking bill that would eventually force the drinking age to twenty-one in all of the states.

Proponents of the bill wanted the legal drinking age raised to twenty-one, while opponents cited many reasons why this should not be done. The opponents had been joined by the Reagan administration in opposing the legislation but the administration changed its position early in 1984.

Those who were in favor of the bill spoke of the varying laws that created "blood borders" as young persons traveled across state lines to purchase alcoholic beverages.

Statistics were produced to show that increases in the legal drinking age had reduced alcohol-related deaths in some instances, yet statistics from Florida and Maine displayed the opposite result.

Among the reasons that prompted foodservice executives to oppose the law was the fact that 1 million youths would lose their jobs since they would not be able to work as bartenders until they reached the age of twenty-one years. Another reason was the loss of tax revenues.

At the time of the hearings, twenty-three states had set the drinking age at twenty-one with four of them having raised it in 1983.

After the arguments, hearings, debates, and other action, the law became effective in June of 1984.

As of May 1, 1986, the District of Columbia plus ten states had not complied with the federal mandate. Another twenty states had failed in one degree or another to comply. Noncompliance cost the states millions of dollars after the October 1, 1986 deadline.

In 1987, by a vote of 7 to 2, the U.S. Supreme Court upheld the constitutionality of the law. The law had been challenged by South Dakota as being in violation of the Twenty-first Amendment, which had given the states powers to control liquor distribution within their respective borders. The main point of the high court was that different drinking ages prompted young persons to cross state borders to purchase where age limits were lower. This in turn created an interstate safety problem which Congress had the power to address. South Dakota and Colorado then set their age limit to 21. The last two holdout states were Ohio and Wyoming. Thus the lawful drinking age in the United States is uniform at twenty-one.

In the following case, a patron sued the tavern owner for injuries caused to him by an intoxicated patron. Pay attention to what the court had to say about the duty of the tavern operator, through himself, his agents, and employees, to protect patrons from each other. This particular tavern is located in what is known as a "tough" part of Seattle.

REIBOLDT V. BEDIENT
Wash. App. 562 P. 2d 991 (1977)

SWANSON, Judge

On the evening of Sunday, September 16, 1973, Wilbur Reiboldt, along with several of his friends, journeyed to the Anchor Inn Tavern in the Pioneer Square area of Seattle to enjoy a program of live music. While Reiboldt was engaged in setting up his recording equipment, he was twice approached by an allegedly intoxicated Indian named Half Moon who tried to solicit free drinks from Reiboldt. On each occasion, Reiboldt informed Half Moon that he was not an employee of the tavern but, rather, was merely a patron. After the second attempt at "bumming" free drinks from Reiboldt, Half Moon attacked Reiboldt by striking him alongside the head. As a result of this blow, Reiboldt was thrust to the floor but managed in a dazed condition to stagger to his feet. Immediately upon reaching his feet, Reiboldt was again struck by Half Moon. This second attack caused Reiboldt to fall to the floor unconscious. At this point, Half Moon allegedly kicked Reiboldt causing him to suffer a broken leg. During the entire incident which, according to the witnesses, lasted from approximately 5 to 15 minutes, Albert R. Bedient, the tavern owner, was tending to his duties behind the bar. His testimony adduced at trial indicated that he had no knowledge of the supposed drunken nature of Half Moon, nor did he know of any complaints registered by any patrons concerning potential violence. Bedient testified that as soon as his attention was drawn to the altercation, he immediately went to the scene, but by the time he got there the fight was over. On the other hand, there was testimony introduced on behalf of Mr. Reiboldt that Bedient knew of Half Moon's intoxicated condition prior to the time of the incident and had, in fact, demanded Half Moon's departure from the Anchor Inn Tavern earlier that same day. There was also testimony which the jury could have believed which indicated that Bedient refused to respond to cries for help from the various patrons of the tavern.

Wilbur Reiboldt subsequently brought this action for personal injuries against Albert Bedient and the Anchor Inn Tavern, alleging that he had sustained serious bodily injuries in Bedient's tavern and that Bedient had been negligent in failing to protect his patrons from harm and injury. The jury returned a verdict of $75,000 in Reiboldt's favor. Bedient then timely sought a judgment notwithstanding the verdict or, in the alternative, a new trial, which was granted. Reiboldt appeals from the order granting a new trial, and Bedient cross-appeals.

Turning first to the claims made by appellant Reiboldt, the trial court gave the following reasons for granting a new trial:

> 1. Defendant's argument on the question of contributory negligence is not valid. There is something to it, but not enough.
>
> 2. This is a very thin case of liability. The only evidence whatever on the subject of negligence was that of Janet Charles. [In lower record.]
>
> 3. The size of the verdict, although not shocking, was astounding. It was at least five times greater than it should have been.
>
> 4. Although the court is hard put to put any single factor down that would warrant the granting of a new trail, it is the feeling of the court that justice has miscarried and that a new trial should be granted.

Reiboldt contends that the reasons stated by the trial court in its order was inadequate to grant a new trial. We agree and reverse.

The entry of a new trial is governed by CR 59. The trial court's order appears to include only two of the possible nine grounds stated in CR 59 for granting a new trial:

(a)(5) Damages so excessive or inadequate as unmistakably to indicate that the verdict must have been the result of passion or prejudice;

(a)(9) That substantial justice has not been done.

However, the order itself fails to comply with the requirements of CR 59(f):

In all cases where the trial court grants a motion for a new trial, it shall, in the order granting the motion, state whether the order is based upon the record or upon facts and circumstances outside the record which cannot be made a part thereof. If the order is based upon the record, the court shall give definite reasons of law and facts for its order. If the order is based upon matters outside the record, the court shall state the facts and circumstances upon which it relied.

The order expresses reasons or opinions which provide little or no assistance respecting appellate review of this case. We can only conclude that the trial judge simply disagreed with the jury, and this is not sufficient.

In order to uphold, as a basis for a new trial, a trial court's belief that the verdict is too high, the order must contain a finding that the amount awarded by the jury was "so excessive . . . as unmistakably to indicate that the verdict must have been resulting of passion or prejudice." CR 59(a)(5). Such a finding is absent from the order under review. As stated in *James v. Robeck,* 79 Wash. 2d 864, 870, 490 P.2d 878, 882 (1971),

[I]t is our opinion that the rule now and for some time prevailing in this jurisdiction requires that the passion and prejudice be of such manifest clarity as to make it unmistakable.

Our review of the record does not support a conclusion that the jury verdict was so high as unmistakably to indicate passion or prejudice. Moreover, there exists a strong presumption of the adequacy of jury verdicts, see RCW 4.76-.030; *Cox v. Charles Wright Academy, Inc.*, 70 Wash.2d 173, 422 P.2d 515 (1967), and the trial court is precluded, absent a showing of passion or prejudice, from substituting its conclusion for that of the jury on the issue of damages.

With regard to the second reason for granting a new trial stated in the order, "the feeling of the court that justice has miscarried," we are hard pressed to accept such a ground as adequate, especially in light of the provisions of CR 59(f) which require that the order granting a new trial "state, whether the order is based upon the record or upon facts and circumstances outside the record which cannot be made a part thereof." If we assume that the order is based upon matters outside the record, the order fails to contain the facts and circumstances upon which it relied, as required by the rule. On the other hand, if we assume that the order is based upon the record, the rule requires that the court give "definite reasons of law and facts for its order." CR 59(f). We must conclude that the order provides no adequate basis for review of the asserted "failure of substantial justice" as a ground for new trial. See *Knecht v. Marzano, supra.*

[Citation omitted.]

Next, we consider the arguments advanced by respondent in his cross-appeal. Essentially, he contends that the trial court erred in failing to direct a verdict in his favor both at the close of the plaintiff's case and at the close of all the evidence. A motion for a directed verdict admits the truth of the evidence of the party against whom the motion is made and all inferences that reasonably can be drawn therefrom. In addition, such a motion therefrom requires that the evidence be interpreted most strongly against the moving party and in the light most favorable to the opposing party. It is also a well-recognized rule in this state that in ruling upon a motion for a directed verdict, no element of discretion is involved and the trial court can grant such a motion only when it can be held as a matter of law that there is no evidence, nor reasonable inference from the evidence, to sustain the verdict. In evaluating the evidence introduced, and all reasonable inferences arising therefrom, the trial court must determine whether the nonmoving party has presented substantial evidence establishing a *prima facie* case in support of its claim. After carefully reviewing the record, we find sufficient evidence which could, if believed by the jury, support plaintiff Reiboldt's theory that the owner of the Anchor Inn breached his duty to exercise reasonable care and vigilance to protect patrons from reasonably foreseeable injury. We find no error in the trial court's denial of respondent's motion for a directed verdict.

Respondent next contends that the trial court erred when it refused to give a requested instruction on contributory negligence. A careful review of the record indicates no evidence upon which to base an instruction on contributory negligence. We find no error.

Finally, respondent argues that the trial court erred when it refused to grant it motion *in limine.* [A motion made to limit testimony; to decide what can or cannot be testified to at trial.]

In *State v. Morgan,* 192 Wash. 425, 430, 73. P.2d 745, 747 (1937), our Supreme Court ruled that

> [i]n the exercise of its sound discretion, the [trial] court could refuse to go into the matter in advance of the offer of evidence, in regular course, during the trial, and no error can be predicated upon this ruling.

It is, therefore, a matter of discretion as to whether or not a motion, prior to trial, to limit the evidence will be granted. Furthermore, in the instant case the respondent cross-appellant had ample opportunity to object to testimony as it was presented that he felt was irrelevant to the issue under litigation. Moreover, respondent Bedient has directed us to only four instances where allegedly prejudicial evidence was offered into evidence. After carefully reviewing each occurrence, we note that the cumulative effect of the supposed extraneous evidence was not prejudicial to respondent's case. Furthermore, in all the instances cited to us by the respondent, the trial court sustained objections to the introduction of irrelevant testimony when asked to do so. We cannot say that the trial court abused its discretion in this matter.

The order granting a new trial is reversed, and the cause is remanded for reinstatement of the verdict and entry of a judgment consistent with the verdict.

CALLOW and ANDERSEN, JJ., concur.

All in all, a bad day for the tavern owner because of his failure to exercise reasonable care, through his agents and employees, to protect patrons from foreseeable injury.

Many other novel legal matters have come up in the operation of taverns and more can be expected in the future. An example was the question of whether a bar operator had a duty to accede to a robbery in order to prevent patrons from being injured or killed.

Duty to Comply with Robber?

The Court of Appeals of Arizona has held that a barkeeper's primary duty of making his premises reasonably safe for his patrons does not encompass an additional duty not to increase the risk of criminal activity by complying with demands of a robber. It therefore upheld the trial court in denying damages for injury and death to patrons which occurred when a bartender, confronted with an armed robber demanding that he turn over the money in the cash register, replied "go ahead and shoot me, you are not getting my money." The robber complied, killing the bartender with four shots, injuring one patron and killing another. The Court pointed out that a contrary holding would dissuade proprietors from offering resistance to armed robbers because of the constant fear of civil suit, and would not provide the desired assurance that the risk to an invitee would be substantially reduced; the only persons who would clearly benefit from the imposition of such a duty would be the criminals themselves.[23]

QUESTIONS

1. Explain why there is a legal difference today between the laws of inns and the laws of restaurants and taverns.
2. *Per curium* means "by the court." What is the legal importance of knowing if an opinion was written by the entire court or by only one judge?
3. The law has traditionally placed a premium upon definitions. Give one reason why it is important, as a matter of law, to know if a business establishment is a restaurant or not?
4. What was a "dram shop" under early English law? What is a "dram-shop law" today?
5. The laws that regulate the consumption of alcoholic beverages are being developed in two primary places. What are they?
6. What did the federal laws on the drinking age finally accomplish in the United States?
7. Why did dram-shop laws that create third-party liability not develop until this century?
8. Why was the original Magna Carta written on sheepskin and in Latin? Would the copy purchased by the Texas businessman be written on sheepskin and be in Latin?

Would he have had the authenticity of that item established before he paid $1.5 million for it?

9. What did "cooperage" mean in an earlier England? Might a person today whose name is Cooper have roots back to those years?
10. Why did early bars become places to post legal notices, proclamations, and other information?

ENDNOTES

1. *Coffman v. Kennedy,* 141 Cal Rptr. 267 (Cal. App. 1977).
2. *Grasser v. Fleming,* 253 N.W. 2d 757 (Michigan, 1977).
3. *Las Vegas Review Journal,* July 13, 1983.
4. *Las Vegas Review Journal,* December 6, 1982.
5. *Nevada v. Rosenthal,* 559 P. 2d 830 (1977), at p. 40-41.
6. Uniform Commercial Code, Article 2, section 314.
7. UCC, *supra.*
8. *Grasser v. Fleming, supra.*
9. *Rapport v. Nichols,* 31 N.J. 188, 156 A. 2d 1 (1959).
10. Rapport, *supra.*
11. Rapport, *supra.*
12. N*evada Beverage Index*, 1983, p. E-17.
13. National Safety Council, *Accident Facts*, p. 49, 1959 Edition.
14. Rapport, *supra.*
15. *Thomas v. Bohelman,* 86 Nev. 10, 13, 462 P. 2d 1020, 1022 (1970), emphasis added.
16. *Rapport,* supra.
17. *Berkeley v. Park,* 47 Misc. 2d 381, 262 N.Y.S. 2d 290 (Sup. Ct. Otsego Co. 1965).
18. Section 11-101, McKinney Sup. 1978.
19. *Mitchell v. Shoals, Inc.,* 280 N.Y.S. 2d 113 (1967).
20. *Konig v. N.C.O. Ry.,* 36 Nev. 181, 214-215, 135 P. 1, 141, 153 (1913).
21. Nevada Beverage Index, *supra* at p. E-20.
22. N.Y. Alco. Bev. Cont. Law, section 65(c) McKinney Supp. 1982.
23. *Bennett v. Estate of Baker,* 557 P. 195.

23

Travel Agents and Agencies

Ramses II, the Pharaoh of the exodus, was a great builder. His father began and he completed the sprawling palace on the bank of the River Nile that the Egyptians called "The Great House," or in their own language, pharaoh. *In time the kings of Egypt, being inseparable from this great house, took on its name and thus became the Pharaohs.*

Ramses' lust for stone, size, and rock-ribbed immortality knew no limits. He built that giant statue of himself in the desert that Shelley described in "Ozymandias." He built walled cities, colonnaded temples, and even islands in the Nile. He carved tombs out of the red rock of the Nile escarpments until he was well into his eighties, he built with fury, frenzy, and unremitting compulsion.

The Jews, Howard Fast

OVERVIEW

Here we shift our attention to a segment of the HRI industry that has been growing in legal importance during the past decade. This has been true because lawyers have begun to shift losses and travel disappointments at far-off destinations back to those who sold the vacation package that went sour.

A helpful way to begin is by examining two paragraphs from a law book written by a leading plaintiff's attorney who is specializing in travel litigation. In these paragraphs we have an opportunity to see one professional discussing legal strategy with other professionals. The footnotes are credited to that author also.

> In discussing reported travel cases, it should be noted that many courts focus on establishing the nature of the relationship between the parties. Once such a relationship is identified, the courts will then find duties and standards which traditionally flow from such

McPherson County Courthouse, McPherson, Kansas.

> relationships. Four different relationships are usually found. First, some courts have found that the travel agent is the agent of the supplier, wholesaler, or tour operator.[1] Second, some courts have found the travel agent to be the agent of the traveler.[2] Third, some courts have viewed the relationship between the traveler and travel agent as contractual in nature with the travel agent as the principal.[3] Fourth, some courts have viewed the travel agent as a broker in the business of assisting in the creation of bilateral contracts.[4] This latter relationship has been referred to as transactional analysis.[5]
>
> The focus on traditional relationships has generated much judicial confusion and has often generated unjust decisions. Travel cases should be decided on an *ad hoc* basis relying upon transactional analysis of the facts.[6] The facts of the case should include not only what transpired between the traveler and the middleman but also (1) facts establishing the functional relationship between the travel entities involved,[7] (2) facts demonstrating the knowledge which the middleman possesses or should possess,[8] and (3) facts and admissions identifying the standards of care which are applicable, whether self-imposed through education[9] or trade associations[10] or imposed by statute[11] and by the courts.[12]

Thus we see a legal travel expert discussing his craft with his contemporaries. With this as a beginning point, let's make some observations about travelers and their needs.

Travelers vary from person to person in their wishes, needs, wants, and travel objectives. Some are truly seasoned travelers; others are novices in the travel realm. Many lack the most basic information about visas and health requirements to travel in foreign nations, and most cannot speak a second language. Thus they are in need, as a class, of information about customs in the states and in foreign nations; they need help with currency exchange, and advice about clothing and climatic conditions. There is an obvious need for someone to provide such information and assistance. This has come to pass in the last decade through the expanding services being offered by travel agents and agencies.

The services that have been provided to travelers have been quite good in most instances. Yet some of those services have formed the basis for lawsuits. Lawyers look for anything that may imply or establish a special promise by a travel agent to an injured traveler. An example would be an oral representation about the quality of the trip package that was purchased, or perhaps some symbol, desk sign, button, or patch that would lead the traveler to believe that the travel agent was the agent of someone else.[13] All of this is part of a legal warfare that is being waged against travel agents.

In the past, travel agents operated with little fear of the consequences of their acts because seldom did an injured traveler come after them for compensation. This was so because there had been no concentrated legal effort to bring them into litigation or to have them answer for the defaults of others. This has now changed and a new field of litigation is opening up against travel agents and their agencies. So long as travel agents were permitted to run their operations without fear of legal liability, the legal picture developed one way. Now that the fear of money loss is a strong reality, the legal picture is taking on new forms. It is to those new patterns that we want to direct our attention.

A topic of growing interest in the travel and lodging industry is the legal liability of those who serve as "travel conduits" between one who is planning to travel and those who provide the travel, lodging, and entertainment at the destination. Such persons, or firms, are known as "travel agents"—although the use of the word "agents" leaves a lot to be cleared up in the legal sense.

In the customary situation, the traveler (who in most instances is a consumer, yet may be combining business with a pleasure trip) seeks the advice and services of the travel agent. The traveler sets forth the proposed trip, providing a general idea of time, destination, and desired price range, and what he or she wants to accomplish on the trip. The travel agent then makes arrangements with a wholesale travel agent, and air, rail, or sea carriers; then coordinates with innkeepers at the destination and makes the necessary reservations there. In addition the travel agent often sets up tour plans for the traveler. For these services, the travel agent charges a fee, usually a percentage of the deposits required by wholesale travel agents, inns, and others. These deposits are eventually forwarded to the wholesale agent and those at the destination, minus the agreed percentage retained by the travel agent as per the agreement between the travel agent and the wholesale agent.

Thus we find at least four and perhaps five persons or firms involved in this process:

1. The direct-sale travel agent who deals with the traveler face to face.
2. The wholesale travel agent who is contacted by the direct sales agent. (In many instances, wholesale agents are bypassed.)
3. The innkeeper.
4. The airline, railroad, or shipping line, or a combination of them, referred to as "carrier."
5. Tour operators at the destination, whom we will call "guides."

Obviously, in such a multiple-party undertaking many things can go wrong. Funds may not be forwarded as promised; lodging may not be available upon arrival; guides may fail to materialize as planned; carriers may not meet the required timetables; and worst of all, injury or death may occur to the traveler in the process.

SOME BASICS

First, it is helpful to examine some of the legal basics involved in this relationship. We will then look at cases in which disputes have arisen.

"Sale" or Not?

To begin with, does an agent "sell" a traveler a trip package within the "UCC Sales" meaning of that word? This is an important question. In the absence of the furnishing of food or drink, the answer appears to be "no." A "service" rather than a "sale" is provided. Next, what standard of care is a travel agent held to?

Standard of Care

Both direct-sale and wholesale travel agents are held by the courts to the standards of knowledge and skill that could be expected of the reasonable person who is engaged in that business. Failure to meet these standards could result in legal liability just as in other areas of inn law.

Prior Experience

If an agent has had unfavorable experiences with those at the destination, that information should be made available to the traveler. If the agent has had no previous experience, a duty exists to make reasonable inquiry about accommodations at the destination as part of the service to the traveler. In the travel industry, some parts of the world are known as "hot spots."

Failure to Make Inquiry

Failure to make inquiry about destinations and travel routes that travelers are being sent to could and often is held by the courts to be negligence. After all, this is part of the services that the travel agent is providing. This is true even though there is usually no direct money payment by the traveler to the travel agent. If it is found in court that this negligence is the proximate cause of the loss suffered by the traveler during the trip, the legal results are obvious.

Travel agents have a duty at law to confirm reservations that are being made for the traveler. In addition they are being held responsible to confirm the contractual obligations of tour operators and wholesale travel agents. This latter duty approaches strict liability because there are few excuses acceptable for failure to do so. A travel agent is no longer a ticket seller—although that is what they were until about two decades ago—and they are moving into a closer legal relationship with those whom they serve. While such increasing obligations place additional costs on the travel agent, these burdens must be taken into consideration as part of the costs of doing business.

Constructive Fraud

Several courts have held that a special relationship exists between a travel agent or agency and the traveler.[14] Because of this relationship, it is possible for a case to be brought against the travel agent for constructive fraud. This type of fraud was defined in *Brown v. Lockwood.*[15]

> Constructive fraud may be defined as a breach of a duty which, irrespective of moral guilt and intent, the law declares fraudulent because of its tendency to deceive, to violate a confidence or to injure public or private interests which the law deems worthy of special protection. . . . The elements of a cause of action to recover for constructive fraud are the same as those to recover for

> actual fraud with the crucial exception that the element of *scienter* upon the part of the defendant, his knowledge of the falsity of his representation, is dropped and is replaced by a requirement that the plaintiff prove the existence of a fiduciary or confidential relationship warranting the trusting party to repose his confidence in the defendant and therefore to relax the care and vigilance he would ordinarily exercise in the circumstances. The law regards the making of a misrepresentation by a defendant who possesses a position of superiority and influence over the plaintiff by reason of the confidential relationship between them as a breach of duty actionable as constructive fraud. . . .

Since the courts are finding a special relationship between travelers and travel agents, what is the duty of the agent to enter the relationship in the beginning?

Duty to Accept?

While an innkeeper must accept all guests, the same is *not* true of the travel agent. A travel agent may turn down potential travelers as he or she may choose.

Not an Insurer

In addition, a travel agent is not an insurer of the safety of the traveler—and certainly does not want to be. But as previously mentioned, if the agent knows of risks or has reason to know of them, they must be brought to the attention of the traveler. The failure to do so may create responsibility on the part of the agent to the traveler who suffers a loss because of those risks.

The problems that we have been discussing have resulted in new regulations on the travel agent business.

REGULATION OF THE INDUSTRY

The travel-agent industry came in for some black eyes in the early 1970s. The result was an increased demand for controls. In the past, due to a relatively low demand for such services, there was little regulation. Today there is the American Society of Travel Agents, that has served the industry well for many years and has done all it could to protect travel agents, as well as travelers. At the federal level, the Federal Trade Commission (FTC) and others had powers—but seldom used them. Such agencies are now active in controlling the activities of travel agents directly and indirectly. This is a direct outgrowth of the consumer protection movement that became so prevalent in the past decades.

New Controls

Late in 1977, the Civil Aeronautical Board issued a proposal that would require the following on all charter travel tours:

1. All payments made in checks, credit-card charges, or money orders would be made payable to an escrow bank—not to the travel agent or tour operator.
2. Advance payments would be banned.

Federal regulation 14 CFR 378a now requires a tour operator to buy a surety (guarantee) bond to make certain of contract performance. Each bond so issued must state that it is issued "subject to 14 CFR 378a."

These bonds are required to ensure the financial responsibility of the tour operator in supplying ". . . the transportation, and all other accommodations, services, and facilities in accordance with the contract between the tour operator . . ." and the tour participants.

Agents or Not?

If a direct sale agent is a true legal "agent" (see Chapter 8) then so long as the identity of the principal (such as a wholesale travel agent, innkeeper, carrier, or guide) is disclosed, there is no contractual obligation on the part of the agent. An agent is not responsible for contracts negotiated for the principal so long as the principal is disclosed.

However, as one examines the basic requirements of an agency relationship, it becomes clear that travel agents often *do not* meet the requirements of a true legal agency. These requirements are four in number:

1. Both the principal or agent must agree to the relationship.
2. The principal must have the right to control the agent.
3. A fiduciary relationship must exist between them.
4. The agent must have the power to bind the principal.

An examination of these requirements makes it clear that in the usual travel situation, at least one and often more of them are not present. The cases that have attempted to construe this topic have not been satisfactory to date.

If a direct sale travel agent does *not* disclose the wholesale agent, the contract of the traveler and the sales agent would be binding upon the agent. This follows the traditional legal liability of an agent who acts for an undisclosed principal. In the following case, the judge placed the matter squarely into the law of agency and held the travel agent responsible for the reservations that went bad.

BUCHOLTZ V. SIROKIN TRAVEL, LTD.
80 Misc. 2d 333, 363 N.Y.S. 2d 415 (1974).

Before HOGAN, P. J., and FARLEY and GAGLIARDI, JJ.
PER CURIAM.

Judgment affirmed without costs.

In this Small Claims action, plaintiff seeks to cast defendant travel agency into damages for reservations that went awry. Since it is undisputed that the travel agency had utilized the services of a wholesaler who had put together a "package tour," defendant contends on this appeal that the wholesaler alone is liable for any default in performance.

Allocation of responsibility in the case before us should proceed upon the principles of agency law. In our opinion, where, as here, there is no proof of an independent relationship between the retail travel agent and the wholesaler, the travel agent should be considered the agent of the customer. If, in using a wholesaler to make the travel arrangements, the travel agent acts with the consent, express or implied, of the principal-customer, then, if reasonable diligence has been used in its selection, the travel agent will not be responsible for any dereliction of duty on the part of the wholesaler. If, on the other hand, the travel agent acts without such consent, he will be responsible to the customer for any damage sustained as a result of the acts of the wholesaler.

The court below, in applying these principles, found that the plaintiff did not consent to the employment of the wholesaler. Although its opinion did not so state, the record indicates that the court also declined to hold that knowledge of the practice of employing wholesalers should be imputed to the plaintiff. We see no reason to disturb this determination. The record supports a finding that plaintiff was not informed of the existence of the wholesaler until after the reservations were agreed upon and it cannot be said that knowledge of this practice is so pervasive among the public as to compel a finding of implied consent.

We find no merit in defendant's remaining contention.

All concur. [Examine Figure 23.1.]

This decision seems clear on its face, yet, as a matter of law, it is not that simple. In this case, the court finds the traveler to be the principal. In practice this normally isn't so because the direct travel agent *is the agent of the wholesale travel agent* and that makes a big difference. Yet the court holds that the travel agent is the agent of the traveler, who is the principal. However, the traveler did not consent to the use of the wholesale travel agent and this fact had a key bearing on the outcome of the case.

The legal question raised in the McQuade case that follows is "To what extent must the travel agent go in disclosing its principal?" In this case we see the consequences that can follow for failing to so disclose.

E.A. MCQUADE TRAVEL AGENCY, INC., V. DOMECK
190 So. 2d 3, Dist. Ct. App. Fla. (1966).

Plaintiffs filed this suit against defendant to recover damages for breach of contract. Plaintiffs alleged that, in consideration of $2,677.50 paid to defendant, defendant agreed to sell plaintiffs two tickets on a certain cruise to Europe. Defendant answered alleging that it received the monies for the benefit of and transmittal to Caribbean Cruise Lines, Inc., a foreign corporation.

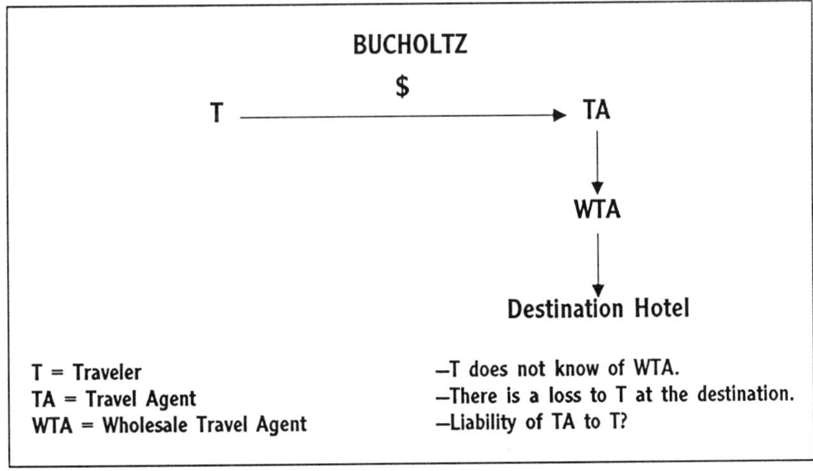

FIGURE 23.1

This cause came before the trial court on stipulated statement of facts to the effect that, on May 12, 1964, the defendant agreed to sell plaintiffs two tickets on a European cruise of the M/S Riviera which was to leave on September 11, 1964; that plaintiffs paid defendant the sum of $2,667.50 on or prior to July 23, 1964. All payments were made to E.A. McQuade Travel Agency, but the tickets were not delivered to the plaintiffs. It is also stipulated that there was no discussion between the plaintiffs and the defendant as to the person or corporation for which the defendant acted as agent, if any, or as to what disposition would be made of the money paid to defendant.

Prior to August 15, 1964, defendant forwarded $2,406.75 to Caribbean Cruise Lines, Inc., the company that was offering the cruise to Europe. On or about August 15, 1964, the plaintiffs and the defendant were informed that the M/S Riviera would not be making the scheduled cruise and that Caribbean Cruise Lines, Inc., had filed bankruptcy.

The plaintiffs requested the defendant to return the money which they had paid for the tickets they did not receive. The defendant has offered to pay to the plaintiffs $266.75 which was its commission but declined to pay any additional monies. [Examine Figure 23.2.]

The original complaint contained a prayer for judgment in the amount of $2,057.50 plus costs. Prior to trial plaintiffs amended their complaint to reflect the exact amount they had paid defendant to be $2,667.50.

The trial court held the defendant liable because it failed to disclose its principal and awarded the plaintiffs $2,057.50 plus costs.

The main question presented for our determination is whether the defendant sufficiently disclosed the identity of its principal, Caribbean Cruise Lines, Inc., by merely revealing the name of the cruise ship, M/S Riviera.

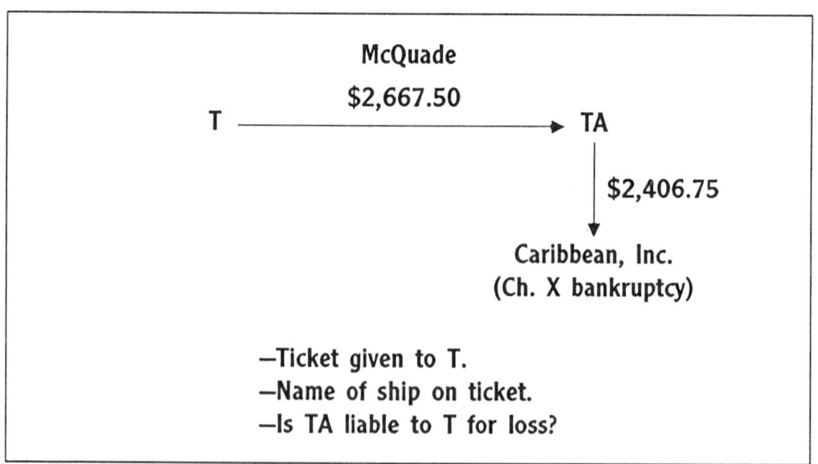

FIGURE 23.2

In our research we failed to find a Florida decision directly on the question of disclosure of principal by an agent. However, the law in other states is well established that the disclosure of agency is not complete for the purpose of relieving the agent from personal liability unless it embraces the name of the principal. The disclosure of the name of the ship is merely the disclosure of a trade name, and is not a disclosure of the identity of the principal. The liability of an agent acting for an undisclosed principal is fully discussed in *Unger v. Travel Arrangements, Inc.*, 1966, 25 A.D.2d 40, 266 N.Y.S.2d 715, a decision involving the same cruise.

We agree with the trial court that the defense of agency does not relieve the defendant from liability. The record supports the trial court's finding that the defendant was an agent of an undisclosed principal and therefore can be held liable. *Hohauser v. Schor,* Fla.App.1958, 101 So.2d 169. We hold that there is sufficient evidence to support the trial court's holding that the defendant breached its contract with plaintiffs by failing to furnish the promised tickets.

The court has carefully considered the other points raised on appeal by appellant and finds them without merit.

Accordingly, we affirm as to liability and reverse as to amount of damages with direction that the judgment be amended to award damages to the plaintiffs in the amount of $2,667.50, plus costs.

SMITH, C. J., and WALDEN, J., concur.

One suggested solution to the generally unsatisfactory attempt to apply agency law to the travel agent and agency is to find that a *double agency* exists. The first comes about between the travel agent and the traveler. The second then comes into being between the travel agent and the wholesale travel agent.

Dual Agents

First, there is the agency between the travel agent and the traveler. As soon as all legal obligations are met by the first agent, such as contacting the wholesale agent, arranging for tickets, and paying over deposits, the first agency has been completed and liability ends there for the first agent. The second agency now comes into being between the traveler and wholesale agent.

In the Levine case, the court found that there were two agencies, one of which came into being and was completed before the other one arose. Examine Figure 23.3. After the purpose of the first agency was completed, the second agency then came into being. The facts in the case explain how this came about.

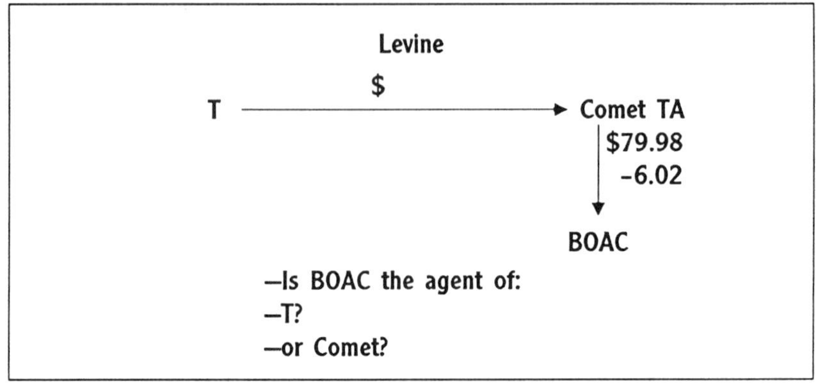

FIGURE 23.3

LEVINE V. BRITISH OVERSEAS AIRWAYS CORPORATION
66 Misc. 2d 820, 322 N.Y.S. 2d 119 (1971)

BENTLEY KASSAL, Judge.

Plaintiffs move for summary judgment against defendants, British Overseas Airways Corporation ("BOAC") and Leo Lazar d/b/a/ Comet Travel Agency ("Comet") to recover the sum of $86 as a refund for a portion of two airline tickets returned unused to BOAC. Comet failed to appear in this action. BOAC does not dispute that plaintiffs are entitled to the refund, but asserts in opposition to this motion that "pursuant to airline custom and regulation," it paid the claimed amount, less the travel agent's commission, to Comet, as "agent" for plaintiffs, and is thus no longer liable to plaintiffs. BOAC's answer however, does not refer to Comet as plaintiffs' agent but states that BOAC paid the money to Comet pursuant to the said IATA regulations, contract and industry custom.

The essential facts are not in dispute; the issue to be resolved is whether Comet was plaintiffs' agent in this transaction, and, if so, whether payment to Comet discharged BOAC from further liability for the refund.

The facts are these: On September 3, 1970, plaintiffs purchased two round-trip BOAC tickets from Comet for this trip—New York/London/Amsterdam/Copenhagen/Stockholm/London/New York. On September 30, 1970, pursuant to BOAC instructions, plaintiff Robert Levine sent the two unused portions of the tickets directly to BOAC for a refund. His accompanying letter is as follows: "We are enclosing herewith two (2) tickets (BEA No. 6942777 and No. 6942778), each for a refund in the sum of $43. Kindly forward your check in the sum of $86 to me at your earliest convenience, and oblige."

BOAC, having determined that plaintiffs were entitled to a refund, sent back a form letter acknowledging plaintiffs' request and advising them that the claim had been processed through "your travel agents," who would make the final settlement with them. Simultaneously, BOAC sent a check to Comet, made to Comet's order, for $79.98, the refund due, less Comet's retained commission of $6.02. This check was negotiated by Comet on October 13, 1970, but no payment has ever been received by plaintiffs.

In January, plaintiffs again wrote to BOAC to demand the refund. On January 19,1971, the day this action was instituted, BOAC wrote Comet enclosing a photocopy of its check and requesting that plaintiffs be paid. Since that time, BOAC has repeatedly contacted Comet to make payment to plaintiffs, without avail.

In its answer BOAC does not cite any specific regulations of the International Air Transport Association, a voluntary association of international air carriers, or any binding custom, to substantiate its claim that it has satisfied its obligation of payment by making the refund to the travel agent. Nor do I have knowledge of any IATA regulations regarding such refunds.

It is understandable, however, that BOAC and other airlines may have adopted this practice for their own benefit as the most convenient and feasible method of repayment since the travel agent retains a commission on the sale. But such practice, established unilaterally, could not bind plaintiffs or exonerate BOAC from liability to plaintiffs, simply on the ground of its being their own usual procedure. Plaintiffs returned their tickets directly to BOAC, not through their travel agent. They were not in the travel business, and no custom existed between them and BOAC or any other airline as to any further involvement of the travel agent beyond the initial purchase and issuance of the original BOAC tickets. Furthermore, the instructions in plaintiffs' letter are explicit to that effect. "Kindly forward your check in the sum of $86 *to me . . .*" [emphasis added]. Thus, the fact that BOAC might have followed its usual "custom" will not immunize it from liability to plaintiffs, especially in view of plaintiffs' express instructions.

The other theory on which BOAC relies is one of agency. It claims that its obligation has been discharged because a travel agent is the agent of the traveler and thus payment to the agent constitutes payment to the traveler, his principal. Plaintiffs, on the contrary, consider Comet to be BOAC's agent.

When a person goes to a travel agency to book transportation and other arrangements with a vague request such as "Get me a flight to London on the 15th and hotel reservations", it may very well be in that situation that the travel agent, who is essentially a "broker", becomes the traveler's agent; under those circumstances, he is not the agent of the airline, even though he may have a supply of blank official tickets supplied by them. At most, the travel broker is an agent for an undisclosed principal and the agent alone is responsible to the traveler; the airline only becomes liable if it ratifies the transaction made by the broker.

In my opinion, once plaintiffs' initial purchase of the tickets from Comet had been satisfactorily completed, any possible agency relationship which may have existed between them was thereupon terminated. Having used only a portion of their tickets, plaintiffs were entitled to a refund, whether they had purchased their tickets from Comet or across a BOAC counter. They chose to deal directly with BOAC, as a disclosed principal, to ask for a refund. They did not deal with Comet and it was not necessary for plaintiffs to return tickets through the travel agency, as BOAC's acceptance implies; nor was it "necessary" for BOAC to return this money via Comet, except for their own convenience and-sole-benefit for accounting purposes to avoid the extra step of having to collect the commission Comet had retained on the ticket sale. Plaintiffs never authorized BOAC to remit the refund in this manner; Comet was not authorized to receive this payment; plaintiffs in no way held out Comet as their agent for this purpose.

Assuming *arguendo* that an agency relationship between plaintiffs and Comet continued after the initial sale of the tickets, this would not *per se* justify BOAC's refund payment since "an agent has no authority to receive payment merely because of the fact that he represented a principal in the transaction out of which the debt arose . . ." Restatement Agency 2d sec. 71, Comment; see also 12 Am.Jur.2d, Brokers sec. 79. Payment to a party who has no authority, actual or apparent, to receive it does not discharge the debtor.

Accordingly, summary judgment is granted against defendant, British Overseas Airways Corporation and against defendant Leo Lazar d/b/a Comet Travel Agency, by default, and judgment may be entered in favor of the plaintiffs for the relief demanded in the complaint.

These cases illustrate the legal complexities as well as the uncertainties that come into play when the courts apply agency law to travel agents and agencies. It is never certain what is going to happen in the end. Therefore, travel agents and agencies are looking for ways to limit their liability. It is not unlike the situation that existed centuries ago when innkeepers began to look for ways to limit the strict liability placed upon them by the common law.

AS INDEPENDENT CONTRACTORS

Direct-sale travel agents are taking legal steps to make it clear that they are *not* agents of the wholesale travel agents or those at the destination. This is being done by the use of conspicuous disclaimers in the contract with the traveler. Thus the direct sales agent is bound by the contract to make the arrangements agreed upon, but makes no promises or warranties as to performance by others or quality of accommodations. This limits the legal liability of the direct-sales agent, leaving the liability based solely upon the traveler-direct sales agent contract. After all reservations are properly made, failure of those services would be the responsibility of others. On the other hand, if the traveler specifies a specific *quality* of accommodations and the direct sales agent fails to obtain them, or forgets to do so, then contractual liability would exist.

If a direct sale agent makes express promises to the traveler as to quality of service and the like, these promises become part of the contract and would be binding upon the agent. A better practice would be to use the disclaimer rather than shouldering the additional contract burdens. This is a matter for the direct sales agent to decide. But as we have seen before, such disclaimers do not always work.

MEASURE OF DAMAGES

In those cases where liability attaches to a travel agent, the question arises as to what the extent and measure of damages should be. On this point, it must be recognized that not only can a disappointed traveler receive damages for him or herself, but also for the accompanying spouse and children.[16]

> . . . [W]here a person had entered into a contract for the benefit of himself and others who were not parties to the contract, he could sue on the contract for damages for the loss suffered not only by himself, but also by the others in consequence of a breach of the contract. . . .
>
> Jackson was, therefore, entitled to damages not only for the loss in the value of the holiday and the discomfort, vexation, and disappointment which he himself suffered by reason of Horizon's breach of contract but, also for the discomfort, vexation, disappointment suffered by his wife and children.

The Odysseys case that follows is a leading case on damages and it lays down principles that are being followed in travel cases. However, it must be noted that this case was tried before a judge and not a jury. The recovery allowed by the judge was conservative and essentially equals the contract price for the trip lost. Plaintiffs' lawyers have now come to realize that, in such cases, not only is the contract price of the trip involved but also the loss of the trip itself, the ruined vacation, and other measurable factors.

Travel lawyers recognize that such cases must be tried before juries and *not* judges because juries are able to relate to disappointments suffered by others in ruined travel situations. In a case similar to Odysseys, where the contract amount was $1,003, the jury returned a verdict of $15,000 for the traveler.[17] Judges tend to be more conservative because they center their rulings on legal points and not on the personal issues. On the other side of the coin, the one being sued will opt for a trial by judge and not jury where that can be arranged. All that is required in most courts is the agreement of the parties. But, for the reasons stated above, it is going to be difficult to get such an agreement from plaintiffs' lawyers in travel cases.

ODYSSEYS UNLIMITED, INC., V. ASTRAL STAR TRAVEL SERVICE
77 Misc. 2d 502, 354 N.Y.S. 2d 88 (1974).

JOSEPH LIFF, Justice.

Following an earlier practice, in the summer of 1972 the Paterson and Majewski families began to plan a joint vacation over the Christmas holiday. In doing so they relied upon Astral Travel Service ("Astral") an agency with which they had previously dealt. They looked forward to spending a few days with their five children in the Canary Islands, of course not anticipating the discomfort, inconvenience and disappointment they would suffer.

Astral (a retail travel agent) suggested to Dr. Paterson and Mr. Majewski a package tour prepared by Odysseys (a wholesale agency). The tour, entitled "Xmas Jet Set Sun Fun/Canary Isle," was scheduled to depart December 26, 1972 by jet for Tenerife, Canary Isles, Puerto de la Cruz, staying at the "delux Semiramis Hotel" and returning on January 1, 1973 by jet. Majewski and Paterson accepted this trip costing $1,375.90 and $1,076.80 respectively and made their down payments to Astral. Astral withheld its commission and forwarded the balance along with the reservations to Odysseys who in turn confirmed the reservations to Astral's Mr. Howard Pollack. Exhibit B is a handsome colored brochure illustrating the Hotel Semiramis, its location, accommodations, etc., etc. designed to excite the eye of any one contemplating a trip abroad. An information sheet furnished details of the trip and referred to the accommodations at the "Five-Star Hotel Semiramis."

On December 26, 1972 the group flew off to the Canary Islands. They arrived at the airport in Tenerife at about dawn and waited about two hours (one-half hour was spent in a bus) before they were taken to the Hotel Semiramis. At this point the passengers had been en route some thirty hours. While at the airport they saw Mr. Newton, President of Odysseys, who accompanied the group tour. (The inference may reasonably be drawn that he went along because he anticipated the difficulties which were shortly to be encountered.) Two hundred fifty weary but expectant guests arrived at the

Semiramis and were presented with a letter from the hotel advising them that there was no space available and that he was looking for others. For about four hours, two hundred fifty people (including bag and baggage except for what was strayed) were in the lobby of the Semiramis until they were divided into groups and directed to other hostelries. The Paterson and Majewski families were brought to the Porto Playa Hotel which was not fully ready for occupancy because it was under construction and without the recreational facilities and conveniences available at the Hotel Semiramis. Portions of the Porto Playa Hotel were enclosed in scaffolding. Paterson and Majewski testified that work was done in their rooms, water supply uncertain, electric connections incomplete, etc., etc. throughout their stay.

The Court is convinced that prior to the group's departure Mr. Newton was aware that there were no reservations at the Semiramis Hotel for his charges. He testified that on either December 18th or 19th, 1972 he knew of the overbooking at the hotel. Paterson and Majewski stated that Newton told them at the hotel that the reservations were in jeopardy and would not be honored but he did not share his knowledge. In his letter of January 12, 1973 addressed to tour members, Mr. Newton confirms the fact that he had been aware of some "problem with overbooking by that hotel" (Semiramis Hotel) and states that his agent (Viajes Aliados, S. A.) "had the foresight to have arranged for alternate accommodations." He is at the least disingenuous in asserting that he had assurance from the Spanish National Tourist Office that the Semiramis Hotel would have accommodations for the group because that office informed him that the Hotel Semiramis was "instructed to receive all the members of your group for whom reservations were made." However, the reservations for the tour were not confirmed and, therefore, the hotel was not obligated to accommodate the members of the group.

Majewski and Paterson sue in contract and negligence seeking recovery of their payments for their trip and for their ordeal. Their claims spring from a breach of contract by Astral for its failure to furnish the hotel accommodations agreed upon. Majewski and Paterson are entitled to recover from Astral for the breach of contract. Damages in the usual breach of contract action should indemnify a party "for the gains prevented and losses sustained by the breach; to leave him in no worse, but put him in no better, position than he would have been had the breach not occurred" (2 N.Y. PJI 907; see also 13 N.Y.Jur., Damages §38; 25 C.J.S. Damages §74). However, when a passenger sues a carrier for a breach of their agreement concerning accommodations the "[i]nconveniences and discomforts which a passenger suffers . . . are to be considered in the assessment of the damages" (N.Y. Damages Law §624). "[D]amages arising from a breach of the contract to carry, which results in inconvenience and indignity to the passenger while in transit, are not limited to the price of passage" (*Lignante v. Panama Railroad Co.*, 147 App.Div. 97, 99-100, 131 N.Y.S. 753, 754; see also *Aplington v. Pullman Co.*, 110 App.Div. 250, 97 N.Y.S. 329) and "the discomfort and inconvenience to which" a passenger was put by the breach of the carrier's contract "was within the contemplation of the parties and a proper element of damage" *(Campbell v. Pullman Company,* 182 App.Div. 931, 169 N.Y.S. 1087; see also *Owens v. Italia Societa Per Azione,* 70 Misc.2d 719, 723, 334 N.Y.S.2d 789 [Civil Court of the City of New York] aff'd 75 Misc.2d 104,347 N.Y.S.2d 431 [Appellate Term, First Dept.]). Although these cases concerned accommodations with common carriers the principle should be applied to the relationship between travel agent and clients. The agent should be "held responsible to: (a) verify or confirm the reservations and (b) use reasonable diligence in ascertaining the responsibility of any intervening 'wholesale or tour organizer'" *(Bucholtz v. Sirokin Travel Ltd.,* 74 Misc. 2d 180, 182, 343 N.Y.S.2d 438, 442). Because the contract was violated and the accommodations contracted for not furnished a more realistic view for awarding damages to Majewski and Paterson would include not only the difference in the cost of the accommodations but also compensation for their inconvenience, discomfort, humiliation and annoyance.

Paterson and Majewski are entitled to return of the total sum each paid for the trip as damages to them and their family for the inconvenience and discomfort they endured.

The tour included a period from December 26th to January 1st. The party landed on its easterly journey on the 27th December. When the Majewskis and Patersons became aware of their predicament they made heroic efforts to return immediately but heavy bookings in the holiday season made that impossible. They were constrained to remain and to suffer the results of Mr. Newton's callousness. Had their dealings been directly with the plaintiff we would have considered the imposition of additional damages. However, their negotiations and dealings were with Astral who might have exerted greater efforts to see that arrangements were properly made.

In all of the circumstances we think that it would be appropriate to make the Patersons and Majewskis whole in pocket. Accordingly, they are awarded judgment against Astral in the amounts of $1,076.80 to Paterson and $1,375.90 to Majewski.

On Astral's cross-claim against Odysseys for breach of contract, concerning the Majewski and Paterson claims if successful, Astral is entitled to a judgment against Odysseys in the amount of $2,452.70 less $308.30 which Astral retained as its commission, because Odysseys failed to perform its contract and it was Odysseys which was responsible for the fate which befell Majewski and Paterson.

In an unrelated matter Astral counterclaimed against Odysseys seeking return of a $1,345.00 deposit for a group tour also to the Canary Islands but via Iberia Airlines and with a stay at the San Felipe Hotel. Astral gave this sum to Odysseys as a deposit for a group tour of fifty persons since it was allegedly required by the San Felipe Hotel to "firm up your confirmation" (Exhibit L). Odysseys indicated that this deposit was non-refundable (Exhibits

L and N). Having received cancellations by members of the group that was to take this trip, Astral was unsuccessful in attempts to substitute their vacationers and requested a refund of the deposit paid. Odysseys' proof failed to show that it suffered any loss by the cancellation or that it paid any part of the deposit to the hotel. We also found that Odysseys asked for the deposit because it was required by the hotel but no part of it was ever paid over to the hotel. Accordingly, Astral is entitled to a return of their deposit and may enter judgment against Odysseys for said amount.

Disclaimers

As mentioned before the Odysseys case, travel agents and agencies are turning to the use of disclaimers to limit their liability for defaults by others in the travel chain. As a principle of law, parties of equal bargaining power can reach any reasonable agreement and the courts will uphold them. But there is also a rule of law that says that, if the bargaining power of the parties is *not* equal, the courts will take that fact into consideration when it comes time to decide whether the agreement should be upheld. Thus, in looking at disclaimers used by travel agents and agencies, the courts will look to:

1. Readability.
2. Equal bargaining power—or the lack of it.
3. Notice to the traveler.
4. Unconscionability.[18]

The leading case on disclaimers as used by travel agents is found in *Klakis v. Nationwide Leisure Corporation* that follows. This dissenting opinion was adopted by a subsequent decision handed down by the court in 1980.[19] The case itself was eliminated because it is a legal maze of motions, orders, and opinions that are of little value to us.

MARION KLAKIS ET AL. V. NATIONWIDE LEISURE CORPORATION
73 A.D. 2d 521, 422 N.Y.S. 2d 407 (1979).

Plaintiff's purchased from defendant Nationwide Leisure Corporation (hereinafter "Nationwide") a chartered tour to Nassau which was scheduled to leave Kennedy Airport at 6:00 A.M. on January 22, 1978, and to return there at 1:30 P.M. on January 26, 1978. The tour included round trip chartered jet flights on defendant Capitol International Airways (hereinafter "Capitol"), a certified supplemental air-carrier. In the complaint, plaintiffs charge that the flight left Kennedy one day later, on January 23, 1978, rather than January 22nd, as scheduled, and that as a consequence of the delays in their travel, they received, instead of the advertised four nights and five days, a stay of only three nights and two days. Insofar as here pertinent, the complaint states three causes of action against all the defendants. The first cause of action alleges fraud, the second breach of contract, and the third seeks rescission.

The disclaimer of liability contained in Nationwide's brochure which was incorporated in the agreement between plaintiffs and Nationwide to the effect that Nationwide "shall not be responsible in any way for any delays, changes in departure time," while it may be viable regarding incidental delays and changes, is not a defense to delay of sufficient magnitude to vitiate the contract for the simple reason that such delay strikes at the heart of the performance bargained for under the agreement. The principal herein, Nationwide, assumed a specific duty by contract, to wit, to afford to plaintiffs a five days and four nights tour. Under the circumstances herein, Nationwide as principal might well be liable to plaintiffs for the failure of performance occasioned by the delays caused by the independent contractor Capitol (See, *Dorkin v. American Express Co.*, 74 Misc.2d 673, 675, 345 N.Y.S.2d 891, 892). No explanation is presented on this record by defendants relevant to the delays in air transportation experienced by plaintiffs regarding the return flight to New York. Thus a viable claim for breach of contract against Nationwide and Capitol respecting the delays encountered by plaintiffs in returning to New York remains.

THE OCCASIONAL TRAVEL AGENT

Assume that a tourist destination has a visitor's center on the outskirts of town. The purpose of the center is to assist motorists in becoming oriented to what is available in town and to assist them in obtaining hotel or motel accommodations. Such centers are found at Las Vegas, other key tourist destinations, and at almost all interstate entrances to the various states. Are such centers engaged in the travel agency business and if so, what rules govern the operations? If not, what then?

For finding rooms for tourists, the inn pays a fee to the center, such as $5.00 per room placed. This activity raises legal questions. First, what is the liability of the tourist center, if any, if it is unable to find accommodations for a traveler who wants to use their services? The answer is probably "no liability at all" for there would be no contractual agreement between anyone.

Now change the facts. The tourist center asks a motel for a room for a traveler and the motel refuses to make the reservation. Does liability now attach to anyone? The answer probably depends upon the availability of rooms at the motel. If rooms had been available and the reservation was refused, was the common-law duty to receive violated? The problem here is that the motel refused the tourist center, who is not a traveler. Yet at the same time, they refused the traveler.

If the motel had been full, the refusal would have been lawful and that would be the end of it.

What happens now if the tourist center takes cash from the traveler, say $10.00, with the promise to find a room elsewhere? Again the tourist center fails to find a room. This changes the facts and there would be liability on the tourist center because of the breach of contract and damages would be recoverable.

Change the facts one more time. The center locates a room, gets the tourist checked in, and then the tourist declares the room to be unsatisfactory. Is this a breach of contract as to the center—or is it a breach of contract as to the motel or hotel?

Without arriving at answers, let it suffice to say that the activities of the tourist centers at the edge of town raise legal questions for which there are no ready answers.

QUESTIONS

1. Explain why a travel agent fills a positive need for travelers.
2. What is the legal problem that becomes involved when a travel agent passes on to someone else the services that the traveler thought were going to be performed by the agent?
3. What is the legal error in disclosing only the name of a ship to a traveler who buys a ticket for a cruise on that ship?
4. What is "constructive fraud"?
5. Who is entitled to damages when a family of five has a vacation trip ruined because of the negligence of a travel agent?
6. What is the problem encountered by the courts when they try to apply agency law to travel agent cases?
7. Give an example of how one can be an undisclosed principal in a travel agency case.

8. How is a travel agent normally paid for his or her services?
9. The Levine case involved less than $100. Can you suggest how such a case got into an upper New York court in 1971?
10. True or False. One possible solution to the traveler–travel agent legal problems is for the courts to find two agencies instead of one.

ENDNOTES

1. See *Rappa v. American Airlines, Inc.*, 87 Misc. 2d 759, 386 N.Y.S. 2d 612 (1976).
2. New York: *Odysseys Unlimited, Inc. v. Astral Travel Service*, 77 Misc. 2d 502, 354 N.Y.S. 2d 88 (1974); *Seigel v. Council of Long Island Educators, Inc.*, 75 Misc. 2d 750, 348 N.Y.S. 2d 816 (1973); *Bucholtz v. Sirokin Travel Service, Ltd.*, 74 Misc. 2d 180, 343 N.Y.S. 2d 438, *aff'd* 80 Misc. 2d 333, 363 N.Y.S. 2d 415 (1974).

   Pennsylvania: *Slade v. Cheung and Risser Enterprises, Inc.*, 10 Pa. D. & C. 3d 627 (Pa. C. P. 1979).
3. Illinois: *Simpson v. Compagnie Nationale Air France*, 42 Ill. 2d 496, 248 N.E. 2d 117 (1969).
   New York: *Levine v. British Overseas Airways Corp.*, 66 Misc. 2d 766, 322 N.Y.S. 2d 119 (1971).
   Pennsylvania: *Slade v. Cheung and Risser Enterprises, Inc.*, 10 Pa. D. & C. 3d 627 (Pa. C. P 1979).
4. *Ibid.*
5. See Wohlmuth, "The Liability of Travel Agents: A Study in the Selection of Appropriate Legal Principals," 40 *Temp. L. Q.* 29, 51 (1966).
6. See *Slade v. Cheung and Risser Enterprises, Inc.*, 10 Pa. D. & C. 3d 627 (Pa. C. P 1979). See also, Wolmouth, N. 5 *supra*, 40 *Temp. L. Q.* at p. 56. "Even if the travel agent could be considered an agent, it merely clouds the issue to treat him as such for the purpose of liability. The issue is: Should the travel agent be held liable to the client under various circumstances? This question, aside from the problem of negligence, can best be answered by treating the travel agent as one who contracts with his client and, then, by determining what the travel agent expressly, impliedly, and as a matter of legal imposition, undertakes to do in his relations with his client."
7. See §5.02 *supra.*

8. See §5.04[4] *supra.*
9. See §5.04[2] *supra.*
10. See §5.04[3] *supra.*
11. See §5.04[5] *supra.*
12. Thomas A. Dickerson, *Travel Law,* Law Journal Seminars-Press, New York, sec. 5.05, using the author's footnotes.
13. *Maggio v. Maggiore,* 44 A.D. 2d 883, 351 N.Y.S. 2d 408 (1954).
14. *United Airlines v. Lerner,* 87 Ill. App. 3d 801, 401 N.E. 3d 225, *Slade v. Cheung,* 10 Pa. D. and C. 3d 627 (Pa. C. P. 1979), *Rosen v. Porter,* 62 Ill. App. 3d 762, 379 N.E. 2d 407 (1978).
15. 76 A.D. 2d 721, 432 N.Y.S. 2d 186, at pages 193–94 (1980).
16. *Jackson v. Horizon,* 175 All. E.R. 92.
17. *Scher v. Liberty Travel,* 38 A.D. 2d 581, 328 N.Y.S. 2d 836 (1971).
18. *Majestic,* 166 U.S. 375, 17 S. Ct. 597, 41 L. Ed. 1039 (1897).
19. *Dupack v. Nationwide,* 73 A.D. 2d 903, 424 N.Y.S. 2d 436 (1980).

24

Common Carriers

"As a general rule, statutes in derogation of the common law are to be strictly construed; however, a different rule applies to remedial statutes in derogation of the common law since where a statute is both remedial and in derogation of the common law it is usual to strictly construe the question whether it modifies the common law but to liberally construe its application."[1]

"There are three points to be considered in the construction of all remedial statutes; the old law, the mischief, and the remedy; that is, how the common law stood at the making of the act; what the mischief was, for which the common law did not provide; and what remedy the parliament hath provided to cure this mischief. And it is the business of the judges so to construe the act as to suppress the mischief and advance the remedy."[2]

OVERVIEW

An important part of the travel chain is found in the means of transportation by which travelers get from one point to another. While a considerable amount of travel is carried out by private vehicle, a substantial part is carried out by public transportation. The laws that regulate these "common carriers" form the basis of this chapter.

An important part of travel and lodging law is found in those rules and statutes that regulate cruise ships, passenger trains such as Amtrak, airlines, and other carriers. These rules, statutes, and treaties are of relatively recent origin although the original control of common carriers came to us out of the early common law. The rules of cruise ships can be traced back for centuries when the sailing ships plied the high seas. In this chapter we will look first at the principles that regulate ship travel and then examine airline cases. The law is in a state of flux and changes will be forthcoming in the future—particularly in air travel. First, let's take a look at the law that regulates cruise ships.

CRUISE SHIPS

Contract of Carriage

When a breach of contract of common carriage occurs, compensatory damages are available to the traveler who can prove those damages. Punitive damages *cannot* be recovered unless the breach is accompanied by an intentional, wanton, and willful act of the carrier or its agents. If a willful act of an employee is outside the scope of employment, then punitive damages cannot be recovered from the common carrier.[3] In most states, punitive damages cannot be recovered in a breach of contract case unless the acts also constitute an independent cause of action in tort.[4]

Contractual Duty

A common carrier has a contractual duty, once the contract of carriage arises, to transport passengers, exercising the highest degree of vigilance and care for their comfort and safety.[5] This duty extends to employees and agents of the carrier even when such acts are outside the scope of employment. But observe that we are talking about *contractual duties*—not tort duties. It must be remembered that the damages recoverable are only compensatory and not punitive when the act of the employee is outside the scope of the employment. If an employee of a common carrier acts within the scope of his or her employment and insults or harms a traveler intentionally, then punitive damages can be recovered from the common carrier upon proper proof in court.

The act must be authorized by the carrier or ratified by the carrier later. In other words, the act of the employee must be that of the carrier. As a general principle, a criminal act committed by an employee outside of the scope of employment does not render the employer liable—unless ratification takes place. In some states, employers cannot ratify an unlawful act of an employee. In the following case, the plaintiff brought suit for compensatory and punitive damages because of an assault by an employee against her during a cruise. Punitive damages that had been awarded to the injured plaintiff were set aside by the upper court as being contrary to the rule of common carriers.

COMMODORE CRUISE LINE LTD. V. KORMENDI
Fla. App. 344 So.2d 896 (1977)

Before HENDRY, C.J., and BARKDULL and NATHAN, J.J.
PER CURIAM

Appellant, defendant below, appeals from a final judgment entered pursuant to a jury verdict which awarded plaintiffs both compensatory and punitive damages for an assault and battery alleged to have been committed upon Ilona Kormendi by an employee of appellant during a cruise on appellant's ship; and from a post judgment "order denying defendant's motion to alter or amend final judgment and/or to set aside the judgment and/or for new trial."

Appellee, traveling without her husband, was allegedly assaulted and battered by an employee of appellant. The incident was alleged to have occurred one evening, during a Caribbean cruise on appellant's ship, while appellee was a passenger. The assailant apparently attempted to rob appellee's cabin, but was taken by surprise by appellee's presence in said cabin. A scuffle ensued after which the knife-wielding individual ran from the scene. This retreat was, however, not taken before appellee identified the person as a black man in crewman's garb. A subsequent investigation by the ship's captain and officers transpired; however, the identity of the assailant was never discovered.

The cause proceeded to trial upon the theory of breach of contract of common carriage. At trial there was ample testimony to suggest that the aforementioned investigation to ascertain the identity of the assailant was far from adequate, as there were no black passengers aboard the ship during the cruise and only two black crewmen.

At trial's conclusion, a jury returned a verdict for appellees and against appellant in the sum of Eighty-five Thousand Dollars ($85,000.00) compensatory damages and Two Hundred Thousand Dollars ($200,000.00) punitive damages. Post-trial motions were filed by appellant and denied by the court and this appeal follows.

Appellant raises two points on appeal. The first point challenges the sufficiency of the evidence in support of appellees' claim for assault and battery. After reviewing the record, we are of the opinion that there was substantial competent evidence adduced that would support a verdict for appellees.

Appellant's second point concerns the correctness of an award of punitive damages. It is appellant's contention that, pursuant to a cause of action based upon a breach of contract of common carriage, punitive damages are only awardable against an employer when its employee commits an intentional, willful, wanton or malicious act while within the scope of his employment. *Subjudice,* no contention or argument was made by appellees that the assault occurred while within the official duties of the employee and therefore, appellant argues, it was error to allow punitive damages.

For the reasons that follow, we agree with appellant's contention and reverse.

Under Florida Law, punitive damages are not generally recoverable for breach of contract unless the acts constituting the breach also amount to an independent cause of action in tort, sustained by proper allegation and proof of an intentional wrong, insult, abuse or gross negligence.

Furthermore, under Florida law, a contractual duty arises between a passenger and common carrier obligating the carrier to transport the passenger to his or her destination, exercising the highest degree of care and vigilance for the passenger's safety. *Hall v. Seaboard Air Line Ry. Co.,* 84 Fla. 9, 93 So. 151 (1921); 5 Fla. Jur. *Carriers,* §108. The carrier's duty is transferred by and through its employees and any willful misconduct by its employees are actionable as against the carrier-employer. *Hall, supra,* 14 Am. Jur. 2d *Carriers,* §1059.

In addition, in comparison to an ordinary master-servant relationship, a common carrier is liable to a passenger for the wrongful acts of his or her employees during the contractual period, notwithstanding the fact that said acts are not within the scope of the employees' employment. Compare *Reina v. Metropolitan Dade County,* 285 So. 2d 648 (Fla. 3d DCA 1973), where the contract of carriage had terminated before the employee–bus driver assaulted the former passenger.

The only question, then, for our determination, is whether the expanded liability of a common carrier for damages occasioned by a breach of contractual duty owed by its employee to a passenger includes liability for punitive damages, over and above compensatory damages, notwithstanding the fact that the complained of act or acts were committed by the employee outside the scope of his employment.

While case law and authority for awarding punitive damages against a common carrier and in favor of a passenger for the wrongful acts of an employee done within the scope of the employee's employment are ample, *Miami Transit Co. v. Yellen,* 156 Fla. 351, 22 So. 2d 787 (1945); *Atlantic Greyhound Lines v. Lovett,* 134 Fla. 505, 184 So. 133 (1938); 5 Fla. Jur. *Carriers,* §144; our research and research of counsel have failed to reveal authority from within this state for the question posed above.

Research of the law in other jurisdictions which have considered the question does reveal the following. In order for a common carrier to be liable to a passenger for punitive damages, the insulting, abusive or intentional wrong must be committed by the employee while discharging duties within the scope of his employment, or the act must be authorized by the employer or subsequently ratified by him.

In that the assault was not committed by the employee while discharging duties within the scope of his employment, it was therefore incumbent upon appellees to allege and prove at trial that the act was subsequently ratified or initially authorized by appellant. This was never done, however, *assuming arguendo,* that the theory of ratification was attempted by appellees, this would be to no avail. The law is clear that unless the original act under scrutiny is done on the behalf of the employer, no ratification can take place. In addition, the Florida Supreme Court has stated that a criminal act committed outside the scope of a servant's authority cannot be ratified by the master. *Mallory v. O'Neill,* 69 So.2d 313 (Fla. 1954).

In conclusion, we hold that where, as here, a passenger injured by an employee of a common carrier files suit based upon a breach of contract of carriage, punitive damages can only be awarded to the passenger upon a proper allegation and proof that the complained of act was committed by the employee while within the scope of his employment or, when the act was initially authorized by the carrier or subsequently ratified by him.

Accordingly, it was error to award punitive damages to appellees and therefore, the judgment appealed must be reversed and remanded with instructions to the trial judge to deduct the award of punitive damages from the total recovery. Once done, the final judgment as modified is affirmed.

Affirmed in part; reversed and remanded in part.

Cruise Ships—An Observation

One of the leading hotel colleges in the United States books passage on cruise ships and then conducts classes on board during the cruise. Some samples of these classes include "The economic and political implications of tourism in the Caribbean," "Hospitality protocol," and "Variations in casino play and management."

A poster circulated throughout the campus of this particular university announces "Come Join Us—Sign up for a Nautical Course—January 1-8, 19XX. A six-day Cruise on the S/S Rhapsody." In the upper-left hand corner of this poster, in small type, is found "Paquet—French Cruises." Payment is to be made to the Board of Regents of the university.

Now assume that Joe Student signs up, pays the $799.00 "double occupancy," and then suffers a loss of goods or is injured during the cruise. He would certainly have the right to sue the shipowner, assuming that the cause of the loss was due to the negligence of the shipowner, or act of an employee of the ship. Such suits must normally be brought where the ship is registered—often a foreign nation. But could Joe Student sue the Board of Regents of the university? This is much preferable to having to take it to some other nation where the owners of the ship can be found.

Under the ruling of the McQuade case, in Chapter 23, the answer would be "yes." While the name of the ship had been disclosed, the complete name, address, and capacity of the shipowner was not. Thus the Board of Regents would, in all probability, be held to be the agent of an undisclosed principal. Therefore, under agency law the agent assumes personal liability for all contracts (and resulting torts) that have been entered into while carrying forth the authority granted by the principal.

This undesirable legal result could be avoided in a simple manner. The owner of the ship, the legal capacity, and the address of the owner should be set forth on all ads, tickets, brochures, and other written information about the cruise. In addition, that information should be placed in **CONSPICUOUS** type so that it will be noticed. In doing this, the principal has been disclosed and, under agency law, the agent (Board of Regents) incurs no personal liability for any subsequent breach of contract, tort, or other loss.

As to the use of disclaimers on cruise ship contracts, there is little chance of their being successful. The courts have passed on their use negatively[6] and the U.S. Code covers them specifically:[7]

> It shall be unlawful for the manager, agent, master, or owner of any vessel transporting passengers between ports of the United States or between any such port and a foreign port to insert in any rule, regulation, contract, or agreement any provision or limitation (1) purporting in the event of loss of life or bodily injury arising from the negligence or guilt of such owner or his servants, to relieve such owner, master, or agent from liability, or from liability beyond any stipulated amount, for such loss or injury, or (2) purporting in such event to lessen, weaken, or avoid the right of any claimant to a trial by court of competent jurisdiction on the question of liability for such loss or injury, or the measure of damages therefor. All such provisions or limitations contained in any such rule, regulation, contract, or agreement are declared to be against public policy and shall be null and void and of no effect.

Turning from our look at the law of cruise ships, let's examine the laws that come to the front in the operation of airlines. This is an area in which the rules, regulations, and common-law holdings are vast indeed. Thus it is necessary to limit our discussion to representative laws and regulations. A helpful place to begin is by a look at airline reservations.

RESERVATIONS—AIRLINES

Damages

When breach of an airline reservation occurs, recoveries have been permitted for compensatory damages (actual loss) as well as punitive damages. In one case a federal judge permitted a "bumped" traveler to recover punitive damages, basing the decision on federal law.[8]

The Archibald case shows the 1972 view of the courts on this subject.

ARCHIBALD V. PAN AMERICAN WORLD AIRWAYS
460 F. 2d 14 (1972)

CHOY, Circuit Judge.

Mr. and Mrs. George B. Archibald appeal a district court order directing a verdict for Pan American World Airways, Inc. (Pan Am). The District Court found that the Archibalds had failed to present a *prima facie* case of undue or unreasonable preference or unjust discrimination in violation of 49 U.S.C. §1374(b). We reverse and remand.

On August 2, 1968, the Archibalds made two economy reservations for Pan Am's Flight 801 on August 6 from Tokyo to Guam. Pan Am accepted and confirmed the reservations, and told the Archibalds no further confirmation was necessary. On August 6, the Archibalds checked in at the airport nearly an hour early, and received seat assignments. When they attempted to board the plane, however, they and 28 other passengers were asked to step aside. Many of these passengers eventually enplaned, but the Archibalds and a dozen others did not. Three passengers who did go aboard made their reservations after the Archibalds had made theirs.

Pan Am then told the remaining passengers that the flight had been oversold, and that they would not be able to go. The airline provided hotel accommodations for the bumped passengers, tendered a voucher for payment of denied boarding compensation which Mr. Archibald did not cash, and put the Archibalds on the next available flight to Guam.

49 U.S.C. §1374(b) reads, in pertinent part:

"No air carrier or foreign air carrier shall make, give, or cause any undue or unreasonable preference or advantage to any particular person . . . in any respect whatsoever or subject any particular person . . . to any unjust discrimination or any undue or unreasonable prejudice or disadvantage in any respect whatsoever."

This section creates a private federal cause of action for unreasonable preferences and unjust discrimination. *Fitzgerald v. Pan American World Airways, Inc.*, 229 F.2d 499 (2nd Cir. 1956). An injunction against prospective or continuing discrimination is usually refused out of deference to administrative remedies before the Civil Aeronautics Board. *Mortimer v. Delta Air Lines*, 302 F. Supp. 276, 282 (N.D. Ill., 1969); *Wills v. Trans World Airlines, Inc.*, 200 F. Supp. 360, 366 (S.D.Cal., 1961). However, purely nominal compensatory damages are available, including an award for humiliation and hurt feelings when the facts warrant, and the extent and nature of the affront are established. *Flores v. Pan American World Airways, Inc.*, 259 F. Supp. 402, 404 (D.P.R., 1966). See *Wills, supra,* 200 F. Supp. at 366-367, in which the plaintiff received $1.54 for pecuniary loss and $5,000 in punitive damages. Punitive damages over and above actual injury are awardable if the defendant acted "wantonly, or oppressively, or with such malice as implies a spirit of mischief or criminal indifference to civil obligations." *Wills, supra,* at 367-368.

Decisional law has not yet clearly established what constitutes a *prima facie* case under §1374(b). Actual discrimination or preference must be shown. *Flores, supra.* Other elements of a plaintiff's case are found in the three reported decisions involving passengers with reservations who were not allowed to board planes. In *Mortimer,* an economy passenger was bumped to make room for a first class passenger. While its opinion dealt with jurisdictional issues, the court commented, "In order to succeed in an action under this section, it must be alleged, as it is here, and proven that the plaintiffs right to fair, equal and nondiscriminatory treatment has been violated." 302 F. Supp. at 281.

In *Wills,* an economy passenger was sacrificed in favor of a first class passenger with a later reservation in direct violation of the airline's own bumping policy. The court held that the plaintiff was "entitled to priority in flight accommodations over all passengers who had made later reservations than he and yet were permitted to board the flight. . . . By disregarding plaintiff's priority, the defendant airline unjustly and unreasonably discriminated against him, and thus violated the Act." 200 F. Supp. at 365. And in *Stough v. North Central Airlines, Inc.*, 55 Ill.App.2d 338, 204 N.E.2d 792 (1965), the court affirmed a jury verdict that the airline had not discriminated against two passengers with reserved seats who (in accordance with company safety regulations) were not allowed to board a plane which departed with empty seats.

These three cases demonstrate that while overselling does not *per se* give rise to a §1374(b) action, substantial overselling is evidence of malice to be considered in assessing punitive damages. See *Wills, supra,* 200 F.Supp. at 367-368. Some overselling is an economic necessity for an airline in view of inevitable cancellations and no-shows. However, when a flight is thus oversold, the airline must fill the plane in a reasonable and just manner. *Stough* and *Wills* indicate that bumping which is outwardly discriminatory or preferential may be legitimated by proof that the airline adhered to its established policy and that the policy is reasonable. This policy is within the peculiar knowledge of the airline, which is most able to present evidence justifying the selection of one passenger over another. The passenger cannot reasonably be expected to divine at the gate, or discover later, what the airline's policy is and whether it has been obeyed. The passenger is able to prove that he possessed a confirmed reservation and a resultant right to a seat, and that this priority was not honored. This suffices to establish that a preference or discrimination has occurred. It is not unreasonable then to place upon the airline the burden of proving that the discrimination or preference was reasonable by demonstrating company policy and why, in each particular case, one passenger was chosen over another.

The Archibalds proved that they had a priority right to an economy seat because they held confirmed reservations on Flight 801, and that Pan Am allowed three passengers with later reservations to board the plane. With this, they established a *prima facie* case that Pan Am had unjustly and unreasonably discriminated against them. Since Pan Am had not demonstrated, if it could, the reasonableness of its preference of the three passengers over the Archibalds, a directed verdict for the airline was inappropriate at that stage of the trial.

Reversed and remanded.

Bumping of passengers is almost always caused by overbooking of a flight. Some overbooking by airlines can be justified on pure economic grounds. This assumes that alternate service is available for all who need it and within a reasonable time. In the airline industry, because of the constant no-shows, an exception to the general contract obligation to hold a seat should be applied in the courts. But as the Archibald case showed us, this was not the case.

Overbooking Today

Under the Deregulation Act of 1978, the Civil Aeronautics Board (CAB) did away with the tariff system as it related to flight delays. There was one exception to this, however, and it had to do with oversales of seats or overbooking. Under current regulations,[9] control is still maintained to balance the interests of both airlines and passengers. The procedure now followed is that passengers are asked to give up their seats for appropriate compensation. The regulations require that notice be given of this practice. The best way to understand airline overbooking is to read the terms found on U.S. airline tickets. Examine Figure 24.1. As to deregulation in general, the CAB had been active, until it was replaced.

During 1980 and 1981, the CAB took several actions to assist carriers as well as travel agents to prepare for airline deregulation that came in 1983. They encouraged small carriers to enter the market, permitted discount air fares, eliminated the filing of tariffs which the airlines had relied on so long for lost baggage and delayed flights, and returned the airlines to common-law control.

Now that airline deregulation is a reality, much of the regulation of airlines is coming from the courts because the airlines no longer have tariffs for protection. A look at some holdings in court cases will illustrate the point.

Court Changes in Regulation

The doctrine of *res ipsa loquitur* was applied to the airline industry when it was in its infancy. This has changed due to the deregulation of the airlines. It is not so important now to keep the "big brother eye" upon them as it was in earlier decades. The airline industry has done much to control itself, thus bringing the safety level of flying to an all-time high. Yet many problems still exist and one of them is flight delays.

Flight delays can lead to recovery in court for discomfort and inconvenience. One court said it this way:[10]

> . . . [I]n an appropriate case damages for mental distress can be recovered in contract, just as damages for shock can be recovered

NOTICE—OVERBOOKING OF FLIGHTS

Airline flights may be overbooked, and there is a slight chance that a seat will not be available on a flight for which a person has a confirmed reservation. If the flight is overbooked, no one will be denied a seat until airline personnel first ask for volunteers willing to give up their reservation in exchange for a payment of the airline's choosing. If there are not enough volunteers the airline will deny boarding to other persons in accordance with its particular boarding priority. With few exceptions, persons denied boarding involuntarily are entitled to compensation. The complete rules for the payment of compensation and each airline's boarding priorities are available at all airport ticket counters and boarding locations.

FIGURE 24.1 (Taken from an airline ticket of a major air carrier).

RED BRICK TAVERN on Route 40 in Ohio.

> in tort. One such case is a contract for a holiday, or any other contract to provide entertainment and enjoyment. If the contracting party breaks his contract, damages can be given for the disappointment, the distress, the upset and frustration caused by the breach. I know it is difficult to assess in terms of money, but it is no more difficult than the assessment which the courts have to make every day in personal injury cases for loss of amenities. Taking the present case, Mr. Jarvis has only a fortnight's holiday in the year. He books it far ahead and looks forward to it all the time. He ought to be compensated for the loss of it.

Antitrust cases are making their appearance in airline cases. "Airline trade associations, ATA and IATA, monitor the sale of air transportation by travel agents and tour operators. ATA and IATA have the power to withdraw an agency appointment if the travel agent or tour operator fails to adhere to association rules. On occasion, travel agents and tour operators have commenced antitrust actions against these trade associations. These actions usually allege a conspiracy to restrain trade and drive the plaintiff out of business. All of these actions had been limited if not dismissed because of the doctrine of primary jurisdiction of the Civil Aeronautics Board. This defense, however, became no longer available in 1983, and the courts will, no doubt, see a goodly number of antitrust cases in the travel field."[11]

As a common carrier, an airline is almost an insurer of the baggage that it carries,[12] subject to The Warsaw Convention that we will examine in a moment. An air carrier that violates the racial laws or fails to follow its boarding plans can be sued for actual plus punitive damages.[13] Leaving this examination of actions by the courts, it is useful to learn something about The Warsaw Convention. If it is applicable, it provides protection to the airlines and strips passengers of considerable legal protection.

The Warsaw Convention

A major treaty was enacted at Warsaw, Poland, in 1929 that had and continues to have a major effect upon "international carriage by air." It has no application to flights *inside* of a single nation. Of all legal conventions, this one has been the most widely accepted, with over 100 nations being signatory to it today. The original articles of The Warsaw Convention were signed by twenty-three nations on October 12, 1929. The first ratifying nations were Brazil, France, Latvia, Poland, Romania, Spain, and Yugoslavia. The pact took effect on February 13, 1933, in those nations. It went into force in the United States on October 29, 1934, because our nation did not sign it until later.

Purpose of the Treaty

The convention was created to limit the liability of the fledgling airlines. Written in French, it replaced common-law liability with the limits on liability contained within the treaty. The limit on liability for death was set at $8,000 or 125,000 francs. The treaty provided that this sum was to be paid by use of the French franc of 65½ milligrams gold of fineness of nine hundred thousandths, and provisions were made to convert this standard to any national currency.

Montreal Agreement of 1966

In 1966, at a meeting of the signatory nations held at Montreal, Canada, the limit on liability was raised to $75,000. This was not an amendment of the original treaty but a mere contract by the signing parties and it applies only to American citizens.

Montreal Protocol of 1975

The treaty was updated again in Montreal in 1975. Figure 24.2, taken from an airline ticket, explains the terms of the convention.

These and other limitations on liability have been the subject of litigation and some examples are offered. In the first case, limitations similar to those found in Figure 24.2 were challenged and formed the basis of the opinion of the judge. (This was not an international flight so The Warsaw Convention did not apply.)

ADVICE TO INTERNATIONAL PASSENGERS ON LIMITATION OF LIABILITY

Passengers on a journey involving an ultimate destination or a stop in a country other than the country of origin are advised that the provisions of a treaty known as The Warsaw Convention may be applicable to the entire journey, including any portion entirely within the country of origin or destination. For such passengers on a journey to, from, or with an agreed stopping place in the United States of America, the Convention and special contracts of carriage embodied in applicable tariffs provide that the liability of certain carriers, parties to such special contracts, for death of or personal injury to passengers is limited in most cases to proven damages not to exceed U.S. $75,000 per passenger, and that this liability up to such limit shall not depend on negligence on the part of the carrier. The limit of liability of U.S. $75,000 above is inclusive of legal fees and costs except that in case of a claim brought in a state where provision is made for separate award of legal fees and costs, the limit shall be the sum of U.S. $58,000 exclusive of legal fees and costs. For such passengers traveling by a carrier not a party to such special contracts or on a journey not to, from, or having an agreed stopping place in the United States of America, liability of the carrier for death or personal injury to passengers is limited in most cases to approximately U.S. $10,000 or U.S. $20,000.

The names of carriers, parties to such special contracts, are available at all ticket offices of such carriers and may be examined on request. Additional protection can usually be obtained by purchasing insurance from a private company. Such insurance is not affected by any limitation of the carrier's liability under The Warsaw Convention or such special contracts of carriage. For further information please consult your airline or insurance company representative.

NOTICE OF BAGGAGE LIABILITY LIMITATIONS

Liability for loss, delay, or damage to baggage is limited as follows unless a higher value is declared in advance and additional charges are paid: (1) For most international travel (including domestic portions of international journeys) to approximately $9.07 per pound ($20.00 per kilo) for checked baggage, and $400 per passenger, for unchecked baggage; (2) for travel wholly between U.S. points to $750 per passenger on most carriers (a few have lower limits). Excess valuation may be declared on certain types of valuable articles. Carriers assume liability for fragile or perishable articles. Further information may be obtained from the carrier.

FIGURE 24.2

GREENBURG V. UNITED AIRLINES, INC.
414 N.Y.S. 2d 240,
98 Misc. 2d 544 (1979).

BERNARD FUCHS, Judge.

Plaintiff is a school teacher who flew with defendant on vacation from New York City to San Francisco and checked her bags for the flight. The bags never arrived. She sues for their value and for damages incident to the baggage loss.

At trial, which was to the Court, there was no serious contest of liability. As a common carrier defendant bears an insurer's responsibility for the loss. 7 N.Y.Jur., Carriers §434. Defendant's principal reliance was placed on the tariff which limits its liability for lost baggage in most cases to $750.00. Local and Joint Passenger Rules Tariff P. R.6, C.A.B. No. 142, Rule 370.

The tariff itself sets forth the following exception to its limitation of liability: "The above maximum liability shall be waived for an individual claimant where it can be shown that with respect to that claimant the carrier failed to provide notice of limited liability for baggage in accordance with Section 221.176 of the Civil Aeronautics Board's Economic Regulations."

The clear policy of the C.A.B.s Economic Regulations at Section 221.176 is to require conspicuous display of the limited liability notice. They specify the size of type and language of the notice and require it to be posted on signs.

A notice of limited liability for baggage is printed on the sixth page of plaintiff's six page ticket. That page, measuring 3¼ inches vertically by 7⅜ inches horizontally is dense from edge to edge (no margins) with 24 lines of material.

Three of those lines are distinct from the rest in capital letters of bold faced type. One of the bold faced lines is centered at the top and reads "ADVICE TO INTERNATIONAL PASSENGERS ON LIMITATION OF LIABILITY." About 2¼ inches down the page, in similar type at the end of the first of only two paragraphs, appear the words "SEE CONDITIONS OF CONTRACT ON REVERSE SIDE OF PASSENGER COUPON." The latter statement ends near the right edge and is followed, in the same lettering, by a line directly under and appearing to continue as part of it reading "NOTICE OF BAGGAGE LIABILITY LIMITATIONS."

Any reasonable person, let alone a harried tourist, would conclude that the described page, under its top line, applies solely to international passengers. The format is perfectly calculated to obscure from a domestic traveler's view the presence there of an applicable limit of baggage loss liability. Even the second paragraph where the loss limitation finally appears applies only to international travel until the domestic passenger's eye, if it persists through the upper mass of irrelevant material, falls at last on the fourth of its six lines.

A notice so elusive cannot fulfill the office provided for it in the tariff. In order to succeed defendant's communication must be positioned and identified so as to penetrate the traveling public's reasonably focused consciousness. Instead, defendant has set before the traveler a morsel of nourishment hidden in a banquet of dust. Authority and principle combine to deny it effect.

In *Lisi v. Alitalia-Linee Aeree Italiane*, 370 F.2d 508 (2d Cir., 1966), *aff'd* 390 U.S. 455, 88 S.Ct. 1193, 20 L.Ed.2d 27 (1968), *rehear den.*, 391 U.S. 929, 88 S.Ct. 1801, 20 L.Ed.2d 671 (1968), limited liability under The Warsaw Convention for wrongful death and personal injuries was disallowed because defendant's notice of the limitation (in tickets and baggage checks) was printed too small to notify passengers adequately. Our own Court of Appeals reached the same conclusion in *Egan v. Kollsman Instrument Corp.*, 21 N.Y.2d 160, 287 N.Y.S.2d 14, 234 N.E.2d 199, *cert. den.*, 390 U.S. 1039, 88 S.Ct. 1636, 20 L.Ed.2d 301 (1967), again because the carrier had failed to provide "conspicuous notice" of its limited liability. The rationale of those decisions, equally applicable in the present case, is that an inadequately communicated notice cannot alert a passenger to seek alternate protections such as insurance coverage.

Failure to deliver (or timely to deliver) a ticket bearing notice of limited liability is equally fatal to a carrier's defense against death claims exceeding The Warsaw Convention ceiling and for the same reason. *Martens v. Flying Tiger Line, Inc.*, 341 F.2d 851, *cert. den.*, 382 U.S. 816, 86 S.Ct. 38, 15 L.Ed.2d 64 (2d Cir., 1965); *Warren v. Flying Tiger Line, Inc.*, 352 F.2d 494 (9th Cir., 1965). Nothing in *Martin v. Trans-World Airlines, Inc.*, 219 Pa.Super. 42, 280 A.2d 647 (1972) limits the application of those authorities in the present case. As a seasoned traveler using terminals posted with conspicuous signs, that plaintiff was or should have been aware of the liability limitation notwithstanding an obscure notice on the ticket and baggage cheek.

Plaintiff testified to the loss of a long list of clothing and personal items both new and used which she had packed for use in the climates of California, Washington and Alaska (not a flight destination) over a five week period. Her claimed cost of those items and of one new suitcase is in evidence. In the Court's judgment the proven value of the lost goods was $1,869.00. See *Lake v. Dye,* 232 N.Y. 209, 133 N.E. 448 (1921); *Warren's Negligence,* Vol. 7B, ch. 16, *Personal Property,* 1.05 (1968). Plaintiff should also recover $80.00 spent over four days in San Francisco travelling repeatedly to the airport in search of her baggage.

Defendant has already paid its claimed maximum liability of $750. Accordingly, plaintiff is granted judgment in the net amount of $1,199 with interest from the date of loss, July 31, 1978, and costs of the action.

The tariff discussed in the Greenburg case is now moot because of deregulation.

In *Maugnie v. Compagnie National Air France*,[14] "An airline passenger brought an action against an air carrier to recover damages for personal injuries sustained when she slipped and fell as she proceeded down a passenger corridor leading from the carrier's gate to the main area of an airline terminal. The United States District Court for the Central District of California, William Matthew Byrne, Jr., J., held that, since the passenger had deplaned and reached a safe point inside the airport when the accident occurred the injuries complained of were not suffered "on board the aircraft or in the course of any operation of . . . disembarking" within the meaning of that phrase as used in The Warsaw Convention and that the passenger therefore could not recover. The passenger appealed. The Court of Appeals, Richey, District Judge, held that the district court's conclusion was correct.

Under The Warsaw Convention, damages for mental injury must flow from some bodily injury and not from mental distress alone.[15]

Once it is determined that an airline cannot rely on the protections of The Warsaw Convention, common-law principles of liability control.

The Convention provides for a two-year period of limitation from the date of destination arrival–or the date that arrival should have occurred. Failure to give notice of this time limitation does not extend it.[16]

Under the Convention, carriers are liable for any delays involving passengers and their luggage.[17] A court has held that this duty includes efforts to get passengers on other flights.[18] A defense provided by the Convention is that "the carrier shall not be liable if it takes all measures to avoid damage."[19] The first cases that follow involve The Warsaw Convention. The final case involves negligence of the airline in question. All contain information about the control of common carriers.

In the first case, a passenger who lost luggage on an international flight claimed that there was "willful misconduct" on the part of the airline. If the court so finds, Article 25(1) of the Convention will not apply and the airline will be responsible for the full value of the lost luggage. Otherwise the limitations of the Convention apply.

The Cohen Case

The case had its beginning in July 1974, when Charles and Hermaine Cohen left New York to begin a 28-day tour of South America.

(A detailed and personal account of their adventures and subsequent court trials can be found in *How to Stand up For Your Rights & Win!*, by Roy M. Cohn, a Simon and Schuster Fireside Book, New York, beginning on page 154. That account is worth reading.) On one leg of their tour, their flight to Rio de Janeiro was diverted to São Paulo, Brazil. Upon transfer to another flight at São Paulo, the Cohens became concerned that their luggage would not be transferred to the new flight. After being assured that the transfer had been made, they went on to Rio. At that point, they found that their luggage was on a New York-bound jet. Because of their itinerary they were not booked on that flight, still having eighteen days left on the tour. They demanded that their luggage be unloaded but the airline personnel refused, telling them that the jet would be back in two days and that they could recover their luggage then.

Because of the timetable of the remaining tour, they had to continue on their travels without their luggage, forcing them to buy clothes and other effects. During the balance of their trip they suffered inconvenience, embarrassment, and discomfort because they were not able to adequately replace their clothing and other effects.

On their return to New York, they were told by the airline, Varig, that their luggage had disappeared. Varig offered them $640.00, taking credit for $60.00 that was advanced to them by the airline in Rio, for a total of $700.00. This was the amount that the airline was obligated to pay under the 250 francs per kilo rule of The Warsaw Convention.

The Cohens refused the $640.00 and sued. A New York jury awarded them $6,440.65 with the award split one-half for the lost baggage and one-half for the discomfort and mental suffering. The jury found that the refusal to unload was willful and thus The Warsaw Convention limitation did not apply. The airlines appealed and in the case that follows, what the appellate court did to the jury verdict can be seen.

COHEN V. VARIG AIRLINES, INC.
390 N.Y.S. 2d 515 (1976)

Carriers

In action by airline passengers against airline to recover value of lost baggage checked with airline, there was insufficient evidence to support trial court's finding that airline's refusal to unload all luggage from its plane constituted "willful misconduct," so as to abrogate limitation of liability provision of Warsaw Convention.

Before DUDLEY, PJ., and RICCOBONO and TIERNEY, JJ.
PER CURIAM:

Judgment entered December 15, 1975 (Danzig, J.) modified by decreasing the total recovery to the sum of $700.00, with interest and costs; as modified, affirmed without costs.

There was insufficient evidence in the record to support the trial court's finding that the act of defendant in refusing to unload all luggage from its plane in Rio de Janeiro constituted "willful misconduct" within the purview of Article 25(1) of The Warsaw Convention *(Grey v. American Airlines, Inc.,* 227 F.2d 282 [2d Cir.]).

DUDLEY, P.J., and TIERNEY, J., concur.
RICCOBONO, J., dissents in the following memorandum.
RICCOBONO, Justice (dissenting):

I dissent and vote to affirm for the reasons set forth in the opinion of Danzig, J., at Trial Term, except as indicated at the end of this memorandum.

In my view, there was sufficient evidence in the record for the Trial Court to find in the unique and unusual factual pattern under review that the act of defendant, by its employee, in refusing to remove plaintiff's luggage from its plane in Rio de Janeiro constituted "willful misconduct" within the purview of Article 25(1) of The Warsaw Convention *(Grey v. American Airlines, Inc.,* 227 F.2d 282 [2d Cir.]). Moreover, I agree with Trial Term that New York law governed the elements of damages to be recovered by plaintiffs.

Plaintiffs' recovery was not limited by defendant's filed tariff to the loss of their personal property. Individuals and corporations engaged in quasi-public business may not contract to absolve themselves from liability for their own willful misconduct or gross negligence.

Tishman & Lipp, Inc. v. Delta Airlines, 275 F. Supp. 471 (S.D.N.Y.), *aff'd* 413 F.2d 1401, (2nd Cir.), relied on by appellant is not applicable. Plaintiffs' luggage contained the usual apparel and accoutrements of vacationers, not thousands of dollars worth of jewelry.

The award to plaintiff Hermaine K. Cohen, however, was excessive. Contrary to the finding below her medicines were not in the lost luggage; she had them with her. I would therefore reduce her award for distress and inconvenience by $250.00.

The Cohens were not finished yet and they appealed this ruling to the intermediate appellate court of New York. That court reinstated the jury verdict for the loss of the luggage but refused to reinstate the jury award for the mental suffering. The latter part of the ruling was based on a long-standing rule in New York that recovery cannot be had for mental injury in the absence of physical injury independent of the mental injury. Such had not been the case here. The Cohen cases represents a leg in the development of the "laws of lost luggage," under The Warsaw Convention.

Our next to the last case provides one more example of what not to do with disclaimers. This was an unfortunate situation since not only Mrs. Seiter but scores of others died in the crash in question.

The Warsaw Convention was recognized by the court and given proper deference. But when it came to the question of whether or not Mrs. Seiter had proper notice of the limitation on liability, the court ruled in her estate's favor.

EGAN V. KOLLSMAN INSTRUMENT CORP.
287 N.Y.S. 2d 14 (1967)

FULD, Chief Judge.

Mrs. Eileen M. Seiter was killed when the American Airlines plane on which she was a passenger crashed as it approached LaGuardia Airport on February 3, 1959. Her administrators have brought this action for wrongful death and American has raised as an affirmative defense the limitation of liability provisions of The Warsaw Convention (49 U.S.Stat., pt. 2, p. 3000, hereinafter referred to as the "Convention"). Two questions are presented by this appeal: Was the final leg of the flight–from Chicago to New York City–to be deemed "international transportation" for purposes of the Convention so as to render it applicable to the present action and, if it was, had the carrier sufficiently complied with the Convention's notice requirements to permit it to limit its liability?

Mrs. Seiter had purchased an airline ticket for a round trip between New York City and Vancouver, Canada. The ticket scheduled her on successive flights of Northwest Airlines and United Airlines with stopovers at Seattle (west and eastbound) and at Chicago (eastbound). On the face of the ticket, below the name of the passenger, the following footnote appeared in exceedingly small, almost unreadable (4½ point) print:

> "Carriage/Transportation under this Passenger Ticket and Baggage Check, hereinafter called 'ticket', is subject to the rules relating to liability established by the Convention for the Unification of Certain Rules relating to International Carriage/Transportation by Air signed at Warsaw, October 12, 1929, if such Carriage/Transporta-

tion is 'international carriage/transportation' as defined by said Convention."

Mrs. Seiter arrived in Vancouver on January 26, 1959, as scheduled, but on February 3, when she was ticketed to return to New York, she discovered that all flights out of Vancouver had been canceled because of inclement weather. Instead of waiting for the next available flight, she proceeded to Seattle by bus, obtaining a refund check from Northwest Airlines for that portion of her journey when she reached that city.

Mrs. Seiter reached Seattle in time to permit her to take off on the Northwest flight to Chicago for which she had been originally scheduled. Reaching Chicago too late to make her scheduled connection to New York City, she presented her ticket to Northwest Airlines and received a new one for passage on an American Airlines flight to La Guardia Airport. The new ticket—under the heading "COMPLETE ROUTING THIS TICKET AND CONJUNCTION TICKET(S)"—specified the origin and destination as "NY" and expressly recited that it was "ISSUED IN EXCHANGE FOR" the original ticket, the fare being listed at the figure which had initially been paid for the entire round trip. Mrs. Seiter boarded respondent American's aircraft which, as stated above, crashed while attempting to make a landing at La Guardia.

The present action, for wrongful death, was brought against American Airlines and two other defendants—one the manufacturer of an assertedly defective altimeter and the other the assembler of the aircraft. We are, however, concerned solely with the sufficiency of American's (third) affirmative defense which asserts an "exemption from and limitation of liability in accordance with all of the applicable provisions of said Convention."

As both courts below recognized, answer to the underlying question—whether the flight from Chicago to New York City was "international transportation" under the Convention—depends upon the nature of the contract between the carrier and its passenger.[20] When it provides for "international" transportation, "whether or not there be a break in the transportation" (art. 1, subd. [2]), all flights taken under it are governed by the Convention.

The Convention's emphasis on the contract actually "made" appears to have been specifically designed to prevent any subsequent intervening circumstances from affecting the result. The reason is manifest; as one commentator put it, "[t]his prescription possesses, for the parties involved, the appreciable advantage of settling in advance the application of The Warsaw Convention, thus becoming independent of fortuitous events."

The contract embodied in the original ticket issued in this case was undoubtedly for international transportation since, in the words of the Convention (art. 1, subd. [2]), it provided for "an agreed stopping place within a territory . . . of another power." Whether or not Mrs. Seiter might have been able to rescind this contract and enter into a wholly new one of an entirely domestic character in Seattle, the simple fact is that she chose not to do so.[21] The remainder of her journey–from Seattle to Chicago and from Chicago to New York–was performed under the original contract; and since, as already noted, it provided for international transportation, it was subject to the Convention.

The plaintiff contends, however, that in view of the bus trip from Vancouver, the later flights were not performed by "successive air carriers" as required by the Convention (art. 1, subd. [3]) and that, in order for a subsequent domestic flight to be subject to the Convention, the international transportation must be "completely by air." It may well be true–although we need not now consider the matter–that, had the parties initially agreed that the journey from Vancouver to Seattle would be by bus, the Convention would not have been applicable to the later flights. But Northwest was unquestionably named as a successive air carrier on the ticket originally issued pursuant to that contract and, so long as the flight was performed under it, the Convention applies.

This brings us to the plaintiffs' further argument that, even if The Warsaw Convention applies, the carrier is not entitled to invoke the provisions limiting its liability because the ticket delivered to Mrs. Seiter did not give sufficient notice that the rules of the Convention relating to the limitation of liability were applicable.

Under article 3 (subd. [1], par. [e]) of the Convention, an airline is required to deliver a passenger ticket which contains a "statement that the transportation is subject to the rules relating to liability established by this convention."[22] The ticket before us did contain, in footnotes on the several coupons, such a statement but, as is apparent from inspection, it is in such exceedingly small and fine print as almost to defy reading.[23] Thus, although there was literal compliance with the prescription of article 3, the question arises whether such compliance satisfies the Convention's demands when viewed in the light of its over-all purposes. We do not believe that it does. In our judgment, a statement which cannot reasonably be deciphered fails of its purpose and function of affording notice and may not be accepted as the sort of statement contemplated or required by the Convention.

An examination of the ticket forms which the respondent used, in the light of that policy, can only lead one to conclude that Mrs. Seiter was not sufficiently apprised of the consequences which would result from the fact that her flight happened to carry her outside of the United States. Despite the fact that the Convention was applicable to her journey, the carrier's failure to give the requisite notice prevents it from asserting a limitation of liability.

In the final case, an airline was sued for scald burns received by a passenger while in flight. Notice how the "directed verdict" was set aside since the upper court felt that there were questions of fact for a jury to decide. The court also distinguished negligence of the pilot, if any, from that of the stewardess.

RUDEES V. DELTA AIRLINES, INC.
553 S.W 2d. 84 (Tenn. 1977)

MATHERNE, Judge.

While riding as a fare-paying passenger on a regularly scheduled flight of the defendant airline, the plaintiff sustained personal injuries when a stewardess spilled scalding coffee on his lap. The plaintiff sued for damages, and the trial judge, at the conclusion of the plaintiff's proof, directed a verdict for the defendant. The plaintiff appeals, assigning that action of the trial judge as error.

The plaintiff boarded the defendant's DC-9 airplane at Memphis for a flight to Atlanta, Georgia. The passengers were asked to keep their seat belts fastened due to the possibility that the plane might encounter air turbulence. At a point approximately 100 miles from Atlanta, a stewardess came down the aisle of the airplane carrying at waist level an open tray which contained several cups of scalding coffee. The plaintiff was seated on an aisle seat with his seat belt fastened; he had not ordered coffee. The airplane apparently hit some clear air turbulence which made the stewardess sway in the aisle and spill the contents of the cups on the plaintiff's lap. This resulted in rather severe burns to the plaintiff's thighs and groin area.

The defendant, on motion for directed verdict, argued that the plaintiff had not proved any negligence on its part. Counsel for the defendant argued, and the trial judge apparently agreed, that the plaintiff could not recover because he failed to prove that the pilot was negligent or that the defendant knew or should have known about the air turbulence.

The foregoing argument overlooks the basis of the lawsuit. The plaintiff alleged that the stewardess was negligent: (1) in spilling the coffee; (2) in her manner of carrying scalding coffee down the aisle of the plane; (3) in carrying the coffee in uncovered containers; and (4) in attempting to serve scalding coffee during flight. The issue is the negligence of the stewardess; therein lies the lawsuit.

Facts were proved from which the jury could have found the proximate cause of the plaintiff's injuries was the negligence of the stewardess as charged. We hold that reasonable minds could well differ on this issue and that the trial judge erred in directing a verdict for the defendant.

The judgment of the trial court is reversed, and this lawsuit is remanded for a new trial.

CARNEY, P.J., and NEARN, J., concur.

QUESTIONS

1. What did airline deregulation do to international airline liability?
2. What does the law require before one can recover punitive damages?
3. What was the legal issue in the Commodore case?
4. What was "The Warsaw Convention"? What was its purpose?
5. Why was "willful misconduct" so important in the Cohen case?
6. What is a "directed verdict"? What is it used for?
7. Can there be a directed verdict in a case where there is in fact a jury question? Why?
8. Why is the question of whether or not there was negligence one that a jury must determine?
9. What is an "affirmative defense"? If you do not know, ask.
10. True or False. The Warsaw Convention was designed to protect international airlines only.

ENDNOTES

1. *Albuquerque Hilton, Inc., v. Mary Haley*, 565 P. 2d 1027 (1977).
2. 1. *Cooley's Blackstone,* page 86.
3. *Commodore Cruise Line, Ltd. v. Kormendi.*
4. *Country Club of Miami Corporation v. McDaniel,* 310 So. 2d 436 (Fla. 3d. DCA 1975).
5. *McManigal v. Chicago Motor Coach Company,* 18 Ill. App. 2d 183, 151 N.E. 2d 410 (1958).
6. *Moore v. American,* 30 F. Supp. 843 (S.D.N.Y. 1935).
7. 46 U.S.C. sec. 183c.
8. Civil Aeronautics Act of 1938, section 8404 (b). "No air carrier shall, . . . cause any undue . . . preference . . . to any person . . . in any respect whatsoever" (in the granting of air seats). Also see *Nader v. Allegheny Airlines,* civ. act No. 1346-72 (D.C. 1973).
9. C.A.B. Econ. Reg., Part 250-Oversales (Reg. ED 1306).
10. *Jarvis v. Swan Tours,* 1973 Q.B. 233.
11. Dickerson, *supra* sec. 2.09(3).

12. *Greenburg v. United*, 98 Misc. 2d 544, 414 N.Y.S. 2d 240 (1979).
13. *Mahaney v. Compagnie*, 15 Aviation Cases 17, 655 (S.D.N.Y. 1979).
14. 549 F. 2d 1256.
15. *Rosman v. Trans World*, 34 N.Y. 2d 385, 358 N.Y.S. 2d 97, 314 N.E. 2d 848 (1974).
16. *Bergman v. Pan American World Airways, Inc.*, 32 A.D. 2d 95, 299 N.Y.S. 2d 982 (1969).
    "It follows that the carrier may not avail itself of those provisions of the Convention which exclude or limit liability. Is a statute of limitations a provision that excludes or limits liability? We think not. . . . Firstly, because a statute of limitations never limits liability, nor does it exclude it. . . . If by virtue of any state of facts the statute is tolled or waived, the liability is unaffected. . . ." 299 N.Y.S. 2d at 984.
17. Art, 20(1).
18. *Murry v. Capitol*, 424 N.Y.S. 2d 89.
19. Art. 20(1).
20. Article 1 of the Convention, which bears on its applicability, reads as follows:
    "(1) This convention shall apply to all international transportation of persons, baggage, or goods performed by aircraft for hire. It shall apply equally to gratuitous transportation by aircraft performed by an air transportation enterprise.
    "(2) For the purposes of this convention the expression 'international transportation' shall mean any transportation in which, according to the contract made by the parties, the place of departure and the place of destination, whether or not there be a break in the transportation or a transshipment, are situated either within the territories of two High Contracting Parties, or within the territory of a single High Contracting Party, if there is an agreed stopping place within a territory subject to the sovereignty, suzerainty, mandate or authority of another power, even though that power is not a party to this convention. Transportation without such an agreed stopping place between territories subject to sovereignty, suzerainty, mandate, or authority of the same High Contracting Party shall not be deemed to be international for the purposes of this convention.
    "(3) Transportation to be performed by several successive air carriers shall be deemed, for the purposes of this convention, to be one undivided transportation, if it has been regarded by

the parties as a single operation, whether it has been agreed upon under the form of a single contract or a series of contracts, and it shall not lose its international character merely because one contract or a series of contracts is to be performed entirely within a territory subject to the sovereignty, suzerainty, mandate, or authority of the same High Contracting Party."

21. That she took out a $50,000 insurance policy in Seattle has, as Special Term declared, "little bearing on [the passengers] intent relative to termination of the contract for international transportation or of the character of the trip from Seattle to New York in terms of internal or international passage." Mrs. Seiter may have purchased the $50,000 policy because she desired coverage in addition to the $25,000 of insurance (to cover the round trip) which she had procured before leaving New York, in view of the forecast of bad weather. Its purchase certainly created no inference that she considered the round trip at an end.

22. Article 3 provides:
"(1) For the transportation of passengers the carrier must deliver a passenger ticket which shall contain the following particulars:
(a) The place and date of issue;
(b) The place of departure and of destination;
(c) The agreed stopping places provided that the carrier may reserve the right to alter the stopping places in case of necessity, and that if he exercises that right, the alteration shall not have the effect of depriving the transportation of its international character;
(d) The name and address of the carrier or carriers;
(e) A statement that the transportation is subject to the rules relating to liability established by this convention.
(2) The absence, irregularity, or loss of the passenger ticket shall not affect the existence or the validity of the contract of transportation, which shall none the less be subject to the rules of this convention. Nevertheless, if the carrier accepts a passenger without a passenger ticket having been delivered he shall not be entitled to avail himself of those provisions of this convention which exclude or limit his liability."

23. One court has described the notice in this way (*Lisi v. Alitalia-Linee Aeree Italiane*, D.C., 253 F.Supp. 237, 243, *affd.* 2 Cir., 370 F.2d 508)):
"The footnotes printed in microscopic type at the bottom of

the . . . coupons, as well as condition 2(a) camouflaged in Lilliputian print in a thicket of 'Conditions of Contract' crowded on [the outside back cover], are both unnoticeable and unreadable. Indeed, the exculpatory statements on which defendant relies are virtually invisible. They are ineffectively positioned, diminutively sized, and unemphasized by bold face type, contrasting color, or anything else. The simple truth is that they are so artfully camouflaged that their presence is concealed."

24. The language of the statement which was mandated by the CAB was similar to that provided for in the amendment to article 3 appearing in the so-called Hague Protocol to the Convention executed in 1955. (See 3 CCH Aviation L. Rep., par. 27,106). This Protocol was never ratified by the Senate, apparently because its most significant feature, increasing the maximum liability to $16,000, was considered inadequate. It is of more than passing interest that in 1965 our Government in a Notice of Denunciation declared that it opposed the Convention's low limits on liability and indicated an intention to withdraw from the Convention unless an agreement were reached (among the world's international air carriers) to raise the limit to $75,000 and that in May of 1966 such an agreement was executed. (See 3 CCH Aviation L.Rep., par. 27,130; The Warsaw Convention–Recent Developments and the Withdrawal of the United States Denunciation, 32 J. Air L. & Com. 243.)

Selected Bibliography

The Association of Trial Layers of America. *Everyday Law,* December, 1988.

Black, Henry Campbell. *Black's Law Dictionary.* 5th ed. St. Paul, MN: West Publishing Co., 1979.

"Bogies's Faces Lawsuit." *Las Vegas Sun,* April 26, 1984, 8C.

Bowman, Robert J. *The House of Blue Lights.* New York: St. Martin's Press, 1988.

Bryan, J., and J. V. Murphy. *The Windsor Story.* New York: Dell Publishing Co., 1980.

Cooley's Blackstone. 1850.

Dickerson, Thomas A. *Travel Law.* New York: Law Journal Seminars-Press, 1986.

Douglas, William O. Eighth Annual Benjamin Cardoza Lectures.

Eiler, James O. *Hotel and Casino Law Letter* 2, no. 1 (November, 1983).

Florida Hotel and Motel News, March, 1983, 26.

Goodwin, John R., *Business Law.* 3rd ed. Homewood, IL: Richard D. Irwin, Inc., 1980.

Greene, Robert W. *The Sting Man.* New York: Ballantine Books, 1981.

Hospitality Law 5, no. 7 (July 1990): 4.

Hotel and Casino Law Letter 2, no. 2 (April 3, 1983).

Jackson, Donald Dale. *Gold Dust.* New York: Alfred A. Knopf, 1980.

"Law as a Liberal Art Versus Law as a Professional Discipline: A False Dichotomy," *American Business Law Journal* 15, no. 1 (Spring, 1977): 68.

Lodging, May, 1982, 2.

Lodging Hospitality, March, 1988, 24.

Marshall, Anthony G., and Elio C. Bellucci. "Innkeeper's Security: Quo Vadis." *Florida Hotel & Motel News,* March, 1983.

McGinnis, Joe. *Going to Extremes.* New York: The New American Library, 1980.

Murray, William. *When the Fat Man Sings.* New York: Bantam Books, 1986.

National Law Journal, May 11, 1981, 36.

Newman, Christopher. *Sixth Precinct.* New York: Facett Gold Medal, 1986.

New York Times, June 7, 1981, 15.

New York Times, July 19, 1981, 1.

Parker, Robert B. *Taming a Seahorse.* New York: Delacorte Press—Seymore Lawrence, 1986.

Roberts, Kenneth. *Northwest Passage.* Greenwich, CT: Fawcett Publications, 1960.

Sanders, Lawrence. *The Third Deadly Sin.* New York: Berkeley Books, 1980.

Shepherd, Donald, and Robert R Slatzer. *Bing Crosby, the Hollow Man.* New York: Pinnacle Books, 1980.

Sherry, John E.H. *The Laws of Innkeepers.* rev. ed. Ithaca, NY: Cornell University Press, 1981.

Silyenat, James R. rev. ed. of *The Tides of Power* by Bob Eckhart and Charles Black. New Haven, CT: Yale Press, 1978.

Sinclair, Upton. *The Jungle.* New York: New American Library, 1960.

Successful Hotel Marketer 3, no. 19: 2.

Tapply, William. *Dead Winter.* New York: Delacorte Press, 1987.

Tapply, William. *Vulgar Boatman.* New York: Charles Scribner's Sons, 1988.

Vallen, Jerome J., et al. *The Art & Science of Managing Hotels/Restaurants/Institutions.* Rochelle Park, NJ: Hayden Book, 1980.

Weekly Newsletter, Motel/Hotel Insider, May 19, 1980.

Index to Cases

Note: Text page numbers in this index are indicated by boldface type.

Index to Words and Topics